Data Envelopment Analysi
Theory, Methodology, and

Data Envelopment Analysis:
Theory, Methodology, and Application

Abraham Charnes
University of Texas at Austin

William W. Cooper
University of Texas at Austin

Arie Y. Lewin
Duke University

Lawrence M. Seiford
University of Massachusetts

Kluwer Academic Publishers
Boston/Dordrecht/London

Distributors for North America:
Kluwer Academic Publishers
101 Philip Drive
Assinippi Park
Norwell, Massachusetts 02061 USA

Distributors for all other countries:
Kluwer Academic Publishers Group
Distribution Centre
Post Office Box 322
3300 AH Dordrecht, THE NETHERLANDS

Library of Congress Cataloging-in-Publication Data
Data envelopment analysis: theory, methodology and application / by
   Abraham Charnes . . . [et al].
       p.   cm.
     Includes bibliographical references and index.
     ISBN 0-7923-9479-8.—ISBN 0-7923-9480-1
     1. Social sciences—Statistical methods.   2. Data envelopment
analysis.   I. Charnes, A. (Abraham), 1917–1993.
   HA31.38.D38   1993   94-22053
   300′.1′5195—dc20   CIP

Printed on acid-free paper.

Printed in the United States of America

This book is dedicated to George Kozmetsky
for his early championing of DEA and for his
lifelong commitment to nurturing creativity.

Contents

Department of Agricultural Economics
and Rural Sociology
The Pennsylvania State University
103 Armsby Building
University Park, PA   16802-5600

TOC
Ch 2,3,7] Scanning

Preface

This book represents a milestone in the progression of Data Envelopment Analysis (DEA). It is the first reference text which includes a comprehensive review and comparative discussion of the basic DEA models. The development is anchored in a unified mathematical and graphical treatment and includes the most important modeling extensions. In addition, this is the first book that addresses the actual process of conducting DEA analyses including combining DEA and parametric techniques.[1]

The book has three other distinctive features. It traces the applications-driven evolution and diffusion of DEA models and extensions across disciplinary boundaries. It includes a comprehensive bibliography to serve as a source of references as well as a platform for further developments. And, finally, the power of DEA analysis is demonstrated through fifteen novel applications which should serve as an inspiration for future applications and extensions of the methodology.

The origin of this book was a Conference on New Uses of DEA in Management and Public Policy which was held at the IC[2] Institute of the University of Texas at Austin on September 27–29, 1989. The conference was made possible through NSF Grant #SES-8722504 (A. Charnes and W. W. Cooper, co-PIs) and the support of the IC[2] Institute. The purpose of the conference was to: (a) provide opportunities for further contacts between persons already working in DEA; (b) provide a common background, including knowledge of computer codes, for conference participants; and, (c) disseminate knowledge about DEA and its uses. In

---

[1] To accelerate diffusion of DEA instruction in undergraduate and graduate courses, authors of textbooks may obtain permission to incorporate any of these chapters by writing to Kluwer Academic Publishers.

pursuit of the latter goal, selections from this conference are contained in the novel applications chapters.

Unfortunately the production of this book was delayed by several unforeseen circumstances, perhaps the most important of which was the illness of Professor A. Charnes. Although he never saw the final product (Professor Charnes died on December 19, 1992) he remained enthusiastic about this project to the end.

Finally, the editors wish to note the unfailing support of George Kozmetsky, to whom this book is dedicated, and the IC^2 Institute which made possible the publication of the soft cover edition.

Our intention is that this book serve as an introduction to DEA for new users as well as a reference for persons already knowledgeable in DEA. In this way we hope that the book also provides a basis for participating in future endeavors and extensions of activities which have emerged from these uses.

W. W. Cooper
University of Texas, Austin TX

Arie Y. Lewin
Duke University, Durham, NC

Lawrence M. Seiford
University of Massachusetts, Amherst, MA

Data Envelopment Analysis:
Theory, Methodology, and Application

I CONCEPTS, MODELS, AND COMPUTATION

1 INTRODUCTION

1. Introduction

The story of data envelopment analysis (DEA) begins with Edwardo Rhodes's Ph.D. dissertation research at Carnegie Mellon University's School of Urban and Public Affairs (now the H. J. Heinz III School of Public Policy and Management). Under the supervision of W. W. Cooper, Edwardo Rhodes was evaluating Program Follow Through—the educational program for disadvantaged students (mainly black or Hispanic) undertaken in U.S. public schools with support from the Federal Government. The analysis involved comparing the performance of a matched set of school districts that were participating and *not* participating in Program Follow Through.

Program Follow Through recorded the performance of schools in terms of outputs such as "increased self-esteem in a disadvantaged child" (as measured by psychological tests) and inputs such as "time spent by mother in reading with her child." It was the challenge of estimating the relative "technical efficiency" of the schools involving multiple outputs and inputs, without the usual information on prices, that resulted in the formulation of the CCR (Charnes, Cooper, and Rhodes) ratio form of

3

DEA and the publication of the first paper introducing DEA in the *European Journal of Operations Research* in 1978 (Charnes, Cooper, and Rhodes, 1978). CCR used the optimization method of mathematical programming to generalize the Farrell (1957) single-output/input technical-efficiency measure to the multiple-output/multiple-input case by constructing a single "virtual" output to a single "virtual" input relative-efficiency measure. Thus DEA began as a new Management Science tool for technical-efficiency analyses of public-sector decision-making units (DMUs). In this regard, the emergence of DEA was an extension of the historical focus of OR/MS methodologies on the development and application of heuristics and optimization techniques to resource allocation problems.

This chapter has been organized to accomplish several purposes. First, we present a conceptual introduction to DEA. Second, and more importantly, we expand the purpose, applications, and future promise of DEA beyond its initial definition and use as a methodology for efficiency calculations. We believe that DEA provides a new approach to organizing and analyzing data—"discerning new truth." It has become an alternative and a complement to traditional central-tendency analyses, and it provides a new approach to traditional cost-benefit analyses, frontier etimation, policy making, learning from outliers (e.g., best practices), and inducing theory from external observations. Third, we trace the evolution of DEA, and in the last section of this chapter, we present the structure of the book and introduce the novel applications from contributing authors.

2. Data Envelopment Analysis: The Concept

DEA involves an alternative principle for extracting information about a population of observations such as those shown in figure 1–1. In contrast to parametric approaches whose object is to optimize a single regression plane through the data, DEA optimizes on each individual observation with an objective of calculating a discrete piecewise frontier determined by the set of Pareto-efficient DMUs. Both the parametric and nonparametric (mathematical-programming) approaches use all the information contained in the data. In parametric analysis, the single optimized regression equation is *assumed* to apply to *each* DMU. DEA, in contrast, optimizes the performance measure of each DMU. This results in a revealed understanding about each DMU instead of the depiction of a mythical "average" DMU. In other words, the focus of

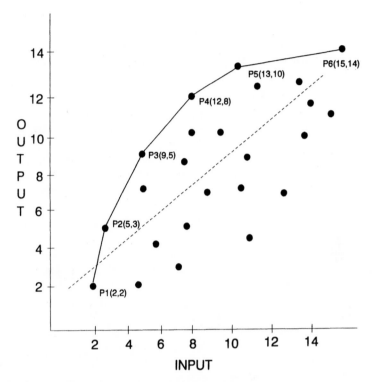

Figure 1-1. Comparison of DEA and regression.

DEA is on the *individual* observations as represented by the n optim-
izations (one for each observation) required in DEA analysis, in contrast to the focus on the *averages* and estimation of parameters that are
associated with single-optimization statistical approaches.

The parametric approach requires the imposition of a specific
functional form (e.g., a regression equation, a production function, etc.)
relating the independent variables to the dependent variable(s). The
functional form selected also requires specific assumptions about the
distribution of the error terms (e.g., independently and identically
normally distributed) and many other restrictions, such as factors earning
the value of their marginal product. In contrast, DEA does not require
any assumption about the functional form. DEA calculates a maximal
performance measure for each DMU relative to all other DMUs in the
observed population with the sole requirement that each DMU lie on or

below the extremal frontier. Each DMU not on the frontier is scaled against a convex combination of the DMUs on the frontier facet closest to it.

Charnes, Cooper, and Rhodes (1978) extended Farrell's (1957) idea linking the estimation of technical efficiency and production frontiers. Their CCR model generalized the single-output/input ratio measure of efficiency for a single DMU in terms of a fractional linear-programming formulation transforming the multiple output/input characterization of each DMU to that of a single "virtual" output and virtual input. The relative technical efficiency of any DMU is calculated by forming the ratio of a weighted sum of outputs to a weighted sum of inputs, where the weights (multipliers) for both outputs and inputs are to be selected in a manner that calculates the Pareto efficiency measure of each DMU subject to the constraint that no DMU can have a relative efficiency score greater than unity.

The solid line in figure 1–1 represents a frontier derived by DEA from data on a population of DMUs, each utilizing different amounts of a single input to produce various amounts of a single output. It is important to note that DEA calculations, because they are generated from actual observed data for each DMU, produce only *relative* efficiency measures. The relative efficiency of each DMU is calculated in relation to all the other DMUs, using the actual observed values for the outputs and inputs of each DMU. The DEA calculations are designed to maximize the relative efficiency score of each DMU, subject to the condition that the set of weights obtained in this manner for each DMU must also be feasible for all the other DMUs included in the calculation. DEA produces a piecewise empirical extremal production surface (e.g., the solid line in figure 1–1), which in economic terms represents the *revealed* best-practice production frontier—the maximum output empirically obtainable from any DMU in the observed population, given its level of inputs.

For each inefficient DMU (one that lies below the frontier), DEA identifies the sources and level of inefficiency for each of the inputs and outputs. The level of inefficiency is determined by comparison to a single referent DMU or a convex combination of other referent DMUs located on the efficient frontier that utilize the same level of inputs and produce the same or a higher level of outputs. This is achieved by requiring solutions to satisfy inequality constraints that can increase some outputs (or decrease some inputs) without worsening the other inputs or outputs. The calculation of potential improvement for each inefficient DMU does not necessarily correspond to the observed performance of any actual DMU making up the piece wise production frontier or to a deterministic projection of an inefficient DMU onto the efficient frontier. The calculated improvements (in each of the inputs and outputs) for inefficient DMUs are *indicative* of potential improvements obtainable because the projections are based on the *revealed* best-practice performance of "comparable" DMUs that are located on the efficient frontier.

We wish to conclude this section by noting that, initially, DEA relative-efficiency solutions were of interest to operations analysts, management scientists, and industrial engineers largely because of three features of the method:

1. characterization of each DMU by a single summary relative-efficiency score;
2. DMU-specific projections for improvements based on observable referent revealed best-practice DMUs; and
3. obviation by DEA of the alternative and indirect approach of specifying abstract statistical models and making inferences based on residual and parameter coefficient analysis.

The attraction of DEA to traditional frontier econometricians (see Schmidt, 1986, for early concerns) emerged from the new insights obtained in production frontier analysis involving their existence and the variance around them. For example, the BCC model (discussed in chapter 2) relaxed the constant-returns-to-scale requirement of the original CCR ratio model and made it possible to investigate local returns to scale. Thus it became evident that DEA can complement information about average returns to scale from econometric models with DMU-specific scale-efficiency information for each DMU on the frontier. Similarly, DEA solutions can provide DMU-specific information for most productive scale size (Banker, 1984) and allocative efficiency (Banker and Mainderata, 1988) in contrast to only average most-productive scale and average allocative efficiency obtained from traditional econometric frontier analysis.

3. DEA as a New Way for Organizing and Analyzing Data

The orientation of DEA on deriving the best-practice frontier and on optimizing the individual DMU affords new ways of organizing and analyzing data and can result in new managerial and theoretical insights. It should be noted that DEA calculations

1. focus on individual observations in contrast to population averages;
2. produce a single aggregate measure for each DMU in terms of its utilization of input factors (independent variables) to produce desired outputs (dependent variables);
3. can simultaneously utilize multiple outputs and multiple inputs with each being stated in different units of measurement;
4. can adjust for exogenous variables;
5. can incorporate categorical (dummy) variables;
6. are value free and do not require specification or knowledge of a priori weights or prices for the inputs or outputs;
7. place no restriction on the functional form of the production relationship;
8. can accommodate judgment when desired;
9. produce specific estimates for desired changes in inputs and/or outputs for projecting DMUs below the efficient frontier onto the efficient frontier;
10. are Pareto optimal;
11. focus on revealed best-practice frontiers rather than on central-tendency properties of frontiers; and
12. satisfy strict equity criteria in the relative evaluation of each DMU.

To illustrate unexpected managerial insights obtainable from DEA calculations, consider the distribution of observations in figure 1–2, which displays a population of DMUs in terms of efficiency scores and output levels. A ranking of the DMUs on the basis of the output measure alone would have ranked DMUs 28 and 29 in the top four and DMU 6 as fourth from the bottom. The DEA analysis, however, indicate that DMUs 28 and 29 have the potential to improve output by 12.5% and 6%, respectively, whereas DMU 6 is performing as well as can be expected. In terms of rewarding good performance or reallocating resources, the DEA solutions shown in figure 1–2 should result in different managerial actions. DMUs 5 and 6, for example, clearly distinguish themselves from the other DMUs in the bottom of the distribution (1, 2, 3, 7, 8, 22, 26) and should be rewarded. Most important, management needs to make a distinction between the two groups, even though the output performance of both groups is poor. Similarly, DMUs 28 and 29, which are performing at a high level but not at their DEA potential, ought be given goals toward improving their performance.

The discussion of the DEA solutions plotted in figure 1–2 illustrates

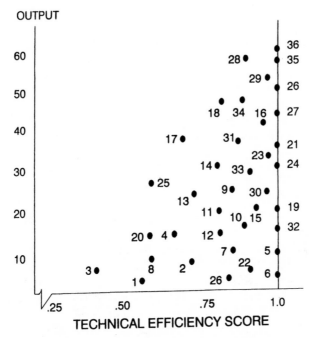

Figure 1–2. Distribution of DEA efficiency scores by output (adapted from Lewin and Morey, 1981).

that by the use of another methodology, unanticipated insights may be obtained and may thus redirect managerial action. In a broader sense, the DEA framework creates a new approach for learning from outliers and for inducing new theories of best practice. Statistical methodology texts and seminars on doctoral research methods stress the importance of examining and understanding outlier data. However, Lewin (1992) noted that "in practice because of a research tradition that places great value on fitting models that account for the greatest amount of variance, researchers have honed their arguments for discarding or discounting outlier data" (p. 15). There are, of course, other explanations as to why researchers might ignore data that raise questions or contradict the prediction of a particular theory or model (see, for example, Mitroff and Linstone, 1993; Charnes, Cooper, and Sueyshi, 1988).

The observations in figure 1–1 serve to illustrate the importance of learning from outliers. Fitting a regression plane that maximizes the explained variance is understandable from the perspective of explaining central tendencies. However, if the objective is to develop a central-tendency explanation (theory or model) of best practice, then it could be argued that a regression plane should be estimated for the observations located on and near (but below) the efficient frontier. In other words, the DEA approach provides an analytical tool for determining effective and ineffective performance (in particular when multiple measures of performance and various discretionary and exogenous variables are involved) as the starting point for inducing theories about best-practice behavior. The resulting explanations could be in the form of central-tendency models (see, for example, chapter 17 for a two-stage analysis) or in the form of comparative ethnographic research whose aim is to induce grounded theory (Eisenhardt, 1989).

Finally, we wish to note the observation by Seiford and Thrall (1990) that "DEA proves particularly adept at uncovering relationships that remain hidden for other methodologies" (p. 8). For example, in their study of 114 North Carolina hospitals, Banker, Conrad, and Strauss (1986) have demonstrated the possibilities of returns to scale in individual hospitals. Prior regression-based studies of the same populations (same input/output variables) reached the conclusion that no returns to scale were present. In another context, the DEA results of Leibenstein and Maital (1992) have lent further support to DEA serving as a means for discerning new truth. Leibenstein and Maital's (1992) DEA results were able to empirically apply DEA to directly estimate X-inefficiency. In particular, their study of Boston Bruins' Offensive Efficiency is the first to demonstrate that gains from decreasing X-inefficiency (moving inefficient DMUs onto the frontier) can be more significant than gains from increases in allocative efficiency (movement of efficient DMU to the optimal point on the frontier). The DEA results of Leibenstein and Maital (1992) should reopen the controversy in microeconomics surrounding the existence and magnitude of X-inefficiency. In this case, DEA was ideally suited as an empirical approach because it directly estimates which DMUs are maximizing (in a relative sense) some objective function (e.g., profits).

4. Milestones in the Evolution of DEA

Between 1978 and 1992, over 400 articles, books, and dissertations were published involving DEA (see chapter 22, this volume). The rapid development of DEA was to a large extent the result of two related factors. As has been the case with other Operations Research methodologies, the development of DEA was informed by problems that arose in the process of applying the method. It was through such a process that various extensions to DEA—returns to scale, dummy or categorical variables, discretionary and nondiscretionary variables, longitudinal analysis, incorporating judgment (e.g., managerial preferences, expert opinion), and most productive scale and allocative efficiency—came about (see chapters 2, 3, and 4).

Interaction and exchanges with the traditional parametric frontier analysis community (see, for example, Lewin and Lovell, 1990) has been influential in directing attention to the issue of robustness and sensitivity analyses and has also resulted in hybrid (e.g., two-stage) methodological applications utilizing both nonparametric and parametric methods (see, for example, chapters 6 and 17).

Figure 1–3 represents our attempt at plotting major milestones in the evolution of DEA. Our unfolding historical time line captures the publication of key papers (e.g., model extensions, noteworthy applications), specific events in the emergence of the DEA/frontier-analysis community (e.g., conferences, special issues), and the publication of books on DEA or textbook chapters that highlight the application of nonparametric methods in frontier analysis.

Figure 1–3 does not incorporate the enormous range of applications involving DEA. The extensive but probably incomplete bibliography included in this volume (chapter 22) is intended to document the diffusion and growth of DEA. The bibliography is evidence of DEA applications involving a wide range of contexts, such as education (public schools and universities), health care (hospitals, clinics, physicians), banking, armed forces (recruiting, aircraft maintenanced), auditing, sports, market research, mining, agriculture, siting and spatial studies, retail outlets, organization effectiveness, transportation (ferries, highway maintenance), public housing, index number construction, benchmarking, etc.

The diffusion of DEA applications and methodological extensions, as measured by the cumulative growth in the number of published papers, dissertations, book chapters, working papers, and books, is also shown in figure 1–3. The cumulative growth in the number of publications has been accelerating rapidly. Another indication of the diffusion of DEA-related research and applications can be gained from an analysis of paper presentations in meetings of professional societies. For example, in the 1991 Spring TIMS/ORSA meeting and the 1991 Fall ORSA/TIMS meeting, more papers involving applications of DEA were presented in non-DEA dedicated session than in sponsored DEA sessions.

It seems to us that in the relatively short span of 14 years (1978–1992), It can be said that DEA has arrived. It has established itself as

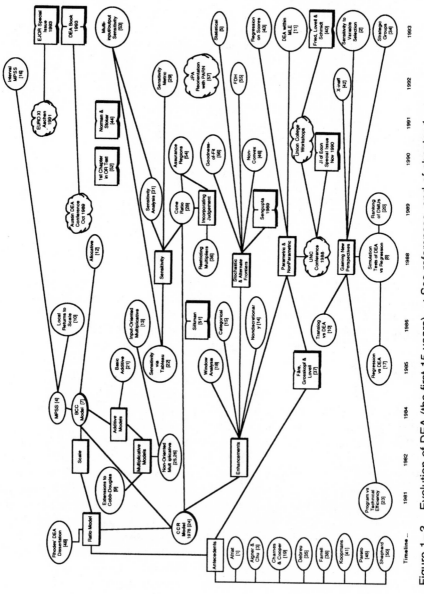

Figure 1-3.   Evolution of DEA (the first 15 years).   : See references, end of chapter 1.

an important analytical tool whose acceptance among researchers and practitioners within the communities of management science, econometrics, and industrial engineering is no longer in doubt. However, the ultimate potential of DEA is yet to be realized.

5. Structure of this Book

Our purposes for this book were to establish a reference source for DEA that accomplishes the following seven objectives:

1. promotes DEA as a new approach to organizing and analyzing data beyond its origin in efficiency analyses;
2. presents an integrated framework and standardized notation for understanding basic DEA models and their extensions;
3. develops a deeper understanding of computational issues involved with solving various DEA formulations;
4. provides insights into the DEA process, its usage, and its interpretations;
5. highlights the range of potential uses of DEA through examples of novel applications;
6. provides an updated comprehensive bibliography;
7. facilitates the diffusion of DEA by making chapters 1–4 and 21 available for inclusion in operations research, econometric, and statistics textbooks under normal provisions that maintain original copyright status.

This chapter presents the conceptual introduction to DEA, promotes its uses as a new approach to organizing and analyzing data, and traces its evolution. Chapter 2 introduces the notation of DEA and its underlying framework of four basic models. The framework makes it clear that the choice of DEA formulation requires 1) a choice of orientation—minimization of inputs or maximization of outputs or no orientation and 2) a scale assumption—constant returns to scale (CRS) or variable returns to scale (VRS).

Chapter 3 presents key extensions of DEA, such as incorporating 1) nondiscretionary variables (inputs or outputs), 2) categorical inputs and outputs (dummy variables), and 3) judgment, such as managerial preferences or expert opinion. The chapter also discusses the use of DEA in longitudinal analysis. Chapter 4 by Agha Iqbal Ali discusses the computational characteristics of DEA in the context of the models and their extensions presented in chapters 2 and 3. Part I concludes with a brief chapter summarizing the capabilities of several production-quality DEA software packages, some of which are commercially available.

Part II of the book consists of 15 novel applications intended to showcase the range, power, elegance, and insights obtainable via DEA analysis or in conjunction with more traditional statistical methods. Most of these novel applications were first presented at the Conference on New Uses of DEA in Management, 27–29 September 1989, at the IC^2 Institute at the University of Texas at Austin.

Finally, part III provides an updated (to 1992) DEA bibliography (chapter 22) as well as a chapter (21) whose primary focus is on the DEA process and uses. In particular, chapter 21 addresses caveats associated with DEA use as an exploratory data analysis methodology and uncovers relationships that have remained unobserved during the use of other methods, new hybrid uses combining statistical and DEA formulations, and various issues of interpretation and implications for policy making or managerial action.

6. Overview of Contributed Chapters

Unlike most proceedings, the papers (presented at the conference and those submitted following the conference) included as chapters in part II were only accepted following a rigorous peer review process. Each paper was reviewed by at least two referees and then revised accordingly. The result is a select collection of outstanding, novel applications. Chapter 17 by Lovell, Walters, and Wood makes use of both statistical and DEA analyses. In their study of educational performance using cohort data on high-school sophomores, they show how both types of analysis can be used to obtain insights and perspectives that would not otherwise be available. In particular, they use a series of DEA models to evaluate the efficiency of the schools attended. One class of DEA models evaluates short-term performance, and another evaluates longer-range effects as the cohorts move along. These results are then complemented by statistical methods in a longitudinal study of "accomplishments." In this case, the accomplishment record is found to be better than the output record (as measured by academic performance), and this raises the possibility that public schools may be doing a better job than the usual records show in preparing students for their subsequent careers.

In chapter 7 on health service performance, Byrnes and Valdmanis decompose efficiency into components that they identify with allocative, technical, and scale efficiencies. Using price-cost data, they are able to rank the hospitals covered in their study by using total costs as a common ordering principle. The total inefficiency identified—which was found to be substantial—is corroborated by the customarily used ratio approached (e.g., cost per discharge), but Byrnes and Valdmanis find that the latter approach is less informative in locating sources and amounts of inefficiency.

In contrast to Byrnes and Valdmanis, who covered 123 hospitals in their study, Chilingerian (chapter 9) concentrates his attention on a single hospital. This permits him to focus on the individual physicians (36 in number) practicing in this hospital, who 1) account for some 20% of the expenditures but also 2) control decisions that account for some 80% of the total expenditures. Applying DEA to data on the performance of each physician, Chilingerian (like Byrnes and Valdmanis) obtains results from his use of DEA that are found to be much more informative than the information to be found in ratio (averaging) approaches.

It is also possible to join parametric and nonparametric approaches to obtain new amalgams. One such possibility is described by Banker and Johnston (chapter 6). Banker and Johnston extend the usual DEA models and introduce developments that make it possible to use standard statistical characterization, including tests of significance, on the results they secure from their use of DEA to study the different strategies used by various U.S. airlines in response to deregulation.

DEA can also offer possibilities for use in index number construction. Chapter 18 by Lovell and Zieschang describes experiments using DEA to deal with appearing and disappearing commodities—a problem that has become severe in constructing price indexes for products like electronic computer components, which are subject to very rapid change. In this study, Lovell and Zieschang turn to uses of dual variable values with results that compare favorably with the commonly used "reservation-price" and "link-to-show-no-charge" approaches. More experimentation is needed, as Lovell and Zieschang note, but at least they have opened a path to possible new approaches which, inter alia, may make it possible to relax conditions—such as an already attained efficiency or an already attained equilibrium—that are assumptions underlying other approaches, as in the use of "superlative" and "hedonic" indexes.

Färe, Grosskopf, Lindgren, and Roos (chapter 13) approach the need for relaxing the assumptions of an already achieved technical efficiency in yet other ways. In particular, they use a radial measure of efficiency from which they construct an index of productivity for Swedish hospitals along lines suggested by Malmquist indexes. Inter alia (although Färe et al. do not stress this point), this opens new possibilities for consideration in managerial (and public policy) decision by directing attention to the possible removal of inefficiencies, including waste, as well as by altering the technologies (including managerial performance) that may also affect productivity. Thus, a possibility for improvement is brought into view that is not apparent in customary indexes of productivity that do *not* distinguish between productivity increases resulting from 1) improvements in technology and 2) improvements in performance with existing technologies.

Other policy issues are covered in the studies of ferry transport in Norway, reported in chapter 15 by Førsund and Hernaes and in the study of highway maintenance patrols in Canada by Cook, Kazakov, and Roll (chapter 10). In both cases, private-enterprise as well as public-organization performances are evaluated by DEA. Both chapters are directed toward improving the control of these activities, but an interesting by-product occurs, because neither study finds evidence that the private-enterprise activities are more efficient than their publicly controlled counterparts. Similar findings are reported by Gary Ferrier in his study of dairy cooperatives (chapter 14).

As reported in Charnes, Cooper, and Rhodes (1978, 1979), DEA was originally developed in response to a need for improved methods for evaluation and controlling public sector activities. However, in chapter 12, Desai, Haynes, and Storbeck show how DEA can be used to improve location decisions for both private and public enterprises in situations where multiple outputs as well as multiple inputs need to be taken into account.

Other applications to private-enterprise activities include the study of strategic leaders in the U.S. brewing industry by Day, Lewin, Li, and Salazar (chapter 11). As the authors note, one purpose of this study is to use DEA's frontier (= outlier) properties in order to determine whether strategic groups can be identified in the manner suggested by Porter (1980). Applying DEA to a longitudinal analysis of the U.S. brewing industry, these authors find that there is sufficient turbulence over time in the data to indicate that Porter's concept of "strategic grouping" is, at best, of limited value.

Much of the discussion of DEA carries with it an assumed independence in the activities of the DMUs being evaluated. That is, it is assumed that each DMU is in control of its own inputs and outputs. Such an assumption is not always appropriate, however, as is made clear in chapter 8 by Charnes, Cooper, Golany, Phillips, and Rousseau, who treat the highly competitive business of marketing carbonated beverages. Here some of the activities of each DMU may take the form of advertising, which is directed to acquiring market share from other DMUs. To accommodate this kind of behavior, advertising by Pepsi-Cola, say, is treated as input to Coca Cola, and vice versa. Time-dependent consequences of competitive behavior are also taken into account, as in, for instance, the case of market share, where market shares in earlier periods are represented as inputs and market shares in later periods are represented as outputs. This chapter extends the concept of DMUs to include RUs (response units) consisting of groups of households, etc., that are targets of marketing activities. In this way, possibilities are opened for uses of DEA to replace the assumption of a single sales-response curve with more general *families* of response curves that generate the observations to which frontier boundaries can be assigned by DEA. Finally, as the authors of chapter 8 report, DEA's ability to deal with multiple outputs and inputs can be used in place of the usual approach, in which sales responses are analyzed relative only to a single (summary) input like "advertising" or "sales effort."

Chapter 16 by Golany and Roll opens yet another alternative to cone-ratio and assurance-region approaches by moving from the dual to the primal DEA model in order to incorporate known standards (as in industrial engineering) to serve as constraints for the efficiency evaluations. In doing this, Golany and Roll also open a way to extend industrial engineering concepts by associating them with a methodology that can be applied in multiple output–multiple input contexts.

Public- and private-industry applications do not exhaust the possibilities of DEA, as Mark Mazur shows in chapter 19. He applies DEA to evaluate the performance of individual batters and pitchers in big-league baseball. The ability of DEA to accommodate different types of inputs and outputs allows him to take explicit account of data on runs batted in as well as batting averages and home runs for his evaluation of hitters, and on walks and strikeouts as well as numbers of games won, lost, and saved by pitchers.

"Sensitivity analyses," which test the extent to which results might vary with perturbations in the data, are used in both engineering and operations research, as well as in other disciplines. Sensitivity analysis is the subject of chapter 20 by Thompson, Dharmapala, and Thrall. In most of the other approaches, attention has been focused on the sensitivity of DEA results to variation in one data point or only a few data points, as is also the case when examining the effects of removing or censoring "outliers" in the course of a statistical study. Thompson, Dharmapala, and Thrall provide a new approach to this topic in which *all* data may be varied simultaneously and the process of variation is allowed to continue until a first change of results occurs. Here the definition of a "change of results," as taken from DEA, means that the status of some DMU is changed from "efficient" to "inefficient," or vice versa. Finally, to facilitate further study of these DEA properties, Thompson, Dharmapala, and Thrall also provide a set of mathematical appendices as well as an extensive set of references for those who want to undertake further work on this topic.

References for figure 1-3: Evolution of DEA

1. Afriat, S. Efficiency Estimation of Production Functions. *International Economic Review* (1972), 13:568–598.
2. Ahn, T., Seiford, Lawrence M. Sensitivity of DEA to Models and Variable Sets in a Hypothesis Test Setting: The Efficiency of University Operations. In Yuji Ijiri (ed.), *Creative and Innovative Approaches to the Science of Management*. New York: Quorum Books (1993).
3. Aigner, D. J., Chu, S. F. On Estimating the Industry Production Function. *The American Economic Review* (1968), 58:826–839.
4. Banker, R. D. Estimating Most Productive Scale Size Using Data Envelopment Analysis. *European Journal of Operational Research* (1984), 17(1): 35–44.
5. Banker, R. D. Maximum Likelihood, Consistency and Data Envelopment Analysis: A Statistical Foundation. *Management Science* (forthcoming). (See also [6].)
6. Banker, R. D. Stochastic Data Envelopment Analysis. Working Paper (1990). Carlton School of Management, Univ. of Minnesota.
7. Banker, R. D., Charnes, A., Cooper, W. W. Some Models for Estimating Technical and Scale Inefficiencies in Data Envelopment Analysis. *Management Science* (1984), 30(9):1078–1092.
8. Banker, R. D., Charnes, A., Cooper, W. W., Maindiratta, A. A Comparison of DEA and Translog Estimates of Production Frontiers Using Simulated Observations From a Known Technology. In A. Dogramaci, R. Färe (eds.), *Applications of Modern Production Theory: Efficiency and Productivity*. Boston: Kluwer Academic Publishers (1988).
9. Banker, R. D., Charnes, A., Cooper, W. W., Schinnar, A. A Bi-extremal Principle for Frontier Estimation and Efficiency Evaluation. *Management Science* (1981), 27(12):1370–1382.
10. Banker, R. D., Conrad, R. F., Strauss, R. P. A Comparative Application of DEA and Translog Methods: An Illustrative Study of Hospital Production. *Management Science* (1986), 32(1):30–44.
11. Banker, R., Johnston, H. Evaluating the Impacts of Operating Strategies on Efficiency in the U.S. Airline Industry. Chapter 6, this book.

12. Banker, R. D., Maindiratta, A. Nonparametic Analysis of Technical and Alloctive Efficiencies in Production. *Econometrica* (1988), 56(6):1315–1332.

13. Banker, R. D., Maindiratta, A. Piecewise Loglinear Estimation of Efficient Production Surfaces. *Management Science* (1986), 32(1):126–135.

14. Banker, R. D., Morey, R. Efficiency Analysis for Exogenously Fixed Inputs and Outputs. *Operations Research* (1986), 34(4):513–521. (See also [47].)

15. Banker, R. D., Morey, R. The Use of Categorical Variables in Data Envelopment Analysis. *Management Science* (1986), 32(12):1613–1627.

16. Banker, R. D., Thrall, R. Estimation of Returns to Scale Using Data Envelopment Analysis. *European Journal of Operational Research* (1992), 22(1).

17. Bowlin, W. F., Charnes, A., Cooper, W. W., Sherman, H. D. Data Envelopment Analysis and Regression Approaches to Efficiency Estimation and Evaluation. *Annals of Operations Research* (1985), 2:113–138.

18. Charnes, A., Clark, T., Cooper, W. W., Golany, B. A Developmental Study of Data Envelopment Analysis in Measuring the Efficiency of Maintenance Units in the U.S. Air Forces. In R. Thompson, R. M. Thrall (eds.), *Annals of Operation Research* (1985), 2:95–112.

19. Charnes, A., Cooper, W. W. Management Models and Industrial Application of Linear Programming. *Managements Science* (1957), 4(1):38–91.

20. Charnes, A., Cooper, W. W., Divine, D., Ruefli, T. W., Thomas, D. Comparisons of DEA and Existing Ratio and Regression Systems for Effecting Efficiency Evaluations of Regulated Electric Cooperatives in Texas. *Research in Governmental and Nonprofit Accounting* (1989), 5: 187–210.

21. Charnes, A., Cooper, W. W., Golany, B., Seiford, L., Stutz, J. Foundations of Data Envelopment Analysis for Pareto-Koopmans Efficient Empirical Production Functions. *Journal of Econometrics (Netherlands)* (1985), 30(1/2):91–107.

22. Charnes, A., Cooper, W. W., Lewin, A. Y., Morey, R. C., Rousseau, J. Sensitivity and Stability Analysis in DEA. *Annals of Operations Research* (1985), 2:139–156.

23. Charnes, A., Cooper, W. W., Rhodes, E. Evaluating Program and Managerial Efficiency: An Application of Data Envelopment Analysis to Program Follow Through. *Management Science* (1981), 27(6):668–697.

24. Charnes, A., Cooper, W. W., Rhodes, E. Measuring the Efficiency of Decision Making Units. *European Journal of Operational Research* (1978), 2(6):429–444. (See also [23].)

25. Charnes, A., Cooper, W. W., Seiford, L., Stutz, J. A Multiplicative Model for Efficiency Analysis. *Socio-Economic Planning Sciences* (1982), 16(5): 223–224. (See also [26].)

26. Charnes, A., Cooper, W. W., Seiford, L., Stutz, J. Invariant Multiplicative Efficiency and Piecewise Cobb-Douglas Envelopments. *Operations Research Letters* (1983), 2(3):101–103.

27. Charnes, A., Cooper, W. W., Sun, D. B., Huang, Z. M. Polyhedral Cone-

Ratio DEA Models with an Illustrative Application to Large Commercial Banks. *Journal of Econometrics* (1990), 46:73–91.

28. Charnes, A., Cooper, W. W., Wei, Q. L., Huang, Z. M. Cone Ratio Data Envelopment Analysis and Multi-Objective Programming. *International Journal of Systems Science* (1989), 20(7):1099–1118. (See also [27].)

29. Charnes, A., Haag, S., Jaska, P., Semple, J. Sensitivity of Efficiency Calculations in the Additive Model of Data Envelopment Analysis. *International Journal of Systems Science* (1992), 23(5):789–798.

30. Charnes, A., Neralić, L. Sensitivity Analysis of the Additive Model in Data Envelopment Analysis. *European Journal of Operations Research* (forthcoming).

31. Charnes, A., Neralić, L. Sensitivity Analysis in Data Envelopment Analysis 1. *Glasnik Matematički* (1989), 24(44, 1). (See also [30, 32, 33].)

32. Charnes, A., Neralić, L. Sensitivity Analysis in Data Envelopment Analysis 2. *Glasnik Matematički* (1989), 24(44, 2/3).

33. Charnes, A., Zlobec, S. Stability of Efficiency Evaluations in Data Envelopment Analysis. *Zeitschrift für Operations Research* (1989), 33:167–179.

34. Day, D., Lewin, A. Y., Salazar, R., Li, H. Strategic Leaders in the U.S. Brewing Industry: A Longitudinal Analysis of Outliers. Chapter 11, this book.

35. Debreu, G. The Coefficient of Resource Utilization. *Econometrica* (1951), 19:273–292.

36. Dyson, R. G., Thanassoulis, E. Reducing Weight Flexibility in Data Envelopment Analysis. *Journal of the Operational Research Society* (1988), 39(6):563–576.

37. Färe, R., Grosskopf, S., Lovell, C. A. Knox. *The Measurement of Efficiency of Production*. Boston: Kluwer Academic Publishers (1985).

38. Farrell, M. J. The Measurement of Productive Efficiency. *Journal of Royal Statistical Society* (1957), A, 120:253–281.

39. Ferrier, G., Lovell, C. A. Knox. Measuring Cost Efficiency in Banking. *Journal of Econometrics* (1990), 46:229–245.

40. Fried, H., Lovell, C. A. K., Schmidt, S. (eds.) *The Measurement of Productive Efficiency: Techniques and Applications*. Oxford: Oxford University Press (1993).

41. Koopmans, T. C. Analysis of Production as an Efficient Combination of Activities. In T. C. Koopmans (ed.), *Activity Analysis of Production and Allocation*. New York: Wiley (1951).

42. Leibenstein, H., Maital, S. Empirical Estimation and Partitioning of X-Ineffiency: A Data-Envelopment Approach. *American Economic Review* (1992), 82(2):428–433.

43. Lovell, C. A. K., Walters, L., Wood, L. Stratified Models of Education Production Using Modified DEA and Regression Analysis. Chapter 17, this book.

44. Norman, M., Stoker, B. *Data Envelopment Analysis: The Assessment of Performance*. New York: John Wiley & Sons (1991).

45. Pareto, V. *Manuel d'economie politique*, 2nd ed. Paris: Marcerl Giard (1927).
46. Petersen, N. C. Data Envelopment Analysis on a Relaxed Set of Assumptions. *Management Science* (1990), 20(3):305–314.
47. Ray, S. C. Data Envelopment Analysis, Nondiscretionary Inputs and Efficiency: An Alternative Interpretation. *Socio-Economic Planning Sciences* (1988), 22(4):167–176.
48. Rhodes, Edwardo. Data Envelopment Analysis and Approaches for Measuring the Efficiency of Decision-making Units with an Application to Program Follow-Through in U.S. Education. Pittsburgh, PA: Ph.D. dissertation, School of Urban and Public Affairs, Carnegie-Mellon University (1978).
49. Sengupta, J. K. *Efficiency Analysis by Production Frontiers: The Nonparametric Approach.* Boston: Kluwer Academic Publishers (January 1989).
50. Shepherd, R. W. *Theory of Cost and Production Functions.* Princeton, NJ: Princeton University Press (1970).
51. Silkman, Richard H. (ed.) *Measuring Efficiency: An Assessment of Data Envelopment Analysis.* Publication No. 32 in the series New Directions for Program Evaluation, A Publication of the American Evaluation Association. San Francisco: Jossey Bass (1986).
52. Anderson, David R., Sweeney, Dennis J., Williams, Thomas A. *An Introduction to Management Science: Quantitative Approaches to Decision Making*, 6th ed. St. Paul, MN: West Publishing (1991).
53. Thompson, R. G., Dharmapala, P. S., Thrall, R. Sensitivity Analysis of Efficiency Measures With Applications to Kansas Farming and Illinois Coal Mining. Chapter 20, this book.
54. Thompson, R. G., Langemeier, L., Lee, C., Lee, E., Thrall, R. The Role of Multiplier Bounds in Efficiency Analysis with Application to Kansas Farming. *Journal of Econometrics* (1990), 46:93–108.
55. Tulkens, H. On FDH Efficiency Analysis: Some Methodological Issues and Applications to Retail Banking, Courts, and Urban Transit. *Journal of Productivity Analysis* (forthcoming).
56. Varian, H. Goodness-of-fit in Optimizing Models. *Journal of Econometrics* (1990), 46:125–140.
57. *Journal of Productivity Analysis.* Reorientation: Knox Lovell appointed Editor-in-Chief; Equal emphasis on parametric and nonparametric productivity analysis; Affiliation with Productivity Analysis Research Network (PARN) (1992).

2 BASIC DEA MODELS

1. Introduction

Data Envelopment Analysis (DEA) is a body of concepts and methodologies that have now been incorporated in a collection of models with accompanying interpretive possibilities as follows:

1. the CCR ratio model (1978)
    - (*i*) yields an objective evaluation of overall efficiency and
    - (*ii*) identifies the sources and estimates the amounts of the thus-identified inefficiencies;
2. the BCC model (1984) distinguishes between technical and scale inefficiencies by
    - (*i*) estimating pure technical efficiency at the given scale of operation and
    - (*ii*) identifying whether increasing decreasing, or constant returns to scale possibilities are present for further exploitation;
3. the Multiplicative models (Charnes et al., 1982, 1983) provide
    - (*i*) a log-linear envelopment or

      (*ii*) a piecewise Cobb–Douglas interpretation of the production process (by reduction to the antecedent 1981 additive model of Charnes, Cooper, and Seiford); and

4. the Additive model (as better rendered in Charnes et al., 1985) and the extended Additive model (Charnes et al., 1987)

      (*i*) relate DEA to the earlier Charnes–Cooper (1959) inefficiency analysis and in the process

      (*ii*) relate the efficiency results to the economic concept of Pareto optimality as interpreted in the still earlier work of T. Koopmans (1949) in the volume that published the proceedings of the first conference on linear programming.[1]

While each of these models addresses managerial and economic issues and provides useful results, their orientations are different and, more importantly, they generalize and provide contact with these disciplines and concepts. Thus, models may focus on increasing, decreasing, or constant returns to scale as found in economics that are here generalized to the case of multiple outputs. They may determine an efficient frontier that may be piecewise linear, piecewise log-linear, or piecewise Cobb–Douglas with, again, generalization to the multiple output–input situations being achieved in the process. They may utilize non-Archimedean constructs, and they may focus on either input reduction or output augmentation to achieve efficiency.

Somewhat surprisingly, little reported research has aimed at relating these different models and their possibilities.[2] This chapter seeks to achieve comparisons by focusing on the above basic mathematical models. In particular, we examine the CCR ratio model, the BCC model, the Additive model, and the Multiplicative models. Primal and dual characterizations for each model are presented, and comparisons between models are developed via geometric portrayals of the corresponding envelopment surfaces, returns-to-scale properties, projections onto the efficient surface, and invariance of measurement units. Additional extensions with accompanying theory are discussed in chapter 3.

In the discussion to follow, we assume that there are n decision-making units (DMUs) to be evaluated. Each DMU consumes varying amounts of m different inputs to produce s different outputs. Specifically, DMU_j consumes amounts $X_j = \{x_{ij}\}$ of inputs ($i = 1, \ldots, m$) and produces amounts $Y_j = \{y_{rj}\}$ of outputs ($r = 1, \ldots, s$). For these constants, which generally take the form of observations, we assume $x_{ij} > 0$ and $y_{rj} > 0$.[3] The $s \times n$ matrix of output measures is denoted by Y, and the $m \times n$

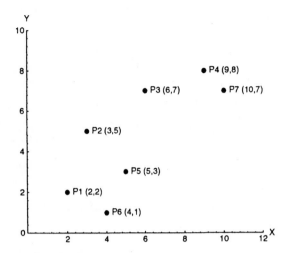

Figure 2–1.   Example DMUs.

matrix of input measures is denoted by X. To illustrate the discussion to follow, we will employ the example presented in figure 2–1, which consists of seven DMUs, each consuming a single input (x) to produce a single output (y), which are assigned the coordinate values associated with the points $P_1, \ldots, P_7$, which represent the corresponding DMUs—namely, $DMU_1, \ldots, DMU_7$.

Essentially, the various models for DEA each seek to establish which subsets of n DMUs determine parts of an *envelopment surface*. As will be seen, the geometry of this envelopment surface is prescribed by the specific DEA model employed. To be efficient, the point P_j corresponding to DMU_j must lie on this surface. Units that do not lie on the surface are termed inefficient, and the DEA analysis identifies the sources and amounts of inefficiency and/or provides a summary measure of relative efficiency. Details will now be developed for identifying the envelopment surface, called the efficient frontier, which serves to 1) characterize efficiency and 2) identify inefficiencies.

The development of the models in this chapter is as follows. Section 2 starts with the Additive model. The Multiplicative models are examined in section 3. Sections 4 and 5 discuss the BCC and CCR models, respectively. The original ratio form characterizations are given in section 6. We conclude with a summary of model features in section 7.

2. The Additive Model

The model that we use to introduce the concepts that guide a DEA analysis is the additive model of Charnes, Cooper, Golany, Seiford, and Stutz (1985), as given in the following pair of dual linear programming problems.[4] (Here the names Primal and Dual are interchanged from those in earlier published papers.)

| **Additive Primal** | **Additive Dual** |
| (ADD$_P$) | (ADD$_D$) |

$$\min_{\lambda, s^+, s^-} \; z_o = -\vec{1}s^+ - \vec{1}s^-$$

$$\text{s.t.} \quad Y\lambda - s^+ = Y_o$$

$$-X\lambda - s^- = -X_o$$

$$\vec{1}\lambda = 1$$

$$\lambda, s^+, s^- \geq 0$$

$$\max_{\mu, v, u_o} \; w_o = \mu^T Y_o - v^T X_o + u_o$$

$$\text{s.t.} \quad \mu^T Y - v^T X + u_o \vec{1} \leq 0$$

$$-\mu^T \leq -\vec{1}$$

$$-v^T \leq -\vec{1}$$

The primal problem[5] on the left is referred to as the *envelopment form*, while the dual problem on the right is the *multiplier form*. Both problems always have solutions; hence, the duality theorem of linear programming can be used to guarantee that $z_o^* = w_o^*$, where the superscript (*) denotes an optimum value. One may solve either of these equivalent linear programming problems by means of standard linear programming algorithms and obtain a solution to the other problem as well without extra effort. The optimal value, $z_o^*(= w_o^*)$, yields an efficiency rating that measures the distance that a particular DMU being rated lies from the frontier. Thus, DMU_o is efficient if and only if $z_o^* = w_o^* = 0$. The DMU_o is inefficient if it does not lie on the frontier, i.e., if any component of the slack variables, s^{+*} or s^{-*} is not zero; the values of these nonzero components identify the sources and amounts of inefficiency in the corresponding outputs and inputs.

This process is repeated n times, once for each DMU_j that is to be rated. That is, in principle, we solve ADD_P with $(X_o, Y_o) = (X_j, Y_j)$ for $j = 1, \ldots n$. The objective function values obtained effectively partition the set of DMUs into two subsets: DMUs for which $z_o^* = 0$ are *efficient* and determine the envelopment surface, while DMUs for which $z_o^* < 0$ are *inefficient* and lie beneath the surface.

Table 2–1 lists optimal values obtained from the above dual linear programs for the DMUs in figure 2–1 with the following results. DMU_1, DMU_2, DMU_3, and DMU_4 have an objective function value of zero, and

Table 2–1. Solution Values for the Additive Model

DMU	Primal Problem (ADD_p)				Dual Problem (ADD_D)			
	z_j^*	s^+	s^-	λ	w_j^*	μ	v	u_o
1	0	0	0	$\lambda_1 = 1$	0	1	3	4
2	0	0	0	$\lambda_2 = 1$	0	1	1	-2
3	0	0	0	$\lambda_3 = 1$	0	3/2	1	$-9/2$
4	0	0	0	$\lambda_4 = 1$	0	3	1	-15
5	-4	2	2	$\lambda_2 = 1$	-4	1	1	-2
6	-5	4	1	$\lambda_2 = 1$	-5	1	1	-2
7	-4	0	4	$\lambda_3 = 1$	-4	3/2	1	$-9/2$

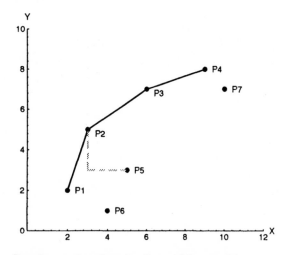

Figure 2–2. Envelopment surface for the additive model.

are thus efficient. These efficient DMUs determine the piecewise linear envelopment surface composed of the three facets shown in figure 2–2. DMU_5, DMU_6, and DMU_7 are inefficient, with objective function values of $z_5^* = -4$, $z_6^* = -5$, and $z_7^* = -4$, and thus lie below the envelopment surface. Associated with each inefficient DMU_j, (X_j, Y_j), is an optimal comparison point $(\hat{X}_j, \hat{Y}_j)$ on the envelopment surface that may be expressed as a convex combination of the DMUs, i.e., $(\hat{X}_j = \Sigma \lambda_k^* X_k, \hat{Y}_j = \Sigma \lambda_k^* Y_k$ with $\Sigma \lambda_k^* = 1$, $\lambda_k^* \geqslant 0$, $\forall k$).[6] Optimal values for the slack variables obtained from solving the primal problem ADD_P measure the $L1$ distance from (X_j, Y_j) to this projected point $(\hat{X}_j, \hat{Y}_j)$ on the frontier. As discussed in Charnes et al. (1985), the Additive model selects the point on the envelopment surface that maximizes the $L1$ distance in the "northwesterly" direction. Specifically, for a particular DMU_o, the primal problem ADD_P picks the most extreme of all convex combinations of DMUs with output levels $Y\lambda \geq Y_o$ and input levels $X\lambda \leq X_o$. Thus for DMU_5 with coordinates (5, 3) in our example, this farthermost point (with nonegative slacks) occurs at DMU_2 with coordinates (3, 5) for an $L1$ distance of 4 obtained from a nonzero input slack of $5 - 3 = 2$ and an output slack of $5 - 3 = 2$.

The dual (multiplier form) problem, ADD_D, yields an alternate geometric interpretation. Here one seeks the closest supporting (facet-defining) hyperplane, i.e., $\mu Y_o - v X_o + u_o = w_o$ with maximal w_o.[7] An efficient point (X_o, Y_o) will lie on the facet-defining hyperplane with equation $u^* Y_o - v^* X_o + u_o^* = 0$.[8] Figure 2–3 shows a supporting hyperplane for (efficient) DMU_3 with equation $\frac{3}{2}y - 1x - \frac{9}{2} = 0$, where these coefficient values are obtained from the row for DMU_3 in table 2–1. For inefficient DMUs, the objective function value, w_o^*, measures the distance to the closest supporting hyperplane. For example, the supporting hyperplane $(\frac{3}{2}y - 1x - \frac{9}{2} = 0)$ for DMU_3 and the parallel hyperplane $(\frac{3}{2}y - 1x - \frac{9}{2} = -4)$ that passes through DMU_7 are an $L1$ distance of 4 units apart.

As may be evident from the geometry of the envelopment surface, the Additive model has, as a consequence, variable returns to scale. This is a consequence of the presence of the convexity constraint $(\vec{1}\lambda = 1)$ in the primal problem or, equivalently, the presence of the associated uncon-

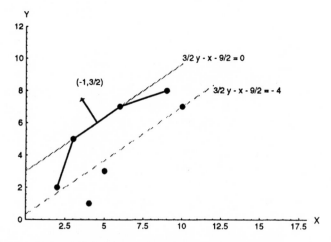

Figure 2–3.   Facet-defining hyperplane for the additive model.

strained variable u_o in the dual. The basis for this relationship will be more fully developed in the following sections.[9]

It should be obvious that the optimal objective function values for the Additive model (for inefficient DMUs) are dependent upon the units of measurement. However, it is possible to obtain unit independence by normalization, as discussed in chapter 3. An interesting additional consequence of the convexity constraint[10] established by Ali and Seiford (1990) is translation invariance of the envelopment surface. Specifically, replacing the values y_{rj} and x_{ij} by the new (translated) values

$$\hat{y}_{rj} = y_{rj} + c_r \quad r = 1, \ldots, s$$

$$\hat{x}_{ij} = x_{ij} + d_i \quad i = 1, \ldots, m$$

(with c_r, $d_i > 0$) results in equivalent linear programming problems. Thus, for the Additive model, the classification of DMUs as efficient or inefficient is invariant with respect to an affine *translation* of the data.

3. Multiplicative Models

In contrast to the piecewise linear envelopment afforded by the majority of DEA models, multiplicative DEA models have been developed that allow a piecewise log-linear or a piecewise Cobb–Douglas envelopment. In addition to properties that relate this extension to the usual simple functional form in econometrics, the resulting multiplicative measures of efficiency have other advantages with natural extensions to multiple outputs and inputs.

As can be readily verified from the formulation given below, the Units Invariant Multiplicative model of Charnes, Cooper, Seiford, and Stutz (1983) results from the application of the Additive model to the logarithms of the original data values. Hence all interpretations and comments from the previous section again apply, but now in the transformed space $(\mathrm{Log}(X), \mathrm{Log}(Y))$.

Invariant Multiplicative Primal ($\mathbf{InvMult_P}$)	**Invariant Multiplicative Dual** ($\mathbf{InvMult_D}$)

$$\min_{\lambda, s^+, s^-} \quad z_o = -\vec{\mathbf{1}} s^+ - \vec{\mathbf{1}} s^-$$

s.t.
$$\overrightarrow{\mathrm{Log}(Y)}\, \lambda - s^+ = \overrightarrow{\mathrm{Log}(Y_o)}$$
$$\overrightarrow{\mathrm{Log}(X)}\, \lambda + s^- = \overrightarrow{\mathrm{Log}(X_o)}$$
$$\vec{\mathbf{1}} \lambda = 1$$
$$\lambda, s^+, s^- \geq 0$$

$$\max_{\mu, v} \quad w_o = \mu^{\mathrm{T}} \overrightarrow{\mathrm{Log}(Y_o)} - v^{\mathrm{T}} \overrightarrow{\mathrm{Log}(X_o)} + u_o$$

s.t.
$$\mu^{\mathrm{T}} \overrightarrow{\mathrm{Log}(Y)} - v^{\mathrm{T}} \overrightarrow{\mathrm{Log}(X)} + u_o \vec{\mathbf{1}} \leq 0$$
$$-\mu^{\mathrm{T}} \leq -\vec{\mathbf{1}}$$
$$-v^{\mathrm{T}} \leq -\vec{\mathbf{1}}$$
$$\mu_o \text{ free}$$

However, two additional observations are worthwhile. First, the translation invariance property of the Additive model, valid for the transformed data $(\text{Log}(X), \text{Log}(Y))$, is equivalent to scale (units) invariance for the original data (X, Y). Second, the piecewise linear envelopment of the Additive model in the transformed space yields a piecewise Cobb–Douglas envelopment surface in the original data space of observations. For example, the facet joining DMU_1 and DMU_2 in the transformed space with equation

$$\alpha(\text{Log}(2), \text{Log}(2)) + (1 - \alpha)(\text{Log}(3), \text{Log}(5)), \quad 0 \leqslant \alpha \leqslant 1$$

is mapped in the original data space to the facet with the equation

$$(2^{\alpha}3^{1-\alpha}, 2^{\alpha}5^{1-\alpha}), \quad 0 \leqslant \alpha \leqslant 1.$$

The entire piecewise Cobb–Douglas envelopment surface for the units invariant multiplicative model is given in figure 2–4.

An interesting multiplicative model (which actually predates the previous model in the literature) results from the removal of the convexity constraint. This multiplicative model, originally developed in Charnes, Cooper, Seiford, and Stutz (1982), is given by the following dual linear programs:

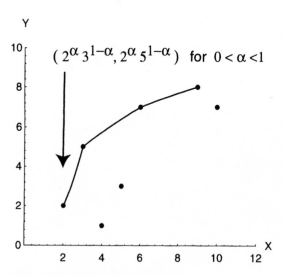

Figure 2–4.   Cobb–Douglas envelopment surface.

Variant Multiplicative Primal	**Variant Multiplicative Dual**
(VarMult$_P$)	**(VarMult$_D$)**

$$\min_{\lambda, s^+, s^-} \quad z_o = -\vec{\mathbf{1}}\,s^+ - \vec{\mathbf{1}}\,s^-$$

$$\text{s.t.} \quad \text{Log}(\vec{Y})\lambda - s^+ = \text{Log}(\vec{Y_o})$$

$$\text{Log}(\vec{X})\lambda + s^- = \text{Log}(X_o)$$

$$\lambda, s^+, s^- \geq 0$$

$$\max_{\mu, v} \quad w_o = \mu^{\mathsf{T}}\text{Log}(\vec{Y_o}) - v^{\mathsf{T}}\text{Log}(\vec{Z_o})$$

$$\text{s.t.} \quad \mu^{\mathsf{T}}\text{Log}(\vec{Y}) - v^{\mathsf{T}}\overrightarrow{\log(X)} \leq 0$$

$$-\mu^{\mathsf{T}} \leq -\vec{\mathbf{1}}$$

$$-v^{\mathsf{T}} \leq -\vec{\mathbf{1}}$$

Notice that the formulation is identical to the preceding Invariant Multiplicative model except for the absence of the convexity constraint ($\vec{\mathbf{1}}\lambda = 1$) in the normalized primal and the absence of the associated dual variable u_o in the dual. The effect of this modification is more easily seen from the dual side. The absence of u_o, (i.e., $u_o \equiv 0$) forces supporting hyperplanes (in the transformed space) to pass through the origin; as a result, both the number of efficient DMUs and the number of facets of the envelopment surface are reduced. More importantly, since supporting hyperplanes must pass through the origin, the model is restricted to piecewise constant returns to scale in the transformed data space. These connections between the convexity constraint, supporting hyperplanes, and returns to scale will be discussed more fully in the context of the remaining two models.

4. The BCC Model

We have seen that an inefficient DMU can be made fully efficient by projection onto a point $(\hat{X}_o, \hat{Y}_o)$ on the envelopment surface. The particular point of projection, $(\hat{X}_o, \hat{Y}_o)$, selected is dependent upon the DEA model employed. As shown below, it will also be dependent on the orientation. For instance, in an input orientation with the BCC model of Banker et al. (1984), one focuses on maximal movement toward the frontier through proportional reduction of inputs, whereas in an output orientation one focuses on maximal movement via proportional augmentation of outputs.

4.1. BCC Input Orientation

The dual linear programs for the BCC model with an input orientation are given below.

Input-Oriented BCC Primal (BCC$_P$-I)	Input-Oriented BCC Dual (BCC$_D$-I)

$$\min_{\theta, \lambda, s^+, s^-} \quad z_o = \theta - \varepsilon \cdot \vec{1} s^+ - \varepsilon \cdot \vec{1} s^-$$

$$\max_{\mu, v} \quad w_o = \mu^T Y_o + u_o$$

s.t.
$$Y\lambda - s^+ = Y_o$$
$$\theta X_o - X\lambda - s^- = 0$$
$$\vec{1}\lambda \geq 1$$
$$\lambda, s^+, s^- \geq 0$$

s.t.
$$v^T X_o = 1$$
$$\mu^T Y - v^T X + u_o \vec{1} \leq 0$$
$$-\mu^T \leq -\varepsilon \cdot \vec{1}$$
$$-v^T \leq -\varepsilon \cdot \vec{1}$$
$$u_o \text{ free}$$

Several new constructs appear in this BCC model formulation. The variable θ appears in the primal problem, and the constant ε, a non-Archimedean (infinitesimal) constant, appears both in the primal objective function and as a lower bound for the multipliers in the dual problem. The (scalar) variable θ is the (proportional) reduction applied to all inputs of DMU_o (the DMU being evaluated) to improve efficiency. This reduction is applied simultaneously to all inputs and results in a radial movement toward the envelopment surface. The presence of the non-Archimedean ε in the primal objective function effectively allows the minimization over θ to preempt the optimization involving the slacks. Thus, the optimization can be computed in a two-stage process with maximal reduction of inputs being achieved first, via the optimal θ^*; then, in the second stage, movement onto the efficient frontier is achieved via the slack variables (s^+ and s^-).[11] Evidently the following two statements are equivalent:

1. A DMU is efficient if and only if the following two conditions are satisfied:
    (a) $\theta^* = 1$;
    (b) all slacks are zero.
2. A DMU is efficient if and only if $w_o^* = z_o^* = 1$.

The nonzero slacks and the value of $\theta^* \leq 1$ identify the sources and amount of any inefficiencies that may be present.

Figure 2–5 illustrates the situation for the example DMUs of figure 2–1. In an input orientation, the objective is to produce the observed outputs with a minimum resource level. For DMU_5, using BCC$_P$–I with $(X_o, Y_o) = (5, 3)$ determines a convex combination of the vectors (X_i, Y_i), $i = 1, \ldots 5$ that is not below $y = 3$ $(= Y_o)$ and that allows as much shrinkage of X_o as possible. From table 2–2, the minimal value of θ^* is 7/15 for $\lambda^* = (2/3, 1/3, 0, 0, 0, 0, 0)$. Thus condition 1(a) for

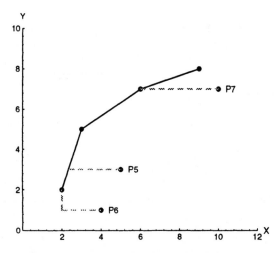

Figure 2–5. Envelopment surface for the BCC-Input model.

Table 2–2. Solution Values for the Input-Oriented BCC Model

DMU	θ^*	s^+	s^-	λ	w_j^*	μ	v	u_o
				Primal Problem (BCC_p-I)		*Dual Problem (BBC_D-I)*		
1	1	0	0	$\lambda_1 = 1$	1	1/6	1/2	2/3
2	1	0	0	$\lambda_2 = 1$	1	1/3	1/3	$-2/3$
3	1	0	0	$\lambda_3 = 1$	1	1/4	1/6	$-3/4$
4	1	0	0	$\lambda_4 = 1$	1	1/3	1/9	$-5/3$
5	7/15	0	0	$\lambda_1 = 2/3, \lambda_2 = 1/3$	7/15	1/15	1/5	4/15
6	1/2	1	0	$\lambda_1 = 1$	$\frac{1}{2} - \varepsilon$	ε	1/4	$\frac{1}{2} - 2\varepsilon$
7	3/5	0	0	$\lambda_3 = 1$	3/5	3/20	1/10	$-9/20$

efficiency as given above fails to be satisfied. The input shrinkage to $\frac{7}{15}X_5 = \frac{7}{15} \times 5 = \frac{7}{3}$ and all slacks zero projects DMU_5 onto the point $(\hat{X}_5, \hat{Y}_5) = (2\frac{1}{3}, 3) = (X\lambda^*, Y\lambda^*)$. DMUs 1–4 are efficient ($\theta^* = 1$, $s^+ = 0, s^- = 0$) and determine the piecewise linear envelopment surface, with $(\hat{X}_5, \hat{Y}_5)$ lying on the segment connecting P_1 and P_2.

It should be noted that while the envelopment surfaces for the BCC model and the Additive model are identical, the objective function values (efficiency scores) and, more importantly, the efficient projections[12] differ. This is perhaps most evident for DMU_6. The use of $BCC-I$ yields a projection onto $(2, 2)$, the point associated with P_1 on the envelopment surface. This differs from the Additive model of section 2, where the projection point is $(3, 5)$ for P_6 and the projection path has an $L1$ distance of 5 as obtained from the slacks $s^{+*} = 4$ and $s^{-*} = 1$. (Compare figures 2–2 and 2–5.) In the present ($BCC-I$) case, the projection path consists of input reduction by $\theta^* = 1/2$ and final movement to the frontier through the slack value $s^{+*} = 1$. Note, however, that the Additive and BCC models both characterize P_6 as inefficient. More generally, as shown in Ahn et al. (1988), a DMU is characterized as inefficient in one of these models if and only if it is characterized as inefficient by the other model as well. Differences in the actual efficiency scores/projections simply reflect the metrics used in the two models.

4.2. BCC Output Orientation

As can be seen from the formulation below, the essential difference between the previous input-oriented BCC model and the output-oriented BCC model is that the LP now *maximizes* on ϕ to achieve proportional output augmentation. Here the normalizing constraint for the multiplier form (the dual problem) now involves μY_0, while vX_0 appears in the objective function. (The cause for this rearrangement will become evident in section 6 on ratio forms.)

Output-Oriented BCC Primal
(BCC$_P$–O)

$$\max_{\phi,\lambda,s^+,s^-} z_o = \phi + \varepsilon \cdot \vec{1}s^+ + \varepsilon \cdot \vec{1}s^-$$

s.t. $\phi Y_o - Y\lambda + s^+ = 0$

$X\lambda + s^- = X_o$

$\vec{1}\lambda = 1$

$\lambda, s^+, s^- \geq 0$

Output-Oriented BCC Dual
(BCC$_D$–O)

$$\min_{\mu,v,v_o} q_o = v^T X_o + v_0$$

s.t. $\mu^T Y_o = 1$

$-\mu^T Y + v^T X + v_0 \vec{1} \geq 0$

$\mu^T \geq \varepsilon \cdot \vec{1}$

$v^T \geq \varepsilon \cdot \vec{1}$

v_o free

In an output orientation, the focus shifts from input resource minimization; the objective is to maximize output production while not exceeding the given resource levels. The interpretation is similar to that applied in section 4.1. for the input orientation: the above output-oriented model,

BCC_P-O, attempts via ϕ^* to achieve as much expansion of Y_o as the constraints will allow.

We turn now to interpreting the multiplier problem in BCC_D-O above to illustrate what is occurring in the dual space. In the dual problem BCC_D-O, the objective is to find a supporting hyperplane (i.e., a hyperplane that lies on or above all the DMUs) that minimizes the vertical distance from the hyperplane to the DMU being analyzed. In this interpretation, v_o plays the role of a y intercept. From table 2–3, the closest supporting hyperplane for DMU_5 has the equation $\frac{1}{3}y - \frac{2}{9}x + 1 = 0$, which forms the facet of the envelopment surface joining DMU_2 and DMU_3. The objective function value $w_5^* = 19/9$ is the maximal proportional increase in output levels, i.e., ϕ^*Y_o. As illustrated in figure 2–6, DMU_5 is projected onto the point $(5, 6\frac{1}{3})$. Solving BCC_D-O for the other DMUs yields the envelopment surface in figure2–6, where the remaining inefficient points are projected onto those segments of supporting hyperplanes that envelop the convex hull. We again emphasize that this proportional output augmentation *by itself* may not be sufficient to achieve efficiency. Additional movement to the envelopment surface may be necessary and is accomplished via positive input and/or output slack values. Thus for DMU_7 the efficient projection to $(X_7, Y_7) \rightarrow (\hat{X}_7, \hat{Y}_7) = (X_7 - s^{-*}, \phi^*Y_7 + s^{+*}) = (9, 8)$ requires both an output augmentation portion (with $\phi^* = 8/7$) *and* the slack value $s^{-*} = 1$.

Finally, the reader should note in figure 2–5 and 2–6 that while the envelopment surfaces are identical for both the input and the output orientations for the BCC model, an inefficient DMU is projected to *different* points on the envelopment surface. For example, with an input orientation, DMU_5 was projected onto the point $(2\frac{1}{3}, 3)$ while in the

Table 2–3. Solution values for the output-oriented BCC model

| DMU | Primal Problem (BCC_p-O) | | | | Dual Problem (BCC_D-O) | | | |
	ϕ^*	s^+	s^-	λ	q_j^*	μ	v	v_o
1	1	0	0	$\lambda_1 = 1$	1	1/2	3/2	2
2	1	0	0	$\lambda_2 = 1$	1	1/5	1/5	2/5
3	1	0	0	$\lambda_3 = 1$	1	1/7	2/21	3/7
4	1	0	0	$\lambda_4 = 1$	1	1/8	1/24	5/8
5	19/9	0	0	$\lambda_2 = 1/3, \lambda_3 = 2/3$	19/9	1/3	2/9	1
6	17/3	0	0	$\lambda_2 = 2/3, \lambda_3 = 1/3$	17/3	1	2/3	3
7	8/7	0	1	$\lambda_4 = 1$	$\frac{8}{7} + \varepsilon$	1/7	ε	$\frac{8}{7} - 9\varepsilon$

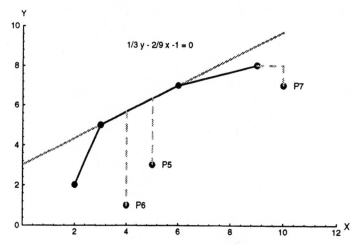

Figure 2–6. Envelopment surface for the output-oriented BCC model.

output orientation, DMU_5 was projected onto $(5, 6\frac{1}{3})$. This simply reflects
the focus of the orientation, i.e., whether the emphasis is on input
reduction or output augmentation. Efficiency characterizations are
otherwise the same: an optimal objective function value of one with all
slacks identically zero. In particular, a DMU is characterized as efficient
with an output orientation if and only if it is characterized as efficient with
an input orientation applied to the same data.

5. The CCR Model

The CCR model of Charnes, Cooper, and Rhodes (1978) also admits
both input and output orientations, and the formulation is similar to that
for the BCC model. However, the envelopment surface for the CCR
model, as seen from figures 2–7 and 2–8 below, is different from the
envelopment surfaces of the previously described models.

5.1. CCR Input Orientation

In the dual linear programs for the input-oriented CCR model given
below, the reader should note that neither the convexity constraint
$(\vec{1}\lambda = 1)$ nor the variable u_o appears in the formulation.

(Input-Oriented CCR Primal)	(Input-Oriented CCR Dual)
(CCR$_P$–I)	(CCR$_D$–I)

$$\min_{\theta, \lambda, s^+, s^-} \quad z_o = \theta - \varepsilon \cdot \vec{1}s^+ - \varepsilon \cdot \vec{1}s^-$$

$$\max_{\mu, v} \quad w_o = \mu^T Y_o$$

s.t. $\quad Y\lambda - s^+ = Y_o$

$\qquad \theta X_o - X\lambda - s^- = 0$

$\qquad \lambda, s^+, s^- \geqslant 0$

s.t. $\quad v^T X_o = 1$

$\qquad \mu^T Y - v^T X \leqslant 0$

$\qquad -\mu^T \leqslant -\varepsilon \cdot \vec{1}$

$\qquad -v^T \leqslant -\varepsilon \cdot \vec{1}$

The absence of the convexity constraint enlarges the feasible region for CCR_P from the convex hull considered in the BCC_P model to the *conical* hull of (or the convex cone generated by) the DMUs. The result, as can be seen from the values for z^* in table 2–4, is a reduction in the number of efficient DMUs; in fact, only DMU_2, receives an efficiency rating of 1.

The effect of enlarging the feasible region to the conical hull is easily visualized as follows. The interpretation for the envelopment problem CCR_P-I with $(X_o, Y_o) = (6, 7)$ is the selection of a point in the cone $\{(X\lambda, Y\lambda) \mid \lambda \geqslant 0\}$ that allows maximal input reduction of X_o. This point will lie on the ray through (X_2, Y_2), and therefore $\theta_3^* = 7/10$. Hence DMU_3 is projected onto the boundary point $(4\frac{1}{5}, 7)$. From the optimal λ^* values in table 2–4, it is readily apparent that each DMU is projected onto this ray through (X_2, Y_2), and thus the envelopment surface for $CCR-I$ is the ray $\{\alpha(X_2, Y_2) \mid \alpha \geqslant 0\}$, as illustrated in figure 2–7.

The comments of section 4.1 regarding the role of the non-Archimedean constant, ε, continue to apply for the CCR model. More importantly, we again emphasize that proportional input reduction with θ^* may not *by*

Table 2–4. Solution Values for the Input-oriented CCR Model

DMU	Primal Problem (CCR_p–I)				Dual Problem (CCR_D–I)		
	$z_j^* = \theta^*$	s^+	s^-	λ	w_j^*	μ	v
1	3/5	0	0	$\lambda_2 = .4$	3/5	3/10	1/2
2	1	0	0	$\lambda_2 = 1$	1	1/5	1/3
3	7/10	0	0	$\lambda_2 = 1.4$	7/10	1/10	1/6
4	8/15	0	0	$\lambda_2 = 1.6$	8/15	1/15	1/9
5	9/25	0	0	$\lambda_2 = .6$	9/25	3/25	1/5
6	3/20	0	0	$\lambda_2 = .2$	3/20	3/20	1/4
7	21/50	0	0	$\lambda_2 = 1.4$	21/50	3/50	1/10

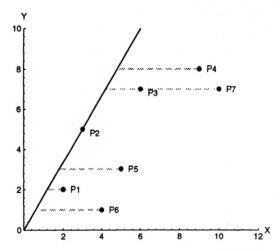

Figure 2–7.   Envelopment surface for the input-oriented CCR model.

itself be sufficient to achieve efficiency. This may not be manifest, since for any two-dimensional example the slack values will always be zero. However, the reader should be forewarned that in higher-dimensional (multiple-input multiple-output) examples, positive input and output slacks are frequently necessary to reach the envelopment surface and achieve full efficiency. In particular, it may be necessary to augment some outputs *and* reduce some inputs in order to achieve efficiency.

Table 2–5.   Solution Values for the Output-Oriented CCR Model

DMU	*Primal problem (CCR$_p$–O)*				*Dual problem (CCR$_D$–O)*		
	$z_j^* = \phi^*$	s^+	s^-	λ	q_j^*	μ	ν
1	5/3	0	0	$\lambda_2 = 2/3$	5/3	1/2	5/6
2	1	0	0	$\lambda_2 = 1$	1	1/5	1/3
3	10/7	0	0	$\lambda_2 = 2$	10/7	1/7	5/21
4	15/8	0	0	$\lambda_2 = 3$	15/8	1/8	5/24
5	25/9	0	0	$\lambda_2 = 5/3$	25/9	1/3	5/9
6	20/3	0	0	$\lambda_2 = 4/3$	20/3	1	5/3
7	50/21	0	0	$\lambda_2 = 10/3$	50/21	1/7	5/21

5.2. CCR Output Orientation

For the output-oriented CCR model, maximal output augmentation is again accomplished through the variable ϕ applied to the output vector Y_o of the DMU being analyzed (see solutions, table 2–5). While an interpretation similar to that employed in section 5.1 for the input orientation could be applied here for the variable ϕ, we instead examine the dual problem, CCR_D-O.

Output-Oriented CCR Primal **(CCR_P–O)**	**Output-Oriented CCR Dual** **(CCR_D–O)**
$\max\limits_{\phi,\lambda,s^+,s^-} \quad z_o = \phi + \varepsilon \cdot \vec{1}s^+ + \varepsilon \cdot \vec{1}s^-$	$\min\limits_{\mu,v} \quad q_o = v^T X_o$
s.t. $\quad \phi Y_o - Y\lambda + s^+ = 0$	s.t. $\quad \mu^T Y_o = 1$
$X\lambda + s^- = X_o$	$-\mu^T Y + v^T X \geq 0$
$\lambda, s^+, s^- \geq 0$	$\mu^T \geq \varepsilon \cdot \vec{1}$
	$v^T \geq \varepsilon \cdot \vec{1}$

Recall that in section 4.2 the variable v_o for BCC_D-O played the role of a y-intercept. For the above CCR_D-O formulation (since $v_o \equiv 0$), the supporting-hyperplane interpretation requires supporting hyperplanes to pass through the origin. This yields the efficient frontier given by the ray $\{a(X_2, Y_2) \mid a \geq 0\}$, as illustrated in figure 2–8.

The reader should again note that while the two orientations yield identical envelopment surfaces, an inefficient DMU is projected to different points on the frontier under the input and output orientations. Nevertheless, the same result holds as for the *BCC* model. That is, a DMU is characterized as efficient in an input-oriented *CCR* model if and only if it is characterized as efficient in the corresponding output-oriented *CCR* model. On the other hand, the relations between the *CCR* and *BCC* models are somewhat different. If a DMU is characterized as efficient in the *CCR* model, it will also be characterized as efficient with the *BCC* model; the converse does not necessarily hold, as indicated by what happened in going from table 2–2 to table 2–4 (see Ahn et al. 1988, for an analytical development).

6. Ratio Form Characterizations

To facilitate comparisons between the basic DEA models, the previous sections have focused on dual linear programming characterizations. The

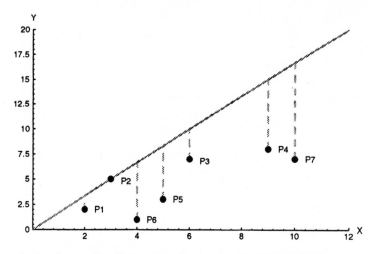

Figure 2–8. Supporting Hyperplane for the output-oriented CCR model.

CCR and BCC models have alternate ratio characterizations. These ratio forms have a strong intuitive appeal, since they extend the engineering-ratio approach for efficiency measures (from the single-input, single-output case) to multiple-input, multiple-output situations. In fact, the LP characterizations presented in sections 4 and 5 for the CCR and BCC models were originally derived from the ratio forms.

6.1. CCR Ratio Form

The essential characteristic of the CCR ratio construction is the reduction of the multiple-output–multiple-input situation (for each DMU) to that of a single "virtual" output and a single "virtual" input. For a DMU, the ratio of this single virtual output to single virtual input provides a measure of efficiency that is a function of the multipliers. This ratio, which is to be maximized, forms the objective function for the particular DMU_o being evaluated, so that symbolically

$$\max_{u,v} h_o(u, v) = \frac{\Sigma_r u_r y_{ro}}{\Sigma_i v_i x_{io}} \tag{2.1}$$

Of course, without further additional constraints, equation (2.1) is unbounded. The additional set of (technological) constraints (one for each DMU) reflects the condition that the ratio of virtual output to virtual input of every DMU should be less than or equal to unity. The mathematical programming problem for the CCR (input-oriented) ratio form is

$$\max_{u,v} \frac{\sum_r u_r y_{ro}}{\sum_i v_i x_{io}}$$

$$\frac{\sum_r u_r y_{rj}}{\sum_i v_i x_{ij}} \leq 1, \quad \text{for } j = 0, 1, \ldots, n \qquad (CCR\text{--}IR)$$

$$\frac{u_r}{\sum_i v_i x_{io}} \geq \varepsilon, \quad \text{for } r = 1, \ldots, s$$

$$\frac{v_i}{\sum_i v_i x_{io}} \geq \varepsilon, \quad \text{for } i = 1, \ldots, m$$

The above ratio form yields an infinite number of optimal solutions; if (u^*, v^*) is optimal, then $(\beta u^*, \beta v^*)$ is also optimal for $\beta > 0$. One can define an equivalence relation that partitions the set of feasible solutions of $(CCR\text{--}IR)$ into equivalence classes. The transformation developed by Charnes and Cooper (1962) for linear fractional programming selects a representative solution (i.e., the solution (u, v) for which $v^T X_o = 1$) from each equivalence class and yields the following equivalent linear programming problem:[13]

$$\max_{\mu,v} \quad \omega_o = \sum_r \mu_r y_{ro}$$

$$\text{s.t.} \qquad \sum_i v_i x_{io} = 1$$

$$\sum_r \mu_r y_{rj} - \sum_i v_i x_{ij} \leq 0 \qquad (CCR_D\text{--}I)$$

$$\mu_r \geq \varepsilon$$

$$v_i \geq \varepsilon$$

whose LP dual problem is

$$\min_{\theta, \lambda, s_r^+, s_i^-} \quad z_o = \theta - \varepsilon \sum_r s_r^+ - \varepsilon \sum_i s_i^-$$

$$\text{s.t.} \qquad \sum_j \lambda_j Y_j - s^+ = Y_o$$

$$\theta X_o - \sum_j \lambda_j X_j - s^- = 0 \qquad (CCR_P\text{--}I)$$

$$\lambda_j, s_r^+, s_i^- \geq 0$$

The reader should verify that these LP problem formulations are equivalent to those given in section 5.1.

6.1.1. CCR Output Ratio Form. Alternately, one could have started with the output side and considered instead the ratio of virtual input to virtual output as given by

$$\min_{u,\, v} \quad \frac{v^T X_o}{\mu^T Y_o}$$

$$\text{s.t.} \quad \frac{v^T X_j}{\mu^T Y_j} \geq 1 \quad j = 1, \ldots, n \qquad (CCR\text{-}OR)$$

$$\frac{u}{\mu^T Y_o} \geq \varepsilon \vec{\mathbf{1}}$$

$$\frac{v}{\mu^T Y_o} \geq \varepsilon \vec{\mathbf{1}}$$

Again, the Charnes–Cooper (1962) transformation for linear fractional programming yields model $CCR_D\text{-}O$ with its associated dual problem, $CCR_P\text{-}O$.

Output-Oriented CCR Primal $(CCR_P\text{-}O)$	Output-Oriented CCR Dual $(CCR_D\text{-}O)$
$$\max_{\phi,\lambda,s^+,s^-} \quad z_o = \phi + \varepsilon \cdot \vec{\mathbf{1}}s^+ + \varepsilon \cdot \vec{\mathbf{1}}s^-$$	$$\min_{\mu,v} \quad q_o = v^T X_o$$
$$\text{s.t.} \quad \phi Y_o - Y\lambda + s^+ = 0$$	$$\text{s.t.} \quad \mu^T Y_o = 1$$
$$X\lambda + s^- = X_o$$	$$-\mu^T Y + v^T X \geq 0$$
$$\lambda, s^+, s^- \geq 0$$	$$\mu^T \geq \varepsilon \cdot \vec{\mathbf{1}}$$
	$$v^T \geq \varepsilon \cdot \vec{\mathbf{1}}$$

6.2. BCC Ratio Form

The BCC ratio form differs from the CCR form only by the addition of a variable $\tilde{u}_o$ in the input orientation and a variable $\tilde{v}_o$ in the output orientation. The formulations are given below.

The BCC Ratio Model (INPUT Orientation)

$$\max_{u,\bar{v},\bar{u}_o} \quad \frac{uY_o + \bar{u}_o}{vX_o}$$

$$\text{s.t.} \quad \frac{uY_j + \bar{u}_o}{vX_j} \leqslant 1 \quad j = 1, \ldots, n$$

$$u/vX_o \geqslant \varepsilon \cdot \vec{\mathbf{1}}$$

$$v/vX_o \geqslant \varepsilon \cdot \vec{\mathbf{1}}$$

The BCC Ratio Model (OUTPUT Orientation)

$$\min_{u,v,\tilde{v}_o} \quad \frac{vX_o + \tilde{v}_o}{uY_o}$$

$$\text{s.t.} \quad \frac{vX_j + \tilde{v}_o}{uY_j} \geqslant 1 \quad j = 1, \ldots, n$$

$$u/uY_o \geqslant \varepsilon \cdot \vec{\mathbf{1}}$$

$$v/uY_o \geqslant \varepsilon \cdot \vec{\mathbf{1}}$$

Again, the Charnes–Cooper transformation of Fractional Programming applied to *BCC–IR* and *BCC–OR* yield the pairs of linear programs presented in sections 4.1 and 4.2.

The reader should note that, for the BCC and CCR Ratio formulations, a change in orientation simply amounts to inverting the ratio. The effect is less obvious for the linear programming formulations of the BCC and CCR models, since the Charnes–Cooper transformation in fractional programming selects the denominator of the ratio for the normalizing constraint and uses the numerator of the ratio as the objective function of the equivalent linear program. Thus, the effect of passing from an input to an output orientation for the BCC and CCR models is the observed rearrangement of normalizing constraint and objective function for the (multiplier side) linear program, as noted in section 4.2.

7. Summary of Model Features

The discussion in the preceding sections has focused on the geometry involved in the basic DEA models. It should serve to underscore that different results may be achieved not only with the selection of different models but also with the different orientations within a model.

The crucial choices for the basic models examined are the envelopment surface and the projection path to the envelopment surface for the inefficient DMUs. Essentially, an analyst must choose between the piecewise constant returns-to-scale surface (of the CCR model) and the variable returns-to-scale surface (given by the BCC or Additive models). For a given envelopment, the second choice is the projection path to a point on the efficient frontier. For the CCR and BCC models, this reduces to selecting between an input or output orientation. If variable returns-to-scale production possibilities are chosen, however, the choices are three: an input-oriented radial metric or an output-oriented radial metric with the BCC model or the $L1$ metric of the Additive model. As described in section 4, the envelopment surface is identical for all three choices (see figures 2–2, 2–5, and 2–6); the comparison point (efficient projection) for an inefficient DMU, however, is different for the three models.

We also emphasize that an important effect of model selection is the types of returns-to-scale properties associated with these different model choices. As demonstrated in earlier sections, restrictions on returns to scale can be interpreted equivalently in terms of a restriction on λ or a restriction on supporting hyperplanes. For the piecewise linear envelopment surfaces (CCR, BCC, and Additive models), no restriction on $\Sigma\lambda$, corresponds to piecewise constant returns to scale, since all supporting hyperplanes must pass through the origin. The (convexity constraint) restriction $\Sigma\lambda_i = 1$ admits variable returns to scale, since supporting hyperplanes are not restricted to pass through the origin.

Table 2–6 summarizes the features for the basic DEA models. As we have observed, model selection carries with it an implicit choice among three different envelopment surfaces.

1. The CCR model results in a piecewise linear, constant returns-to-scale envelopment surface.
2. The BCC and Additive models yield in a piecewise linear, variable returns-to-scale envelopment surface.
3. The Multiplicative models yield piecewise log-linear envelopment surfaces.

The units-invariance property of the objective function values for the BCC and CCR models is a consequence of the theoretical properites of ε, the non-Archimedean infinitesimal. In principle, the product of ε and the sum of the slacks is not dependent upon the units of measurement, since the purpose of this term in the objective function is to distinguish between efficient and inefficient DMUs on the boundary. Numerical difficulties

Table 2–6. Comparison of Basic DEA Models

Model	Returns to Scale	Envelopment Surface	Projection Map	Envelopment Metric (Range)	Units Invariant	Involves Non-Archimedean
Additive	Variable	Piecewise Linear	$Y_o \to Y_o + S^+$ $X_o \to X_o - S^-$	$L1$ $(z \leq 0)$	No	No
Invariant Multiplicative	Variable (Log-linear)	Piecewise Cobb–Douglas	$Y_o \to Y_o e^{s^+}$ $X_o \to X_o e^{-s^-}$	e^{L1} $(e^{s^+} \geq 1,\ 0 < e^{s^-} \leq 1)$	Yes	No
Variant Multiplicative	Constant (Log-linear)	Piecewise Log-linear	$Y_o \to Y_o e^{s^+}$ $X_o \to X_o e^{-s^-}$	e^{L1} $(e^{s^+} \geq 1,\ 0 < e^{s^-} \leq 1)$	No	No
BCC Input	Variable	Piecewise Linear	$Y_o \to Y_o + s^+$ $X_o \to \theta X_o - s^-$	Radial (Inputs) $(0 < \theta \leq 1)$	Yes	Yes
BCC Output	Variable	Piecewise Linear	$Y_o \to \phi Y_o + s^+$ $X_o \to X_o - s^-$	Radial (Outputs) $(\phi \geq 1)$	Yes	Yes
CCR Input	Piecewise Constant	Piecewise Linear	$Y_o \to Y_o + s^+$ $X_o \to \theta X_o - s^-$	Radial (Inputs) $(0 < \theta \leq 1)$	Yes	Yes
CCR Output	Piecewise Constant	Piecewise Linear	$Y_o \to \phi Y_o + s^+$ $X_o \to X_o - s^-$	Radial (Outputs) $(\phi \geq 1)$	Yes	Yes

can arise, however, in computation, with the selection of an arbitrarily small number (10^{-6}) to approximate ε. The correct algorithmic implementation requires a two-stage (preemptive) approach. These issues are discussed in chapter 4.

In summary, the choice of a particular DEA model determines 1) the implicit returns-to-scale properties; 2) the geometry of the envelopment surface (with respect to which efficiency measurements will be made); and 3) the efficient projection, i.e., the inefficient DMU's path to the efficient frontier. Due to the potential consequences on the study and the results obtained, selection of a basic DEA model for an analysis should be made only after careful consideration.

We conclude this chapter by stressing that our coverage has been limited to a basic subset of the DEA models that have appeared in the literature.[14] While some additional models that arise as natural extensions to those already covered are discussed in chapter 3, an exhaustive treatment of all DEA models with their variations falls outside the scope of these introductory chapters.

Notes

1. This is the work that M. J. Farrell (1957) cites as the source of his (activity analysis) characterizations.

2. Notable exceptions are Ahn, Charnes, and Cooper (1988) and Ahn and Seiford (1990).

3. This assumption can be relaxed (see Charnes et al., 1986 and Ali and Seiford, (1990).

4. It should be noted that X, Y, X_o, and Y_o, consist of the observed output and input values for the DMUs and are therefore constant. The variable sets for the linear programs are $\{\lambda, s^+, s^-\}$ and $\{\mu, v, u_o\}$, respectively.

5. s^+ and s^- are the slack vectors for the outputs and inputs, respectively, and $\vec{1}$ is a vector of ones.

6. This comparison point can be equivalently expressed by the efficient projection $(X_j, Y_j) \rightarrow (\hat{X}_j, \hat{Y}_j) = (X_j - s^{-*}, Y_j + s^{+*})$, which gives $(\hat{X}_j, \hat{Y}_j)$ as a point on the efficient frontier. Note that both of these expressions reduce to the identity mapping for (efficient) DMUs on the envelopment surface, since an efficient DMU has $s^{-*} = s^{+*} = 0$.

7. Via the duality theorem of linear programming, w_o is bounded above by zero, hence we are maximizing a nonpositive quantity.

8. Note that $(-v^*, \mu^*)$ is the normal to this hyperplane and $u_o^* = 0$ if and only if the plane passes through the origin.

9. A complete discussion is also given in Seiford and Thrall (1990).

10. The convexity constraint $\vec{1}\lambda = 1$ appears, for example, in the envelopment form problem for the Additive model.

11. See the discussion by Ali (chapter 4, this volume) for the way this preemption is observed without any need to specify the value of the non-Archimedean constant, ε.

12. For the BCC input orientation, the efficient projection is given by $(X_o, Y_o) \rightarrow (\hat{X}_o, \hat{Y}_o) = (\theta^* X_o - s^{-*}, Y_o + s^{+*})$ or, equivalently, $(\hat{X}_o, \hat{Y}_o) = (X\lambda^*, Y\lambda^*)$.

13. The change of variables to (μ, v) is a result of the transformation $\left(\mu \equiv \dfrac{u^T}{vX_o}, \right.$ $\left. v \equiv \dfrac{v^T}{vX_o} \right)$.

14. Hybrid models that combine portions of the envelopment surfaces from the BCC and CCR models can be obtained by replacing the convexity constraint $(\vec{1} \cdot \lambda = 1)$ with either $(\vec{1} \cdot \lambda \leq 1)$ or $(\vec{1} \cdot \lambda \geq 1)$. For complete details, the reader is referred to section 4.3 in Seiford and Thrall (1990).

3 EXTENSIONS TO DEA MODELS

1. Introduction

The basic DEA models discussed in the previous chapter are associated with the way the returns-to-scale, the geometry of the envelopment surface, and the efficient projections are identified. This array of choices provides considerable flexibility, which can be further increased by incorporating refinements or extensions to the basic theory. These valuable additions to the methodology of DEA allow one to fine tune an analysis to reflect managerial or organization factors, sharpen efficiency estimates, and/or overcome inconsistencies.

A number of useful enhancements have appeared in the literature, and a comprehensive treatment is beyond the scope of this text. We limit our coverage to four of the more important extensions that illustrate the adaptability of the basic DEA methodology. Although our presentation formulates an extension in terms of a particular DEA model, the reader should note that the extensions are applicable to any of the DEA models. The four extensions discussed below allow an analyst to treat both nondiscretionary and categorical inputs and outputs, to incorporate

49

judgment or ancillary managerial information, and to investigate efficiency change over multiple time periods.

2. Nondiscretionary Inputs and Outputs

The model formulations of chapter 2 implicitly assume that all inputs and outputs are discretionary, i.e., controlled by the management of each DMU and varied at its discretion. Thus, failure of a DMU to produce maximal output levels with minimal input consumption results in a decreased efficiency score. In any realistic situation, however, there may exist exogonously fixed or nondiscretionary inputs or outputs that are beyond the control of a DMU's management.[1] Instances from the DEA literature include snowfall or weather in evaluating the efficiency of maintenance units, soil characteristics and topography in different farms, number of competitors in the branches of a restaurant chain, local unemployment rates confronted by different U.S. Army recruitment units, age of facilities in different universities, and number of transactions (for a purely gratis service) in library performance.

For example, Banker and Morey (1986a) illustrate the impact of exogonously determined inputs that are not controllable in an analysis of a network of fast food restaurants. In their study, each of the 60 restaurants in the fast food chain consumes six inputs to produce three outputs. The three outputs (all controllable) correspond to breakfast, lunch, and dinner sales. Only two of the six inputs, expenditures for supplies and expenditures for labor, are discretionary. The other four inputs (age of store, advertising level, urban/rural location, and drive-in capability) are beyond the control of the individual restaurant manager. Their analysis clearly demonstrates the value of accounting for the nondiscretionary character of these inputs explicitly in the DEA models they employ; the result is identification of a considerably enhanced opportunity for targeted savings in the controllable inputs and targeted increases in the outputs.

The key to the proper mathematical treatment of a nondiscretionary variable lies in the observation that information about the extent to which a nondiscretionary input variable may be reduced is not meaningful for the DMU manager. Our initial formulation is in terms of the Additive model, but we remind the reader of our earlier comment that the extension is applicable (with slight modification) to any of the DEA models.

Suppose that the input and output variables may each be partitioned into subsets of discretionary (D) and nondiscretionary (N) variables. Thus,

$$I = \{1, 2, \ldots, m\} = I_D \cup I_N, \, I_D \cap I_N = \emptyset$$

and

$$O = \{1, 2, \ldots, s\} = O_D \cup O_N, \, O_D \cap O_N = \emptyset$$

The basic model formulation for the Additive model (with nondiscretionary variables) is given by

$$\min_{\lambda_j, s_r^+, s_r^-} - \left(\sum_{r \in O_D} s_r^+ + \sum_{i \in I_D} s_i^- \right)$$

$$\sum_{j=1}^{n} y_{rj} \lambda_j - s_r^+ = y_{ro} \qquad r = 1, \ldots, s$$

$$-\sum_{j=1}^{n} x_{ij} \lambda_j - s_i^- = -x_{io} \qquad i = 1, \ldots, m$$

$$\sum_{j=1}^{n} \lambda_j = 1$$

$$\lambda_j \geq 0, \qquad j = 1, \ldots, n$$

$$s_r^+ \geq 0, \qquad r = 1, \ldots, s$$

$$s_i^- \geq 0, \qquad i = 1, \ldots, m$$

where the index sets $r \in O_D$ and $i \in I_D$ are confined to the discretionary outputs and inputs.

Essentially, one omits the nondiscretionary input excesses and output slacks (those for I_N and O_N) from the objective function when the efficiency scores are computed, since they are beyond the control of the DMU manager. They are, however, incorporated in the constraints so that their presence is taken into account, as in the choice of the reference DMUs from which the pertinent relative efficiencies are secured.

In the case of the input- or output-oriented CCR and BCC models, the treatment of nondiscretionary inputs and outputs is similar. In particular, for an input orientation, it is not relevant to maximize the proportional decrease in the *entire* input vector. Such maximization (actually, the minimum value of θ) should be determined only with respect to the subvector that is composed of *discretionary* inputs. Thus the formulation for the input-oriented BCC model with nondiscretionary variables is given by

$$\min_{\theta, \lambda_j, s_r^+, s_i^-} \theta - \varepsilon \left(\sum_{r \in O_D} s_r^+ + \sum_{i \in I_D} s_i^- \right)$$

$$\sum_{j=1}^{n} y_{rj} \lambda_j - s_r^+ = y_{ro} \qquad r = 1, \ldots, s$$

$$\theta x_{io} - \sum_{j=1}^{n} x_{ij} \lambda_j - s_i^- = 0 \qquad i \in I_D$$

$$- \sum_{j=1}^{n} x_{ij} \lambda_j - s_i^- = -x_{io} \quad i \notin I_D$$

$$\sum_{j=1}^{n} \lambda_j = 1$$

$$\lambda_j \geq 0, \qquad j = 1, \ldots, n$$

$$s_r^+ \geq 0, \qquad r = 1, \ldots, s$$

$$s_i^- \geq 0, \qquad i = 1, \ldots, m$$

It is to be noted that the θ to be minimized appears only in the constraints for which $i \in I_D$, whereas the constraints for which $i \notin I_D$ operate only indirectly (as they should) because the input levels x_{io} are not subject to managerial control.

The necessary modifications to incorporate nondiscretionary variables for an output orientation as well as those for the other DEA models are straightforward and left to the reader. However, we should point out that there is an underlying and subtle issue associated with the concept of controllable outputs that is obscured by the symmetry of the input/output model formulations. Specifically, switching from an input to an output orientation is not as straightforward as it may appear and frequently causes interpretational difficulties for outputs not directly controllable, i.e., those outputs influenced only through associated input factors. An example of such an output would be sales that are influenced by advertising, market size, etc., but are not directly controllable. This issue will be discussed further in chapter 21.

3. Categorial Inputs and Outputs

Our previous development assumed that all inputs and outputs were continuous variables. However, ordinal variables frequently arise in realistic situations; some inputs or outputs may reflect the presence or absence of a particular capability (e.g., a drive-in facility) or may have a more natural representation as discrete levels (e.g., population categories). The importance of properly incorporating these discrete ordinal variables (dummy variables) into the basic DEA models was first argued by Banker and Morey (1986b):

> . . . suppose we are attempting to estimate the resources (such as labor and capital) that a branch of a bank needs to obtain a given level of deposits, given a population base of say 100,000, with a specific income, age, and other demographic characteristics. Then in DEA the branch in question might well be compared to a composite branch built from a branch with a population of 80,000 and another with a population of 120,000, both weighted equally. While this may seem like a very reasonable approximation, it is clear that the branches employed for this comparison would be less controversial if we were to insure that the peer group consisted only of branches with a population of 100,000 or less. We may allow a branch operating in an even more difficult situation, such as a branch with a population base of say only 80,000, to be included in the peer group, but not one with a larger population, since we might be unwilling to assume that the marginal productivity associated with this factor were the same for a branch with a population of 120,000 as that for the branch with a population of 100,000.
>
> The above considerations become even more important when one realizes that some factors in such relative efficiency analysis are 0–1 variables: some branches of a bank may have a drive-in capability and some others may not; some branches may have automatic tellers and some may not. What is desired for the above situations is a method for insuring that the composite reference members be constructed from DMUs which are in the same category or possibly from those in a category which is deemed to be operating in an even more difficult or unfavorable situation.

The principle expressed in the last sentence is conceptually quite simple. However, as Kamakura (1988) points out, it can be difficult to express correctly in terms of a model formulation. Banker and Morey (1986b) propose a mixed-integer LP formulation for discretionary categorical variables that incorrectly prescribes categories that are undefined or meaningless.

Instead of focusing on an LP model formulation, a better and more easily applied approach is to adapt the LP solution algorithm. This has the additional advantage, which can be significant in extensions, of allowing *multiple* categorical variables.

Suppose that an input variable can assume one of L levels $(1, 2, \ldots, L)$. These L values effectively partition the set of DMUs into categories. Specifically, the set of decision-making units $D = \{1, 2, \ldots, n\} = D_1 \cup$

$D_2 \cup \ldots \cup D_L$, where $D_k = \{i \mid i \in D$ and input value is $k\}$ and $D_j \cap D_k = \emptyset$, $j \neq k$. We wish to evaluate a decision-making unit with respect to the envelopment surface determined for the units contained in its and all preceding categories. The following model specification allows decision-making unit $DMU_o \in D_K$, $K \in \{1, \ldots, L\}$ to be evaluated with respect to the units in $\cup_{k=1}^{K} D_k$.

$$\min_{\lambda_j, s_r^+, s_i^-} \quad - \left(\sum_{r=1}^{s} s_r^+ + \sum_{i=1}^{m} s_i^- \right)$$

$$\sum_{j \in \cup_{k=1}^{K} D_k} y_{rj} \lambda_j - s_r^+ = y_{ro} \qquad r = 1, \ldots, s$$

$$- \sum_{j \in \cup_{k=1}^{K} D_k} x_{ij} \lambda_j - s_i^- = -x_{io} \qquad i = 1, \ldots, m$$

$$\sum_{j \in \cup_{k=1}^{K} D_k} \lambda_j = 1$$

$$\lambda_j \geq 0, \qquad j \in \cup_{k=1}^{K} D_k$$

$$s_r^+ \geq 0, \qquad r = 1, \ldots, s$$

$$s_i^- \geq 0, \qquad i = 1, \ldots, m$$

Thus, the above specification allows one to evaluate all units $l \in D_1$ with respect to the units in D_1, all units $l \in D_2$ with respect to the units in $D_1 \cup D_2, \ldots$, all units $l \in D_C$ with respect to the units in $\cup_{k=1}^{C} D_k, \ldots$, and all $l \in D_L$ with respect to the entire set of in $D = \cup_{k=1}^{L} D_k$. Although our presentation is for the Additive model, it should be obvious that categorical variables can be easily incorporated in this manner for any DEA model. In addition, the above formulation is easily implemented in the underlying LP solution algorithm via a candidate list.

The preceding development rests on the assumption that there is a natural nesting or hierarchy of the categories. Each DMU should be compared only with DMUs in its and more disadvantaged categories, i.e., those operating under the same or worse conditions. If the categories are not comparable (e.g., public universities vs. private universities), then a separate analysis should be performed for each category.[2]

4. Incorporating Judgment or A Priori Knowledge

Perhaps the most significant of the proposed extensions to DEA is the concept of restricting the possible range for the multipliers. In the basic

DEA models of the previous chapter, the only explicit restriction on multipliers is positivity (guaranteed by the lower bounds of either ε or 1). This flexibility is often presented as advantageous in applications of the DEA methodology; a priori specification of the multipliers is not required, and each DMU is evaluated in the best possible light.

In some situations, however, this *complete* flexibility may give rise to undesirable consequences, since it can allow a DMU to appear efficient in ways that are difficult to justify. Specifically, the model often assigns unreasonably low or excessively high values to the multipliers in an attempt to drive the efficiency rating for a particular DMU as high as possible.

Three situations for which it has proven beneficial to impose various levels of control are the following:

1. the analysis ignores additional information that cannot be directly incorporated into the model or that contradicts expert opinion;
2. management has strong preferences about the relative importance of different factors and what determines best practice; and
3. for a small sample of DMUs, the method fails to discriminate, and all are efficient.

Imposing additional restrictions on the values that the multipliers can assume increases the power and flexibility of DEA and thus yields sharper efficiency estimates by incorporating expert information, managerial preference, or other judgment into the analysis.

Proposed techniques for enforcing these additional restrictions include imposing upper and lower bounds on individual multipliers (Dyson and Thanassoulis, 1988; Roll, Cook, and Golany, 1991); imposing bounds on ratios of multipliers (Thompson et al., 1986); appending multiplier inequalities (Wong and Beasley, 1990); and requiring multipliers to belong to given closed cones (Charnes et al., 1989).

To illustrate the general approach, suppose we wish to incorporate additional inequality constraints of the following form:

$$\mu \mathbf{a}_k^o + v \mathbf{a}_k^i \leq 0, \qquad k = 1, \ldots, K$$

where $\mathbf{a}_k^o$ is the s-vector of coefficients for the output multipliers, μ, and $\mathbf{a}_k^i$ is the m-vector of coefficients for the input multipliers. v.

Such constraints, of course, may be included in any of the DEA models. Here we consider their inclusion in the basic Additive model.

$$\max_{\mu,v,u_o} \quad w_o = \mu^T Y_o - v^T X_o + u_o$$

$$\text{s.t.} \quad \mu^T Y - v^T X + u_o \vec{1} \leq 0$$

$$\mu^T A^o + v^T A^i \leq 0$$

$$-\mu^T \leq -\vec{1}$$

$$-v^T \leq -\vec{1}$$

$$u_o \text{ free}$$

Each of the thus-introduced constraints corresponds to a variable z_k in the associated (dual) envelopment program. The K-vector of variables corresponding to the additional constraints is denoted $\mathbf{z}$. The coefficients of each of the K constraints are given by columns of the (s, k) matrix $\mathbf{A}^o$ and the (m, k) matrix $\mathbf{A}^i$.

$$\min_{\lambda, s^+, s^-, z} \quad z_o = -\vec{1} s^+ - \vec{1} s^-$$

$$\text{s.t.} \quad Y\lambda - s^+ + \mathbf{A}^o \mathbf{z} = Y_o$$

$$-X\lambda - s^- + \mathbf{A}^i \mathbf{z} = -X_o$$

$$\vec{1}\lambda = 1$$

$$\lambda, s^+, s^- \geq 0$$

The elements of the vectors $\mathbf{A}^o \mathbf{z}$ and $\mathbf{A}^i \mathbf{z}$ have been characterized in the literature as *residues*. They should not be confused with the standard slack variables that are also present. The residues allow adjustments to the efficiency score. Thus, introducing such restrictions on the multipliers has the effect of altering the envelopment surface.

The elegant Cone Ratio CCR model formulation of Charnes, Cooper, Wei, and Huang (1988) generalizes the CCR model of Charnes, Cooper, and Rhodes (1978) discussed in the previous chapter by requiring multipliers to belong to closed cones. The two dual problems are

Cone Ratio Primal   **Cone Ratio Dual**

$$\min_{\theta, \lambda, s^+, s^-} \quad \theta \qquad\qquad\qquad \max_{\mu,v} \quad \mu^T Y_o$$

$$\text{s.t.} \quad -\theta X_o + X\lambda \in V^* \qquad\qquad \text{s.t.} \quad v^T X_o = 1$$

$$-Y\lambda + Y_o \in U^* \qquad\qquad\qquad v^T X - \mu^T Y \in K$$

$$\lambda \in -K^* \qquad\qquad\qquad\qquad -\mu^T \in U$$

$$-v^T \in V$$

where $V \subset E_+^m$, $U \subset E_+^s$ are acute closed convex cones and V^* and U^* are the negative polar cones of V and U, respectively (see Yu, 1974).

If V and U are polyhedral cones represented in sum form (see Charnes et al., 1990) then the above Cone Ratio model is equivalent to a CCR model with transformed data. Specifically, if $V = \{A^T\alpha: \alpha \geqslant 0\}$ and $U = \{B^T\gamma: \gamma \geqslant 0\}$, then $V^* = \{v: Av \leqslant 0\}$ and $U^* = \{u: Bu \leqslant 0\}$. It is easily shown that the above Cone Ratio model coincides with a CCR model evaluating the same DMUs but with transformed data $\bar{Y} = BY$ and $\bar{X} = AX$. The important advantage of the sum form for polyhedral cones is thus revealed. Preprocessing (transforming) the data reduces the problem to the original CCR form, thus allowing access to existing DEA software codes without modification.

5. Window Analysis

In the examples of the previous sections, each DMU was observed only once, i.e., each example was a cross-sectional analysis of data. In actual studies, observations for DMUs are frequently available over multiple time periods (time series data), and it is often important to perform a panel data analysis where interest focuses on changes in efficiency over time. In such a setting, it is possible to perform DEA over time using a moving average analogue, where a DMU in each different period is treated as if it were a "different" DMU. Specifically, a DMU's performance in a particular period is contrasted with its performance in other periods in addition to the performance of the other DMUs.

The *window analysis* technique that operationalizes the above procedure is best illustrated with the study of aircraft maintenance operations, described in Charnes et al. (1985). There data were obtained for 14 ($n = 14$) tactical fighter wings in the U.S. Air Force over seven ($P = 7$) monthly periods. To perform the analysis using a three-month ($w = 3$) window, one proceeds as follows.

Each DMU is represented as if it were a different DMU for each of the three successive months in the first window (M1, M2, M3), and an analysis of the 42 ($= nw = 3 \times 14$) DMUs is performed. The window is then shifted one period, and an analysis is performed on the second three-month set (M2, M3, M4) of 42 DMUs. The process continues in this manner, shifting the window forward one period each time and concluding with the final (fifth) analysis of 42 DMUs for the last three months (M5, M6, M7). (In general, one performs $p - w + 1$ separate analyses, where each analysis examines nw DMUs.) Table 3-1 illustrates the results of this analysis.

Table 3–1.   Window Analysis with Three-Month Window

Wing	Month 1	Month 2	Month 3	Month 4	Month 5	Month 6	Month 7
Wing-A	97.89	97.31	98.14				
		97.36	97.53	97.04			
			96.21	95.92	94.54		
				95.79	94.63	97.64	
					94.33	97.24	97.74
Wing-B	93.90	95.67	96.14				
		96.72	96.42	94.63			
			95.75	94.14	93.26		
				94.54	93.46	96.02	
					93.02	96.02	94.49
Wing-C	93.77	91.53	95.26				
		91.77	95.55	94.29			
			93.21	95.04	94.83		
				93.20	93.09	92.21	
					93.59	92.32	92.83
Wing-D	99.72	96.15	95.06				
		97.91	95.70	100.0			
			94.79	100.0	94.51		
				99.71	94.39	94.76	
					94.95	94.67	89.37
Wing-E	100.0	100.0	100.0				
		100.0	100.0	100.0			
			98.97	99.05	100.0		
				99.37	100.0	100.0	
					100.0	100.0	100.0
Wing-F	97.42	93.48	96.07				
		93.60	96.24	93.56			
			94.46	91.75	92.49		
				91.73	92.32	92.35	
					92.68	91.98	99.64
Wing-G	90.98	92.80	95.96				
		93.67	96.80	99.52			
			93.34	94.48	91.73		
				91.94	89.79	95.58	
					89.35	95.14	96.38

Table 3–1. *Continued*

Wing	Month 1	Month 2	Month 3	Month 4	Month 5	Month 6	Month 7
Wing-H	100.0	100.0	100.0				
		100.0	100.0	100.0			
			100.0	100.0	100.0		
				100.0	100.0	100.0	
					100.0	100.0	100.0
Wing-I	99.11	95.94	99.76				
		96.04	100.0	100.0			
			98.16	98.99	94.59		
				98.97	94.62	99.16	
					94.68	98.92	97.28
Wing-J	92.85	90.90	91.62				
		91.50	92.12	94.75			
			90.26	93.39	93.83		
				92.92	93.84	95.33	
					94.52	96.07	94.43
Wing-K	86.25	84.42	84.03				
		84.98	84.47	93.74			
			83.37	82.54	80.26		
				82.39	80.14	79.58	
					80.96	78.66	79.75
Wing-L	100.0	100.0	100.0				
		100.0	100.0	99.55			
			100.0	99.39	97.39		
				100.0	96.85	100.0	
					96.66	100.0	100.0
Wing-M	100.0	100.0	100.0				
		100.0	100.0	100.0			
			100.0	100.0	100.0		
				100.0	100.0	98.75	
					100.0	98.51	99.59
Wing-N	100.0	100.0	98.63				
		100.0	100.0	100.0			
			99.45	100.0	100.0		
				100.0	100.0	100.0	
					100.0	100.0	100.0

The structure of table 3–1 portrays the underlying framework of the analysis. For the first "window," wing A is represented in the constraints of the DEA model as though it were a different DMU in months 1, 2, and 3. Hence, when wing 1 is evaluated for its month 1 efficiency, its own performance data for months 2 and 3 are included in the constraint sets along with similar performance data of the other wings for months 1, 2, and 3. Thus the results of the "first window" analysis consist of the 42 scores under columns Month 1–Month 3 in the first row for each wing. For example, wing 1 had efficiency ratings of 97.89, 97.31, and 98.14 for its performance in months 1, 2, and 3, respectively. The second row of data for each wing is the result of analyzing the second window of 42 DMUs, which result from dropping the month 1 data and appending the month 4 data.

The arrangement of the results of a window analysis as given in table 3–1 facilitates the identification of trends in performance, the stability of reference sets, and other possible insights. For example, "row views" clarify performance trends for wings E and M. Wing E improved its performance in month 5 relative to prior performance in months 3 and 4 in the third window, while wing M's performance appears to deteriorate in months 6 and 7. Similar "column views" allow comparison of wings (DMUs) across different reference sets.

The utility of table 3–1 can be further extended by appending columns of summary statistics (mean, median, variance, range, etc.) for each wing to reveal the relative stability of each wing's results. Finally, a Facet Participation Table, which records the number of times an efficient DMU appears in the efficient reference set for other DMUs, is valuable in window analyses. (See chapters 8 and 11 for details of additional applications.)

The window analysis technique represents one area for further research extending DEA. For example, the problem of choosing the width for a window (and the sensitivity of DEA solutions to window width) is currently determined by trial and error. Similarly, the theoretical implications of representing each DMU as if it were a different DMU for each period in the window remain to be worked out.

6. Summary

The extensions to DEA described in this chapter provide valuable techniques that not only allow one to fine tune the frontier but also make it possible to formulate DEA models that incorporate the modeling features of parametric analysis techniques. Thus the extensions make it possible to formulate DEA models that incorporate dummy variables and discretionary and nondiscretionary variables, and these can incorporate judgment or managerial preferences by constraining the multipliers. They also permit time series portrayals for studying trends and increasing the degrees of freedom by repeated uses of limited bodies of data. Other extensions and enhancements of the DEA methodology involve calculations of DMU-specific most-productive scale size (Banker, 1984), allocative efficiency (Banker and Mainderata, 1988), incorporation of ordinal relationships (Ali, Cook and Seiford, 1991), and sensitivity analysis (Charnes et al., 1985, 1992; Thompson et al., chapter 20, this volume), as well as the introduction of stochastic attributes of DEA (Sengupta, 1987; Banker, 1993).

Notes

1. Ray (1988) argues that technical inefficiency is simply the result of a failure to incorporate all relevant nondiscretionary variables.

2. In such an analysis, the managerial inefficiencies should be removed by projection onto the frontier for the category before comparison. The first example of this technique is the Program Follow Through evaluation of Charnes, Cooper, and Rhodes (1981).

4 COMPUTATIONAL ASPECTS OF DEA

Agha Iqbal Ali

1. Introduction

The increased application of data envelopment analysis (DEA) over the past decade has been accompanied by a growing awareness of computational subtleties of the mathematical models that compose the methodology. In this chapter, we introduce elements of the computational characteristics of DEA in the context of the basic DEA models that were presented in chapter 2.

Research-oriented interest in computational DEA has led to the development of computational tools that facilitate DEA applications. Many early applications had to resort to the rather tedious, cumbersome, and potentially problematic process of using standard linear programming software, solving a linear program for each DMU separately, and subsequently compiling the results. Today, computational tools, in the form of specialized software for DEA, are available to facilitate computation, thus freeing the researcher to focus on the application itself.

At this point, it is necessary to distinguish between a DEA model and an application model. A researcher who uses the DEA methodology, as opposed to one who develops either theoretical or computational DEA methodology, is primarily concerned with the development of the application model. Specifically, the researcher is concerned with the selection of the n DMUs, the s outputs, the m inputs, and a DEA model that is consistent with hypotheses that are maintained about the application area. Refinement of an application model, an integral part of model development, is motivated by questions regarding the appropriateness of a variable being defined as input or output as well as those regarding the appropriateness of a particular DEA model. Specialized DEA software packages frequently include data and model management capabilities and thus give the researcher the capability to select a specific DEA model for the application, based on properties of DEA models such as the form of envelopment surface and the evaluation principle or metric. In addition, since computation in specialized software is DEA specific, several DEA analyses that might be required to refine the application model can be easily performed.

Interestingly enough, it was initial applications of DEA that revealed computational inaccuracies and subtleties, often elusive, that occur when using standard linear programming software for DEA computation. To facilitate DEA applications, two major computational issues are paramount: accuracy and ease of use. Accuracy is an issue because the solution of mathematical programs arising in DEA requires a substantially different focus than is typical for the solution of linear programming problems. Beyond the usual criteria, such as user friendliness, input requirements, report generation, ease of use for DEA also includes the criterion of streamlined computation. By streamlining DEA computation, the fact that in any analysis a sequence of n mathematical programs is solved is made transparent to the user. This chapter introduces the reader to the characteristics of DEA models that necessitate specialized computation with respect to both of these issues: 1) the accurate solution of a DEA model for a single decision-making unit (DMU); and 2) constructs that afford efficiency in computation when solving a sequence of n mathematical programs. In addition, we also discuss, in general, the use of specialized software including interpretation of output obtained by such software.

In section 2, we review DEA models from the computational point of view. In section 3, three computational characteristics of DEA mathematical programs that underscore the importance of accuracy in computation are discussed. These characteristics are potential sources of inaccuracy and lack of robustness if one uses standard linear programming software that has not been specialized for DEA. In section 4, we discuss elements of DEA computation, focusing on constructs and mechanisms (many of which are standard in computational mathematical programming) that allow efficient DEA computation. Section 5 briefly introduces the framework for DEA software and the essential features of such software.

2. DEA Analyses

DEA analyses presume the selection of a specific DEA model for analysis of a particular data set represented by an $(s \times n)$ matrix of outputs, $\mathbf{Y}$, and an $(m \times n)$ matrix of inputs, $\mathbf{X}$. As in the chapter on basic DEA models, $x_{il} > 0$, $y_{rl} > 0$, denote, respectively, the ith input and r^{th} output of DMU_l, and X_l and Y_l denote, respectively, the vectors of input and output values for a DMU_l, $l = 1, \ldots, n$. The computational view of the DEA models differs from the application view of DEA models. In an application view, one is concerned, beyond the selection of the DMUs and the selection of the particular variables that constitute inputs and outputs, with the selection of a particular DEA model. As discussed in earlier chapters, DEA models differ in the assumed form of the underlying envelopment surface as well as the particular envelopment metric. The models that assume a piecewise linear envelopment surface can be further classified with respect to the assumed returns to scale, which may be either constant (CRS) or variable (VRS). Further classification is based on orientation: a model may not have any orientation, may be input orienting, or may be output orienting. The classification is represented pictorially in figure 4–1.

Determination of whether or not a decision-making unit, DMU_l, for some l, lies on (determines) the envelopment surface usually requires the solution of a mathematical program.

$$\boxed{(Y_l, X_l)} \rightarrow \boxed{\text{DEA MODEL (Y, X)}} \rightarrow \boxed{(\hat{Y}_l, \hat{X}_l)}$$

DEA models, as pictorially represented above, may be thought of as a projection mechanism. Regardless of the specific DEA model, the solution to the mathematical program for DMU_l, as represented by (Y_l, X_l), obtains a projected point $(\hat{Y}_l, \hat{X}_l)$. When $(\hat{Y}_l, \hat{X}_l) = (Y_l, X_l)$, DMU_l, is, of course, efficient and on the envelopment surface. For an inefficient DMU_l the point $(\hat{Y}_l, \hat{X}_l)$ is on the envelopment surface, and can always be represented in terms of efficient DMUs. In general, because of different

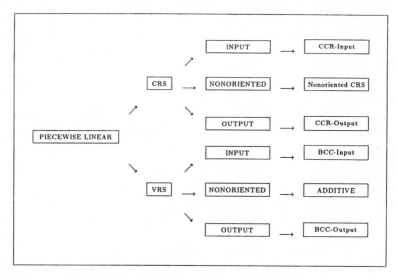

Figure 4–1.   Classification by returns to scale and orientation.

orientations or evaluation metrics, different models obtain different projected points for inefficient units. Regardless of the specific DEA model, the projected point is always represented, in terms of efficient DMUs, by the following expression:

$$(\hat{Y}_l, \hat{X}_l) = \left(\sum_{j=1}^{n} \lambda_j^l Y_j, \sum_{j=1}^{n} \lambda_j^l X_j \right)$$

The projected point is always a nonnegative linear or convex combination of the (efficient) DMUs that have $\lambda_j^l > 0$. Letting $\Lambda^l = \{j \mid \lambda_j^l > 0\}$,

$$((\hat{Y}_l, \hat{X}_l)) = \left(\sum_{j \in \Lambda^l} \lambda_j^l Y_j, \sum_{j \in \Lambda^l} \lambda_j^l X_j \right)$$

Overall inefficiency, then, is represented by the discrepancy between $(\hat{Y}_l, \hat{X}_l)$ and (Y_l, X_l), as given by

$$\hat{y}_{rl} - y_{rl}, \qquad r = 1, \ldots, s$$

$$x_{il} - \hat{x}_{il}, \qquad i = 1, \ldots, m$$

Thus, by solving a mathematical program for each $l \in D = \{1, 2, \ldots, n\}$, DEA identifies the set of efficient units, $E^* = \{l \mid \hat{y}_{rl} - y_{rl} = 0, r = 1, \ldots, s; x_{il} - \hat{x}_{il} = 0, i = 1, \ldots, m\}$ and the set of inefficient units $I^* =$

$D - E^*$. Properties that allow identification of membership of DMU_l in E^* or I^* without solving a mathematical program are useful in streamlining the solution of DEA mathematical programs.[1] To illustrate this point, consider the mathematical statement of the additive model:

$$ADD_P: \quad \min \ - \sum_{r=1}^{s} s_r - \sum_{i=1}^{m} e_i$$

$$\sum_{j=1}^{n} y_{rj}\lambda_j - s_r = y_r, \qquad r = 1, \ldots, s$$

$$- \sum_{j=1}^{n} x_{ij}\lambda_j - e_i = -x_i, \qquad i = 1, \ldots, m$$

$$\sum_{j=1}^{n} \lambda_j = 1$$

$$\lambda_j \geq 0, \qquad j = 1, \ldots, n$$

$$s_r \geq 0, \qquad r = 1, \ldots, s$$

$$e_i \geq 0, \qquad i = 1, \ldots, m$$

Since a projected point, $(\hat{Y}_l, \hat{X}_l)$, can be expressed entirely in terms of efficient units, the program is equivalently stated by replacing the summation $\Sigma_{j=1}^{n}$ in the constraints by $\Sigma_{j \in E^*}$. Such equivalent formulation is possible for all DEA models. In practice, of course, E^* is not available a priori. However, as each mathematical program in D is solved, more information about E^* and I^* is obtained in that either the subset of DMUs known to be inefficient, $I \subseteq I^*$, or the subset of DMUs known to be efficient, $E \subseteq E^*$, is augmented. By successively incorporating this information, the explicit mathematical program that is used for computation has progressively fewer variables, since the summation in the constraints needs only be $\Sigma_{j \in D-I}$. Computation is streamlined, since the mathematical programs explicitly handled are smaller.

A property that identifies inefficient units is that of total domination. This property finds application, as will be discussed in section 4, in determining $I \subseteq I^*$ prior to solution of DEA mathematical programs.

Definition 4-1. If $x_{ik} \leq x_{il}$, $i = 1, \ldots, m$ and $y_{rk} \geq y_{rl}$, $r = 1, \ldots, s$ with $x_{ik} < x_{il}$ for some $i = 1, \ldots, m$ and/or $y_{rk} > y_{rl}$ for some $r = 1, \ldots, s$ then DMU_l is *totally dominated* by DMU_k.

Lemma 4-1. If DMU_l is totally dominated by some other DMU_k, then $l \in I^*$.

Note that a DMU that totally dominates another DMU need not be efficient. Inefficient units that are not totally dominated are, in fact, totally dominated by a linear or convex combination of efficient DMUs. If all inefficient units were totally dominated, then DEA computations would be very simple. For example, a data set with a large percentage of inefficient units, most of which are totally dominated, would be easily analyzed with streamlined computation. By identifying totally dominated units prior to computation, the size of each of the n mathematical programs would be reduced substantially. Two properties that allow identification of efficient units are summarized by the following two lemmas (Ali, 1992).

Lemma 4–2. For models *BCC* and *ADD*,

1. If DMU_{k_i} is the unique DMU with $x_{ik_i} = \min_{j=1,\ldots,n} x_{ij}$, then it is a member of E^*; and
2. If DMU_{k_r} is the unique DMU with $y_{rk_r} = \max_{j=1,\ldots,n} y_{rj}$, then it is a member of E^*, for $r = 1, \ldots, s$.

Lemma 4–3. DMU_k, where

$$\frac{\sum_{r=1}^s y_{rk}}{\sum_{i=1}^m x_{ik}} = \max_{j=1,2,\ldots,n} \frac{\sum_{r=1}^s y_{rj}}{\sum_{i=1}^m x_{ij}}$$

is a member of E^*.

Lemma 4–2 may be thought of as an "efficient by virtue of specialization" property that holds for the VRS envelopment form. Lemma 4–3 may be thought of as an "efficient by virtue of overall performance" property. These two properties are applied, as will be discussed in section 4, to determine $E \subseteq E^*$ prior to solution of DEA mathematical programs. In addition, computations can be further streamlined by augmenting this set during the course of a DEA analysis. We illustrate this with respect to model ADD_P. Note that this model has $m + s + 1$ basic variables, of which some f are $\lambda_{F_1}, \lambda_{F_2}, \ldots, \lambda_{F_f}$, and $m + s - f + 1$ are from among s_r and e_i. We refer to the set $\Lambda^l = \{F_1, F_2, \ldots, F_f\}$ as the *reference set* for DMU_l. The DMUs in the reference set are efficient, as stated in the following lemma (Rhodes, 1978; Charnes, Cooper, Golany, Seiford, and Stutz, 1985):

Lemma 4–4. In the optimal solution to a DEA model for DMU_l, each DMU_k in the reference set, Λ^l, is efficient.

The DMUs that compose the reference set for DMU_l lie on a *facet of the envelopment surface*, and the projected point $(\hat{Y}_l, \hat{X}_l)$ also lies on this facet. Note that when $f = m + s$, the facet is a *face of the envelopment surface*. Thus, after the solution of a DEA mathematical program for DMU_l, E can be augmented by up to $m + s$ DMUs, since the number of DMUs that compose a reference set, f, can be at most $m + s$. Augmentation of the set E in this manner is most beneficial for data sets with a major percentage of efficient DMUs. The use of E in streamlining computation will be further discussed in section 4. We point out that the size of E^* relative to D depends on the particular data set. No conclusive statements about the percentage of DMUs found to be efficient can be made based on n, s, and r.

While some computational characteristics are common across all DEA models, "orienting" models share some additional computational characteristics. The orienting models CCR (Charnes, Cooper, and Rhodes, 1978) and BCC (Banker, Charnes, and Cooper, 1984) are entirely different in form from ADD (Charnes, Cooper, Golany, Seiford, and Stutz, 1985), which is not orienting. The statements of the input-orienting models for the CRS and VRS envelopment forms, respectively, follow:

$$CCR_P\text{-}I: \quad \min \theta - \sum_{r=1}^{s} \varepsilon s_r - \sum_{i=1}^{m} \varepsilon e_i$$

$$\sum_{j=1}^{n} y_{rj}\lambda_j - s_r = y_{rl}, \quad r = 1, \ldots, s$$

$$x_{il}\theta - \sum_{j=1}^{n} x_{ij}\lambda_j - e_i = 0, \quad i = 1, \ldots, m$$

$$\lambda_j \geq 0, \quad j = 1, \ldots, m$$

$$s_r \geq 0, \quad r = 1, \ldots, s$$

$$e_i \geq 0, \quad i = 1, \ldots, m$$

$$BCC_P\text{-}I: \quad \min \theta - \sum_{r=1}^{s} \varepsilon s_r - \sum_{i=1}^{m} \varepsilon e_i$$

$$\sum_{j=1}^{n} y_{rj}\lambda_j - s_r = y_{rl}, \quad r = 1, \ldots, s$$

$$x_{il}\theta - \sum_{j=1}^{n} x_{ij}\lambda_j - e_i = 0, \quad i = 1, \ldots, m$$

$$\sum_{j=1}^{n} \lambda_j = 1$$

$$\lambda_j \geq 0, \quad j = 1, \ldots, n$$
$$s_r \geq 0, \quad r = 1, \ldots, s$$
$$e_i \geq 0, \quad i = 1, \ldots, m$$

Computational mechanisms for orienting models differ from those for nonorienting models. This difference can be anticipated, given that the projections are effected differently for the two types of models. We illustrate this by using model-specific representations of the projected point that depend on whether or not the DEA model is orienting, and if so, what the orientation is. These representations make use of the slack output and excess input variables, s_r^l, $r = 1, \ldots, s$, e_i^l, $i = 1, \ldots, m$. For ADD_P, which does not have any orientation and for which the entire inefficiency is accounted for by slack outputs and excess inputs, the projected point is given by

$$\hat{y}_{rl} = y_{rl} + s_r^l, \quad r = 1, \ldots, s$$
$$\hat{x}_{il} = x_{il} - e_i^l, \quad i = 1, \ldots, m$$

The reader will note that the slack output and excess input variables play a different role in orienting models. In nonorienting models, these variables account for total inefficiency. In orienting models, they do not. For the above input-orienting formulations, CCR_P-I and BCC_P-I, inefficiency is partly accounted for by the proportional reduction (by a factor of $(1 - \theta)$) of all inputs and partly by the (residual) excess inputs and slack outputs. Thus the projected point is expressed as

$$\hat{y}_{rl} = y_{rl} + s_r^l, \quad r = 1, \ldots, s$$
$$\hat{x}_{il} = \theta x_{il} - e_i^l, \quad i = 1, \ldots, m$$

Similarly, for the output-orienting formulations, CCR_P-O and BCC_P-O, inefficiency is partly accounted for by the proportional augmentation of all outputs (by a factor of $(\phi - 1)$) and partly by the (residual) excess inputs and slack outputs. Thus the projected point is given by

$$\hat{y}_{rl} = \phi y_{rl} + s_r^l, \quad r = 1, \ldots, s$$
$$\hat{x}_{il} = x_{il} - e_i^l, \quad i = 1, \ldots, m$$

We illustrate the difference, with respect to projection mechanism, between orienting and nonorienting models with the same form of envelopment by examining ADD_P, which has no orientation, and the input-oriented formulation BCC_P-I. Of all the potential points on the envelopment surface to which an inefficient DMU may be projected, the Additive model obtains one for which the objective $-(\Sigma_{r=1}^{s} s_r + \Sigma_{i=1}^{m} e_i)$ is minimized, i.e., $(\Sigma_{r=1}^{s} s_r + \Sigma_{i=1}^{m} e_i)$ is maximized. For ADD_P, this is equivalent to maximizing $(\Sigma_{r=1}^{s}(\hat{y}_{rl} - y_{rl}) + \Sigma_{i=1}^{m}(x_{il} - \hat{x}_{il}))$. The input orientation of BCC_P-I, on the other hand, obtains a projected point so that $\min_{i=1,\ldots,m}(x_{il} - \hat{x}_{il})$ is maximized.

The computational difference between orienting and nonorienting models is also seen in model representation. The orienting models of chapter 2 effect an envelopment metric that orients the projection and employ a non-Archimedean infinitesimal, ε. The primary focus in input-orienting models is to minimize the extent to which inputs can be proportionally reduced, as given by θ. Note that inputs are proportionally reduced by a factor of $(1 - \theta)$. The secondary objective is to minimize the quantity $-(\Sigma_{r=1}^{s} s_r + \Sigma_{i=1}^{m} e_i)$. Similarly, for output-orienting models the primary focus is to maximize the extent to which outputs can be proportionally augmented, as given by ϕ. Again, the outputs are proportionally augmented by a factor of $(\phi - 1)$.

The returns-to-scale possibilities (CRS or VRS) represented by the form of envelopment used also affects the computational characteristics of these models. In terms of model representation, models that differ only in the returns-to-scale possibilities allowed differ only in a single constraint. When the difference in models is only that of envelopment surface, the production possibility set for CRS models is larger than that for VRS counterparts. This finding can be, initially, counterintuitive; the CRS model, CCR_P, is less contrained than the VRS model, BCC_P. Note that the mathematical representation of BCC_P has one more constraint than that of CCR_P. However, the more constrained the model, the less its chance of being declared inefficient. In fact, the number of inefficient DMUs obtained using a CRS model is at least that obtained using a VRS model. For the input-oriented formulation CCR_P-I, the optimal basis consists of $m + s$ basic variables that consist of θ, some f variables λ_{F_1}, $\lambda_{F_2}, \ldots, \lambda_{F_f}$, and $m + s - f$ variables from among s_r and e_i. Note that since θ is always basic, the size of the *reference set*, $\Lambda^l = \{F_1, F_2, \ldots, F_f\}$, for DMU_l is at most $m + s - 1$. For BCC_P-I, the corresponding VRS model, the size of the reference set for a DMU is at most $m + s$. Required computations for a VRS versus a corresponding CRS can differ substantially, since the form of the envelopment affects not only the relative sizes of E^* and I^* but also the manner in which efficient constructs evolve during the course of DEA analysis.

3. Computational Characteristics of DEA Mathematical Programs

The characteristics of the mathematical programs arising in DEA necessitate that particular attention be paid to computational robustness and accuracy of computation. DEA models involve constraint matrices that are 100% dense; in addition, the data can have a wide range and can exhibit degeneracy. This section discusses computational characteristics of DEA that impact numerical stability and accuracy and, consequently, demonstrate the need for specialized computational mechanisms for DEA models.

3.1. Data Values and ILL-Conditioning

In the course of developing a DEA application, one frequently encounters data with wide ranges in their values; one input or output variable may have values that are in the units and tens, whereas another input or output variable has values in the hundreds of thousands and millions. Such a wide range in the values of the input and output variables can cause computational difficulties if the user does not have the facility to fine-tune the tolerances that are used within the solution mechanism employed to solve the DEA mathematical programs. Computational difficulties can arise because the data matrix is potentially ill conditioned when the range of values of the input and output variables is wide. A user could obviously resort to rescaling the data. Scaling any of the input measures or the output measures is possible and easy to accomplish. However, scaling can have drawbacks. The primary drawback is that scaling can destroy lower-order digits in the data, potentially destroying the ability to accurately discriminate between different units.[2] Another drawback is that scaling does not remove all sources of ill-conditioning.

Another source of ill-conditioning is due to a wide variation in the values for a *particular* input or output measure across the n units. Ill-conditioning arising from such a phenomenon is not alleviated by data scaling. Ali and Seiford (1990) suggest the use of a displacement of data for handling data that exhibit a wide range or contain zero values. It is shown that an affine displacement (additive translation) does not alter the afficient frontier for VRS models (such as ADD or BCC).

The data in table 4–1 (Charnes, Cooper, and Li, 1990) are not ill conditioned. However, if the values of the variable INV had been in the units and tens, the potential for ill-conditioning would exist. Similarly, if

Table 4–1. Data Set with 28 DMUs, 3 inputs, and 3 outputs[a]

DMU	G.I.O.V.	P & T	R.S.	LABOR	W.F.	INV
1	6785798	1594957	1088699	483.01	1397736	616961
2	2505984	545140	835745	371.95	355509	385453
3	2292025	406947	473600	268.23	685584	341941
4	1158016	135939	336165	202.02	452713	117424
5	1244124	204909	317709	197.93	471650	112634
6	1187130	190178	605037	178.96	423124	189743
7	658910	86514	239760	148.04	367012	97004
8	993238	1411954	353896	184.93	408311	111904
9	854188	135327	239360	123.33	245542	91861
10	606743	78357	208188	116.91	305316	91710
11	736545	114365	298112	129.62	295812	92409
12	454684	67154	233733	106.26	198703	53499
13	494196	78992	118553	89.70	210891	95642
14	842854	149186	243361	109.26	282209	84202
15	776285	116974	234875	85.50	184992	49357
16	490998	117854	118924	72.17	222327	73907
17	482448	67857	158250	76.18	161159	47977
18	515237	114883	101231	73.21	144163	43312
19	625514	173099	130423	86.72	190043	55326
20	382880	74126	123968	69.09	158436	66640
21	867467	65229	262876	77.69	135046	46198
22	830142	128279	242773	97.42	206926	66120
23	521684	37245	184055	54.96	79563	43192
24	869973	86859	194416	67.00	144092	43350
25	604715	55989	127586	46.30	100431	31428
26	601299	37088	224855	65.12	96873	28112
27	145792	11816	24442	20.09	50717	54650
28	319218	31726	169051	69.81	117790	30976

[a] For a discussion of variables and associated units of measurement, see Charnes, Cooper, and Li (1990).

the range of values for the variable W.F. were from the tens to the millions, such potential would, again, exist.

3.2. Values of Multipliers

Even when the data matrix is not ill conditioned, a mismatch in admissible values for the variables of the mathematical program and the tolerances

Table 4–2.   Range of Measures for the 28-DMU Data Set

Measure	Low Value	High Value
G.I.O.V.	145792.00	6785798.00
P & T	11816.00	1594957.00
R.S.	24442.00	1088699.00
LABOR	20.09	483.01
W.F.	50717.00	1397736.00
INV	28112.00	616961.00

employed in the solution mechanism can lead to inaccurate results.

In orienting models, due to the presence of the normalizing constraint $\Sigma_{i=1}^{m} v_i x_{il} = 1$ ($\Sigma_{r=1}^{s} \mu_r y_{rl} = 1$ for output orientation) in the dual program, values for the multipliers μ_r, $r = 1, \ldots, s$, and v_i, $i = 1, \ldots, m$, are inversely proportional to the values of the input and output variables. Thus, the larger the input and output values, the smaller the values for the multipliers. Table 4–2 provides the range of values for the measures in table 4–1. From this range, we can see that the value of the multiplier for the variable LABOR will be larger in magnitude than the values of other multipliers. The fact that these other multiplier values can be small creates a potential for confounding the testing of optimality: when reduced costs, which are computed using these multipliers (dual variables), are much smaller than the employed pricing tolerance, they are erroneously considered to be zero. The algorithm then terminates prematurely.

There are many computational mechanisms for avoiding such potential loss of accuracy. The most common approach is to restate the normalizing constraint by replacing the right-hand-side value of 1 in the normalizing constraint by 100 or 1000. The effect of this replacement is that all values for multipliers are 100 or 1000 times what they would be with a right-hand-side value of 1.[3]

3.3. Degeneracy in DEA Models

In linear programming, a basis, corresponding to a feasible solution, is said to be degenerate when at least one of the basic variables has a value of zero. LP bases corresponding to feasible solutions for any of the DEA models can be degenerate. In each of the DEA models, when the mathematical program is solved for an efficient DMU_l, then each feasible basis is degenerate. For example, in input-orienting models, only the variables θ and λ_l have nonzero values. All other basic variables have a value of zero, making the basis degenerate. In the additive model, λ_l is the only variable with a nonzero value. Mathematical models that exhibit degeneracy can require a significant amount of computation before optimality conditions are verified and an optimal solution obtained. This is because degenerate simplex pivots are performed during which no improvement in the value of the objective occurs. While such behavior may not be noticeable when performing analyses with small data sets, it becomes evident when the number of inputs and outputs $(m + s)$ is larger than 10. As the number of input and output measures $m + s$ increases, the potential for encountering a very large number of degenerate pivots also increases. It may even be noticeable with fewer inputs and outputs. The deterioration becomes worse as the number of constraints (number of inputs plus number of outputs) increases, because basic solutions have a larger number of variables at a level of zero.

There are many well-established mechanisms to avoid the potential for "cycling" of simplex iterations. For classes of mathematical programs that exhibit degeneracy, in addition to anticycling mechanisms, it is desirable to reduce the actual number of degenerate pivots to improve efficiency in computation. Degenerate pivots can be controlled by a number of different computational mechanisms. We shall illustrate the phenomenon of degenerate pivots by examining the effect of tie-breaking rules for the ratio test of the simplex procedure.

Recall that for the simplex method, a degenerate pivot occurs when the minimum ratio is zero or else there is a tie for a nonzero minimum ratio. That is, for a given entering variable, a number of the currently basic variables are admissible leaving variables. The three rules for determining the leaving variable that we examine are 1) the first encountered basic variable for which the ratio is zero, 2) the first encountered basic variable s_r or e_i that yields a ratio of zero, and 3) the first encountered basic variable λ_j with a ratio of zero.

A comparison of the first and third rules is given in table 4–3 for models ADD_P and BCC_P-I using three "real-world" data sets, labeled, S81, U533, and M100, respectively. The table reports the total number of iterations required to solve the n mathematical programs for each of the data sets, along with the CPU seconds required for solution. When the second rule was used, the analysis for each of these data sets was aborted after one hour of CPU time.[4] To see why degenerate pivots are pervasive with the second rule, suppose a variable $\lambda_l \notin \Lambda^l$ is basic at some iteration.

Table 4–3.   Degeneracy in DEA Models

					Tie-Break Rule 1		Tie-Break Rule 3	
Data Set	n	s	m	I*	Pivots	CPU Seconds[a]	Pivots	CPU Seconds[a]
Additive								
S81	81	4	11	28	2207	22.1	1041	11.7
U533	533	4	3	442	17386	166.2	8920	94.8
M100	100	8	6	20	13448	157.7	2146	24.8
BCC-Input								
S81	81	4	11	28	9124	104.9	2771	33.35
U533	533	4	3	442	24172	277.0	15677	198.9
M100	100	8	6	20	49345	627.2	3686	49.1

[a] IBM9370 at Engineering Computing Services, The University of Massachusetts at Amherst.

The second rule would tend to retain this variable as basic as long as a slack output or excess input variable were a potential leaving variable and thus might impede convergence to optimality.

The first rule also has a tendency to produce a large number of degenerate pivots relative to the third rule. Note that rule 3 requires substantially fewer pivots than rule 1. For data set M100, the difference between the number of pivots required by the two rules is most striking. We refrain from making a conclusive statement about the efficacy of one rule over another rule based on only three data sets. Our purpose here is to demonstrate the effect of degeneracy on computation. We note that the tendency for degeneracy is more marked for the data sets S81 and M100; they have, respectively, 15 and 14 inputs and outputs and have a relatively small percentage of inefficient units. Data set U533 has only 7 inputs and outputs and a relatively large percentage of inefficient units. It is apparent that marked reduction in overall computational effort is obtained when computational mechanisms are specialized for DEA computation, such as the use of the tie-break rule 3) for the ratio test.

3.4. The Non-Archimedean Models as Linear Programs

Two major issues arise when considering the use of commercially available software for linear programs for performing DEA. The first of these is that it becomes a cumbersome task, since the software package must be invoked separately for each of the linear programs to be solved. In recent years, it has become a less cumbersome task, since many commercial linear programming systems allow the simplex procedure to be invoked as a subroutine.

The second issue is more involved: solving the non-Archimedean models as linear programs, with an explicit value for ε, can lead to inaccurate results. Commercial implementations of the simplex method for the solution of linear programs use specific values for error tolerances (Murtagh, 1981). It is because of the inability of such software to recognize the computational characteristics of a specific application that suboptimal solutions can result. Accurate computation is a necessary concern, particularly for models involving use of the non-Archimedean infinitesimal. This is because of potential nonconvergence to optimality due to tolerances employed. The accurate solution of non-Archimedean models requires that they be solved using the methodologies that do not require explicit specification of ε.

One of the first specialized software systems specifically designed for performing DEA (Bessent, Bessent, Kennington, and Regan, 1982) was for the model CCR_P-I. The implementation treated the non-Archimedean model as a linear program, with an explicit value of 10^{-6} for the infinitesimal ε. Of course, if the value of ε used is "small enough," then accurate results would be obtained. However, what "small enough" is depends on the particular data set. Note that if $\varepsilon \geqslant \min_{j=1,\ldots,n} 1/(\Sigma_{i=1,\ldots,m} x_{ij})$, then the linear programs CCR_D-I and BCC_D-I[5] have unbounded objective function values (Ali and Seiford, 1990). If the value for ε is chosen to be smaller, finite objective values are obtained; however, the values are a function of the specific value used for ε. Readers will immediately draw the parallel between ε used here and M used for the solution of linear programming problems using the Big-M method. However, there is a major distinction that must be borne in mind. When the value of M is not large enough, the problem is declared infeasible. If there was a doubt as to whether the problem was truly infeasible, the value of M could be increased and the problem solved again. However, as long as the chosen value of ε is small enough to produce finite results, there would be no indication of whether or not the solution obtained is in fact the optimal solution to the original non-Archimedean problem. In addition, if the value is too small, serious computational limitations arise because of zero tolerances. For example, the value of the reduced costs for selecting a variable to enter the basis may become legitimately close to zero. However, because of tolerances employed, the variable may not be deemed a candidate for basis entry when it should. Thus, premature termination may occur and true optimality will not be obtained.

The implication in terms of lack of computational robustness and accuracy of solving the non-Archimedean models as linear programs, not only because a numerical value is used for ε but also because of tolerances employed, is illustrated using the 28-unit data set. Table 4–4 reports the optimal objective values obtained when the model for the CCR_P is solved

Table 4–4. Sensitivity to ε—Optimal Objective Values Using the 28-DMU Data Set

	Tolerance 10^{-12}				Tolerance 10^{-6}	
DMU	$\varepsilon = 10^{-5}$	$\varepsilon = 10^{-6}$	$\varepsilon = 10^{-7}$	$\varepsilon = 10^{-8}$	$\varepsilon = 10^{-7}$	$\varepsilon = 10^{-8}$
1	$-\infty$	$-\infty$	1.00000	1.00000	1.00000	1.00000
2	$-\infty$	$-\infty$	0.66063	0.71462	0.73667	0.75059
3	$-\infty$	$-\infty$	0.65048	0.65668	0.66335	0.67023
4	$-\infty$	$-\infty$	0.51739	0.52131	0.51739	0.52131
5	$-\infty$	$-\infty$	0.57284	0.57966	0.57686	0.58164
6	$-\infty$	$-\infty$	0.91282	1.00000	1.00000	1.00000
7	$-\infty$	$-\infty$	0.47122	0.48728	0.48310	0.48728
8	$-\infty$	$-\infty$	1.00000	1.00000	1.00000	1.00000
9	$-\infty$	$-\infty$	0.62458	0.62533	0.62790	0.62801
10	$-\infty$	$-\infty$	0.52593	0.53781	0.53133	0.54154
11	$-\infty$	$-\infty$	0.66870	0.69390	0.69093	0.69390
12	$-\infty$	$-\infty$	0.62947	0.65105	0.62947	0.65105
13	$-\infty$	$-\infty$	0.45197	0.45331	0.45197	0.45331
14	$-\infty$	$-\infty$	0.71270	0.71828	0.71270	0.71828
15	$-\infty$	$-\infty$	0.86284	0.86524	0.86284	0.86524
16	$-\infty$	$-\infty$	0.59350	0.59750	0.59350	0.59750
17	$-\infty$	$-\infty$	0.63129	0.63544	0.63415	0.63544
18	$-\infty$	$-\infty$	0.66710	0.67048	0.66710	0.67048
19	$-\infty$	$-\infty$	0.65816	0.66010	0.65816	0.66010
20	$-\infty$	$-\infty$	0.56298	0.56724	0.56425	0.56724
21	$-\infty$	$-\infty$	1.00000	1.00000	1.00000	1.00000
22	$-\infty$	$-\infty$	0.78598	0.78800	0.78598	0.78800
23	$-\infty$	1.00000	1.00000	1.00000	1.00000	1.00000
24	$-\infty$	$-\infty$	1.00000	1.00000	1.00000	1.00000
25	$-\infty$	0.98995	1.00000	1.00000	1.00000	1.00000
26	$-\infty$	1.00000	1.00000	1.00000	1.00000	1.00000
27	$-\infty$	0.50144	0.53239	0.53541	0.63239	0.53541
28	$-\infty$	0.55436	0.68995	0.70315	0.68995	0.70315

Note: $-\infty$ implies termination due to unboundedness.

as a linear program with four different explicit values for ε (10^{-5}, 10^{-6}, 10^{-7}, 10^{-8}) and a tolerance of 10^{-12}, and with two explicit values for ε (10^{-7}, 10^{-8}) and a tolerance of 10^{-6}. The sensitivity to the specific value for ε is apparent. With a tolerance of 10^{-12}, unit 25 is found to be inefficient with $\varepsilon = 10^{-6}$ and efficient for smaller values of ε. The sensitivity to the tolerance employed is apparent by comparing the objective values obtained with pricing tolerances at 10^{-12} and 10^{-6}. The latter value (10^{-6}) is more representative of default tolerances used in commercial software for linear programs. Note that entirely different optimal values are obtained for DMUs 2 and 3. This sensitivity is due to the fact that reduced costs of nonbasic variables can become close to the particular tolerance employed depending on 1) the value of ε used and 2) the range of data values for the measures of inputs and outputs.

4. Efficient DEA Computation

DEA is computationally intensive precisely because it requires the solution of n mathematical programs, one for each of the DMUs. The programs for each of the n DMUs are solved successively, as summarized in the algorithmic specification for DEA analysis below.

Algorithm: Data Envelopment Analysis
Initialize $\mathbf{Y}$, $\mathbf{X}$, n, m, s.
         $l \leftarrow 1$.
Define   Initialize DEA MODEL($\mathbf{Y}$, $\mathbf{X}$) for (Y_l, X_l).
Solve   Obtain ($\hat{Y}_l$, $\hat{X}_l$) from DEA MODEL($\mathbf{Y}$, $\mathbf{X}$) for (Y_l, X_l).
         Record Solution for DMU_l.
Increment $l \leftarrow l + 1$.
         If $l > n$ Output results and terminate, otherwise go to *Define*.

The computational efficiency of the algorithm is essentially determined by the efficiency of solution for the individual mathematical programs. This section discusses issues related to *efficient computational methodology* for performing DEAs.

Computations for the solution of each mathematical program can be streamlined by introducing constructs that reduce the required number of simplex pivots as well as the time per pivot. *Restricted pricing* and *candidate lists* can be implemented by maintaining and updating the subsets of DMUs $E \subseteq E^*$ and $I \subseteq I^*$, which are known to be, respectively, either efficient or inefficient. Both these constructs affect the pricing operation of simplex calculations directly. The reduction of the overall computational effort for DEA is also addressed by dynamically determining the order in which the programs for DMUs in the comparison set, D, are solved. Such dynamic ordering capitalizes on the similarity between successive programs by using advanced starting bases.

Data preprocessing identifies a subset $E \subseteq E^*$ of DMUs known to be efficient and a subset $I \subset I^*$ of DMUs known to be inefficient. A straightforward application of the total domination property of lemma 4–1 serves to identify I, and a straight-forward application of lemmas 4–2 and 4–3 serves to identify E. One of these sets is iteratively augmented by $\{l\}$ after the program for DMU_l is solved. In addition, using lemma 4–4, E can also be augmented by the reference set for DMU_l (that is, $E \leftarrow E \cup \Lambda^l$).

The *pricing* operation of the simplex method used to solve the mathematical programs is central to the efficiency of the simplex method. This operation is streamlined using *restricted basis entry*. That is, the variables that are explicitly priced are those in $D - I$, since any variable λ_j such that $j \in I$ will never be in an optimal solution for any DMU_j. If the number of totally dominated units is relatively large, the value of restricted basis entry is obvious. Even when the number of totally dominated units is zero, restricted basis entry is useful, particularly in the latter half of a DEA analysis. Pricing is further streamlined by using E as a candidate list. When the simplex method is invoked for DMU_l, only the variables in the candidate list are priced. This process serves to quickly locate at least some of the DMUs that compose reference set for DMU_l. Thus, the combination of restricted basis entry and candidate lists streamlines pricing regardless of the relative sizes of E^* and I^*. Their use not only allows reduction of the overall computations in pricing but also serves to reduce the number of iterations required to achieve optimality.

Rather than solving the programs for DMUs in the comparison set in the order that the data are arranged, it is computationally beneficial to use a dynamically determined ordering. One such dynamic ordering is determined by solving programs for (unprocessed) DMUs in E. The ordering is dynamic in the sense that E is iteratively modified by application of lemma 4–4. Further, when judiciously implemented, it serves to augment E quickly. Such dynamic ordering also serves to streamline computation in yet another manner, namely, the use of *advanced starting bases*. The optimal basis for a mathematical program for DMU_l can be used as an advanced starting basis for each unprocessed DMU_k where $k \in \Lambda^l$, the reference set for DMU_l. When an advanced basis is in fact optimal for DMU_k, then optimality of the program for DMU_k is proven without performing a single simplex pivot.

The benefits of using such computational constructs to streamline computation for DEA are reported in Ali (1992). We include some of the computational results from that study to illustrate their effect in streamlining DEA computation. Table 4–5 reports the number of DMUs, outputs, inputs, the number of inefficient units, $(i = |I^*|)$, the number of totally dominated units (d), the total number of simplex iterations used for all n units (the sum of the number of simplex iterations for each of the programs for n units), the number of times an advanced basis is employed, the number of CPU seconds used for data preprocessing, the total number of CPU seconds, and the CPU seconds per LP. As expected, execution time increases as problem size increases. As a fraction of the number of efficient units, the number of times an advanced basis is employed is significant. For data set 3, of the 30 efficient units, the mathematical programs for 18 are aided by the use of advanced bases. For data set 3, the number of pivots per DMU is slightly larger than 20 (5369/246).

Table 4–6 reports relevant statistics with and without the use of the computational constructs discussed in this section. The last column in the table quantifies the reduction in computation time obtained by the use of these constructs. Reduction in computational effort is more significant for larger data sets. For data set 4, which has 533 DMUs, reduction in computational effort is by a factor of 6—in other words, a reduction to only 16% of the effort that was required without the use of these efficient constructs. For all data sets, the total number of simplex pivots and the total number of variables for which the pricing operation is performed are reduced significantly. For example, for data set 4, the number of pivots decreases from 30,325 to 16,641. Similarly, substantially less effort is required for the pricing operation. For data set 4, the number of variables priced reduces from 16,762,794 to 1,458,434, or a reduction of about 91%.

5. DEA Software Features

In order to facilitate the use of data envelopment analysis, DEA software offers the ability to select any one of the several DEA models. Such software incorporates constructs that facilitate the solution of a sequence of linear programs. Because of specialized computational mechanisms, it circumvents the possibility of nonconvergence to optimality and produces accurate results.

DEA software breaks down the process of applying DEA into four steps:

Table 4–5. Summary of Computational Experience

Data Set	DMUs	Outputs	Inputs	CPU Seconds[a]				Preprocess	Total	per Lp
				i	d	Iter	Advanced			
1	81	3	3	63	17	1148	12	.22	5.10	.062
2	153	2	4	146	20	1387	4	.69	8.06	.052
3	246	4	3	216	28	5369	18	2.00	39.06	.158
4	533	4	3	503	139	16641	20	10.59	141.47	.265

[a] IBM9370, Engineering Computing Services, University of Massachusetts at Amherst.
i:Number of inefficient units; d:Number of dominated units.

Table 4–6. Effect of Streamlining

Data Set	Without Efficient Constructs			With Efficient Constructs			Improvement Ratio
	Number of Iterations	Number of Priced	CPU Seconds	Number of Iterations	Number of Priced	CPU Seconds	
1	1327	122098	9.11	1148	42695	5.10	.55
2	2736	468468	27.65	1387	74865	8.06	.29
3	6380	1697384	104.96	5369	397814	39.06	.37
4	30325	16762794	882.04	16641	1458434	141.67	.16

1. Data management

2. Model selection

3. Solution

4. Report generation

Data management allows preparation of data files and usually includes the ability to edit data in some fashion. Once data are resident within the software, the latter three steps, which pertain to actual DEA analysis, can be performed. As an example, let us suppose that we wish to use DEA to help in assessment of highway patrol units, as in the study by Cook, Roll, and Kazakov in chapter 10. We will assume the data resident within the software is as given in table 4–7.

Model selection refers to the selection of the particular variables that compose the m inputs, the s outputs, and the comparison set D of DMUs. Often, model selection allows the ability to scale and or translate the values of a particular input or output. Model selection also allows the selection of a particular DEA model to be used for the analysis from a menu. To perform an analysis for only those units in region 20, in our example, the comparison set consists of the 14 units in the region. Further, we may select a set of three outputs (AREA, TRAFFIC, SAFETY) and a set of two inputs (MAINTAIN, CAPITAL) for our illustrations using a VRS input-oriented model (i.e., model BCC_P-I).

After model selection, the approriate reference set, data, and model parameters are extracted, the analysis performed, and reports generated. Various kinds of reports are produced by DEA software; no standard format is used for report generation. In the rest of this section, we discuss the type of information provided by example reports. (Note that available software does not produce reports using this exact format.) There are several tabular reports that can immediately be used to identify efficiency classification of DMUs. Table 4–8, for example, reports total inefficiency as represented by the discrepancy between the original data for a DMU and the obtained projected point. Efficient DMUs are easily recognized to be those for which the original data and the projected point are the same. For our sample analysis, 8 of the 14 DMUs are efficient.

Individual reports summarize the analysis for each DMU. A generic report that would be obtained for the second unit in our analysis of region 20, i.e., DMU P:20-2, is illustrated in figure 4–2. The report identifies the DEA model and the size of the comparison set for the analysis. For each output and input variable, the original data, the projected point, and the difference between these is given in the columns DATA, PROJECTED,

Table 4–7. Highway Patrol Data[a]

DMU	AREA	TRAFFIC	PAVEMENT	SAFETY	MAINTAIN	CAPITAL	CLIMATE	REGION
P: 2–17	347	805	284	371	890	147	813	2
P:2–18	815	884	223	541	822	1578	1123	2
P:3–8	492	189	104	420	457	115	699	3
P:8–4	490	204	385	253	489	6	887	8
P:8–22	396	593	89	637	654	15	622	8
P:8–25	438	512	108	445	634	165	822	8
P:20–1	686	39	99	161	665	35	601	20
P:20–2	746	192	98	322	1636	1866	611	20
P:20–3	808	250	215	330	1482	35	631	20
P:20–4	561	62	288	232	423	7	650	20
P:20–5	740	19	99	132	459	140	703	20
P:20–6	1044	56	291	140	569	7	705	20
P:20–7	1332	141	195	409	640	29	686	20
P:20–8	1065	121	90	203	754	1597	649	20
P:20–9	435	71	272	187	499	618	575	20
P:20–10	634	59	339	276	398	705	659	20
P:20–11	922	161	168	326	1155	27	678	20
P:20–12	1259	187	100	289	889	474	677	20
P:20–13	638	154	272	213	549	146	650	20
P:20–14	1398	75	102	148	883	148	580	20

[a]Subset of data from Cook, Roll, and Kazakov (chapter 10, this volume). AREA: area served factor; TRAFFIC: average traffic served; PAVEMENT: pavement rating change factor; SAFETY: accident prevention factor; MAINTAIN: maintenance expenditures; CAPITAL: capital expenditures; CLIMATE: climatic factor; REGION: region of patrol unit. The first number in the DMU name is the region.

Table 4-8. Highway Patrol DEA Output: Total Excess Inputs and Slack Outputs

	Outputs			Inputs	
DMU	AREA	TRAFFIC	SAFETY	MAINTAIN	CAPITAL
P:20-1	.00	29.35	84.84	−208.33	−10.96
P:20-2	426.36	.00	.00	−663.44	−1578.72
P:20-3	.00	.00	.00	.00	.00
P:20-4	.00	.00	.00	.00	.00
P:20-5	.00	.00	.00	.00	.00
P:20-6	.00	31.87	148.56	−15.60	−1.97
P:20-7	.00	.00	.00	.00	.00
P:20-8	.00	.00	147.46	−188.58	−1376.17
P:20-9	187.29	.00	74.02	−78.55	−97.28
P:20-10	.00	.00	.00	.00	.00
P:20-11	.00	.00	4.62	−253.25	−1.71
P:20-12	.00	.00	.00	.00	.00
P:20-13	.00	.00	.00	.00	.00
P:20-14	.00	.00	.00	.00	.00

```
NAME: P:20-2                                    MODEL: VRS/Input
Unit: 2                              No. Units in Comparison Set: 14

                    DATA     PROJECTED    INEFFICIENCY    PRICE
Outputs...
AREA        (D)     746.00    1172.36         426.36       EPS
TRAFFIC     (D)     192.00     192.00            .00      .00527
SAFETY      (D)     322.00     322.00            .00      .00075
Inputs....
MAINTAIN    (D)    1636.00     972.56        -663.44      .00061
CAPITAL     (D)    1866.00     287.28       -1578.72       EPS


    Theta:     .59448    Virtual input:   1.252
    Phi:      1.00000    Virtual output:  1.000
    Sigma:    1248.370

    Analysis of Projection _____
                    Proportional    Residual..
    AREA                .00            .00
    TRAFFIC             .00            .00
    SAFETY              .00            .00
    MAINTAIN         663.44            .00
    CAPITAL          756.71         822.01


    Reference Set _____
    P:20-7     .19839
    P:20-12    .57739
    P:20-3     .22422
```

Figure 4-2. DEA report.

and INEFFICIENCY. The values of μ_{area}, $\mu_{traffic}$, μ_{safety}, $v_{maintain}$, and $v_{capital}$ are given in the column PRICE.

The projected point for unit 2 is summarized by Theta = .59488 and the sum of slacks by Sigma = 1248.37. Part of the inefficiency is due to reducing the inputs by a factor of (1-.59488), and the rest is aggregated in Sigma. Finally, the projected point is a convex combination of the units 3, 7, and 12 in the reference set.

A tabular presentation of efficiency scores also allows immediate identification of efficient and inefficient units. Such a report is illustrated in table 4–9, which tabulates values of θ and Σ $(= \Sigma_{r=1}^{s} s_r + \Sigma_{i=1}^{m} e_i)$. Since the values of individual slack output and excess input variables may also be of interest, these values are reported in table 4–10. However, note that it is not always possible to identify units that are efficient or inefficient solely on the basis of table 4–10. In the event that all inefficiency is entirely explained by θ, these slack output and excess input variables would be zero.

6. Summary

Given the ever-growing use of the DEA methodology, specializing computation specifically for DEA is relevant, since it greatly facilitates

Table 4–9.   Highway Patrol DEA Output: Efficiency Scores

DMU	θ	Σ
P:20-1	.68672	114.186
P:20-2	.59448	1248.370
P:20-3	1.00000	.000
P:20-4	1.00000	.000
P:20-5	1.00000	.000
P:20-6	.97259	180.427
P:20-7	1.00000	.000
P:20-8	.74989	1124.205
P:20-9	.84259	261.311
P:20-10	1.00000	.000
P:20-11	.93655	184.582
P:20-12	1.00000	.000
P:20-13	1.00000	.000
P:20-14	1.00000	.000

Table 4-10. Highway Patrol DEA Report: Output Slacks and Excess Inputs

DMU	Outputs			Inputs	
	AREA	TRAFFIC	SAFETY	MAINTAIN	CAPITAL
P:20-1	.00	29.35	84.84	.00	.00
P:20-2	426.36	.00	.00	.00	822.01
P:20-3	.00	.00	.00	.00	.00
P:20-4	.00	.00	.00	.00	.00
P:20-5	.00	.00	.00	.00	.00
P:20-6	.00	31.87	148.56	.00	.00
P:20-7	.00	.00	.00	.00	.00
P:20-8	.00	.00	147.46	.00	976.75
P:20-9	187.29	.00	74.02	.00	.00
P:20-10	.00	.00	.00	.00	.00
P:20-11	.00	.00	4.62	179.97	.00
P:20-12	.00	.00	.00	.00	.00
P:20-13	.00	.00	.00	.00	.00
P:20-14	.00	.00	.00	.00	.00

application of the methodology. Efficient DEA computation is possible and is achieved by employing appropriate theory and computational mechanisms. Issues of accurate and robust computation are pertinent primarily because of the computational characteristics of the mathematical programs that compose the methodology. The potential for inaccuracy due to such characteristics is circumvented by using appropriate computational mechanisms.

The use of a particular methodology is inherently tied to the availability of tools that facilitate its application. Neccessary criteria for computational tools for DEA include the following:

1. *Computational precision.* All "real arithmetic" should be carried out in double precision.
2. ε *for non-Archimedean models.* The non-Archimedean models should not be solved as linear programs with explicit value for ε.
3. *Avoidance of degeneracy.* When the number of inputs and outputs is larger than 10, the potential for cycling and/or slow convergence to a solution is significant.
4. *Tolerances.* Tolerances used for simplex calculations should be chosen in accordance with the range of values of the data set being analyzed.

In this chapter we have limited our discussion to essential characteristics of DEA models. The computational mechanisms remain the same when solving models that include restrictions specifying bounds or other relationships on the variables μ and v, or models that include categorical or non discretionary variables. However, the reader should be aware that these extensions can introduce their own additional computational characteristics.

Acknowledgments

This chapter has benefited from careful readings and incisive comments by Arie Lewin, Larry Seiford, and two anonymous reviewers.

Notes

1. Such properties do not obviate the need for solution of a mathematical program for each DMU in D. The programs still need to be solved to obtain other information. For example, even if a unit is known to be inefficient, the projected point generally needs to be obtained by means of a mathematical program.

2. When it is necessary to scale data, it should be borne in mind that all DEA models are not units-invariant with respect to the obtained projected point.

3. The reader will recall the fact that the effect of scaling the right-hand-side vector in a linear program by a positive scalar s is that the optimal solution vector is scaled by s. That is, if $\mathbf{x}^*$ is optimal for $\{\min \mathbf{cx} | \mathbf{Ax} = \mathbf{b}, \mathbf{x} \geq \mathbf{0}\}$, then $s\mathbf{x}^*$ is optimal for $\{\min \mathbf{cx} | \mathbf{Ax} = s\mathbf{b}, \mathbf{x} \geq \mathbf{0}\}$.

. 4. The analysis was actually run to completion for data set S81. With model BCC_P-I and rule 2, the analysis was completed after 3529640 iterations, requiring over 47 hours on a personal computer.

5. These models appear in chapter 2.

5 DEA SOFTWARE PACKAGES

1. Introduction

It is probably a truism that the lack of simple access to reliable DEA software packages has hampered the diffusion and wider application of DEA analyses. Although, in principle, DEA solutions can be obtained with convential linear programming software, in reality this task can be time-consuming. In principle, DEA solutions require the calculation of as many linear programs as there are DMUs. When using ordinary linear programming software packages, this task can become daunting even for small problems (e.g., 100 DMUs). DEA calculations with standard LP software packages are also prone to inaccurate classification of the improperly efficient and nearly efficient DMUs because of the need to calibrate, perhaps by trial and error, the appropriate magnitude of the non-Archimedean infinitesimal[1] that introduces lower-bound constraints on all variables (see Charnes, Cooper, and Rhodes, 1979; Lewin and Morey, 1981; see also chapter 4 of this volume and Ali and Seiford (1993) for a comparison of results with different values for the non-Archimedean infinitesimal). Specialized DEA codes eliminate the need to calibrate the non-Archimedean infinitesimal by a preemptive approach. In addition, specialized DEA codes automate the recursive running of LP programs, the scaling of data, and the choice of models (orientation and returns to scale). Most of the empirical DEA papers to date (including many of the chapters in this book) do not provide information on how the DEA calculations were made (e.g., standard LP packages or specialized DEA code). At this stage in its development, the maturation of DEA practice and its wider acceptance will, in our judgment, be facilitated by 1) standardizing DEA notation and reference to models (e.g., as developed in chapters 2 and 3) and 2) providing adequate information regarding the method of computation.

It is because of the paucity of information about the availability of production-quality DEA software that we are providing information on the DEA codes known to us. In the next section, we provide summary descriptions of five specialized DEA software packages that are currently available. For each software package, we contacted the developer and requested information regarding platforms, capabilities, and contacts for additional information. The responses to the questionnaire follow.

2. BYU-DEA

Name of DEA Code: BYUDEA

DEA code runs on what machine/operating system?
   IBM PC & Compatibles

What is the computational precision? 10^{-6}

For which additional platforms/operating systems is your software available?
   We also have a VAX version that we use for large applications.

Is documentation available?   Yes, but it is brief.

Which DEA models does it solve?   CCR, BCC, Multiplicative

Can it perform window analysis?   No

Does it handle:
   Nondiscretionary variables?   Yes
   Categorical variables?   Yes
   Restrictions on the multipliers (cone ratio/assurance region techniques)?
   Yes

Does it incorporate epsilon for non-Archimedean models? If so, how?
Indirectly through the superefficiency option. A superefficient DEA value > 1 indicates a frontier point without slack; a superefficiency DEA value = 1.0 indicates a frontier point with positive slack.

Does it incorporate an anticycling technique?
Yes, it has a lexicographic ratio test, to avoid cycling.

Person to contact for additional information? (name, address, phone, fax, email)

Donald L. Adolphson
Marriott School of Management
Brigham Young University
Provo, Utah 84602
(801) 378-2433
(801) 378-5984 (FAX)
ADOLPHSD@msm1.byu.edu

Lawrence C. Walters
Marriott School of Management
Brigham Young University
Provo, Utah 84602
(801) 378-7495
(801) 378-5984 (FAX)
larry@ipm.byu.edu

3. IDEAS

Name of DEA Code: IDEAS

DEA code runs on what machine/operating system?
IBM PC-Compatible 286 and above with MS DOS 3.1 and above

What is the computational precision? REAL*8

For which additional platforms/operating systems is your software available?
Customization for large data sets and different hardware platforms is available.

Is documentation available? Yes

Which DEA models does it solve? CCR, BCC, Multiplicative, Additive

Can it perform window analysis? Automatically? No

Does it handle:
Nondiscretionary variables? Yes
Categorical variables? Yes
Restrictions on the multipliers (cone ratio/assurance region techniques)? Yes

Does it incorporate epsilon for non-Archimedean models? If so, how?
  Through a two-stage approach in two different ways

Does it incorporate an anticycling technique?
  Yes

Person to contact for additional information? (name, address, phone, fax, email)
  Agha Iqbal Ali
  1 Consulting
  PO Box 2453
  Amherst MA 01004-2453
  413-256-1211

4. PIONEER

Name of DEA Code: PIONEER

DEA code runs on what machine/operating system? Any Unix-based system; MS DOS version under development. Parallel processing version available for Sequent computers.

What is the computational precision? Double

For which additional platforms/operating systems is your software available?
  See above

Is documentation available? Under development

Which DEA models does it solve? CCR, BCC, Multiplicative, Additive

Can it perform window analysis? Yes

Does it handle:
  Nondiscretionary variables? Not yet
  Categorical variables? Not yet
  Restrictions on the multipliers (cone ratio/assurance region techniques)?
  Under development

Does it incorporate epsilon for non-Archimedean models? If so, how?
  Through a two-phase approach

Does it incorporate an anticycling technique? Yes

Additional Features:

PIONEER is designed for solving large-scale problems, and has been applied to data sets of over 8000 DMUs.

Person to contact for additional information? (name, address, phone, fax, email)

Dr. Richard Barr
email: barr@seas.smu.edu
Dept. Computer Science and Engineering
Science Info Center 306
Southern Methodist University
Dallas, TX 75275
Phones:
(214) 768-2605 office
(214) 768-3085 fax @ office
(214) 826-3289 fax @ home

5. Warwick-DEA

Name of DEA Code: Warwick DEA Software

DEA code runs on what machine/operating system?
Under DOS on IBM compatible PCs

What is the computational precision?
Single, but double precision available

For which additional platforms/operating systems is your software available?
None at present for the up-to-date version. (Older version ran under UNIX and on IBM mainframes. New version is not yet upgraded to these systems).

Is documentation available?   Yes

Which DEA models does it solve?

CCR, BCC, Additive

Targets models (nonradial models (see Thanassoulis and Dyson, *EJOR* 56:80–97), model m3)

Mixed Targets model (as targets model, but a radial improvement of specified size is given top priority)

Can it perform window analysis?   No

Does it handle:

Nondiscretionary variables?   Yes, BCC model only (at present)

Categorical variables?   No

Restrictions on the multipliers (cone ratio/assurance region techniques)?
Yes—restrictions on raw weights as well as virtual inputs and outputs

Does it incorporate epsilon for non-Archimedean models? If so, how?
It uses two-phase optimization

Does it incorporate an anticycling technique?   Yes

Additional Features:

For BCC models, the omega range is given to enable the user to ascertain the nature of returns to scale.

For efficient DMUs, the maximum weight for each input–output variable is given such that the efficiency is not affected.

The user can incorporate weights during radial as well as nonradial (additive solution) phases.

The user can assess the efficiency of a DMU without including it in the reference set of DMUs ("superefficiency").

Software is available in versions that utilize a Math co-processor.

Person to contact for additional information? (name, address, phone, fax, email)
Dr. Emmanuel Thanassoulis
Warwick Business School
Warwick University
Coventry CV4 7AL, UK
Tel +44 203 523 523 Ext 2145
Fax +44 203 524 539
E-Mail orset@wbs.warwick.ac.uk

Notes

1. It should be emphasized that the non-Archimedean infinitesimal is *not* a number, and hence, in principle, cannot be approximated by any finite-valued number. Standard LP packages require the user to internally represent this infinitesimal by a small number. The correct approach, as implemented in most DEA codes, is to employ a two-phase optimization. See Ali and Seiford (1993).

II NOVEL APPLICATIONS

6 EVALUATING THE IMPACTS OF OPERATING STRATEGIES ON EFFICIENCY IN THE U.S. AIRLINE INDUSTRY

Rajiv D. Banker and Holly H. Johnston

1. Introduction

The purpose of this chapter is to introduce a new methodology within the framework of data envelopment analysis (DEA) that can be used to evaluate the impacts of operating strategies on efficiency and relate efficiencies to the competitive position of the firm. In management science, there has been an increasing emphasis on the potential use and effectiveness of broad competitive or business strategies, such as those set forth by Miles and Snow (1978), Miller and Friesen (1984), and Porter (1980, 1985). There is also an ongoing interest in evaluating the effectiveness of operating strategies that are intended to enhance competitive position by constributing to efforts to improve productivity and throughput, reduce inventory holding costs, and otherwise reduce costs and enhance revenues. If the absolute and relative impacts of these strategies are to be examined empirically, then there is a need for quantitative measures that capture the constructs involved and models that capture the causal relationships between variables reflecting operating strategies, efficiency, and competitive strategy or position. Such models should also be useful for management by enhancing its ability both to assess the

97

realized impacts of operating and business strategies ex post and to predict the likely impacts of proposed alternative strategies.

DEA provides methods for estimating production frontiers and measuring productivity that require a minimal set of assumptions regarding technology and minimum extrapolation from observed data. DEA does not require assumptions regarding cost minimization or profit maximization or equivalence between technologies across firms. Also, in applied econometrics, DEA is being found to be fairly robust to the specification of functional form (see Gong and Sickles, 1990). As a result, DEA may provide a particularly robust methodology for use in research involving production frontiers as well as operating and business strategies that are difficult to capture empirically, particularly for industries that are in disequilibrium and have rapidly changing technologies and competitive and regulatory environments.

With respect to DEA itself, there is a need for models that control for relationships between the best-practice frontier and differences in the enveloped production frontiers that are reflected in the measures of technical efficiency. DEA provides a linear piecewise estimate of the production-possibility frontier in terms of input and output quantities. The frontier is the tightest-fitting envelope of the data, and technical efficiency is measured in terms of deviations from it. With pooled cross-sectional, time series data, DEA provides an estimate of the long-run industry or sample best-practice frontier. The frontier envelops a potentially large number of related frontiers with differing (and often unobservable) parameters, depending on the relationships between input and output quantities that hold for different firms and different points in time. Individual firms may have different versions of technology in place at any given point in time, and each firm may have a somewhat different version of its own technology in place at each successive point in time. A firm may be on its own best-practice frontier, given the technology that it has in place, and be considered technically inefficient with respect to the sample frontier. Alternatively, it may be on a sample (cross-sectional frontier during an early time period, before certain technological or organizational advances that enable the frontier to expand, and therefore may be treated as technically inefficient with respect to the long-run frontier. The observed deviations from the frontier are due to differences in specific characteristics of the technology (such as process configuration, the extent to which firms can exploit potential sources of economies, and management strategies), as well as to pure technical inefficiency (the failure to be on any frontier) and any measurement error that may be present. Thus, it would be useful if models could be developed within the

DEA framework to capture the relationships not only between input and output quantities but also between the production correspondence or efficiency and these operating characteristics and other factors, such as exogenous events, which influence efficiency.

In this chapter, we begin to develop a class of models within a DEA, maximum likelihood (MLE) framework to address these two needs. We begin, in section 2, by developing measures of cost efficiency and revenue-generating efficiency that are based on DEA measures of technical efficiency and can be related respectively to Porter's generic low-cost leadership and product differentiation strategies. The measures can be plotted with reference to each other and their frontiers to analyze the realized strategic positioning of firms graphically.[1] This approach is illustrated in section 3 with an application to the U.S. domestic airline industry during the transition following deregulation, a period of considerable change with respect to technology and competitive environment, as well as interest from the standpoint of management and public policy. The analysis provides a set of substantive results that complement earlier industry findings by Bailey and Williams (1988). The rest of the chapter is devoted to sketching out a multivariate modeling approach for statistically estimating the relationships between operating strategies, industry-wide and firm-specific events, and technical efficiency in the use of inputs and generation of revenue. To the extent that the measures of cost and revenue-generating efficiency capture elements of Porter's low-cost and differentiation strategies, the models can also be used to infer the relationships between operating strategies and events and realized competitive position.

To motivate the models from a methodological perspective, we begin section 4 by drawing upon a paper by Banker (1993), which provides a statistical foundation for DEA. Banker presents conditions under which DEA estimators of production frontiers and technical efficiency are consistent and/or MLE. The approach involves attributing probability density functions (p.d.f.'s) to DEA measures of efficiency, and the results hold for a broad class of distributions, including the lognormal, exponential, and half-normal. This chapter represents a first step in our long-term research. The goal is to develop a class of models that provide MLE for functions describing the relationships between the characteristics of the enveloped production frontiers, strategic or operating choice variables, exogenous and endogenous events, and efficiencies. This chapter presents the basic modeling approach and a preliminary, illustrative application to the airline industry. In section 4, we sketch out two alternative modeling approaches, using the half-normal distribution to illustrate them, and note some of the methodological issues that will be involved in implementing the approach. Next, since it would be useful to be able to work with the normal distribution and appeal to the equivalence of ordinary least squares (OLS) and MLE, as a logical first step, in section 5 we explore a model utilizing the lognormal distribution and transformations to the normal. The model involves some theoretical and empirical disadvantages as well as the initially apparent advantages and is intended only to provide an illustrative application. The substantive results are not intended to provide a basis for policy or managerial decisions. Section 6 contains a few brief concluding remarks.

2. Evaluating Business Strategy: Measures of Cost and Revenue-Generating Efficiency

DEA is usually used to evaluate productivity, an important component of a firm's overall cost advantage and a successful low-cost strategy. However, in industries where there are material differences in input prices between firms, it is also important to measure advantages in terms of input prices to capture the firm's total cost advantage. The measures of technical and aggregate cost efficiency in the use of inputs developed in this section are intended to accomplish this. A successful differentiation strategy involves realizing higher output prices. This may be accomplished by providing a service that consumers perceive to be of high quality and for which consumers are therefore willing to pay a premium. In the case of a focus or niche-differentiation strategy, this can also be accomplished by achieving geographically based monopoly power. In a DEA framework, these can be examined via the ratio of the revenue of the firm to the maximum revenue generated by any firm in the industry, while controlling for output levels.

To capture the ability of the firm to differentiate its product and/or achieve monopoly power and thereby achieve higher price realizations, for each firm j and time period t, we solve the BCC_P-O program in chapter 2, section 4.2, substituting total revenues for the output quantity in the model and the vector y_{rjt} of output quantities for the inputs in the model. The reciprocal ϕ'_{jt} ($0 < \phi'_{jt} \leq 1$) of the resulting efficiency scalar ϕ_{jt} provides a measure of *revenue-generating efficiency (RGE)*. It can be interpreted as the proportion of revenues actually achieved out of the maximum revenues possible, given the firm's vector of actual outputs.

To capture the ability to implement a low-cost strategy, we develop a measure of *aggregate cost efficiency (ACE)*, capturing both productivity in the use of inputs and advantages in input prices relative to the industry. For each firm j, input i, and period t, we solve the BCC_P-I program (chapter 2, section 4.1) where x_{ijt} is the quantity of input i for referent firm j during period t and y_{rjt} is the vector of output quantities r produced by firm j during period t. The resulting efficiency scores θ_{ijt} ($0 < \theta_{ijt} \leq 1$) scale the quantities of inputs actually used by the firm to the minimum quantities that could have been used. These scores and data on actual inputs and prices are then combined, assuming separability, into a measure of ACE as in

$$ACE_{jt} = \frac{\Sigma_{ijt} \theta_{ijt} x_{ijt} p_{it}^{min}}{\Sigma_{ijt} x_{ijt} p_{ijt}} \qquad (6.1)$$

where

p_{ijt} = the average price per unit of input i paid by firm j during period t, and

p_{it}^{min} = the minimum price per unit of input i paid by any sample firm during period t.

The maintained assumption of separability is discussed in the following section.[2] ACE_{jt}, then, may be factored into the product of two ratios representing *aggregate input usage efficiency (AIUE)* and *aggregate input price efficiency (AIPE)*, where

$$AIUE_{jt} = \frac{\Sigma_{ijt} \theta_{ijt} x_{ijt} p_{ijt}}{\Sigma_{ijt} x_{ijt} p_{ijt}} \qquad (6.2)$$

and

$$AIPE_{jt} = \frac{\Sigma_{ijt} \theta_{ijt} x_{ijt} p_{it}^{min}}{\Sigma_{ijt} \theta_{ijt} x_{ijt} p_{ijt}} \qquad (6.3)$$

3. Application to the Airline Industry

Next we use the measures described above to examine graphically the strategic positioning of a sample of airlines during part of the transition following deregulation. We begin by describing the industry context, characteristics of production, and categories of inputs and outputs and data used.

3.1. Industry Context

The domestic airline industry provides a particularly rich setting for the empirical study of relationships between cost and revenue structures, operating strategies, efficiency, and business strategies. The industry was formally deregulated by the Airline Deregulation Act of 1978, which called for a six-year phased transition to deregulation, and the transition, in terms of both regulatory policy and industry strategy, continues today.[3] In response to the changing regulatory environment, carriers adopted a variety of competitive and operating strategies, which included adopting hub-and-spoke systems; reconfiguring networks to eliminate unprofitable routes and add more lucrative, feeder and long-haul flight segments; reconfiguring fleets to match aircraft characteristics to route structures; adopting new fuel-efficient aircraft and computerized flight management systems; increasing aircraft utilization rates; and renegotiating labor contracts to obtain more flexible work rules and other reductions in labor costs (Bailey et al., 1985; Graham and Kaplan, 1982; U.S. General Accounting Office, 1985). Many of these strategies were thought to have substantial impacts on productivity and input prices as well as the ability to generate revenues.

Price competition was intense. The industry engaged in its first round of intense fare wars in 1982 and the spring of 1983. Following a brief respite during the second half of 1983, further rounds of competitive fare setting began, although these were less widespread and more route specific. Price competition between the major carriers in major hubs and on transcontinental and eastern corridor routes, as well as between incumbent carriers and low-cost new entrants, was particularly intense. There were also intense, and often bitter, labor–management negotiations and strikes, as well as several bankruptcies, takeover bids and mergers, and changes in top management. Finally, the process of adjustment was complicated by industrywide events such as the August 1981 Professional Air Traffic Controllers Organization (PATCO) strike and subsequent Federal Aviation Administration (FAA) restrictions on slots and operations at the nation's 22 largest airports, and decreases in demand due to the 1981–1982 recession. The combined effects of the carriers' operating strategies and these events should be reflected in the observed repositioning, in terms of overall business strategy, of the carriers throughout the period.

3.2. Characteristics of Production

The production of air transportation services is characterized by multiple outputs, a large number of categories of costs, a large proportion of fixed or capacity costs, and few input substitution possibilities once aircraft have been selected. In this chapter, efficiency scores are calculated for 10 categories of inputs: 1) aircraft and traffic servicing labor (ground labor handling aircraft, passengers, baggage, and cargo), 2) reservations and sales labor, 3) flight crew labor (pilots, copilots, navigators, and flight engineers), 4) flight attendant labor, 5) fuels and oils, 6) maintenance labor, 7) maintenance materials and overhead, 8) ground property and equipment, 9) flight equipment, and 10) general overhead. Labor inputs are expressed in hours, and fuels and oils in gallons. Inputs in the remaining categories are expressed in deflated dollars as described below. Outputs are defined in terms of revenue outputs, that is, revenue passenger miles (RPMs), and categorized according to the type of aircraft used:[4]

- older model, regular-bodied aircraft, including, for example, McDonnell-Douglas DC-119s and Boeing 727s;
- older model, wide-bodied aircraft, including McDonnell-Douglas DC-10s and DC-8s, Lockheed L-1011s, and Boeing 747s; and
- more recently introduced, fuel-efficient models, including Boeing 737s, 757s, and 767s, McDonnell-Douglas Super 80s, and Airbus Industrie A300s.[5]

Choices regarding aircraft should reflect the firm's strategic choices regarding route structure, flight frequency, fleet mix, and load factors.s They also should largely determine the required quantities of other inputs. As a result, the substitution possibilities between input categories, except via the choice of aircraft, are marginal,[6] and, ex post, the production technology, given these strategic choices, may be characterized by fixed proportions.

3.3. Industry Data

The data are from a panel of quarterly data from 1981–Q1 to 1985–Q4, for 12 major national and regional carriers (American, Continental, Delta, Eastern, Northwest, Pan American, Piedmont, Republic, Trans World, United, USAir, and Western). They were developed from traffic and financial statistics from Form 41 Reports submitted by certificated carriers to the Civil Aeronautics Board (CAB) and Department of Transportation (DOT). The financial statistics include detailed revenue and expenditure accounts by functional categories, assets, and liabilities. The traffic statistics include the number of aircraft departures and passenger and ton miles for different categories of passengers and types of cargo. The data also include annual full-time equivalent labor inputs by operating function and annual inventories of carriers' aircraft fleets, which we have supplemented with semiannual and quarterly data from Form 41 Reports, annual fleet data published in *Air Transport World*, and fleet data from carriers' annual reports.[7] The data were cleaned by cross-checking calculations and, where necessary, by obtaining original hard-copy data from the DOT. The unit of analysis is the carrier's domestic operating system.[8]

Inputs representing the flow of services from flight equipment (airframes, aircraft engines, avionics, etc.) were calculated by imputing fairmarket rental values to owned and leased aircraft by aircraft category. Inputs representing the flow of services from ground property and equipment were calculated using the "perpetual inventory" method developed by Christensen and Jorgenson (1969).[9] They include landing fees deflated by the Air Transport Association cost index for landing fees and rental expenses for ground property and equipment deflated by the Producer Price Index for fixed nonresidential structures. Maintenance material and overhead inputs were calculated as the total cost of maintenance of property and equipment, deflated by the Producer Price Index for fabricated metals. General overhead inputs were calculated using the total expenses for supplies, general and administrative personnel, utilities, insurance, communications, and so forth, deflated by the GNP Implicit Price Deflator.

3.4. Graphical Examination of Strategic Positions

Examining sources of economic rents under deregulation, Bailey and Williams (1988) find the industry to be a hybrid of two classes of carriers: 1) former local service carriers, including, for example, USAir and Piedmont, endowed from regulation with regional sources of rents (due to barriers to entry associated with thin routes into small regional hubs) and 2) former trunk carriers, including the four largest carriers, United, American, Eastern, and Delta, as well as the smaller trunk carriers, endowed with scale-based sources of rents (due to opportunities to use large aircraft, hubs, and scale-based pricing techniques and to induce brand loyalty). Plotting the carriers in average revenue yield (revenue per RPM) and decreasing cost per (ASM) space for 1978 and 1984, they compare the carriers' strategic positions at the beginning and end of the CAB's phased transition to deregulation. For 1978, they find two distinct clusters. The former local service carriers exhibit relatively high costs and revenue yields, representing service differentiation and/or the ability to extract local monopoly rents. The former trunk carriers exhibit relatively low costs and yields, representing the ability to exploit scale-based sources of rents. In contrast, for 1984, they find a dispersion of carriers along a continuum between low costs and high yields, with the movement for all but two carriers in the sample indicating trade-offs between differentiated and low-cost positions.

Plotting geometric means of the carriers' *RGE* and *ACE* ratios for 1981 through 1985 with respect to each other and their frontiers (see figures 6–1, 6–2, and 6–3; the corresponding data are provided in table 6–1), we obtain somewhat different but consistent and complementary results.[10] We cover an intersecting period of time and use different measures to operationalize differentiation and low-cost leadership, but obtain similar broad findings. (Bailey and Williams (1988) use measures of revenue and cost per unit output, while we use efficiency-based measures which control for differences in outputs across carriers.) While it is difficult to compare the movements between positions for specific carriers across the two studies because there are not enough data to establish comparable benchmark positions,[11] we also find that

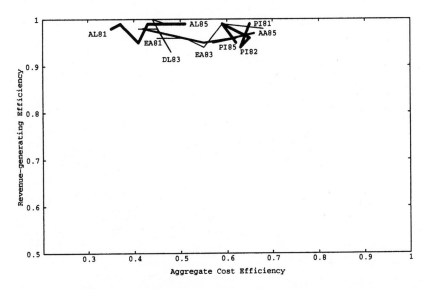

Figure 6–1. Strategic repositioning of U.S. airlines during the transition following deregulation: carriers with high RGE.

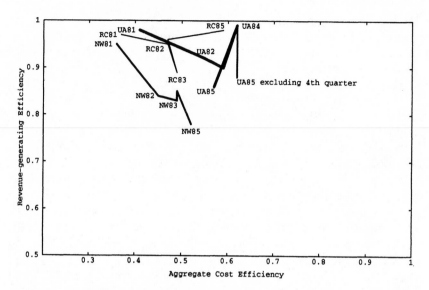

Figure 6–2. Strategic repositioning of U.S. airlines during the transition following deregulation: carriers with lower RGE.

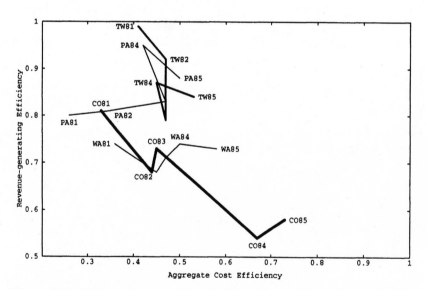

Figure 6–3. Strategic repositioning of U.S. airlines during the transition following deregulation: carriers exhibiting substantial movement.

Table 6-1. Strategic Repositioning of U.S. Airlines During the Transition following Deregulation (Annual Geometric Means of Quarterly Observations)

Carrier	Year	ACE	AIUE	AIPE	RGE
Carriers with High RGE (Figure 6-1)					
American (AA)	1981	.42	.62	.67	.98
	1982	.55	.81	.67	.95
	1983	.62	.87	.71	.96
	1984	.57	.80	.72	.95
	1985	.66	.88	.75	.97
Delta (DL)	1981	.41	.60	.69	.98
	1982	.45	.64	.70	.98
	1983	.48	.67	.72	.93
	1984	.44	.61	.72	1.00
	1985	.47	.64	.73	.99
Eastern (EA)	1981	.45	.65	.69	.96
	1982	.51	.70	.73	.96
	1983	.55	.77	.72	.94
	1984	.59	.80	.74	.99
	1985	.68	.93	.73	.98
Piedmont (PI)	1981	.65	.92	.71	.99
	1982	.63	.87	.73	.94
	1983	.65	.88	.75	.96
	1984	.59	.79	.76	.99
	1985	.62	.79	.79	.95
USAir (AL)	1981	.35	.49	.71	.98
	1982	.37	.52	.71	.99
	1983	.41	.56	.73	.95
	1984	.43	.61	.72	.99
	1985	.51	.71	.71	.99
Carriers with Lower RGE (Figure 6-2)					
Northwest (NW)	1981	.36	.52	.70	.95
	1982	.45	.62	.73	.84
	1983	.49	.66	.74	.83
	1984	.49	.65	.75	.85
	1985	.52	.69	.75	.78
Republic (RC)	1981	.37	.55	.66	.97
	1982	.47	.66	.71	.95
	1983	.49	.65	.75	.89
	1984	.47	.60	.79	.96
	1985	.59	.74	.80	.98

Table 6–1. *Continued*

Carrier	Year	ACE	AIUE	AIPE	RGE
United (UA)	1981	.41	.64	.65	.98
	1982	.55	.84	.66	.92
	1983	.59	.90	.66	.90
	1984	.62	.90	.69	.99
	1985	.57	.77	.75	.86
Carriers Exhibiting Substantial Movement (Figure 6–3)					
Continental (CO)	1981	.33	.47	.71	.81
	1982	.44	.56	.78	.68
	1983	.45	.76	.59	.73
	1984	.67	.73	.92	.54
	1985	.73	.89	.82	.58
Pan American (PA)	1981	.26	.42	.61	.80
	1982	.35	.54	.65	.81
	1983	.47	.71	.65	.83
	1984	.42	.59	.71	.95
	1985	.50	.80	.63	.88
Trans World (TW)	1981	.41	.60	.68	.99
	1982	.47	.67	.71	.92
	1983	.47	.62	.76	.79
	1984	.45	.63	.71	.87
	1985	.53	.75	.71	.84
Western (WA)	1981	.36	.51	.70	.74
	1982	.45	.60	.74	.68
	1983	.47	.61	.76	.71
	1984	.50	.64	.78	.74
	1985	.58	.75	.77	.73

most of the movement appears to represent a trade-off between the two strategic positions.

The results are also complementary in that we can examine the carriers' successive positioning in greater detail. Since we use more frequent observations and measures of efficiency plotted with reference to frontiers, we find somewhat less of a continuum between differentiation and low-cost leadership. We can also see the intermediate adjustment that occurs and observe many more instances (roughly one third of all shifts) in which a carrier's movement indicates simultaneous improvement or deterioration along both strategic dimensions. Also, some carriers are consistently high or low along both dimensions. Finally, our measures are less scale dependent and show that, for most carriers, there is considerable change in *ACE* with respect to the frontier and relatively less in *RGE*.

Several commonalities across carriers are evident. Between 1981 and 1983, most carriers exhibit improvements in *ACE*. This finding is likely to reflect the impacts of early efforts to improve productivity and reduce costs, including early adoption of hub-and-spoke systems, reconfiguration of networks, and increases in aircraft utilization rates. During this period, many carriers also exhibit drops in *RGE*. This finding is likely to reflect the impacts of decreases in demand during the 1981–1992 recession and increasing competition in fare setting, culminating in the 1982–1983 fare wars. Between 1983 and 1984, in the aftermath of the fare wars, most carriers exhibit improvements in *RGE* accompanied by declines in *ACE*. The fare wars had resulted in substantial losses in profitability, and during a period of retrenchment in the second half of 1983, the industry began to show profitability for first time since deregulation. Also, by this time most of the carriers had begun to establish hub-and-spoke systems and modernize their fleets. Finally, between 1984 and 1985, the industry seemed to settle into a more stable phase of continuing readjustment, and most carriers begin to exhibit improvements in *ACE* again.

Several carriers are clustered at relatively high levels of *RGE* (see figure 6–1 or table 6–1). These include two former local service carriers, USAir (AL) and Piedmont (PI), that appeared to have monopoly power in their hubs, suggesting the ability to earn monopoly rents as opposed to premiums for differentiated services. USAir exhibits the lowest *ACE*, due primarily to its low *AIUE*, and achieves some improvements in *ACE* by increasing *AIUE*, while maintaining high *RGE*. Piedmont begins with higher *ACE*, due primarily to high *AIUE*. Its *ACE* then diminishes as it trades off *AIUE* for *AIPE*, and Piedmont suffers net losses in both *ACE* and *RGE*. Three of the four largest former trunk carriers, American (AA), Delta (DL), and Eastern (EA), were also able to achieve high *RGE* and comparable gains in *AIPE*. Most of the remaining carriers exhibit more movement in both *RGE* and *ACE*. The largest former trunk carrier, United (UA), was able to achieve substantial gains in *ACE*, due mainly to gains in *AIUE*, between 1981 and 1983 (see figure 6–2 or table 6–1). Following its retrenchment between 1983 and 1984, it suffered losses in both *ACE* and *RGE* between 1984 and 1985. The net losses in *ACE* during 1985 were due to a drop in *AIUE*, probably due to its second-quarter 29-day pilots' strike. Without the strike, as illustrated by the mean point for the first three quarters of 1985, its losses in *RGE* might still have been substantial, but those in *ACE* might not have been.

The most repositioning is exhibited by Continental (CO) and two primarily international carriers, Pan American (PA) and Trans World (TW) (see figure 6–3 or table 6–1). Continental began the period as a local service carrier with an apparent high-cost, differentiation strategy. Following its takeover by Texas Air in October 1981, ACE increased. However, continuing labor–management relation problems led to strikes by its mechanics beginning in August 1983 and by pilots and flight attendants beginning in October 1983, and Continental filed for bankruptcy in September 1983. Following the resolution of the bankruptcy proceedings in January 1984, Continental emerged with higher $AIUE$ and $AIPE$ and lower RGE, an apparent low-cost strategy. Although it is difficult to determine without additional information, Continental, Pan American, and Trans World appear to be in transition between strategic positions, as opposed to being "stuck in the middle."

4. Modeling the Impacts of Operating Strategies and Events on Efficiency

The differences in positioning observed above should reflect the carriers' choices regarding network structure, fleet and service mix, service quality, pricing, and load factors, as well as the impacts of the PATCO strike and carrier-specific mergers, strikes, and bankruptcies. In the remaining sections, we develop a DEA-based approach to modeling the relationships between these variables and events, and the carriers' RGE and technical efficiency in the use of inputs by input category. We begin by summarizing the Banker (1993) results on the statistical consistency of DEA estimators that first motivated this chapter.

4.1. DEA, MLE, and Consistency

Banker (1993) proves that, if the deviations between the actual and efficient quantities of outputs, given a vector of inputs, are regarded as observations on independently and identically distributed (i.i.d.) random variables generated by a monotonically decreasing $p.d.f.$, then DEA estimators of the best-practice, monotonically increasing, and concave production frontier are MLE. That is, the frontier estimates solving the DEA linear program also solve the corresponding MLE problem, and DEA estimators provide a MLE of the production frontier, a desirable statistical criterion for an estimator.[12] Banker also shows that DEA estimators of the best-practice production frontier are likely to be biased downward from the true production frontier for a finite sample size[13] and proves that asymptotically this bias approaches zero, that is, the DEA estimators are consistent. Banker also shows that if 1) the true production frontier is monotonically increasing and concave, 2) the true inefficiency deviations from the frontier values are independent of the inputs, and 3) the probability of arbitrarily small inefficiency deviations is strictly greater than zero, then the DEA estimators are consistent and the asymptotic distribution of the efficiency scores is the same as the true distribution. Thus, Banker's consistency results hold for a broader class of distributions, beyond those that are monotonically decreasing, as long as the probability of arbitrarily small deviations from the frontier is strictly positive.

4.2. Alternative Modeling Approaches

This section sketches out a complementary set of models that provide MLE of parameters defining the relationships between characteristics of production technologies, operating choice variables, exogenous and endogenous events, and technical efficiencies. Since the Banker proofs involve attributing a *p.d.f.* to the observed distribution of technical efficiencies, it seems logical to use the same classes of density functions to specify these models. This raises methodological issues of choosing *p.d.f.*'s that yield these properties, fit the empirical distributions of efficiencies as closely as possible (without over-fitting), and provide solutions to first-order conditions. These issues have been explored to some extent in the literature, which has developed methods to estimate production frontiers using parametric approaches. Therefore, as we pursue this line of research beyond the initial efforts presented here, in addition to deriving the models directly, we will be able to draw on this work for evidence regarding the statistical and empirical advantages and disadvantages of using different classes of distributions. The half-normal distribution appears to be one of the most promising candidates for a distribution that will satisfy the requirement for a monotonically decreasing *p.d.f.* and for the gamma distribution for a skewed unimodal density function that will support a consistent estimator. Schmidt (1976) used the exponential and half-normal distributions to provide a statistical (MLE) basis for the Aigner–Chu (1968) frontier models. Also, the half-normal, exponential, and gamma distributions have been used in stochastic frontier estimation, for example, by Aigner, Lovell, and Schmidt (1977), Cowing,

Reifschneider, and Stevenson (1982), Meeusen and van den Broeck (1977), and Gong and Sickles (1990).

Next we suggest two alternative modeling approaches, depending on the type of distribution that fits the observed efficiencies and the way the parameters of the distribution are postulated to affect efficiency. One approach is to use a standard regression-type model, with the efficiencies specified as functions of vectors of technology, operating choice, and event variables, and a random disturbance term following the postulated distribution. For example, the true-efficiency deviations and therefore asymptotically the DEA estimators, θ_{ijt}, by input category i, can be hypothesized to be some function $h_i(\bullet)$ of a vector of $k = 1, 2, \ldots, K$ technology, operating choice and event variables, z_{jt}, and a random disturbance ε_{ijt}:

$$\theta_{ijt} = h_i(z_{jt})\,\varepsilon_{ijt} \tag{6.4}$$

If the ε_{ijt} are independently distributed with continuous, individual p.d.f. $f(\varepsilon_{ijt})$, and equation (6.4) is continuous and differentiable, then the individual p.d.f. for θ_{ijt} will be

$$g(\theta_{ijt}) = f(s(\theta_{ijt}))\,ds(\theta_{ijt})/d\theta_{ijt} \tag{6.5}$$

where $s(\theta_{ijt})$ is the inverse function of equation (6.4). The industry joint p.d.f. for input i would be

$$g_i = \Pi_{jt}g(\theta_{ijt}) \tag{6.6}$$

Suppose that the ε_{ijt} are distributed half-normally with parameter σ_i. Then

$$f(\varepsilon_{ijt};\,\sigma_i) = \frac{2}{\sqrt{2\pi}\,\sigma_i}\exp\{-\varepsilon_{ijt}^2/2\sigma_i^2\} \tag{6.7}$$

and

$$\begin{aligned} g(\theta_{ijt}) &= f(\theta_{ijt}/h_i(z_{jt}))\,d(\theta_{ijt}/h_i(z_{jt}))/d\theta_{ijt} \\ &= \frac{2}{\sqrt{2\pi}\,\sigma_i h_i(z_{jt})}\exp\{-(\theta_{ijt}/h_i(z_{jt}))^2/2\sigma_i^2\} \end{aligned} \tag{6.8}$$

To obtain MLE, optimization algorithms and econometric methods appropriate for multivariate models and panel data can be used to choose values for the parameters of $h_i(z_{jt})$ and parameter σ_i that maximize the corresponding joint p.d.f. The θ_{ijt} scale the parameter estimates in $h_i(z_{jt})$ and $g(\theta_{ijt})$. Substituting 1 for θ_{ijt} yields observations that are linear extrapolations onto the frontier given the values of z_{jt}.

An alternative approach would be to assume that just the efficiency scores themselves are distributed according to the postulated *p.d.f.* and that the parameters of the *p.d.f.* are functions of the technology, operating choice, and event variables. The efficiency scores can be transformed as necessary to satisfy the range properties of the random variable. For example, let $\theta'_{ijt} = 1/\theta_{ijt} - 1$ so $0 \leqslant \theta'_{ijt} < \infty$, and suppose that the θ'_{ijt} are distributed half-normally with parameter σ_{ijt}, where

$$\sigma_{ijt} = h_i(z_{jt}) \tag{6.9}$$

Then

$$
\begin{aligned}
f(\theta'_{ijt}; \sigma_{ijt}) &= (2/\sqrt{2\pi}\,\sigma_{ijt})\exp\{-\theta^2_{ijt}/2\sigma^2_{ijt}\} \\
&= (2/\sqrt{2\pi}\,h_i(z_{jt}))\exp\{-\theta^2_{ijt}/2(h_i(z_{jt}))^2\} \tag{6.10}
\end{aligned}
$$

If the θ'_{ijt} can be treated as distributed independently, the industry joint *p.d.f.* for input i would be

$$f_i = \Pi_{jt}f(\theta'_{ijt}; \sigma_{ijt}) \tag{6.11}$$

and parameter estimates in $h_i(z_{jt})$ would be chosen to maximize f_i. The function $h_i(z_{jt})$ substitutes for σ_{ijt}, so the parameters of the explanatory variables directly determine the shape of the distribution. The parameter estimates are scaled differently in this formulation, and, again, linear extrapolations can be used to obtain frontier observations, given the values of z_{jt}.

Ideally, in developing a model for a specific application, one would examine the shapes of the empirical distributions and choose the most appropriate distribution, taking into account the fits of alternative distributions to the empirical distributions, their theoretical properties and the properties desired for the related estimators, and the tractability of working with alternative distributions.

5. Model Assuming the Lognormal Distribution

It would also be useful if a model could be developed within a framework employing the normal distribution in such a way that OLS estimators of the parameters would also be MLE. Therefore, for this chapter, we have chosen to explore some of the issues involved in a model assuming that the inefficiencies are lognormally distributed. This approach is also appealing because the derivation and estimation appear to be fairly simple and straightforward. Since the lognormal distribution is not monotonically increasing, Banker's propositions suggest that the DEA scores themselves can provide consistent but not MLE.

5.1. Derivation

The derivation is for a multivariate model treating inefficiency scores for inputs in I categories and revenue generation as functions of a series of operating choice and event variables as in equation (6.4), under the assumption that the random errors are generated by a lognormal *p.d.f.* For each input category i, $i = 1, 2, \ldots, I$, the efficiency scores $0 < \theta_{ijt} \leq 1$ can be transformed by

$$\theta''_{ijt} = 1/\theta_{ijt} - 1 + \omega \tag{6.12}$$

where ω is some very small amount, so that $0 < \theta''_{ijt} < \infty$ and constitutes a measure of technical inefficiency in the use of input i. Then inefficiency can be posited to be a multiplicative function of the explanatory variables and random error term, such as

$$\theta''_{ijt} = \beta_{i0} \Pi_k z_{kjt}^{\beta_{ik}} \exp\{v_{ijt}\} \tag{6.13}$$

where the β_{ik}, $k = 1, 2, \ldots, K$, *are parameters capturing the relationships between the explanatory variables and inefficiency in the use of input* i, and $\exp\{v_{ijt}\}$ ($\equiv e^{v_{ijt}}$) is a random error term that is assumed to be i.i.d. and lognormally distributed with mean 1, so the expected value of θ''_{ijt} will be

$$E(\theta''_{ijt} | z_{jt}) = \beta_{i0} \Pi_k z_{kjt}^{\beta_{ik}} \tag{6.14}$$

The goal is to be able to estimate equation (6.13) in its linear-in-parameters form and appeal to the equivalence of OLS and MLE.

One can proceed analogously for revenue-generating inefficiency, transforming the original efficiency scores ϕ_{jt} as in

$$\phi''_{jt} = \phi_{jt} - 1 + \omega \tag{6.15}$$

so $0 < \phi'_{jt} < \infty$, and specifying

$$\phi''_{jt} = \gamma_0 \Pi_k^{\gamma_k} z_{kjt} \exp\{\eta_{jt}\} \tag{6.16}$$

where $\exp\{\eta_{jt}\}$ denotes the corresponding random error term.

The lognormal to normal transformation appears to be an appealing way to obtain the required normal distribution as well as to linearize the model in its parameters. However, the transformation introduces bias into the point estimates of the intercepts and the predicted values of the inefficiencies. Since the transformation is nonlinear, the log of the expected value of the lognormal distribution is not equal to the expected value of the corresponding normal distribution. If $\exp\{v_{ijt}\}$ is assumed to be lognormally distributed with mean 1 and variance σ^2, then v_{ijt} is distributed normally with mean $-(1/2)\sigma^2$. The estimates of the slope coefficients will be best linear unbiased, but the estimated value of $\ln \beta_{i0}$ is biased by $-(1/2)\sigma^2$. The expected value of the predicted inefficiencies will be

$$E(\exp\{\ln \hat{\theta}''_{ijt}\}) = \beta_{i0} \Pi_k z^{\beta_{ik}}_{kjt} \exp\{-(1/2)\sigma^2 + (1/2)V(\hat{\theta}''_{ijt})\} \quad (6.17)$$

where $V(\hat{\theta}''_{ijt})$ is the variance of the predicted values of $\ln \hat{\theta}''_{ijt}$ (see Kennedy, 1983). Also, $-(1/2)\sigma^2$ does not approach zero asymptotically (Kennedy, 1983).

5.2. Illustrative Empirical Results

This section presents empirical results from estimating a preliminary version of the above model for the airline industry. The model is composed of 11 equations, 10 specified as in equation (6.13) for input-usage inefficiency and one specified as in equation (6.16) for revenue-generating inefficiency (using the 10 categories of inputs and 3 categories of outputs described in section 3.2). The dependent variables are quarterly DEA scores for each carrier, computed as described in section 2, and transformed as in equations (6.12) and (6.15). The independent variables, additional data, estimation, and findings are described below. Since this is an illustrative application, we will not provide too much detail.

5.2.1. Operating Choice Variables and Events. For all of the input-inefficiency equations except flight equipment, flight crew labor, and fuel, and for the revenue-generating inefficiency equation, the operating choice variables include the percentages of flights through competitive and dominated hubs, the average load factor, and a surrogate measure of service quality. The equation for inefficiency in the use of flight equipment includes the hub concentration variables, load factor, and an aircraft utilization rate. The equation for inefficiency in the use of flight crew labor includes RPM in wide-bodied and fuel-efficient aircraft, load factors, and quality. The equation for fuel inefficiency contains RPM in wide-bodied and fuel-efficient aircraft and load factor. The hypothesized relationships to inefficiency are discussed below.

Hub Concentration. Hub-and-spoke systems have been considered one of the most important strategies adopted by carriers following deregulation, although researchers are only beginning to collect empirical evidence regarding their specific effects. Banker and Johnston (1993) find that carriers can achieve significant economies in the use of flight crew and ground labor by concentrating more flights through their hubs. They also find that carriers that dominate market share in their hubs require significantly less on-ground labor per unit output than carriers with competitive hubs. We attempt to capture the use of hub-and-spoke systems with two variables:

- *Percentage of Flights through Competitive Hubs:* the percentage of the carrier's flights that are routed through its hub airports where the carrier faces substantial competition.
- *Percentage of Flights through Dominated Hubs:* the percentage of the carrier's flights that are routed through its hub airports where the carrier has considerable market power.[14]

We expect to find decreases in input usage inefficiencies with increases in the percentages of flights through hubs, with the coefficients for the percentages through dominated hubs being of greater magnitudes. If carriers can achieve cost savings by routing more flights through hubs, they will be better able to compete in setting fares, implying increases in revenue-generating inefficiency with increases in the concentration of flights through competitive hubs. Also, carriers that can pursue a differentiation strategy or achieve monopoly power in their hubs should be able to achieve higher *RGE* than carriers with competitive hubs. Therefore, the coefficients for dominated hubs should be lower than those for competitive hubs, and perhaps even negative.

Average Load Factor. To increase the proportion of space made available that was actually sold, carriers also sought to increase load factors. Bailey et al. (1985) document the changes in load factors for 1950 through 1982, and Caves, Christensen, and Tretheway (1984) and Kirby (1986) find significant decreases in total costs with increases in load factors. The ratio of RPM to ASM is used to capture this variable. Decreases in input inefficiencies should be associated with increases in load factors. Since revenue-generating inefficiency is measured with respect to RPMs, the coefficient estimate for average load factor in its equation should be insignificant.

Service Quality. An inverse measure of service quality, complaints submitted to the DOT per 1000 passengers carried, is also included. In general, it might be expected that carriers must use more resources per unit output to provide higher-quality service, and, as fewer resources are used, that the proportion of passengers submitting complaints would increase. However, there is also evidence suggesting that improvements in product or service quality may not necessarily require additional inputs. Carriers pursuing differentiation strategies should be providing higher-quality service and therefore exhibit greater *RGE*. However, if some of the carriers in the sample are exploiting local monopoly power to earn economic rents, this effect would be attenuated. Carriers pursuing low-cost strategies should use fewer resources per unit output and generate more complaints per passenger. Therefore, revenue-generating inefficiency and the proportion of complaints should be positively related.

Aircraft Utilization. Another strategy, also documented by Bailey et al. (1985), was increasing aircraft utilization rates, that is, the number of hours per day that available aircraft are actually being used to provide service. The standard measure of aircraft utilization, the ratio of ramp-to-ramp hours to available aircraft days, is included in the equation for inefficiency in the use of flight equipment.[15] Decreases in inefficiency should be associated with increases in aircraft utilization.

Aircraft Characteristics. Banker and Johnston (1993) find that older wide-bodied and newer fuel-efficient aircraft require fewer flight crew labor hours and less fuel per unit output than older regular-bodied aircraft. To capture these impacts, RPMs in these two types of aircraft are included in these two input equations. The results should be consistent with previous findings.

Event Variables. Intercept binary variables intended to capture the effects of the following events are included in all the equations except fuel inefficiency:

- *PATCO Strike and Post-PATCO Strike Restrictions.* We attempt to capture the effects of the PATCO strike and subsequent FAA restrictions with two variables, the first during the third and fourth quarters of 1981 and first quarter of 1982, when slots were frozen and operations capped at approximately 75% of normal levels, and the second during the remaining quarters of 1982, when the FAA was gradually reducing restrictions. With the disruption in operations and outputs capped, the productivity, for example, of ground property and equipment and flight equipment, would be below normal, and input inefficiencies should be greater than usual, particularly during the first three quarters.
- *United Pilots' Strike (1985Q2).* During the second quarter of 1985, United's pilots were on strike for 29 days and United operations were reduced to less than 15% of their normal levels. Inefficiency in the use of many of its inputs should have been greater than normal.
- *Impacts of the United Strike on Other Carriers.* Since United carried a large proportion of industry traffic (approximately 18% in

the preceding quarters) and cut back its operations so deeply, its strike should have had positive impacts on the load factors of many other carriers, and their inefficiencies should be lower than normal.

- *Continental Strikes and Bankruptcy (1983Q4–1984Q1); Northwest Strike (1981Q2); Pan American Strike (1985Q1).* Results similar to those for the United strike should obtain for Continental when it was undergoing strikes and bankruptcy proceedings, Northwest during its 1981 mechanics and ground personnel strike, and Pan American during its 1985 maintenance and ground personnel strike.
- *Impacts of Braniff Bankruptcy on Competitors (1982Q2–1984Q1).* Braniff ceased operations in May 1982, reorganized under federal bankruptcy laws, and returned to operation in March 1984 at reduced levels. Its close competitors, American and Delta at Dallas–Fort Worth, could be expected to achieve gains in productivity via increasing load factors during this period.[16]

The fare wars were most intense during the first and second quarters of 1983, and inefficiency in revenue generation should be higher than usual. Therefore, binary variables for these quarters were also included in the revenue-generation inefficiency equation.

5.2.2. Additional Data. Measures of hub concentration, market share, and monopoly power were developed from Form 41 data, and complaints per 1000 passengers were derived from the monthly *CAB/DOT Consumer Complaint Report*. Information used as the bases for specifying the event variables was taken primarily from government documents and articles in the *Wall Street Journal* and other national newspapers.

5.2.3. Estimation Procedure. Each equation was initially estimated separately, with the data being examined for evidence of collinearity and the residuals for evidence of nonlinearily, nonnormality, serial and contemporaneous correlation, and heteroscedasticity.[17] Although the correlations between some explanatory variables were fairly high and several had trended data, collinearity was not a problem. The condition indices and proportions of variation in the eigenvectors explained by Belsley, Kuh, and Welsch (1980) diagnostics were within acceptable limits. Also, nonlinearity within the relevant ranges was not apparent. However, the postulated distribution for the error terms may not hold very well. Kolmogorov D-test statistics (see Stephens, 1974) for the normality of the residuals reject normality for most equations at fairly high levels. When the normal distribution does not hold, least squares coefficient estimates are unbiased minimum variance, but only from among linear unbiased estimators, and consistent; the estimate of the variance is unbiased and consistent; the estimators are not efficient or asymptotically efficient; and F-and t-statistics may not be valid for finite samples (see Judge et al., 1985).

Serial correlation is to be expected, since there are quarterly observations and the effects of random shocks may be expected to last longer than one quarter. Contemporaneous correlation, between the residuals across equations for each carrier and quarter and between the residuals across carriers for each equation and quarter, could also be expected. Random shocks due to events not captured in the model (internal, such as major changes in management, or external) may have similar or related effects on the inefficiencies of different inputs and revenue generation of a given carrier. Correlation among the residuals across carriers by equation and quarter could be also expected because random shocks in the environment could affect several carriers' inefficiencies in the use of a given input similarly. Finally, heteroscedasticity could be expected if, for example, inefficiencies were proportionally related to the size of operations.

Serial correlation, contemporaneous correlation, and heteroscedasticity were all fairly strong. First-order autocorrelation coefficients, estimated by carrier and equation using a variant of the Prais–Winsten estimator proposed by Park and Mitchell (1980), ranged between .40 and .90. Estimates of contemporaneous correlation between the disturbances across the equations for the input inefficiencies ranged from .11 to .66. With the exception of the equation for maintenance labor inefficiency, Breusch–Pagan (1979) and other test statistics rejected homoscedasticity at highly significant levels.[18] Since we were somewhat constrained in terms of available software and programming time for dealing simultaneously with heteroscedasticity and contemporaneous correlation via seemingly unrelated regression (Zellner, 1962), we estimated each of the equations separately in a manner that would correct for the two more serious problems, namely, serial correlation and heteroscedasticity. We estimated first-order autocorrelation coefficients, by carrier, using the estimator mentioned above, transformed the data, including the first observations for each time series, in the usual manner, and ran a second set of regressions on the transformed data, taking heteroscedasticity into account.[19] Since the process generating differences in the variances of the disturbances was not known, we used White's (1980) procedure to obtain consistent estimators of the variance–covariance matrices. With the contemporaneous correlation remaining, the coefficient estimates of the separate regressions are unbiased and consistent but may be inefficient, and the estimates of their variances may be biased (Parks, 1967).

In sum, the autocorrelation coefficients were likely to have been underestimated, and the effects of the biased estimates of the variances carry through to some extent. The estimators are not efficient or asymptotically efficient due to deviations from normality. Therefore, in interpreting the results, we focus primarily on the coefficients' signs and strongest results and are cautious in making inferences.

5.2.4. Findings and Discussion. The model appears to fit moderately well (see table 6–2). With the exception of maintenance materials and overhead, the percentages of variation in the explained inefficiencies range from approximately 41% for reservations and sales labor to 78% for fuels and oils. The F-statistics are all significant at the .0001 or higher level. As will be seen, their strength is due primarily to the importance of load factors in determining input usage efficiency when it is measured with respect to RPMs. The signs of the coefficient estimates for most of the explanatory variables are in the hypothesized directions. However, the t-statistics are weaker, on the basis of previous experience working

Table 6–2. Determinants of Inefficiency: Summary of Multivariate Regression Results

Inefficiency Category	F-value	df^a	$df_d{}^b$	$pr > F$	R^2	Ajusted R^2
Aircraft & traffic servicing labor	13.804	13	227	.001	.4415	.4095
Reservations & sales labor	12.169	13	227	.0001	.4107	.3769
Flight crew labor	24.864	13	227	.0001	.5874	.5638
Flight attendant labor	24.590	13	227	.0001	.5848	.5610
Maintenance labor	16.843	13	227	.0001	.4910	.4618
Maintenance materials & overhead	4.194	13	227	.0001	.1937	.1475
Ground property & equipment	12.695	13	227	.0001	.4210	.3878
General overhead	27.164	13	227	.0001	.6087	.5863
Flight equipment	20.961	13	227	.0001	.5455	.5195
Fules	213.099	4	236	.0001	.7832	.7795
Revenue generation	55.962	14	226	.0001	.7761	.7623

[a] df_n = degrees of freedom, numerator.
[b] df_d = degrees of freedom, denominator.

with these data, than we would expect to find in a model utilizing a *p.d.f.* that fits the empirical distribution of the inefficiency scores or error terms more closely. The results do demonstrate the promise of the modeling approach, however, and we focus on a few of the strongest below. The results across equations for load factors and hub concentration are presented in table 6–3, and the results for the PATCO and United strikes in table 6–4. The remaining results are provided in tables 6–5 and 6–6 in the appendix.

Load Factor. The coefficients are strongly negative and significant for every input category. This lends support to hypotheses that decreases in input inefficiencies with respect to the production of revenue outputs are associated with increases in load factors. The coefficient in the revenue-generating inefficiency equation is insignificant, as expected, since inefficiency is measured with respect to RPM.[20]

Hub Concentration. The signs of most of the coefficients for the percentages of flights through competitive and dominated hubs are in the expected directions, with those for the aircraft and traffic servicing labor and ground property and equipment equations being significant at moderately high levels. This lends support to hypotheses that decreases in input inefficiencies are associated with increases in the concentration of flights through competitive hubs. The results for concentration through dominated hubs are weaker. They fail to support the hypotheses that carriers that are able to achieve some monopoly power can achieve greater gains in efficiency in the use of on-ground inputs than carriers with competitive hubs.

Strikes and Fare Wars. The results support hypotheses that inefficiency in the use of most inputs was greater during the PATCO strike and the succeeding two quarters. The signs of the coefficients for the next three quarters are also generally consistent with the hypothesized relationships, and their lower point estimates and levels of significance are consistent with diminishing effects. Inefficiency in the use of many inputs and revenue generation was also significantly higher for carriers undergoing strikes and bankruptcies. This is illustrated in table 6–4 for the United strike. Similar results for the remaining strikes are presented in table 6–6 in the appendix. Finally, revenue-generating inefficiency was higher during the 1983 fare wars ($\hat{y} = 1.4743$, $t = 5.285$, $p > |t| = .0000$).

6. Concluding Remarks

In summary, the objective of this chapter has been to introduce a new methodology within a statistical DEA framework that can be used to

Table 6–3. Regression Results: Relationships between Operating Strategies and Inefficiency Load Factors and Hub Concentration

| | Load Factor | | Percentage of Flights through Hubs | | | |
| | | | Competitive | | Dominated | |
Inefficiency Category	Coefficient Estimate	t-statistic	Coefficient Estimate	t-statistic	Coefficient Estimate	t-statistic
Aircraft & traffic servicing labor	-6.8807	-5.828[a]	-.8633	-2.127[c]	.0005	.013
Reservations & sales labor	-6.4916	-7.071[a]	-.0957	-.267	-.0175	-1.030
Flight crew labor	-6.7882	-9.587[a]				
Flight attendant labor	-8.1051	-9.898[a]	-.0490	-.151	-.0283	-1.321
Maintenance labor	-5.4850	-8.051[a]	-.4836	-1.793	-.0105	-.550
Maintenance materials & overhead	-3.6446	-5.548[a]	.5305	.842	.0220	.830
Ground property & equipment	-4.7412	-4.079[a]	-1.3341	-2.477[c]	-.0973	-2.110[c]
General overhead	-9.2000	-6.803[a]	.4818	.953	.0762	1.915
Flight equipment	-5.2694	-7.027[a]	-.3832	-1.062	-.0635	-2.837[b]
Fuels	-11.4128	-12.790[a]				
Revenue generation	-.5130	-.485	.6114	1.689	-.0224	-.744

[a] pr > |t| < .0001.
[b] pr > |t| < .01.
[c] pr > |t| < .05.

Table 6–4. Regression Results: Relationships between Strikes and Inefficiency PATCO Strike and Post-strike Operating Restrictions and United Airlines Pilot Strike

Inefficiency Category	PATCO Strike (1981Q3–1982Q1)		Post-PATCO Strike (1982Q2–Q4)		United Strike (1985Q2)	
	Coefficient Estimate	t-statistic	Coefficient Estimate	t-statistic	Coefficient Estimate	t-statistic
Aircraft & traffic servicing labor	.7255	2.852[b]	.5055	1.411	2.0717	6.836[a]
Reservations & sales labor	.4848	2.592[b]	.3465	1.198	2.0082	8.460[a]
Flight crew labor	.5296	3.838[a]	.2958	1.334	1.2591	3.058[b]
Flight attendant labor	.4350	1.751	.3601	1.369	1.5670	6.374[a]
Maintenance labor	.3685	3.152[b]	.1960	.959	1.2275	5.328[a]
Maintenance materials & overhead	.0943	.597	−.1128	−.427	1.2632	3.855[a]
Ground property & equipment	.6189	3.452[b]	−.2010	−.613	.9437	1.228
General overhead	.8981	2.68[b]	.3145	.893	2.0727	1.868
Flight equipment	.3462	2.232[c]	.0009	.004	1.1427	1.673
Revenue generation	.4456	1.451	.4105	1.152	.9561	1.821

[a] $pr > |t| < .0001$.
[b] $pr > |t| < .01$.
[c] $pr > |t| < .05$.

evaluate the associations between operating strategies, environmental events, and efficiency, and to relate these variables to the competitive position of the firm. DEA may provide a particularly robust basis for this type of modeling effort, particularly for industries (such as the airlines) that are in disequilibrium due to rapidly changing technologies and deregulation. The methodology also relates technology, operating strategy, and event variables that differ between carriers and over time to the technical efficiency scores that have been computed using panel data and are therefore with reference to the long-run best-practice frontier, which envelops the frontiers that obtain for successive time periods and for firms with differing technologies.

Specifically, we have developed and related DEA-based measures of aggregate cost and revenue-generating efficiency to Porter's low-cost and product-differentiation strategies and used them to analyze graphically the realized strategic repositioning of a sample of airlines during a period of considerable environmental change and adjustment. Then, to examine the impacts of the strategic choices statistically, we have operationalized the DEA MLE and the consistency results of Banker to introduce multivariate models of the relationships between technology, operating choice, and event variables and technical efficiency in input utilization and revenue generation. We have sketched out two basic types of models: one relating the explanatory variables to efficiency in a conventional manner involving regression on a vector of explanatory variables and disturbance term following the postulated distribution, and one relating these variables directly to the parameters determining the shapes of the distributions attributed to the efficiency measures. We have illustrated both approaches with the half-normal distribution. We have also begun to explore a model utilizing the lognormal distribution and provided a set of preliminary empirical results that demonstrate the potential usefulness and richness of the approach.

Appendix: Supplementary Tables of Results

Table 6−5.   Regression Results: Relationships between Inefficiency and Service Quality, Aircraft Characteristics, and Aircraft Utilization Rates

Inefficiency Category	Coefficient Estimate	t-statistic
Complaints per Thousand Passengers		
Aircraft & traffic servicing labor	−.2139	−.821
Reservations & sales labor	−.0544	−.393
Flight crew labor	−.0526	−.314
Flight attendant labor	.1853	1.346
Maintenance labor	.2390	1.906
Maintenance materials & overhead	.3537	2.035[c]
Ground property & equipment	1.0382	5.092[a]
General overhead	.6177	3.207[b]
Revenue generation	.4538	2.689[b]
RPM: Wide-bodied Aircraft		
Flight crew labor	−.0293	−1.319
Fuels & oils	.0589	3.792[a]
RPM: New Aircraft		
Flight crew labor	−.0889	−3.083
Fuels & oils	−.0213	−1.468
Aircraft Utilization		
Flight equipment	−2.5337	−2.627[b]

[a] $pr > |t| < .0001$.
[b] $pr > |t| < .01$.
[c] $pr > |t| < .05$.

Table 6–6. Regression Result: Relationships between Inefficiencies and Firm-specific Strikes and Bankruptcies

	Competitor Effects						Firm Effects			
	United Strike (1985Q2)		Braniff Bankruptcy (1982Q2–1983Q4)		Northwest Strike (1981Q2)		Continental Strike & Bankruptcy (1983Q4–1984Q1)		Pan American Strike (1985Q)	
Inefficiency Category	Coefficient Estimate	t-statistic	Coefficient Estimate	t-statistic	Coefficient Estimate	t-statistic	Coefficient Estimate	t-statistic	Coefficient Estimate	t-statistic
Aircraft & traffic servicing labor	−.6503	−1.168	−1.1908	−1.372	.3775	−1.003	3.8486	13.295[a]	−4.1015	−7.568[a]
Reservations & sales labor	−.5151	−1.277	−.5087	−1.232	1.1116	4.245[a]	2.4798	2.154[c]	.8304	.387
Flight crew labor	−.4023	−1.267	−.5853	−1.471	.9494	7.629[a]	−.6976	−.381	2.0579	4.417[a]
Flight attendant labor	−.1462	−.384	−.5416	−1.301	.9901	3.158[b]	−.6556	−.331	.6176	1.115
Maintenance labor	−.5081	−1.929	−.4082	−1.501	.6855	4.319	1.7672	1.796	−2.9677	−17.065
Maintenance materials & overhead	−.3848	−1.353	.6146	2.676[b]	−.4175	−2.532[c]	−.8902	−1.382	.3010	.735
Ground property & equipment	−2.1531	−2.881[b]	1.1747	3.240[b]	.8620	2.751[b]	−.1677	−.439	−.3281	−.525
General overhead	−.1494	−.285	−.1552	−.223	1.6038	3.966[a]	−1.7649	−.513	2.5780	4.573[a]
Flight equipment	−.1674	−.534	.0428	.096	.1523	.392	1.4754	3.312[b]	.327	.808
Revenue generation	−.5553	−1.545	−1.1298	−1.966[c]	−.1627	−.324	−2.3026	−.802	−3.1541	−11.829[a]

[a] pr > |t| < .0001.
[b] pr > |t| < .01.
[c] pr > |t| < .05.

Notes

1. Mintzberg (1978, 1985) distinguishes between a firm's intended strategies and the strategies that are realized or actually emerge from the complex interactions involved in the management process and interactions between the firm and its environment. In this chapter, we focus on the apparent or realized strategies of the firm from the perspective of an outside observer, as opposed to those strategies that may have been intended.

2. Since efficiency is measured one input at a time, no slack appears for that input in an optimal solution to the DEA linear program. See also Banker and Maindiratta (1988). Where separability cannot be maintained, an alternative procedure would be to utilize a DEA program employing multiple inputs and multiple outputs to obtain a single measure of technical efficiency and a program employing input prices as well to obtain an overall measure of aggregate cost efficiency that can be related to Porter's low-cost strategy. We also estimated DEA scores using a BCC_P-I model employing the ten inputs and three outputs. The resulting efficiency scores and $AIUE$ scores are significantly correlated ($\hat{\rho} = .53; pr > |\hat{\rho}| < .0001$).

3. Civil Aeronautics Board (CAB) authority over route entry and exit formally expired at the end of 1981, and its authority over fare levels expired at the end of 1982.

4. A revenue passenger mile is defined as the provision of air transportation services for one revenue passenger and his or her baggage for a distance of one mile.

5. Banker and Johnston (1992) find significant differences in fuel and flight crew labor requirements between these three broad categories of aircraft, but few within them.

6. Caves, Christenson, and Tretheway (1984), Sickles (1985), Sickles, Good, and Johnson (1986), and Good, Nadiri, and Sickles (1989) have found empirical evidence that substitution between broad categories of inputs such as labor, capital, energy, and materials is generally inelastic.

7. Quarterly estimates of full-time equivalent inputs were extrapolated from annual labor input data using the cost shares for separate labor accounts. Quarterly estimates of fleet inventories were extrapolated from annual fleet data, which were made more precise, wherever possible, by taking into account rental values and other supplementary fleet inventory data with a straight-line method.

8. International operations were regulated and deregulated separately, with route and fare agreements largely negotiated by treaty.

9. The "perpetual inventory" method has been applied to the airline industry by Caves, Christensen, and Tretheway (1984), Sickles (1985), and Sickles, Good, and Johnson (1986).

10. We first computed RGE and ACE for each carrier and quarter, and then computed the annual geometric means of these ratios to reduce the number of observations to be plotted. Sicne RGE and ACE are in ratio form, we used geometric rather than arithmetic means.

11. Bailey and Williams (1988) provide two data points per firm, for 1978 and 1984. While we can construct quarterly or annual time series for an intersecting period, we can only do so beginning with 1981.

12. As noted by Schmidt (1976) with respect to the parametric frontier estimators developed by Aigner and Chu (1968) and by Banker (1993) with respect to DEA estimators, the desirable statistical properties of consistency and asymptotic efficiency do not necessarily follow and must be derived separately. This is because one of the regularity conditions usually used to prove that these properties hold for MLE does not hold (the range of the random variable is not independent of the parameters being estimated).

13. The linear piecewise frontier estimated via the DEA model constitutes the tightest-fitting frontier enveloping the data for the best-practice production frontier, which must lie on or below the true frontier.

14. A carrier's hub was considered to be competitive if the carrier had less than 60% of the total number of flights by all carriers through the airport during a quarter, and dominated if the carrier had 60% or more.

15. Ramp-to-ramp hours are measured from the time a flight leaves one gate to the time it arrives at another.

16. With quarterly observations, seasonal dummy variables could also be used to control for or investigate the impacts of seasonality.

17. If collinearity had been a problem, the OLS estimators of the standard errors of the coefficient estimates would have been best linear unbiased (BLUE) but large. The latter are violations of the OLS assumptions that can result in unbiased and consistent but inefficient estimates of the regression coefficients and in biased and inconsistent estimates of their variances.

18. However, these tests are based on the assumption that the disturbances are normally distributed.

19. The Prais–Winsten estimator proposed by Park and Mitchell (1980) is consistent, minimizes the sum of squared residuals conditional on the estimates of the coefficients, and performs very well for short time series and trended data in relation to several other estimators. It also reduces the extent to which the autocorrelation coefficient tends to be underestimated (see Kmenta and Gilbert, 1970; Park and Mitchell, 1980). However, like other estimators, it does underestimate the standard errors, leaving a substantial probability of making a type I error.

20. An alternative way to specify the model would be to measure the efficiencies with respect to a measure of space made available, such as ASM. Load factors are often cited as sources of potentially substantial gains in productivity, and should be in the sense of converting space made available into revenue outputs and reducing what otherwise would be considered wasted or non-value-adding space. Also, large proportions of the inputs are used to produce the capacity to provide services. Measuring *RGE* with respect to RPM has the advantage of enabling us to capture pure price effects, that is, the ability of the firm to earn a premium either for a differentiated product or as a consequence of exerting monopoly power. However, it may also be useful to simultaneously examine the ability of carriers to convert ASM into RPM by increasing load factors.

7 ANALYZING TECHNICAL AND ALLOCATIVE EFFICIENCY OF HOSPITALS

Patricia Byrnes and Vivian Valdmanis

1. Introduction

High health care costs in the United States (11.7% of GNP in 1988) and the effect of these costs on governmental budgets and private industry has stimulated cost consciousness among the purchasers of hospital care. Cost-containment efforts recently enacted by third-party payers (Medicare, some state Medicaid programs, and private payers) as well as increased competition in the hospital market have pressured hospital management to seek more efficient means of providing services.

Analysts of the health care industry, in particular the hospital industry, have long attributed hospital cost growth to the cost-plus or charge-plus payment mechanism used by third-party payers (see, for example, Sloan and Steinwald, 1980). In the past, reimbursements were paid retrospectively based on costs incurred, and hospital managers did not face formal budget constraints or pressures from price competition. Without price competition and with little incentive to contain costs, hospitals competed on the basis of quality of care. Since quality was usually measured in terms of numbers of inputs employed (e.g., advanced medical equipment) and by types of inputs (e.g., registered nurses versus licensed practical nurses), cost inefficiencies tended to arise and to be perpetuated.

With the shift to increased cost awareness, new arrangements such as preferred provider organizations (PPOs) and health maintenance organizations (HMOs) entered the health care market. These types of providers have encouraged market competition in the hospital industry by contracting with hospitals, on the basis of price, to care for patients. Since hospitals, in general, are experiencing low occupancy rates, they are willing to enter into contracts with PPOs and HMOs in return for patient volume. However, in order to remain financially solvent, hospital management must meet these competitive pressures with more cost-efficient production practices.

Data envelopment analysis (DEA) can enable hospital managers to identify both sources of relative cost inefficiency—technical and allocative. Reducing employment of excess inputs would increase technical efficiency, and selecting the cost-minimizing mix of inputs, given relative input prices, would lead to allocative efficiency. Hospitals that attain both types of efficiency can lower their costs and thereby gain an edge in attracting PPO or HMO contracts (as well as other patients) by competing more effectively with relatively cost-inefficient competitors.

DEA has been used by several researchers to study hospital performance (Sherman, 1984; Banker, Conrad, and Strauss, 1986; Grosskopf and Valdmanis, 1987). In these past works, the focus has been on assessing hospital efficiency in technical terms, i.e., the "right" amount of inputs to produce a given level of outputs. With the approach of Farrell (1957), however overall cost-minimizing efficiency includes technical efficiency and allocative efficiency. Allocative efficiency results if the producing unit chooses the cost-minimizing combination of inputs given the relative cost per unit of inputs. As Sexton, Silkman, and Hogan (1986) correctly point out, studies that focus only on technical inefficiencies in production may lead to erroneous conclusions as to the nature of cost-minimizing inefficiency. A more complete analysis of cost inefficiency in the provision of services should include measures of allocative inefficiency.

Many studies of cost inefficiency calculate only the technical-efficiency component, because calculation of the allocative component (and hence, overall cost-minimizing efficiency) requires information on the relative prices of inputs. In the absence of input price information, various ways to include an allocative efficiency measure in DEA have been developed. For example, Charnes, Cooper, Wei, and Hung (1989) developed the cone ratio, and Thompson, Singleton, Thrall, and Smith (1986) applied the assurance region (AR), which contains estimates of allocative inefficiency based on all reasonable price vectors. The benefits of the DEA/cone-ratio and the DEA/AR techniques are especially noted when prices are not available. If information on input prices *is* available, the allocative component of overall efficiency is easily calculated via linear programming techniques (Färe, Grosskopf, and Lovell, 1985).

In this chapter, we respond to the suggestion of Sexton et al. (1986) and also expand on previous research by including measures of allocative efficiency. The linear programming model we employ allows us to compute overall cost-minimizing efficiency and its components, i.e., technical and allocative efficiency. The technical-efficiency component is the CCR input-based linear programming model presented in chapter 2 of this book. In addition, we employ the Färe et al. (1985) linear programming technique to decompose the technical efficiency measures into sources of technical inefficiency: pure technical inefficiency, a nonoptimal scale of operation, and inefficiency due to input congestion. These measures of inefficiency can be used by the hospital manager to determine how well the hospital performs vis-a-vis its competitors.

The following section provides a discussion of the cost-minimizing performance measures and briefly explains how they can be computed using DEA modeling techniques. The third section contains a discussion of the data from our study, and the empirical results are given in section 4. The application of the results to hospital management concludes the chapter.

2. Cost-Efficiency Measures: A DEA Approach

To gauge the cost performance of hospitals, we computed four DEA-type linear programming problems for each hospital in our sample as well as six measures of relative efficiency. The first three measures, based on Farrell's classification, include overall cost-minimizing inefficiency and its components: technical and allocative inefficiency. The other three measures are based on the decomposition of the technical-inefficiency measure into the sources of technical inefficiency. This decomposition is not typically part of DEA; it is a extension intended to characterize the inefficiency scores in terms of the structure of the production technology.[1] All the linear programming problems can be classified as input-oriented DEA-type models, and we therefore use the notation of chapter 2 to briefly describe the sequence of computations.

All six measures of inefficiency are illustrated in figure 7–1, which

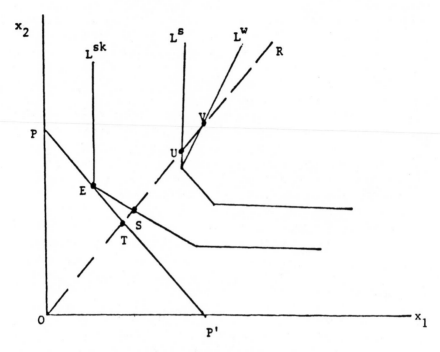

Figure 7–1. Decomposition of the cost-minimizing efficiency measure.

depicts the input-space representation of the production technology. Let
x_1 and x_2 denote the two inputs used in production. We first focus on
overall cost-minimizing efficiency and its components. To compute these
measures, the data are initially enveloped with a restrictive technology
exhibiting constant returns to scale (CRS) and strong disposability inputs
(SDI).[2] In figure 7–1, this technology is denoted L^{sk} and represents the
isoquant or lower bound of the set of all input combinations yielding at
least some given output level. Given input prices, as reflected in the
isocost line labeled PP', the cost-minimizing input combination for the
given output level is at point E.

Farrell proposed measuring the deviation from cost minimization as
the ratio of efficient input usage to actual input usage, given observed
input proportions. In terms of figure 7–1, for a DMU (or hospital in our
example) operating at point R, this overall inefficiency, denoted OE_R,
can be measureed as $\dfrac{OT}{OR}$. To compute this measure, denote the relative
prices of each of the m inputs that hospital R faces as $P_R = (p_{1R},$

$p_{2R}, \ldots, p_{mR}$). For hospital R, the minimum cost, $MC_R(Y, X, P)$, for the technology is the solution to the following linear programming problem:

$$MC_R(Y, X, P) = \text{minimize}_{X_R, \lambda_j} P_R \cdot X_R$$

$$\text{s.t.} \quad Y\lambda \geq Y_R$$

$$X\lambda \leq X_R$$

$$\lambda_j \geq 0 \tag{7.1}$$

The solution equation (7.1) is the estimated minimum cost, $MC_R(Y, X, P)$, for observation R. Denote the actual cost for observation R as $P_R \cdot X_R$. Then the overall efficiency for the inputs is defined as the ratio of minimum to actual observed costs:

$$OE_R(Y, X, P) = \frac{MC_R(Y, X, P)}{P_R \cdot X_R} \tag{7.2}$$

The measure of technical efficiency for a hospital, R, is denoted $TE_R(Y, X)$, and is obtained by solving the following linear programming problem:

$$TE_R(Y, X) = \text{minimize} \; {}_{\lambda_j, \theta} \theta$$

$$\text{s.t.} \quad Y \cdot \lambda \geq Y_R$$

$$X \cdot \lambda \leq X_r \cdot \theta$$

$$\lambda_j, \theta \geq 0 \tag{7.3}$$

The solution is used to determine the amount by which observed inputs can be proportionally reduced, while still producing the given output level.

In figure 7–1, this technical efficiency measure, for hospital R, is $\frac{OS}{OR}$. Note that this technical component is independent of input prices. The price-dependent component, i.e., the allocative efficiency, AE_R, is measured as $\frac{OT}{OS}$ and is computed as

$$AE_R(Y, X, P) = \frac{OE_R(Y, X, P)}{TE_R(Y, X)} \tag{7.4}$$

This allocative measure captures inefficiency due to the fact that hospital R, even if on the isoquant with its factor proportions, did not pick the "right" input combination given relative input prices.

A summary of the Farrell decomposition of relative overall cost-minimizing efficiency is given by

$$OE_R = TE_R \cdot AE_R \tag{7.5}$$

which is confirmed for the example in figure 7–1, since

$$\frac{OT}{OR} = \frac{OS}{OR} \cdot \frac{OT}{OS} \tag{7.6}$$

The decomposition of technical efficiency is accomplished by relaxing the restrictions on the constructed reference technology in which efficiency is gauged. In Farrell's model, CRS and SDI are assumed. Comparing measures of efficiency relative to this frontier and other measures calculated relative to less restrictive technologies yields the decomposition of technical efficiency. This decomposition is illustrated in figure 7–1. The overall technical-efficiency measure computed relative to the CRS–SDI technology, L^{sk}, was given above. Scale inefficiency occurs because the hospital is not operating at the scale of operation consistent with long-run competitive equilibrium, i.e., a point of constant returns to scale. In figure 7–1, for a hospital operating at point R, the scale component is captured by $S = \dfrac{OS}{OU}$, the radial difference in the isoquant that assumes CRS, labeled L^{sk}, and the technology that relaxes the CRS restriction, L^s. The scale-efficiency component is computed by solving the following linear programming problem:[3]

$$W_R(Y, X) = \text{minimize}_{\lambda_j, \theta}\, \theta$$

$$\text{s.t.:} \quad Y \cdot \lambda \geq Y_R$$

$$X \cdot \lambda \leq X_R \cdot \theta$$

$$\sum_{j=1}^{n} \lambda_j = 1$$

$$\lambda_j,\ \theta \geq 0 \tag{7.7}$$

The addition of the constraint that the activity parameters must sum to unity relaxes the CRS restriction and envelops the data more closely than the CRS technology. Using the relationship between this measure and the $TE_R(Y, X)$, the scale-efficiency measure for a hospital R, denoted $S_R(Y, X)$, is defined as

$$S_R(Y, X) = \frac{TE_R(Y, X)}{W_R(Y, X)} \tag{7.8}$$

This measure of scale efficiency measures wasted inputs due to deviation from technically optimal scale, that is, from CRS. If for a given hospital, say hospital S, $S_S(Y, X) = 1$, then $TE_S(Y, X) = W_S(Y, X)$, and the technology exhibits constant returns to scale for that observation. In this case, hospital S is gauged scale efficient. For hospital R in figure 7–1, we have $S_R(Y, X) \leqslant 1$; the two technologies do not coincide, and the hospital is not operating at CRS. The source of scale inefficiency (increasing or decreasing) is determined by examining the basic solution of the linear programming problem and whether the constraint on the activity parameters is binding.

The congestion component is due to production on a backward-bending segment of the isoquant that is in the region where marginal product is negative. This is captured by computing a measure of technical efficiency, the pure technical-efficiency measure, relative to the technology that relaxes the SDI restriction (i.e., allows for backward-bending isoquants). In figure 7–1, the input set with the weak-disposability (WDI) restriction is labelled L^w. The pure technical component shown as $PTE = \dfrac{OV}{OR}$ for observation R is the inefficiency due to production in the interior of the input set L^w, rather than on the isoquant. The congestion component for observation R is given by the ratio $C_R = \dfrac{OU}{OV}$. To compute these two measures, we solve the following linear programming problem:

$$PTE_R(Y, X) = \text{minimize}_{\lambda_j, \theta}\ \theta$$

$$s.t.: \qquad Y \cdot \lambda \geqslant Y_R$$

$$X \cdot \lambda = \delta \cdot \theta \cdot X_R$$

$$\sum_{j=1}^{n} = 1$$

$$\delta \leqslant 1$$

$$\lambda_j,\ \theta,\ \delta \geqslant 0 \qquad\qquad (7.9)$$

In this linear programming problem, the reference technology assumes WDI, i.e., L^w in figure 7–1. The role of the δ parameter is to make feasible non-negative combinations of inputs—for example, the backward-bending portion of that technology in figure 7–1. The congestion measure is defined as

$$C_R(Y, X) = \frac{W_R(Y, X)}{PTE_R(Y, X)} \qquad\qquad (7.10)$$

This measures compares the difference between the backward-bending isoquant, L^w, and the closest non-backward-bending isoquant, L^s. If $C_J(Y, X) = 1$ for a hospital J, then the hospital is not operating on the backward portion of the isoquant. Otherwise, if $G_J(Y, X) < 1$ (as is the case for hospital R in the figure), there are wasted inputs due to congestion.

To summarize, the relative technical efficiency for an observation R is equivalent to

$$TE_R = S_R \cdot PTR_R \cdot C_R \qquad (7.11)$$

which is confirmed for the example in figure 7–1, since

$$\frac{OS}{OR} = \frac{OS}{OU} \cdot \frac{OV}{OR} \cdot \frac{OU}{OV} \qquad (7.12)$$

Substituting equation (7.11) into equation (7.5), we have the complete decomposition of cost-minimizing efficiency:

$$OE_R = S_R \cdot PTE_R \cdot C_R \cdot AE_R \qquad (7.13)$$

The overall cost-minimizing efficiency measure is decomposed into the allocative-efficiency component and three technical-efficiency components. Each measure is less than or equal to unity. A value of unity indicates that actual input usage is equal to efficient usage, in the sense of the measure. Further, efficient input levels are determined by the best-practice observations in the sample. In the next section, the data to implement these measures for a sample of hospitals are presented.

3. Data

The hospital data used in this study are obtained from the California Health Facilities Commission (CHFC) survey for fiscal year 1983. The sample is limited to 123 community (nonteaching) not-for-profit hospitals so that we could control for organizational differences in the hospital industry. For example, teaching hospitals have a different case mix, and public hospitals offer different amenities. We constrained our sample in order to control for quality-of-care differentials, given that hospitals of similar organizational form produce similar types of care (Sherman, 1984).[4]

We also focused on the production of inpatient care, because it composed the largest component of hospital costs. Further, the survey data allow inputs and costs to be separated by inpatient units. Barring systematic errors in accounting practices, we can assess the performance of inpatient services. The cost efficiency of hospital inpatient services was modeled in a multiple-input, multiple-output framework. Descriptive statistics of the input and output variables are given in table 7–1.

The three outputs are medical-surgical acute (ACU) discharges; medical-surgical intensive care (ICU) discharges; and maternity (MAT) discharges. We used discharges rather than length of stay in order to avoid endogenity in the specification of outputs, i.e., confounding apparent differences in efficiency with occupancy rates. Acute and intensive care were studied separately to acknowledge differences in resource use. Because this approach enables us to include multiple outputs directly, we do not have to derive a scalar measure of diagnostic severity within each of our sample hospitals. The mix of these inpatient services differs among the sample hospitals. For example, as revealed by the minimum values for the ICU and MAT variables (see table 7–1), some hospitals did not provide these services as part of their patient mix in 1983.

Six inputs are specified. The five labor inputs are registered nurse (RN), management and administrative personnel (MGT), technical services personnel (TECH), aides and orderlies (AIDE), and licensed practical nurses (LPN). All labor inputs are measured in full-time

Table 7–1. Input, Output, and Price Variables: Descriptive Statistics (Sample Size = 123)

Variable	Mean	Standard Deviation	Minimum Value	Maximum Value
ACU	7779.85	4913.68	367.00	32005.00
ICU	359.80	381.21	0.00	2526.00
MAT	1417.26	1326.48	0.00	6159.00
RN	281383.44	231645.58	12200.00	1288208.00
MGT	29073.38	32296.27	2.00	225948.00
TECH	17384.70	38095.52	2.00	384211.00
AIDE	82118.44	63762.18	2520.00	333766.00
LPN	65238.05	53207.83	3538.00	354187.44
BEDS	267.77	152.32	38.00	943.00
RN Wage	13.15	1.25	7.98	16.58
MGT Wage	14.53	1.30	11.02	20.27
TECH Wage	10.69	3.00	5.69	26.81
AIDE Wage	7.05	1.01	5.42	9.75
LPN Wage	8.94	0.91	6.92	13.50
Capital Price	3184.64	1860.57	611.38	12159.52

equivalence hours. Because data for licensed practical nurses (LPNs) were not available from the survey, the LPN hours were estimated using the RN hours for each hospital and a county-specific index of the fraction of LPN hours to RN hours. The capital input we used in this study is the average staffed beds (BEDS). Following Pauly and Wilson (1986), staffed beds were used instead of licensed beds, since the former are fully staffed and operational to serve patients. Since RNs, LPNs, and aides exhibit at least partial substitutibility, i.e., RNs can perform the tasks of LPNs and aides and to a certain extent LPNs and aides can perform the duties of RNs, the standard allocative-efficiency model, as specified here, can be applied.

Descriptive statistics of the input prices used are also given in table 7–1. The wage rates for all labor types (including LPNs) are reported in the survey. We assumed that due to the monopsony power of hospitals over health care workers (e.g., nurses), the ex post wage rate that hospitals pay is equivalent to the wage rate reported. The input price for capital was defined as depreciation divided by number of staffed beds.[5] By using this specification, the price of capital is not assumed to be fixed across hospitals, as was done in earlier studies, e.g., Cowing and Holtman (1983) and Eakin and Kniesner (1988).

From the data, we were able to determine input shares as well as the operating costs for the sample hospitals. These data are summarized in table 7–2. The cost of registered nurses accounts for over half, on average, of total costs. Capital costs account for the next largest share— 14% of hospital operating costs, on average. Aides' and orderlies' salaries account for 11%, whereas management salaries account for 7% and

Table 7–2. Descriptive Statistics of Total Cost and Input Shares

Cost/Input Share	Mean	St. Dev.	Min Value	Max Value
RN	0.56	0.09	0.32	0.78
MGT	0.07	0.05	0.00[a]	0.28
TECH	0.03	0.05	0.00[a]	0.47
AIDE	0.11	0.07	0.01	0.31
LPN	0.09	0.03	0.03	0.16
BEDS	0.14	0.07	0.04	0.36
Total cost (Mil. dollars)	6.31	4.74	0.41	29.09

[a] Less than 1%.

technician salaries 3% of total costs. The calculated total operating cost in 1983 was, on average, over 6 million dollars for the sample hospitals.

4. Empirical Results

Using the specification described in the previous section, we can compute relative measures of overall cost-minimizing efficiency, allocative efficiency, and technical efficiency, including the components of scale congestion and pure technical efficiency. Given that efficiency is denoted by a measure equal to unity, excess costs due to inefficiency are calculated as one minus the performance measure multiplied by actual costs.

Summary statistics for each relative performance measure are given in table 7–3. Average overall efficiency defined in this total cost-minimizing framework is approximately 0.61. On average, inefficient hospitals would have needed to lower operating costs by 39% in order to perform as well as other similar, best-practice hospitals in the sample. Only 6 of the 123 hospitals operated at minimum costs.

The relative level of the allocative and technical measures provides evidence as to the source of deviations from cost-minimizing efficiency. For the sample as a whole, the primary source of inefficiency is allocative inefficiency. These hospitals employed the "wrong" input mix, given input prices, so that their costs were 27% higher than the cost-minimizing level.[6] Conversely, almost 40% of the sample hospitals were technically efficient. Technically inefficient hospitals, however, could have reduced inputs by 16%, on average, and still have produced the same level of inpatient services.

The source of relative technical inefficiency can be determined for

Table 7–3. Summary of Efficiency Measure Results

Efficiency Measure	Mean	St. Dev.	Median	Minimum Value	Number Efficient
Overall	0.61	0.18	0.59	0.31	6
Allocative	0.73	0.15	0.73	0.37	6
Technical	0.84	0.17	0.86	0.10	49
Pure techanical	0.94	0.13	1.00	0.48	93
Congestion	0.95	0.10	1.00	0.51	83
Scale	0.94	0.09	0.98	0.58	49

these hospitals. Statistics for these measures are also provided in table 7–3. The decomposition of the technical-efficiency measure shows that for over 60% of the sample, scale inefficiency is the primary cause of technical inefficiency.[7] We also used this method to determine the type of scale inefficiency affecting these hospitals, whether increasing or decreasing scale inefficiency. These results are reported in table 7–4. A third of the sample exhibited decreasing returns to scale (DRS), whereas 27% of the sample hospitals exhibited increasing returns to scale (IRS).

Since scale refers to size, we include in table 7–4 the descriptive statistics of variables indicating hospital size, including total number of discharges, number of beds, and the average cost per discharge. The 49 scale-efficient hospitals are midsized hospitals in terms of averages, cost per discharge. The variation of average cost per discharge across hospitals of different sizes suggests that the sample hospitals follow the traditional U-shaped average cost curve.

Before empirical analysis can be applied, hospital management must be convinced that these measures do, in fact, reflect inefficiency. Hence, we have validated these efficiency measures by comparing them to more traditional measures of cost performance. Table 7–5 is a comparison of average product (output per unit of input) and average cost of efficient and inefficient hospitals in our sample. Since the best-practice hospitals in our sample have lower average costs and higher average products, we conclude that the findings using DEA corroborate more traditional measures of cost efficiency.

By using the DEA approach, we are also able to determine what the cost-minimizing input shares of the hospitals would be, had they all operated as efficiently as the the best practice in the sample. Table 7–6 provides a description of the estimated efficient shares of each input at minimum cost. These values can be compared to average actual input shares of each hospital, as provided in table 7–2. A comparison of these tables reveals that, on average, labor costs could be decreased if the share of registered nurses were decreased and the share of each of the other

Table 7–4. Summary of Returns-to-Scale Results (Sample Size = 123)

RTS	Number of Observations	Average Discharges	Average Beds	Cost per Discharge
IRS	33	6,078	202	822.66
CRS	49	9,140	230	588.21
DRS	41	12,854	366	663.24

Table 7–5. Characteristics of Efficient/Inefficient Hospitals

	Number of Observations	Cost per Discharge	Discharge per Beds
Allocative			
Efficient	6	415.5	42.5
Inefficient	117	689.5	35.5
Technical			
Efficient	49	588.2	40.5
Inefficient	74	734.3	32.8

Table 7–6. Descriptive Statistics of Efficient Input Cost Shares

Input Type	Mean	St. Dev.	Min Value	Max Value
RN	0.52	0.07	0.33	0.71
MGT	0.07	0.01	0.03	0.12
TECH	0.01	0.01	0.00	0.11
AIDE	0.10	0.04	0.07	0.30
LPN	0.10	0.02	0.06	0.15
BEDS	0.19	0.08	0.06	0.45

nonmanagement labor inputs were increased. For example, increasing the number of LPNs and aides relative to RNs would lower costs. Using RNs for specialized patient care while increasing the use of LPNs for more general nursing services (i.e., simple patient care such as bathing patients, taking blood readings, and the like) should be a focus of management control in the sample hospitals.

Capital was underutilized by the hospitals in the sample. This result is surprising, given the hypothesized effect of nonprice competition on the management decisions (Sloan and Steinwald, 1980) and recent evidence that occupancy rates have been falling. One possible explanation is that the capital price variable is not specified correctly. In fact, using depreciation costs ignores actual replacement costs, and hence the price of this input may be understated. Another explanation for this result could be found in how "beds" were defined. Staffed beds, not licensed beds, were used as the measure of capital, implying that these beds are operational only because there are sufficient nurses hired to adequately care for the patients. Therefore, their under-utilization would mean that commensurate nursing staff were also underutilized. To increase the number of beds, as defined, would require hiring more nurses. As previously stated, the measures derived from this analysis can be used to adjust hospital costs to efficient levels. For example, the mean actual cost for the hospitals in our sample is $6.31 million. If each hospital were operating as efficiently as the best practice of the sample, the average cost would be $3.5 million, a decrease of 39%. The average costs per inpatient discharge would fall from 675 to $380 if all relative inefficiencies could be eliminated.

5. Summary and Applications for Hospital Management

This study examined the decomposition of overall efficiency into its component parts—technical and allocative efficiency—for a sample of nonprofit hospitals operating in California. DEA techniques were used to arrive at these measures of relative efficiency. This chapter expands on earlier DEA analysis of hospital performance by incorporating price measures as well as physical unit measures. We also derive information on the sources of technical efficiency: scale, input congestion, and underutilization of inputs (pure technical inefficiency). The empirical results show that hospitals in our sample suffer from allocative inefficiency to a greater degree than from technical inefficiency. Estimates of the cost savings possible from reduced inefficiencies of providing inpatient care range from 32% to 40% of operating costs. In other words, if hospitals in our sample were required to perform as efficiently as similar, best-practice hospitals, costs per inpatient discharge would fall, on average, by 39%.

The pressures imposed on hospital managers from cost-containment efforts and price competition has stimulated a demand for managerial tools that would identify efficiency in hospital service production. This study illustrates the types of information that can be gleaned using the DEA model and its extensions.

There are at least three ways hospital managers could use this information. First, the information provided here would allow managers to discern whether too many inputs were being used in the production of hospital care or whether the wrong input mix, given the relative prices of inputs, was being used.

Second, managers could use this information to determine how competitive they are in the market for patients. Relatively efficient hospitals could use this information as a marketing tool to attract PPO or HMO contracts. With increasing price competition, hospitals will be wanting PPO and HMO patients in order to increase census and patient load.

Third, hospital managers could apply the resulting measures to determine what price they could offer to PPOs and HMOs. This price would consist of the cost per discharge, given relatively efficient production practices (with adjustments for case mix and capital replacement costs).

These are illustrative examples of how management could use the DEA approach for internal control, marketing, and rate setting. In actual application, management decisions would need to be based on more finessed and precise definitions of the inputs and outputs than those used in this analysis. However, with the growing market pressures on hospitals and public interest in health cost-containment policies, changes in hospital management will occur, including an increased role of efficiency in decision making. With this increased emphasis on efficiency of hospital operations, the quality of data also will need to improve. Since reimbursements (most notable the Diagnostic Related Groups (DRGs)) rely on accurate data, hospitals have increased incentives to collect more detailed data regarding their patients and costs. DEA techniques, as demonstrated in this chapter, will serve as a powerful tool for more effective management and dissemination of these types of data.

Acknowledgments

Both authors contributed equally to this chapter. In addition, we wish to acknowledge the reviewers for their constructive comments and suggestions on earlier drafts.

Notes

1. See Byrnes, Färe, Grosskopf, and Lovell (1988) for another application of the technical-efficiency decomposition.

2. This is the same technology representation as the input-oriented CCR model. Strong disposability of inputs requires that the isoquants have no backward-sloping segments, i.e., marginal physical products of each input are nonnegative.

3. This is the input-oriented BCC problem.

4. All nonteaching, not-for-profit hospitals in the survey that reported complete and consistent data were included in the sample. For a more detailed description of the CHFC survey and the sample selection, see Byrnes and Valdmanis (1987).

5. It would have been preferable to adjust for the age of the hospital and equipment—

for example, by dividing cumulative depreciation by net depreciation. However, the survey data did not provide this information. We discuss the limitations of our capital and capital price specifications in the presentation of empirical results.

6. This assumes that the measured input prices are the same as those the hospital decision maker faces. Additional analysis using DEA/cone-ratio or DEA/AR methods could provide bounds to these computed levels of allocative inefficiency.

7. The average level of the three components is within two percentage points; however, over 60% of the hospitals are relatively congestion free and did not waste inputs, in the pure technical sense, relative to similar hospitals in the sample.

8. Our results are similar to the Banker et al. (1986) sample results. They found that increasing returns prevailed in hospitals with less than 200 beds. For our sample, the number of beds in hospitals characterized by increasing returns is 202, on average.

8 A MULTIPERIOD ANALYSIS OF MARKET SEGMENTS AND BRAND EFFICIENCY IN THE COMPETITIVE CARBONATED BEVERAGE INDUSTRY

Abraham Charnes, William W. Cooper,
Boaz Golany, D. B. Learner, Fred Y. Phillips,
and John J. Rousseau

1. Introduction

Measurement and evaluation of sales response, in a multiattribute sense, for a product in the usual marketing environment of competing brands has been and continues to be an exceedingly complex and difficult task. It is made more so by the inability to obtain either comprehensive data or sample data that are free from noise factors, not all of which are recognized a priori or a posteriori. For example, even a casual review of the marketing literature would lead one to conclude that even in a heavily researched area such as the advertising–sales response curve there is little conclusive evidence as to the shape of these curves, and that all such investigations are limited by vitrue of ignoring interactions of marketing mix variables. These studies also, of course, treat only one response variable at a time.

In the extant data envelopment analysis (DEA) work, management and control of inputs and their conversion into outputs are in the hands of the individual decision-making units (DMUs). These DMUs are and continue to be the sources of all sample observations and all input–output conversion patterns that serve to determine the aggregate production function and the relative efficiencies of the DMUs in such a production environment. Yet, the results of the analyses project the relative inadequacies in *real-world* rather than theoretical terms for the individual units so that corrective action may be undertaken with them individually to improve the existing aggregate production function.

In this chapter, we describe a series of DEA applications in which similar methods were employed to break ground in radically different conceptual and practical situations in marketing. Instead of DMUs, we consider *response units* (RUs), such as regional marketing areas, groups of households, etc., that respond to the inputs (advertising, promotion, product/brand qualities) set in place by the competing product manufacturers. The "decision making" on most of the inputs is in the hands of the manufacturers. The conversion into desired outputs is the response elicited from these units. Thus we have a simultaneous bombardment of RUs with competing inputs. The outputs desired by the competing manufacturers are elicited responses from the RUs.

Therefore, we can conceive of this situation as a production process involving the marketing areas or RUs in place of DMUs. Thereby, if we can create a similar mathematical structure to that of DEA, we should have on the dual side an efficiency analysis of elicited response from the marketing areas. But how shall we account for the denigrating interaction of competing brand inputs?

The competitive effects in the marketing scenarios we are interested in can be described via an analogy from Game Theory. Consider a two-player situation where one player corresponds to the brand being evaluated and the second player corresponds to all other competing brands. Assuming a relatively modest overall growth in market volume, the "game" is almost zero-sum. Actions taken by one player that result in gains to that player also result in equivalent losses to the other player. For example, unretained customers of the first player (lost market-share points) are gained by the second player (the collection of its competitors).

In the evaluation of a brand, therefore, we can capture the effects of its competition by including competitors' activity as an input. For such a scenario, we introduced the device of complementing (or taking the reciprocal of) the input factor that corresponds to the competition, since lesser *competitive* input should tend to increase (or, at least, not decrease) the outputs of the brand being evaluated (see Charnes et al., 1984). Competitive effects, therefore, were represented by the complement (or reciprocal) of competitors' aggregate expenditures. With this device, we anticipated isotonicity of the aggregate production function, a most important desideratum of the mathematical structure (see Charnes, Cooper, et al., 1985).

In the following, we illustrate these concepts with reference to national marketing of the carbonated beverages product category, using the additive model of chapter 2, section 2 (ADD$_P$). We employ Areas of Dominant (Television) Influence (ADIs) as the marketing areas, and brands within ADIs as the basis for defining response units. The word *brand* refers to a particular product offering, e.g., Diet Coke in two-liter packages. We employ the *window analysis* approach developed in Charnes, Clark, et al. (1985), with the same response unit in a different time period being treated as if it were a different response unit. By moving the window forward from period to period, we obtain robust time series estimates of the efficiency of elicited response in each marketing area.

Numerous experiments were conducted using a variety of data sets appropriate for the different kinds of marketing efficiency evaluations that we introduce below. According to the varied needs and interests of different levels of management, we devised alternative means of presentation that identify sources of inefficiency and point out ways for possible corrective actions. The results presented below serve only to illustrate the application procedures employed and the innovative reporting and analysis capabilities that were devised, and we do not attempt to discuss in any detail the complete and voluminous experimental results.

Although a few passing observations are made concerning the carbonated beverages market, the primary focus of this chapter is the possibilities for DEA in uncovering significant aspects of sales response to marketing activities, and the noted extensions in the application environment.

2. Background

The work described here spanned a period of almost two years from mid-1983 to early 1985. During this period, the authors explored many aspects of DEA's extension (from its origins in the not-for-profit enterprises) to competitive situations, and the application of these extensions to the marketing of carbonated beverages. We chose the carbonated beverage market for this study for a variety of reasons.

- When this study was launched, in February 1983, the beverage market was undergoing some upheaval due to the introduction by major manufacturers of many new brands, including caffeine-free and diet drinks with a new a sweetener. This made the market interesting and promised some insight into how DEA would handle new product introductions, which are usually accompanied by heavy advertising and promotions.
- The beverage market is characterized by a high degree of competition, resulting in heavy advertising and promotion even during "normal" periods. How efficiently promotional money is spent has material implications for the profitability of the product and its manufacturer.
- Many brands in this market are distributed nationwide, permitting analysis at various hierarchical levels, e.g., at the national level, among regions representing aggregated markets, and among individual market areas.
- Detailed marketing expenditure and purchase information for this category were available for current years. These data originated from separate (independent) sources such as the Arbitron Ratings Company, the Census Bureau, etc.

3. Innovations in DEA Application

This section describes the different conceptual and practical situations that were addressed in our experiments and illustrates the types of reporting mechanisms that were devised for display and interpretation of results at different levels of management.

3.1. Marketing Efficiency and RUs

Figure 8–1 below shows four general types of scenarios that were considered in these applications to evaluating marketing efficiency. The precise definition of response unit varies according to the scenario analyzed.

To measure *market efficiency*, an RU is defined as a particular brand within a specific geographical (market) area. It is analyzed with other RUs representing the same brand in many other geographical areas. By extension, in measuring *aggregate-brand market efficiency*, an RU is defined as a meaningful aggregation of several brands (e.g., all diet

	Single Brand	Multiple Brands	Aggregated Brands
Single Market	X	Brand Efficiency	X
Multiple Markets	Market Efficiency	X	Aggregate-Brand Market Efficiency
Aggregated Markets	X	Aggregate-Market Brand Efficiency	X

Figure 8-1.   Marketing efficiency evaluation scenarios.

beverages) in a specific market. It is analyzed together with other RUs representing this came collection of brands in many other markets.

To measure *brand efficiency*, an RU is defined as a brand in a particular market competing against other brands in the same market. *Aggregate-market brand efficiency* measures the performances of multiple brands within some aggregation of individual markets that might compose a region or the total national market.

Market areas were defined in terms of *areas of dominant influence* (ADI), the term that Arbitron Ratings Company uses for a television market. An ADI is an unduplicated geographic area to which counties are assigned on the basis of their highest share of viewing of originating stations and satellite stations reported in combination with them. Some counties may be divided into two or more separate areas due to topography, with the resulting subdivisions assigned to different ADIs. In the United States, there are over 200 television markets encompassing over 3000 counties. We chose the ADI definition of market area because TV advertising, along with price promotions, is the major component of marketing expenditure in the carbonated beverage product category.

The RUs were further defined by quarter. Thus, we had eight data points (nine in the Los Angeles ADI) for most product offerings in each market over the two years for which analyses were performed.

3.2. Defining Input/Output Factors

The choice of input and output factors was determined by the authors' experience in drawing and executing marketing plans and by the availability of data. In any application, two general classes of inputs need be considered: discretionary and nondiscretionary inputs (see the early definitions in Charnes and Cooper, 1985; Charnes, Cooper, et al., 1985). In our context, discretionary inputs, such as advertising expenditure, are those inputs whose values can be varied directly by the brand manufacturer in order to try to elicit a desired response. Nondiscretionary inputs, such as market size and competitive activity, are those inputs that contribute to defining the marketing environment, and hence influence market response, but are not under the direct control of the brand manufacturer.

The set of input factors reflected the major components of a typical marketing plan and, on the output side, the goals of the marketing plan, i.e., the criteria for evaluating it. The selection of inputs was determined by the fact that the efficiency evaluation was focused on brand manufacturers and not retailers. Thus, only inputs that described the direct influence of the manufacturer on consumers (mainly, advertising and promotion) were included as resource inputs. Other important marketing factors (e.g., shelf positioning), which reflect retailers' activities, were therefore omitted from the analysis. Still, a crucial marketing consideration remains, namely, the price of the product. However, unlike prior inputs, price does not reflect actual usage of resources; rather, it is an outcome of a managerial decision. Hence, this input was included only in some of the experiments, and the results were compared to other input–output mix definitions in which related measures (e.g., revenues or margin) were put on the output side. Three nondiscretionary factors were considered: the first two reflected the sales' potential, and the third accounted for competition, as explained earlier.

The output variables captured the multiple dimensions of response, going beyond typical marketing-mix studies that use only sales volume or market share. Market share was used here with extra caution, because market shares have to sum to 100% across all DMUs. Referring again to the Game Theory analogy, a market share point gained by any brand must have been lost by the collection of its competitors. However, when DEA is used to project inefficient units onto the efficiency frontier, one is likely to find that the sum of the projected market shares is larger than 100%. Since DEA optimization is applied to each unit individually, it is impossible to maintain the market share consistency requirement across all units. Thus, market share projections could only be interpreted as an optimistic forecast for potential growth.

After some months of experimentation, the following set of factors was selected for our subsequent analyses:

Discretionary inputs
Resource inputs
- network TV advertising ($000s)
- deal value (cents off)
- local (spot) TV advertising ($000s)

Costless ("managerial decision") inputs
- price per ounce (expressed as its inverse, oz./$)

Nondiscretionary inputs
- average temperature (°F) in the sales region
- market size (in 1000s of households)
- competitive spot/network TV advertising (inverse of the expenditure in $000s)

Outputs
- sales volume (000s of ounces)
- volume sold on deal (000s of ounces)
- number of buying households (000s)
- average frequency of purchase
- market share (%)

Data on the outputs and some of the input variables were obtained from the MRCA Information Services National Consumer Panel database.[1] These estimates of purchases by all U.S. households are projections from purchase data collected weekly from a panel of over 7500 households. The figures on advertising through network and spot television were made available by the Broadcast Advertisers Research (BAR) Inc. BAR estimates expenditures using actual advertisements that are aired in each market and estimates of the costs of these spots. Data on other media (print, radio, billboards) were available, but since expenditures on these are relatively minor for the category, they were not used.

3.3. Experiments

Many different experiments were conducted in our investigations into the different kinds of marketing efficiency. For example, in several *brand efficiency* studies, all brands, and then a group of the largest 32 brands, were evaluated in the New York and Los Angeles markets separately. An *aggregate-market brand efficiency* experiment used more than 80 brands over the total national market, although not all were on the market throughout the two-year period. In three *market efficiency* studies, Pepsi-Cola and Coca-Cola were evaluated separately and then jointly in each of the 74 major ADI markets as determined by population size. An *aggregate-brand market efficiency* experiment combined Pepsi and Coke (all packages) for analysis in each of the 74 ADIs.

Different experiments used different combinations of, or variations on, the above set of inputs and outputs. For example, in some instances the "sales volume" output was subdivided according to whether children were present in the buying households; price per case was used instead of price per ounce; and number of purchase occasions replaced average purchase frequency. The first runs did not include temperature and market share factors. An evident efficiency bias toward southern ADIs was remedied by including mean temperature as an input. Market share, when included, did not markedly change the distribution of relative efficiency scores, but did change the facet participation table (see below). We later incorporated feedback of the previous period's market share (output) as an input variable for the current period. In the multiperiod situation, the firm both produces and consumes market share. It consumes market share in the sense that market leadership directly drives profitability and indirectly drives consumer awareness and hence further sales.

DEA window analysis, and the several kinds of facet tables we devised, provided a general picture of the market and presented the performance of all units in summary form. To aid in assessing the results, we devised detailed reports that identify sources of inefficiency and point out ways for possible corrective actions. The limited set of results presented below are only illustrative of the application procedures employed and the different reporting and analysis capabilities that were devised, and we do not attempt to discuss in any detail the complete results of the experiments.

3.4. Window Analysis

Window analysis (see Charnes, Clark, et al., 1985) considers RUs defined by the same brand in different time periods as separate observations. Out of a total of n quarters, DEA is performed on all RUs defined in the earliest $k < n$ contiguous quarters, that is, quarters 1 through k. It is then performed on quarters 2 through $k + 1$, 3 through $k + 2$, and so on. Each RU is thus analyzed several times with slightly different comparison sets. In general, we found that $k = 3$ or 4 tended to yield the best balance of informativeness and stability of the efficiency scores. The $k = 4$ quarter window also facilitates yearly planning and helps detect seasonal effects. The three-period windows were also used primarily in order to allow new brands on the market to appear in at least one window. These experiments were, we believe, the most comprehensive use of window analysis to date. They enabled us to

- determine most appropriate window length and number of windows;
- test stability of efficiency ratings;
- detect trends and seasonal effects in the efficiency performance of individual RUs;
- analyze time-lagged effects of specific variables, e.g., previous periods' advertising;
- allow for variable number of RUs in a market, e.g., as a result of new market entries or discontinued brands;
- increase the "sample size" by replicating RUs across quarters;
- flag possible errors in the data;
- further distinguish efficient RUs by their "consistency of efficiency" as revealed by the window table (see table 8–1); and
- create the facet participation table (see table 8–5 below).

Table 8–1 provides an illustrative partial window analysis table for seven brands (with brand names replaced by numbers) taken from a much larger brand efficiency analysis in the Los Angeles market from the spring of 1982 through the fall of 1983 (labeled Q1 through Q7). Here the window length was three quarters, providing five window runs. Four columns added on the right of the table provide diagnostics for the stability of each brand's efficiency ratings. The first two of these columns contain the mean efficiency rating and variance over the 15 evaluations of each brand. The third column shows the largest difference in efficiency scores recorded for a single period, and the fourth column gives the

Table 8–1. Partial Window Analysis Table of Brands in the Los Angeles Market

RU	Q1	Q2	Q3	Q4	Q5	Q6	Q7	Mean	Var	Col. Range	Total Range
1	.90	.75	1.00					.94	.11	.12	.25
		.76	.88	1.00							
			.93	1.00	1.00						
				1.00	1.00	.95					
					1.00	.96	1.00				
2	1.00	.82	.79					.89	.09	.03	.21
		.81	.80	1.00							
			.81	1.00	.88						
				1.00	.88	.87					
					.92	.90	.92				
3	.97	1.00	1.00					1.00	.00	.00	.03
		1.00	1.00	1.00							
			1.00	1.00	1.00						
				1.00	1.00	1.00					
					1.00	1.00	0.98				
4	1.00	.87	.83					.94	.07	.02	.17
		.87	.83	.96							
			.85	.94	1.00						
				.94	1.00	1.00					
					1.00	1.00	1.00				
5	.92	.88	.89					.89	.01	.03	.09
		.90	.89	.88							
			.91	.89	.86						
				.90	.87	.89					
					.89	.92	.83				
6	1.00	1.00	.84					.88	.13	.09	.26
		1.00	.84	.91							
			.86	1.00	.82						
				1.00	.87	.74					
					.84	.75	.79				
7	1.00	1.00	1.00					1.00	.00	.00	.00
		1.00	1.00	1.00							
			1.00	1.00	1.00						
				1.00	1.00	1.00					
					1.00	1.00	1.00				

difference between the maximum and minimum scores over all evaluations. Table 8-1 shows fair stability of efficiency scores, which was the usual case for the window analysis runs.

3.5. RU Summary

The familiar RU efficiency summary table remains an important management report. It shows the dimensions and magnitudes of possible improvements in performance, and identifies the RU's efficient role models (i.e., the facet members). Table 8-2 shows the efficiency summary for a brand designated as RU 3 in a brand-efficiency study of the 32 largest brands in the New York market during Fall 1983.

For this analysis, each output (i.e., total volume, deal volume, buying households, and purchase frequency) was subdivided according to whether children were present or absent in the household, since this distinction is relevant to total soft drink volume per household and to

Table 8-2. Brand Efficiency Analysis of 32 Brands in the New York Market, Fall 1983 (Efficiency Summary for RU 3)

	Value Measured	Value if Efficient	Potential Improvement
Outputs			
Total Volume Absent	221,936	289,783	67,847
Total Volume Present	81,250	146,035	64,785
Deal Volume Absent	119,624	163,925	44,301
Deal Volume Present	33,506	81,105	47,599
No. Buying HH Absent	667	1317	651
No. Buying HH Present	464	701	237
Purch. Frequency Absent	2,446	2,527	81
Purch. Frequency Present	1,089	1,600	511
Inputs			
Average Price	6.7	6.7	0.0
Deal Value	25.2	20.8	4.4
Spot TV Expenditure	116.0	116.0	0.0
Network Expenditure	1390.5	1390.5	0.0
Efficiency = 0.75			
Facet Members:	RU 35	RU 15	RU 4	RU 1
Lambda Values:	0.20	0.55	0.15	0.10

consumption patterns for diet drinks. The brand corresponding to RU 3 is inefficient and needs to improve its performance in both target groups, although the percentage improvement possible in both total volume and volume sold on deal is greater in households with children. Increase in volume to households without children is to be achieved primarily through higher penetration, whereas households with children have to be persuaded to buy the brand more often. Different strategies are therefore called for with respect to the two segments.

This type of report can also be used to compare a brand's performances in its major markets or to compare its performance against competitors within and across markets. Table 8–3 is taken from a market efficiency analysis of a brand (labeled brand A) across the 74 major ADIs. In table 8–3, the performance of brand A in market RU 9 is compared to its performances in the other 73 ADIs, and is rated efficient. However, when brand A in RU 9 is evaluated with respect to itself *and* its major competitor, brand B, in all ADIs, it is no longer fully efficient (see table 8–4). The competing brand B in market RU 9 now evaluates brand A in RU 9, as does the competing brand in RU 15. Thus, when competing

Table 8–3. Market Efficiency Analysis of Brand A in 74 ADIs, Fall 1983 (Efficiency Summary for RU 9)

	Value Measured	Value if Efficient	Potential Improvement
Outputs			
Total Volume Absent	818.5	818.5	0.0
Total Volume Present	683.2	683.2	0.0
Deal Volume Absent	594.9	594.9	0.0
Deal Volume Present	337.3	337.3	0.0
No. Buying HH Absent	389.4	389.4	0.0
No. Buying HH Present	268.6	268.6	0.0
Purch. Frequency Absent	665.2	665.2	0.0
Purch. Frequency Present	454.2	454.2	0.0
Inputs			
Average Price	734.0	734.0	0.0
Deal Value	49.4	49.4	0.0
Spot TV Expenditure	66.0	66.0	0.0
Competition	278.0	278.0	0.0
Temperature	63.3	63.3	0.0
Efficiency = 1.00			

Table 8–4. Joint Market Efficiency Analysis of Brands A and B in 74 ADIs, Fall 1983 (Efficiency Summary for Brand A in RU 9)

	Value Measured	Value if Efficient	Potential Improvement
Outputs			
Total Volume Absent	818.5	2066.0	1247.5
Total Volume Present	683.2	1503.5	820.3
Deal Volume Absent	594.9	1526.8	931.9
Deal Volume Present	337.3	1046.8	709.5
No. Buying HH Absent	389.4	655.7	266.3
No. Buying HH Present	268.6	557.2	288.6
Purch. Frequency Absent	665.2	1458.2	793.0
Purch. Frequency Present	454.2	1006.9	552.7
Inputs			
Average Price	734.0	666.0	68.0
Deal Value	49.4	48.8	0.6
Spot TV Expenditure	66.0	34.0	32.0
Competition	278.0	175.0	103.0
Temperature	63.3	63.3	0.0
Efficiency = 0.68			
Facet Members:	RU 9-B	RU 15-B	

brands are included in the analysis, deficiencies in the marketing programs of each brand are highlighted. This result indicates that one should look to the marketing activities of brand B in order to improve the efficiency of brand A in RU 9.

3.6. Facet Participation Table

All evaluations in DEA are effected by reference to subsets of units that are rated as fully efficient. This rating is the maximum obtainable by the unit being evaluated with respect to the efficient units. The DEA optimization picks reference sets (facets) that are most like the unit being evaluated. The units whose input–output vectors appear in all optimal bases for RU_o are its facet members. These are necessarily efficient and they envelop RU_o.

When a DEA is performed for a single period, one might suspect that some of these facet members appear there only by chance and that they will not be in the facet in other time periods. With a window analysis, each RU is evaluated mk times, where m is the number of windows and k is the number of periods in a window. Thus we have mk lists of facet members (with their corresponding optimal λ values) for each RU.

We can collect these results in two ways: 1) by counting the number of times an efficient RU appears in the facets of all RUs (including its own) and 2) by summing over all facets the optimal λ values corresponding to each efficient RU. The facet participation table (see table 8–5) provides an example of the first method. In this example of brand efficiency, the 32 largest brands were analyzed over nine quarters in the Los Angeles ADI. The window size was four quarters, providing six window runs, so that the maximum number of times an efficient brand could appear in the facets of each brand was 24. Of the 32 brands (the rows of the table), 12 were efficient in at least one quarter (the columns of the table).

Examining the table row by row reveals for each brand the efficient brands that are most important in determining its own efficiency. A column of the table shows the number of times the corresponding efficient brand appeared in the facets of each brand. Note that brands 19 and 30 were consistently efficient. The final row of column totals allows us to rank order the efficient brands by their overall influence on the reference set and thus to gain more insight into the geometric properties of the empirical production function. The theoretical maximum column total in table 8–5 is 768 (= 32 × 24). In general, RUs with high counts tend to be located near the center of the production frontier while others with low counts are located near the edges.

Additional insight may be obtained from the second method (summing optimal λ values), which provides a means for assessing the relative importance or strength of the efficient RUs in the evaluation process. Whereas the simple count considers an efficient RU with a low λ value and another with a higher λ value as being equally important in evaluating an inefficient RU, here we obtain a finer distinction between them based on the values of λ.

From the perspective of an inefficient RU looking to its role models for guidelines for ways to improve performance, greater attention might be paid to those facet members with the highest λ values in a particular evaluation, or to those of its facet members with the largest sums of λ values across the total of its evaluations. Efficient RUs with the largest sums of λ values across all facets most strongly evaluate all other RUs and may be considered as the best of the best industrywide.

Table 8–5. Facet Participation Table: Window Analysis Brand Efficiency (32 Brands in the Los Angeles Market over Nine Quarters)

Brand	*Efficient Brands*											
	1	3	7	8	14	17	18	19	20	22	24	30
1	12	1	7	5	1	3	5	11	6	3	3	3
2	6	3	9	0	4	11	4	12	4	0	4	2
3	4	18	8	2	10	1	2	14	5	0	0	3
4	9	2	5	2	0	11	4	0	3	4	3	15
5	0	6	3	3	5	13	0	10	1	0	1	6
6	2	2	3	5	1	12	1	2	4	2	4	13
7	5	6	21	4	9	1	3	8	5	1	1	3
8	0	6	2	11	1	6	1	3	1	0	1	7
9	0	3	1	5	5	11	0	3	2	0	0	7
10	1	3	3	5	1	12	1	7	0	1	4	7
11	0	1	7	8	4	7	1	4	0	0	0	14
12	1	1	6	8	1	15	1	9	0	3	2	1
13	1	0	4	6	0	5	2	2	0	0	2	3
14	0	6	1	3	23	1	0	10	1	0	0	7
15	0	0	1	3	0	3	0	4	0	1	3	11
16	0	0	4	3	0	15	0	6	0	0	3	10
17	0	3	7	6	6	20	1	1	4	1	1	12
18	4	1	4	1	1	2	12	4	5	4	1	12
19	0	5	3	1	5	2	0	24	8	0	0	1
20	5	2	3	0	3	1	1	6	21	2	2	12
21	1	1	4	3	3	15	0	8	2	0	3	7
22	10	2	0	5	0	1	4	4	4	15	1	4
23	0	0	3	4	1	11	0	8	0	0	1	7
24	2	0	1	1	2	7	1	5	1	0	8	3
25	0	4	6	3	4	13	0	12	4	0	3	4
26	2	0	1	3	0	2	1	12	0	3	2	13
27	3	2	6	10	2	12	3	12	0	4	7	1
28	5	4	4	3	2	7	1	6	9	1	4	9
29	4	2	6	8	3	15	3	6	1	2	8	3
30	2	2	0	1	2	2	2	0	7	3	0	24
31	10	0	0	0	0	0	1	0	3	5	0	12
32	0	0	7	4	0	5	0	3	0	0	2	4
Total	89	86	140	126	99	242	55	206	101	55	74	240

3.7. Histogram of Facet Appearances

Charnes, Cooper, and Rhodes (1978, 1980) initiated study of the distribution of efficiency scores for a given set of DMUs. They constructed empirical density functions and began statistical study through the use of a class of gamma functions as a canonical form for comparison of efficiency distributions. We approached the same issue through the facet appearance "scores" rather than the efficiency scores. In figure 8–2, we take marginal totals from a facet participation table (similar to table 8–2) to construct a frequency histogram of facet appearances. The facet participation table was obtained from a market efficiency experiment with Coca Cola in 74 ADIs, using window analysis from the second quarter of 1982 through the fourth quarter of 1983. The general shape of the histogram proved stable in several other experiments not reported here.

The histogram of figure 8–2 shows that 27 ADIs appeared in the facets of inefficient markets 25 times, 7 ADIs appeared 75 times, 1 ADI appeared 525 times, etc. This representation forms a basis for identifying the most robustly efficient markets, i.e., markets that appear as reference markets most often. One way of making this determination is to establish a cut-off point in terms of the number of facet appearances and then select those markets that meet or exceed this standard. One purpose in identifying the most frequently efficient ADIs is to choose test markets

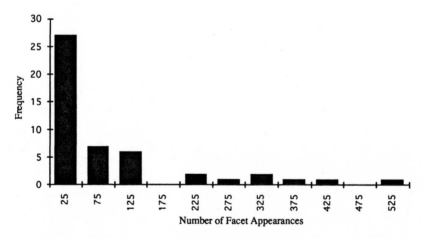

Figure 8–2.   Histogram of facet appearances by markets: Coca Cola in 74 ADIs, 1982–1983.

for new products. Thus, test market results from efficient markets may be taken as representing the best possible performance of the new brand.

3.8. Thematic Map

Another device for summarizing the efficiency measures was a colored map of the ADIs in the U.S.[2] The colors correspond to efficiency classifications, with efficiency ratings categorized into four groups (0–80, 81–90, 91–99, and 100). The efficiency scores on which this map was based were the mean scores for each of the 74 major ADIs obtained from a market efficiency window analysis of Coca Cola for the period 1982–1983.

The purpose of such a map is to provide a geographical distribution of efficiency scores that may assist decision makers in identifying possible geographical patterns, which in turn may constitute additional insight into causes of inefficiency. The idea is to present an overall picture to complement the detailed efficiency breakdown provided by other devices such as those presented in figure 8–2 and tables 8–1 to 8–5. Consequently, the map does not distinguish among units that are in the same category (e.g., ADIs in the 0–80 class), although significant efficiency differences may exist among them. This device, which combines a succinct summary with a powerful visual appeal, is aimed at executive levels of management whose interest lies in overall company performance rather than in individual, unit-by-unit evaluation.

3.9. Lagged Effects of Advertising

Recognizing that advertising can have a residual effect on consumer behavior long after its date of insertion, we experimented with using a function of the previous period's advertising expenditure and the current period expenditure as an input. Different weighting schemes were tried, for example, (0.25) (previous quarter Ad.$) + (0.75) (current quarter Ad.$). Expecting the lagged effect to last no more than three months, we did not attempt lags of more than one quarter. None of the weighting schemes used had much differential impact on the values and distribution of efficiency scores, except for brands where advertising was highly variable from season to season.

4. Summary of Application Innovations

We have described a series of multiperiod DEA applications to the marketing of carbonated beverages that marked the methodology's first extension to for-profit situations with explicit consideration of competitive effects. Special problems of structuring DMUs and input–output variables in such situations were also described. (Figure 8–3 shows an expanded list of input–output variable candidates for marketing applications.) The applications made thorough use of window analysis, and additional novel data representations were devised.

Four kinds of competitive marketing scenario were distinguished, each of which implied its own efficiency issues. In analyzing brand efficiency, different brands compete in an individual market or some aggregation of markets. Market efficiency is characterized by competition among many area/regional managers of the same brand or a meaningful collection of brands. Our replication of RUs over successive time periods indicates a fifth kind of competitive scenario, namely that of a brand or market manager competing against him/herself, either to improve over time or to meet a prescribed plan.

Novel data representations included the facet participation table and a graphic frequency distribution of facet appearances. Geographic analysis was introduced into DEA, indicating the most efficient spatially defined RUs and building an "efficiency map" of the region or nation. Further, special treatment was effected for demographic analysis, breaking down variables such as sales volume, market penetration, etc. by demographic categories, e.g., income, education, and number of children in the household.

Other innovative application devices included

- Feedback of the previous period's market share (output) as an input variable for the current period;
- Lagged advertising inputs;
- The use of microcomputer exploratory data analysis tools;
- The concept of costless "managerial decision" variables. These are input variables that may increase in numerical value without incurring incremental cost to the firm. They include the price that is set for a product, its package size, etc.;
- Identification of efficient frontier facets with market segments. This is useful, for example, in selecting "standard" markets for experimental design decisions. Other useful notions of segmentation include efficient vs. inefficient brands or markets, both globally and with respect to RUs defining or associated with a facet (i.e.,

Inputs/Resources	Outputs/Objectives
Advertising Expenditures	Revenue
by Media	Volume—units[a]
by Market (ADI)	Distribution—by channel[a]
	H/H Penetration[a]
	Targel Group (demo) Penetration[a]
Media Reach, Frequency	Packages Sales—units, dollars
Ditto	
Cume	
Gross Rating Points	
Ditto	
Promotion Expenditure	Market Share[a]
Type	Total
Duration	Buying H/H's
Value	Last period's share
Total deal expenditure last period	
Distribution	Volume/Buying H/H[a]
Channel Share by H/H[a]	Volume/1000 H/H's[a]
Level	
Store Location	Source(%) of Volume[a]
Price	Own Brands
Field Selling Expenditures	Competitors Brands
# Salesman	Repeat Rate[a]
# Sales Calls	Share of AD $[a]
Trade Promotions	Share of Promotion $[a]
Type	
Duration	
Value	Ad recall?
Package	# Households—by type[a]
Type	# Outlets—by type[a]
Size	Segmented per capita purchasing[a]
Outlet	Shares[a]
Type	Volumes[a]
Size	BDI/CDI[a]

[a] Prior period nondiscretionary constraints (inputs).

Figure 8–3. Marketing variables for inclusion in DEA.

enveloped by RUs defining the facet); and RUs associated with one facet vs. RUs associated with another facet; and

- Use of inverse or complementary quantities for the own-price inputs of an RU and the competitive input of its competitors.

A great deal of experimental data from these DEA applications have yet to be analyzed, and many other patterns and regularities were noted but not subject to research follow-up.

5. Additional Insights into the Soft Drinks Market

This application of DEA to the highly competitive soft drinks market provided several additional insights into the structure and functioning of the market that may also shed some light on other competitive situations. Indeed, we expect that much of what we have learned is equally valid for many other high-turnover consumer products in competitive markets. Unlike the axiom of classical equilibrium economics by which competition drives inefficient firms out of the market, our longitudinal studies showed that (technical) inefficiencies among brands persisted, although their magnitude varied over time.

The county map of the U.S. showing the market efficiency of Coca Cola based on the additive DEA model, showed that fully efficient ADIs are few and widely dispersed. Thus, no particular geographic concentration of efficient performance could be discerned.

During the two-year period studied, our analysis of competing brands in the Los Angeles ADI revealed that some brands were able to sustain a higher product price simultaneously with a higher purchase frequency by households with children. Most of the efficient brands were in this group, with the remaining efficient brands being so rated on dimensions other then price/frequency performance. Detailed analysis also revealed potential efficiencies/inefficiencies that might be associated with advertising. Several brands did not advertise at all in Los Angeles. Of these, the brand RC Regular achieved the highest market share and was rated efficient. Coca Cola, which was the advertising leader, achieved about the same market share but was rated as less than fully efficient. No clear relationship between advertising and purchase frequency among households with children could be detected. The most frequently purchased brand was Cragmont, a private-label brand that does not advertise. For all of Coca Cola's advertising expenditure, its purchase frequency was about half that of Cragmont.

Our analysis also confirmed that trade-offs between inputs and between outputs are not only possible but also prevalent. For example, Shasta and Seven-Up were both rated as efficient, but they achieved their efficiency ratings with very different input–output mixes. Seven-Up's advertising expenditure was three times that of Shasta, and it had a higher purchase frequency than did Shasta, but Shasta achieved more total volume.

6. Concluding Remarks

Our experience with private-sector applications of management science techniques led to the recognition that different levels of management have different focuses and objectives, and consequently require different types of presentations addressing different aspects of the company's operations. This requirement expressed itself in, among other ways, the kinds of issues raised by investigating the different types of marketing efficiency presented in figure 8-1. Executives at the headquarters level were more interested in Aggregate Market–Brand Efficiency and Aggregate Brand–Market Efficiency, whereas regional (midlevel) managers were concerned with Market Efficiency and Brand Efficiency issues. Accordingly, we devised alternative means of presenation, each specifically tailored for the needs of the relevant management level involved. The varying degrees of detail required at different managerial levels therefore demanded the evaluation of several different data sets spanning the two-year analysis period.

The experiments outlined above were a prelude to initial formulations and other ongoing research in effectiveness analysis, and provided a springboard for constructing resource allocation, redistribution, and planning models[3] based on the results of the efficiency analysis. We believe this promises to be a most fruitful extension of DEA for application in both the public and private sectors.

Acknowledgments

We wish to acknowledge the support and insightful suggestions of Arie Lewin, Lawrence Seiford, and two anonymous reviewers on the first version of this chapter.

Notes

1. MRCA Information Services, 2215 Sanders Rd., Northbrook, IL 60062.
2. This map could not be reproduced here for technical reasons.
3. See Golany, Learner, Phillips, and Rousseau (1990a, 1990b) and Golany, Phillips, and Rousseau (1989).

9 EXPLORING WHY SOME PHYSICIANS' HOSPITAL PRACTICES ARE MORE EFFICIENT: TAKING DEA INSIDE THE HOSPITAL

Jon A. Chilingerian

1. Introduction

Perhaps it is no longer startling to Americans that more than $2 billion a day is spent on their medical care. But two additional facts may be surprising. First, although physicians account for less than 20% of those expenditures, they control up to 80% of the expenditure decisions (Eisenberg, 1986). Second, research has begun to reveal wide variations in the way physicians practice medicine (Eisenberg, 1986). Moreover, these findings have led some to speculate that rising hospital costs may be more the result of clinical inefficiency owing to excessive physician utilization of hospital resources than of waste owing to managerial inefficiency (Eisenberg, 1986; Chilingerian and Sherman, 1987; Young and Saltman, 1983; Aaron and Schwartz, 1984; Enthoven, 1980).

Despite a growing interest in the clinical efficiency of physicians outside the hospital, hospital managers have not focused on this issue. Understanding why requires a look at the problem of management control inside the hospital (Harris, 1977; Young and Saltman, 1983).

Hospitals have been acknowledged as among the most complex organizations (Drucker, 1988). The provision of clinical services in a hospital is composed of highly complex, highly divergent activities, e.g., examinations, diagnoses, treatment therapies, medications, and nursing care. In every phase of the medical care process, there are different providers who specialize in delivering services to patients—i.e., physicians, nurses, technicians, assistants, interns, and residents. However, it is the physician who is ultimately in charge of the patient's recovery and therefore decides on a unique bundle of hospital products and services. The physician not only oversees the production of clinical services but also controls the clinical production process and has the sole right to decide on the particular bundle of services that a patient will receive.

While the quest for the efficient and productive provision of hospital services has been a recurring theme of hospital managers, hospital managerial attention has, by and large, been relegated to matters such as shared service arrangements to lower input prices (Chilingerian and Sherman, 1987), the productivity of labs (Paschke et al., 1984), nurse staffing levels, and so on, while ignoring how physicians allocate expensive hospital resources to patients. Since physicians are not salaried employees, hospitals have had to rely on cooperative, as opposed to hierarchical, relations with them. Moreover, physicians have never cooperated with corporate and management controls that have intruded on their decision-making sovereignty. Thus, hospitals have relinquished control over clinical service production to the attending physicians.

Today, the situation is changing. For example, many hospital managers have adopted information systems with software that reports on the resources used by individual physicians. Some hospitals have begun providing physicians with comparative feedback on the average length of stay, average ancillary charges, and morbidity and mortality of their patients in relation to the hospital average. Now that the clinical data are available, better evaluation techniques and performance indicators are needed.

Whether physician efficiency succeeds in becoming a critical health policy issue for the 1990s depends on resolving the unique problems associated with measuring it. For example, evaluating physicians' clinical efficiency requires the ability to find "best practices"—i.e., the minimum set of inputs to produce a successfully treated patient. Despite the growth of interest among health services managers to monitor and assess the performance of physicians and their impact on clinical service delivery, few evaluation techniques have overcome physician objections to such studies.

This chapter reports on a pilot study of physician efficiency inside the hospital.[1] It is shown that data envelopment analysis (DEA) can be adapted to resolve many of the problems associated with measuring physician efficiency. Moreover, DEA will be demonstrated using real clinical data to explore some of the factors that are associated with physician efficiency. This chapter will 1) review the literature, 2) demonstrate how and why DEA can be applied to physicians, and 3) interpret the results of a pilot study by identifying some factors that may influence physician efficiency.

2. Theoretical Issues and Prior Expectation

2.1. Studies of Physician Behavior

Technical inefficiency in the provision of hospital services occurs because of excessive physician utilization. Previous research on physician utilization has found relationships between the use of resources and such factors as the type of practice, case mix, physician age, and physician specialty. Eisenberg (1986) suggests that models of physician performance should consider practice style, personal characteristics of the physician, patient characteristics, and the general context of the practice setting (see figure 9–1). He argues that these factors can affect the length of stay, number of tests used, medications prescribed, and so on. This study was organized with the conceptual model displayed in figure 9–1 in mind.

2.1.1. Prepaid Group Practices versus Fee-For-Service. According to Luft (1980), HMOs give providers an incentive to use resources more efficiently. The results of more recent studies of prepaid group practices continue to support the idea that lower use of hospital services is partly the result of the way that HMOs "encourage" physicians to practice medicine (Hlatky et al., 1983; Brewster and Bradbury, 1984).

H1: Physicians affiliated with an HMO will tend to be technically efficient more frequently than physicians affiliated with more traditional types of practice settings (e.g., fee-for-service).

While some studies have found lower rates of diagnostic testing for HMO-based versus fee-for-service types, other studies have found no differences in the use of tests when case mix or type of insurance are controlled for (Yelin, 1985). Thus, one would expect to observe a tendency for technical efficiency when the case mix is younger, less complicated, or less severe.

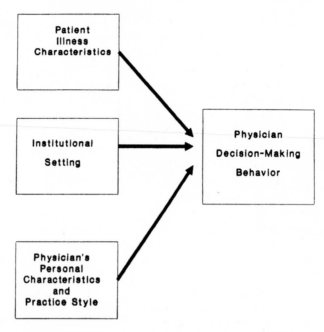

Figure 9-1.   Factors affecting physician decision-making behavior.

H2:   Physicians with a case mix that is, on average, younger and less complex will tend to be technically efficient more frequently than physicians with an older, sicker average case mix.

2.1.2. Age.   The literature suggests that younger physicians utilize more diagnostic services than older, more clinically mature physicians— clinicians tend to reduce utilization as they age (Childs and Hunter, 1972).[2]

H3:   Older physicians with an equivalent case mix will tend to be technically efficient more frequently than younger physicians.

2.1.3. Subspecialists.   According to prevailing views, when case mix was controlled for, physicians who specialize have been associated with less efficient use of input resources than those who do not (Eisenberg and Nicklin, 1981; Fishbane et al., 1981).

H4: Physicians without board-certified subspecialties will tend to be technically efficient more frequently than physicians with board-certified subspecialties.

3. Evaluating Physician Efficiency using Data Envelopment Analysis

There are conceptual, methodological, and practical problems associated with measuring physician efficiency. First, conceptualizing physician efficiency involves identifying *all* the appropriate outputs and inputs.[3] Identifying inputs and outputs raises two questions—1) For which resource inputs and outputs should physicians be held accountable? and 2) Can we define the physician's clinical output while holding quality constant (Cromwell, 1974)?

A second conceptual problem involves specifying the technical relationship among inputs. In analyzing clinical processes, it has been pointed out that it is possible for physicians to substitute inputs—e.g., ancillary services for days of hospital stays and vice versa—when caring for patients with similar illnesses (Eisenberg, 1986). Within the boundaries of "good clinical practice," there is room for a variety of methods of clinical production, and therefore, a variety of "best-practicing" physicians. Consequently, an evaluation model should be able to distinguish a "best practice" within a clinical method from a legitimate clinical alternative.

Methodological problems also exist. First, there is the problem of making valid comparisons. Comparability problems arise due to differences in the level of activity among physicians. Since some physicians admit as few as one patient per month while more active physicians admit several patients per day, studies must be limited to only the most active members of a hospital's medical staff.

Another methodological problem results when the "more active" physicians vary in the complexity, severity, and demographics of their mix of patients. While case-mix differences may average out at the hospital level, they explain differences in efficiency at the individual physician level. Hence, the mix of patients is an important determinant of why physicians utilize longer hospital stays and expensive ancillary services for their patients. Therefore, in order to compare physician efficiency, it is necessary either to adjust a physician's outputs for variations in the mix of their patients (i.e., older patients, more complex diagnoses, more severe conditions) or to limit comparisons to physicians with "equivalent" patients (Flood and Scott, 1987). Limiting comparisons to physicians with similar patient mix leads to the statistical problem of handling small numbers.

Finally, even if conceptual agreement and a sound methodological approach existed, attending physicians object to being held accountable for their clinical efficiency. Physicians are the hospital manager's most influential stakeholder. The community hospital's survival depends on physician loyalty and patronage. If a management control system

> intervenes in patient-related decisions, many doctors will quite likely attempt to subvert the system, perceiving it as an affront to their medical autonomy (Young and Saltman, 1983, p. 129).

Therefore, the objective of the evaluation model selected should make sense to the physician, be congruent with a physician's professional values, and be perceived as fair.

In sum, to measure physician efficiency, an approach is needed that can meet five basic requirements. First, the measure should include all major inputs and outputs and pinpoint how each contributes to overall performance. Second, it should be able to account for physicians utilizing different clinical methods (i.e., substitution among hospital inputs) versus overuse of resources within a clinical method (i.e., technical inefficiency). Third, it should be able to account for case mix. Fourth, the measure should not only inform us about extreme cases, but also help us to explore the nature of "best practices" (i.e., efficient input–output relations). Finally, and most importantly, it should be clinically reasonable to physicians.

3.1. Measurement of Physician Efficiency: Ratios versus DEA

To compare an individual physician's performance in relation to a peer group, a method of ranking physicians is needed. Traditionally, two simple ratios described and evaluated physician performance in the hospital: average length-of-stay and average dollars of ancillary services.[4] However, in light of the five requirements just discussed, these measures have become increasingly inapplicable to the study of individual physician performance.

The first problem with these traditional ratios is their inability to collapse all the relevant inputs and outputs into a single measure of productive efficiency. To evaluate physician performance with two inputs and two outputs, four ratios are needed: e.g., average length-of-stay for output A, average length-of-stay for output B, and so on; average ancillary services for output A; average ancillary services for output B. A second problem with ratios is their inability to deal with substitution among hospital inputs. There is potential for misinterpretation of single-factor ratios like average length-of-stay when other inputs (viz., ancillary services) are ignored. Higher-than-average lengths-of-stay are not necessarily the result of inefficiency. It is possible that higher utilization is the result of taking a different clinical path—i.e., one that trades shorter lengths-of-stay for increased use of ancillary services.

Third, to control for case-mix differences among physicians, researchers are often forced to patition individual physicians into small comparison groups (i.e., $n \leq 12$). With small numbers, the group means become dependent on how spread out the individual averages are. In other words, if these averages are not normally distributed, the mean becomes difficult to interpret. To evaluate individual performance, standards (or rules) are needed. For example, a typical rule might be *"Pay attention if averages exceed one or two standard deviations from the mean."* With a small sample size, few physicians will be one standard deviation from the mean in either direction. While this suggests little variability in performance, it is an artifact of the measure.

To make valid comparisons of physician performance using ratio analysis, there are three research strategies: shift the unit of analysis from the individual physician to a theoretically meaningful aggregate (e.g., specialists versus generalists, or HMO versus fee-for-service), undertake large samples, or introduce outside standards. Although national or regional standards could be established for physicians, these would require developing a clinical theory of hospital-based clinical practice. Given the dominant position of physicians inside the hospital, outside standards are more easily challenged than comparisons with one's peers.

In summary, though ratios are a clear and simple calculation, they are weakened when study samples must be partitioned into smaller comparison groups. Since they describe a statistical relation between a single input and an aggregate output, higher-than-average utilization may be due to a more complicated output mix. Moreover, they can neither define efficient relationships nor differentiate between clinical methods and practicing a clinical method inefficiently.

DEA, on the other hand, has several distinct advantages over the ratio approach. First, DEA can assimilate multiple input–output data into a single measure of efficiency. Second, DEA focuses attention on the nature of efficient input–output relationships by considering how inputs are substituted as well as the rates of output transformation. Since the evaluation measure compares physicians who have taken an "equivalent" clinical process (i.e., similar patient mix and combination of inputs) to care for their patients, the results of DEA are fair. Third, as a nonparametric approach, DEA can handle smaller comparison groups without the measurement problem associated with common averages. Whether or not DEA will be perceived as fair and clinically relevant remains to be determined.

3.2. Choice of DEA Models

To locate best-practicing physicians, the CCR_D-I (input-oriented CCR dual) model, which estimates a piecewise linear envelopment surface with constant returns to scale, was selected (see chapter 2). Although a hospital's production function may exhibit variable returns to scale, there are economic reasons for expecting that a physician's clinical production function exhibits constant returns to scale (Pauly, 1980). Physicians are taught that similar patients with common conditions should be taken through the same clinical process.[5] Thus, if physicians want to treat twice as many low-severity patients with a common diagnosis, they would expect to use twice as many resources; consequently, scaling up the quantity of patients should result in a doubling of the inputs. Since hospitals gladly allow physicians who double or triple their admissions to use as many inputs as physicians need, and since there is no reason to believe that the act of increasing caseloads has a scale effect on the productivity of the inputs, variable returns to scale did not seem justified.[6]

The CCR_D-I model has a strong intuitive appeal when applied to physicians. The model answers the following question: Given the quantity of patients treated and discharged by this physician, could the inputs be reduced? Since the model holds the clinical output level constant while minimizing clinical inputs, it accommodates a quality-constant definition of output (Cromwell, 1974). Thus, the model could be used not only to monitor variations in the utilization of resources and to identify which clinical inputs might be reduced, but also to help researchers understand why medical practices vary (Eisenberg, 1986).

4. Data and Methods

4.1. Sample Population

This study took place in a single hospital[7] and consisted of any internist or surgeon who treated and discharged 35 or more cases over a three-month period in 1987.[8] When the data were collected, the 24 internists discharged a total of 1199 patients and the 12 surgeons 793 patients.

The data were generated from a computerized patient classification system known as MedisGroups (Brewster et al., 1985). MedisGroups is a severity classification system based on an "objective illness measure"—the patient's key clinical findings at the time of admission. The assignment of a patient into a severity group depends entirely on the clinical findings from a patient's physical exams, laboratory, radiology, pathology tests, and so on. The test results reported in the medical record are translated by a medical algorithm (developed by practicing physicians) into one of five mutually exclusive severity groups. Each severity class defines a relative degree of organ failure ranging from 0–4, where zero means no abnormal findings and 4 means life-threatening findings indicative of organ failure (see Brewster et al., 1985). Thus the average weighted severity of the case mix of each physician can be obtained from the MedisGroups system.

Table 9–1 describes the characteristics of the sample. The average age of the physician was 44, and that average physician produced 29 low- and 18 high-severity cases, with a 91% satisfactory outcomes (i.e., absence of morbidity or mortality). The average length of stay was 7.2 days per patient, and the average total charges per patient for ancillary services was $3595.

4.2. Defining the Inputs and Outputs

The two major hospital services categories commonly used by every physician are length of stay and ancillary services. The costs generated by a patient's length-of-stay encompass admission, medical records, discharge process, meals, laundry, medical supplies, and nursing care. Since there are so many different types of ancillary services, with varying levels of technological sophistication, the total charge for ancillary services was used in the present study. Since a single hospital was studied, cost-accounting differences and cost-to-charge ratios were implicitly held constant; the result was a reasonably good proxy for the sum of the weighted ancillary services used.

Customarily, two criticisms have been leveled at definitions of physician output defined in terms of the number of cases. First, an adjustment is needed for mix, or complexity, of a physician's cases (Fetter and Freeman, 1986); second, another adjustment is needed for intradiagnostic

Table 9–1. Summary of Input and Output Measures and Factors Affecting Physician Decision-Making Behavior (n = 36)

	Mean	Std. Dev.	Minimum	Maximum
Outputs				
Low-severity cases	29	19	7	88
High-severity cases	18	6	5	28
Inputs				
Average length of stay	7.2	2.8	3.2	18.0
Total ancillary services ($)	3595	1114	2176	6244
Explanatory variables				
Average age of patients	61	9	41	77
Physician's area of specialization	.42	.5	0.0	1.0
Average weighted severity	1.3	.37	.6	2.2
Relative weight of caseload	1.16	.29	.6	2.07
Physician's age	44	8	33	58
HMO affiliation	.361	.487	0.0	1.0
Fraction of caseload with satisfactory outcomes, i.e., absence of morbidity and mortality	.91	.06	.78	.98

severity (Conklin et al., 1984). Thus, a physician's output cannot be adequately defined without measures of case-mix complexity and severity.

It makes no sense to evaluate the efficiency of a medical service process that results in morbidity, mortality, or readmission to the hospital for the same condition, so every discharge was then classified into two outcomes:

1. Satisfactory—patients who had recovered and were discharged in a healthier state were classified as having had a satisfactory outcome;

2. Unsatisfactory—the presence of morbidity or mortality in each patient's case was classified an unsatisfactory outcome.

The 24 internists discharged 1080 satisfactory and 119 unsatisfactory cases. The 12 surgeons discharged 752 satisfactory and 41 unsatisfactory cases.

Next, two outputs were classified for each physician, based on the presence of a satisfactory outcome: the quantity of low-severity cases and the quantity of high-severity cases using the MedisGroups system mentioned above.[9] Appendix A displays the inputs and outputs used in the DEA model.

4.3. Classifying the Physician Evaluations into Equivalent Comparison Groups

The first task in evaluating internists and surgeons was to assign each type to a relatively homogeneous category.[10] The diagnosis-related group (DRG) system classifies each patient discharge into one of 470 illness categories or "product lines." Each DRG has an assigned value or weight that reflects the relative complexity associated with the DRG, and a higher case-mix value is associated with greater resource consumption. The case mix of each physician was analyzed and classified in terms of the type and quantity of DRGs treated by each physician, and indexed by an average relative weight.

Among the internists, two significantly different comparison groups emerged: Group 2 consisted of a case mix of higher-than-average complexity ($n = 12$, relative weight > 1.0); Group 1 consisted of physicians with a case mix of lower-than-average complexity ($n = 12$, relative weight ≤ 1.0). The 12 surgeons were also classified into two groups: high complexity ($n = 6$, relative weight ≥ 1.48) and low complexity ($n = 6$, relative weight < 1.48).

A separate CCR_D–I model was run for each of the four comparison groups (see figure 9–2). For each inefficient physician, the linear programming formulations were used to project an efficient practice style, even if hypothetically. (The net input/output adjustments suggested by this analysis are referred to as "slack" in table 9–4 below.)

4.3.1. Explanatory Variables. Physician characteristics and information on outcomes were collected for each of the 36 physicians. *These variables were not incorporated as inputs in the DEA model*; rather, they were used to explain why some physician practices appeared to be less efficient. These variables were classified as follows: 1) physician's age, 2)

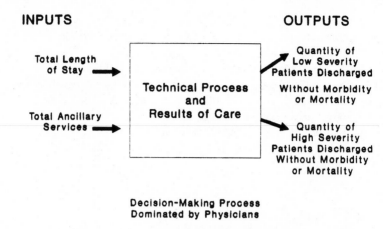

Figure 9-2.   Application of a DEA model to measure physician efficiency.

physician's subspecialty, 3) institutional affiliation, and 4) effectiveness score. Every physician was either an employee of a local prepaid group practice HMO, or they belonged to a more traditional practice (fee-for-service). These variables were coded as dummy variables (0 = 30–40 years old, 1 = 41 + years; 1 = board-certified subspecialist; 0 = internist or general surgeon; 1 = affiliated with HMO, 0 = fee-for-service). An effectiveness score was also calculated for each physician by subtracting the number of cases of morbidity and mortality from the total number of cases and dividing by the total number of cases. The DEA scores were transformed into a binary variable, where a DEA score of 100% = 1 was coded as "efficient," and a DEA score of less than 100% = 0 was coded as "inefficient."

5. Results and Discussion

5.1. DEA Findings

Turning first to the results for the sample of 36 physicians, tables 9–2 and 9–3 indicate that DEA found 13 efficient and 23 inefficient physicians. The average efficiency score for every physician was 89% out of 100%, with a range of 61% to 100%. To check the findings, tables 9–2 and 9–3 compare DEA with the usual ratios used to evaluate performance: average length of stay and average total ancillary charges. DEA iden-

Table 9-2. A Comparison of DEA With Ratio Analysis: Surgeons

Physician ID surgeons	DEA Efficiency Score	Average Length of Stay (days)	Average Ancillary Services ($)	Effectiveness Rating
Group 1: Surgeons with less complex cases (DRG relative weight ≤ 1.48)				
S1	100%	4.00[a]	2176.62[a]	98%
S2	76%	6.44[a]	3096.85	98%
S3	72%	5.69	5362.22[a]	96%
S4	81%	5.77	4182.82	90%
S5	100%	4.46	3234.67	97%
S6	97%	5.10	3800.97	91%
		Mean = 5.24	Mean = 3942	
		S.D. = .9	S.D. = 1085	
Group 2: Surgeons with more complex cases (DRG relative weight > 1.48)				
S7	98%	6.15	4798.31	91%
S8	100%	7.33[a]	6196.07[a]	86%
S9	100%	5.78[a]	4158.67[a]	97%
S10	90%	6.52	5967.95[a]	95%
S11	91%	7.13	4883.21	96%
S12	100%	6.52	4399.14	92%
		Mean = 6.57	Mean = 5067	
		S.D. = .58	S.D. = 832	

[a] Greater than one standard deviation from the mean.

tified six best practices and 14 inefficient physicians that were not detected by the ratios. For example, physician M9 was within one standard deviation from the mean length of stay and mean ancillary charges, but in comparison with best practices was rated only 76% efficient.

DEA also rated physician S8 100% efficient, though that physician had higher-than-average ratios. The reason S8 was considered a best practice while performing so far above the mean is that S8 had a disproportionate number of high-complexity cases (over 30%). Any physician with such a high proportion of high-severity cases would utilize higher-than-average days of stay and ancillary services, a fact that the simple ratios had failed to detect. On the other hand, in no case did DEA evaluate a physician as inefficient when lower-than-average ratios were present. Thus, DEA not only found the outliers, but it was able to find inefficiencies for physicians well within the standards set by the ratios.

Table 9-3. A Comparison of DEA With Ratio Analysis: Internists

Physician ID Internists	DEA Efficiency Score	Average Length of Stay (days)	Average Ancillary Services ($)	Effectiveness Rating
Group 1: Internists with less complex cases (DRG relative weight ≤ 1.0)				
M1	100%	6.24	3497.36	96%
M2	82%	5.62	3039.47	82%
M3	63%	18.14[a]	4072.04[a]	88%
M4	87%	6.86	2965.64	84%
M5	84%	8.07	3270.02	91%
M6	100%	10.43	2488.12[a]	80%
M7	100%	6.08	2852.36	97%
M8	100%	8.40	2463.74[a]	83%
M9	76%	8.69	3535.24	91%
M10	88%	9.32	2957.32	86%
M11	100%	4.51	2741.06	90%
M12	91%	14.27[a]	3373.12	98%
	Mean =	8.9 Mean =	3104	
	S.D. =	3.9 S.D. =	468	
Group 2: Internists with more complex cases (DRG relative weight > 1.0)				
M13	97%	6.14	2765.68	92%
M14	100%	3.22[a]	2568.78	93%
M15	68%	5.12	5039.07[a]	96%
M16	100%	6.05	2485.49	79%
M17	72%	8.26	3507.59	79%
M18	61%	9.05[a]	6243.79[a]	92%
M19	98%	6.94	2654.00	89%
M20	91%	7.63	3117.45	95%
M21	79%	6.51	2796.41	78%
M22	95%	10.53	2700.42	91%
M23	74%	8.53	3520.30	91%
M24	100%	4.72[a]	2514.64	92%
	Mean =	6.9 Mean =	3326	
	S.D. =	2.04 S.D. =	1165	

[a] ••.

DEA not only rates efficiency but also locates the source(s) of inefficiency and estimates the amounts of inefficiency. DEA located physician S2 as 76% efficient compared with physician S1. (By scanning the input–output data in appendix A, this was not obvious.) The meaning of the inefficiency score is revealed in table 9–4. If S2 was as efficient as S1, S2 could have treated three more low-severity patients, reduced total length of stay by 87 days, and reduced ancillary services by $30,300. Since S2 treated 41 patients (see appendix A), this would amount to an average reduction of two days of stay and $739 per patient—a goal that on its face appears reasonable.

Table 9–4.   Slack Analysis of Inefficient Physicians[a]

		Increased Outputs		Reduced Resources	
Physician ID	DEA Efficiency Score	High-Severity Cases	Low-Severity Cases	Days of Stay	Total Ancillary Services ($)
S2	76%	0	3	87	30,300
S3	72%	0	2	85	168,800
S4	81%	3	0	61	49,700
S6	97%	3	0	4	8,600
S7	98%	0	0	5	21,800
S10	90%	0	2	67	183,100
S11	91%	0	0	30	23,500
M2	82%	0	0	69	37,400
M3	63%	0	0	604	72,900
M4	87%	0	0	131	19,800
M5	84%	0	0	63	23,800
M9	76%	0	0	112	45,700
M10	88%	0	0	138	12,800
M12	91%	0	0	374	11,900
M13	97%	0	0	14	3,300
M15	68%	0	4	110	152,400
M17	72%	0	0	133	45,400
M18	61%	0	0	136	132,500
M19	98%	0	0	43	1,700
M20	91%	0	0	45	10,000
M21	79%	0	0	73	21,300
M22	95%	0	0	279	6,900
M23	74%	0	0	136	40,000
Total		6	11	2799	1,123,600
% Improvement		.5%	2%	29%	13%

[a] The DEA linear programming formulation projects the value of the imputs and outputs if a physician "could" practice as efficiently as the best-practicing physician within a given cone (see chapter 2).

Table 9–4, which summarizes the organizational slack found by DEA, reveals a potential increase of 17 cases and a reduction in resources of 2799 days and over $1.0 million of ancillary services. For many community hospitals, if half of that savings could be achieved, the result would be an operating surplus on the revenue and expense statement.

5.2. Factors Associated With Technical Efficiency

In order to explore the factors associated with the efficiency ratings, a series of parametric (T-Tests) and nonparametric (Mann–Whitney) tests were performed on the efficient (physicians with a DEA score of 100%) and inefficient physicians.[11] Table 9–5 displays tests for the hypotheses. While there was a significantly higher proportion of efficient physicians who were affiliated with the prepaid group-practice HMO,[12] hypotheses 2 to 4 were not supported. So, for the technically efficient versus inefficient physicians, there was no significant difference in the physician's age, subspecialty, case mix (severity and complexity), average age of the patient population, effectiveness, or the quantity of high- versus low-severity cases. Thus it appears that HMO-based physicians were more likely to be operating on the efficient production surface.

To shed more light on the finding that the HMO-based physicians were more efficient, parametric and nonparametric tests were performed on the data controlling by type of physician (internists versus surgeons). If H1 is correct, then HMO surgeons and internists should both have a significantly higher efficiency rating. The mean efficiency rating for the physicians affiliated with an HMO was 97.7%, and for those not affiliated, 87.8%—a significant difference ($t = 2.74$, $p < .01$). However, when type of physician is controlled for, significant differences between HMO-based and fee-for-service physicians hold for internists ($t = -2.20$, $p < .04$) but not surgeons (see table 9–6).[13]

If it is true that HMO physicians are more efficient than the others, then their lengths of stay and use of ancillary tests should also be significantly lower. Again, these expectations were supported for the internists but not for the surgeons (table 9–6). The HMO-based internists had significantly lower average lengths of stay (6 versus 9 days), and lower average ancillary charges ($2781 versus $3525). Besides institutional affiliation, other factors may determine efficiency. The literature above mentions the case mix and age of the patient as most relevant. Neither of these factors changed the result.[14]

Although an initial look at these results suggests some differences in

Table 9–5. Summary of Tests Comparing the Differences Between Efficient and Inefficient Physicians Found by DEA

Variable	Mean	t-Test t-value (prob > t)	Mann–Whitney U (prob > U)
Low-severity cases			
Efficient	31	−.58	143
Inefficient	27	(.57)	(.83)
High-severity cases			
Efficient	18	−.08	149
Inefficient	18	(.94)	(.97)
Total volume of cases			
Efficient	52	−.58	140
Inefficient	48	(.57)	(.75)
Relative weight			
Efficient	1.16	.05	126
Inefficient	1.17	(.96)	(.4388)
Average weighted severity			
Efficient	1.3	−.03	142
Inefficient	1.3	(.97)	(.79)
Average age of patient mix			
Efficient	61	−.05	146
Inefficient	61	(.96)	(.9)
Effectiveness rating[a]			
Efficient	1.28	−.31	130
Inefficient	1.27	(.76)	(.51)
Physician's age			
Efficient	46	−1.21	116
Inefficient	43	(.273)	(.27)
Physician's subspecialty			
Efficient	.54	−1.08	121
Inefficient	.35	(.29)	(.27)
Affiliation with HMO			
Efficient	.61	−2.53	90
Inefficient	.22	(.016)[b]	(.02)[b]

[a] Since the true population proportions are unknown, the proportions were transformed via the arc-sin transformation before the t-test was begun (see Winer, 1962).

[b] $p < .05$.

Table 9-6. Summary of Tests Comparing the Differences Between Fee-for-Service and HMO Physicians Found by DEA for Internists and Surgeons

Variable	Mean	t-Test t-value (prob > t)	Mann–Whitney U (prob > U)
Interns (n = 24)			
Efficiency score			
Fee-for-service	84%	−2.20	33.5
HMO	94%	(0.39)[a]	(.03)[a]
Average length of stay			
Fee-for-service	9.1	2.77	26
HMO	6.1	(0.12)	(.01)[a]
Average ancillary charge			
Fee-for-service	3525	2.56	29
HMO	2781	(.021)[a]	(.02)[a]
Effectiveness rating			
Fee-for-service	.89	.68	.64
HMO	.88	(.51)	(.72)
Relative weight			
Fee-for-service	1.02	−.25	61.5
HMO	1.04	(.8)	(.62)
Average weighted severity			
Fee-for-service	1.43	−1.34	53
HMO	1.58	(.19)	(.31)
Average age of patients			
Fee-for-service	65	−1.14	49.5
HMO	67	(.27)	(.23)
Surgeons (n = 12)			
Efficiency score			
Fee-for-service	91%	−1.2	9
HMO	97%	(.26)	(.39)
Average length of stay (days)			
Fee-for-service	5.8	−1.08	8
HMO	6.3	(.31)	(.31)
Average ancillary charge ($)			
Fee-for-service	4192	−.92	10
HMO	4841	(.4)	(.52)
Effectiveness rating			
Fee-for-service	.94	−.49	12.5
HMO	.94	(.64)	(.85)

Table 9-6. *Continued*

Variable	Mean	t-Test t-value (prob > t)	Mann–Whitney U (prob > U)
Relative weight			
Fee-for-service	1.36	−1.44	7.5
HMO	1.65	(.22)	(.27)
Average weighted severity			
Fee-for-service	.89	−.85	9.5
HMO	.97	(.43)	(.45)
Average age of patients			
Fee-for-service	52	−.36	12.5
HMO	53	(.73)	(.85)

[a] $p < .05$.

the decision-making efficiency of HMO-based physicians, there are certain issues that remain unanswered. This investigation has not taken into account the overlap that exists in being young or being a specialist in an HMO. Further tests are needed to ensure that belonging to an HMO is really associated with physician efficiency.

5.3. Controlling by Subspecialty and Physician Age

Tables 9-7 to 9-9 investigate the relation between efficiency and institutional affiliation, controlling for the presence of a subspecialty and the age of the physician. Table 9-7 indicates that for physicians without a subspecialty, there are no significant differences in efficiency between the HMO and fee-for-service physician. Internists with a subspecialty who were affiliated with the HMO were somewhat more efficient, but the difference was not significant ($p = .1$).

Finally, Table 9-8 indicates no significant efficiency differences between HMO and fee-for-service physicians over 40 years old; however, younger HMO-based internists were significantly more efficient than their fee-for-service counterparts. Table 9-9 displays the parameter estimates and shows the log-linear coefficients and the odds of being efficient rather than inefficient for some of the key terms in the model (for an explanation of the model, see appendix B). For the average physician, the odds

Table 9–7. Frequency Distribution of Physician Efficiency by Institutional Affiliation and Subspecialty Training

Decision-Making Efficiency	Physicians with Subspecialty			Physicians without Subspecialty		
	Fee-for Service	HMO	Total	Fee-for Service	HMO	Total
Efficient	2	5	7	3	3	6
Inefficient	6	2	8	12	3	15
Total	8	7	15	15	6	21
	Fisher's Test = .1			Chi-square = .71		

$^a p = .4.$

Table 9–8. Frequency Distribution of Physician Efficiency by Institutional Affiliation and Physician's Age

Decision-Making Efficiency	Physicians 30 to 40 Years Old			Physicians 41+ Years Old		
	Fee-for Service	HMO	Total	Fee-for Service	HMO	Total
Efficient	1	4	5	4	4	8
Inefficient	11	2	13	7	3	10
Total	12	6	18	11	7	18
	Fisher's Test = .02[a]			Fisher's Test = .35		

$^a p < .05.$

of being inefficient were much better than being efficient (1.65 to 1). However, HMO affiliation improved the odds of being technically efficient.[15] The odds of an HMO physician in this sample being efficient rather than inefficient (other things being equal) are 2.27 to 1, and the odds of a fee-for-service physician being efficient are .44 to 1. Moreover, belonging to an HMO *and* being young boosted a physician's odds of being efficient rather than inefficient (1.66 to 1 versus .61 to 1).

Table 9-9. A Log-Linear Model of Physician Efficiency

	Parameter Estimates ×2	Odds of Being Efficient versus Inefficient
Performance		
Efficient	−.374	.69
Inefficient	+.374	1.45
Affiliation–performance interaction		
Fee-for-service × Efficient	−.8176	.44
HMO × Efficient	+.8176	2.27[a]
Physician's age–performance interaction		
40 and younger × Efficient	−.218	.80
Over 40 × Efficient	+.218	1.24
Type of physician–performance interaction		
Surgeon × Efficient	+.1842	1.20
Internist × Efficient	−.1842	.83
Affiliation–age–performance interaction: 40 and under × Efficient		
HMO	+.49	1.63
Fee-for-service	−.49	.61

[a] $p < .05$.

6. Conclusions

It was found that the physicians who used more resources efficiently did so with equivalent case-mix complexity and severity, and average patient age. Even more important, they did so with equivalent outcomes in terms of morbidity and mortality. The analysis also identified some key factors that contribute to the association between a physician's institutional affiliation and decision-making efficiency. Belonging to an HMO may increase a young physician's chances of being efficient. In order to know the order of relative importance of these conditions, the effect of each condition must be weighed while holding the other conditions constant. If the sample size were larger, these issues could be answered more definitively by either regression analysis or log-linear modeling.

There are some interesting interpretations of the analysis. Recall the propositions from the literature review that suggested that older physicians will be more efficient. The HMO did not achieve any significant result with these already-more-efficient classes of physicians. But the HMO was able to keep the most inefficient physicians, the younger physicians, in check.

A second interpretation of the analysis is that, over time, the HMO exercises greater influence over a physician's decision-making efficiency. Hence, the younger physicians are recruited into the HMO as less efficient performers, and as they become socialized by the HMO, their behavior converges with the older, more efficient physicians. This interpretation would explain why the younger HMO physicians were rated as more efficient than the fee-for-service physicians.

A third interpretation also takes time into account as habituation facilitates learning. The argument is that, over time, every physician gets to know their patients better. So in five or ten years, they know their patients and their patients' families so well that they can rule out certain procedures and tests. Somehow, HMOs bring younger physicians along much faster.

Interviews with several physicians reveal that degree of patient uncertainty—meaning a lack of sure knowledge about the patient's past medical history—can play an important role in inefficient decision-making behavior. Physicians may act more efficiently in treating patients they know better. As one physician observed:

> I act differently when I know the patient. I'll hold off treatment and tests longer if I know the patient.

It also might be interpreted that physicians who achieve better outcomes[16] can conserve resources and serve the same number of patients if there is some mechanism of control. In this study, the mechanism of social control appears to be membership in an HMO.

6.1. Can HMOs Really Control Physician Behavior in "Open" Hospitals?

According to Luft (1980), HMOs assume the financial risk and/or gain associated with hospital resource consumption. The theory is that since HMOs are exposed to risk, their managers pay more attention to physicians' resource-utilization behavior—i.e., they offer financial incentives to physicians to use resources more efficiently, and they screen and socialize their employees better. However, with the exception of the "Kaiser-controlled" hospitals, no studies have found strong effects of the prepaid group-practice HMO on physician behavior. The findings from the present DEA study indicate that HMO control may extend inside the community hospital that openly grants admitting privileges to local physicians.

There are three problems with the current study. First, a longitudinal study with a larger sample size is needed to confirm the findings presented here. Window analysis can be used to validate the efficiency ratings of physicians while obtaining longitudinal information about significant variances in scores at different points in time (e.g., two or more quarters of information). Employing this method in future studies would provide assurance of the stability of physician scores (for more details, see Golany and Roll, 1989). Second, until the results of this study are investigated by clinically trained researchers, the implications are mere speculation.

Third, some critics may argue that evaluating the decision-making efficiency of high-quality outcomes is flawed because it is tantamount to sampling on the dependent variable. While that criticism may be valid, it does not apply to this type of evaluation. If the quality of physician outputs is inconsistent, then there is no reason to measure decision-making efficiency. Increasing the quantity of *all* outcomes includes writing death certificates more efficiently. On the other hand, increasing the quantity of satisfactory outcomes—without increasing costs—challenges physicians to think about learning practice patterns that find the "quick route to health." Because it also involves learning new and better practices, this approach poses a challenge that the medical profession cannot afford to ignore.

6.2. Using DEA to Evaluate Physicians

DEA is an attention-directing managerial technique. By evaluating the relative efficiency of physicians, it locates trouble spots in practice styles and in the service delivery system. In the future, DEA could be used either to evaluate the practice patterns of physicians before allowing them into a hospital or HMO or to evaluate physicians hired on a trial basis (Chilingerian and Sherman, 1990). Thus, DEA opens up the strategic possibility of targeting the customer market for efficient physician services.

In this study, DEA helped to uncover a factor that explained physician decision-making efficiency—that is, affiliation with an HMO. However, if (as this study showed) HMO physicians are more efficient in providing hospital services, then there is a need to investigate how their organization accomplishes that result. In other words, the managerial behavior and the process of control inside the HMO needs to be understood.

In future studies, an additional benefit of using DEA will be to provide an objective technique for selecting a case for further ethnographic and qualitative study. For example, if researchers want to study the process of control in a service organization, prior to commencing the study, DEA could be used to locate best and worst practices. If DEA could be used to select cases for comparative analysis of decision-making processes (see Lewin and Minton, 1986), the implications go beyond health care and apply to any professionally dominated service organization.

Acknowledgments

I would like to thank Stuart Altman, Sarita Bhalotra, Robert C. Bradbury, Dianne Chilingerian, Mitchell Glavin, Susan A. Goldberger, David Rosenbloom, Sanford Weiner, Arie Y. Lewin, and the two anonymous reviewers for their helpful comments.

Appendix A: Summary of Physician Inputs and Outputs

| | Outputs | | Inputs | |
	Low-Severity Discharges	High-Severity Discharges	Total Length of Stay (days)	Total Ancillary Services($)
Surgeon				
S1	47.00	11.00	232.00	126244.0
S2	36.00	5.00	264.00	126971.0
S3	45.00	9.00	307.00	289560.0
S4	44.00	13.00	329.00	238421.0
S5	76.00	21.00	433.00	304763.0
S6	22.00	7.00	148.00	110228.0
S7	30.00	9.00	240.00	187134.0
S8	19.00	11.00	220.00	185882.0
S9	70.00	16.00	497.00	357646.0
S10	88.00	18.00	691.00	632603.0
S11	33.00	15.00	342.00	234394.0
S12	45.00	21.00	430.00	290343.0
Internist				
M1	32.00	11.00	281.00	157381.0
M2	30.00	26.00	382.00	206684.0
M3	22.00	20.00	889.00	199530.0
M4	24.00	18.00	343.00	148282.0
M5	21.00	20.00	363.00	147151.0
M6	13.00	28.00	532.00	126894.0
M7	13.00	22.00	219.00	102685.0
M8	13.00	16.00	294.00	86196.00
M9	21.00	28.00	469.00	190903.0
M10	17.00	15.00	345.00	109421.0
M11	26.00	20.00	230.00	139794.0
M12	24.00	16.00	585.00	138298.0
M13	14.00	20.00	227.00	102330.0
M14	26.00	12.00	132.00	105320.0
M15	47.00	18.00	348.00	342657.0
M16	7.00	27.00	260.00	106876.0
M17	17.00	23.00	380.00	161349.0
M18	14.00	21.00	344.00	237264.0
M19	12.00	19.00	243.00	92890.00
M20	12.00	24.00	290.00	118463.0
M21	14.00	15.00	241.00	103467.0
M22	23.00	25.00	558.00	143122.0
M23	18.00	21.00	367.00	151373.0
M24	21.00	15.00	184.00	98071.00

Appendix B: Explanation of the hierarchical log-linear model used in this chapter

Log-linear models are considered a substitute for multiple regression when dealing with categorical data. Since the efficiency scores and explanatory variables in this chapter were analyzed in contingency tables, log-linear models could be used to test hypotheses about efficient and inefficient physicians and to estimate the odds of being efficient for different types of physicians.

When using a log-linear model, the variables in the contingency table are treated as independent variables, and the number of cases in each cell becomes the dependent variable (Everitt, 1980). In general, the model for the log of the observed frequency of the ith row and the jth column is

$$\text{Log}_e F_{ij} = U + U_{1i} + U_{(2)j} + U_{12(ij)}$$

U represents an overall mean effect, and U_{1i} represents the effect of the ith efficiency category (efficient/inefficient), $U_{(21)j}$, the effect of the jth institutional affiliation category (HMO/fee-for-service), and $U_{12(ij)}$ the interaction effect between levels i and j of the efficiency and institutional affiliation variables. The parameter estimates obtained from fitting log-linear models were used to quantify the effects of explanatory variables on the DEA score.

From these parameter estimates, one can derive a logit equation that predicts the $\log(F_1/F_2)$, where F_1 is the number of physicians in a given subgroup who are efficient and F_2 is the number of inefficient physicians in that subgroup. The log F_1/F_2 is equivalent to log $(F_1) - (F_2)$, which estimates the odds of being efficient rather than inefficient.

After the log-linear model was run, the parameter estimates were examined and coefficients were obtained by multiplying the estimates by 2. The coefficients were translated into odds by taking the antilogs. Table 9-9 shows these coefficients and the antilogs (referred to as "odds") for some of the key terms in the model (for a more detailed explanation, see Everitt, 1980; Knoke and Burke, 1980).

Notes

1. Physician efficiency, as it is used here, is defined as admitting and discharging the highest quantity of patients from the hospital without morbidity and mortality using the minimum number of resource inputs.

2. On the other hand, Pineault (1977) reported that when uncertainty was low, older

physicians tended to use fewer technical services than younger physicians; however, when uncertainty was high, the reverse was found.

3. In this chapter, *physician efficiency* refers to the efficiency of clinical decision making in the provision of acute hospital care.

4. The average length-of-stay is computed as a ratio of the total number of days of hospital stay used by a physician divided by the total number of patients. Average ancillary dollars is a ratio of the total ancillary charges divided by the total number of patients.

5. Here, the clinical process refers to a series of adaptive decisions made by the physician, such as admitting the patient, ordering lab tests, treatments, consultations and drugs, monitoring physiologic signs, and discharging the patient.

6. The question of returns to scale should be addressed in future research.

7. There is an advantage to studying physician efficiency in a single hospital. Since one of the significant resource inputs is ancillary services, and since every hospital faces different wage rates, laboratory fees, medical supply prices, all these factors are held constant (Garber et al., 1984). Comparing physicians in different hospitals can be misleading if some ancillary services are more efficient than others. By comparing physicians in the same institution, they all face the same systemic disadvantages.

8. The decision to look at physicians with at least 35 patients was suggested to me by a physician working in the quality-assurance area.

9. MedisGroups' five severity groups were collapsed into two output categories: the quantity of low- versus high-severity cases. The high-severity cases were defined as having significant, severe, and critical clinical findings upon admission, with organ failure present or a likelihood of going into organ failure if not treated (MedisGroups categories 3 and 4). The low-severity cases were defined as patients with either few or no abnormal clinical findings upon admission (categories 0, 1, and 2).

10. It is important to note that prior to computing the average weighted severity and average relative weight of each physician's case mix, all the cases with morbidity and mortality were removed. This was done so that only the quality outcomes would be evaluated.

11. The nonparametric test statistics were chosen to avoid making the incorrect assumption that the measures are independent and normally distributed.

12. Chi-square tests were used to determine whether the frequency of a score of 100% differed between HMO and fee-for-service, and between physicians with and without a subspecialization. The obtained chi-square between efficiency and the HMO affiliation was significant ($x^2 = 4.1$, $dF = 1$, $p = .0427$).

13. Part of the reason for this finding may be the smaller number of surgeons in the sample ($n = 12$) and the small number of HMO surgeons ($n = 3$).

14. Several Tobit models were run, with DEA score as the dependent variable and case mix, age, subspecialty, and HMO affiliation as independent variables. Each model found that affiliation with the HMO was the only significant variable.

15. These antilogs represent the relative odds, and do not suggest that a greater number of HMO physicians will be efficient.

16. Recall that an effectiveness score of greater than 90% meant that fewer than 10% of a physician's patients experienced mortality or morbidity.

10 ON THE MEASUREMENT AND MONITORING OF RELATIVE EFFICIENCY OF HIGHWAY MAINTENANCE PATROLS

Wade D. Cook, Alex Kazakov, and
Yaakov Roll

1. Introduction

This chapter describes the application of data envelopment analysis
(DEA) tools to the measurement of relative efficiency of highway maintenance patrols in Ontario, Canada. The system has evolved as a result of
a two-year study carried out for the Ontario Ministry of Transportation,
with the purpose of implementing it on a provincewide basis.

Most of the routine maintenance activities on Ontario's highways fall
under the responsibility of the 244 patrols (approximately similar in size)
scattered through the province. Each such patrol is responsible for some
fixed number of lane-kilometers of highway, as well as those activities
associated with that portion of the network. More than 100 different
categories of operations or activities exist, and are grouped under the
headings *surface, shoulder, right of way, median,* and *winter operations.*

Various statistics (such as *road side* maintenance operations accomplished, by highway class) are maintained, but there is presently no
formal process for evaluating patrol activities. Several objectives led to
the decision to launch a patrol efficiency-measurement project. First, it
was felt that the Ministry needs a management tool by which to assess

quantitatively the relative efficiency of the different patrols. Second, a desire was voiced to be able to evaluate the impact of various "external" (e.g., regional) factors as well as maintenance policy options (e.g., extent of privatization) on patrol efficiency. Furthermore, since observed accomplishments influence budgetary decisions, a better understanding of efficiency would give management a yardstick for measuring what accomplishments can be expected within a given budget limit.

While there are various possible approaches to the problem of measuring efficiency in this context, the DEA framework is particularly appropriate for a number of reasons. First, the prospect of obtaining production standards in the usual engineering sense seems doubtful. The number of different "products" and the different environmental and soil conditions mitigate against a conventional industrial engineering approach. Second, DEA is capable of handling noneconomic factors, such as number of accidents, cars/day, average age of pavement, etc. and allows for measurement of such factors on different scales. This approach seems particularly suited to the maintenance area, since factors such as traffic intensity, safety parameters, and average age of pavements are important parts of the picture.

In the sections to follow, the application of DEA to the maintenance efficiency problem is discussed. A central theme of this chapter is to provide a case-specific description of the *process* of factor development and of the issues addressed; therefore, full details of this process are provided. Next, the models applied are described and the outcomes of a trial run presented. This run covered four maintenance districts in which a total of 62 patrols operate. (The data for the various analysis factors corresponding to these patrols are available from the authors.) The potential for various further analyses is then demonstrated, followed by some concluding comments.

2. The Model

To address the needs of the agency, analyses of efficiency at various levels are required. In particular, it is necessary to understand not only how well a maintenance patrol is performing within a district setting but also how that patrol compares to others, both regionwide and provincewide. (The province is divided geographically into five distinct regions, each of which is further subdivided into districts. The total number of districts in Ontario is 18.) Furthermore, within any district, there is a desire to examine both technical and managerial efficiency and to evaluate characteristics such as privatization, impact of truck traffic, and so on.

The factors used to evaluate patrol performance are discussed in detail in the following section. Briefly, these are as follows:

Outputs
1. Assignment size factor (ASF)
2. Average traffic served (ATS)
3. Rating change factor (RCF)
4. Accident prevention factor (APF)

Inputs
1. Maintenance expenditure (MEX)
2. Capital expenditure (CEX)
3. Climatic factor (CLF)

Very early in the study, it was realized that the regular (unbounded) model yields efficiency ratings that credit patrols with a higher level of performance than can be considered justified. Since complete flexibility in choice of weights is permitted, the model will often assign unreasonably low or excessively high weights (multipliers) to some factors in the process of trying to drive the efficiency rating for the patrol in question as high as possible. Moreover, the weight assigned to a factor such as capital expenditure by one patrol may differ drastically from the corresponding weights for other patrols. Thus, in order to exercise some reasonable level of control over the manner in which importance weights are assigned, bounds need to be imposed in the model.

Using the notation of the input-oriented CCR DEA model (see chapter 2, section 5.1) the following bounded version was constructed for the maintenance patrol problem.

$$\max_{\mu,\, v} \omega_o = \mu^T Y_o \tag{10.1}$$

subject to

$$v^T X_o = 1 \tag{10.2}$$

$$\mu^T Y - v^T X \leq 0 \tag{10.3}$$

$$\mu_r - T_o P1_r \leq 0, \quad \forall\, r \tag{10.4a}$$

$$-\mu_r + T_o P2_r \leq 0, \forall\, r \tag{10.4b}$$

$$v_i - T_o Q1_i \leq 0, \quad i = 1 \text{ and } 3 \tag{10.5a}$$

$$-v_i + T_oQ2_i \leq 0, \quad i = 1 \text{ and } 3 \tag{10.5b}$$

$$-0.5v_1 + v_2 \leq 0 \tag{10.6a}$$

$$0.2v_1 - v_2 \leq 0 \tag{10.6b}$$

where

Y_{rj}, X_{ij} = observed values of output and input factors in patrol j
$P1_r$, $P2_r$ = upper and lower bounds on factor weights for outputs r
$Q1_i$, $Q2_i$ = upper and lower bounds on factor weights for inputs i
T_o = transformation coefficient (fractional to linear formulation)

Note that in the case of the second input (CEX), the bound takes the form of a ratio to the weight accorded to the first input (MEX). This represents the feeling (by the maintenance branch) that when both factors are measured in the same monetary units, capital expenditure should not be given a weight higher than half that given to the direct patrol expenditures. On the other hand, the weight for CEX should not be less than 0.2 of the weight for MEX (for a similar approach, see Thompson et al., 1990).

Geometrically, the imposition of such bounds amounts to bending out the isoquant frontier, as illustrated in the appendix. A full discussion of bounding in DEA and the associated geometric interpretations are provided in Roll et al. (1991).

3. Factors Considered

In a preliminary study of potential factors that could be utilized to best represent causes and effects relating to patrol performance, four outputs and three inputs have been chosen. Following is a brief description of the various factors and the way numerical values for these have been determined.

3.1. ASF—Area Served Factor

This factor was chosen to measure the *extent* of the work load for which the patrol has responsibility. The ASF factor value is calculated from the formula

$$ASF = \sum_i [L_i(TLE)_i(A_j + C) + L_i(S_iB_j + D)]$$

where

L_i = length of road section i
TLE_i = two-lane equivalent of road section i
S_i = shoulder width of road section i
A_j = coefficient for road surface type j (the one in road section i)
B_j = coefficient for shoulder type j (the one in road section i)
C = coefficient for winter operations
D = coefficient for other operations (ROW, median, etc.)

A, B, C, and D are coefficients (based on Ministry of Transportation data) representing the relative total effort required for each component of the maintenance task.

3.2. ATS—Average Traffic Served

This factor is intended to be a measure of the overall benefit to the users of the highway system in a patrol. The formula for computing ATS is given by

$$ATS = 10^{-3} \sum_i L_i (AADT)_i$$

where L_i is the length of road section i, $AADT_i$ is the Annual Average Daily Traffic, and 10^{-3} is a scaling factor designed to bring ATS within a reasonable range for analysis. There is some argument for adjusting $AADT_i$ to account for the percentage of commercial vehicles. An earlier analysis has shown, however, that such an adjustment has very little influence on efficiencies.

3.3. RCF—Pavement Rating Change Factor

This factor measures the actual change in Pavement Condition Rating (PCR) of the various road sections, relative to a "standard" change for the same period. For determining the standard change in road rating, a Pavement Rating Characteristic Curve was defined that links expected PCR values to pavement age. The factor is calculated from

$$RCF = 100 \left[\sum_i A_i \frac{R_{oi} - R_{si}}{R_{oi} - R_{1i}} \right]^{1/2}$$

where

A_i = area of road section i (km TLE), relative to total area covered by the patrols

R_{oi} = PCR reading of road section i, at beginning of period (year)

R_{1i} = PCR reading of road section i, at end of period

R_{si} = expected PCR rating at end of year

The coefficient 100 here is a scaling factor needed to bring the numerical values within the desired range.

3.4. APF—Accident Prevention Factor

Much of the work of maintenance staff arises due to the need to prevent accidents (surface and shoulder repairs, washouts, etc.). In this regard, accident prevention can be viewed as a reason for or goal of maintenance. A reasonable measure of accident prevention should be directly proportional to traffic level (ATS) and inversely proportional to the observed number of accidents. The chosen form is given by

$$APF = 100\frac{ATS}{C}$$

where 100 is a scaling factor and C is the "adjusted" number of road accidents, during the observed period, on all road sections serviced by a patrol. Adjustment of the number of accidents is done by utilizing various available accident-circumstance descriptors, and accounting for the degree to which maintenance patrols might be involved with these events.

3.5. MEX—Maintenance Expenditures

MEX is the total of all expenditures linked directly to the patrol. It includes both "in-house" work as well as maintenance activities performed by private contractors.

3.6. CEX—Capital Expenditures

CEX is the total of all capital expenditures made toward improving the existing highway infrastructure. These would include resurfacing, shoulder paving, repairs to structures, dome construction, etc.—all activities that complement maintenance efforts. Excluded are new link and new structure construction, since these do not directly complement maintenance. Five-year average figures were taken.

3.7. CLF—Climatic Factor

What can often be an overriding consideration in the performance of a patrol is the environmental circumstances in which that patrol must operate. In particular, the climatic differences that exist between, say, patrols in Kenora (north) and those in London (south) may explain differing work loads or pavement conditions, etc. The amount of snowfall, for example, will clearly influence the level of winter maintenance (snow removal and salting) needed. The extent of spring breakups will directly influence the need for summer road-surface work.

Four subfactors were taken into account in arriving at an overall climatic factor: snowfall, major temperature cycles, minor temperature cycles, and rainfall.

Snowfall, rainfall and temperature data are recorded by environmental stations throughout the province. Software designed by the Research and Development Branch extracts the relevant information from environment data files and computes for each station the four subfactor values D_{ij} (higher values denoting more severe conditions). Here i is the station number and j is the subfactor number. The overall climatic factor for a patrol is computed from

$$CLF_k = \sum_i P_{ki}\left(\sum_j (W_j/D_{ij})\right),$$

where

k = patrol index
P_{ki} = weight of station i in calculating the climatic factor of patrol k
W_j = relative importance weight of climatic factor j

It should be noted that the weights W_j were chosen while taking into account the numerical scales of each of the climatic factors (e.g., the snowfall numbers are much greater in size than the major cycle numbers). In addition, the weights were selected with attention to the resultant CLF measure being relatively of the same order of magnitude as the other efficiency factors.

4. Analysis of Efficiency

A total of 62 patrols lying in four districts (districts 2, 3, 8, and 20) are geographically spread across the province. Data corresponding to the seven factors for each of the 62 patrols is used in the analysis of patrol maintenance.

In order to set reasonable bounds on the multipliers, a full set of runs with the unbounded model was first done and the corresponding multipliers noted. As usual, multipliers for the same factors varied widely in the different rows. In the case of μ_1 or ASF, for example, the 62 runs resulted in values of μ_1 as low as virtual zero and as high as 1546 (in the particular scale used).

There is no clear-cut objective procedure that will provide the "right" bounds on factor multipliers. The procedure followed in our case relied rather on managerial judgment as to the relative importance of the various factors and on the acceptable flexibility in the respective multipliers. Additional practical considerations stem mainly from the quality of the data used. Thus, determining the weights consisted of choosing from the range of weights obtained in the unbounded runs. Two considerations may enter the decision process in making this choice:

1. The first consideration is whether to accord a factor a relatively high range of weights or a relatively low one. This should be determined by management's concept as to the role a specific task plays in the general performance of a patrol (in the case of outputs), and by how important a factor is deemed in a patrol's ability to perform these tasks (for inputs).

    An additional point here is the quality of data on which the numerical values given to the various factors are based. Naturally, the less reliable the data are, the lower is the weight one would tend to give this factor (so that it does not distort the entire efficiency picture).

2. The second consideration pertains to the width of the range. It is argued that for a factor where there is either certainty about the scale being utilized or about the importance that should be accorded to that factor, then a narrow or tight range should apply. Such would be the case for a factor like MEX. Actually, there should not be a large amount of flexibility available for the importance weight for such a factor. On the other hand, CLF is a factor whose scale of measurement is open to question, since the significance of climatic influences is not clearly under-

stood. Therefore, for this somewhat vague factor, a wide (flexible) range is permitted. The above considerations, resulted in the following assumptions:

Factor	Level	Flexibility
ASF (μ_1)	Up	Narrow
ATS (μ_2)	Up	Wide
RCF (μ_3)	Up	Narrow
APF (μ_4)	Up	Tight
MEX (v_1)	Up	Tight
CLF (v_3)	Down	Wide

It is noted that no bounds have been set on CEX (v_2). Instead, a relation was imposed between v_2 and v_1, namely, $0.2v_1 \leqslant v_2 \leqslant 0.5v_1$.

Table 10–1 displays the ranges or bounds chosen for each of the factors. The efficiencies obtained when running the model with and without these bounds are shown in columns 1 and 2 of table 10–2.

5. Further Analyses

5.1. District Runs

In order to extract maximum information for effective managerial control, the DEA model was run for each district separately. The resultant set of efficiencies, when only patrols in the same district are considered, appears in column 3 of table 10–2. It is noted that (due to the smaller comparison group) these district efficiencies are higher than the corresponding values obtained when the entire set of patrols was considered. It is also the case

Table 10–1. Bounds on Factor Weights

Factor	ASF	ATS	RCF	APF	MEX	CEX	CLF
Notation[a]	$\mu1$	$\mu2$	$\mu3$	$\mu4$	$v1$	$v2$	$v3$
Upper bound	800	1000	1000	600	2000	[b]	1400
Lower bound	400	200	200	200	1000		200

[a] All weights are in $1/10^6$.

[b] Bounds on $v2$ were replaced by the constraints $0.2 \, v_1 \leqslant v2 \leqslant 0.5 \, v1$.

Table 10–2.   Efficiency Ratings for Individual Patrols

		Efficiencies					Efficiencies		
DMU		Unbounded	Indiv. Weights Entire Sample	Indiv. Weights Within District	**DMU**		Unbounded	Indiv. Weights Entire Sample	Indiv. Weights Within District
D	P	(1)	(2)	(3)	D	P	(1)	(2)	(3)
2	1	.725	.724	.825		5	1	1	1
	3	.768	.741	.878		6	1	.849	.912
	5	.663	.614	.795		7	.876	.824	.906
	6	.700	.671	.791		8	1	.949	.984
	7	.650	.622	.725		9	1	.836	.945
	9	.739	.679	.751		10	1	.980	1
	10	.841	.756	1		12	1	.903	.955
	11	.948	.836	1		13	1	.869	.939
	13	.951	.912	1		14	1	.879	.956
	15	1	1	1		15	1	1	1
	16	1	.761	.776		16	.871	.825	.883
	17	1	.891	.931		17	.942	.872	.897
	18	.857	.774	.839		18	1	.763	.870
						19	.826	.753	.885
3	1	.855	.722	.988		21	1	.848	.935
	2	.787	.744	1		22	1	1	1
	3	.756	.642	.793		25	.817	.799	.875
	4	.761	.752	1					
	5	1	.641	1	20	1	.583	.526	.526
	6	.990	.874	1		2	.739	.369	.370
	7	1	.945	1		3	.989	.541	.541
	8	.840	.811	.982		4	1	.914	.974
	9	.944	.786	.991		5	.770	.674	.674
	10	.613	.562	.693		6	1	.948	.966
	11	.802	.729	.923		7	1	1	1
	12	1	.705	.941		8	.781	.597	.600
	13	.921	.677	.881		9	.915	.625	.635
	14	.457	.430	.608		10	1	.890	.921
						11	.819	.586	.586
8	1	.867	.672	.246		12	.927	.762	.768
	2	.885	.353	.353		13	.933	.795	.843
	3	1	.940	1		14	1	.849	.849
	4	.998	.881	.925					

that some patrols that were inefficient in the earlier analysis obtained a rating of 1.0 in the district setting, since those efficient patrols in *other* districts against which comparison was made have been removed from the peer group.

Because significant differences may exist from one district to another (e.g., climatic and highway-type differences), the intradistrict efficiency measures of column 3 in table 10–2 may provide a fairer appraisal of performance. At the same time, it is desirable to detect any district-to-district differences, obtainable from interdistrict comparisons.

Overall district performance can be viewed in a number of ways. Two useful measures that can be derived are referred to as technical efficiency and managerial efficiency.

5.1.1. Technical Efficiency. With this measure, we compare best performance in a district to best performance in the entire set. This measure is taken as an indicator of the technical potential of a district. Simply speaking, technical efficiency is a measure of the distance of the district frontier from the overall frontier. One technique for obtaining this measure is to bring all points in a district to the district frontier by applying the adjustment method proposed in Channes, Cooper, and Rholdes (1978). A somewhat simpler approach is to correct the district efficiencies by dividing the overall efficiency of each patrol (column 2 of table 10–2) by the relative efficiency within the district (column 3). The resulting quotients are approximations of individual patrol efficiencies if they were brought to the district frontiers. Taking the average of all corrected efficiencies within a district is then a measure of technical efficiency. These values are shown in column 2 of table 10–3. It is noted, for example, that the best performance of district 20 (.986) is near the best for the entire group. District 3, on the other hand, has its best performers only at 79% of the overall best performance.

5.1.2. Managerial Efficiency. This measure refers to the actual performance of patrols within a district. The most reasonable measure to take is the average of the actual efficiencies for the patrols in a district. Column 1 in table 10–3 provides the average of efficiencies when the comparison group is the overall set. Column 3 is the average when the comparison group is only that set of patrols within the district. Naturally, the latter average (column 3) is larger than the former (column 1).

It is noted that the overall efficiency of a district (the efficiency relative to the entire group) is *approximately* equal to the product of the managerial efficiency within it (column 3) and the technical efficiency of the

Table 10–3.   District Efficiencies

District	# of Patrols	(1) Ave. Eff. Relative to Overall Frontier	(2) Eff. of Dist. Front. Relative to Over. Front	(3) Ave. Eff. Relative to District Frontier
2	13	.762	.884	.862
3	14	.716	.790	.903
8	21	.847	.938	.904
20	14	.720	.986	.732

district (column 2)—i.e., thevalue in column 1 is approximately equal to the product of the values in column 3 and column 2. Exact equality fails here because of the manner in which the averages are obtained.

5.2. Analysis of Various Characteristics

Over and above the input parameters chosen for the analysis of patrols, there are other influences (on performance) that deserve attention. These influences can be thought of as *characteristics* or circumstances that can·affect the efficiency with which a patrol operates. Three particular characteristics have been chosen:

1. % privatizaiton
2. traffic level
3. serves vs. does not serve the 401 (the main traffic artery of Ontario)

The method applied to examine a characteristic was 1) to define levels for that characteristic, 2) to separate out those patrols corresponding to the various levels, and 3) to do separate analyses on each of the subgroups. In the present situation, only two levels will be chosen for the study of each characteristic. So, for the case of % privatization, for example, all patrols below some percentage will be separated from those patrols above that percentage. This percentage level can be viewed as a *threshold* distinguishing high from low privatization units. The way in which such analyses were carried out is demonstrated for the first of the three characteristics.

The percentage of privatization is defined as the proportion of the total maintenance budget for the patrol that is utilized on privatized jobs. This proportion was determined from the budget codes in the data file from which the financial information had been extracted.

In the analyses carried out, the influence of the privatization characteristic was examined within each of the four districts under study. Because there are substantial efficiency differences from one district to another, it is advisable to separate out this influence first, and then look at the privatization effects. For this reason, different thresholds for distinguishing between high and low privatization have been chosen for each district. These were taken, approximately, at the district-average % privatization (see table 10–4).

As an example of this type of analysis, consider the results for district 8 as displayed in table 10–5. When efficiency analyses within each subgroup render results that are on average not different from the ones relative to the entire group, then this characteristic presumably has no impact on performance. When some differences do occur, we can draw some conclusions.

For example, in the case of low privatization in district 8, the average efficiency rating of .9592 is not significantly different from the average for these patrols when analyzed relative to the entire district (.9463). This finding can only be explained by the fact that very few high-privatization patrols were on the efficient frontier. Thus, low-privatization patrols tend to perform better than high-privatization patrols, since more of the former than the latter were on the frontier. On the other hand, the average efficiency rating for high-privatization patrols increased from .8474 to .8773. This means that a substantial improvement in the performance picture for high-privatization patrols occurs when the efficient low-privatization patrols are removed from the analysis. Thus, a

Table 10–4. Thresholds for % Privatization

		District			
		2	3	8	20
% privatization	max.	31.4	38.6	32.0	43.3
	average	22.1	24.2	10.2	25.2
	min.	15.1	14.6	.4	9.4
Threshold (%)		22	25	10	25
Patrols above		7	6	9	5
Patrols below		6	8	12	9
Total		13	14	21	14

Table 10–5.   District 8 (Subgroup A: Above 10%; Subgroup B: Below 10%)

	Number of DMUs	Average efficiencies	
		District analysis	Subgroup analysis
Subgroup A (high privatization)	9	.8474	.8773
Subgroup B (low privatization)	12	.9463	.9592
Total/Average	21	.9039	

possible inference that one might make in the case of district 8 is that patrols practicing a low-privatization policy tend to perform on average better than is true of those with high privatization.

The general inferences that could be drawn from these analyses are as follows:

1. Privatization impacts are different from district to district. Overall, there is no conclusive evidence that (in this particular case) privatization increases efficiency.
2. There appears to be no marked effect of the volume of traffic on patrol performance.
3. Patrols not serving highway 401 are performing marginally better than patrols serving that artery.

The way in which a particular characteristic affects performance should always be examined within the wider context of all existing factors. Thus, in this special case, subdivision by a certain characteristic within districts does not always have to point to the same general conclusion for each of those districts. The different sets of other factors may influence differently the impact of the examined characteristic.

It must be emphasized that what is being measured is efficiency, i.e., the ratio of outputs to inputs. Consequently, obtaining results on the impact of a certain characteristic does not provide direct information as to whether that characteristic necessitates more effort. Rather, the results point to the ratio between that extra effort (as the case may be) and the corresponding compensation (e.g., budget) for it. For example, in the "serves 401" analysis, the lower efficiencies for those patrols that deal with the 401 seems to indicate that while a greater effort may be needed to maintain freeways, apparently the corresponding patrols are overcompensated for this.

6. Concluding Comments

With regard to the case described above, the following points pertaining to applications of the DEA approach must be emphasized:

1. It is, obviously, of extreme importance to choose the correct factors that would enter the analysis—both effects (outputs) and conditions (inputs) contributing to the possibility of getting these effects. However, it may be equally important to carefully build the necessary relationships between measurable data and factors that enter the DEA model. Out of the seven different factors that were chosen in our case, only one (MEX—direct expenditure for each patrol) used observed data in their raw form. All other factors had to be modified in some way, or obtained from suitable combinations of a set of observable data. Two typical examples are the pavement rating change factor (RCF) and the climatic factor (CLF).

2. While serving as a basis for all subsequent analyses, the regular (unbounded) version of DEA does not always satisfactorily capture real-life situations. In practice, management will not accept a set of efficiency ratings where some factors are (virtually) not counted at all and other factors get unduly high weights (see Sherman, 1988). Thus, some bounds have to be imposed on the variation of factor weights.

Deciding on such bounds poses a difficult problem to the efficiency analyst. The relative position of such bounds, the range allowed between upper and lower bounds, etc. may significantly affect the final outcome.

The authors are of the opinion that no "mechanical" systematization of the process of choosing bounds would serve its purpose. What is required is a thorough knowledge of the process in which DMUs are engaged, a clear vision of the purposes for which efficiency is measured, and sound managerial considerations, in order to be able to determine limits within which factor weights may vary.

If we carry the idea of a bounded DEA model to its extreme, we find ourselves looking for a common set of weights where no variation at all is allowed. Such an approach deprives DEA of one of its most important characteristics, namely, the recognition that the same factors may carry a different importance under different circumstances. However, the gap between normal DEA efficiency (e.g., that obtained with a bounded model) and that obtained with a CSW may indicate the extent to which particular circumstances affect the potential for high performance.

3. In addition to the basic runs, DEA enables a series of diverse analyses such as the impact of organizational divisions, specific characteristics or programs, etc. These different analyses complement the basic efficiency outcomes, providing possible explanations for efficiency gaps and offering a better understanding of the performance of the entire system.

Appendix: Graphical Representation of Bounds on Factor Weights

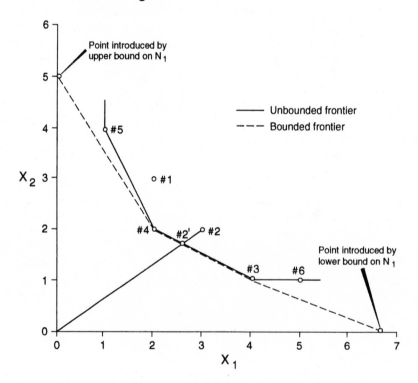

11 STRATEGIC LEADERS IN THE U.S. BREWING INDUSTRY: A LONGITUDINAL ANALYSIS OF OUTLIERS

Diana Day, Arie Y. Lewin, Hongyu Li, and Ronald Salazar

1. Introduction

For over 15 years now, both strategy research and industrial organization (IO) economics research have been working on the development of a theory of strategic groups. Hunt (1972), Newman (1973, 1978), and Porter (1973, 1979; also see Caves and Porter, 1977) originally established some of the key concepts and hypotheses in strategic group research. However, empirical support to validate strategic groups or test hypotheses about strategic group theory has been mixed. For example, an important hypothesis in strategic group research argues that there are performance differences between strategic groups. This hypothesis found support with Oster (1982) and was partially supported in Dess and Davis (1984); however, Porter (1973, 1979), Caves and Porter (1977), Caves and Pugel (1980), and Cool and Schendel (1987), among others (e.g., Frazier and Howell, 1983), did not support this hypothesis.

There are several explanations for these conflicting results. First, most studies use only one performance criterion; however, most firms have multiple performance criteria (Drucker, 1954; March and Simon, 1958; Cyert and March, 1963; Simon, 1964). In addition, the key goal or objective varies from firm to firm; therefore, depending on the performance criteria used, different strategic groups will emerge. Second, more simply, it could be that the wrong method for identifying the groups was used and hence that the results on hypotheses tests about performance differences are not accurate (Barney and Hoskisson, 1990). Third, as systems theory suggests, two firms can achieve the same performance goals using different strategies (Ashby, 1969; see Nayyar, 1989, for other theoretical explanations of this phenomenon). Under those conditions, one should find no differences in performance outcomes between groups. On the other hand, as was pointed out before, two firms may use the same strategy to achieve different objectives. Finally, due to various considerations such as luck, etc., two firms trying to achieve the same objective with the same strategy may have differing levels of success. If we use as the definition of strategic groups that those pursuing the same strategy will be assigned to the same group, then unless those in the same group are somehow buffered from direct competition because they compete in different geographic markets, etc., each strategic group should resemble a microcosm of a typical industry structure. Hence, some groups will have only one player who has a monopoly position within that market. Others will have a small number of players with an oligopolistic structure. If most of the strategic groups are oligopolistic in structure, then their internal rivalry should be low (Porter, 1979), and, hence, all groups may have similar performance outcomes. Furthermore, if we assume for a moment that one strategic group pursues low-cost leadership while another pursues a differentiation strategy, then assuming that each strategy is equally viable (i.e., valuable), performance results will not differ by group.

The topic of strategic group research has spawned over 45 published studies, including 13 unpublished dissertations, since Hunt originally introduced the concept. However, today much confusion still surrounds the key theoretical issues in strategic group research. Why has the concept of strategic groups been so seductive? Perhaps its seductiveness is due to its sheer simplicity and intuitive appeal. It appears to explain so much, but its predictions are often rather disappointing (i.e., Kool and Schendel, 1987). Perhaps this inconsistency can be attributed to the atheoretical nature of the empirical research (Harrigan, 1985) and to the use of research methods that are inappropriate to testing the key hypotheses from strategic group theory (Barney and Hoskisson, 1990). As Kool and Schendel (1987) state, "a systematic procedure to operationalize the concept needs to be developed."

2. Theoretical Review

2.1. Defining Strategic Groups

Kool and Schendel (1987) insist that "if a cumulative stream of research is to be built, the strategic group concept needs to be more carefully defined." Hence, we must first develop an appropriate and defendable definition from the literature.

Hunt (1972) originated the term *strategic groups* in his study of white goods industries. He defined a strategic group as

> a group of firms within an industry that are highly symmetric . . . with respect to cost structure, degree of product differentiation, degree of vertical integration, and the degree of product diversification . . . formal organization, control systems, and management rewards and punishments . . . and the personal views and preferences for various possible outcomes. . . .

His justification for the identification of these groups was that doing so "minimized economic asymmetry within each group" (Hunt, 1972, p. 57). Hence, one of the key goals in the introduction of the strategic group concept was to parcel out some of the heterogeneity in the structure–conduct–performance paradigm at the industry level. Caves and Porter (1977) further refined the concept by introducing the notion of mobility barriers (see also Caves, 1980, 1984). They defined mobility barriers as intra-industry barriers similar to entry barriers between industries so that firms cluster in strategic groups within an industry and these groups are separated by mobility barriers. They argued that some strategic groups have been able to construct high-mobility barriers that protect them from entry not only from those outside the industry but also from those competing within the industry but outside their particular strategic group (Caves and Porter, 1977). This suggests that mobility barriers are a necessary condition for the existence of strategic groups. Without mobility barriers, any grouping of businesses can at best be characterized as an "archetype" (Hambrick 1983a, 1983b; Miller and Friesen, 1977, 1970, 1988), but without the protective barriers one can draw no implications about the economic differences either across or within groups.

Hatten and Hatten (1978, 1985) further defined the concept by arguing that an industry encompasses both direct and indirect competitors. Cool and Schendel (1987) present arguments for a definition of strategic groups as a set of firms competing within an industry on the basis of similar combinations of scope and resource commitments. For purposes of theoretical development, we will define strategic groups as

> a set of firms competing directly or indirectly within an industry on the basis of similar combinations of scope and resource commitments resulting in similar degrees of product differentiation, vertical integration and diversification, and similar cost structures, who are protected by mobility barriers from other groups within and outside the industry.

2.2. Previous Research on Strategic Groups

McGee and Thomas (1986) provide one of the first comprehensive reviews of the literature on strategic groups. In their review, they argue that theoretical concepts such as mobility barriers, isolating mechanisms, and controllable variables offer much sounder bases for strategic group identification than those used in prior research. They conclude by examining the implications that strategic group theory has for 1) the structure–performance linkage, 2) firm mobility, 3) patterns of rivalry, 4) industry evolution, and 5) firm growth.

Nayyar (1989) extends McGee and Thomas's (1986) review by focusing on a number of additional weaknesses in the literature on strategic groups that McGee and Thomas overlook. He points out that a number of McGee and Thomas's dimensions for group identification are inappropriate, while others that are quite important are left out. Furthrmore, he goes through a more thorough discussion of how groups pursuing different strategics can have similar outcomes. He suggests that a more interesting question for strategic group research is "how can researchers theoretically predict how many groups with what combination of the 'sources of asymmetry' will exist in any given industry" (Nayyar, 1989, p. 102). Arguments are made for looking at the bases of diversification and the specific industries in which a firm competes to define strategic groups. Finally, he points out that using performance or output measures as dimensions to define strategic groups results in a tautology when one is testing for performance differences between strategic groups.

Thomas and Venkatraman's review (1988) classified strategic group research using "operationalization of strategy" and the approach to group development to create a taxonomy, evaluate research, and identifying new research directions for this stream of research. Finally, Barney and Hoskisson (1990) provide a critical review of previous strategic group research, arguing that neither the assertion about the existence of strategic groups nor assertions about performance differences have really been tested with the empirical research to date.

In most previous research, strategic groups have been identified either by inspection (Hunt, 1972; Porter, 1973, 1979; Caves and Porter, 1977; Caves and Pugel, 1980; Harrigan, 1980; Miller, 1981; Oster, 1982; Frazier and Howell, 1983; Lahti, 1983; Lubatkin and Pitts, 1983; Kogut, 1984; Lecraw, 1984; Trembley, 1985; de Bondt, 1988) or by cluster analysis (Hatten and Schendel, 1977; Hatten, Schendel, and Cooper, 1978; Ramsler, 1982; Hayes, Spence, and Marks, 1983; Hergert, 1983; Hawes and Crittenden, 1984; Harrigan, 1985; Amel and Rhoades, 1987; Cool and Schendel, 1987; Fiegenbaum, Sudharshan, and Thomas, 1987; Amel and Rhoades, 1988; Mascarenhas and Aaker, 1989). In addition, other approaches to strategic groups involved analysis of variance (Tassey, 1983; Cool and Shendel, 1988), regressions (Caves, 1984; Primeaux, 1985; Fombrum and Zajac, 1987), chi squares tests (Hatton and Hatton, 1985) and three-mode factor analysis (Baird, Sudharshan, and Thomas, 1988). The use of inspection to identify strategic groups is obviously simplistic and can easily lead to erroneous conclusions, as several critics have previously noted (Harrigan, 1985; Kool and Schendel, 1987; Venkatraman, 1988). Using cluster analysis is also a problematic approach, however, as Barney and Hoskinsson (1990) discuss in detail. Cluster analysis (e.g., factor analysis, multidimensional scaling, and principal component analysis) is a descriptive methodology that will produce grouping of firms regardless of whether strategic groups really exist in an industry or not. In addition, it is unlikely that clustering methodologies will identify the single firm as defining its own strategic group. Most important, clustering methods will not group firms on the basis of the pattern of relationships between strategy variables and performance measures, but only on the basis of relationships among strategic variables.

Strategic groups as a concept were first investigated by IO researchers with the hope of finding some explanation for why there seemed to be such high variance in profitability among firms within industries (Hunt, 1972; Newman, 1973, 1978; Porter, 1973, 1979; Caves and Porter, 1977; Caves and Pugel, 1980; Hergert, 1983; Hatten, 1974; Hatten and Schendel, 1977; Hatten, Schendel, and Cooper, 1978; Lahti, 1983; Hawes and Crittenden, 1984). However, since much of the empirical research on strategic grouping of firms does not incorporate linkages between strategy and performance (i.e., to explain intra-industry profit variability), it did not serve the original intent of this research nor does it encompass the complete definition of strategy. Chandler (1962, p. 13) defines strategy as "the determination of the basic long-term goals and objectives of an enterprise, and the adoption of courses of action and the allocation of resources necessary for the carrying out of these goals." Furthermore, strategy research basically assumes that firms attempt to maximize performance (typically profitability or sales) with the minimum necessary resources. By identifying strategic groups only on the basis of input variables or industry demographics, this research has ignored both the underlying economic rationale for this theory and strategic research in general.

2.3. Identifying Strategic Groups With DEA

As has already been discussed, the assumption that firms have strategies implies that managers possess some causal model (however incomplete) that relates resource allocation decisions and other exogenous variables (e.g., demographic and economic parameters) to the attainment of a goal function. The typical goal function would consist of multiple measures of performance such as profits, sales, market share, rate of return on assets, rate of return on equity, quality, customer satisfaction, etc. Most empirical research on firm behavior assumes that firms maximize a single-value goal function and also specify a functional form relating inputs to outputs. The DEA methodology has certain strengths that match especially well with the problems, of determining strategic groups and of testing concepts of strategic group theory. DEA applies to the comparison of entities that transform multiple resources into multiple outputs. In particular, the method is applicable when these entities can be assumed to be homogeneous in terms of the industry, outputs produced, and inputs utilized, and when the entities can be assumed to be maximizing outputs and minimizing inputs. DEA does not require a priori judgments by the researcher about the relative importance of the various outputs nor does it require knowledge of input prices.

DEA calculates the relative efficiency of each entity in converting inputs into outputs as if each entity was allowed to select prices (i.e., weights) on inputs and outputs that maximized its score subject to an equity constraint. The DEA calculations define a production frontier on which are located all Pareto-optimal entities. Each entity not on the frontier is dominated by an entity or combination of entities that define a facet of the frontier and that form a reference set. This latter feature of DEA provides the basis for grouping strategic groups for the purposes of the present research. A strategic group resulting from DEA analysis consists of all firms that share the same reference firm or firms located on the frontier. A second requirement is the ability to perform longitudinal analyses of the industry as means for establishing the validity of the strategic group concept. The longitudinal analysis is based on the window-analysis approach described in chapter 3 and in Charnes, Clark, Cooper, and Golany (1985). However, our objective here is not to study and explain the performance of U.S. brewers over time (this will be reported on in another paper), but to determine what strategic groups emerge and to evaluate the persistance and stability of strategic group memberships over time.

2.4. DEA Window Analysis

Most DEA analyses are cross sectional, comparing the performance of DMUs in the same time period. One approach to performing the longitudinal analysis is to compare cross-sectional runs across the number of time periods in the study. This approach introduces variability into the analysis because it treats the performance of a DMU in each time period as independent from performance in the previous period. Also, with this approach it is not feasible to ascertain trends in performance or to observe persistence of efficiency or inefficiency, the window analysis approach corrects for some of these problems. The underlying assumption is that of a moving-average analysis, except that each DMU's score is represented in the window n times (where n represents the number of times periods in window) instead of being represented by a single summary score. Charnes, Clark, Cooper, and Golany (1985) discuss the trend analysis of the efficiency scores and their managerial applications. It should be noted, however, that choosing the number of time periods to be included in the window is at present a matter of judgment.

2.5. Why Study Strategic Groups in the U.S. Brewing Industry?

Defining the boundaries of an industry is a difficult problem in the context of strategic group theory. In the case of the beer industry, the boundaries can encompass the beverage industry as a whole, alcoholic beverages (beer, wine, liquor), or the beer industry itself. For the time period (1960–1974) under study, we believe that the beer industry in the U.S. can be studied within its own boundaries.

From a market perspective, it appears that beer and soft drinks are not close substitutes for one another, and neither are beer and hard liquor. The same holds true for beer and wine. Because of legal constraints in some states, the distribution channels for beer, wine, and hard liquor are different. The brewing technology for beer, although widely disseminated and well understood, is significantly different from wine making, soft drink production, or the distilling and blending of hard liquor. Finally, during the time period under study, there were very few U.S. brewers (if any) that were also competing in "hard" liquor or in other beverage categories. Thus it seems to us that the boundaries for the U.S. brewing industry could be identified and agreed upon. A second important reason for choosing the U.S. brewing industry pertains to data availability and to the existence of strategic group research on the U.S. brewing industry in the extant literature (Hatten, 1974; Hatten and Schendel, 1977; Hatten, Schendel, and Cooper, 1978; Hatten and Hatten, 1985, 1987; Patton, 1976; Kaithahn, 1974). It was hoped that these studies could be used to evaluate the reasonableness of the DEA analyses as well as help to account for any contrarian observations.

2.6. U.S. Brewing Industry Data

Previous researchers (Hatten, 1974; Patton, 1976; Salazar, 1987, 1989) have described the relationship between performance and predictor variables in the U.S. brewing industry. We have utilized a subset of brewing industry data (1952–1988) described by Salazar (1989) for the models described below. The number of firms considered here was limited by the requirement of a consistent sample across time periods and because industry participants changed dramatically in later time periods. The findings are based upon data for 11 firms (identified in table 11–1) for the period 1960 to 1970. Every firm included was a publicly traded, major producer of beer in the U.S. These firms were selected because of their use in other studies of the industry and on the basis of data availability.

Patton's (1976) work suggests that the three principal performance objectives of firms in the brewing industry during the subject time period were profitability, market share, and production efficiency. In addition, content analysis of annual reports indicated that some firms explicitly measured their performance in terms of rate of return on assets and/or on equity. Each of these goals is desirable and amenable to our use, because each is intended to be maximized for every given level of input. We have specified seven different models suggestive of these strategic goals.

The seven models were identical in terms of the inputs to be mini-mized. The measures used for inputs were selected to represent impor-

Table 11–1. Brewers Included (1960–1970) in the Analysis

Name	Abbreviation
Anheuser-Busch	ABUD
Associated Breweries	ASSC
Fallstaf	FALS
Grain Belt Breweries	GRBT
Heileman	HLMN
Lone Star	LONE
Lucky Lager	LUCK
Olympia Breweries	OLYM
Pabst	PBST
Ranier	RAIN
Schlitz	SLTZ

tant resources commitments to the production process that each firm would wish to minimize for a given level of output. These were 1) the direct costs of brewing, 2) the resource commitment to marketing expenditures, and 3) the total commitment of resources to production capacity. Direct costs of brewing consist of material costs and labor cost. The resource commitment to marketing is derived following Hatten (1974) from accounting expenditures for marketing expressed in dollars (MKTEXP). The resource commitment to capacity is represented by total plant and equipment and is reflected in the total rated annual barrel production capacity.

The seven models are named for the outputs to be maximized. The measures used for outputs were numbers of barrels produced, operating income, rate of return on equity, and rate of return on assets. In addition, three other output models were also analyzed. For each of the seven models summarized in table 11–2, the analysis was run for both three-year and four-year moving windows. In other words, for each model, nine three-year windows and eight four-year windows were analyzed.

3. Analysis of Results

For the purposes of this chapter, we are interested in observing the grouping of firms in the U.S. brewing industry in terms of firms that define a facet on the efficient frontiers (dominant firms) and those other

Table 11-2. Summary of Models Used In Analyses

Model	Output Measure
1	Barrels Produced (Barrels)
2	Operating Income (OPINC)
3	Rate of Return on Equity (ROE)
4	Rate of Return on Assets (ROA)
5	Barrels and OPINC
6	Barrels and ROE
7	Barrels and ROA

firms for which the dominant firm(s) serves as a DEA reference. Figures 11-1 to 11-7 summarize the resulting strategic grouping of firms for the seven different DEA models. Overall, these data are not very supportive of the concept of strategic groups in the U.S. brewing industry during the period under study. For example, figure 11-1 summarizes the results for BARREL model (maximization of barrels brewed). Each row in the table shows by window the group of firms for whom a specific firm is the frontier reference. Thus, for example, ABUD seems to be in its own reference group, and the GRBT strategic group includes, in the first window, ASSC, HLMN, LONE, LUCK, OLYM, PBST, and RAIN. However, a closer inspection reveals that many firms have overlapping group memberships within a window and that group memberships change across windows. When the overlapping group memberships within windows are eliminated, no clear patterns emerge, and it must be concluded that for the seven models analyzed the 11 firms do not compete within clearly identifiable, stable strategic groups.

At first glance, these results seem counterintuitive. The time period under analysis has been characterized by concerns with production efficiencies. Thus, brewers should be minimizing production costs and maximizing capacity utilization. Such a strategy is best captured by model 1 (see figure 11-1), which maximizes barrels sold. For this model, only two clearly dominant firms emerge. The first is GRBT and the second is PBST (see figure 11-8). However, PBST has no clear strategic group associated with it, while GRBT defines a group variously made up of ASSC, LONE, HLMN, and LUCK. Hatten (1974, p. 188) stated that ABUD, GRBT, and PBST were the industry leaders in production efficiencies, which our analysis confirms for GRBT and PBST. However, the DEA results suggest that ABUD is among the near efficient producers with summary relative efficiency scores ranging from .91 to 1.00 and

	1 (60, 61, 62)	2 (61, 62, 63)	3 (62, 63, 64)	4 (63, 64, 65)	5 (64, 65, 66)	6 (65, 66, 67)	7 (66, 67, 68)	8 (67, 68, 69)	9 (68, 69, 70)
ABUD	ABUD	ABUD	ABUD	ABUD	ABUD	ABUD	ABUD	ABUD SLTZ	ABUD SLTZ
ASSC				ASSC	ASSC LUCK	ASSC	ASSC	ASSC	ASSC
FALS	FALS	FALS	FALS	FALS					
GRBT	ASSC LUCK GRBT OLYM HLMN PBST LONE RAIN	ASSC OLYM GRBT RAIN LONE LUCK	ASSC LONE FALS LUCK GRBT OLYM HLMN PBST RAIN	ASSC LONE FALS LUCK GRBT OLYM HLMN RAIN	ASSC LONE FALS LUCK GRBT OLYM HLMN RAIN	ASSC LONE FALS LUCK GRBT OLYM HLMN RAIN	ASSC LONE FALS LUCK GRBT OLYM HLMN RAIN	GRBT LUCK LUCK	GRBT LONE LUCK
HLMN	HLMN	HLMN	HLMN				HLMN	ASSC FALS HLMN	ASSC FALS HLMN
LONE						LONE	LONE	LONE	LONE
LUCK						LUCK	LUCK	LUCK OLYM	LUCK OLYM
OLYM	OLYM	OLYM						OLYM	OLYM
PBST	FALS PBST LUCK SLTZ OLYM	FALS PBST LUCK SLTZ OLYM	ABUD PBST FALS SLTZ LUCK	ABUD PBST FALS SLTZ OLYM	ABUD PBST FALS SLTZ OLYM	ABUD OLYM ASSC PBST FALS SLTZ	ABUD PBST FALS SLTZ OLYM	ABUD PBST ASSC SLTZ FALS	ABUD PBST ASSC SLTZ FALS
RAIN	RAIN	RAIN	RAIN	RAIN	RAIN	RAIN	RAIN	OLYM RAIN	LUCK RAIN OLYM
SLTZ	SLTZ	ABUD SLTZ	SLTZ			SLTZ			

Figure 11–1.   Strategic group analysis, model 1. Output measure: Barrels.

A. Multiple Membership

	1 (60, 61, 62)	2 (61, 62, 63)	3 (62, 63, 64)	4 (63, 64, 65)	5 (64, 65, 66)	6 (65, 66, 67)	7 (66, 67, 68)	8 (67, 68, 69)	9 (68, 69, 70)
ABUD	ABUD	ABUD	ABUD SLTY	ABUD SLTZ	ABUD	ABUD SLTZ	ABUD SLTZ	ABUD SLTZ	ABUD SLTZ
GRBT	GRBT HLMN RAIN	GRBT HLMN LONE LUCK RAIN	GRBT LONE RAIN	GRBT RAIN	GRBT RAIN	GRBT HLMN LONE LUCK OLYM RAIN	GRBT HLMN LONE LUCK RAIN	GRBT LUCK	GRBT LUCK
HLMN	HLMN HLMN	HLMN	HLMN OLYM	FALS HLMN LONE LUCK OLYM PBST	ASSC FALS HLMN LONE LUCK PBST	ASSC FALS GRBT HLMN LONE LUCK OLYM PBST ABUD SLTZ	ASSC FALS GRBT HLMN	ASSC FALS HLMN	ASSC FALS HLMN PBST
OLYM	FALS LUCK OLYM SLTZ	FALS OLYM SLTZ	OLYM	ASSC OLYM ABUD	OLYM	OLYM		OLYM	OLYM
PBST	FALS PBST SLTZ	PBST ABUD	FALS PBST ABUD SLTZ	FALS PBST SLTZ	FALS PBST ABUD SLTZ	FALS PBST SLTZ	FALS PBST	FALS PBST	FALS PBST
RAIN	ASSC RAIN	RAIN	RAIN	RAIN	ASSC RAIN	ASSC RAIN	RAIN	LUCK RAIN	ASSC LUCK RAIN
SLTZ	SLTZ	FALS SLTZ	SLTZ						
LONE	ASSC LONE LUCK PBST	ASSC LONE LUCK	ASSC FALS LONE LUCK PBST	ASSC LONE	ASSC LONE LUCK	LONE LUCK	FALS HLMN LONE LUCK OLYM PBST ABUD SLTZ	FALS HLMN LONE LUCK OLYM PBST SLTZ	LUCK OLYM SLTZ

Figure 11–2.   Strategic group analysis, model 2. Output measure: operating income.

B. No Multiple Membership

	1 *(60, 61, 62)*	*2* *(61, 62, 63)*	*3* *(62, 63, 64)*	*4* *(63, 64, 65)*	*5* *(64, 65, 66)*	*6* *(65, 66, 67)*	*7* *(66, 67, 68)*	*8* *(67, 68, 69)*	*9* *(68, 69, 70)*
ABUD	ABUD							ABUD	ABUD
GRBT	GRBT	GRBT	GRBT	GRBT	GRBT			GRBT	GRBT
HLMN				HLMN LUCK	HLMN	ASSC		ASSC	HLMN
HLMN				HLMN LUCK	HLMN	ASSC		ASSC	HLMN
OLYM	OLYM	OLYM			OLYM				
PBST		PBST			SLTZ				
RAIN	RAIN							RAIN	RAIN
LONE	LONE	ASSC	ASSC LUCK				OLYM	LONE	

Figure 11–2. *Continued*

A. Multiple Membership

	1 (60, 61, 62)	2 (61, 62, 63)	3 (62, 63, 64)	4 (63, 64, 65)	5 (64, 65, 66)	6 (65, 66, 67)	7 (66, 67, 68)	8 (67, 68, 69)	9 (68, 69, 70)
GRBT	GRBT RAIN	GRBT LONE RAIN	GRBT RAIN	GRBT RAIN	GRBT RAIN	GRBT LUCK RAIN	GRBT LUCK OLYM RAIN	GRBT LUCK	GRBT LUCK
HLMN	HLMN	HLMN	HLMN OLYM	FALS HLMN OLYM	FALS HLMN	HLMN LUCK	HLMN LUCK	ABUD ASSC FALS HLMN OLYM PBST SLTZ	ABUD ASSC FALS HLMN LUCK OLYM PBST SLTZ
LONE	ABUD ASSC FALS LONE LUCK OLYM PBST SLTZ	ABUD ASSC FALS LONE LUCK OLYM PBST SLTZ	ABUD ASSC FALS LONE LUCK OLYM PBST SLTZ	ABUD ASSC FALS LONE LUCK PBST SLTZ	ABUD ASSC FALS LONE LUCK OLYM PBST SLTZ	ABUD ASSC FALS LONE LUCK OLYM PBST SLTZ	ABUD ASSC FALS LONE LUCK OLYM PBST SLTZ	LONE LUCK OLYM	HLMN LONE OLYM
OLYM	OLYM	OLYM	LUCK OLYM	LUCK OLYM	LUCK OLYM	OLYM	OLYM		
RAIN	ASSC RAIN	RAIN	RAIN	RAIN	RAIN	RAIN	RAIN	LUCK RAIN	LUCK RAIN

B. No Multiple Membership

	1 (60, 61, 62)	2 (61, 62, 63)	3 (62, 63, 64)	4 (63, 64, 65)	5 (64, 65, 66)	6 (65, 66, 67)	7 (66, 67, 68)	8 (67, 68, 69)	9 (68, 69, 70)
GRBT	GRBT	GRBT	GRBT	GRBT	GRBT	GRBT	GRBT	GRBT	GRBT
HLMN	HLMN	HLMN	HLMN	HLMN	HLMN	HLMN	HLMN	ABUD ASSC FALS HLMN PBST SLTZ	ABUD ASSC FALS PBST SLTZ
LONE	ABUD FALS LONE LUCK PBST SLTZ	ABUD RALS LUCK PBST SLTZ	ABUD ASSC FALS LONE PBST SLTZ	ABUD ASSC LONE PBST SLTZ	ABUD ASSC LONE PBST SLTZ	ABUD ASSC FALS LONE PBST SLTZ	ABUD ASSC FALS LONE PBST SLTZ	LONE	LONE
RAIN								RAIN	RAIN

Figure 11–3.   Strategic group analysis, model 3. Output measure: ROE.

A. Multiple Membership

	1 (60, 61, 62)	2 (61, 62, 63)	3 (62, 63, 64)	4 (63, 64, 65)	5 (64, 65, 66)	6 (65, 66, 67)	7 (66, 67, 68)	8 (67, 68, 69)	9 (68, 69, 70)
GRBT	GRBT LONE RAIN	GRBT LONE RAIN	GRBT HLMN LONE RAIN	GRBT HLMN RAIN	GRBT HLMN RAIN	GRBT LONE LUCK OLYM RAIN	GRBT HLMN LONE LUCK RAIN	GRBT HLMN LUCK	GRBT HLMN LUCK
HLMN	HLMN	HLMN	HLMN LONE OLYM	ABUD OLYM ASSC PBST FALS SLTZ HLMN LONE LUCK	ABUD OLYM ASSC PBST FALS SLTZ HLMN LUCK	HLMN LUCK	HLMN LUCK		
LONE	ASSC SLTZ FALS LONE LUCK OLYM PBST	ASSC SLTZ FALS LONE LUCK OLYM PBST	ABUD PBST ASSC SLTZ FALS LONE LUCK OLYM	ASSC LONE	ASSC LONE	ABUD PBST ASSC SLTZ FALS LONE LUCK OLYM	ABUD OLYM ASSC PBST FALS SLTZ HLMN LONE LUCK	ABUD OLYM ASSC PBST FALS SLTZ HLMN LONE LUCK	ABUD OLYM ASSC PBST FALS SLTZ HLMN LONE LUCK
OLYM	ABUD OLYM PBST SLTZ	ABUD OLYM SLTZ	OLYM	ASSC OLYM	ASSC OLYM				
RAIN	ASSC RAIN	RAIN	RAIN	RAIN	RAIN	RAIN	RAIN	LUCK RAIN	LUCK RAIN

Figure 11–4.   Strategic group analysis, model 4. Output measure: ROA.

B. No Multiple Membership

	1 (60, 61, 62)	2 (61, 62, 63)	3 (62, 63, 64)	4 (63, 64, 65)	5 (64, 65, 66)	6 (65, 66, 67)	7 (66, 67, 68)	8 (67, 68, 69)	9 (68, 69, 70)
GRBT	GRBT	GRBT	GRBT	GRBT	GRBT	GRBT	GRBT	GRBT	GRBT
HLMN	HLMN	HLMN		ABUD FALS LUCK PBST SLTZ	ABUD FALS LUCK PBST SLTZ	HLMN			
LONE	ASSC FALS LUCK	ASSC FALS LUCK PBST	ABUD SLTZ ASSC FALS LUCK PBST		LONE	ABUD ASSC FALS PBST SLTZ	ABUD SLTZ ASSC FALS OLYM PBST	ABUD PBST ASSC SLTZ FALS LONE OLYM	ABUD PBST ASSC SLTZ FALS LONE OLYM
OLYM	ABUD	ABUD							
RAIN	RAIN							RAIN	RAIN

Figure 11–4. *Continued*

A. Multiple Membership

	1 (60, 61, 62)	2 (61, 62, 63)	3 (62, 63, 64)	4 (63, 64, 65)	5 (64, 65, 66)	6 (65, 66, 67)	7 (66, 67, 68)	8 (67, 68, 69)	9 (68, 69, 70)
ABUD	ABUD	ABUD	ABUD	ABUD	ABUD	ABUD	ABUD	ABUD SLTZ	ABUD SLTZ
ASSC			ASSC	ASSC	ASSC	ASSC	ASSC	ASSC	ASSC
FALS	FALS	FALS	FALS	FALS					
GRBT	ASSC GRBT LUCK RAIN	ASSC GRBT LONE LUCK RAIN	ASSC PBST FALS RAIN GRBT LONE LUCK	ASSC RAIN FALS GRBT LONE LUCK	ASSC RAIN FALS GRBT LONE LUCK	GRBT HLMN LONE OLYM RAIN	GRBT HLMN LONE OLYM RAIN	GRBT LUCK	GBT LUCK
HLMN	HLMN	HLMN	HLMN	HLMN OLYM	HLMN	ASSC LONE LUCK FALS GRBT HLMN	ASSC LONE FALS GRBT HLMN	ASSC FALS HLMN	ASSC FALS HLMN OLYM
LONE	ASSC LONE LUCK	ASSC LONE LUCK	ASSC LONE LUCK	ASSC LONE LUCK	ASSC LONE	LONE LUCK	LONE LUCK	FALS LONE	LONE
LUCK	LUCK	LUCK			LUCK	LUCK	LUCK	LUCK	LUCK
OLYM	LUCK OLYM PBST	LUCK OLYM	OLYM	OLYM	OLYM	OLYM		OLYM	OLYM

Figure 11–5. Strategic group analysis, model 5. Output measure: Barrels, OP Inc.

	1 (60, 61, 62)	2 (61, 62, 63)	3 (62, 63, 64)	4 (63, 64, 65)	5 (64, 65, 66)	6 (65, 66, 67)	7 (66, 67, 68)	8 (67, 68, 69)	9 (68, 69, 70)
PBST	FALS LUCK PBST SLTZ	FALS LUCK PBST SLTZ	ABUD SLTZ FALS LUCK PBST	ABUD FALS PBST SLTZ	ABUD FALS PBST SLTZ	ABUD SLTZ ASSC FALS PBST	ABUD SLTZ ASSC FALS PBST	ABUD SLTZ ASSC FALS PBST	ABUD SLTZ ASSC FALS PBST
RAIN	RAIN	RAIN	RAIN	ASSC RAIN	LONE RAIN	RAIN	RAIN	LUCK RAIN	LUCK RAIN
SLTZ	SLTZ	SLTZ	SLTZ			SLTZ			

B. No Multiple Membership

	1 (60, 61, 62)	2 (61, 62, 63)	3 (62, 63, 64)	4 (63, 64, 65)	5 (64, 65, 66)	6 (65, 66, 67)	7 (66, 67, 68)	8 (67, 68, 69)	9 (68, 69, 70)
ABUD	ABUD	ABUD							
GRBT	GRBT	GRBT	GRBT	GRBT	GRBT LUCK			GRBT	GRBT
HLMN	HLMN	HLMN	HLMN	HLMN	HLMN			HLMN	HLMN
LONE	LONE							LONE	LONE
OLYM	OLYM	OLYM	OLYM		OLYM		OLYM	OLYM	
PBST	PBST	PBST		PBST SLTZ	PBST SLTZ	PBST	PBST SLTZ	PBST	PBST
RAIN	RAIN							RAIN	RAIN

Figure 11–5. *Continued*

A. Multiple Membership

	1 (60, 61, 62)	2 (61, 62, 63)	3 (62, 63, 64)	4 (63, 64, 65)	5 (64, 65, 66)	6 (65, 66, 67)	7 (66, 67, 68)	8 (67, 68, 69)	9 (68, 69, 70)
ABUD	ABUD	ABUD	ABUD	ABUD	ABUD	ABUD	ABUD SLTZ	ABUD SLTZ	ABUD SLTZ
ASSC				ASSC	ASSC	ASSC	ASSC	ASSC	ASSC
FALS	FALS LUCK SLTZ	FALS	FALS	FALS					
GRBT	ASSC GRBT LONE TAIN	ASSC GRBT RAIN	ASSC GRBT LUCK RAIN	ASSC GRBT RAIN	GRBT HLMN RAIN	GRBT LONE RAIN	GRBT LONE RAIN	GRBT LUCK	GRBT LUCK
HLMN	HLMN	HLMN	HLMN	FALS HLMN LUCK OLYM	FALS HLMN	GRBT HLMN LONE	ASSC FALS GRBT HLMN LONE	ASSC HLMN	ASSC HLMN
LONE	ASSC LONE LUCK	ASSC LONE LUCK	ASSC FALS LONE LUCK	ASSC LONE LUCK	ASSC LONE LUCK	ASSC FALS LONE LUCK OLYM	FALS LONE LUCK	FALS LONE	ASSC FALS LONE SLTZ
LUCK						LUCK	LUCK	LUCK	LUCK
OLYM	OLYM PBST	FALS LUCK OLYM	OLYM	FALS OLYM	FALS OLYM	OLYM	OLYM	OLYM	OLYM

Figure 11–6. Strategic group analysis, model 6. Output measure: ROA, Barrels.

	1 (60, 61, 62)	2 (61, 62, 63)	3 (62, 63, 64)	4 (63, 64, 65)	5 (64, 65, 66)	6 (65, 66, 67)	7 (66, 67, 68)	8 (67, 68, 69)	9 (68, 69, 70)
PBST	FALS LUCK PBST SLTZ	FALS PBST SLTZ	ABUD FALS LUCK PBST SLTZ	ABUD FALS PBST SLTZ	ABUD FALS PBST SLTZ	ABUD ASSC FALS PBST SLTZ	ABUD ASSC FALS PBST SLTZ	ABUD ASSC FALS PBST SLTZ	ABUD ASSC FALS PBST
RAIN	RAIN	RAIN	RAIN	RAIN	RAIN	RAIN	RAIN	RAIN	RAIN
SLTZ	SLTZ	SLTZ	SLTZ			SLTZ			

B. No Multiple Membership

	1 (60, 61, 62)	2 (61, 62, 63)	3 (62, 63, 64)	4 (63, 64, 65)	5 (64, 65, 66)	6 (65, 66, 67)	7 (66, 67, 68)	8 (67, 68, 69)	9 (68, 69, 70)
ABUD	ABUD	ABUD							
GRBT	GRBT	GRBT	GRBT	GRBT	GRBT			GRBT	GRBT
HLMN	HLMN	HLMN	HLMN	HLMN		HLMN	HLMN	HLMN	HLMN
LONE	LONE LUCK	LONE	LONE	LONE	LONE LUCK		LONE	LONE	LONE
OLYM	OLYM	OLYM	OLYM		OLYM	OLYM	OLYM	OLYM	OLYM
PBST		PBST	PBST	PBST	PBST SLTZ	PBST	PBST	PBST	PBST
RAIN							RAIN	RAIN	RAIN

Figure 11-6. *Continued*

A. Multiple Membership

	1 (60, 61, 62)	2 (61, 62, 63)	3 (62, 63, 64)	4 (63, 64, 65)	5 (64, 65, 66)	6 (65, 66, 67)	7 (66, 67, 68)	8 (67, 68, 69)	9 (68, 69, 70)
ABUD	ABUD	ABUD	ABUD	ABUD	ABUD	ABUD	ABUD	ABUD SLTZ	ABUD SLTZ
ASSC		ASSC	ASSC	ASSC	ASSC	ASSC	ASSC	ASSC	ASSC
FALS	FALS LUCK PBST SLTZ	FALS LUCK SLTZ	FALS	FALS					
GRBT	ASSC GRBT RAIN	ASSC GRBT RAIN	ASSC GRBT LUCK RAIN	ASSC GRBT RAIN	GRBT RAIN	GRBT RAIN	GRBT RAIN	GRBT GRBT LUCK RAIN	GRBT LUCK
HLMN	HLMN	HLMN	HLMN OLYM	HLMN OLYM	HLMN	GRBT HLMN	ASSC FALS GRBT HLMN	ASSC FALS HLMN SLTZ	ASSC FALS HLMN OLYM
LONE	ASSC LONE LUCK	ASSC LONE LUCK	ASSC LONE LUCK	ASSC FALS LONE LUCK	ASSC FALS LONE LUCK	ASSC FALS LONE LUCK	FALS LONE LUCK	LONE	LONE
LUCK					LUCK	LUCK	LUCK	LUCK	LUCK
OLYM	LUCK OLYM	LUCK OLYM	OLYM	OLYM	OLYM	FALS OLYM	OLYM	OLYM	OLYM
PBST	FALS LUCK PBST SLTZ	PBST SLTZ	ABUD FALS LUCK PBST SLTZ	ABUD FALS PBST SLTZ	ABUD FALS PBST SLTZ	ASSC FALS PBST SLTZ	ABUD ASSC FALS PBST SLTZ	FALS PBST SLTZ	FALS PBST SLTZ
RAIN	RAIN	RAIN	RAIN	RAIN	RAIN	RAIN	RAIN	RAIN	RAIN
SLTZ	SLTZ	SLTZ	SLTZ			SLTZ			

Figure 11–7.   Strategic group analysis, model 7. Output measure: ROA, Barrels.

B. No Multiple Membership

	1 (60, 61, 62)	2 (61, 62, 63)	3 (62, 63, 64)	4 (63, 64, 65)	5 (64, 65, 66)	6 (65, 66, 67)	7 (66, 67, 68)	8 (67, 68, 69)	9 (68, 69, 70)
ABUD	ABUD	ABUD				ABUD	ABUD	ABUD	ABUD
FALS	FALS	FALS							
GRBT	GRBT	GRBT	GRBT	GRBT	GRBT			GRBT	GRBT
HLMN	HLMN	HLMN	HLMN	HLMN	HLMN	HLMN	HLMN	HLMN	HLMN
LONE	LONE	LONE	LONE	LONE LUCK	LONE LUCK	LONE	LONE	LONE	LONE
OLYM	OLYM	OLYM	OLYM		OLYM	OLYM	OLYM	OLYM	OLYM
PBST	PBST	PBST	PBST	PBST SLTZ	PBST SLTZ	PBST	PBST SLTZ	PBST	PBST
RAIN	RAIN						RAIN	RAIN	RAIN

Figure 11–7. *Continued*

	1 (60, 61, 62)	2 (61, 62, 63)	3 (62, 63, 64)	4 (63, 64, 65)	5 (64, 65, 66)	6 (65, 66, 67)	7 (66, 67, 68)	8 (67, 68, 69)	9 (68, 69, 70)
ABUD	ABUD								
GBRT	ASSC GRBT LONE	ASSC GRBT LONE	ASSC GRBT LONE	GRBT HLMN LONE LUCK	GRBT HLMN LONE LUCK	GRBT HLMN	GRBT	GRBT	GRBT
HLMN	HLMN	HLMN						HLMN	HLMN
LONE								LONE	
PBST	PBST	PBST	PBST	PBST SLTZ	SLTZ PBST	PBST	PBST SLTZ	PBST	PBST
RAIN								RAIN	RAIN

Figure 11–8. Strategic group analysis, model 1 (no multiple membership). Output measure: Barrels

averaging .96, which explains and supports the conclusion reached by Hatten (1974).

An analysis of the consistently dominant (i.e., DEA-efficient) firms for each model across all windows indicates that GRBT, a small regional brewer, consistently defines the frontier for each primary facet (Barrels, Operating Income, ROE, and ROA), and HLMN, a large regional brewer, defines the frontier for two facets (ROE and ROA). In addition, LONE, also a small regional brewer, is on a segment of the ROE and ROA frontiers, while PBST, as mentioned earlier, also defines a segment of the production frontier (Barrels). These results are consistent with other financial analyses of the brewing industry (Hatten, 1974; Patton, 1976) and merely support the reasonableness of DEA calculations.

It should also be noted that the choice of the number of time periods in a window for DEA window analysis is entirely ad hoc.. As noted earlier, the seven models were analyzed for three- and for four-year windows, and the results were essentially identical. These results indicate that the analysis of data in this chapter is robust and not sensitive to the choice of the number of years in the moving window.

The results reported here do not negate the concept of strategic groups in general. They do question the operationality of the strategic-group construct for the brewing industry during the years 1960 to 1970. It should also be noted that due to missing or incomplete data, not all firms are represented (e.g., Miller, Hamm, Carling, Rheingold, Stroh, Genessee, Ballantine, Pearl, C. Schmidt, etc.), and that if the missing firms could be included, different results would obtain.

The findings do illustrate that by use of another methodology, contrary results may be obtained, thus redirecting the discussion of strategic groups. The DEA window analysis makes it possible to evaluate the homogeneity and mobility-barrier criteria. It also demonstrates the possibility of firms defining their own strategic groups and that the membership of a strategic group is a function of the model specified. Ideally, the model for each firm should correspond to the actual strategy of that firm.

12 A SPATIAL EFFICIENCY FRAMEWORK FOR THE SUPPORT OF LOCATIONAL DECISION

Anand Desai, Kingsley Haynes,
and James Storbeck

1. Introduction

A cursory examination of the location literature suggests that a substantial number of spatial analysts have steadily moved away from simple programming models with a single objective to more complicated models with multiple objectives. Often, this movement has been undertaken in the name of promoting *realistic* models that support the multidimensional situation in which actual siting decisions take place.

This chapter proposes still further movement to a multiobjective perspective. It utilizes data envelopment analysis (DEA) in order to improve the analytical support of locational decisions. More specifically, the development of a DEA framework for measuring *relative spatial efficiency* is suggested for conceptual reasons, dealing with the problematic character of the notion of accessibility, as well as for methodological reasons, dealing with the characterization of what constitutes an acceptable solution in many decision settings.

1.1. Conceptual Rationale

Though some notion of accessibility has been the key construct of most location studies, spatial analysts have not yet reached general agreement as to what constitutes access or how it should be measured. As Fisher and Rushton (1979) have noted, numerous objectives have been proposed in order to define the optimum location of services, such as minimum aggregate distance, minimum average distance, minimum maximum distance, minimum distribution costs subject to variable capacity limits or service area thresholds, and maximum population coverage subject to resource restrictions, among others. Each of these objectives implies a different notion of access and very different measurement criteria. A common problem in planning, then, is the lack of agreement as to which of these measures is most appropriate for a given scenario.

Given the difficulty of selecting *the* best measure of access, Fisher and Rushton (1979) suggested that location analysts should develop siting processes where solutions are mapped in a multidimensional space defined by several alternative criteria. Furthermore, they proposed the use of the notion of *spatial efficiency*, which was defined as

> ... the access or distribution costs associated with a given locational arrangement ... in comparison with those costs associated with the best known alternative arrangement (p. 84).

The authors rationalized the use of such relative measures as a practice that would facilitate flexibility in the planning of service hierarchies in less developed areas. Unlike the typical location planning process that identifies objectives and criteria a priori, a multiobjective analysis based on spatial efficiency would suspend commitment to a particular objective form and allow the analyst "to consider the relative merits of the objectives and criteria themselves."

1.2. Methodological Rationale

Over the years there have been a number of successful attempts to determine appropriate facility sites by means of the mathematical expression of planning objectives. Of course, one problem associated with such expressions is the reduction and subsequent *loss of information* in the process of translating verbal planning statements into strictly defined mathematics. Indeed, this problem is significant when one realizes that a decision maker's acceptance of model outcomes in such analyses relies heavily upon their understanding of the underlying assumptions and their concurrence with the choice of mathematical objectives (Rushton, 1987). In the support of *actual* decisions, then, analytical techniques are needed that 1) capture much of the information from the original problem setting, 2) preserve and present numerous decision alternatives, and 3) frame model results in terms that are important to the decision maker.

Consequently, many spatial analysts have turned to multiobjective programming (MOP) models that are particularly responsive to tasks 1 and 2 above. By articulating problems in terms of multiple goals, many researchers have attempted to capture more fully the essential aspects of locational planning situations and to offer the decision maker alternative solutions that are "equally good" along *several* dimensions. Embedded in the traditional MOP approach, however, is an implicit reduction of information at the reporting stage, in that most analytical results are framed in terms of the *nominal* classification of *inferior* and *noninferior* solutions. In seeking the so-called Pareto-optimal set, many analysts have simply discarded "inferior" solutions when reporting their results, focusing on the "best possible" or "noninferior." In so doing, they may have failed in many instances to report results that are important to the decision maker. In some more complex decision settings, for example, a decision maker may be less interested in asking the question "Is this solution inferior?" and more interested in asking "How inferior is this solution?" The latter question implies that a decision maker may find a solution that is slightly inferior along technical dimensions, but highly acceptable for other non-technical reasons.

Nonetheless, deviations from the traditional development of MOP can be found. Church and Huber (1979), for example, developed a programming approach for finding "close-to-optimal" solutions, given the existence of the noninferior set. Their approach was to find *near optima* within a given region of objective space. Also working within the multiobjective frame, Brill et al. (1982) proposed an MOP-based methodology for generating alternative solutions that are feasible and "significantly different" from previously generated solutions. While these authors acknowledge the utility of generating the noninferior set with multiobjective programming models, they state that "it is important to examine other solutions as well if there are important unmodeled issues" (p. 221). With similar motivation, Schilling et al. (1982) suggest the use of display techniques (based on objective space and decision space) when performing multiobjective analysis. Again, the concern of these authors is for the (conscious or unconscious) *exclusion* of certain objectives in the analysis.

One should note that, in the above examples, these authors are addressing the most common shortcoming of traditional MOP modeling efforts—the presentation of the *noninferior set* as that which is most important to solving the planner's dilemma. Subsequently, these researchers are developing ways to supplement the information that may be deemed insufficient for real-world decision settings. In each case, then, they are attempting to provide analytical models that *better support actual decisions*.

1.3. Relative Spatial Efficiency

The need for a measure of relative spatial efficiency is clear. This chapter proposes a DEA framework for measuring the relative spatial efficiency (RSE) of siting decisions. While it is similar in structure to the RSE model first developed by Desai and Storbeck (1990), the present effort departs from that previous model in important ways. By choosing measures of access that are quite disparate, this analysis shows how spatial efficiency analysis can be used to support both facility *sizing* and *siting* decisions. Still consistent with the original Fisher and Rushton proposal, however, our DEA modeling approach can be seen as a "broadened" multiobjective perspective that allows the articulation of multiple inputs and outputs and the examination of trade-offs between them. Moreover, in its construction of a ratio-scale-based definition of "inferior" and "noninferior," this framework produces analytical models that better support a wide range of actual locational decisions.

Given the above setup, then, we are interested in comparing the access costs of a given locational configuration with those of the best-known alternative. The access costs of a given siting decision, therefore, serve as "inputs" to the locational decision-making process and to the DEA model. For our study, the output of the incremental siting decision is defined quite simply as the benefit of having an additional facility. More elaborate cost measures (i.e., outputs) are certainly possible within this framework, but are not undertaken for reasons of graphical display and ease of exposition. Naturally, the model forms, which are relatively straightforward, are easily expanded to address more complex planning situations.

In order to demonstrate the flexibility of this DEA approach to spatial efficiency, we incorporate two very different measures of access—a *system*-defined measure of overall total person-miles traveled (commonly known as a *p-Median* objective), and an *individually* defined measure of population coverage within local trading areas (commonly known as a *weighted covering* objective). The former objective was chosen because it is sensitive to the number of facilities being sited in a region, and the latter because it can be used to express demand sensitivity to the size of a facility. With these two criteria, then, we can more readily examine trade-offs between the spacing and sizing of service facilities.

Working within this DEA framework, we now turn to a simple example of measuring the RSE of siting decisions. In the next section, the planning scenario under consideration is detailed and a more complete rationale for the inputs to the DEA model is given. In section 3, we briefly discuss the particular form of DEA used in this analysis, the various types of efficiency achieved, and the results of the analysis. Conclusions are reached in the final section of the chapter, and directions for future locational modeling developments are suggested.

2. A Planning Scenario: System Expansion

We are considering two alternatives for improving a system of community mental health services in Franklin County, Ohio: the expansion in size of an existing facility versus the creation of a new community center of the same scale as the current sites. The pertinent planning issue, therefore, is to determine when is it preferable to expand an existing facility and when would it be advisable to add a new facility.

Using data supplied by the Franklin County Mental Health Board (1988), we first aggregate the populations of 458 census areas into zipcode populations, since the needs of clients from these groupings are typically monitored by the Board, providing the basis for many of the Board's statistical analyses. For our purposes here, we consider only two decision criteria, namely, demand covered within the service areas of the treatment sites and total distance traveled by those outside of the service areas to the community centers. The travel distance is obtained simply by computation of the *p-Median* objective for those beyond the maximum service area distance for each given system configuration. Unlike most location studies, which compute person-miles traveled for all persons in a region, we limit such computations to sites outside the covered areas in order to assess the impact of a particular siting configuration upon *uncovered* demand (Church, Current, and Storbeck, 1991). The demand covered within facility service areas is computed on the basis of a nonlinear function, indicating decreasing attractiveness for a center with increasing distance (figure 12–1a). Furthermore, this coverage function is

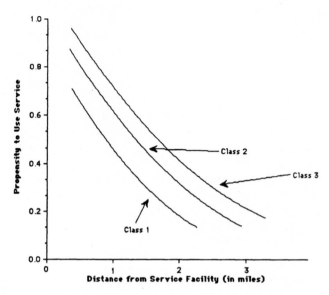

Figure 12–1a.   Relationship between usage and distance for selected facility classes.

shown to shift upward (in a northeasterly direction) with increasing size of the facility. Such relationships indicate that consumer utilization of services increases with the size (or *attractiveness*) of the facility, but decreases (at differing rates for different sizes) with distance. It is common in market-area analyses to estimate these utilization rates from past records or surveys of the clientele. For this study, we use a *weighted covering* step function to approximate the service areas implied by these nonlinear attendance functions (Church and Roberts, 1983; Ghosh and McLafferty, 1987). In the example of figure 12–1b, about 67% of the people within $1\frac{1}{2}$ miles of the facility tend to use its services, 30% in the second interval to $2\frac{1}{2}$ miles, and about 12% of those in the third interval. Note that the larger-sized facility has a greater range. Also, at any given distance within this range, the likelihood of the service being used is greater than that for the smaller facility.

We begin our analysis with the existing configuration in which treatment centers are located at eight nodes in the region; the population for each of the 40 nodes (i.e., zipcode centroids) is given in the appendix. The total distance for this configuration of eight sites is 13973.54 personmiles, and the total (weighted) demand *uncovered* is 492278.56.

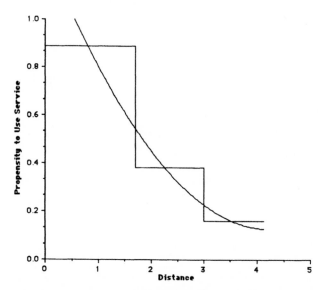

Figure 12–1b. Coverage-step-function approximating spatial demand curve.

Table 12–1. Extent of Service Area and Estimated Utilization Rates For Selected Facility Sizes

Facility Size Class	Service Area Radius by Access Interval			Utilization Rates by Access Interval		
	1	2	3	1	2	3
1	2 mi.	4 mi.	6 mi.	.80	.45	.10
2	2 mi.	4 mi.	8 mi.	.90	.55	.15

Obviously, our desire in this analysis is to present solutions that minimize these two measures.

Using the attractiveness functions suggested in table 12–1, we first compute the effect of expanding the existing treatment centers. Figure 12–2a shows the amount of population not covered and the distance traveled in person-miles as the existing treatment centers are expanded. Clearly, some expansion scenarios are more desirable than others, the most desirable being those which move toward the origin of the graph. In this example, expansion of facilities at 43205 or 43223 are superior

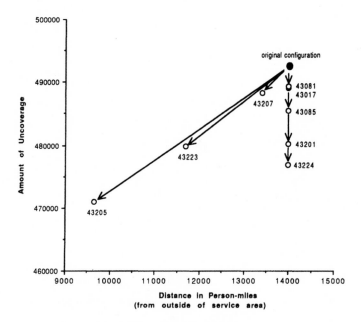

Figure 12–2a. Expansion DMUs in attribute space.

to other such decisions, with the former dominating all expansion possibilities with the minimum distance traveled and the minimum noncoverage. These two treatment centers are located in the southeast and southwest corners, respectively, of Franklin County, where service gaps currently exist. Expansions in the central part of the county (i.e., 43201 and 43224) would increase service coverage, but would do little in terms of improving the extent of distance traveled by outlying clients. It is worth noting that facility expansions in northern Franklin County would have relatively small impacts on the two accessibility criteria, since three of the current facilities already cover the outlying populations to a great extent in that part of this service region.

The question now becomes one of choosing between the expansion of an existing facility and the addition of a new one. To evaluate the relative merit of each node as a potential site for locating a new treatment center, we compute the average total distance and the extent of noncoverage for the configuration consisting of a new center at that site, in addition to the existing facilities at eight other sites. In order to show how DEA can evaluate these siting decisions (and can combine these evaluations with those of the expansion possibilities), we now turn to an explication of the RSE framework and the subsequent analysis of the Franklin County data.

3. The DEA Framework and Analysis

The traditional MOP solution of this location decision problem would correctly identify the undominated configurations as the optimal location decisions. However, in so analyzing the data, a considerable amount of potentially useful information is lost by not evaluating the relative merits of the dominated configurations. In addition, one could not easily develop an MOP model that readily combines analysis of both the expansion and siting scenarios, since these have very different problem characteristics (i.e., facility sizes, utilization rates, number of centers).

Within this context, the RSE framework provides a natural extension to the more traditional mathematical programming formulations of the location decision problem. Since the DEA model is not responsible for the generation of the feasible set of decisions but merely for the evaluation of it, scenarios of greatly differing types can be examined along common dimensions—e.g., travel distance and extent of coverage. Clearly, the decision to locate a new treatment center or to expand an existing one will not be made solely on the basis of the two criteria under consideration in this example. However, even in this case, we propose to demonstrate that the DEA formulation of the problem provides a richer analysis of spatial accessibility and allows insights that are not obvious from the MOP formulation of the location problem.

In keeping with the simplicity of our example, we use the basic CCR$_P$-I (Charnes, Cooper, and Rhodes, 1978, section 5.1 of chapter 2) formulation of DEA to measure the relative merits of all the possible facility spacing/sizing decisions in which we either add a new site or carry out the expansion of the existing centers. The data used in the analysis are given in table 12-A1 in the appendix. The input data consist of the total distance traveled (by those outside of service areas) and the extent of noncoverage for each configuration of a new facility and the eight existing facilities, yielding 32 data points (or decision-making units (DMUs)). Nine additional data points, representing no change, as well as the eight different expansion scenarios of the existing treatment centers make up the total data set of 41 configurations. Thus, each DMU consists of a configuration of nine treatment sites of eight sites wherein the center at one of the current locations has been expanded (see figure 12-2b). As stated above, we use distance and the extent of noncoverage

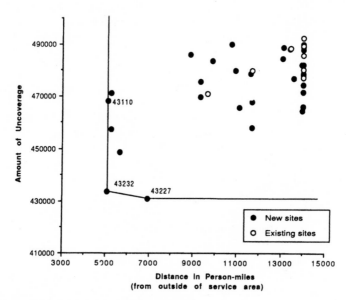

Figure 12-2b.   DMU map in attribute space.

as inputs of the process and unity as the normalized measure of output for each DMU.

The analysis of these data yielded two noninferior DMUs (i.e., 43227 and 43232). These *perfectly efficient* DMUs are the locational configurations obtained by siting a new treatment center at the corresponding zipcode sites (see figure 12–3). These two sites are particularly strong in terms of offering substantially increased coverage of east-side populations that were previously residing in one of the existing service gaps. An additional site at 43110, though not perfectly efficient, proved to be an excellent alternative, primarily in terms of minimum travel distance, with an RSE score of .995. It typified three other such east-side locations, which had RSE scores greater than .95.

The DEA procedure further revealed the *relative weights* that would be assigned to the accessibility measures at a noninferior DMUs. In our two-dimensional context, the specific relative weights are in the form of the slopes of the lines that join adjacent efficient DMUs and thereby define the (piecewise linear) best-practice frontier. Figure 12–3, for example, shows that if a decision maker weights the coverage criterion much more heavily than that of distance, an additional center at node 43227 is the preferred course of action. This result is further supported

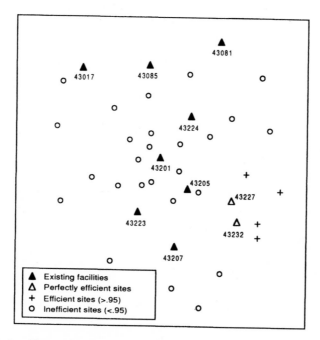

Figure 12–3. Map of Franklin County sites.

analytically by the slope of the horizontal facet connected to that node's solution, which implies a coverage-to-distance weighting ratio equal to ∞:1. If the decision maker's preference for the coverage criterion is revised downward, however, the locational configuration of DMU 43232 is now of interest, and the connecting facet becomes the relevant frontier. A further downward revision of that weight, so that the ratio becomes 1:∞, moves the decision maker's consideration to the vertical facet defined by 43232, suggesting that distance, rather than coverage, is of primary importance.

An MOP formulation of this problem would require that different sets of weights be iteratively assigned to the accessibility criteria; a solution at each iteration then consists of the nondominated DMU that corresponds to the given set of weights. DEA, on the other hand, conducts an exhaustive search of the relative weights and selects those weights that yield the complete set of noninferior DMUs. DMUs not on the frontier are inefficient, in an RSE sense, and their distance from the frontier is an indicator of their inefficiency. Consequently, the noninferior DMUs, and the sections of the frontier bounded by them, partition the data into *comparison groups*, whose efficiency scores are computed in reference to that facet. The reference set associated with each DMU is identified in table 12–A2 in the appendix.

Group I scores, for example, are determined with reference to the horizontal facet defined by DMU 43227. Since this DMU represents the locational decision with the best measure of coverage, the efficiencies for this group are computed in reference to a trade-off function, which implies that the coverage input is of primary importance. Moreover, since each DMU has a projection on the efficient frontier along the ray from the origin, then given the magnitudes of the two inputs, this group's projections will appear to be nearly vertical, intersecting the facet to the right of the defining DMU. Consequently, these RSE scores are achieved virtually in sole reference to DMU 43227. As one can determine from figure 12–3, the projections of most of this group's DMUs will be at varying distances from 43227 along that horizontal facet. Hence, in choosing among inefficient DMUs, it is possible to select DMUs not only on the basis of their RSE scores but also on the basis of their *similarity* to the efficient DMUs. Determining the identity of the efficient DMU that is most similar to a given inefficient DMU is straightforward in that the solution to the mathematical program provides the relative weights corresponding to each of the efficient DMUs.

Group II RSE is measured with reference to the facet bounded by noninferior DMUs 43227 and 43232, which represent siting solutions that offer the best coverage and the best distance, respectively. There is but one DMU in this group (43109), yielding an RSE score of .966; its efficiency is computed with reference to the facet that represents only a slight trade-off between distance and coverage. The intersection on the facet near 43232 suggests that 43109 is most like the "best distance" DMU and that its score reflects that profile.

Group III efficiencies are computed in relation to the vertical facet bounded on one side by DMU 43232, a siting decision that represents the best possible distance. Like those of group I, the RSE scores for this group must be interpreted differently from those of group II, since they are computed with reference to a facet not fully bounded by actual data points. Specifically, the RSE score for DMU 43110 suggests that its ray from the origin would intersect the frontier at some point in the vertical facet. A DMU at this point on the vertical facet will have an RSE score of unity; however, it is not truly efficient, since it is *dominated* by DMU 43232, and the amount of noncoverage could be readily lowered by moving to that DMU *without trading off distance*. DMU 43232, therefore, would be a better solution than DMU 43110's projection on the efficient frontier. Clearly, the RSE scores for this group must be interpreted carefully. These scores are exaggerated since, for all DMUs in this group, it is possible to lower coverage without having to trade off distance. Such is the case for group I scores; in that case, however, it is possible to lower distance without having to trade off coverage. Thus, with the projections on the frontier in group II, it was not possible to stay on the frontier without trading off one input for the other, whereas for DMUs in groups I and III, there is a slack along each of the dimensions that must be eliminated before the DMU can be truly efficient. In distinguishing between the efficiencies of these points, we have provided an intuitive explanation of the difference; for a formal characterization and discussion of the different types of efficiencies, see Charnes, Cooper, and Thrall (1986).

One might notice that the RSE scores in this study are relatively high in value, varying from .875 to 1.000. Obviously, this somewhat small range in values is due to the nature of the traditional accessibility measures used in the analysis (i.e., distance in person-miles and number of persons not covered). Had we moved the "zero" point for these measures, greater variation in RSE values would have been noted. Still, the importance of our spatial efficiency assessments resides in the distribution and rank order of scores, not in their magnitude. Summary statistics on the scores of the DMUs in each of the three comparison groups identified in this analysis are given in table 12-2. In addition to informing the analyst about the distribution of the DMUs in the attribute space, this partitioning of the data also serves to identify structural similarities in the data. For instance, in figure 12-3, which is a map of all the sites, one might note that group II and III decisions, which can be characterized as minimum distance sites, are found in the far eastern edge of Franklin County. These decisions also have the highest RSE scores among inefficient sites. The lower-scored group I decisions, including

Table 12-2. Summary Statistics for RSE Scores by Comparison Group

Comparson Group	Reference Set	N	Mean Score	Standard Deviation
I	43227	35	0.899	0.017
II	43227, 43232	1	0.966	—
III	43232	3	0.978	0.015
All Data		41	0.911	0.034

expansion scenarios, tend to be found in the northern, southern, and central portions of the county. The higher-scored decisions (e.g., siting at 43221) in this group are found in the western part of the county. The primary reason for the within-group disparity of RSE scores is proximity of a decision (i.e., siting or expansion) to existing system service facilities.

Oftentimes, other considerations, not explicitly included in the analysis, can restrict the range of potential feasible locations, with the result that none of the noninferior DMUs is a feasible choice. The best DMU, under such restrictions, (for instance, zoning regulations or preference functions) must then be selected from the remaining DMUs by searching through the relevant comparison group. Some of these restrictions can be explicitly incorporated in the initial DEA model in the form of additional constraints. The construction of *assurance regions* (Thompson, Singleton, Thrall, and Smith, 1986) and the more general cone-ratio approaches (Charnes, Cooper, Huang, and Sun, 1990) provide ways of imposing additional restrictions on the choice set.

4. Summary and Conclusions

Underscoring the movement of spatial analysts to multiobjective perspectives in location research, this chapter has proposed a particular multiobjective perspective for the measurement of *relative spatial efficiency*. Specifically, DEA has been suggested as a research framework that greatly improves the analytical support of locational decisions. Furthermore, our research demonstrates how disparate measures of accessibility, defined at the system and individual levels, can be integrated into a coherent characterization of RSE. Moreover, when compared to other MOP models of facility siting, the DEA approach better presents decision-relevant alternatives. This superiority is due to DEA's development of a ratio-scale-based definition of inferior solutions, rather than a simple classification into groups of inferior and noninferior DMUs.

Though the model presented above is somewhat simple for illustrative purposes, more elaborate versions of RSE are certainly possible, given the flexibility of the DEA framework. Indeed, the measurement of spatial efficiency could be tailored for a number of different decision contexts and could easily include multiple outputs, aspatial costs and benefits, and the inclusion of stated preferences, among other planning and evaluation considerations. Such elaborations are being explored by the present authors in future research.

Finally, we would emphasize the importance of this relative efficiency framework to the support of actual decisions. In the example scenario, the decision maker was presented with two different kinds of alternatives—those of facility siting and facility sizing. While the former entails a purely locational decision, the latter is essentially an aspatial decision, but one that has spatial implications. Because of its focus on relative efficiency, DEA is able to evaluate and compare both types of decisions. MOP techniques for locational siting are not as flexible, in that they could not easily incorporate facility *expansion* decisions into their set of alternatives. Furthermore, in terms of Fisher and Rushton's (1979) proposal a decade ago, it is this kind of flexibility in DEA that allows us to suspend commitment to a particular objective form and consider the relative merits of various criteria in the locational planning process.

Appendix: Input Data, RSE Scores, and Comparism Group Membership

Table 12–A1.   Input Data

DMU	Distance	Non-coverage	Remarks
00001	13973.54	492278.56	original configuration
43223	11684.22	479768.63	expansion
43201	13973.54	480142.06	.
43017	13973.54	488987.94	.
43085	13973.54	485455.25	.
43207	13392.57	488269.94	.
43205	9661.20	470936.13	.
43224	13973.54	476919.50	.
43081	13973.54	489216.19	expansion
43119	9315.76	475430.69	new
43123	13563.96	476667.94	.
43026	13032.51	484339.19	.
43228	9315.76	469685.81	.
43204	11114.37	465567.75	.
43222	13921.51	481910.88	.
43215	13973.54	481910.88	.
43212	11684.22	467725.13	.
43210	13973.54	465877.06	.
43220	13947.53	464265.69	.
43221	11684.22	457793.19	.
43202	13973.54	471530.94	.
43002	13973.54	487561.63	.
43214	13973.54	478442.75	.
43137	13973.54	489848.56	.
43217	13372.17	487918.38	.
43125	9885.46	483265.38	.
43206	13973.54	477758.13	.
43209	10722.71	489715.50	.
43227	6952.71	430797.69	.
43110	5100.83	468003.44	.
43232	5075.82	433788.56	.
43109	5638.64	448573.81	.
43068	5238.76	471040.38	.
43203	13973.54	492278.56	.
43211	13973.54	477018.88	.
43219	11601.95	478564.63	.
43230	10933.06	479596.13	.
43213	5238.76	457394.31	.
43004	8864.55	485970.38	.
43229	13973.54	474089.75	.
43054	13076.44	488642.50	new

Table 12–A2. RSE Scores and Comparison Group Membership

Configuration Identifier	RSE Score	Reference Set Configurations	
		43227	43232
43221	0.941	×	
43220	0.928	×	
43204	0.925	×	
43210	0.925	×	
43212	0.921	×	
43228	0.917	×	
43205	0.915	×	
43202	0.914	×	
43229	0.909	×	
43119	0.906	×	
43123	0.904	×	
43224	0.903	×	
43211	0.903	×	
43206	0.902	×	
43219	0.900	×	
43214	0.900	×	
43230	0.898	×	
43223	0.898	×	
43201	0.897	×	
43215	0.894	×	
43222	0.894	×	
43125	0.891	×	
43026	0.889	×	
43085	0.887	×	
43004	0.886	×	
43002	0.884	×	
43217	0.883	×	
43054	0.882	×	
43207	0.882	×	
43017	0.881	×	
43081	0.881	×	
43209	0.880	×	
43137	0.879	×	
43203	0.875	×	
00001	0.875	×	
43109	0.966	×	×
43110	0.995		×
43213	0.969		×
43068	0.969		×

13 PRODUCTIVITY DEVELOPMENTS IN SWEDISH HOSPITALS: A MALMQUIST OUTPUT INDEX APPROACH

Rolf Färe, Shawna Grosskopf, Björn Lindgren,
and Pontus Roos

1. Introduction

The purpose of this chapter is to study productivity change in Swedish hospitals during the time period from 1970 to 1985. By comparing annual changes in the productivity of individual hospitals, it is possible both to identify general trends in the productivity of the hospital industry as a whole and to identify individual hospitals exhibiting patterns of change in productivity that differ from the rest of the industry. A careful analysis of the results of this exercise should add to our knowledge about the factors determining the pattern of hospital productivity in Sweden.

Hospitals typically produce multiple outputs using multiple inputs. However, the exact nature of this very complex technology is to a large extent unknown. In addition, Swedish hospitals operate in a nonmarket environment: market prices of outputs are unavailable, and it cannot be taken for granted that hospitals behave as cost minimizers. These facts have to be reflected in the analytical approach to be chosen.

In a recent paper, Caves, Christensen, and Diewert (1982a) develop productivity indices for making comparisons under very general conditions.[1] In particular, they develop an output-based and an input-based productivity index in the spirit of Malmquist (1953), i.e., they make use of the output and the input distance functions, respectively, to define the two indices. They ". . . require that the framework hold for very general structures of production, yet be empirically implementable using only observed prices and quantities of outputs and inputs" (Caves, Christensen, and Diewert, 1982a, p. 1393). Their approach requires, however, that (for the output-based measure) firms are revenue maximizers and that (for the input-based measure) firms are cost minimizers.

In this chapter, we employ a Malmquist output-based productivity index. However, our data set does not admit prices, nor can we assume that Swedish hospitals are revenue maximizers. Thus, we need to generalize the method suggested by Caves, Christensen, and Diewert (1982a). In short, we calculate the distance functions directly in the "goods" space by means of linear programming, thereby circumventing the need for price information and allowing for inefficiency, while preserving the requirement that the framework holds for very general production structures.

Our calculations exploit the fact that the output distance functions used to construct that Malmquist index are reciprocal to Farrell (1957) outputoriented technical-efficiency measures. They therefore bear a close relationship to the CCR output-oriented DEA model. This link to efficiency allows us to decompose productivity changes into changes in efficiency and change in the best-practice frontier (technical change), an idea used by Nishimizu and Page (1982) in a parametric context.

The pattern of productivity change in the Swedish hospital sector is complex. We find considerable variation across individual hospitals in our sample. Productivity changes reflect both efficiency change and change in best sample practice. We find evidence of both regress and progress.

This chapter proceeds as follows. In section 2, we begin with some background concerning the Swedish health care and hospital sectors that motivates our work, and we highlight the distinguishing features of our sample. The Malmquist output-based productivity index to be used here will be defined in section 3. In section 4, we show how to calculate distance functions as solutions to linear programming problems. A discussion of our data and its construction constitutes section 5. In section 6, we present and discuss our results.

2. Background

Efficiency in health care has been a neglected goal for public policy in many countries. Traditionally, in Sweden, a seemingly ever-increasing demand for health care has been met merely by putting more resources into the health sector, the increase being financed by higher tax rates and general economic growth. These two traditional methods of increasing health care production are now approaching their limits of application. Almost all political parties in Sweden argue for reductions in tax rates, and the annual growth rate of the Swedish economy was less than 2% during the 1980s. Consequently, in recent years, the efficiency of health care delivery has begun to receive greater attention. The possibilities of improving the utilization of existing resources and increasing productivity over time are issues that have been brought into sharper focus.

Health care accounted for 11.1% of total employment in Sweden in 1985; the annual increase in the number of man-hours worked was 3.6% in the 1970s and 2.4% in the 1980s, respectively. Most (i.e., 93%) of all health care personnel are publicly employed. In fact, every third public employee works in the health care sector. So, in Sweden, health care is not only financed through government but also largely provided by public producers, the exception being dental care, where 50% of the services are provided by private dentists. The Swedish system is not a national health service. However, there are 26 county councils that are by law responsible for health care delivery within their geographical boundaries. The county councils are also empowered to impose a proportional income tax on their residents. The budgets of different health care providers are negotiated and allocated in advance by the county council administration on a one-year basis. These "fixed" budgets are not based on the actual flow of patients but on some politically determined decision-making process. Normally, however, hospitals have run deficits that have led more or less automatically to increased budgets in the following years. Hospitals can survive without revenue maximization or cost minimization, so they are free to adopt several possible behavioral strategies.

Publicly employed doctors and other health care personnel are salaried; only private physicians and dentists are paid on a fee-for-service basis. Salaries follow a uniform scheme, and general pay increases are centrally negotiated between the Federation of County Councils and the central trade unions of the various types of health care personnel. Other input prices—for instance, drug prices—are centrally determined as well. So, on the whole, input prices are the same all over Sweden. Direct consumer charges are low, but they too are uniform across the country, being regulated by central government authorities.

Another distinct feature of the Swedish health care system is its concentration on hospitals as the key means of delivery not only for inpatient but also for outpatient care. In fact, almost 50% of all physician visits take place at the hospitals. Thus, hospital-based health care accounted for 72% of total health care costs in Sweden in 1985. (It should be observed that hospital costs also include all physician costs—there are no "independent" doctors working in Swedish public hospitals.)

To summarize, the Swedish hospital sector is an important component of the Swedish health care sector. County councils are responsible for health care delivery, and hospitals' budgets are negotiated with these governments, with no apparent attempts to link budgets to cost control or productivity. Services are essentially free (but financed by a local income tax), and input prices are negotiated centrally. Thus attempts to measure productivity that require assuming optimizing behavior and information on prices where those prices are assumed to reflect opportunity cost are inappropriate. The Malmquist index, which presumes no optimizing behavior and does not require price data, provides an appropriate tool to measure productivity in this case.

3. A Malmquist Output-Based Productivity Index

For each time period t, $t = 1, \ldots, T$, the production technology S^t models the transformation of inputs $x^t \varepsilon R_+^M$ into outputs $y^t \varepsilon R_+^M$, where $S^t = \{(x^t, y^t): x^t \text{ can produce } y^t\}$. The technology is assumed to satisfy properties sufficiently strong to allow the definition of a meaningful output distance function.[2]

The output distance function is defined at t as

$$D_o^t(x^t, y^t) = \inf\{\theta: (x^t, y^t/\theta)\varepsilon S^t\}. \tag{13.1}$$

This function is a complete characterization of the technology. It satisfies certain properties; in particular, it is homogeneous of degree $+1$ in outputs. We note that $(x^t, y^t)\varepsilon S^t$ if and only if $D_o^t(x^t, y^t) \le 1$.

In order to define a Malmquist output-based productivity index in the spirit of Caves, Christensen, and Diewert (1982a), we also need to relate an input–output vector (x^t, y^t) at time period t to the technology S^{t+1} at the following period. Thus we define

$$D_o^{t+1}(x^t, y^t) = \inf\{\theta: (x^t, y^t/\theta)\varepsilon S^{t+1}\}. \tag{13.2}$$

One may define $D_o^t(x^{t+1}, y^{t+1})$ in a similar fashion[3]; in this case, an observed input–output vector produced in period $t + 1$ is compared to technology in the previous period t. The value of the mixed-period distance functions will be less than or equal to unity if and only if the observations being assessed are "feasible," i.e., are members of technology in the other period. Clearly, if technical progress occurs over time,

$(x^{t+1}, y^{t+1}) \notin S^t$, and $D_o^t(x^{t+1}, y^{t+1}) > 1$. This may cause computational problems, an issue which is discussed below.

We now define our Malmquist output based productivity index as

$$M_o^{t+1}(x^{t+1}, y^{t+1}, x^t, y^t) = \left[\frac{D_o^t(x^{t+1}, y^{t+1})}{D_o^t(x^t, y^t)} \frac{D_o^{t+1}(x^{t+1}, y^{t+1})}{D_o^{t+1}(x^t, y^t)} \right]^{1/2}. \quad (13.3)$$

The index in equation (13.3) differs slightly from the formulation of the Malmquist productivity index proposed by Caves, Christensen, and Diewert (1982a). The index in equation (13.3) is the geometric mean of two of their Malmquist productivity indexes. In addition, in their work, Caves, Christensen, and Diewert assume that $D_o^t(x^t, y^t)$ and $D_o^{t+1}(x^{t+1}, y^{t+1})$ equal 1, i.e., in Farrell's terminology, there is no allowance for technical inefficiency. Here, we relax that assumption, and allow for inefficient observations.

An equivalent way of stating the Malmquist output-based productivity index is

$$M_o^{t+1}(x^{t+1}, y^{t+1}, x^t, y^t) = \frac{D_o^{t+1}(x^{t+1}, y^{t+1})}{D_o^t(x^t, y^t)} \left[\frac{D_o^t(x^{t+1}, y^{t+1})}{D_o^{t+1}(x^{t+1}, y^{t+1})} \frac{D_o^t(x^t, y^t)}{D_o^{t+1}(x^t, y^t)} \right]^{1/2}$$

$$(13.4)$$

or

$$M = E \cdot P$$

where

$$E = \frac{D_o^{t+1}(x^{t+1}, y^{t+1})}{D_o^t(x^t, y^t)}$$

$$P = \left[\frac{D_o^t(x^{t+1}, y^{t+1})}{D_o^{t+1}(x^{t+1}, y^{t+1})} \frac{D_o^t(x^t, y^t)}{D_o^{t+1}(x^t, y^t)} \right]^{1/2}$$

which is illustrated in figure 13.1. The two ratios in the square bracket can be thought of as measures of technical progress as measured by shifts in the frontier measured at period $t + 1$ (OA/OD) and period t (OC/OE) and then averaged geometrically. The terms outside the bracket represent the changes in efficiency between the two periods (OB/OA and OF/OE).

This decomposition of productivity change into technical change and change in efficiency is similar in spirit to that suggested by Nishimizu and Page (1982). In contrast to the appproach taken here, they employ a parametric specification of technology, specifying a deterministic scalar-valued frontier production function like that proposed by Aigner and Chu

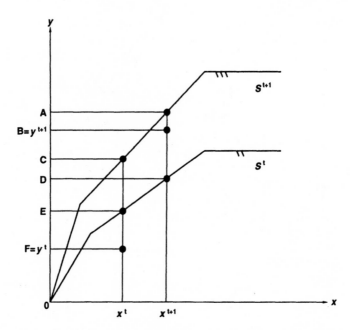

Figure 13–1.   Illustration of the Malmquist output-based productivity index.

(1968). The approach taken here allows for production of multiple outputs and does not require specification of a particular functional form for technology, both of which we feel are important considerations in the analysis of the hospital sector.

4. Calculating Distance Functions:
The Linear Programming Model

We calculate the distance functions that constitute the Malmquist index as solutions to linear programming problems. We begin by specifying the technology that will serve as constraints to the linear programming problems used to calculate the distance functions composing the Malmquist index. We assume that there are $k = 1, \ldots, K$ observations of $n = 1, \ldots, N$ inputs $x_n^{k,t}$ in each period $t = 1, \ldots, T$, which are employed to produce $k = 1, \ldots, K$ observations of $m = 1, \ldots, M$ outputs denoted $y_m^{k,t}$ in each period $t = 1, \ldots, T$. We assume that the number of observations does not change over time, i.e., $K^t = K$ for all t. Then we can describe the technology in period t as follows:

$$S^t = \{(x^t, y^t): \sum_{k=1}^{K} \lambda^{k,t} x_n^{k,t} \leq x_n^t, \quad n = 1, \ldots, N$$

$$\sum_{k=1}^{K} \lambda^{k,t} y_m^{k,t} \geq y_m^t, \quad m = 1, \ldots, M$$

$$\sum_{k=1}^{K} \lambda^{k,t} \leq 1; \quad \lambda^{k,t} \geq 0, \quad k = 1, \ldots, K\} \quad (13.5)$$

where $\lambda^{k,t}$ is an intensity variable, familiar from activity analysis. These intensity variables serve to form the convex combinations of observed inputs and outputs, thus forming the technology or reference set.

Next, suppose we wish to measure the relative productivity change of observation k' between period t and period $t + 1$. We begin by calculating $D_o^t(x^{k',t}, y^{k',t})$ as the solution to the following programming problem:

$$D_o^t(x^{k',t}, y^{k',t}) = \min_{\theta, \lambda} \theta \quad (13.6)$$

subject to

$$\sum_{k=1}^{K} \lambda^{k,t} x_n^{k,t} \leq x_n^{k',t}, \quad n = 1, \ldots, N$$

$$\sum_{k=1}^{K} \lambda^{k,t} y_m^{k,t} \geq y_m^{k',t}/\theta, \quad m = 1, \ldots, M$$

$$\sum_{k=1}^{K} \lambda^{k,t} \leq 1; \quad \lambda^{k,t} \geq 0, \quad k = 1, \ldots, K.$$

This problem can be rewritten to reveal its relation to the traditional Farrell output-oriented measure of technical efficiency as well as the standard DEA models as follows:

$$[D_o^t(x^{k',t}, y^{k',t})]^{-1} = \max_{\phi, \lambda} \phi \quad (13.6a)$$

subject to

$$\phi y_m^{k',t} - \sum_{k=1}^{K} \lambda^{k,t} y_m^{k,t} \leq 0, \quad m = 1, \ldots, M$$

$$\sum_{k=1}^{K} \lambda^{k,t} x^{k,t} \leq x_n^{k',t}, \quad n = 1, \ldots, N$$

$$\sum_{k=1}^{K} \lambda^{k,t} \leq 1,$$

$$x^{k,t} \geq 0, \quad k = 1, \ldots, K.$$

In equation (13.6a), it is obvious that the output distance function as calculated here is the reciprocal of an output-oriented Farrell measure of technical efficiency calculated relative to technology satisfying nonincreasing returns to scale. The model in equation (13.6a) bears a resemblance to the output-oriented DEA model (CCR_p–O of chapter 2, section 5.2), but has a different objective function—there are no slack variables or non-Archimedeans in equation (13.6a). In addition, the intensity variables are restricted to sum to less than or equal to one; the CCR formulation imposes constant returns to scale.

We impose nonincreasing returns to scale in order to guarantee that equation (13.7) below has a solution, even when an observation (x^{t+1}, y^{t+1}) is not a member in S^t, which will be the case if technical progress occurs. By imposing nonincreasing returns, we guarantee the existence of a solution, as well as some flexibility in modeling scale properties, since the alternativeis the more restrictive use of constant returns to scale.[4]

$D_o^t(x^{k',t+1}, y^{k',t+1})$ can be calculated as follows:

$$D_o^t(x^{k',t+1}, y^{k',t+1}) = \min_{\theta,\lambda} \theta \qquad (13.7)$$

subject to

$$\sum_{k=1}^{K} \lambda^{k,t} x_n^{k,t} \leq x_n^{k',t+1}, \quad n = 1, \dots, N$$

$$\sum_{k=1}^{K} \lambda^{k,t} y_m^{k,t} \geq y_m^{k',t+1}/\theta, \quad m = 1, \dots, M$$

$$\sum_{k=1}^{K} \lambda^{k,t} \leq 1; \quad \lambda^{k,t} \geq 0, \quad k = 1, \dots, K.$$

Problem (13.7) can be rewritten as the following linear programming problem:

$$[D_o^t(x^{k',t+1}, y^{k',t+1})]^{-1} = \max_{\phi,\lambda} \phi \qquad (13.7a)$$

subject to

$$\phi y_m^{k',t+1} - \sum_{k=1}^{K} \lambda^{k,t} y_m^{k,t} \leq 0, \quad m = 1, \dots, M$$

$$\sum_{k=1}^{K} \lambda^{k,t} x_n^{k,t} \leq x_n^{k',t+1}, \quad n = 1, \dots, N$$

$$\sum_{k=1}^{K} \lambda^{k,t} \leq 1; \quad \lambda^{k,t} \geq 0, \quad k = 1, \dots, K$$

Note that $D_o^t(x^{k',t}, y^{k',t})$ and $D_o^t(x^{k',t+1}, y^{k',t+1})$ differ in that the observation being assessed is by construction an element of the technology in the former problem but not necessarily in the latter problem. This implies that $D_o^t(x^{k',t}, y^{k',t}) \leq 1$, whereas $D_o^t(x^{k',t+1}, y^{k',t+1}) \gtreqless 1$. $D_o^{t+1}(x^{k',t+1}, y^{k',t+1})$ and $D_o^{t+1}(x^{k',t}, y^{k',t})$ are defined analogously, and we have $D_o^{t+1}(x^{k',t+1}, y^{k',t+1}) \leq 1$. Recall that Caves, Christensen, and Diewert (1982a) assume that $D_o^t(x^{k',t}, y^{k',t}) = D_o^{t+1}(x^{k',t+1}, y^{k',t+1}) = 1$, which we relax here (see above).

One of our inputs, nonlabor input, is given in value terms, rather than in quantities. However, since our measures are independent of unit of measurement, we may (conceptually) multiply the nonlabor input constraint by prices to obtain value. Since each hospital faces the same input prices in Sweden, the solutions to our programming problems and our index are unaffected.[5] For details, see Färe and Grosskopf (1985).

5. Data

The data in this study consist of annual observations of outputs and inputs from small and middle-sized Swedish public hospitals. No teaching hospitals are included in the sample. The time period is 1970 to 1985.

Small hospitals have 3 to 4 departments for short-term care, and middle-sized hospitals have 6 to 8 departments. All hospitals also have one department for long-term chronic care.

We specify three separate proxies for hospital outputs: short-term inpatient care, long-term chronic care, and ambulatory care. Short-term inpatient care is measured in discharges and long-term chronic care in bed days. We have used doctor visits as a proxy for ambulatory care.

We include three separate proxies for hospital outputs rather than one aggregate proxy (such as admissions or bed days). We have used discharges rather than bed days as our proxy for inpatient care in order to distinguish between intensity of care in inpatient versus long-term chronic care. Bed days gives a useful measure of the hotel-type services that constitute a large part (of the cost) of long-term chronic care. Doctor visits was our best available proxy of ambulatory care. These proxies, while imperfect, are consistent with those recommended by Breyer (1987).

All output data were obtained from each individual hospital. The total number of discharges and visits per hospital have been aggregated from the data available from individual departments.

In addition to our three output proxies (inpatient discharges, long-term patient bed days, and number of doctor visits), we have two input proxies: real labor input and a proxy for real nonlabor input. The non-labor input proxy does not include capital. Details of how these input proxies were constructed are found below. Some idea of the range and patterns found in our data for these 17 hospitals over the 1970–1985 period may be gained by referral to table 13–1. Mean, minimum, and maximum values of our three output and two input proxies are displayed for 1970, 1975, 1980, and 1985. The general pattern is one of increasing "production" and increasing resource use.

The hospital accounting system in Sweden does not include direct information on the flow of labor input (numbers of hours worked). As a consequence, real labor input was estimated for each hospital and each year. This estimation has been done in two steps. First, average labor expenditure per hour is estimated for four types of labor in the hospital sector. Then a labor expenditure index is estimated for each hospital, which is used to deflate annual total labor expenditure.

The data for this procedure are from annual reports to the county council, in which each hospital reports total labor expenditure in March for each type of labor. In the report, average labor expenditure is esti-

Table 13–1. Mean, Minimum, and Maximum Values of Inputs and Outputs: Selected Years

		1970	1975	1980	1985
Inpatient Discharges	Min	350	367	348	369
	Mean	1001	1195	1254	1355
	Max	1946	3060	2818	2890
Long-term Bed Days	Min	0	105	197	101
	Mean	296	453	545	579
	Max	698	1157	1390	1607
Doctor Visits	Min	188	202	222	268
	Mean	596	705	817	823
	Max	1207	1380	1926	1918
Real Labor Input	Min	471	633	950	995
	Mean	1342	1876	2543	2448
	Max	2662	4004	6266	5408
Real Other Input	Min	485	773	1066	1066
	Mean	1558	2204	3042	3440
	Max	3019	5296	8100	8242
Mumber of Hospitals		17	17	17	17

mated for full-time equivalent employment in the health care sector in general (not just hospitals); however, it is possible to identify labor mainly employed in the hospital sector. We have calculated average labor expenditure per year for four groups of labor: doctors, other medical labor, service labor, and administrative labor.

Annually, the Statistiska Centralbyrån (Central Statistical Bureau, SCB) asks a sample of employed personnel in the health care sector how many hours they have been working during a given two-week period in the period January–March. From the SCB report, it is possible to distinguish between medical labor (doctors excluded), service labor, and administrative labor. The SCB report includes average number of hours worked per week. We assume that the SCB data are also relevant for the hospital subsector. Average number of hours worked per week is multiplied by average number of working weeks per year (52 minus holidays and vacation) to arrive at an estimate of the average number of hours worked per year.

The sample in the SCB annual investigation is not useful for estimation of hours worked by doctors because the sample is too small. Instead we have used information from studies done by Landstingsförbundet (The Federation of Swedish County Councils), Läkarförbundet (The Swedish Medical Association), and Socialstyrelsen (The Swedish National Board of Health and Welfare), in which every doctor working at a hospital is asked to report the hours worked during a given two-week period. This survey is not undertaken annually. The average number of hours worked per year by an average doctor in the hospital sector is estimated for the period 1970 to 1985 from observations for year 1970, 1972, 1974, 1977, 1979, 1982, and 1985.

Table 13–2 displays estimated average numbers of hours worked per year for a full-time equivalent employee for the years 1970 to 1985.

From the hospital accounting system, it is possible to determine total labor expenditure per year for doctors, medical labor, service labor, and administrative labor. Estimated average labor expenditure per hour for each type of labor in the hospital sector has been used to calculate average labor expenditure per hour for all personnel for each hospital, which is our estimate of the average wage. Table 13–2 shows the result for each hospital year from 1970 to 1985. The relatively small differences across hospitals indicate that the mix of labor is roughly constant across our sample.

Real labor input is calculated for each hospital by deflating hospital total labor expenditure with average hospital labor expenditure per hour.

Nonlabor inputs includee food, drugs, medical supplies, laundry, and

Table 13–2.   Estimated Average Number of Hours Worked per Year by Doctors, Medical Labor, Service Labor, and Administrative Labor in the Hospital Sector, 1970 to 1985 (hours per ful-time equivalent)

Year	Doctors	Medical Labor	Service Labor	Administration Labor
1970	2086	1862	1906	1725
1971	2064	1834	1858	1725
1972	1980	1795	1814	1684
1973	1967	1762	1776	1647
1974	1954	1728	1752	1610
1975	1936	1718	1718	1608
1976	1918	1704	1694	1605
1977	1901	1699	1666	1600
1978	1785	1617	1617	1575
1979	1699	1575	1593	1575
1980	1686	1532	1579	1570
1981	1673	1485	1560	1557
1982	1664	1490	1546	1530
1983	1656	1418	1537	1485
1984	1647	1542	1528	1463
1985	1638	1570	1523	1440

other goods and services. Capital services are excluded. There exists no quantity or price index for hospital nonlabor inputs. What is officially published is a "price" index for drugs used in hospitals; however, this drug index is not really an index over time, since the base in the index changes over time. Here we have used the consumer price index to deflate nonlabor hospital expenditures. Real nonlabor input is measured in 1980 prices.

The lack of data on capital service is, of course, a serious problem in a sector where capital has been dramatically affected by (and has contributed to) technical advance. Unfortunately, accounting practices in the Swedish hospital sector do not allow us to provide a reasonable proxy for capital services.

6. Results and Discussion

We calculated the Malmquist output-based productivity index (M) for each of the 17 hospitals in our sample, as well as the two components of the Malmquist index: efficiency change (E) and frontier shifts (P) (see equation 13.4). These indices were calculated for all adjacent periods from 1970 to 1985. In order to more easily interpret these results, we took the natural logarithms of the indexes and their components, which allows us to interpret these as percent changes.

Table 13–3 displays percent changes in relative output efficiency for each individual hospital, as represented by the natural logarithm of the term outside the bracket in equation (13.4) of our Malmquist output-based productivity index. The results indicate considerable variation across hospitals and across time. Three hospitals (numbers 3, 9, and 12) were efficient (and therefore showed no change in efficiency) in all periods from 1970 to 1985. For the other hospitals, we found periods with positive, negative, or no changes in efficiency. Furthermore, our results showed that many hospitals improved their efficiency between 1978 and 1979 and only a few hospitals had negative changes in efficiency from 1982 to 1983 and from 1983 to 1984. For any two periods, our results showed that half or almost half of the hospitals had changes in efficiency between two periods.

These results are similar to those found by Pedersen, Olesen, and Petersen (1987) for Danish hospitals. Pedersen et al. used DEA to calculate the efficiency of 96 Danish hospitals in 1983. Six separate proxies were used for outputs: five for short-term inpatient care and one proxy for ambulatory care. Total hospital expenditure was used as a proxy for real input (capital costs were excluded). Assuming nonincreasing returns to scale, the results of this input-based study showed that 27 hospitals were efficient and that 20% of the hospitals could reduce inputs by more than 20% without any reduction in output.

Table 13–4 presents the natural logarithm of calculated technical progress/regress as measured by average shifts in the best-practice frontier from period t to $t + 1$ (see equation (4)). According to our results, there were periods with progress and periods with regress for each individual hospital. Regress was most frequent in the middle and end of the 1970s and during the years 1982 to 1985. Our results showed progress in the best-practice frontier for all hospitals between 1981 and 1982, and progress for 14 hospital from 1980 to 1981. In total, for all hospitals and all periods, we found progress in the best-practice frontier in 108 cases and regress in 142 cases.

Table 13–5 displays calculated changes in the Malmquist-based productivity index. From table 13–5 we observe that no hospital had a clear-cut positive or negative productivity change. According to our results, many hospitals had negative productivity changes in the middle and the

Table 13–3.   Changes in Hospital Relative Efficiency Between Time Period t and $t + 1$(%), Years 1970 to 1988[a]

Hospital	1970–1971	1971–1972	1972–1973	1973–1974	1974–1975	1975–1976	1976–1977	1977–1978	1978–1979	1979–1980	1980–1981	1981–1982	1982–1983	1983–1984	1984–1985	Increase
1	−6.5	+5.2	−6.4	+7.2	−7.0	−3.0	−1.4	+1.9	+7.4	−9.8	+3.1	−0.1	−3.5	+0.1	−3.2	6
2	−1.6	+1.6	a[b]	a	a	a	a	−0.3	−0.3	a	a	a	a	a	a	1
3	a	a	a	a	a	a	a	a	a	a	a	a	a	a	a	—
4	a	a	a	a	−2.7	+2.7	−2.5	+1.7	+0.8	a	a	a	a	a	−0.1	3
5	a	a	−4.8	+4.8	−1.3	+1.3	−11.3	−4.3	10.3	5.3	a	a	a	a	a	4
6	+4.6	−17.1	+17.1	−13.5	−8.7	−5.4	−8.3	+6.8	+7.8	−0.6	−3.2	−1.8	+1.9	+2.6	+22.4	6
7	−1.1	+0.9	+0.2	+0.4	+3.5	−9.2	−4.5	−10.1	+10.1	−0.8	−11.9	−1.8	+1.7	+4.6	+9.6	9
8	a	+3.4	−1.1	+6.5	a	a	a	a	a	a	−4.5	−2.5	+5.4	+1.7	−1.1	4
9	a	a	a	a	a	a	a	a	a	a	a	a	a	a	a	—
10	−0.8	+5.6	−2.7	−2.1	−2.3	+0.3	+1.5	−0.2	−1.1	−1.3	+3.9	+0.2	+10.3	+6.4	−5.1	7
11	a	a	a	a	a	a	a	−6.6	+6.6	a	−3.9	+3.9	a	a	−6.4	2
12	a	a	a	a	a	a	a	a	a	a	a	a	a	a	a	—
13	a	a	a	a	a	a	a	a	−5.6	+5.6	a	a	−0.2	+0.2	a	2
14	−0.6	−1.2	+0.5	−7.0	−0.9	+0.9	+1.6	+0.6	+2.0	+10.2	−2.8	−2.5	+5.4	a	a	7
15	+9.5	a	a	a	−4.3	+0.8	+3.5	a	a	a	a	−8.5	+7.6	−5.0	+3.5	5
16	+15.8	a	a	a	a	−0.2	−4.4	−6.0	+6.5	−1.0	+4.9	a	a	a	a	3
17	a	a	−0.6	+0.6	a	a	−1.0	−9.8	+11.0	a	a	a	a	a	a	2
Positive changes	3	5	3	5	1	5	3	4	10	3	3	2	6	6	3	
Negative changes	5	2	5	3	7	4	7	7	2	5	5	6	2	1	5	
No changes[b]	9	10	9	9	9	8	7	6	5	9	9	9	9	10	9	

[a] Changes calculated from

$$\ln M = \ln E + \ln P$$

where

M is Malmquist output = based productivity, index year $t + 1$

E is $D_0^{t+1}(x^{t+1}, y^{t+1})/D_0^t(x^t, y^t)$

P is $\left[\dfrac{D_0^{t+1}(x^{t+1}, y^{t+1}) \cdot D_0^t(x^t, y^t)}{D_0^{t+1}(x^{t+1}, y^{t+1}) \cdot D_0^{t+1}(x^t, y^t)} \right]^{1/2}$

[b] "a" means no change in relative, efficiency.

Table 13–4. Average Productivity Shifts in Hospital Best-Practice Frontier Between Time Period t and $t + 1$(%), Years 1970 to 1985[a]

Hospital	1970–1971	1971–1972	1972–1973	1973–1974	1974–1975	1975–1976	1976–1977	1977–1978	1978–1979	1979–1980	1980–1981	1981–1982	1982–1983	1983–1984	1984–1985	Increase
1	+4.3	-1.2	+1.0	-4.4	-6.3	-4.5	+3.3	-1.6	-13.5	-0.4	-0.4	+5.6	-2.6	-4.0	-1.0	4
2	+3.2	-3.2	+1.9	+3.5	-0.2	-6.1	-6.0	+0.8	-2.5	-1.3	+4.6	+7.5	+0.5	-4.0	-3.5	7
3	+14.8	-3.2	-3.3	+0.9	+12.2	+5.1	+4.8	+2.4	-14.1	-9.4	+1.8	+3.7	+4.6	-1.5	+4.0	10
4	+2.3	-1.7	+0.3	-2.9	-5.2	+2.1	-3.7	+3.3	-3.3	-2.8	+0.9	+7.8	-2.0	+2.8	-6.4	7
5	+2.4	-1.5	+0.2	+0.7	+6.6	+9.3	+11.5	+3.9	-12.6	-8.6	+1.7	+5.6	-2.9	-0.9	-2.9	9
6	+4.7	-22.0	+0.1	-9.8	-11.9	-4.3	+0.4	-0.4	-3.5	-2.1	+1.3	+7.9	-3.7	-1.4	+0.2	6
7	+6.9	-4.1	+1.1	-2.7	-8.1	-1.6	-2.6	+1.2	-8.8	-0.1	+5.3	+5.6	-4.7	-2.1	-5.4	4
8	-0.8	-0.2	+2.4	+3.2	-1.1	-7.8	-5.5	+0.4	-5.3	-0.2	+0.6	+1.8	-3.4	-2.9	+1.8	6
9	+1.0	-2.8	-4.8	-2.3	-6.0	-7.5	+0.6	-2.2	-3.0	-3.6	+3.3	+8.2	-6.1	-2.9	-1.6	4
10	+16.0	-14.3	+0.9	-2.7	-10.8	-3.5	-4.9	-1.6	-0.1	-6.8	+6.2	+8.2	-5.3	+2.0	-4.3	5
11	-6.6	-5.1	+3.2	+1.9	-4.2	-7.7	-7.8	+3.9	-5.1	-4.7	+1.9	+6.7	+1.6	-5.7	+0.5	7
12	-0.6	+3.0	-0.4	-0.7	-5.4	+7.6	+4.1	+0.4	-1.3	-0.6	+2.8	+1.6	-0.6	-0.1	+3.0	7
13	+4.2	-8.2	+3.1	+5.5	-4.6	-1.7	-7.4	-5.1	-2.0	-3.4	+5.4	+0.3	-2.4	-1.3	+3.9	6
14	-0.8	-3.7	-4.6	+2.0	-6.1	-1.0	-3.1	+2.4	-5.9	-1.7	+5.2	+0.8	+0.8	+0.1	-4.1	6
15	+4.8	-4.8	+5.8	+1.4	-9.4	-9.2	+0.2	-1.1	-7.9	+7.9	-4.8	+1.6	-2.1	-2.7	+0.6	7
16	+6.6	+3.8	-0.7	+1.7	-7.4	-0.9	-5.9	+0.6	-5.2	-4.4	+8.3	+4.5	-2.7	-4.1	-4.9	6
17	+6.9	-4.2	+0.7	-2.1	-6.9	-3.8	-1.7	+2.3	+1.2	+6.2	-4.7	+9.3	-2.9	-2.6	-7.6	6
Grpwij	13	2	12	9	2	4	7	11	1	2	14	17	4	3	7	108/142
Regress	4	15	5	8	15	13	10	6	16	15	3	0	13	14	10	

[a] see footnote a, table 13–3.

Table 13–5. Malmquist Output-Based Productivity Index, Annual Growth Rates (%)[a]

Hospital	1970–1971	1971–1972	1972–1973	1973–1974	1974–1975	1975–1976	1976–1977	1977–1978	1978–1979	1979–1980	1980–1981	1981–1982	1982–1983	1983–1984	1984–1985	Increase #
1	-2.2	+4.0	-5.4	+2.8	-0.7	-7.5	+1.9	+0.3	-6.1	-10.2	-2.7	+5.5	-6.1	-3.9	-4.2	6
2	+1.6	-1.6	+1.9	+3.5	-0.2	-6.1	-6.0	+0.5	-2.2	-1.3	+4.6	+7.5	+0.5	-4.0	-3.5	7
3	+14.8	-3.2	-3.3	+0.9	+12.2	+5.1	+4.8	+2.4	-14.1	-9.4	+1.8	+3.7	+4.6	-1.5	+4.0	10
4	+2.3	-1.7	+0.3	-2.9	-7.9	+4.8	-6.2	+5.0	-2.5	-2.8	+0.9	+7.8	-2.0	+2.8	-6.5	7
5	+2.4	-1.5	-4.6	+5.5	+5.3	+10.6	+0.2	-0.4	-2.3	-3.3	+1.7	+5.6	-2.9	-0.9	-2.9	7
6	+4.7	-39.1	+17.0	-23.3	-20.6	-7.9	-7.9	+6.4	+4.3	-2.7	-1.9	+6.1	-1.8	+1.2	+22.6	7
7	+11.5	-3.2	+1.3	-2.3	-4.6	-10.8	-7.1	-8.9	+1.3	-0.9	-6.6	+3.8	-3.0	+2.5	+4.2	6
8	-1.9	+3.2	+2.3	+9.7	-1.1	-7.8	-5.5	+0.4	-5.3	-0.2	-3.9	-0.7	+2.0	-1.2	+0.7	6
9	+1.0	-2.8	-4.8	-2.3	-6.0	-7.5	+0.6	-2.2	-3.0	-3.6	+3.3	+8.2	-6.1	-3.9	-1.6	4
10	+15.2	-8.7	+1.8	-4.8	-13.1	-3.2	-3.4	-1.8	-1.2	-8.1	+10.1	+8.4	+5.0	+8.4	-9.4	5
11	-6.6	-5.1	+3.2	+1.9	-4.2	-7.7	-7.8	-2.7	+1.5	-4.7	-2.0	+10.6	+1.6	-5.7	+5.9	5
12	-0.6	+3.0	-0.4	-0.7	-5.4	+7.6	+4.1	+0.4	-1.3	-0.6	+2.8	+1.6	-0.6	-0.1	+3.0	7
13	+4.2	-8.2	+3.1	+5.5	-4.6	-1.7	-7.4	-5.1	-7.6	-2.2	+5.4	+0.3	+2.6	-1.1	+3.9	7
14	-1.4	-4.9	-4.1	+5.0	-7.0	-0.1	-1.5	+3.1	-3.9	-8.5	+2.4	-1.5	+6.2	+0.1	-4.1	5
15	+14.3	-4.8	+5.8	-18.8	-13.7	-8.4	+3.6	-1.1	-7.9	+7.9	-4.8	-6.9	+5.5	-7.7	+4.1	6
16	+22.4	+3.8	-0.7	+1.7	-7.4	-0.9	-10.3	-5.4	+1.3	-5.4	-13.2	+4.5	-2.7	-4.1	-4.9	6
17	+6.9	-4.2	+0.1	-1.5	-6.9	-4.0	-2.7	+7.5	+12.2	+6.2	-4.7	+9.3	-2.9	-2.6	-7.6	5
Increase	12	4	9	8	2	4	6	8	5	4	11	14	7	5	7	106/255
Decrease	5	13	8	9	15	13	11	9	12	13	6	3	10	12	10	

[a] see footnote a, table 13–3.

end of the 1970s. Between 1980 and 1982, on the other hand, positive productivity changes were observed for many hospitals.

During the period 1970 to 1985, many new rules and changes in rules regarding legal or contractual conditions for taking time off from work were introduced. For example, in 1978, holidays increased from four weeks per year to five weeks (for doctors from five to six weeks), a new rule was introduced entitling parents to stay home for temporary care of sick children in 1977, for trade union activities in 1974 and 1977, and for care of newborns in 1978. In 1972, weekly work hours decreased by 2.5 hours to 40 hours per week. The stipulated number of hours worked per week for doctors decreased between 1970 and 1985 from an average of 49 hours in 1970 to an average of 41 hours in 1985.

At the end of the 1970s, a new recommendation regarding hospital personnel was introduced. This new recommendation was that any hospital or single department ought to have a sufficiently large number of employees to cover for employees on temporary leave of absence.

These new rules and changes in rules and recommendations regarding hospital personnel certainly affected hospital inputs and may have affected output. Depending on the type of rule or whether the hospital followed central recommendations or not, the effects on output could differ for ondividual hospitals and thus affect their relative efficiency and productivity.

With the input variables given, more short-term care admissions, doctor visits, or bed days in long-term care represent increases in hospital output. According to our results, most hospitals experienced technical advance in the early 1980s. During these years the pressure from politicians and managers on hospitals and individual hospital departments to produce more from a given input increased. One way for departments to produce more would be to discharge patients earlier.

Hospitals, however, reported decreases in average length of stay in almost every time period, not only in the early 1980s. Furthermore, we found that hospitals with reported decreases (increases) in average length of stay experienced regress (increase) in their best-practice frontiers. We conclude that earlier discharge of patients is not the main source of the productivity gain exhibited by many hospitals in the early 1980s. Instead, changes in politicians' and managers' behavior might have had an impact on, for example, the motivation of employees to use alternative medical techniques or a better organization of production. These issues deserve further study.

In order to get some feeling for our results in a long-term framework, we also calculated Malmquist productivity changes and the component

efficiency and technical change components for each hospital between our
two endpoint years, 1970 and 1985. Taking the logarithm of the 15th root
of these changes gives us an estimate of the average annual steady growth
rate required to account for the changes between 1970 and 1985. These
are displayed in table 13–6. Long-term average annual productivity
growth was negative for 13 of our 17 hospitals. Thirteen of 17 experienced
average annual technical regress, and only 5 out of 17 exhibited average
annual gains in efficiency.

Table 13–6. Steady-Growth Long-Run Average Annual Changes: 1970–1985
(%)[a]

Hospital	Average Annual Efficiency Change	Average Annual Technical Change	Average Annual Productivity Growth
1	−1.1	+0.1	−1.0
2	a[b]	+0.2	+0.2
3	a	+2.2	+2.2
4	a	−0.5	−0.5
5	a	+1.1	+1.1
6	−1.3	−2.4	−3.7
7	−0.2	−1.2	−1.5
8	+0.4	−2.2	−1.7
9	a	−0.9	−0.9
10	+1.2	−2.1	−0.9
11	−0.4	−0.7	−1.2
12	a	−0.1	−0.1
13	a	−0.9	−0.9
14	a	−0.8	−0.8
15	+0.4	−1.3	−0.9
16	+0.6	−1.5	−0.8
17	+1.1	−1.1	a
Increase	5	4	3
Decrease	4	13	13
No Change[b]	8	0	1

[a] Calculated using data from 1970 and 1985 only. Again we have $\ln M = \ln E + \ln P$, but
here,

$$E \text{ is } [D_o^{1985}(x^{1985}, y^{1985})/D_o^{1970}(x^{1970}, y^{1970})]^{1/15}$$

$$P \text{ is } \left[\frac{D_o^{1970}(x^{1985}, y^{1985})}{D_o^{1985}(x^{1985}, y^{1985})} \cdot \frac{D_o^{1970}(x^{1970}, y^{1970})}{D_o^{1985}(x^{1970}, y^{1970})} \right]^{1/2 \ 1/15}$$

[b] "a" means no change.

These rather negative results confirm the general pattern found in an earlier study (Lindgren and Roos, 1985). Changes in productivity for individual hospitals were calculated by a type of Paasche quantity index in five-year periods starting in 1960. Between 1970 and 1975 as well as between 1975 and 1980, Lindgren and Roos (1985) found progress in 8 cases and regress in 40 cases of a sample of 24 middle- and small-sized Swedish hospitals. The calculations, however, assumed cost-minimizing or revenue-maximizing behavior, and therefore also technical efficiency.

Since there are well-founded reasons to believe that neither cost-minimization nor revenue maximization has been a major objective of Swedish hospitals, the Lindgren and Roos (1985) results may be biased. Given that they also ignore technical efficiency, their productivity trends do not necessarily reflect technical change.

The relatively negative productivity trends found in this study may also reflect the fact that we have not been able to include any measures of change in quality of inputs or outputs. Recall as well that our nonlabor input proxy does not include equipment or building services. It is difficult to predict the effect of this omission.

To summarize: in this chapter we have introduced a modification of the Malmquist productivity index suggested by Caves, Christensen, and Diewert (1982). We have shown how this nonparametric index of productivity change may be decomposed into changes in efficiency and technical change. We have also shown how to calculate this index based on linear programming methods that exploit the reciprocal relationship between the output distance functions, which are the basis of the Malmquist indexes, and Farrell efficiency measures.

This approach has several advantages over traditional growth accounting or Törnqvist, Paasche, or Laspeyres index-type productivity measures. This index allows for, and measures, technical inefficiency. It does not presume optimizing behavior (this is implicit in methods that rely on factor shares to aggregate inputs and outputs). It also does not require data on prices. It readily allows for multiple outputs without aggregation.

These characteristics have led us to develop and use this index for analysis of the Swedish hospital sector. While primarily illustrative, our results suggest that there is wide variation in performance over the 1970–1985 period for the 17 hospitals in our sample. We find that technical inefficiency exists and that technical regress is fairly common. With further analysis and more refined data, these indexes could prove to be useful management and policy tools, especially in service sectors like the Swedish hospital sector, where traditional empirical tools may not be appropriate.

Notes

1. See also Caves, Christensen, and Diewert (1982b) and Caves, Christensen, and Swanson (1981).

2. See Shephard (1970) or Färe (1988) for such properties.

3. Analogous to equation (13.2), $D_o^t(x^{t+1}, y^{t+1}) = \inf\{\theta: (x^{t+1}, y^{t+1}/\theta)\varepsilon S^t\}$.

4. Given our output-oriented measures, the imposition of nonincreasing returns guarantees a solution to the programming problem in equation (13.7). No problem of existence of solution arises for $D_o^t(x^t, y^t)$ or $D_o^{t+1}(x^{t+1}, y^{t+1})$, since the data being assessed are always an element of the relevant technology. For example, $(x^{k',t}, y^{k',t})$ is included in the left-hand sides of the constraints in equation (13.6), which form the reference technology (in this case, S^t).

If we wish to define Malmquist indexes based on input distance functions, the assumption of nonincreasing returns is no longer sufficient to guarantee solutions to the mixed period ("out of sample") problems. Constant returns to scale are, however, sufficient in that case.

We note that the possibility of nonexistence occurs in the mixed-period problems precisely because the observation under evaluation is not included in the sample of observations forming the reference technology (i.e., it is not included in the summation terms in equation (13.7), for example). This is in contrast to standard DEA formulations and is what allows us to identify both technical change and the frontier in each period without having to resort to window techniques. Our approach also avoids misidentification of technical change, which may occur if we "pool" our data; if nonneutral technical change occurs and frontiers intersect, the convexity of the pooled or intertemporal reference set would obscure those changes.

5. To see this, consider the Mth output constraint from equation (13.6a), $\phi y_M^{k',t} - \Sigma_{k=1}^K \lambda^{k,t} y_M^{k,t} \leqq 0$. If we multiply all y's by a scalar p, then we have $\phi p y^{k',t} - \Sigma_{k=1}^K \lambda^{k,t} p y_M^{k,t} \leqq 0$. Since p is a scalar if all firms $k = 1, \ldots, K$ face the same price, the p's cancel and the solution values of ϕ and λ are unaffected. Note that in the mixed-period problems, this requires that all hospitals face the same prices, and that those prices are the same in the two periods, t and $t + 1$.

14 OWNERSHIP TYPE, PROPERTY RIGHTS, AND RELATIVE EFFICIENCY

Gary D. Ferrier

1. Introduction

Proprietary firms and cooperatives compete in many agricultural markets, especially in the dairy, cotton, and grain and oilseeds markets. While both types of firms are privately owned, the rights of ownership differ considerably between the two. The most notable difference is in owners' abilities to transfer ownership. The theoretical literature on property rights suggests that differences in the rights of ownership will have implications upon the efficiency with which a decision-making unit (DMU) operates. The effect of property rights on efficiency, however, is ultimately an empirical question. This chapter uses data envelopment analysis (DEA) to compare the levels of technical and scale efficiency for a sample of proprietary and cooperative fluid-milk processors in the U.S. to determine the effect of the attenuated rights of cooperative ownership upon productive efficiency.

Because of the large amount of government support that cooperatives receive and their economic importance in agricultural markets, knowledge of the comparative relative efficiencies of cooperative and proprietary firms is important. Though privately owned, cooperatives receive considerable public assistance in the form of preferential tax treatment,[1] research, management, and educational assistance from the U.S. Agricultural Cooperative Service, etc. In addition, cooperatives are important players in the U.S. economy: in 1989, farmer cooperatives had a business volume of \$71.1 billion,[2] and in 1990, 14 cooperatives were among the *Fortune* 500.

Private ownership is usually equated with the goal of profit maximization. Cooperatives, while privately owned, do not necessarily seek to maximize profit.[3] Regardless of firm objectives, both forms of organization should be concerned with technical efficiency—minimizing the resources used to produce a given level of output. In addition, scale efficiency is of interest when considering the potential for increased productivity in the long run. Thus, comparing the relative technical and scale efficiencies of cooperative and proprietary forms of ownership will provide valuable information about their advantages or disadvantages in production.

2. Property Rights and Productive Efficiency[4]

Neoclassical economic theory is based on particular beliefs concerning property rights and the ability to exchange resources. Specifically, it assumes that all resources are fully allocated and privately held, and that resources can be voluntarily exchanged with no information or transaction costs. In reality, these assumptions typically are not met—alternative systems of property rights exist, as do positive information and transaction costs.

The property rights model (Alchian, 1965) drew attention to the restrictive character of the neoclassical theory's assumptions. In particular, property rights theory argues that different institutional settings (such as ownership type) provide decision makers with different rights to the use of economic resources, thus imposing different constraints upon them. These constraints will affect the costs and rewards of production and might systematically affect the behavior of consumers and firms.

Consider the case of cooperatives. Cooperatives and proprietary firms differ in four important ways. First, a cooperative is created to serve the needs of its members; a proprietary firm is organized to maximize profits. Therefore, the two types of firms have different overall goals. Second, cooperatives and proprietary firms differ in their sources of control. Cooperatives are controlled by members who have an obligation to patronize them; proprietary firms are controlled by investors who may or may not be customers of the firm. The control is manifested through voting at annual meetings. Cooperatives give a single vote to each member regardless of ownership share; at proprietary firms, votes are allocated proportionally with investment. Third, the distribution of a cooperative's "profits" (net margin over cost) is based on patronage; proprietary profits are distributed on the basis of ownership shares. Fourth, and perhaps most important, while ownership of proprietary firms is easily transferred, ownership in cooperatives is nontransferable. When a cooperative purchases tangible assets, it issues equity shares equal to the value of the purchase to its members. By law, shares in the cooperative cannot appreciate in value, can earn no more than a "fair" rate of return, and can only be sold when the cooperative, not the member, redeems them.[5]

These differences could have large effects upon incentives, and therefore efficiency. For example, without transferability of ownership, the returns to innovation and monitoring cannot be captured by one innovator. These functions are costly to perform, while the benefits must be shared as a public good with all patron-members. As a result, free-rider problems may reduce the level of entrepreneurship in the cooperative. In addition, nontransferability of ownership creates a "portfolio problem" (Jensen and Meckling, 1979). Cooperative patron-members may not have the opportunity to specialize in the kind of risk offered by the market or to diversify against risk.

Numerous empirical studies have investigated the comparative efficiency of different ownership structures.[6] These studies have focused almost exclusively on the issue of private versus public ownership,[7] and have not produced strong evidence for the superiority of either form of organization. Unfortunately, most of the previous research on this topic has been flawed by its failure to control for relevant factors (such as input subsidies to public firms) or the use of inappropriate methods. For example, many studies have compared the efficiency of public versus private ownership by estimating "average" parametric production or cost functions that include a dummy variable to capture the effects of ownership. First, the failure to use a production or cost *frontier* could bias the results of these studies. Second, results of a parametric method are dependent on the choice of functional form. Finally, Mester (1989) has shown that "intercept tests" based on a dummy variable are valid only under fairly restrictive conditions, which usually are not met.

At least two previous studies (Färe, Grosskopf, and Logan, 1985; Byrnes, Grosskopf, and Hayes, 1986) have compared public versus private performance using DEA. Both studies involved firms operating in monopoly markets. Färe et al. found evidence that public electric utilities had higher overall efficiency measures than did private utilities; Byrnes et al. found no difference in the technical efficiency scores of public and private water utilities.

3. Measuring Technical and Scale Efficiency[8]

This section describes the DEA models used to derive input-oriented measures of technical and scale efficiency for each DMU in the data sample. The first step is to describe the technology that will serve as the point of reference for measuring relative efficiency. The technological relationship between inputs and outputs can be represented by the following piecewise linear input correspondence set:

$$L(Y) = \{X: \lambda \cdot M \geqslant Y, \lambda \cdot H \leqslant X, \vec{1}\lambda = 1, \lambda \geqslant 0\}, \qquad (14.1)$$

where $Y = (y_1, \ldots, y_s)$ is a vector of outputs, $X = (x_1, \ldots, x_m)$ is a vector of inputs, M is an $(n \times s)$ matrix of s observed outputs for each of n firms, and H is an $(n \times m)$ matrix of m observed inputs for each of n firms. For some observed pair of input and output vectors X and Y, the constraint $\lambda \cdot H < X$ states that the convex combination of DMU inputs is larger than the observed vector of inputs, while the constraint $\lambda \cdot M > Y$ says that a convex combination of DMU observed outputs must be greater than the observed vector of outputs. The input correspondence set includes all input vectors X that are capable of producing the output vector Y; as such, the set serves as the reference technology relative to which technical efficency will be measured.

The Farrell (1957) input measure of technical efficiency (TE) is given by

$$\text{TE}(X, Y) = \min\{\theta: \theta \cdot X \in L(Y)\}, \qquad (14.2)$$

where $L(Y)$ is given by equation (14.1). The Farrell input measure of technical efficiency may be calculated for each DMU as the solution to the input-oriented BCC primal model (Banker, Charnes, and Cooper, 1984) presented in chapter 2:

$$\min_{\theta, \lambda, s^+, s^-} z_o = \theta - \varepsilon \cdot \vec{1}s^+ - \varepsilon \cdot \vec{1}s^- \qquad (14.3)$$

subject to

$$Y\lambda - s^+ = Y_o$$

$$\theta X_o - X\lambda - s^- = 0$$

$$\vec{1}\lambda = 1$$

$$\lambda, s^+, s^- \geqslant 0,$$

where the subscript "o" denotes the DMU whose efficiency is being evaluated. Note that the convexity constraint allows for variables' returns to scale to be exhibited by the data.

The solution to equation (14.3), in particular θ^*, gives the technical efficiency for each DMU; i.e.,

$$TE(X, Y) = \theta^*. \tag{14.4}$$

This measure gives the proportion by which the observed DMU could radially contract its input usage and still produce at least its observed vector of output.

Scale efficiency can be used to determine how close an observed DMU is to the most productive scale size (Førsund and Hjalmarsson, 1979; Banker, 1984; Banker and Thrall, 1992). It may be calculated as the ratio of the measure of technical efficiency calculated under the assumption of constant returns to scale (CRTS) to the measure of technical efficiency calculated under the assumption of variable returns to scale (VRTS) (Banker, Charnes, and Cooper, 1984; Färe, Grosskopf, and Lowell, 1985). A measure of technical efficiency under VRTS is already given by the BCC model in equation (14.3). An input measure of technical efficiency under CRTS is given by the solution to the input-oriented CCR primal model (Charnes, Cooper, and Rhodes, 1978) discussed in chapter 2:

$$\min_{\theta, \lambda, s^+, s^-} z_o = \theta - \varepsilon \cdot \vec{1}s^+ - \varepsilon \cdot \vec{1}s^- \tag{14.5}$$

subject to

$$Y\lambda - s^+ = Y_o$$

$$\theta X_o - X\lambda - s^- = 0$$

$$\lambda, s^+, s^- \geq 0.$$

Notice that the difference between the BCC and CCR models is that the latter does not include the convexity constraints. This enlarges the feasible region for the solution, and characterizes the data as satisfying constant returns to scale.

Finally, scale efficiency (SE) for each DMU is given by

$$SE(X, Y) = \frac{\theta^*_{CCR}}{\theta^*_{BCC}}, \tag{14.6}$$

where θ^*_{CCR} is the solution to equation (14.5) and θ^*_{BCC} is the solution to equation (14.3).

A DMU may be scale inefficient if it exceeds the most productive scale size (thus experiencing decreasing returns to scale), or if it is smaller than the most productive scale size (thus failing to take full advantage of

increasing returns to scale). Färe, Grosskopf, and Lovell (1985) show that
the source of scale inefficiency (increasing or decreasing returns to scale)
may be found for each DMU by comparing the measures of technical
efficiency found under assumptions of CRTS (the CCR model in equation
(14.5)), VRTS (the BBC model in equation (14.3)), and nonincreasing
returns to scale (NIRTS) (the BCC model in equation (14.3)) with the
strict inequality on the convexity constraint replaced by a weak inequality).
As a result of this comparison, RTS can be characterized as being either
increasing, constant, or decreasing.

4. The Data and Results

The data used to empirically test the effect of different property rights on
relative firm efficiency consist of plant-level observations of cooperative
and proprietary U.S. fluid-milk processing firms for 1972.[9] Complete data
were available for 84 cooperative fluid-milk processing plants operating in
1972. A random sample of 84 proprietary fluid-milk processing plants was
selected for the same year. To satisfy disclosure restrictions, the data on
cooperatives and proprietary firms were separately rank ordered and then
aggregated into 28 groups of three plants for each type of firm.[10] The data
set thus consist of 56 DMUs, 28 cooperatives, and 28 proprietary firms.

One output and two inputs are specified in the analysis. Two output
measures are available, namely, value of shipments (VS) and value added
(VA). VS is the net selling value of all products shipped by a DMU. VA
is equal to VS less the cost of materials, supplies, fuels, purchased
electricity, and contract work.[11] VS was chosen as the better of the two
candidates because cooperatives do not purchase raw milk for processing;
rather, raw milk is provided to cooperatives by members, and therefore
the "price" of raw milk used to calculate VA for cooperatives may not
represent the true market price. The two inputs used in the analysis are
labor and capital. The quantity of labor is measured by hours of production labor; capital is measured by each DMU's total assets at year's end.

Descriptive statistics for the input and output variables, by ownership
type, appear in table 14–1. The largest DMUs are proprietary firms; the
smallest DMUs are cooperatives. On average, however, the cooperatives
are only slightly smaller than their proprietary counterparts. Because
there is only a single output and two inputs, it is possible to plot the
inputs used per unit of output.[12] Such a plot appears in figure 14–1. From
figure 14–1 it is evident that there is a high degree of disparity in DMU
input requirements.

Table 14–1. The data[a]

	Mean	Standard Deviation	Maximum Value	Minimum Value
Proprietary Firms				
Value of Shipments	16740.2	21380.7	95433.0	883.0
Hours of Labor	179.9	172.1	636.0	20.0
Total Assets	3345.3	3872.6	14821.0	157.0
Cooperatives				
Value of Shipments	16306.1	17239.8	65930.0	819.0
Hours of Labor	161.8	133.6	462.0	18.0
Total Assets	2813.9	2925.2	12356.0	126.0

[a] Value of Shipments and Total Assets are in thousands of dollars; Hours of Labor is in thousands of hours.

A DMU is technically efficient if and only if the solution to equation (14.3) is $\theta^* = 1$ and $s^{-*} = s^{+*} = 0$. Eight of the 56 DMUs were found to be technically efficient, including five of the cooperatives and three of the proprietary firms. Descriptive statistics of the technical and scale efficiency measures for the 56 DMUs in the sample are found in table 14–2. While the cooperatives achieve a higher average level of technical efficiency, both the cooperative and the proprietary fluid-milk processors show a relatively high degree of technical inefficiency. The average technical efficiency for cooperatives is 0.711, and for proprietary firms it is 0.617. A nonparametric test of the difference in mean levels of technical efficiency across ownership types indicates that the difference is statistically significant at the 2% level. The average levels of technical efficiency suggest that wasted or inefficiently employed resources raise the cost of production for cooperatives by 41% and for proprietary firms by 62%.

A DMU is scale efficient if it receives a value of $SE(X, Y) = 1$. Only three cooperatives were scale efficient, while no proprietary firms were scale efficient. Scale efficiency averaged 0.848 for cooperatives and 0.836 for proprietary firms. This difference is not statistically significant. The mean measures of scale efficiency imply that cooperatives and proprietary firms could reduce input usage by 17.9% and 19.6%, respectively, by adopting the most productive scale size. Most of the scale inefficiency is due to operating at a too small level of output—19 cooperatives and 22 proprietary firms operate in regions of increasing returns to scale. This is made more clear with the help of figure 14–2, which plots scale efficiency against output (value of shipments). Figure 14–2 implies the classic

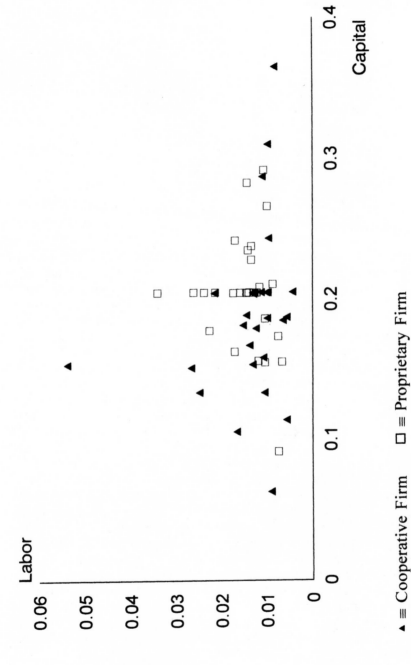

▲ ≡ Cooperative Firm   □ ≡ Proprietary Firm

Figure 14–1.   The "unit isoquant."

Table 14–2. Efficiency Measures

	Mean	Standard Deviation	Maximum Value	Minimum Value
Proprietary Firms				
Technical Efficiency	0.617	0.166	1.000	0.398
Scale Efficiency	0.836	0.156	0.999	0.382
Cooperatives				
Technical Efficiency	0.711	0.174	1.000	0.483
Scale Efficiency	0.848	0.157	1.000	0.410

U-shaped average cost curve of economic theory—scale efficiency increases initially as output increases, reaches a maximum, and then begins to decline.

One possible explanation for the relatively low technical-efficiency measures is found in the nature of the fluid-milk processing market. The market is characterized by large fluctuations in both output demand and raw milk supplies during the year. The firms must employ enough capital and labor needed to process fluid-milk during the peak periods; underutilization of capacity in the off-peak periods may be what is being measured as technical inefficiency. The scale inefficiency may be due to the firms' need to locate near their suppliers. Limited transportation possibilities for raw milk may limit the size of the firm.

5. Conclusion

DEA models were used to empirically compare the relative technical and scale efficiencies of proprietary and cooperative firms. Property rights theory would predict proprietary firms to be more efficient than cooperatives due to the former firms' owners' ability to transfer their ownership rights. Instead, it was found that cooperatives achieved a higher average level of technical efficiency. The average level of scale efficiency was similar for the two types of firms. Thus, it does not appear that cooperatives are at a productive disadvantage relative to their proprietary counterparts as a consequence of the attenuated property rights of its owners.

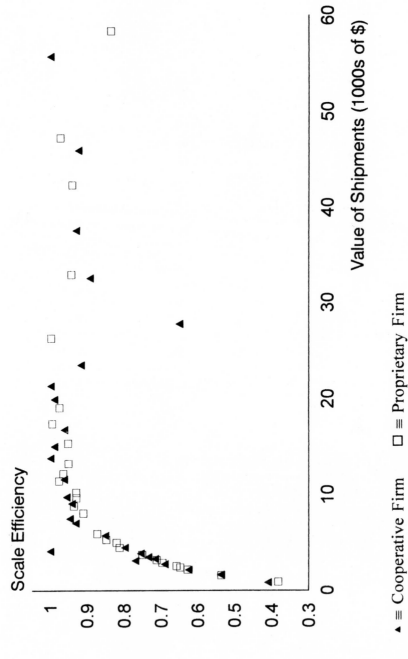

Figure 14-2. Scale efficiency and capacity.

Notes

1. Corporate income is subject to taxation at the corporate and personal levels—so-called double taxation. The income of cooperatives is only taxed at the personal level. Taxing cooperative income only at the personal level is thought to provide cooperatives with a cost-of-capital advantage. See Caves and Petersen (1986).

2. *Farmer Cooperatives*, February 1991, p. 5.

3. See LeVay and Bateman (1980) and LeVay (1983) for discussions of the objectives of cooperatives and justifications for government support of cooperatives.

4. See DeAlessi (1980) for a more thorough overview of the property rights literature.

5. Redemption usually only occurs at the time of a member's death or retirement.

6. See Vickers and Yarrow (1988) and Boardman and Vining (1989) for a more thorough review and references.

7. Exceptions are Porter and Scully (1987) and Hollas and Stansell (1988). Using a parametric frontier to estimate efficiency, Porter and Scully use the same data set as in the present study (though the output measure differs) to find cooperatives to be less efficient than proprietary firms. Hollas and Stansell examine the comparative *price* efficiency of proprietary, cooperative, and municipal electricity suppliers using a profit function. They conclude that while none of the ownership types consistently maximizes profits, the proprietary firms perform better than the others.

8. This section treats the general case of multiple inputs and multiple outputs. The empirical implementation of the models, however, uses only a single output.

9. Some of these data were originally published and analyzed in Porter and Scully (1987). Additional data were generously provided by Professor Porter.

10. For each type of firm, the three smallest plants were first aggregated, then the next three smallest plants, etc. This process maintains the confidentiality of the plants involved, but still allows for an examination of scale efficiency and returns to scale.

11. As might be expected, VS and VA are highly correlated with one another. The Pearson product-moment correlation between VS and VA is 0.884, and the Spearman rank correlation coefficient is 0.929.

12. Plotting the "unit isoquant" in this manner is valid only under constant returns to scale in production. Nonetheless, it does help to illustrate the differences among DMU performances.

15 A COMPARATIVE ANALYSIS OF FERRY TRANSPORT IN NORWAY

Finn R. Førsund and Erik Hernaes

1. Introduction

The trunk road system in Norway has to be supplemented by a number of ferries due to the long coastline with its numerous islands and fjords. There are about 150 ferry distances, serviced by about 250 ferries. In 1988, the cost of running these ferries amounted to about 40% of the maintenance of public roads.

Provision of ferry services takes place within a natural monopoly market because of the high fixed costs. Most of the ferries are run by private companies, but at a loss. The deficits are coverered rather automatically by the Directorate for Road Transport (DRT). In 1988, the deficits amounted to NOK 500 million ($71 million). Presently, the authorities specify in great detail the kind of services that are provided, taking the distribution of demand into consideration, in addition to setting prices. This is one way of preventing producers from reducing supply and or quality and obtaining monopoly profits. As long as the companies consider the chances of a surplus to be small, they have then virtually no incentives to economize. In fact, only 2 of the 150 ferry distances are run at a profit.

In the ferry business, the decision-making unit (DMU) for operating the ferries is a ferry company. The subsidies are paid to 23 ferry companies for running the ferry distances. It is up to the companies what type of ferries to use and how to run them as long as the demand-based minimum requirements of DRT are met. A company may run a ferry on several distances during a year.

It seems reasonable to assume that change of incentives could produce cost savings. An incentive would arise if companies were given a lump-sum subsidy, together with an agreement on transport services provided (to prevent monopoly profits). Cutting costs would then increase profits (including subsidy) if the company was allowed to keep all or a part. To launch such a system, one would need an initial assessment of "reasonable" costs. The aim of the present chapter is to provide the first "physical" stage of such a yardstick. Hence, we aim at estimating input requirements by an efficient producer.

DRT has already put some effort into "cost simulation" in order to reach an estimate of an obtainable cost function. In the terminology of Førsund and Hjalmarsson (1987), this approach is called the "engineering approach." In the case of the ferries, this estimate of required input was, however, far below (in the range of one half of) the average observed level (measured in cost), and the question of whether this difference is due to imperfect simulation or wasteful production is as yet unresolved.

Our way of approaching the problem is to seek out the most efficient of the observed ferries. It is worth noting that none may actually be efficient, in the "blueprint" sense (Førsund and Hjalmarsson, 1987). The best-practice production function will be piecewise linear and calculated as a DEA model with variable returns to scale on a cross-section data set.

2. Methodology

Measuring efficiency of micro units requires two basic ingredients:

- The benchmark for efficiency evaluation
- Definitions of the efficiency measures

2.1. Establishing the Benchmarks

The benchmark, usually called the frontier or best-practice tenchnology, must represent efficiency at least at the level of observed best practice. No true observation should be more efficient than shown by the frontier.

We have applied the nonparametric DEA models of chapter 2, sections 4.1–4.2 and 5.1–5.2, to establish benchmarks.[1] Since the main point is the scale properties adapted, we shall also refer to the BCC and CCR models of chapter 2 as the Variable Returns to Scale (VRS) model and Constant Returns to Scale (CRS) model, respectively.[2]

2.2. The Farrell Efficiency Measures

Having chosen how to establish the benchmark technology, the next question is how to measure efficiency. The distance from an observed unit to the frontier can be measured in a number of ways. The original proposals of Farrell (1957) are to measure the relative distance to the frontier, keeping the inputs fixed in the observed proportions.[3] The efficiency measures adopted in the sequel are the Farrell efficiency measures as generalized to variable returns-to-scale technologies in Førsund and Hjalmarsson (1974, 1979, 1987). This system of efficiency measures is set out below and illustrated by using observation P5 in figure 15–1. This figure combines the envelopment surfaces of figures 2–5 to 2–8 in chapter 2 for the same data set. The definitions are made with reference to the VRS envelopment surface P1, P2, P3, P4.

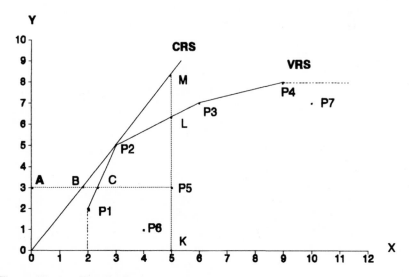

Figure 15–1.   Farrell efficiency measures.

E_1 = input-saving technical efficiency = AC/AP5
E_2 = output-increasing technical efficiency = KP5/KL[4]
E_3 = gross scale efficiency = AB/AP5 = KP5/KM[5]
E_4 = pure scale efficiency (input corrected) = E_3/E_1 = AB/AC
E_5 = pure scale efficiency (output corrected) = E_3/E_2 = KL/KM

Changing the unity constraint on the weights in the BCC models (chapter 2, sections 4.1–4.2) into an inequality constraint of equal to or less than 1 yields a frontier technology exhibiting nonincreasing returns to scale (see Grosskopf, 1986). In figure 15–1, the graph of this technology is OP2P3P4. We have chosen to work with VRS technology as the main assumption, realizing that convex combination of existing ferries may lead to unrealistic "designs." But CRS is clearly even more unrealistic for small boats, and will only serve as reference for scale calculations.

2.3. Scale Efficiency

Since scale turns out to be important for efficiency, as treated here, and scale measures are not covered in full detail in chapter 2, we will expand on these measures. The interpretation of the scale measures is different from the technical-efficiency measures. The measure E_3 is the ratio of the minimal input coefficents (or maximal productivities) at the frontier to the observed input coefficients of a unit. The pure measures E_4 and E_5 have the same interpretation. Thus, the scale measures do not directly show input saving or output increasing as E_1 and E_2 do. To realize the frontier minimal input coefficients, (in general) both output and input have to change.

Calculation of scale-efficiency measures are, of course, only relevant when specifying variable returns to scale frontier. Any scale inefficiency is due to either decreasing or increasing returns to scale. Note that it is nonsensical to ask what the scale properties of the observations are, because we do not make any assumptions about the technologies of the observations. It is only relevant to ask about scale properties of points on the frontier. We have identified two interesting frontier points for each observation, moving in input-saving and output-increasing directions, as shown in figure 15–1 for observation P5.[6]

To determine the scale properties of the frontier reference points, one can, for *unique* solutions, most conveniently inspect the sum of weights, λ, for the solutions with CRS frontier (see Banker, 1984; Banker et al., 1984). If the sum of weights is less than one, we have increasing returns.

A sum less than one means that the best-practice points determining the CRS frontier technology are scaled downwards when defining the reference points on the CRS frontier.

Consider the data points P1–P7 illustrated in figure 15–1. Unit P2 is the only one with positive weight when solving the CCR input-orientation problem (chapter 2, section 5.1), specifying CRS. In order to scale point P2 down to the reference point B, the optimal weight must be OB/OP2 < 1.[7]

If the sum of weights is greater than one, this implies that we have decreasing returns at the adjusted point. The reference point is in general found by scaling up from observed points defining the CRS technology. Solving the CCR output-orientation problem (chapter 2, section 5.2), the point P2 is scaled up to the reference point M, applying the weight 0M/0P2 > 1.[8]

If both E_1 and E_2 are calculated for the VRS frontier, we may have different scale properties at the corresponding reference points, as is the case for unit P5 in figure 15–1. One way of getting only one expression for scale properties is to determine the "average" scale property over the part of the envelopment surface between the reference points for inefficient units, using the relationship established in Førsund and Hjalmarsson (1979, 1987):

$$\varepsilon = \ln E_2 / \ln E_1,$$

where ε is the average scale elasticity. The nature of the average returns to scale is then determined by

$$E_1 > E_2 \Rightarrow \text{increasing average returns to scale}$$
$$E_1 < E_2 \Rightarrow \text{decreasing average returns to scale}[9]$$

2.4. Special Features of DEA

By placing the benchmark technology as a linear faceted convex "lid" over the observations, increasing returns can only be experienced from the "start"[10] of the output ranges. When specifying VRS, there must be at least one unit on the frontier that has constant returns. Very efficient large units would come out as having CRS, and for other units increasing returns would then be prevalent, while efficient units of medium size divide the set in "smaller" units having increasing returns and "larger" units having decreasing returns.[11] If the true technology is increasing returns, imposing convexity results in negative bias of efficiency scores.

Dropping the convexity assumption, the "staircase" or Free Disposal Hull (FDH) approach of Henry Tulkens and associates (Deprins, 1984) may be used to envelop the data. Keeping the convexity assumption of output- and input-possibility sets, which is violated by FDH, but allowing for increasing returns Petersen (1990) has shown how DEA can be accommodated.

A general feature of the DEA approach when specifying VRS is that units at both ends of the size distribution may be identified as efficient simply for lack of other comparable units.[12] In figure 15-1, units P1 and P4 will both be efficient. It is a general identification problem whether scale inefficency of technically efficient units is real or is due to the VRS specification and the method of enveloping the data.

A special technical feature of the DEA method should also be mentioned. Units located at the horizontal and vertical extensions of Farrell's original unit isoquant, or in general on the corresponding extensions of the multidimensional envelopment surface, will get efficiency values of one. For instance, in figure 15-1, a unit located on the vertical extension from unit P1 to the abscissa axis will get the technical efficiency score of one even though unit P1 uses the same amounts of inputs, but produces more output. Thus, units placed on "vertical" or "horizontal" edges of the frontier technology are not efficient in the Pareto sense. As pointed out in chapter 2, problems of this nature are revealed when in the solution for units with technical efficiency scores of one, we also find slacks in the input or output constraints. Instead of employing the technique of the non-Archimedean constant as in the models of chapter 2 (sections 4 and 5), we have used the two-stage procedure of finding the true efficient units by running the Additive model of chapter 2 (section 2) (see chapter 4 for a discussion and a method of finding the Pareto-efficient units).

3. Data

3.1. Data Sources

We have used two main sources of data. The most important is yearly accounts over the years 1984–1988 of costs associated with the running of each ferry. All ferries making up a part of the main road system of Norway, which is the responsibility of the Government, are covered by the data. These data are reported by ferry companies to the authorities (DRT), as a basis for the support given to the companies. As noted in the introduction, most of the ferry transport runs at a loss,[13] which is covered by central authorities.

The accounting data cover all expenses related to the running of ferries: wages and social costs, fuel, maintenance, and insurance. It is hard to find out how capital costs are reported. In principle, the costs should cover depreciation and "normal" remuneration on own capital. In practice, it seems that capital costs are generally only reported insofar as they consist of interest on debt. Return on owners' capital is hardly reported. In addition to data in value terms, there is also information for each ferry about the time in service and the total number of kilometers run per year.

The other important data source is the ship register of ferries held by DRT, which contains information on the type, size, vintage, purchase price, speed, etc. of ferries. We linked the two data sets, obtaining time series data for each ferry for the period 1984–1988. In this chapter, we will only utilize the data set for 1988, due to the construction of the maintenance variable as explained below.[14]

3.2. Output

Given the data available at this stage, we have defined output of a ferry as the product of the total length run in 1988 multiplied by the capacity in standardized cars of the ferry. Output is termed PK.

Other aspects of ferry service output are the number of ports to call on and the length of crossing. If long distances are easier to service (per km) than short distances, since the latter require much maneuvering, unit fuel consumption will differ, as it will due to systematic different exposure to rough weather. Our data do not as yet allow identification of which distances the ferries have sailed, but only the total number of kilometers.

We find it reasonable to assume that inputs (costs) are associated only with running a certain type of ferry, and not with the actual load. Given this assumption, the analysis of efficient allocation of ferries can be broken down into two stages: first, best practice in providing output, and second, optimal allocation of ferry capacity. In this chapter, we analyze the production stage only.

Finally, some remarks on waiting time are in order. We are now analyzing production in terms of unit-kms per time unit, so we do not distinguish between a large ferry running at long intervals and a small ferry running frequently. In the latter case, average waiting time for cars and passengers will be shorter. If efficiency varies with capacity of the ferry, one will therefore have to take the value of time into consideration when allocating transport capacity to ferry distance.

3.3. Inputs

In this analysis, we will distinguish between "ordinary" inputs: capital, labor, fuel, and materials on the one hand, and factors that may explain variation in the relationship between inputs and output on the other hand. The latter group consists of the ferry company (one company may run a number of ferries), type of ferry, and vintage, i.e., building year of ferry.

For each ferry in the cross section, capital is, of course, given. However, since we want to study efficiency also with respect to capital, and since companies may choose which ferry to run specific distances in the short run, we have found it relevant to include capital as a variable. The frontier is then of the ex ante type (see Førsund and Hjalmarsson, 1987).

Capital input can be measured in physical or value terms. In value terms, we have experimented with estimating market value from the insurance premium. From an insurance company, we have been informed about the usual practice in setting the premium. This premium consists of two parts. The first is related to the size of the ferry, through a factor that is set according to past performance of the ferry (company). Variation in behavior will influence this component. The second is related to an assumed market value, through a constant that is the same for all ferries. We are missing sufficient information to separate the two parts, but we have information about the ratio between insurance premium and assumed market value. Assuming that the information on the ratio is better than the implied market value, we did run a regression of this ratio on the ratio of premium and historic price and age.[15] From estimated coefficients, the market value is predicted for each ferry and termed UC.

Secondly, the procedure for setting market value (reported from the insurance company) is implemented directly for each ferry. This procedure is also not totally convincing. It runs as follows: for the first five years, the value of the ferry is constant in real terms; thereafter, the value falls with same rate as inflation, for about 10 years; and thereafter for another 10 years, the value is reduced by inflation and another 40%. This measure was also predicted for each ferry, and termed MV.[16]

As a physical measure of capital, we used capacity of the ferry in number of (standardized) cars, PB.

In principle, data allow the input of labor to be measured in two ways.

First, total wages are reported. If labor is heterogeneous, it will create problems to use wages as a measure. Even in the presence of cost minimization (which we assert is far from certain, given the incentive structure) and identical production functions for all units, total labor cost will vary across units if the prices of different types of labor vary across ferries, e.g., due to variations in local labor markets.

Alternatively, one could use reported crew size and number of shifts. Unfortunately, the latter piece of information is missing for many ferries. In addition, overtime is not included. Furthermore, there is no information on composition of crew.[17]

After checking the relationship between wages and crew size, we have chosen to work with total wages, WG, as an indicator of labor input.[18]

Input of fuel constitutes around 15% of total cost, excluding capital costs. Companies report cost of fuel per ferry, and from DRT we have obtained information about fuel prices paid by companies in 1988. This price varies a great deal across companies, and we have used the reported company price to convert the value of fuel into liters per year per ferry, termed FU. This procedure rests on the assumption that the reported price from a company applies to all ferries run by this company (there are 23 ferry companies and about 250 ferries).

Maintenance and repair vary a great deal from year to year, since major replacements are required at fixed intervals, e.g., every four years. Furthermore, repairs may occur lagged in relation to distance sailed. For each ferry, we calculated average cost per kilometer over a five-year period, and multiplied by kilometers in 1988. The predicted "cost incurred" in 1988 was termed MN.

At this stage, it was important to check the methods and explore the basic production of transport services with ferries in "normal" traffic. Therefore, we have excluded ferries with incomplete information about any of the variables, as well as ferries in service less than five years, since these had not yet had any chance to go through a full maintenance cycle. Also excluded were ferries without positive inputs of all types. This leaves us with 138 out of the original 236 ferries in service in 1988. The ferries included in our data set represent 65% of total cost in 1988, excluding capital cost.

3.4. Empirical Survey of the Data Set

An overview of the variables we use is given in table 15–1, together with some empirical measures. As noted in the column labeled "Average," the

Table 15-1. Summary Statistics of Output and Inputs

Output and inputs	Total	Average	Stand.d.	Max.	Min.
Output					
PK Total transport (1000 car-kms)	306,616	2,222	1,872	9261	6
Inputs					
Capital measure PB Car capacity	5,307	39	22	140	12
Capital measure MV Market value (NOK 1000)	1,357,862	9,840	10,050	50,890	549
Capital measure UC Insurance premium (NOK 1000)	2,576,139	18,668	11,808	51,228	2042
WG Wage sum (NOK 1000)	438,194	3,175	1,357	7,141	1
FU Fuel (1000 litres)	73,100	529	346	1,810	6
MN Maintenance (NOK 1000)	111,987	811	392	2,215	10

estimated value of capital ranges on average from approximately NOK 9.8–18.7 million between the two value approaches. These figures clearly illustrate the problem of measuring capital. The empirical correlations between the variables are set out in table 15–2. Note that the correlation between output (PK) and size of ferry (PB) is high, and that the capital measures are also fairly well correlated.

A successful DEA analysis depends crucially on the quality of the data. Also, for the understanding and interpretation of results, we feel that it is important to get a real "feel" for the data. The distributions of partial productivities give insights about the structure, as well as revealing any outlier problem of significance for the efficiency analysis. Partial productivity numbers, e.g., labor productivity, are often used in practice, and it is therefore of interest to compare DEA results with partial approaches. The distributions are given in figures 15–2 to 15–4.[19] These *Salter diagrams* (Forsund and Hjalmarsson, 1987) should be read in the following way. Each histogram represents one unit. The size of ferries measured by output is represented by the width of the histogram. Size is normalized by dividing individual output levels with total output. The measuring units for the input coefficients on the ordinate axis follow from

Table 15-2.   Partial Correlation Coefficients between Variables

	PK	WG	FU	MN	MV	PB	UC
PK	1	0.70	0.83	0.69	0.83	0.89	0.67
WG		1	0.80	0.63	0.59	0.67	0.66
FU			1	0.73	0.66	0.73	0.75
MN				1	0.48	0.57	0.53
MV					1	0.85	0.69
PB						1	0.71
UC							1

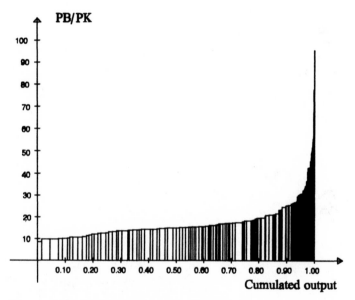

Figure 15-2.   Capital input coefficent distribution.

the units given in the first column in table 15-1. The units are entered according to increasing value of input coefficients.

All distributions show considerable skewness with pronounced "worst-practice" tails, and have the shape of a mirror image of a J on its back. The histogram representation allows us to locate small and large units (in terms of output[20]).

The distribution of the capital input coefficients with car capacity as capital measure is shown in figure 15-2. The "best-practice" tail composes about 10% of output and consists of large ferries. The loop of the J starts at about 80% of total output. The last part of the tail, representing about 10% of output, consists of small units only.[21]

The wage productivity distribution in figure 15–3 shows that the largest ferries, in terms of output, have the lowest wages per unit of output.[22] This finding may reflect manning rules giving larger ferries, in terms of capacity, a cost advantage, but it could also be due to distance covered. There is an efficient tail of about 8% of capacity output for large ferries with small wage coefficients and an upper tail starting at about 80% capacity for mainly small ferries with high and steeply rising wage coefficients.

The fuel input coefficient distribution in figure 15–4 follows the same pattern as the two previous distributions with reference to the location of small and large units, but the J-shape is not so pronounced; the efficient tail, composing about 15% of output, shows a greater difference. We have, then, slowly rising scores of medium-sized ferries representing output from 15% to 70% and a more steeply rising tail of mainly small ferries representing 30% of output.[23]

The maintenance coefficient distribution in figure 15–5 shows clearly that largest ferries have the smallest coefficients. The efficient tail consists

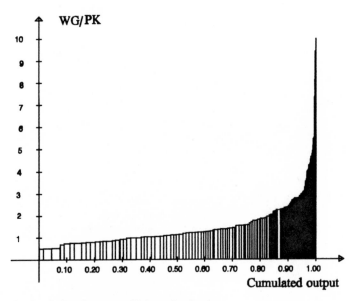

Figure 15–3.   Labor input coefficient distribution.

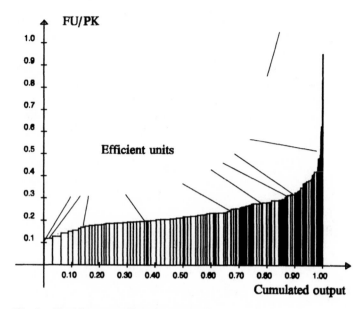

Figure 15–4.   Fuel input coefficient distribution.

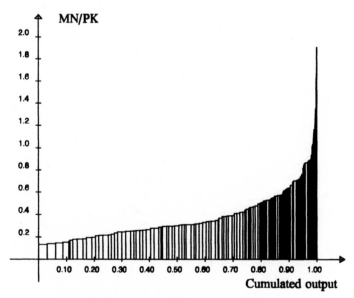

Figure 15–5.   Maintenance input coefficient distribution.

of the four largest units, representing about 10% of output.[24] About 20% of the output at the worst-practice tail is produced by mainly small ferries with steeply rising coefficients.

Without calculating any precise measures the general impression from the partial distributions is that size in terms of output has a systematic positive relationship with partial productivity. There is no apparent best-practice outlier problem, except for labor, where the two very small units have coefficients much smaller than the other best-practice units. The outliers are mainly at the worst-practice end.

4. Empirical Results

The VRS models (chapter 2, sections 4.1–4.2 and 5.1–5.2) have been solved for the 138 ferries in the final data base for the three alternative definitions of capital. We have preferred to concentrate on the most reliable capital measure, namely, the physical measure.

The output of data from DEA models is rather huge, representing a problem of conveying main results.[25] We have preferred to concentrate on the distributions of all five efficiency measures defined in section 2. These are set out in figures 15–6 to 15–11. The figures should be read in the following way. Each histogram represents one unit. The size of ferries measured by output is shown by the width of the histogram. Size is normalized by dividing each ferry's output with total output. The efficiency scores are measured as the height of the histogram on the ordinate axis. The units are ordered according to increasing value of E_1 to E_5, the efficiency scores.

The input-saving efficiency measure E_1 is shown in figure 15–6. Let us start by looking at the right-hand tail of efficient units. There are in fact 12 units that are efficient,[26] representing about 10% of total output. Moving to the left, efficiency falls in two steps with reference to slope of inclination, taking us down to an efficiency score value of 0.80 and then to 0.70, representing 0.65 and 0.20, respectively, on the cumulated output axis. At the tail of least-efficient units, there is a rapid fall from 0.70 down to 0.45. The figure 0.45 means that this least-efficient ferry could produce the observed output with only 45% of observed inputs if operating with frontier efficiency. With reference to the connection between size and efficiency, we see that we have both large and small ferries as efficient, but with a clear tendency for the smallest ferries to be concentrated at the tail of the distribution with least efficient units.[27] Table 15–3, showing correlation coefficients between output and efficiency

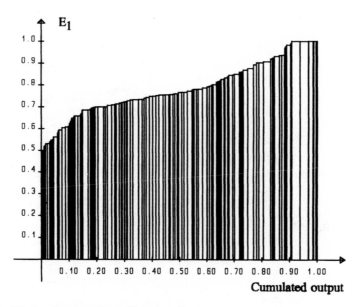

Figure 15–6.   Input-saving efficiency, E_1.

Table 15–3.   Partial Correlation Coefficients Between Size and Efficiency Measures[a]

	PK	E_1	E_2	E_3	E_4	E_5
PK	1	0.20	0.44	0.68	0.70	0.49
E_1		1	0.85	0.57	0.11	−0.37
E_2			1	0.83	0.54	−0.09
E_3				1	0.86	0.45
E_4					1	0.71
E_5						1

[a] Running regressions between the efficiency measures and output, PK, yield positive coefficients significant at level 0.02 for E_1 and level 0.000001 and less for the other coefficients.

measures, reveals a correlation coefficient of 0.20 between output and input-saving efficiency.

Inspecting the distribution of output-increasing efficiency, E_2, in figure 15–7, we see that the shape of the distribution is very similar to the distribution for E_1. The interpretation of an efficiency score is now the

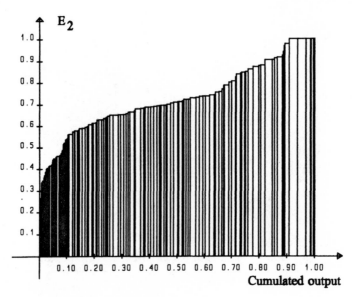

Figure 15-7. Output-increasing efficiency, E_2.

ratio of observed output to potential output at the frontier employing the observed amounts of inputs. One difference is that the least-efficient tail now represents only 10% of output and encompasses the lion's share of the small ferries. There is also here a rapid deterioration in efficiency from 0.55 to 0.23 for the tail of least-efficient ferries. The positive correlation between size and efficiency is more pronounced, with a correlation coefficient of 0.44.

The distribution for gross scale efficiency is shown in figure 15-8. We have a group of five scale-efficient units with about 8% of total output. Note that both large (the two largest[28]) and small units (disappearing as vertical lines) are scale efficient. Even with only one output, the faceted surface of the frontier implies that optimal scale, i.e., a scale elasticity of one, is not unique with respect to output. The smallest ferries are now among the least efficient, and almost all belong to the least-efficient tail of about 20% of total output, with the range between 0.19 and 0.55. Size is obviously positively correlated with gross scale efficiency. Table 15-3 shows the correlation coefficient to be 0.68.

As pointed out in section 2, the scale-efficiency measure, E_3, for the VRS technology can be interpreted as the input-saving efficiency measure for the CRS technology. Recalling figure 15-1, we have that small units

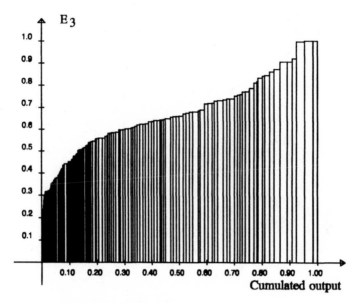

Figure 15–8.   Gross scale efficiency, E_3.

such as unit P1 that are efficient under VRS become inefficient when assuming CRS. The importance of the choice of technology is clearly demonstrated for small units in our data set.

Removing technical inefficiency and concentrating on pure scale efficiency, the two efficiency distributions are shown in figures 15–9 and 15–10. Moving to the frontier in the input-saving direction, the resulting distribution for E_4 is shown in figure 15–9. The efficient units have about 25% of output, and then there is a gradual decrease in efficiency down to the level 0.80, representing about 0.20 on the cumulated output axis. The least-efficient tail consists exclusively of small units representing about 10% of output. The correlation coefficient between output and pure scale efficiency (input corrected) has increased to 0.70 from 0.68 for the gross scale measure.

Moving to the frontier in the output-increasing direction yields a distribution, shown in figure 15–10, somewhat different in shape than the other. Units with efficiency scores above 0.90 compose about 80% of output, with the least-efficient tail of rapidly falling efficiency values again representing about 20% of output. The small units are also now concentrated at the least-efficient tail, but are also spread out over higher-efficiency values. The correlation coefficient shown in table 15–3 between

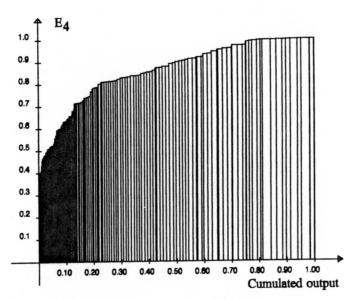

Figure 15–9.   Pure scale efficiency, E_4, input adjusted.

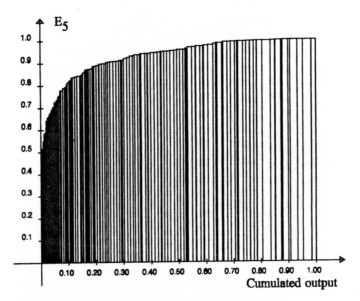

Figure 15–10.   Pure scale efficiency, E_5, output adjusted.

output and pure scale efficiency (output corrected) drops to 0.49 from 0.70 for the input-corrected measure.

A summary impression of the levels of the efficiency distributions is provided in figure 15–11. The distributions for E_1, E_2, and E_3 have shapes of a mirror image of a lying S, and are below the E_4 and E_5 distributions per construct. It also follows that the gross efficiency curve must be below the others, because it reflects both technical and scale inefficiency. The location of the E_2 curve below the E_1 curve implies that concentrating on realizing more output from the inputs yields the highest increase in efficiency. The pure scale-efficiency curve E_5 tells us that if ferries realize the output-increasing potential, ferries representing about 20% of output are really too small. The correlation coefficients between the measures show rather high positive values between E_1, E_2, and E_3, weak correlation between E_1 and E_4, and negative correlation between E_2 and E_4, E_5.

The ultimate purpose of calculating the efficiency distributions is to get ideas for productivity improvement when we look more closely at differences between best-practice units and the inefficient units. In table 15–4, the frequency of occurrence of efficient ferries in the 138 reference sets

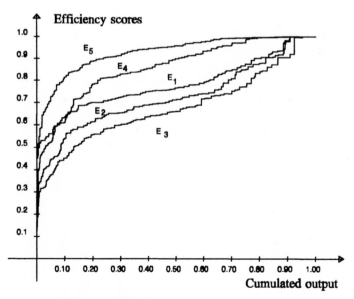

Figure 15–11.   Efficiency distributions E_1–E_5.

Table 15–4. Frequency of frontier Units in Reference Sets (Absolute Numbers, Physical Capital Measure)

Frontier Units	Output $(10^6$ car-kms)	E_1 (VRS)	E_2 (VRS)	$E_3 = E_1(CRS)$ $= E_2(CRS)$
1	0.08	5	7	13
18	1.37	41	20	—
20	2.55	14	9	—
47	0.08	15	6	—
49	0.08	53	34	6
50	0.01	65	51	—
72	0.06	1	2	—
73	4.66	102	98	74
74	0.06	4	4	—
76	0.22	54	63	46
111	9.26	83	109	129

are set out. Table 15–4 should reveal the best-practice ferries of greatest interest as benchmarks. Ferries no. 111 and 73 are the most dominating ones in all specifications. They are both larger than average; no. 111 is in fact the largest ferry in the sample, about four times the average size, while no. 73 is about twice the average size. When restricting the best-practice technology to be CRS, no. 111 has a frequency of 129 and no. 73 has a frequency of 74. When specifying VRS, more units, of course, appear on the frontier. Since new units will tend to be smaller ones, it is not surprising that no. 73 gets higher frequencies in both directions, namely, 102 and 98, while the frequencies for no. 111 go down to 83 and 109 in the input-saving and output-increasing direction, respectively. Since no. 111 is the largest unit, it is to be expected that this unit is in more reference sets the larger the inefficient units. It is remarkable that small units like nos. 76, 1, and 49 are efficient in both specifications. Being efficient in the CRS case also implies that these units are scale efficient in the VRS case. The units located on the CRS frontier must, of course, also be on the VRS frontier.

The smallest ferry, by a large margin, appears efficient (but not scale efficient) in the VRS case. This finding may be due to the method discussed in section 2 and illustrated by unit P1 in figure 15–1.[29] As suggested in section 2, when a large unit is efficient, increasing returns dominate, here only six reference points have decreasing returns in the input-saving direction, and nine in the output-increasing direction and nine average returns are less than one.[30] To utilize fully all the DEA results, the reference set of each of the 138 ferries should be inspected and key characteristics of these units compared with the observation at hand. The size of weights show the most relevant units with which to compare. In addition to the efficiency scores themselves, the slacks on the input constraints reveal special sources of inefficiency; i.e., the appearance of a positive slack indicates that the use of this input is a special source of inefficiency. However, a complete presentation is outside the framework of this chapter.

Summary results for structural efficiency are reported in table 15–5. Based on the individual measures of the distributions above, the total input-savings potential and the total output-increasing potential can be calculated by carrying out the proper weighted aggregation as defined in table 15–5. Results for the two other capital measures are also shown. The numbers for the market value and the physical-capacity input measures do not differ too much, while the insurance premium measure

Table 15–5. Structural Efficiency: Potential Input in Relation to Observed Input and Observed Output in Relation to Potential Output

	Capital Measure		
Structural Efficiency Measures S_1 and S_2	PB (Capacity)	MV (Market)	UC (Insurance)
$S_{1i} = \dfrac{\Sigma_j (x_{ij} E_{1ij}(t) - s_{ij}^-)}{\Sigma x_{ij}}$			
$s_{ij}^- = $ slack on input constraint no. i			
$t = VRS$			
$i = WG$	46	53	45
$i = FU$	66	65	55
$i = MN$	74	66	48
$i = PB$	73	—	—
$i = MV$	—	70	—
$i = UC$	—	—	51
$S_2 = \dfrac{\Sigma y_j}{\Sigma_j \left(\dfrac{y_j}{E_{2j}(t)} + s_j^+ \right)}$			
$s_j^+ = $ slack on the output constraint			
$t = CRS$	62	68	57
$t = VRS$	68	70	58

yields higher total gains. The main explanation is a more skewed distribution of the latter measure. The number 68 in the last row and first column means that observed output is 68% of potential output, given the observed levels of inputs used by each unit. Total output could be increased by $(100/68 - 1)100\% = 47\%$ if all the ferries adopted the frontier technology. The differences between the VRS and CRS technologies are small. The impact of small units moving from the top to the bottom parts of the distributions is almost negligible for the sector as a whole.

The total potential savings of inputs is around 25% to 30% $(100 - 75/70)$ for PB and MV as capital measures and around 40% for UC. The influence on total savings of different factor proportions is almost negligible. The level of input saving is, in the aggregate, considerably smaller than the level for potential increase in output. This means that ferries of suboptimal scale size dominate, as shown in the figures.

4.1. DEA and Partial Productivities

When calculating partial productivity measures as shown in figures 15–2 to 15–5, one naturally tends to focus on best practice. A simultaneous analysis as provided by DEA may give quite a different ranking between units. As an example, the frontier units are indicated in the fuel input coefficient distribution in figure 15–4. The units are spread out over the entire distribution, with two small units at the best-practice frontier and one with a fuel coefficient about eight times higher than the least productive shown in figure 15–4. The latter unit is best practice with respect to labor. A general lesson to be learned is that best-practice units of the partial distributions will tend to be members of the set of frontier units. But it is an empirical question how many there will be from the range of best-practice units, and there will be other units also not predictable from a partial approach.

5. Explanations of Efficiency Scores

5.1. Type of Ferry

There are two main types of ferries: "fjord-ferries" and "pendulum-ferries." The latter are bidirectional ferries, built for lighter crossings. Fjord-ferries are constructed for rougher crossings. One would expect them to be less efficient, since transport under more difficult conditions is not specified as a separate output. To check on this, we calculated the output-based structural-efficiency measure for the two types of ferries. Pendulum-ferries turned out to be slightly more efficient, and more so if CRS is assumed. They are generally larger (with a capacity of 50 cars compared to 29 for fjord-ferries). Allowing variable returns to scale, the difference depends strongly on capital measure, being larger if we use MV (market value). Using capacity as the capital input measure, hardly any difference remains, leaving us with the conclusion that efficiency variation between ferry types is due mainly to higher price of the ferry itself per unit of capacity.

5.2. Vintage

Technical progress represents a potential for newer ferries to be more efficient than old ones. The building years of the ferries are in the data set. Running simple regressions of the efficiency measures on building year, it turns out that there is no significant relationship between technical efficiencies E_1 and E_2, but there is between the scale measures E_3, E_4, and E_5.[31] Checking further, there is a positive correlation of 0.60 (and a significant regression coefficient) between size and building year, and we know that there is a positive relation between output and efficiency for all measures. Recall that our scale measures have the interpretation of potential productivities compared with observed ones. The tentative conclusion is then that technical progress has no impact on technical efficiency due to operational inefficiency, but a positive impact on productivities showing up as improved scale efficiency. However, due to the correlation between size and building year, we cannot separate a pure size effect from technical progress.

5.3. Company

To capture any influence of ferry companies on the operation of ferries, we aggregate ferry efficiency scores into company results. A company efficiency distribution of the output-increasing type for the VRS frontier can be constructed by dividing the sum of actual output for all ferries owned by a company by the sum for the same ferries of potential (best-practice) output for each ferry. A small company turned out to be most efficient, with its ferry or ferries at about 90% efficiency. The majority of large companies follow. The small companies are concentrated at the least-efficient end, as in the complete distribution in figure 15–7. If we interpret only the performance of the best company (90%) to be feasible, this still gives a rate of aggregate actual output to potential output of 70/90, or 77%. Hence, most of the variation in efficiency is "explained" by company variation. This indicates that a closer look at differences between companies might be worthwhile.

6. Concluding Remarks

From an efficiency analysis point of view, the results so far indicate a substantial variation in efficiency across ferries, with a total potential for input saving in the range of 25% or an output increase of almost 50%. These results hold true for both types of ferries, namely, fjord-ferries and pendulum-ferries. Most of the variation in efficiency and potential saving remains on the company level. Efficiency varies positively with output, which is positively correlated with the capacity size of ferries. There is a positive relation between scale efficiency and building year, indicating a positive effect of technical change working through improving productivities, but this cannot be separated from a pure size effect.

Policy implications of our results should be drawn with great care. The role of exogeneous demand must be stressed. If demand is not sufficient, it is unrealistic to prescribe more output to realize scale economies as the solution to the inefficiency problem. But given demand, our efficiency distributions can be used to find the most efficient operation at that scale.

In the planned second stage of this project, the authorities will typically be faced with a situation where they know transport demand at a given sailing distance. Since the distance is given, they will in principle also have information about ports to call on and how the distance is exposed to rough weather. The latter is indirectly captured by the type of ferry—fjord-ferry and pendulum-ferry.

If the authorities want to intervene in the market by subsidizing, we have an optimizing problem in setting the form and size of the subsidy. The initial size of the subsidy would then be important. A high initial subsidy in the case where initial costs were quite high could give high profits for the company. It seems likely, however, that the authorities would want to reduce subsidies in such cases later on, when profits begin to show. Anticipation on the part of the producers of such a reduction might well discourage the company from economizing. One way out this dilemma for the authorities would be to set the initial subsidy "right."

Still, the problem of choosing a strategy for changing subidies raises a principal-agent problem that should be pursued. In practice, it seems likely that the lack of incentives on the part of the producers may well have created a lot of slack and large variation across ferries and transport distances. To use observed cost structures, one may well end up "freezing" an inefficient production system.

Finally, if one wants a yardstick for giving support to specific distances, one would also need to take into account the value of waiting time for cars and passengers, if large ferries (with infrequent departures) were found to be be cheapest, and hence would set the standard for the subsidy allocated to the distance.

Acknowledgments

We are indebted to two referees for perceptive and constructive comments that greatly improved this chapter.

Notes

1. See Forsund (1992) for a comparison of parametric and non parametric deterministic frontiers on the same data set as utilized here.

2. The CCR model of chapter 2, section 5, can be seen as an ingenious way of solving the seminal efficiency model of Farrell (1957), by applying linear programming (LP) and calculating the efficiency score for one unit at a time instead of first establishing all the facets of the frontier as Farrell did. Applying LP was suggested in the discussion of Farrell's paper by Dr. A. J. Hoffman, and the first LP model was actually set up in Boles (1966). Rolf Färe kindly provided the latter reference.

3. The efficiency scores calculated by DEA models are based on this definition.

4. The symbols e_1 and e_2 are actually used by Farrell for input-saving and output-increasing efficiencies. Our definition E_1 corresponds to θ in chapter 2 and E_2 corresponds to $1/\phi$.

5. Note that the gross scale efficiency measure for the VRS frontier coincides with the input-saving measure equal to the output-increasing measure for the CRS frontier.

6. Note that if we move P5 to the frontier, keeping output fixed, the point C exhibits increasing returns to scale, while if we move to the frontier, keeping inputs fixed, point L exhibits decreasing returns to scale.

7. From table 2–4 in chapter 2, we see that the weight is 0.6.

8. From table 2–5 in chapter 2, we have that the weight is 5/3.

9. From tables 2–4 and 2–5 in chapter 2, we have for unit P5 that $E_1 = 7/15$ and $E_2 = 9/19$, implying $E_1 < E_2$ and $\varepsilon < 1$. Inserting the numbers in the equation for ε yields $\ln E_2/\ln E_1 = 0.98$.

10. The meaning of "start" is not necessarily small output levels. A starting facet may extend to high output values.

11. Note that the concept of large and small when we have multiple outputs is not quite clear-cut. Scale properties are usually evaluated along rays with fixed proportions between the outputs. When changing output proportions, scale properties may well change, even if the units keep their "size."

12. See Berg et al. (1991) and (1992) for an application to banks where this feature was prominent.

13. Only two ferry distances of the 150 run a surplus, and data for the ferries running the profitable distances are not reported to DRT.

14. See Førsund (1993) for utilization of the time series cross-section data.

15. The regression equation is

$$\ln(r) = a \ln\left(\frac{x}{v}\right) + bt \ln(s) + C$$

where x is the insurance premium, v is the price paid for the ferry when new, r is the ratio of premium to market price, t is the age in years, and s is the net yearly rate of increase in value common for all ferries (inflation minus depreciation).

16. The second-hand market for ferries is too thin to give reliable information of market value.

17. One (time-consuming) option not taken would be to check individual ferries for minimum crew standards imposed by authorities and actual crew size.

18. As a simple way to check the link between the two alternative, available measures, we ran a regression of total regular wages, excluding overtime and social cost, on crew size multiplied by number of shifts ("man-shifts"), where this was available, for about 100 of the ferries. We also ran wages on man-shifts multiplied by the number of days the ferry had been in service in 1988, divided by 360 (fraction of the year in service). The first regression gave an estimate of NOK 150,000 per man-shift per year and a standard error of about 3000, the latter NOK 1.75 million per man-shift in service per year, with a standard error of NOK 3400. The results indicate that wages are in reasonable accordance with the direct measures of crew size. It should also be noted that wages are negotiated by two nationwide unions.

19. For reasons of readability, a few extreme (low-productivity) very small units representing a negligible output share (less than 0.006) have been deleted in the graphs.

20. Note that we cannot distiguish between small boats running long distances and large boats running short ones in the figures. In order to see this, physical capacity has to be used as size variable. There is a systematic trend of large-capacity ferries producing more output, as seen from the correlation coefficient in table 15–2.

21. The distribution for the insurance-based capital measure, UC, is similar to the one for physical capital, while the market value, MV, distribution differs with a linearly rising shape and no typical location of ferry according to size.

22. Note that there are two small ferries not identifiable in the figure with the lowest wage coefficients.)

23. Note that two small ferries (different from the two with the lowest wage coefficients) not discernible in the figure have the lowest fuel coefficients.

24. There are no small ones at the efficient tail this time.

25. Complete printouts from our interactive DEA program, developed at the Foundation for Research in Economics and Business Administration, Oslo, are available upon request.

26. One unit with score 1 is not Pareto efficient.

27. We shall rely on casual empiricism and simple correlation coefficients instead of developing formal tests, partly due to lack of space and partly due to the fact that formal hypotheses testing is not clear-cut within the deterministic DEA framework.

28. One of them, the Pareto-dominated one in the E_1 and E_2 runs, has now an efficiency score slightly below one.

29. As a sensitivity test, two efficient small ferries, nos. 49 and 50 (the latter being the smallest in the sample), having the smallest labor coefficients, were removed. They appear in 53 and 65 reference sets for E_1, respectively. Scores for other units remain the same, of course. The efficiency scores increase quite modestly, by about 0.02–0.04 for most of the units, except for the few units having large weights. For these, the improvement is typically in the range 0.05–0.10, the small unit taking over as efficient experiencing the highest jump in efficiency (about 0.17).

30. This may indicate that specifying increasing returns as in Petersen (1990) would be relevant. However, the parametric frontier calculated in Førsund (1991) had the text-book shape (of regular ultra passum), but with optimal scale being 40% higher than the largest observation.

31. The regressions run are

$$E_i = \alpha T + \beta, \quad i = 1, \ldots, 5,$$

where E_i is the efficiency measure, T is the year of construction, and α and β are estimated coefficients.

16 INCORPORATING STANDARDS VIA DEA

Boaz Golany and Yaakov Roll

1. Introduction

The engineering approach to efficiency measurement is based on the notion of "standards". In that approach, specific standards are generated for the required input per each kind of output. To this end, traditional techniques of industrial engineering, involving synthetic and statistical approaches, are employed. Thus, these standards are not necessarily observed from the real operations of the units, and in some cases they reflect normative managerial perceptions or targets. The standards are used to determine both optimal output levels and the corresponding minimal inputs. Partial efficiencies are then obtained from the ratios of standard inputs to actual ones, for a given output mix. These partial efficiency figures may be combined into an aggregate efficiency measure, indicating the overall efficiency of the said unit across all the dimensions of its activity (see, e.g., Roll and Sachish, 1981).

In contrast, Charnes, Cooper, and Rhodes (CCR) (1978) developed data envelopment analysis (DEA) as a methodology aimed at evaluating the relative efficiency of decision-making units (DMUs) solely on the basis of their observed performance. Starting from the classical engine-

313

ering definition of efficiency, they express the efficiency of a DMU as a ratio of its weighted sum of outputs to its weighted sum of inputs. An optimization model is run for each DMU to find the weights that will accord it the best possible efficiency rating such that the same weights satisfy a set of normalization constraints for the entire group of observed DMUs.

DEA has gained widespread acceptance as a suitable approach in not-for-profit, public, and service organizations. The methodology suited these situations mainly because the complexity of the units involved, the potentially many interactions among the inputs and outputs, and the presence of qualitative data prevented the use of ordinary efficiency/productivity techniques. However, in certain environments—in particular, in some private-sector applications—one may find accepted standards or benchmarks of performance that need to be taken into account when efficiency is measured. For example, where work methods are designed by engineering departments, one finds standards for labor utilization associated with various products or production processes. Other examples of engineering (or managerial) standards that have been set in environments where DEA was already practiced are hospitals (e.g., Sherman, 1984; Roll and Moran, 1984), power-generating systems (e.g., Golany, Roll, and Rybak, 1994) ana banking (e.g., Parkan, 1987). In addition, it should be noted that the possibility of introducing standard data in DEA was already mentioned in the early work of Charnes, Cooper, and Rhodes (1978, p. 430). However, it was not actively pursued by others in the DEA literature.

The original CCR ratio model offers great flexibility in the evaluation of DMUs. To define the model, one needs only to select the DMUs, the inputs and the outputs. The model is then represented via the pair of dual linear programs (see chapter 2, section 5). No a priori relations (except for a positivity requirement) are assumed to hold for the input–output weights for which the model is solved in its primal representation, and no limitations are placed on the dual side in the selection of DMUs used for the evaluation of any particular DMU.

In recent years, a growing number of researchers have looked into ways to incorporate judgment into DEA. The most notable effort in this direction revolves around limiting the flexibility of the model in assigning values to input–output weights. All the methods suggested in this area, e.g., the Cone Ratio formulation of Charnes et al. (1989), the Assurance Region model of Thompson et al. (1990), and the Factor Weights Bounds of Cook et al. (1991), introduce additional (subjective) judgment into DEA. The motivation to restrict the model's flexibility stems from the realization that in some cases, one has at least partial information on the process of converting inputs to outputs and on the relative importance of the factors, and this information should be included in the model.

The present study suggests an alternative approach for introducing judgment into the DEA methodology by allowing the incorporation of engineering-like standards into the analysis. Thus, observed data from a group of DMUs can be enriched by adding a set of "standard" data to the analysis. In contrast to the weights limitation techniques, which have a direct influence on the model by adding or changing constraints, the incorporation of standards has an indirect effect on the mechanism of efficiency evaluation in DEA. It does not add to or change the structure of the constraints. Rather, it merely enlarges the size of the reference set. In extreme cases, bounds on weights may become so tight as to make the model infeasible, a phenomenon that cannot possibly happen with the standards. It is also interesting to note that the two approaches, standards and weight restriction, affect the efficiency scores in the same direction. The inclusion of standards increases the potential that DMUs previously considered efficient will now be evaluated as inefficient, and that inefficient units will be accorded even lower efficiency scores. Similarly, as bounds on weights become tighter, efficiency scores cannot improve. Therefore, the two approaches can complement each other, and there is no reason not to employ them simultaneously when doing so is desired.

The extension of the reference set by adding standard DMUs should also be viewed in light of the current interest and developments in the area of total quality management (TQM). Specifically, an important feature in TQM relates to setting benchmarks. The idea is that organizations are expected to identify best practices, either within their own operations or throughout their industry, and import these into their environment. In the context of DEA, the identified efficient input–output mixes serve as a benchmark according to which the efficiency of all other DMUs is measured. Consider the case of a bank whose branches are all operating far below the average efficiency achieved by its competitors. Applying DEA to only these branches, we may never uncover the possible improvements in their performance. However, by searching for data on industry benchmarks (e.g., in the banking industry one may find relevant data in the public domain in government publications, such as Federal Reserve and FDIC reports), and using these to extend the reference set by constructing standard DMUs, the bank may find that there is a much larger room for improvement than previously estimated. Even in cases when no exogenous data are readily available for the construction of standards, management can still use benchmarking as a vehicle for performance improvement. By setting goals that are slightly better than current best performance, and entering them as standards into DEA, even the most (relatively) efficient DMUs will be shown potential directions for improvement.

The following section presents the general configuration of standard points vis-à-vis observed points, and some difficulties in establishing standards are discussed. Section 3 provides relative measures of distance between envelopes incorporating standards and those obtained just from the observed points. Additional possibilities for extracting information from standards as well as potential pitfalls resulting from forced comparisons to specific DMUs are demonstrated in section 4. The methodological developments in these sections are accompanied and illustrated by numerical examples taken from the DEA literature. A final section discusses and evaluates the various outcomes.

2. Standards within DEA

Figure 16–1, based on an example given by Charnes, Cooper, and Rhodes (1978), depicts a two-input, single-output case, where the X1 and X2 axes

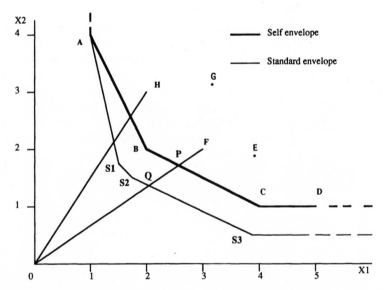

Figure 16–1. Schematic representation of a standard envelope vs. the self-envelope.

represent input per unit output values and the frontier is therefore a unit isoquant. Points A to H represent observed DMUs. The efficient frontier, enveloping the observed points, is given by DMUs A–B–C. Henceforth, this envelope will be referred to as the *self-envelope*. Now suppose that additional information is made available on the standard performance of DMUs of the same kind, and this information is represented by the three standard points S1, S2, S3. Often, these points will be located outside the self-envelope and will form a new standard-envelope, in our case, A–S1–S2–S3. Note that the standards may not cover the entire range of values in each dimension, so the standard envelope may be constructed of both standard and observed points. The relative efficiency of point F is OP/OF with regard to the self-envelope. However, when the standard points enter the analysis, the standard efficiency of point F drops to OQ/OF. Instead of the facet B–C determining the relative efficiency of F, the reference facet is now composed of the two standard points S2 and S3. Thus, in addition to the relative efficiency rating within the analyzed group, an efficiency score is obtained in comparison to a theoretically constructed "engineering" standard. In this way, DEA establishes a contact with accepted industrial engineering practices, where observed performance is compared to potentially possible levels of reference.

Establishing standard DMUs in the context of DEA may prove to be a difficult task (see Sherman, 1984). In ordinary industrial cases, only one standard is set for each dimension of input per unit output. One of the advantages of DEA, however, is that it recognizes the fact that excellence can be achieved by different mixes of inputs and outputs. Hence, it may be necessary to develop several multidimensional standards. Moreover, these should be spread out in such a way as to provide a standard envelope to as many of the observed units as possible, in the relevant ranges of values of their inputs and outputs. The issue of coverage of observed DMUs by standards is treated in the next section.

3. Relative Position of Envelopes

In addition to obtaining efficiency ratings for individual DMUs with respect to the standard envelope, it is of interest to develop an aggregate measure of distance to represent the relative position of the two envelopes. Some of the motivations for measuring this distance are as follows:

- Managers at higher organizational levels may desire to obtain an overall index of actual performance, relative to a standard (supposedly optimal) envelope.

- The introduction of a standard frontier affects individual DMUs to varying degrees. Some remain as efficient as before: others exhibit a decrease in their efficiency. By relating the change in the DMU's evaluation to the overall distance measure, one is able to say how relevant (or effective) were the standards for each particular DMU.

The measurement of distance between envelopes was first carried out by CCR in the context of comparing programs, when the envelope of a subset of DMUs characterized by one program was compared to the envelope of the second program (Charnes, Cooper, and Rhodes, 1981). Another use of comparison between envelopes is demonstrated in Cook et al. (1991). The envelopes can be compared by observing only the projection of the self-efficient points onto the standard envelope or by the projections of all the points (including the self-inefficient ones) onto the standard envelope. The distance between the envelopes or, rather, between the compared points can be measured in many ways, e.g., by using different distance norms. Alternatively, statistical techniques, such as the Minimum Discrimination Information (MDI) statistic (see Charnes and Cooper, 1978), can be applied.

Three simple measures of the relative position of two envelopes are listed below:

1. the average ratio of relative to standard efficiencies across all the observed DMUs (returning to figure 16–1, this measure is the average of all such ratios OQ/OP;
2. the average efficiency of DMUs forming the self-envelope (A, B, C in figure 16–1), with respect to the standard envelope; and
3. the average efficiency of all the observed DMUs with respect to the standard envelope, after they are projected to the self-envelope (see Charnes, Cooper, and Rhodes, 1978, p. 433).

The following (theoretical) example, based on Golany and Roll (1989), serves to illustrate the various relative position measures. Columns 1 to 5 in table 16–1 list the "observed" input and output data for 11 DMUs, as well as corresponding values for two "standard" points. Efficiencies of the observed DMUs (using the CCR_p–I model) with respect to the self-envelope are given in column 6. When the standard points enter the analysis, these efficiencies drop (in this case) to the values listed in column 7. The average ratio of all pairs of efficiencies (column 7 over column 6) in this example is 0.914. It indicates the shortfall of the

Table 16–1. Illustrative Example

| | Data | | | | | Efficiencies | | Relative Position of Envelopes | | |
| | Outputs | | Inputs | | | | | | | |
DMU No.	y_1 {1}	y_2 {2}	x_1 {3}	x_2 {4}	x_3 {5}	Self Enve-lope {6}	Stand. Enve-lope {7}	{7}/{6} all DMUs {8}	{7}/{6} eff. points {9}	Eff. of Adjust. Points Relative to Standards {10}
Observed										
1	0.90	70	10	0.8	54	.784	.681	.868		.869
2	1.00	95	15	1.0	48	.972	.833	.857		.900
3	0.80	75	12	2.1	51	.732	.628	.858		.901
4	0.90	90	10	0.6	42	1.00	.900	.900		.900
5	0.70	80	18	0.5	60	.600	.560	.933	.900	.999
6	1.00	50	7	0.9	52	.911	.907	.996		.995
7	0.80	70	10	0.3	50	.842	.800	.950		1.00
8	0.75	75	12	1.5	55	.638	.573	.898		.906
9	0.65	55	14	1.8	57	.532	.456	.857		.900
10	0.85	90	8	0.9	45	.900	.840	.933		1.00
11	0.95	100	6	0.3	45	1.00	1.00	1.00	1.00	1.00
Standard										
12	1.00	100	7	0.3	42					
13	1.00	95	8	0.3	40					
							Average	0.914	0.950	0.943

analyzed DMUs, as a group, with respect to the standard envelope. When only the efficient frontier of the observed group is considered, i.e., the best practice exhibited by the group, the average ratio (column 9) is 0.950. Following option 3 above, all the observed DMUs are brought to the self-envelope and then assessed relative to the standard envelope. The average efficiency figure by that approach is 0.943, reflecting not only the relative position of the two envelopes but also the particular scatter of the observed points.

Another issue of interest, in this context, is the extent to which the proposed standards cover the entire group of observed DMUs in all the relevant dimensions. Referring again to figure 16–1 the efficiency of point F with respect to the standard envelope is wholly determined by points S2 and S3. The corresponding efficiency of point H, however, is only partially determined by S1. The other component in the facet for point H is point A, originally part of the self-envelope. A numerical measure of the coverage by standards can be obtained by observing the lambda values in the CCR_p–I formulation of chapter 2. Let λ_{kj} be the weight accorded to point k in determining the efficiency of DMU_j. Also, let S be the set of standard points, and O be the set of the observed points. The coverage of DMU_j by the standards can be defined as

$$C_j = \frac{\sum\limits_{k \in S} \lambda_{kj}}{\sum\limits_{k \in S \cup O} \lambda_{kj}} \qquad (16.1)$$

The average of all the C_j values is an indicator of the way the standard points are deployed relative to the observed ones. Table 16–2 presents the coverage values for our example (points 12 and 13 are the standard ones).

In this example, most of the DMUs are fully covered by the standard units, i.e., their efficiency (as given in column 7) is determined by units 12 and 13. This means that the two standard units were successfully selected so as to provide useful benchmarks for the observed DMUs. The two exceptions are DMUs 6 and 11. DMU_{11} is efficient and its rating is not affected by the inclusion of the standards. Thus, we can conclude that this DMU is located at some corner of the frontier (much like point A in figure 16–1). The lambda values for DMU_6 reflect the fact that DMU_{11} is much more important in determining DMU_6's inefficiency than are the standard points 12 and 13. The managerial implication for DMU_6 is that, even in the presence of the standard units, it is DMU_{11} that should be carefully examined to find leads for improving the efficiency of DMU_6.

Table 16–2. Coverage by Standard Units

DMU No.	Eff. DMUs in Std. envelope {11}	Sum of All Lambdas {12}	Sum of $\lambda(12) + \lambda(13)$	Coverage Ratio {13}/{12} {14}
1	12, 13	.900	.900	1.00
2	13	1.00	1.00	1.00
3	13	.800	.800	1.00
4	12	.900	.900	1.00
5	12	.800	.800	1.00
6	11, 12	1.05	.043	.041
7	12	.800	.800	1.00
8	12	.750	.750	1.00
9	13	.650	.650	1.00
10	12	.900	.900	1.00
11	11	1.00	0.00	0.00
			Average	0.8219

4. Model Refinements

In this section we discuss further implications and potential uses stemming from the introduction of standards into DEA. We start by attempting to make contact between two methods of introducing judgment into DEA: the concept of standards and the more well-known approach of limiting the values of the weights. We show how the former can be of assistance when values have to be assigned to bounds on the weights. Later, we caution the reader against potential pitfalls that may be present when comparison to standard units is forced onto the model.

4.1. Standards and Bounds on Virtual Multipliers

The issue of bounds within which virtual multipliers (factor weights) in the CCR_D–I formulation of chapter 2, are allowed to vary has attracted attention in recent years (e.g., Charnes et al., 1989; Dyson and Thanassoulis, 1988; Roll, Cook, and Golany, 1991; Thompson et al., 1990). The motivation for these developments is that under certain circumstances it is impractical to let the factor weights vary freely. Whatever the bounding approach, the difficulty always lies in locating the appropriate bounds for each case, i.e., where to set them and how to determine their range. The information contained in the standard DMUs can serve as a guide for locating such bounds. A feasible technique would be to narrow the bounds within which factor weights are allowed to vary, as long as such narrowing does not affect considerably the efficiency of the standard DMUs.

The bounds on factor weights can be determined in many ways. One possibility is first to define the average ratio of lower to upper bounds across all the factor weights, as in equation (16.2) below:

$$W = \frac{1}{m + s} \cdot \left(\sum_{r=1}^{s} \frac{P_{2r}}{P_{1r}} + \sum_{i=1}^{m} \frac{Q_{2i}}{Q_{1i}} \right) \qquad (16.2)$$

where the notation is as follows:

P_{1r}, P_{2r}: upper and lower bounds (respectively) on weight for output factor r, $r = 1, \ldots, s$

Q_{1i}, Q_{2i}: upper and lower bounds (respectively) on weight for input factor i, $i = 1, \ldots, m$

The range of allowed values for factor weights can thus be represented by W. Then, defining V as the average efficiency of the standard DMUs and W as above, we seek to obtain the largest value of W (narrowest bounds) with minimal resulting deviation of V from unity. The relationship between V and W for the previous numerical example is demonstrated in figure 16–2. It shows that, in our example, one could limit the weights considerably (to a position where the average ratio of the bounds on the weights is $W = 0.69$) while still maintaining full efficiency for all the standard DMUs. Furthermore, by incurring only a 2% reduction in

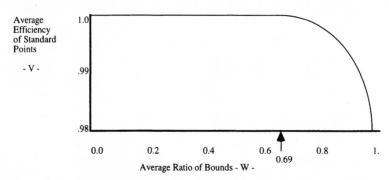

Figure 16–2.   V–W relationship.

the average efficiency scores of the standards ($V = 0.98$), one could tighten the bounds to a single value in every dimension (the so-called CSW—Common Set of Weights in Roll, Cook and Golany, 1991).

The controlled increase of W can be executed in several ways, including trial and error or using shadow price information taken from the DEA model. Another alternative, which was used here to generate the relationship shown in figure 16–2, is to employ differences between bounds rather than their ratios. Then a linear program can be constructed whose constraint set is based on the DEA envelopment constraints, and whose objective is to minimize the sum of differences between the bounds. The following additional notation is used in developing the program:

γ Minimum allowed efficiency for standard DMUs

μ_{rk}, v_{ik} Virtual multipliers for output r and input i, respectively, corresponding to the k_{th} standard DMU

d_i, D_r Ranges of values for v_{ik} and μ_{rk}, respectively

α, β Additional policy parameters

The model to be solved is

$$\text{Min} \quad \sum_{r=1}^{s} D_r + \sum_{i=1}^{m} d_i$$

$$\text{s.t.} \quad \sum_{r=1}^{s} \mu_{rk} \cdot y_{rk} - \gamma \cdot \sum_{i=1}^{m} v_{ik} \cdot x_{ik} \geq 0, \quad k \in S$$

$$\sum_{r=1}^{s} \mu_{rk} \cdot y_{rj} - \sum_{i=1}^{m} v_{ik} \cdot x_{ij} \geq 0, \quad k \in S, \quad j \in S \cup O$$

$$P_{2r} \leq \mu_{rk} \leq P_{1r}, \quad k \in S, r = 1, \ldots, s$$

$$Q_{2i} \leq v_{ik} \leq Q_{1i}, \quad k \in S, i = 1, \ldots, m$$

$$D_r - P_{1r} + P_{2r} = 0, \quad r = 1, \ldots, s$$

$$d_i - Q_{1i} + Q_{2i} = 0, \quad i = 1, \ldots, m \tag{16.3}$$

Notice that in model (16.3), the efficiency of the standard DMUs is not maximized but rather constrained from below by a policy parameter γ. Alternatively, a minor modification to model (16.3) would allow for the efficiency of the standard units to be maximized. This can be accomplished by eliminating the γ parameter and subtracting the sum of the first set of constraints (weighted down so as to become a secondary criterion) from the objective function. Further, note that in model (16.3), the P's and Q's are variables, determining the values of the D's and d's. Variations of model (16.3) may include additional policy parameters specifying lower bounds on the P_{2r} and Q_{2i} values, i.e.,

$$P_{2r} \geqslant a_r, r = 1, \ldots, s; \quad Q_{2i} \geqslant a_i, i = 1, \ldots, m \qquad (16.4)$$

and/or restricting the maximal allowed ratios of lower to upper bound in any factor weight, i.e.,

$$P_{1r} \cdot \beta_r \leqslant P_{2r}, r = 1, \ldots, s; \quad Q_{1i} \cdot \beta_i \leqslant Q_{2i}, i = 1, \ldots, m \quad (16.5)$$

These additional constraints limit the feasible range of values for W, thus bringing the additive formulation offered in model (16.3) closer to the multiplicative structure (equation (16.2)) of W.

4.2. Potential Caveats

The concept of standards of performance, i.e., the best way by which resources may be utilized to achieve desired goals, is closely linked to the notion of model DMUs. The term *model DMUs* is loosely used to describe units whose performance is deemed to be fully satisfactory and hence are accepted as valid standards of reference. Imposing the comparison of all analyzed DMUs to specific points (whether standard or observed ones) may be in conflict with one of the prominent features of DEA, namely, that each DMU is compared to a specific, most suitable reference facet in the envelope. In this section, we wish to demonstrate the potential perils of interfering with this inherent flexibility of DEA.

To illustrate the effect of imposing comparison to model DMUs, consider again the two-input, single-output example given in Charnes, Cooper, and Rhodes (1978) and depicted in figure 16–3. The thick line denotes the regular (unconstrained) envelope of the six points analyzed. Now, suppose that point C is taken as a model unit to which all other points have to be compared (at least partially). This condition can be represented in the CCR$_P$–I formulation by imposing the additional constraint that λ_C (the weight of point C in determining the efficiency of any point) is not less than a specified value π_C. The modified model, solved for DMU$_0$, is

$$\text{Min} \quad \theta_0 - \varepsilon \cdot \left[\sum_{i=1}^{m} s_i^- + \sum_{r=1}^{s} s_r^+ \right]$$

$$\text{s.t.} \quad \sum_{j=1}^{n} Y_{rj}\lambda_j - s_r^+ = Y_{r0}, \quad r = 1. \ldots, s$$

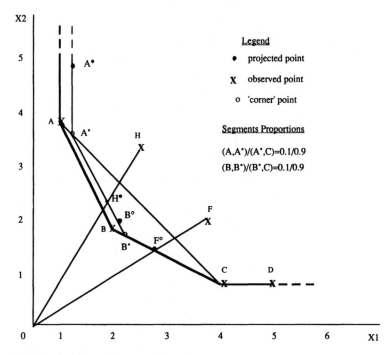

Figure 16–3. Effect of constraining facets.

$$\sum_{j=1}^{n} X_{ij}\lambda_j - \theta_0 X_{i0} + s_i^- = 0, \quad i = 1, \ldots, m$$

$$\lambda_C \geq \pi_C$$

$$\lambda_j, s_i^-, s_r^+ \geq 0$$

Figure 16–3 demonstrates the results of imposing the seemingly mild requirement $\lambda_C \geq 0.1$. This constraint has the effect of shifting the reference envelope inwards to a position given by the thin line. Projected points are represented by thick dots in the figure (these are $A^\bullet$, $B^\bullet$, $H^\bullet$, and $F^\bullet$). Drawing lines through $B^\bullet$ and $H^\bullet$ and through C and $F^\bullet$ yields the intersection (or corner) point B°. Similarly, drawing a vertical line through $A^\bullet$ yields the corner point A°. It is interesting to note that the ratios between the lengths of the line segments (A, A°) and (A°, C) as well as between (B, B°) and (B°, C) are $1:9$. Thus, the new envelope runs parallel to the original one, with the corner points (B°, A°) posi-

5. Conclusions

This chapter has explored the possibilities of including (not yet observed) "standard" points in DEA applications. A straightforward gain from such a step is that a measure of the potential for improvement in the performance of *all* observed DMUs is obtained. Also discussed is the potential use of standard data as a means to link DEA with TQM developments, and ways are suggested in which benchmarks, which possibly are imported from other similar organizations, can be introduced into DEA. In addition, several points, such as simultaneous optimization involving several DMUs, are explored here in a unique way. All these topics may trigger new avenues for research.

Another advantage that stems from the definition of standard DMUs is that such units can be instrumental in setting controls on factor weight variation within DEA. It is important to have a wide (and diverse) set of standard points, accompanying the entire range of activities of the analyzed group. One should, however, be careful not to impair the inherent flexibility of DEA by imposing comparison to any point (observed or standard). Such forced comparison may severely distort the outcome of the analysis.

This chapter leaves open several important issues. One is the difficulty of setting multiple standards (as opposed to the single-standard practice in most engineering applications), and the necessity to lay down specific guidelines for this purpose. Another issue is the need for a much broader analysis of setting constraints on facet selection under different DEA formulations (e.g., Charnes and Cooper, 1985). These also may be fruitful areas for research.

Most applications of DEA in the first decade since its publication were carried out in public or not-for-profit organizations. In these cases, relative efficiencies within the analyzed group of DMUs provide an adequate answer to the efficiency measurement problem. However, DEA is gaining popularity in a wider spectrum of cases, including the private sector. In such environments, efficiency is typically measured with respect to some goals that have not yet been realized. The DEA approach is general enough to enable incorporation of such additional data when they are available. The treatment of standards within the context of DEA broadens the potential applicability of the approach and renders it more attractive to a wider range of users.

Acknowledgments

The authors wish to express their sincere gratitude to Dr. J. J. Rousseau for his constructive comments, which helped revise and improve this chapter, and to Arie Lewin and Lawrence Seiford for their patience, encouragement and support.

17 STRATIFIED MODELS OF EDUCATION PRODUCTION USING MODIFIED DEA AND REGRESSION ANALYSIS

C. A. Knox Lovell, Lawrence C. Walters, and Lisa L. Wood

1. Introduction

In their agenda for research into the determinants of organizational effectiveness, Lewin and Minton (1986, p. 531) called for studies illustrating the "feasibility of using DEA (perhaps in combination with other analytical methods) as a mathematic for relating effectiveness outcomes to features of organization design." In this chapter, we report the initial results of just such a study. The purpose of the study is to investigate the performance of secondary education in the U.S. Performance is defined as the ability of secondary schools to convert human, physical, and financial resources into educational opportunities, and then to combine these opportunities with student input to produce both intermediate- and long-term educational outcomes. At each stage, performance is measured using a modified form of data envelopment analysis (MDEA). The three sets of calculated MDEA scores are then regressed against groups of environmental variables that reflect features of the organizational design and characteristics of the student body of each secondary school in the sample. The modification to DEA and the second-stage regression analysis are structured to take into account the special distributional features of unmodified DEA scores. The empirical results suggest that a two-stage approach that augments MDEA with regression analysis provides a fruitful way of determining effectiveness outcomes and relating them to features of organizational design and the operating environment. Furthermore, regression analysis provides useful information for policymakers interested in how changes in organizational characteristics can improve school performance.

The organizations whose effectiveness we examine are several hundred high schools that participated in the High School and Beyond study initiated in 1980. The model of education production we use is stratified to permit the evaluation of school performance at two distinct levels, and in two ways at the second level. At the first level, performance is measured as the conversion of school resources into an array of services. At the second level, these services are converted by students into both intermediate- and long-term outcomes.

The use of DEA to measure performance of stratified production is reminiscent of the work of Wood (1983), who examined the resource efficiency and effectiveness of public elementary schools in the City of Philadelphia, and of Charnes et al. (1986), who examined the effectiveness of various types of advertising in U.S. Army recruiting. Stratified DEA is particularly attractive, and surprisingly underutilized, in the context of secondary education.

The effectiveness of schools is measured by their MDEA scores. Three sets of scores are computed, one set for each of the various levels of stratification described above. These scores are of considerable interest in and of themselves. However, policy interest centers on the determinants, particularly the manipulable determinants, of these scores, and this makes the second-stage regression analysis important. In this stage, variation in calculated MDEA scores is associated with variation in a variety of environmental variables, some of them policy sensitive. The use of MDEA is motivated by the fact that conventional DEA scores have three significant distributional features. By construction, they are bounded by zero and unity. By virtue of the linear programming computational technique, a mass of observations achieves the upper bound. Typically the scores are skewed. Each of these features makes ordinary least squares (OLS) regression analysis on conventional DEA scores an inappropriate estimation technique.[1] In its stead, we use a technique (the super-efficiency model), due originally to Andersen and Petersen (1993), that is designed to overcome these distributional features of conventional DEA scores. In the first stage, we deal with the problem of the occurrence of a mass of scores at the upper bound by dropping each school from its own reference set. The resulting MDEA scores are bounded below by zero.[2] The natural logarithms of the MDEA scores are unbounded, and are suitable dependent variables in the second-stage OLS regression models.

The stratified model of education production is outlined in section 2. The High School and Beyond data base is described in section 3. The MDEA models and results are presented in section 4. In section 5, the MDEA scores are analyzed using regression analysis. Section 6 concludes with a summary and some suggestions for additional work.

2. A Conceptual Model of Education Production

Since the publication of *Equality of Educational Opportunity* (1966), the relationship between educational resources and student outcomes has been a major area of study among economists and education researchers. With the subsequent publication of *A Nation At Risk* (1983), educational reform became the focus of much attention and heated discussion, and many studies have been issued that attempt to assess the determinants of student achievement. Among these are a long list of attempts at estimating education production functions, with an eye to improving the effectiveness of education through an improved understanding of the underlying production relationships. Recently, however, much of the literature has been called into question. Hanushek (1986, 1989) has published influential reviews of literally hundreds of education production function studies, and concludes that we have generally failed to show any systematic relationship between student outcomes and such things as per pupil expenditures, teacher/pupil ratios, teacher education, teacher experience, and teacher salaries.

While a variety of explanations for this broad failure are possible (Hanushek suggests several), one fundamental shortcoming of many of these studies is their failure to adequately accommodate the multidimensional nature of education. The analytic techniques employed by most of these researchers generally require that either the inputs or the outputs of education be scalar valued. The approach we take in this chapter permits a much richer view of the process of education production.

The approach we propose envisions education as a multistage process, involving multiple inputs and multiple outputs at each stage. Initially, schools garner a wide range of resources—human, physical, and financial —that are organized and expended in the production of intermediate goods, a range of educational services and activities. These services cannot be interpreted as student outcomes, but rather as raw educational materials and activities to which students are exposed. The services thus produced include the courses, extracurricular activities, and instructional time offered by the school.

In the second stage of the educational process, the students combine the school's offerings with personal effort to yield intermediate-term outcomes. Such outcomes include test scores, grades, and more subjective assessments of performance and promise.

In the longer term, the educational services of a school are combined with individual effort and attributes to yield long-term outcomes such as performance in a postsecondary setting, eventual educational attainment, and income levels.

Clearly, this representation of the education process is not complete, but it does represent a richer view than has been traditionally used. It offers the possibility of identifying sources of performance variation in the provision of educational services and in the generation of educational outcomes. Figure 17–1 summarizes the description of the education process articulated here. It is this view of education that provides the basis for the specific models described in section 4.

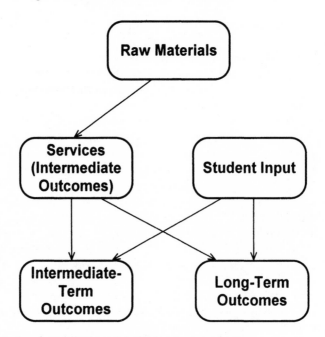

Figure 17–1.   A stratified model of education production.

3. The High School and Beyond Data

The data used in the analysis are taken from the national study generally referred to as High School and Beyond (1987). In this study, a nationally representative sample of 1032 high schools was selected in the 1979–1980 base year. From each selected high school, a random sample of 36 sophomores and 36 seniors was identified. These cohorts of sophomores and seniors continue to be tracked as part of an ongoing data collection effort. The students have now received two follow-up interviews, the first in 1984 and the second in 1986.

The data collected for each student include a wealth of information about their school experience, their family socioeconomic status, and subsequent activities. In addition, substantial information is provided in a supplemental file on the school itself. Finally, a supplemental survey of teachers is also available. The teacher file includes a subjective assessment by each teacher in the school of the status and likely prospects for each student in the sample. All three files were used to compile relevant inputs, outputs, and explanatory variables for the analysis reported here. However, due to both conceptual and data limitations, not all observations were used in all phases of the analysis.

First, only data provided by the sophomores were used in the analysis. The sophomore data are somewhat richer, and it is easier to identify transfer students in the sophomore cohort. All transfer students were omitted from the analysis, since the contribution of schooling for transfer students represents a much more complex issue, and because the data were simply not available for the other schools involved.

Second, since the performance of schools is at issue, it was necessary to aggregate student data to the school level. For a variety of reasons, not all schools were able to provide 36 sophomore respondents as called for in the study design. Some extremely small schools did not have 36 sophomores; others had relatively low response rates. To minimize the effects of extremely small samples from individual schools, only schools with five or more respondents were used in the analysis.

Third, teacher responses were not available for all schools. Since subjective teacher evaluations of student performance provided an important variable, only schools for which these teacher data are available are used.

From these data, three MDEA models of education production were developed, corresponding to the conceptualization of education provided in section 2. The inputs, the outputs, and the number of observations for these models are provided in tables 17–1 through 17–3. The unit of

Table 17–1. Model 1: Resources into Services

Inputs
1. Total number of staff (teachers, aides, student teachers, administrators, and other personnel in the school)
2. Number of volumes in the school library
3. Physical facilities index

Outputs
1. Average # math classes taken × enrollment
2. Average # science classes taken × enrollment
3. Average # vocational education classes taken × enrollment
4. Average # foreign language classes taken × enrollment
5. Extracurricular activity index × enrollment
6. School course offering index
7. Total hours of instruction received by a typical student during the year × enrollment

Number of schools in model 1: 530

---

observation in each MDEA model is a school. Since not all schools provided information on all variables used in each of the three MDEA models, the number of observations varies across models. Nonetheless, each MDEA model contains observations on more than half of the 1032 schools that participated in the High School and Beyond study.

The three inputs for model 1 (table 17–1: Resources into Services) are largely self-explanatory, with one exception. The physical facilities index was created by simply counting the number of identifiable facilities available in the school. The data do not permit refined distinctions between quality or size of facilities, merely an indication of whether each type of facility is available in the school. These identified facilities include

1. indoor lounge for students
2. career information center
3. occupational training center
4. media production facilities
5. remedial reading or math lab
6. subject area resource center (not the library)
7. departmental offices
8. teaching resource center for teachers
9. child or nursery care facility
10. student cafeteria

Thus a school with all ten of these facilities receives a score of 10, while one with only five facilities receives a score of 5. No effort is made to argue that one facility is more critical than another.

The outputs for model 1 require some explanation. The objective here is to capture as fully as possible the range of services provided by the school. These must be divided into services actually utilized by the student samples, and services available, even though they may or may not have been used by the students in the sample.

Outputs 1 to 4 were computed by aggregating student-level data. For each student, the number of classes taken in each of four subject areas was averaged across all students in the sample to obtain the average number of classes taken during a high school career in math, science, vocational education, and foreign language, and this number was multiplied by enrollment. This process resulted in four separate output measures of the total number of classes taken in a school in each of four subject areas.

The extracurricular activities index (output 5) was computed by counting the number of extracurricular activities each sample student was involved in, averaging across respondents within a school, then multiplying by enrollment to arrive at total extracurricular activity participation by school. The activity areas included were sports, cheer leader, pep club, debate, drama, band, chorus, dance, hobby clubs, subject matter clubs, vocational education clubs, community youth clubs, and junior achievement.

In addition to the courses actually taken by sample students, an index of courses offered by the school was computed by counting the types of classes offered by the school. Schools provided yes/no answers to questions about whether particular classes were offered during the base year. The index is a count of the number of yes responses. The courses surveyed include second-year algebra, art, auto mechanics, calculus, chemistry, drama, driver education, economics, ethnic studies, family life, geometry, third-year Spanish, third-year German, third-year French, home economics, physics, psychology, Russian, trigonometry, and either wood or machine shop. Thus a school offering all these courses would receive an index score of 20.

The final output measure for model 1 is the total hours of instruction received by a typical student during the year multiplied by enrollment. Total hours of instruction is computed by multiplying the number of days in the school year, the length of the class period, and the number of periods taken by a typical student.

Table 17–2 describes the inputs and outputs for model 2 (Educational

Table 17–2.   Model 2: Educational Services into Intermediate Outcomes

---

Inputs
   1.   Average # math classes taken
   2.   Average # science classes taken
   3.   Average # vocational education classes taken
   4.   Average # foreign language classes taken
   5.   Extracurricular activity index
   6.   Total hours of instruction received by a typical student during the year
   7.   Average time spent on homework by students

Outputs
   1.   Standardized test score (follow-up year composite)
   2.   Ratio of follow-up test score to base-year test test composite score
   3.   Average high school GPA
   4.   Average teacher's assessment of percent of students who will likely go on
        to college

Number of schools in model 2: 579

Services into Intermediate Outcomes). In this model, 6 of the 7 outputs
from model 1 (i.e., all outputs except the school course offering index),
representing the services provided by the school and participated in by
the students, are taken as inputs to the educational process. However,
in this model, these variables are not multiplied by enrollment because
this model examines schools in terms of the average student. In
addition, student effort is reflected in the average amount of time spent
on homework by the students sampled.

The outputs for the model include the follow-up year test score composite, high school grades, and teacher assessment. As part of the survey,
each student respondent took a standardized test in reading, vocabulary,
and math. The composite score is the average of these scores, and the
school score is the average of all student scores for that school.

Clearly, such a test score reflects not only what the school has contributed to student learning but also the entire array of student background
and family variables. To mitigate these effects somewhat, we follow Desai
(1987) by including as an output the ratio of the follow-up year test score
to the base-year test score. The larger this ratio is, the greater is the test
score improvement by the student. Again, student scores were averaged
to obtain the school score.

High school grades are standardized to a common scale, then averaged
across students within the school.

Table 17–3.   Model 3: Educational Services into Long-Term Outcomes

Inputs
1. Average # math classes taken
2. Average # science classes taken
3. Average # vocational education classes taken
4. Average # foreign language classes taken
5. Extracurricular activity index
6. Total hours of instruction received by a typical student during the year
7. Average time spent on homework by students

Outputs
1. Average postsecondary grades
2. Average 1983 income
3. Average 1985 income
4. Average highest educational level attained

Number of schools in model 3: 585

The final output is a subjective assessment by the teachers within a school of the likelihood that students will go on to college. Each teacher was asked to make an independent assessment of the college potential for each sample student. For teachers who knew the students, responses were aggregated across teachers to obtain an estimate of the likelihood that each student would go on to college. Student scores were aggregated within each school to obtain a measure of the probability of college attendance of students within that school.

Table 17–3 describes the inputs and outputs for model 3 (Educational Services into Long-Term Outcomes). This model makes use of the same inputs as model 2, but the outputs are viewed as longer-term educational outcomes. These include the average postsecondary GPA for those students who went on to college, the average 1983 and 1985 incomes for all students, and the average of the highest educational level attained by the sample students.

These three MDEA models provide the basis for our analysis in section 4.

4. The MDEA Models and the MDEA Results

We now provide a brief summary of the specifications of the MDEA models employed in the analysis. Model 1 is a modification of the input-

oriented BCC primal model (BCC$_P$–I), while models 2 and 3 are modifications of the input-oriented CCR primal model (CCR$_P$–I). Model 1 can
be expressed as

$$\min_{\theta_1, \lambda, s^+, s^-} \quad \theta_1 - \varepsilon \cdot \vec{1}s^+ - \varepsilon \cdot \vec{1}s^-$$

$$\text{s.t.} \qquad \tilde{Y}\lambda - s^+ = Y_0$$

$$\theta_1 X_0 - \tilde{X}\lambda - s^- = 0$$

$$\vec{1}\lambda = 1$$

$$\lambda, s^+, s^- \geq 0$$

where Y_0 is a 7×1 vector of short-term outputs provided by the school
being evaluated, X_0 is a 3×1 vector of inputs utilized by that school, Y is
a $7 \times N_1$ matrix of outputs provided by all schools in the sample, $\tilde{Y} =$
$Y \backslash Y_0$, X is a $3 \times N_1$ matrix of inputs utilized by all schools in the sample,
and $\tilde{X} = X \backslash X_0$. Thus the dimensionality of λ is $(N_1 - 1) \times 1$, N_1 being
the number of schools in the sample for model 1.

Models 2 and 3 are structurally similar to model 1, with the exception
of the convexity constraint $\vec{1}\lambda = 1$, which is dropped. Hence we allow for
variable returns to scale in the short-run model 1, but we impose constant
returns to scale in the intermediate-run model 2 and in the long-run
model 3. Models 2 and 3 are modified input-oriented CCR primal models.
Model 2 can be expressed as

$$\min_{\theta_2, \lambda, s^+, s^-} \quad \theta_2 - \varepsilon \cdot \vec{1}s^+ - \varepsilon \cdot \vec{1}s^-$$

$$\text{s.t.} \qquad \tilde{T}\lambda - s^+ = T_0$$

$$\theta_2 Y_0 - \tilde{Y}\lambda - s^- = 0$$

$$\theta_2 S_0 - \tilde{S}\lambda - s^- = 0$$

$$\lambda, s^+, s^- \geq 0$$

where T_0 is a 4×1 vector of intermediate-term outputs provided by the
school being evaluated, Y_0 is a 6×1 vector of model 1 outputs (deleting
the school offering index), and S_0 is a scalar-valued index of student
input, for the school being evaluated. Thus $\tilde{T} = T \backslash T_0$ is a $4 \times (N_2 - 1)$
matrix of intermediate-term outputs, $\tilde{Y} = Y \backslash Y_0$ is a $6 \times (N_2 - 1)$ matrix
of model 1 outputs, and $\tilde{S} = S \backslash S_0$ is a $1 \times (N_2 - 1)$ vector of student
inputs and the dimensionality of λ is $(N_2 - 1) \times 1$, N_2 being the number
of schools in the sample for model 2.

Model 3 can be expressed as

$$\min_{\theta_3, \lambda, s^+, s^-} \quad \theta_3 - \varepsilon \cdot \vec{1}s^+ - \varepsilon \cdot \vec{1}s^-$$

$$\text{s.t.} \qquad \tilde{Z}\lambda - s^+ = Z_0$$

$$\theta_3 Y_0 - \tilde{Y}\lambda - s^- = 0$$

$$\theta_3 S_0 - \tilde{S}\lambda - s^- = 0$$

$$\lambda, s^+, s^- \geq 0$$

where Z_0 is a 4×1 vector of long-term educational outcomes provided by the school being evaluated, Y_0 is a 6×1 vector of model 1 outputs (again deleting the school offering index), and S_0 is a scalar-valued index of student input, for the school being evaluated. $\tilde{Z} = Z \backslash Z_0$ is a $4 \times (N_3 - 1)$ matrix of long-term educational outcomes, $\tilde{Y} = Y \backslash Y_0$ is a $6 \times (N_3 - 1)$ matrix of model 1 outputs, $\tilde{S} = S \backslash S_0$ is a $1 \times (N_3 - 1)$ vector of student inputs, and the dimensionlity of λ is $(N_3 - 1) \times 1$, N_3 being the number of schools in the sample for model 1.

In conventional DEA models, the data vector of the observation being evaluated is contained in the data matrices that form the observation's reference set. This can lead to a large number of observations having DEA scores of unity. To avoid this possibility, we employ a tie-breaking procedure recommended by Andersen and Petersen (1993). The logic behind their procedure is that it ranks radially efficient observations according to the amount by which their input vectors could be *increased* without them being dominated by a linear combination of other observations. Their procedure is implemented by deleting the observation being evaluated from its own reference set, which explains why the dimensionality of the intensity vector is reduced by one in each model. As a result, the modified DEA scores θ_1, θ_2, θ_3 are bounded below by zero as usual, but are not bounded above by unity. Consequently a school is labeled radially efficient if, and only if, its optimal MDEA score $\theta \geq 1$. And a school is labeled efficient if, and only if, its optimal MDEA score $\theta \geq 1$ and all of its slacks s^+ and s^- are zero.

The data and results of all three models are summarized in tables 17–4 to 17–6. Of primary interest are the distributional characteristics of the MDEA scores in each model. All three distributions are characterized by mild skewness and mild kurtosis. But the large mass of conventional DEA scores located at the upper bound of unity is replaced by a series of MDEA scores above unity, creating the upper tails of the slightly skewed efficiency distributions. Of additional interest are the slacks that exist in the three models. Even after schools are moved to the production

Table 17–4. Summary of Data and MDEA Scores for Model 1 (N_1 = 530) Data

		Mean	SD
Inputs			
1.	Staff	24.45	17.90
2.	Volumes in library	15,608.84	9,178.00
3.	Physical facilities index	4.86	1.95
Outputs			
1.	Avg. # classes taken–math	2,337.50	1,805.47
2.	Avg. # classes taken–science	2,375.95	1,571.67
3.	Avg. # classes taken–voc. ed.	2,469.95	1,756.45
4.	Avg. # classes taken–foreign language	1,127.89	111.42
5.	Extracurricular activity	2,617.52	1,583.34
6.	School course offering	14.49	2.98
7.	Hours of instruction	1,146,620.68	722,726.3

MDEA Score Moments

Mean	0.735	Minimum:	.163
Variance	0.194	Median:	.642
Skewness	3.859	Maximum:	4.405
Kurtosis	23.020		

Slack Analysis

	Frequency	% of N_1	Mean	Min	Max
Inputs					
1	35	6.60	0.058	0.001	0.339
2	60	11.32	0.059	0.002	0.261
3	40	7.55	0.106	0.002	0.331
Outputs					
1	235	44.34	0.050	0.001	0.295
2	88	16.60	0.088	0.003	0.411
3	355	66.98	0.107	0.002	0.499
4	294	55.47	0.078	0.001	0.403
5	267	50.38	0.066	0.001	0.351
6	368	69.43	0.080	0.001	0.401
7	416	78.49	0.091	0.002	0.465

Table 17-5. Summary of Data and MDEA Scores for Model 2 (N_2 = 579) Data

		Mean	SD
Inputs			
1.	Avg. # classes taken–math	1.76	0.81
2.	Avg. # classes taken–science	1.82	0.54
3.	Abg. # classes taken–voc. ed.	1.94	0.77
4.	Avg. # classes taken–foreign language	0.80	0.59
5.	Extracurricular activity	2.17	0.74
6.	Hours of instruction	863.45	130.50
7.	Time on homework	3.94	1.44
Outputs			
1.	Test score	50.19	4.66
2.	Ratio of test scores	1.02	0.036
3.	High school grades	77.23	2.93
4.	Likelihood of college	0.51	0.17

MDEA Score: Moments

Mean	.862	Minimum:	.552
Variance	0.0999	Median:	.821
Skewness	14.569	Maximum:	7.176
Kurtosis	279.082		

Slack Analysis

	Frequency	% of N_2	Mean	Min	Max
Inputs					
1	192	33.16	0.081	0.001	0.506
2	290	50.09	0.122	0.002	0.679
3	346	59.76	0.130	0.001	0.574
4	179	30.92	0.067	0.001	0.340
5	88	15.20	0.087	0.001	0.321
6	15	2.59	0.071	0.005	0.165
7	152	26.25	0.076	0.001	0.308
Outputs					
1	94	16.23	0.077	0.001	0.405
2	299	51.64	0.046	0.001	0.240
3	370	63.90	0.049	0.001	0.207
4	172	29.71	0.041	0.001	0.177

Table 17–6. Summary of Data and MDEA Scores for Model 3 (N_3 = 585) Data

	Mean	SD
Inputs		
1. Avg. # classes taken–math	1.76	0.81
2. Avg. # classes taken–science	1.82	0.54
3. Abg. # classes taken–voc. ed.	1.94	0.77
4. Avg. # classes taken–foreign language	0.80	0.59
5. Extracurricular activity	2.17	0.74
6. Hours of instruction	863.45	130.50
7. Time on homework	3.94	1.44
Outputs		
1. Postsecondary grades	2.78	0.28
2. 1983 income	6,305.13	2,501.03
3. 1985 income	11,482.44	3,427.71
4. Highest level of education	12.35	.445

MDEA Score: Moments

Mean	.7971	Minimum:	.491
Variance	.0408	Median:	.762
Skewness	7.430	Maximum:	3.865
kurtosis	96.1483		

Slack Anaysis

	Frequency	% of N_3	Mean	Min	Max
Inputs					
1	371	63.42	0.110	0.002	0.510
2	336	57.44	0.139	0.001	0.638
3	353	60.34	0.129	0.002	0.625
4	173	29.57	0.072	0.002	0.542
5	54	9.23	0.078	0.005	0.445
6	12	2.05	0.069	0.003	0.335
7	266	45.47	0.096	0.002	0.456
Outputs					
1	64	10.94	0.053	0.002	0.193
2	456	77.95	0.153	0.001	0.541
3	399	68.21	0.154	0.001	0.510
4	199	34.02	0.062	0.002	0.284

frontier, considerable slack remains in all three models, although its magnitude is not large.

The results of model 1 (Resources into Services) suggest that there is wide variation in the efficiency of this short-term transformation process. The median MDEA score is only 0.642, fully 25% of all schools have scores below 0.5, and lots of slack appears.

Schools appear much more similar in their success at actually educating their students. The results of model 2 (Educational Services into Intermediate Outcomes) suggest that while substantial variation continues, average performance increases. The median MDEA score rises to 0.821, and no school has a score below 0.5. Similar results are apparent in model 3 (Educational Services into Long-Term Outcomes), in which the median MDEA score is 0.762 and only one school has a score beneath 0.5. However, slack remains in both models 2 and 3.

Moreover, the simple correlation between the MDEA scores of models 2 and 3 is 0.494, which suggests a strong positive relationship between intermediate- and long-term performance. The simple correlations between MDEA scores of model 1 and those of models 2 and 3 are only 0.029 and −0.024, neither of which approaches statistical significance. This suggests little relationship between short-term resource efficiency and either intermediate- or long-term performance of schools.

Yet the variations in MDEA performance measures remain, and the present climate of education reform and debate could benefit from greater insight into the determinants of success in education. In an effort to explore these issues further, we turn next to a discussion of a regression model that offers potential for further analysis of calculated school performance measures.

5. Explaining the Distribution of MDEA Scores

We now augment the MDEA performance analysis of secondary schools with a regression analysis to explain the variation in the MDEA scores. The purpose of this exercise is twofold: first, from a public policy perspective, we want to see how much of the variation in calculated school performance can be attributed to organizational features of the school that are under the discretion of management, and, second, how much of the variation in school performance can be attributed to noncontrollable characteristics of the school or students.

In our case, because efficient schools were dropped from their own reference sets and reevaluated, MDEA scores are bounded below by zero

but they are not bounded above and there is no mass of MDEA scores
located at the upper bound. The summary statistics in tables 17–4 to
17–6 show that the three sets of MDEA scores are positively skewed,
although not as severely as they would have been had we not dropped
efficient schools from their own reference sets. Nonetheless, in these
circumstances, the use of ordinary least squares (OLS) to estimate an
equation of the general form

$$y = X\beta + u, \qquad (17.1)$$

where y is a vector of MDEA scores, X is a matrix of explanatory
variables, and u is a normally distributed error term with zero mean and
constant variance, produces biased and inconsistent estimates of the
elements of the parameter vector β.[3]

Kalirajan and Shand (1988) and Banker and Johnston (1992) have
addressed this problem by using the transformation $\ln(1 - y/y)$ to convert
conventional efficiency scores bounded by zero and unity to unbounded
dependent variables in a regression analysis. Since our MDEA scores
are only bounded below by zero, a simple logarithmic transformation
achieves the same result. Hence we estimate a model of the general form

$$\ln y = X\beta + u, \qquad (17.2)$$

which on the tenable assumption that $u \sim N(0, \sigma^2)$ may be estimated by
OLS. Variables used in the three regression models are described in table
17–7. Regression results appear in tables 17–8 to 17–10.[4]

5.1. First-Stage Performance

Table 17–8 reports OLS results explaining variation in MDEA scores in
the first-stage model in which school performance is measured by the
ability to convert physical, financial, and human resources into educational opportunities. The OLS regression of calculated MDEA scores
against nine variables succeeds in explaining a significant portion of the
variation in school performance at this stage.

The enrollment variable is positive and highly significant, suggesting
that measured performance increases as school size increases. This
feature of the first-stage model is striking, because allowance for variable
returns to scale was included in the calculation of the MDEA scores in
section 4. Hence, this must be interpreted as the effect of size after
allowing for scale economies in computing the MDEA scores. Large
schools are more efficient than small schools at converting resources

Table 17–7. Variable Definitions for Regression Models

Variable	Definition
LNDEAV1	Natural log of MDEA score for resource efficiency (model 1)
LNDEAC2	Natural log of MDEA score for intermediate outcomes (model 2)
LNDEAC3	Natural log of MDEA score for long-term outcomes (model 3)
LENROLL[a]	School enrollment
ELITE	Dummy variable equal to 1 if school is elite private; 0 otherwise
CATHOLIC	Dummy variable equal to 1 if school is Catholic; 0 otherwise
RURAL	Dummy variable equal to 1 if school in rural area; 0 otherwise
LTCHABS[a]	Categorical variable indicating problem with teacher absenteeism (1 = serious problem, 2 = moderate, 3 = minor, 4 = none)
LSTDABS[a]	Categorical variable indicating problem with student absenteeism (same scale as above)
TAXDST	Dummy variable equal to 1 if school has a separate tax district; 0 otherwise (no separate tax district or private)
UNION	Dummy variable equal to 1 if teachers are unionized; 0 otherwise
GIFT	Dummy variable equal to 1 if school has program for gifted and talented students; 0 otherwise
ENGABIL	Dummy variable equal to 1 if tenth-grade English classes are grouped by ability; 0 otherwise
LDLHS[a]	Proportion of fathers of students in school with less than a high school degree
LBLACK[a]	Proportion of black students in school
LREMREAD[a]	Percent of tenth-grade students taking remedial reading class

[a] Indicates natural logarithm of variable.

into educational opportunities, although the estimated elasticity (0.22) suggests sharply diminishing returns.

The other variable that has a significant impact on school performance is the proportion of students in remedial reading classes. This impact is negative, presumably because these classes consume a disproportionate share of school resources. Elite schools perform significantly better than other schools, but Catholic schools are not significantly different from other schools in terms of performance. Whether or not a school has its own tax district, whether it is in a rural or nonrural location, whether or not teachers are unionized, and problems with teacher absenteeism are not significant determinants of performance. It is somewhat surprising that the presence of a gifted and talented program has no significant

Table 17–8. Regression Results for Resource Efficiency, Model 1 (Dependent Variable: LNDEAV1)

Analysis of Variance

Source	DF	Sum of Squares	Mean Square	F Value
MODEL	9	18.65336747	2.07259639	11.531
ERROR	501	90.05022217	0.17974096	
C TOTAL	510	108.70358964		

ROOT MSE	0.4239587	R-SQUARE	0.1716	
DEP MEAN	−0.422761	ADJ R-SQ	0.1567	
C.V.	−100.283			

Parameter Estimates

Variable	DF	Parameter Estimate	Standard Error	T for HO: Parameter = 0	Prob > |T|
INTERCEP	1	−1.96757	0.22876569	−8.601	0.0001
ELITE	1	0.61423502	0.25209853	2.436	0.0152
CATHOLIC	1	−0.0762427	0.071142763	−1.067	0.2863
RURAL	1	−0.0756507	0.047067	−1.607	0.1086
LENROLL	1	0.22153872	0.02822265	7.850	0.0001
TAXDST	1	−0.0241631	0.03845586	−0.628	0.5301
UNION	1	0.01889879	0.04691135	0.403	0.6872
GIFT	1	−0.0279226	0.0401677	−0.665	0.5066
LREMREAD	1	−0.00890853	0.003230617	−2.758	0.0060
LTCHABS	1	0.02816063	0.07352235	0.383	0.7019

impact on school performance, since a special program for students at the other end of the ability spectrum does have a significant impact.

It is encouraging that some of the determinants of school performance in providing educational opportunities (e.g., school size and remedial reading classes) are subject to manipulation by either school boards or parents.

5.2. Second-Stage Performance

Table 17–9 reports OLS results for the second-stage model, in which six of the outputs of model 1 are combined with student study time to produce intermediate-term educational outcomes. Nine explanatory

Table 17-9. Regression Results for Intermediate Outcomes, Model 2 (Dependent Variable: LNDEAC2)

Analysis of Variance

Source	DF	Sum of Squares	Mean Square	F Value
MODEL	9	0.87472088	0.09719121	2.812
ERROR	549	18.97675433	0.03456604	
C TOTAL	558	19.85147522		

ROOT MSE	0.1859194	R-SQUARE	0.0441	
DEP MEAN	−0.17142	ADJ R-SQ	0.0284	
C.V.	−100.458			

Parameter Estimates

Variable	DF	Parameter Estimate	Standard Error	T for HO: Parameter = 0	Prob > |T|
INTERCEP	1	−0.0916227	0.02623205	−3.493	0.0005
ELITE	1	0.17817252	0.11044436	1.613	0.1073
CATHOLIC	1	−0.0173211	0.03103308	−0.558	0.5770
RURAL	1	−0.0629726	0.01891112	−3.330	0.0009
LDLHS	1	−0.00137455	0.002321059	−0.582	0.5540
GIFT	1	−0.0385138	0.01709012	−2.254	0.0246
ENGABIL	1	−0.0112198	0.01671335	−0.671	0.5023
LBLACK	1	−0.000318512	0.001678973	−0.190	0.8496
LREMREAD	1	0.0002271695	0.001350044	0.168	0.8664
LSTDABS	1	−0.051491	0.02261611	−2.277	0.0232

variables account for a small but significant part of the variation in MDEA scores in the OLS regression.

Results suggest that rural location is once again a hindrance to performance, and the impact is now significant. Elite schools continue to outperform other schools, but not significantly so, Catholic schools are not significantly different from other schools, and schools with gifted and talented programs have lower performance, presumably because these programs divert resources away from the majority of students. Finally, as problems with student absenteeism increase (this variable is categorical, with 1 indicating a serious problem and 4 indicating no problem at all), schools perform better. This result is unexpected and perhaps can be explained by the notion that better-performing schools have more stringent criteria in evaluating problems with student absenteeism than other schools.

The proportion of fathers with less than a high school degree, whether or not schools grouped tenth-grade English classes by ability, the proportion of black students in the school, and the proportion of students in remedial reading classes were not significant determinants of school performance at this stage.

Once again, some variables subject to policy decisions exert a significant impact on school performance as described by model 2 MDEA scores.

5.3. Third-Stage Performance

Table 17–10 reports OLS results that explain variation in third-stage MDEA scores, in which school performance is measured by the ability to

Table 17–10. Regression Results for Long-Term Outcomes, Model 3 (Dependent Variable: LNDEAC3)

Analysis of Variance

Source	DF	Sum of Squares	Mean Square	F Value
MODEL	9	1.08127549	0.120914172	3.873
ERROR	555	17.21514418	0.03101828	
C TOTAL	564	18.29641967		

ROOT MSE	0.1761201	R-SQUARE	0.0591	
DEP MEAN	−0.247342	ADJ R-SQ	0.0438	
C.V.	−71.2052			

Parameter Estimates

Variable	DF	Parameter Estimate	Standard Error	T for HO: Parameter = 0	Prob > |T|
INTERCEP	1	−0.143108	0.02477509	−5.776	0.0001
ELITE	1	0.15326416	0.10460588	1.465	0.1434
CATHOLIC	1	−0.0730158	0.02915971	−2.504	0.0126
RURAL	1	−0.05214991	0.01777476	−2.897	0.0039
LDLHS	1	0.002186196	0.00219736	0.995	0.3202
GIFT	1	−0.0608982	0.01605099	−3.794	0.0002
ENGABIL	1	−0.00989852	0.01580011	−0.626	0.5313
LBLACK	1	0.00004157802	0.001581581	0.026	0.9790
LREMREAD	1	0.0002027794	0.001274131	0.159	0.8736
LSTDABS	1	−0.0471893	0.02137944	−2.207	0.0277

convert educational opportunities and student input into long-term student achievement. Since the focus is on long-term achievement, it is not surprising that explanatory power is fairly low, but nonetheless a significant portion of the variation in calculated MDEA scores is explained by the nine environmental variables.

Operation of a gifted and talented program and a rural location remain negative influences on school performance when performance is measured by long-term student achievement, as does the practice of grouping students according to English ability, although not significantly so. Elite private schools continue to perform better than all other schools, but this variable is no longer statistically significant. In this model, Catholic schools perform significantly below other schools. Finally, as in model 2, as problems with student absenteeism increase, schools perform better.

The proportion of fathers with less than a high school degree, whether or not schools grouped tenth-grade English classes by ability, the proportion of black students in the school, and the proportion of students in remedial reading classes were not significant determinants of school performance in this model.

All in all, the results reported in table 17–10 are similar to those in table 17–9. This should not be surprising, since the intermediate- and long-term MDEA scores to be explained are highly correlated, and since the two sets of explanatory variables are the same. Nevertheless, the similarity of results is encouraging, for it shows that there exists a consistent set of explanatory variables for variation in school performance defined in terms of ability to convert school offerings and student input into a variety of indicators of student achievement.

6. Summary and Conclusions

The purpose of this chapter has been to combine two analytical techniques, DEA and regression analysis, in order to shed new light on the nature and determinants of U.S. secondary school performance. To this end, we have sketched out a stratified model of education production in which school performance is determined by the ability to achieve three objectives. The first objective is a relatively short-term goal of converting resources into educational opportunities for students. The second and third objectives involve the use of educational opportunities and student input to general intermediate-term outcomes such as test scores and long-term outcomes such as income.

School performance measures are obtained using a modified DEA technique that ranks schools on a $(0, +\infty)$ scale rather than on the conventional $(0, +1]$ scale. The chief advantage of the modification is that it eliminates the problem of having a mass of schools concentrated at the upper bound of the performance distribution. The resulting logarithmic MDEA distributions are unbounded and roughly normally distributed, making them appropriate dependent variables in a second-stage OLS regression analysis. The purpose of the regression analysis is to explain the observed distributions of MDEA scores, particularly if the explanation involves policy variables that can be used to enhance school performance.

Results of the first-stage MDEA analysis suggest that schools perform better at meeting their intermediate- and long-term objectives than they do at meeting their short-term objectives. MDEA scores have higher medians and smaller variances in models 2 and 3 than in model 1. This in turn implies that there is greater room for policy impact at the short-term level of education production. This finding is tempered by the fact that other researchers (e.g., Ahn and Seiford, 1990) have found calculated conventional DEA scores in (higher) education to be sensitive to variable selection, and we have not experimented with different inputs and outputs at any of the three levels of education production.

Results of the second-stage regression analysis suggest that we can explain a small but significant part of the variation in MDEA scores in all three levels of education production. Generally speaking, elite schools perform better than other schools, and rural schools perform worse than others. Operations of special programs at either end of the student ability spectrum hinder school performance. Finally, in the short-term model, in which schools convert resources into educational opportunities, school performance is strongly and positively linked with size.

Acknowledgments

This chapter is a much revised and retitled version of a paper originally prepared for the Austin Conference. We are grateful to R. R. Russell, K. Montgomery, E. Rhodes, E. Hanushek, A. Y. Lewin, two readers, and many seminar audiences for helpful comments.

Notes

1. Skewness of DEA scores is rarely reported, an exception being Ahn, Charnes, and Cooper (1988), and even more rarely put to any good use. The mass of DEA scores located at the boundary value of unity receives a variety of responses, ranging from Cameron (1989), who reports without comment 16 of 23 and 9 of 12 observations as having DEA scores of unity, to Andersen and Petersen (1993), who show how to rank observations having DEA scores of unity. Among the researchers who have used regression analysis to attempt to explain variation in DEA scores, Rhodes and Southwick (1989) stand out for their use of a tobit regression model to accommodate the mass of DEA scores located at unity. Ray (1991) uses a variant of corrected ordinary least squares in a second-stage regression model in an effort to explain performance variation in Connecticut public school districts. Finally, Wyckoff and Lavigne (1992) substitute dominance analysis for regression analysis in their effort to explain performance variation in New York public elementary schools.

2. This procedure has no effect on either the frontier against which an observation is evaluated, or the DEA score of the observation being evaluated, if that observation has a conventional DEA score less than unity. For observations having conventional DEA scores of unity, however, frontiers typically become more relaxed, and so scores typically improve. See Andersen and Petersen (1993) for details.

3. Boundedness alone is sufficient to produce this result; see, for example, Maddala (1983).

4. Note that these regressions attempt to explain only the radial component of production inefficiency. The nonradial slack component is small relative to the radial component, and we make no attempt to explain it. The only effort of which we are aware to explain slack in such a way is Sitorus (1966). Fried, Lovell, and Vanden Eeckaut (1993) convert radial inefficiency into variable-specific radial slack, add radial slacks to nonradial slcaks, and regress total (radial plus nonradial) slacks against a vector of explanatory variables, using a seemingly unrelated regressions framework. In this approach, the objective is to explain, simultaneously, total slack in all inputs and outputs.

18 THE PROBLEM OF NEW AND DISAPPEARING COMMODITIES IN THE CONSTRUCTION OF PRICE INDEXES

C. A. Knox Lovell and Kimberly D. Zieschang

1. Introduction

Important and frequently encountered problems in the production of price indexes are the appearance of new commodities that were unavailable when the item pricing sample was first designed, or the disappearance of commodities originally selected for inclusion in the index. There are several traditional methods for "splicing" old commodities out and/or new commodities in, and all hinge on some assumption about the comparability of the new or disappearing items with items continuously available for pricing throughout the period within which price comparisons are to be made. Included among these methods are

1. the *link to show no change* method, whereby a new item's difference in price from an existing item is assumed to be entirely a result of the difference in quality;
2. the *cell relative* method, whereby the price change of a new item at the point of its introduction (or an old item at the point of its disappearance) is assumed to be the same as that of a judgmentally selected group of similar goods;

3. the *resource cost* method, whereby the difference in price of a new
    or disappearing variety with a continuing item is adjusted for
    quality by the relative costs of producing the two items; and
4. the *hedonic* method, whereby the difference in price of a noncon-
    tinuous variety from a continuous item is adjusted using a model-
    based statistical estimate of the difference in the market value of
    measured characteristics of the two items.

All these methods except the resource cost and hedonic are economically
ad hoc (see Triplett, 1983, on the economic foundations of these
methods). It is difficult to evaluate the relative merits of the ad hoc
methods other than, for example, by analyst-specific quasi-statistical
priors about how "smooth" the movements in the aggregate price series
are when each method is applied. The usual implementation of the
hedonic approach requires assumptions about market equilibrium prices
across the quality spectrum that may be difficult to support in some cases,
and good information for resource cost adjustment may be impossible to
obtain (Zieschang, 1985).

Index number theoreticians and practitioners have worried about the
problem of new and disappearing goods in price and quantity indexes
since at least the time of Frisch (1930), whose *determinateness test*
required an index formula to have a positive limit as any component price
or quantity approached zero (see Färe and Lyon, 1981, for a modern
assessment of Frisch's test). Hicks (1940) and Fisher and Shell (1972)
have provided the currently accepted theoretical approach to dealing with
the problem for price indexes. When a good disappears in a Laspeyres-
perspective input price index, the missing price is imputed as the reservation price given the base-period technology, where the reservation price is
defined as the minimum price at which zero quantity of the good is used
in the production of base-period output given comparison period prices of
other goods. A disappearing good in a Laspeyres-perspective output price
index is imputed as its reservation price given the base-period technology,
defined as the maximum price at which no production of the good is
forthcoming given base-period input and comparison period prices
of other outputs. A Paasche output price index would use for the
baseperiod price of new varieties the reservation price at which the
new varieties would just be forthcoming given the comparison period
technology. The Hicks–Fisher–Shell reservation price approach to this
problem is undeniably elegant. However, it has provided little guidance
to index number practitioners, who are faced with attempting to estimate
the unknown reservation prices. The problem is a potentially significant

one if, for example, the price time path of new varieties follows that of the typical new computer model, entering at a high price and rapidly falling thereafter, and may be significantly different from the price paths of existing models, which may experience only slight price declines. Without knowledge of the reservation price, much of this early-product-life price change can be lost, imparting potentially serious bias to a price index—upward bias in this example, and hence downward bias in the growth of implicit quantity indexes computed by using these indexes to deflate value aggregates.

Zieschang (1988) provides a superlative index number approach to the reservation price problem that relies on knowledge of the price-characteristics (hedonic) locus and a certain structural condition satisfied by a firm's technology, given available product description data. The purpose of this chapter is to examine an alternative, programming approach to estimating reservation prices (or at least bounds on them) that does not rely on a hedonic relationship between price and product characteristics. Our approach relies instead on the relationship between output prices and the structure of the production-possibilities frontier. It exploits the duality between the revenue function of interest to Fisher and Shell (1972) and the (output) distance function of Shephard (1970), and it adapts the computational techniques that have evolved in the data envelopment analysis (DEA) literature initiated by Charnes, Cooper, and Rhodes (1978). The problem is examined in the practical setting of finding a method for computing an output price index for the computer equipment industry. We use the Producer Price Index Program of the Bureau of Labor Statistics (BLS) as an illustrative institutional setting for this problem.

2. Some Background on the Producer Price Index

The producer price index (PPI) is built on the concept of a fixed input–output price index elucidated by Fisher and Shell (1972) and Archibald (1977). It thus attempts to approximate a ratio of revenue functions for each covered industry that yield the maximum sales attainable given a fixed vector of inputs and a reference or comparison vector of output prices. If p is an m vector of output prices and T is the set of feasible input output combinations, then the revenue function is

$$R(x, p) = \max\{p'y: (x, y) \in T\}.$$

Fisher and Shell (1972) and Archibald (1977) show that the Laspeyres formula used by the BLS,

$$L(p^0, p^1, y^0, y^1) = \frac{\sum_{i=1}^{m} p_i^1 y_i^0}{\sum_{i=1}^{m} p_i^0 y_i^0} = \sum_{i=1}^{m} \frac{p_i^1}{p_i^0} \cdot s_i^0$$

where

$$s_i^0 = \frac{p_i^0 y_i^0}{\sum_{i=1}^{m} p_i^0 y_i^0}$$

is a lower bound for this conceptual, Laspeyres-perspective industry output price index, given by

$$I(p^0, p^1, x^0) = \frac{R(x^0, p^1)}{R(x^0, p^0)}$$

As with other index numbers, the Laspeyres has the advantage of depending only on observable prices and quantities, rather than the unknown industry production function and input vector. It also requires no recalculation of the shares s_i^0 in its weighted-relative form, saving a great deal of expense and effort, since the weights from the four-digit Standard Industrial Classification (SIC) level and up are obtained from a census of business establishments.

The price relatives p_i^1/p_i^0 are estimated for each i, where i generally corresponds to a four-digit SIC, from a longitudinal sample of prices supplied by a sample of establishments classified in stratum or category i. These business establishments are selected with probability proportionate to a proxy for sales (employment) at the time the establishment sample is drawn from a comprehensive list or frame (the Unemployment Insurance file in most PPI industries). The data the establishment is selected is generally not near the base period some years after a census, because establishment samples are periodically reselected between censuses in the interest of controlling variance as attrition reduces the size of the original samples. The products whose prices enter the index are selected at the time the establishments enter the sample with a technique called *disaggregation* that attempts to select a predetermined number of sample products or "hits" with probability proportionate to sales of each item in the output mix. To estimate the price relative for the ith establishment stratum or category, the product price relatives are averaged, with each product's weight proportional to its establishment's weight in the stratum times the product's weight in the sales of the establishment. For further information on the PPI program, see the *BLS Handbook of Methods* (1988), chapter 16.

Although not used by BLS, the Paasche index formula is used by the Bureau of Economic Analysis for the GNP deflators. It is given by

$$P(p^0, p^1, y^0, y^1) = \frac{\sum_{i=1}^m p_i^1 y_i^1}{\sum_{i=1}^m p_i^0 y_i^1} = \left[\sum_{i=1}^m \frac{p_i^1}{p_i^0} \cdot s_i^1\right]^{-1}$$

where

$$s_i^1 = \frac{p_i^1 y_i^1}{\sum_{i=1}^m p_i^1 y_i^1}$$

The Paasche output price index is an upper bound for the conceptual, Paasche-perspective industry output price index, given by

$$I(p^0, p^1, x^0) = \frac{R(x^1, p^1)}{R(x^1, p^0)}$$

A final index formula variant considered in this chapter is the Fisher Ideal, which is the geometric mean of the Laspeyres and Paasche:

$$F(p^0, p^1, y^0, y^1) = [L(p^0, p^1, y^0, y^1) \cdot P(p^0, p^1, y^0, y^1)]^{1/2}$$

Diewert (1976) has shown the Fisher index to be superlative (exact to a second-order differential approximation for an arbitrary twice-differentiable revenue function) for homogeneous technologies that are invariant across time. Diewert (1992) has extended this result to cover changing homogeneous technologies as well.

We are interested here in the difficulty that arises when products disappear from the sample because they have been discontinued, or when new products appear as 1) commodity analysts attempt to find a substitute commodity from a reporting company for an item that has been discontinued; or 2) a new sample of establishments, and hence products, has been drawn for the industry. The specific problem is to find the shadow or reservation prices at which one unit of the disappearing commodities would still be produced currently, or one unit of the new commodity would have been produced in the base period.

If there are discontinued goods and if the reservation prices for discontinued varieties are known, the Laspeyres index including these prices in the comparison situation, indexed with superscript "1" above, will remain a lower bound to the conceptual Laaspeyres-perspective output price index. If the price change implied by the reservation prices differs from the base-year quantity weighted-average price change of items available in both periods, the Laspeyres index will no longer necessarily have a predictable relationship to the conceptual index. Clearly, if the reservation prices are taken to be zero in the Laspeyres formula, the index will retain its lower bound property, since

$$L(p^0, p^1, y^0, y^1) = \frac{\Sigma_{i \in I_+} p_i^1 y_i^0 + \Sigma_{i \in I_0^1} \hat{p}_i^1 y_i^0}{\Sigma_{i=1}^m p_i^0 y_i^0}$$

$$\geq \frac{\Sigma_{i \in I_+} p_i^1 y_i^0}{\Sigma_{i=1}^m p_i^0 y_i^0}$$

where $\hat{p}_i$ is the reservation price of the ith good, I_+ is the set of indices of goods available in both periods, and I_0^1 is the set of indices of varieties that disappear in the comparison period. This is not the way discontinued varieties are handled in practice, as indicated in the Introduction, but could be taken as a legitimate method of computing a lower bound for the Laspeyres-perspective output price index. If a set of defensible nonnegative, nonzero reservation prices were available, using them in the index would result in a "tighter" lower bound than would obtain if they were assumed zero.

A similar set of remarks holds for the Paasche index in the case of new varieties (the appearance of which by definition has no effect on the Laspeyres index). In this case,

$$P(p^0, p^1, y^0, y^1) = \frac{\Sigma_{i=1}^m p_i^1 y_i^1}{\Sigma_{i \in I_+} p_i^0 y_i^1 + \Sigma_{i \in I_0^0} \hat{p}_i^0 y_i^1}$$

$$\leq \frac{\Sigma_{i=1}^m p_i^1 y_i^1}{\Sigma_{i \in I_+} p_i^0 y_i^1}$$

where $\hat{p}_i$ is the reservation price of the ith good, I_+ is the set of indices of goods available in both periods, and I_0^0 is the set of indices of varieties that are new in the comparison period. The index to the right of the inequality would obtain if reservation prices were taken as zero, and would constitute an upper bound on the Paasche index with nonnegative, nonzero reservation prices, which in turn bounds the Paasche-perspective output price index from above. Our interest is thus in obtaining a set of nonnegative, nonzero imputed prices for new and discontinued varieties that are no greater than the set of reservation prices for the technology relevant to the periods in question.

3. The Computer Equipment Industry

Nowhere has the new and disappearing commodity problem been more manifest than in the computer equipment industry, SIC 3573, which is characterized by products undergoing rapid and significant technological change. The Bureau of Economic Analysis introduced a new price index for this SIC in 1987 that demonstrably improved its price measure for this sector. The previous method for handling the rapid change in characteristics and performance of these products was the link-to-show-no-change method, one of the standard methods cited in the Introduction above. By contrast with the old BEA measure, which indicated very little price change over time, a steady stream of papers using "hedonic" techniques based on statistical estimation of a relationship such as

$$p^t_{3573,i} = h^t_{3573}(a^t_{3573,i}, \beta_{3573}) + \varepsilon^t_{3573,i}$$

with $a^t_{3573,i}$ a vector of product characteristics such as speed, memory, and so on, $\varepsilon^t_{3573,i}$ a random error, and β_{3573} a parameter vector, had showed rapid price declines after accounting for the concurrent increases in quality as measured by product characteristics. A hedonic function is interpreted in this context as a market-equilibrium price locus across a continuous spectrum of characteristics a, and price indexes based on this locus essentially track shifts in the locus through time. This is generally accomplished by using the hedonic function to impute a base-period price for the currently priced package of characteristics (see Triplett, 1986, for a clear explanation of hedonic methods in price indexes). Current BEA methodology now incorporates these hedonic techniques, and its computer price index has fallen rather rapidly since January 1987. BLS is now publishing computer equipment price indexes that also incorporate hedonic methods (Catron, 1988; Sinclair and Catron, 1990).

4. Programming Approaches to the Problem of Imputing Reservation Prices

The technology of computer firms can be represented by a distance function, defined as

$$D(x, y) = [\max\{\phi: \phi y \text{ is producible with } x\}]^{-1}$$

where x is an n-vector of input quantities and y is an m-vector of quantities of output varieties, perhaps defined by their characteristics a. D will be positively linear homogeneous in y by definition, and we assume it is also almost everywhere differentiable, nondecreasing, and convex in y and nonincreasing and quasi-concave in x. A distance function with these properties is dual to the revenue function $R(x, p)$ defined in a previous section via the following operations (see Shephard, 1970):

$$D(x, y) = \max_p \{p'y : R(x, p) \leq 1\}$$

$$R(x, p) = \max_y \{p'y : D(x, y) \leq 1\}$$

Further, if we differentiate D (where differentiable) with respect to y and scale by total revenue, we obtain output prices p, as

$$p = \nabla_y D(x, y) \cdot p'y$$

On this, see Färe and Zieschang (1991). Thus, if some of the elements of p are missing because the associated outputs are zero, we might use the shadow price formula above to impute them for use in an output price index. Our problem now is to obtain the distance function.

Until recently the use of distance functions to characterize the structure of technology has been more popular in theory than in empirical practice. However, in the last few years, Färe, Fukuyama, and Primont (1988) have estimated a translog distance function system, and Färe, Grosskopf, Lindgren, and Roos (this volume) and Färe, Grosskopf, Lovell, and Yaisawarng (1993) have used linear programming techniques to construct, respectively, nonparametric and translog frontiers. The zeros in our data rule out both translog approaches. The nonparametric approach we follow involves characterizing the solution to our problem in the spirit of the Charnes, Cooper, and Rhodes (CCR) (1978) DEA technique. Suppose we know all inputs and outputs of the establishments in our pricing sample. Let y^k be an m vector of outputs and x^k an n vector of inputs for the Kth of K establishments in the pricing sample, and let Y and X be, respectively, $m \times K$ and $n \times K$ matrices containing the output and input vectors for all K establishments. For each establishment in the sample we solve the output-oriented CCR primal problem (BCC_P-O):

$$\max_{\phi^k, \lambda^k, s^{k+}, s^{k-}} \quad \phi^k + \varepsilon \cdot \bar{1}s^{k+} + \varepsilon \cdot \bar{1}s^{k-}$$

$$\text{s.t.} \quad \phi^k y^k - Y\lambda^k + s^{k+} = 0$$

$$X\lambda^k + s^{k-} = x^k$$

$$\lambda^k, s^{k+}, s^{k-} \geq 0$$

where Y and X may contain zeros representing new and disappearing goods. In their original formulation, CCR (1978, p. 430) required Y and X to be strictly postitive matrices; see also Charnes and Cooper (1984, p. 333), and Charnes, Cooper, Golany, Seiford, and Stutz (CCGSS) (1985, p. 98). This requirement is much stronger than the Karlin (1959, p. 338–343)–Shephard (1970, p. 283–292) conditions requiring that Y and X be nonnegative matrices with positive row and column sums. In the new additive DEA formulation of CCGSS (1985), Charnes, Cooper, Learner, Phillips, and Rousseau (1987), and Charnes, Cooper, Rousseau, and Semple (1987, p. 14), the strict positivity requirement is abandoned. Charnes, Cooper, and Thrall (1986) have shown that the CCR model can accomodate zeros in the data matrices Y and X. This is, of course, critically important, since zeros in the data matrices are the central feature of the economic problem we use DEA to address.

The solution contains establishment-specific values for ϕ, λ, and a shadow value or "virtual multiplier" vector. This virtual multiplier vector could be exploited to estimate the shadow prices of commodities produced in zero quantities for some establishments and time periods. In a price index production environment, product output quantities are at least implicitly collected in the form of "quote weights" derived from the establishment/product sample design. However, input quantities are not available, because collecting them is too expensive or places an intolerable reporting burden on voluntary respondents.

To accommodate the circumstances of price index construction, we therefore use the indirect distance function of Shephard (1974) as our representation of the industry technology. The indirect distance function is given as

$$ID(w/c, y) = [\max_\phi \{\phi: C(\phi y, w) \leq c\}]^{-1}$$

where w is a nonnegative $n \times 1$ vector of input prices, and

$$C(y, w) = \min_x \{w'x: D(x, y) \leq 1\}$$

is the cost function of the industry technology.

$ID(w/c, y)$ still requires knowledge of input prices w and total cost of production c. In the application to publically available data on microcomputers below, we assume that input prices are the same for all firms in the industry, and that firms are equally profitable, so that costs are a constant percentage of revenue or sales. We thus use $r = p'y$ as a proxy for total cost, and ignore input prices, which are also unavailable to us, and consider the following output-oriented CCR primal problem for each firm k:

$$\max_{\phi^k, \lambda^k, s^{k+}, s^{k-}} \quad \phi^k + \varepsilon \cdot \bar{1}s^{k+} + \varepsilon \cdot \bar{1}s^{k-}$$

$$\text{s.t.} \quad \phi^k y^k - Y\lambda^k + s^{k+} = 0$$

$$C\lambda^k + s^{k-} = c^k$$

$$\lambda^k, s^{k+}, s^{k-} \geq 0$$

where C is a $1 \times K$ vector whose elements are the total production costs for the firms in the sample: c^k, $k = 1, 2, \ldots, K$.

5. A Programming Model of Microcomputer Production

In our application to microcomputers, we use data from the GML Corporation on company, model, system characteristics, and list price, and data from the Internatioanl Data Corporation (IDC) on aggregate sales by selected companies for the years 1986 and 1987. This yields an initial file of 194 models produced by 24 companies. Data on values of shipments at the model level are usually jealously guarded by computer manufacturers, and were not available to us from a public source. We imputed quantity sold for each model arbitrarily by dividing sales equally between the number of models indicated by GML to be available each year for each company in the IDC sales data and divided by the GML price. We are acutely aware of the potential errors in these imputations, particularly since the sales for some of the largest companies include substantial receipts for equipment other than microcomputers. Given this shortcoming in our quantity data, our results here may best be viewed as a simulation of the programming methodology in a price index production setting. We have somewhat greater confidence in our ability to identify new and disappearing models, however, since this was gleaned from status variables in the GML file for each model. After editing on the basis of product characteristics as described below, our file contained 11 models that were new in 1987 and 7 that were discontinued in that year. In order to obtain some overlap in company production of products, we grouped these models into classes defined on product characteristics.

Although the GML file contains a large number of characteristics, we selected 1) INTEL. presence of Intel 80xx-80xxx central processing unit (CPU), 2) MOTOROLA, presence of Motorola 680xx CPU (the default CPU type is a catchall for other types), 3) BUSWORD, wordsize of the bus in bits, 4) CPUWORD, internal wordsize of the CPU in bits, 5) CLOCK, CPU clock speed in megahertz (MHz), 6) STDRAM, standard random access memory (RAM) in kilobytes, and 7) HDISK, standard megabytes (MB) of hard disk storage. Of the 194 models in our file, 152 produced by 23 of the 24 companies had nonmissing data for all seven characteristics (reducing the number of discontinued models to six). We deleted the incomplete records and weighted up the quantity data on the remaining models to cover the total sales data for each company. A similar weighting process occurs at BLS if it is known that a product is available but price information is not forthcoming from a reporting firm in time for the monthly index production deadline. As noted above, weighting also occurs as a result of the process of sampling products for pricing within company.

In our two-year sample, there are 94 packages of these seven characteristics. The quantities sold of the models in the sample were aggregated within company according to these package classes. The number of product varieties m^k ranges from 1 to 16 across the 23 firms in the sample. Thus the number of constraints in the linear program for the inverse indirect distance function ranged as high as $16 + 1$, where the last constraint is the total cost inequality. The dimension of the multiplier vector $[\lambda' \ \phi']'$ is 23×2 years plus 1, or 47. These problems were easily solved in a few seconds using the LP procedure of the Statistical Analysis System (SAS) running on an Amdahl 5990 (IBM 3090 equivalent) mainframe computer.

6. Reservation Prices from Programming Models

The dual activities computed by each linear program for each output constraint represent the change in the inverse distance function with respect to a perturbation of the associated output. The shadow price of the output is the change in the distance function with respect to the output. The value of ϕ computed for each firm is the value of the inverse distance function for that firm. If the distance function is differentiable, we have the normalized shadow price of the ith output ρ_i as

$$\rho_i = \partial D/\partial y_i = \partial \phi^{-1}/\partial y_i = -\phi^{-2} \cdot [\partial \phi/\partial y_i].$$

Both factors on the far right side are computed in the programs for the firms in the sample, the first factor being the negative of the square of the reciprocal of the maximand and the bracketed quantity being the dual activity or virtual multiplier of the ith output quantity constraint. Following Färe and Zieschang (1991), the nominal shadow price for the ith output of the kth firm is found by multiplying the normalized shadow price by total revenue, $\hat{p}_i^k = (\Sigma_{i=1}^m p_i^k y_i^k) \cdot \rho_i$. If the solution for ϕ contains nonzero slacks, one set of virtual multipliers in the solution may have a zero value for ρ_i. This is of course a perfectly legitimate normalized reservation price in this case, but we may also be interested in the smallest positive value for ρ_i, if it exists, over the programs for all the firms in the sample. An upper bound on the imputed reservation price would be the minimum of this value multiplied by the firm revenue from the period in which the item is unobserved, and the price of the item in the period in which it is observed. We will refer to this technique of computing reservation prices below as *the LP imputation*.

7. Results

Because of the large number of varieties of products (94) relative to the number of firms (23), all but one of our firms were technically efficient, with inverse distance function values of unity. Table 18–1 contains the reservation price results for the new and discontinued varieties in our sample. The first two columns contain the company and model of the variety, the third column contains the list price from the GML file, the fourth column contains the minimum positive revenue-scaled shadow price, and the last column contains the imputed reservation price. For 6 of the 11 new models and 2 of the 6 discontinued models, the LP approach was unable to find a tighter bound on the reservation price than zero. For two of the new models and none of the discontinued models, the LP reservation price imputation lies between zero and the price effective in the period the variety was available. Interestingly, for three of the new models and three of the discontinued models, the maximum reservation price is the same as the price in the available period, implying an imputed price relative of one. This is effectively the link-to-show-no-change method described in the introduction.

In table 18–2 we present the Laspeyres, Paasche, and Fisher price indexes for 1986–1987, using 1) link to show no change, 2) imputation of the LP reservation price, and 3) imputation of a zero reservation price. Not surprisingly, the LP-imputed indexes fall between their "link" and "zero" counterparts for each formula type. It is notable that the estimated price changes are surprisingly small given the rapid price/performance improvements reported in the industry. This can be mostly attributed to imperfections in our data, partly in the quantity fields, as explained above. There is also likely to be a problem with the price data, since they are from published list prices rather than from transaction price data that includes discounts, which along with shipments data also tend to be sensitive information for the companies in this industry. It is likely that discounts from infrequently changed list prices tend to increase as a product ages and must compete with successive generations of higher-performance competitors, a phenomenon that would be only imperfectly reflected in our data.

Table 18–1. Reservation Prices for Microcomputers

Company	Model	List Price	Minimum Positive Shadow Price	Imputed Maximum Reservation Price
New in 1987				
Apple	Macintosh II	$3,899.00	0.00	0.00
Apple	Macintosh SE	$2,600.00	$19,192.43	$2,600.00
Compaq	Deskpro 386	$6,499.00	0.00	0.00
Data General	Dasher 286	$3,395.00	0.00	0.00
Hewlett-Packard	9000 Model 330	$12,700.00	$2,830.51	$2,830.51
Hewlett-Packard	9000 Model 350	$21,900.00	0.00	0.00
IBM	PC XY 286	$2,810.00	0.00	0.00
IBM	Series/1 5170-496	$10,695.00	$23,465.79	$10,695.00
IBM	System/2 Model 30	$1,695.00	0.00	0.00
IBM	System/2 Model 50	$3,595.00	$1,714.09	$1,714.09
Masscomp	MC5550	$29,750.00	$87,635.52	$29,750.00
Discontinued in 1987				
Compaq	Compaq Plus	$3,199.00	$63,830.69	$3,199.00
Compaq	Portable 286/2,3	$5,499.00	$30,139.99	$5,499.00
Hewlett-Packard	9000 Series 500	$28,250.00	0.00	0.00
Masscomp	MC-500	$39,900.00	$41,933.50	$39,900.00
NBI	U! Tech Station	$15,475.00	$2,985.28	$2,985.28
NBI	System One IWS	$13,300.00	0.00	0.00

Table 18-2.   Output Price Indexes for Microcomputers, 1986-1987

Imputation Method	Index
Laspeyres Indexes	
(1) Link to show no change	97.878
(2) LP	97.281
(3) Zero reservation price	97.268
Paasche Indexes	
(1) Link to show no change	98.438
(2) LP	106.552
(3) Zero reservation price	108.080
Fisher Indexes	
(1) Link to show no change	98.150
(2) LP	101.811
(3) Zero reservation price	102.531

8. Concluding Remarks

We have applied the DEA method of determining the "inner technology" implicit in a set of observations on firms, their inputs or costs. And their outputs to the problem of imputing reservation prices in price indexes. Our data set is from a topical industry, microcomputers, and our application of the DEA technique has been successful in illustrating a new method of dealing with the new and disappearing goods problem in producer price indexes. Further refinements of the technique could be made. We stratified or grouped the computer models very little in the interest of isolating the items that were new or discontinued in 1987. Our classification by the seven characteristics that we examined reduced the number of varieties from 153 models to 94 aggregate classes. It may be useful to aggregate further, though proper criteria for the degree of aggregation should include the variability of the resulting shadow price and industry index estimates. Acceptable methods for computing the mean square error of programming frontier estimates have not yet been identified, though a Monte Carlo simulation paper by Gong and Sickles (1992) may point in the right general direction. We refer here to resampling plans such as the Jackknife and Bootstrap (Efron, 1982). Finally, our approach made rather crude use of a wealth of information on product characteristics, one of the strongest features of our data set. It would be interesting to consider a distance function that includes product characteristics as well as output quantities as arguments, rather than merely as variety classification variables. The extended indirect distance function would be $D(w/c, a, y)$, where a is a vector of length $m \cdot J$, where J is the number of characteristics that define a product. The seven characteristics we chose came rather close in this application to being sufficient for unique identification. We might then consider an extended programming problem for each firm that includes constraints not only for the quantities of the varieties it produces but also for their characteristics.

Acknowledgments

Thanks are due to Bert Balk, Netherlands Bureau of Statistics; Rolf Färe, University of Southern Illinois, Carbondale; Marshall Reinsdorf, Office of Economic Research, U.S. Bureau of Labor Statistic (BLS); and William Cooper, University of Texas, for helpful comments and suggestions. We would also like to thank Brian Catron and Jim Sinclair of the Division of Producer Prices and Price Indexes, BLS, for assistance with the data. The views expressed here do not reflect the policy of the Department of Labor or of the Bureau of Labor Statistics, or the views of other staff members of those agencies.

19 EVALUATING THE RELATIVE EFFICIENCY OF BASEBALL PLAYERS

Mark J. Mazur

1. Introduction

Countless hours are spent in debate on innumerable back porches—the topic being the relative merit of baseball players. Much of this debate is poorly focused, since the participants cannot even agree on the relevant dimensions (e.g., is a slick-fielding shortstop more valuable than a slugging leftfielder? than a dominating pitcher?). Moreover, even when the relevant dimensions of comparison can be agreed upon (for example, by limiting the discussion to batting prowess), a relative ranking consensus may not be achieved, since weighting individual items may be pro- blematic (for instance, is a home run worth twice as much as a single? more than twice as much?). However, if agreement can be reached regarding the performance dimensions to be considered, use of data envelopment analysis (DEA) can lead to objective rankings of player performance.

Using baseball players as the subject of this chapter takes advantage of the wealth of statistical data collected and disseminated in each baseball season. This mass of data makes the use of an empirical technique like DEA relatively easy. Another advantage of baseball as subject matter is that each season serves as a self-contained production period, during which various measures of performance are accumulated. Full-time players face all the other teams, eliminating some of the potential for bias that might be present if players only faced some small subset of opponents.[1] Finally, the production of performance statistics on the baseball diamond can be thought of as a production process completely insulated from relative prices. In a typical manufacturing production process, one might expect that changes in relative prices (e.g., an exogenous shock that increases labor costs without a corresponding gain in labor productivity) would cause the producer to attempt to vary the mix of factors used in the production process (e.g., to substitute other factors for labor in the case of a wage increase). However, when examining baseball statistics for a given season, changes in the relative prices (values) of production inputs are expected to be a minor issue. A maintained assumption is that there is little possibility that the value placed on singles will decline relative to home runs during a season and that this change will lead to a player trying to produce more home runs.[2] Rather, one can think of players having the same inputs (the ability to participate in a game) and using these inputs to generate multidimensional outputs (the various performance measures).

One point to be emphasized about this chapter is its demonstration aspect. Since performance in sport can be thought of as taking place in a production environment, it seems natural to address this topic using tools from the field of productivity analysis. The goal of this chapter is to show that DEA can be applied in a nontraditional area (baseball) to generate relative performance rankings among production units (players). One might expect that the methodology used here could be adapted quite easily to other sports in which a relative performance ranking would be desirable. In addition, dimensions other than the ones considered here might optimally be part of a desirable baseball-player ranking scheme that utilized DEA technology.

An outline of this chapter and a brief preview of the results follow. Section 2 describes the data utilized and explains the dimensions considered in the analysis. The issue of scaling the various dimensions so as to provide comparability of efficiency scores over time is also addressed. In section 3, the results from the DEA analysis for individual players are presented in abbreviated form.[3] Maximally efficient frontiers of both pitching and batting performance are traced out, and the players whose performances define these frontiers are noted. To determine the efficiency frontiers, all players are assumed to have the same input (scaled as 1.0). The outputs are taken to be standardized scores on each measure of performance. In addition, some other best and worst statistical performances are noted for each season. These results indicate that DEA can provide an efficient means of summarizing several dimensions of player performance. In order to study whether the DEA performance measures could be related to team performance, a regression analysis is presented in section 4. This analysis shows that team performance, as measured by win/loss records, is strongly related to relative efficiency scores computed for the team as a whole. To some extent, this finding provides support for the validity of using DEA in this context. A final section looks at possible extensions of this line of research.

2. The Data

The basic data sources used in this study were contained in LOTUS worksheets and were purchased from commercial sources.[4] All players who appeared in a major league game in the years 1986, 1987, and 1988 were contained in the original data set. However, many players appeared infrequently, and their performances were not strictly comparable to those of full-time players. In order to concentrate the analysis on those players who appeared on a regular basis, only those with sufficient playing time (as defined by having at least 200 at bats (for batters) or 100 innings pitched (for pitchers)) are included in the subsequent analysis. These restrictions limited the number of batters considered to the range 118–162, and the number of pitchers to the range 62–80. The exact number included depends on the season being examined.

Two distinct areas of baseball performance were analyzed using DEA: batting and pitching. For each of these areas, particular dimensions of performance were subjectively selected to provide the basis for comparisons between players. Traditionally, batting prowess is demonstrated by players leading the league in batting average (BAVG), home runs (HR), and/or runs batted in (RBI). These three dimensions were chosen to define the Triple Crown Frontier (TCF), the measure of batting performance used in this study. Note that performance is increasing in all three of these measures; that is, a higher value of the measure indicates superior performance along the dimension being considered.

For the analysis of pitching prowess, a similar three-dimensional Pitching Dominance Frontier (PDF) was defined. There is little traditional wisdom as to what constitutes adequate statistical measures of pitching performance, so the dimensions analyzed were subjectively chosen. The component dimensions of the PDF frontier were earned run average (ERA), hits to innings pitched ratio (H/IP), and base on balls to strikeouts ratio (BB/SO). In contrast to the batting performance measures, a lower value of these pitching performance measures translates into superior performance along the dimension considered.

DEA provides relative (not absolute) rankings of player performances. In order to provide a consistent basis for scaling the individual dimensions over time (so that different seasons can be meaningfully compared to each other), each dimension is scaled so that the least-favorable observed value for each season generates a score of 0.0 and the most-favorable observed value for each season generates a score of 1.0. For instance, in 1988, the least-favorable observed values for the American League TCF dimensions were BAVG = .159, HR = 0, RBI = 11, and each of these was assigned a standardized score of 0. The corresponding most-favorable observed values were BAVG = .366, HR = 42, RBI = 124, and each of these was assigned a standardized score of 1.0. Intermediate values received a standardized score based on the relative position between the high and low values, that is,

$$INDEX_{ij} = \frac{OBS_{ij} - MIN_i}{MAX_i - MIN_i}$$

where $INDEX_{ij}$ is the standardized score for player j in category i, MAX_i (MIN_i) is the largest (smallest) value in category i, and OBS_{ij} is the observed value for player j in category i, where i = BAVG, HR, RBI. For example, if an American League player had a batting average (BAVG) of .228 for 1988, the standardized score for this player on the BAVG dimension of performance would be

$$INDEX_{BAVG} = \frac{.228 - .159}{.336 - .159} = .3333$$

This standardized score indicates that this particular player's performance on the BAVG dimension falls one third of the way between the worst and best observed performances on this dimension (for the American League in 1988). For each player, three standardized scores were computed (one for each relevant dimension) and utilized in determining that player's position relative to the TCF.

As mentioned earlier, for the dimensions of pitching performance, lower scores indicate more favorable performance. For these dimensions, the standardized performance scores were computed as

$$INDEX_{ij} = \frac{MAX_i - OBS_{ij}}{MAX_i - MIN_i}$$

for the categories i = ERA, H/IP, BB/SO. Just like the batting index numbers, these standardizations also put all measures of performance in the [0, 1] interval. Three standardized pitching performance scores were computed for each player meeting the minimum playing-time requirements. These three-dimensional scores were the inputs used to compute the player's position relative to the PDF.

Rule differences between the leagues (e.g., different sizes of the strike zone, presence or absence of a designated hitter) made it desirable to consider the players from each league separately. In keeping with the notion that a single baseball season is the relevant production period over which performance is observed, each season was evaluated separately. That is, each season was viewed as self-contained, and a separate PDF and TCF were computed for each league.

Team data were also collected for the same categories as individual player data. This required hand collecting the desired items from annual preseason publications (e.g., *The Sporting News Baseball Yearbook*). The pitching performance data for teams were directly comparable to those for individual players and so could be easily incorporated into the analysis, and PDF efficiency scores could be computed for all teams. However, some of the batting performance measures (total HR and RBI) were much larger for teams than for any individual players. Since each team consists of nine batters, dividing aggregate team values by nine for these two categories put the team data on a basis consistent with the individual player data. In this manner, team batting data could be used to compute efficiency scores that would be comparable to the Triple Crown Frontier (TCF) values for individual players.

3. Results

The basic results of combining the observed performance measures on the selected dimensions and computing the TCF for the years 1986–1988 are presented in tables 19–1 through 19–6.[5] Each table presents the players defining the annual frontier for one league and relevant individual statistics. For these six sets of computations, the largest number of players on the TCF was five (American League, 1986) and the smallest was two (National League, 1986). These tables also present the five highest efficiency scores of players whose performance did not place them on the frontier. For contrast, the five lowest Triple Crown efficiency scores in each league are provided for each year analyzed.[6]

Table 19–5 (American League) and table 19–6 (National League)

Table 19–1.   1986 American League triple Crown Frontier

A. Players Defining Frontier (Efficiency Score = 1.0)

Name	BAVG	HR	RBI	Comments
Barfield	.289	40	108	Led in HR
Boggs	.357	8	71	Led in BAVG
Canseco	.240	33	117	Second in RBI, fourth in HR
J. Carter	.302	29	121	Led in RBI
Mattingly	.352	31	113	Second in BAVG, third in RBI

B. Five Highest Efficiency Scores Not on Frontier

Name	Efficiency Score	BAVG	HR	RBI
Gaetti	.9507	.287	34	108
Rice	.9425	.324	20	110
G. Bell	.9404	.309	31	108
Puckett	.9389	.328	31	96
Presley	.8849	.265	27	107

C. Five Lowest Efficiency Scores

Name	Efficiency Score	BAVG	HR	RBI
Romero	.1884	.210	2	23
Motley	.1934	.203	7	20
Rayford	.2000	.176	8	19
J. Cruz	.2155	.215	0	19
Schroeder	.2163	.212	7	19

portray the TCF computations for 1988. In the American League, three players define the TCF, out of 161 players who fit the definition of "full-time player" used in this study. It is conceivable that a single player could define the entire TCF, if that player led the league in all three categories. If, on the other hand, a different player led the league in each of the three categories, then at least three players would define the frontier. In the American League in 1988, Boggs led the league in BAVG and so was on the TCF. Canseco led the league in both HR and RBI, and was also on the TCF. Puckett had a BAVG substantially above that of Canseco, while being only slightly behind in RBI, and so also helped define the TCF. For the American League in 1988, these three players determine the TCF.

Table 19–5 also shows the five players in the American League with

Table 19–2.   1986 National League Triple Crown Frontier

A. Players Defining Frontier (Efficiency Score = 1.0)

Name	BAVG	HR	RBI	Comments
Brooks	.340	14	58	Led in BAVG
Schmidt	.290	37	119	Led in HR, led in RBI

B. Five Highest Efficiency Scores Not on Frontier

Name	Efficiency Score	BAVG	HR	RBI
Hayes	.9868	.305	19	98
Raines	.9838	.334	9	62
Parker	.9720	.273	31	116
Hernandez	.9433	.310	13	81
Sax	.9425	.332	6	56

C. Five Lowest Efficiency Scores

Name	Efficiency Score	BAVG	HR	RBI
Landrum	.0541	.210	2	17
Rose	.1215	.219	0	25
M. Brown	.1308	.218	4	26
Dernier	.1477	.225	4	18
Santana	.1495	.218	1	28

the highest efficiency scores who were not on the TCF. The efficiency scores for these players ranged from .8319 to .9881, as compared with a frontier score of 1.0. These efficiency scores can be thought of as providing an indication of the effectiveness of these players' performances, relative to the performances of those on the TCF.

For contrast, the five lowest efficiency scores computed for the American League in 1988 are also shown in table 19–5. These performances were far below these of the players on the efficiency frontier. The lowest observed efficiency score was for Ken Williams, who had the lowest BAVG of all players in the sample. The efficiency score of .1905 came solely from the HR total (8) which is .1905 of the way between the lowest (0) and highest (42) observed values on this dimension. It is not expected that players with very low efficiency scores would remain as full-time players, unless their efficiency scores improved markedly.

Table 19–6 provides information similar to that in table 19–5, but focuses on the National League. This TCF was defined by four players,

Table 19–3. 1987 American League Triple Crown Frontier

A. Players Defining Frontier (Efficiency Score = 1.0)

Name	BAVG	HR	RBI	Comments
G. Bell	.308	47	134	Led in RBI
Boggs	.363	24	89	Led in BAVG
McGwire	.289	49	118	Led in HR

B. Five Highest Efficiency Scores Not on Frontier

Name	Efficiency Score	BAVG	HR	RBI
Trammell	.9983	.343	28	105
Mattingly	.9840	.327	30	115
Molitor	.9419	.353	16	75
Dw. Evans	.9376	.305	34	123
Puckett	.9288	.332	28	99

C. Five Lowest Efficiency Scores

Name	Efficiency Score	BAVG	HR	RBI
Salazer	.0855	.205	2	21
Pettis	.0988	.208	1	17
Burleson	.1047	.209	2	14
Iorg	.1462	.210	4	30
Tettleton	.1633	.194	8	26

the leaders in each category (Gwynn, BAVG; Strawberry, HR; W. Clark, RBI), along with a fourth player (Galarraga) who had significantly larger totals in RBI and HR than the leader in BAVG, yet who was only slightly off the leader's pace in BAVG. Having a player on the frontier who exhibits strong, but not dominating, performance in any category makes near-frontier level performance more accessible to other players. This last observation can be seen by examining the five highest efficiency scores of players not on the TCF. All five were located more than 95% of the distance from the origin to the frontier (compared to only one American League player, namely, Greenwell). Table 19–6 also presents the five lowest efficiency scores for the National League in 1988. These were somewhat smaller than those for the American League, indicating that in 1988, batting performance in the National League was distributed over a wider range than that in the American League.

In a similar fashion, the results for combining the observed pitching

Table 19–4.   1987 National League Triple Crown Frontier

A. Players Defining Frontier (Efficiency Score = 1.0)

Name	BAVG	HR	RBI	Comments
Dawson	.287	49	137	Led in HR, led in RBI
Guerrero	.338	27	89	Second in BAVG
Gwynn	.370	7	54	Led in BAVG

B. Five Highest Efficiency Scores Not on Frontier

Name	Efficiency Score	BAVG	HR	RBI
Wallach	.9833	.298	26	123
D. Murphy	.9831	.295	44	105
Daniels	.9710	.334	26	64
W. Clark	.9461	.308	35	91
Schmidt	.9159	.293	35	113

C. Five Lowest Efficiency Scores

Name	Efficiency Score	BAVG	HR	RBI
Belliard	.1066	.207	1	15
Garner	.1392	.206	5	23
M. Williams	.1633	.188	8	21
Lindeman	.1813	.208	8	28
Duncan	.1924	.215	6	18

performance measures and computing the PDF are presented in tables 19–7 to 19–12. The largest number of players defining this frontier was six (National League, 1988) and the smallest was three (several cases, including American League, 1986). Again, the five highest efficiency scores of players not on the PDF are provided for each year, as are the five lowest efficiency scores.[7]

Table 19–11 (American League) and table 19–12 (National League) show the PDF computations for the 1988 season. For the American League in 1988, the PDF was defined by five players. The leaders in each of the three individual categories were on the PDF (Anderson, ERA; Candelaria, BB/SO; Robinson, H/IP). In addition, two players who just missed leading the league in any one category performed quite strongly in the other two categories and were also on the frontier (Clemens and Higuera). As in the case of table 19–6, strong but not dominating per-

Table 19-5.   1988 American League Triple Crown Frontier

A. Players Defining Frontier (Efficiency Score = 1.0)

Name	BAVG	HR	RBI	Comments
Boggs	.366	5	58	Led in BAVG
Canseco	.307	42	124	Led in HR, led in RBI
Puckett	.356	24	121	Second in BAVG, second in RBI

B. Five Highest Efficiency Scores Not on Frontier

Name	Efficiency Score	BAVG	HR	RBI
Greenwell	.9681	.325	22	119
Dw. Evans	.8865	.293	21	111
Winfield	.8808	.322	25	107
Hrbek	.8427	.312	25	76
Gaetti	.8319	.301	28	88

C. Five Lowest Efficiency Scores

Name	Efficiency Score	BAVG	HR	RBI
K. Williams	.1905	.159	8	28
Phillips	.2149	.203	2	17
Gerhart	.2306	.195	9	23
B. Ripken	.2408	.207	2	34
Gallego	.2435	.209	2	20

formances by players on the frontier makes relatively high efficiency scores accessible to other players. This is indicated by the five highest efficiency scores for players not on the PDF. All were between .8989 and .9948, meaning that all these performances were at least 89.89% of the distance from the origin to the frontier.

The five lowest pitching efficiency scores for the American League are also presented in table 19-11. These range from .3921 to .4649, indicating that these performances were at least 39% of the distance from the origin to the frontier. These are much higher than the corresponding figures for batting performance. A reason for this disparity could be that the three batting-performance measures are more strongly correlated (at least at the lower levels of observed performance) than the three measures of pitching performance. For instance, a truly weak batter may have few HR and a low BAVG. Consequently, this player might be put in a

Table 19–6.   1988 National League Triple Crown Frontier

A. Players Defining Frontier (Efficiency Score = 1.0)

Name	BAVG	HR	RBI	Comments
W. Clark	.282	29	109	Led in RBI
Galarraga	.302	29	92	Third in HR, sixth in BAVG
Gwynn	.313	7	70	Led in BAVG
Strawberry	.269	39	101	Led in HR

B. Five Highest Efficiency Scores Not on Frontier

Name	Efficiency Score	BAVG	HR	RBI
Dawson	.9884	.303	24	79
Van Slyke	.9782	.288	25	100
Jordan	.9768	.308	11	43
McReynolds	.9726	.288	27	99
Palmeiro	.9575	.307	8	53

C. Five Lowest Efficiency Scores

Name	Efficiency Score	BAVG	HR	RBI
M. Davis	.0772	.196	2	17
Brenley	.1282	.189	5	22
Griffin	.1633	.119	1	27
Jeltz	.1633	.187	0	27
Alicea	.2026	.212	1	24

position in the batting order where it is difficult to drive in runs, leading to a low RBI total. Such a player could have low totals on all three measures of batting performance, and could be quite close to the origin in the three-dimensional space enclosed by the TCF. In contrast, the three pitching-performance categories might be less strongly correlated. While a pitcher with a high value of H/IP may tend to have a high value of ERA, there is no reason to expect much of a correlation between the BB/SO and H/IP ratios. At the lower end of the performance spectrum, then, there appears to be more heterogeneity in the dimensions chosen to evaluate pitching than in those chosen to evaluate batting.

A similar pattern of pitching effectiveness is shown for the 1988 National League season in table 19–12. Six players are on the PDF, the leaders in the three individual categories (Fernandez, H/IP; Magrane,

Table 19–7.   1986 American League Pitching Dominance Frontier

A. Players Defining Frontier (Efficiency Score = 1.0)

Name	ERA	H/IP	BB/SO	Comments
Eichorn	1.72	.669	.271	Lowest ERA
O'Neil	4.33	.590	.647	Lowest H/IP
Saberhagen	4.15	1.058	.259	Lowest BB/SO

B. Five Highest Efficiency Scores Not on Frontier

Name	Efficiency Score	ERA	H/IP	BB/SO
Blyleven	.9913	4.01	.967	.270
Clemens	.9875	2.48	.705	.282
Guidry	.9874	3.98	1.052	.271
Hurst	.9626	2.99	.971	.299
Alexander	.9466	4.46	1.081	.308

C. Five Lowest Efficiency Scores

Name	Efficiency Score	ERA	H/IP	BB/SO
Swift	.2273	5.46	1.287	1.000
Romanick	.2989	5.50	1.170	1.158
Slaton	.3354	5.08	1.150	.930
Butcher	.3837	6.56	1.400	.822
J. Niekro	.3864	4.87	1.112	1.068

ERA; and Ojeda, BB/SO) and three players with sufficiently strong performances in two of the three categories (Cone, Perez, and Scott). The five highest efficiency scores not on the frontier are also shown, ranging from .9516 to .9877. Even though these scores indicate players whose performances were very close to frontier level, some of these players had their performances overshadowed on all three dimensions by someone who was on the PDF. For example, Hershiser (.9855) and Tudor (.9516) both were behind Cone on all three dimensions. The lowest observed efficiency scores are also presented in table 19–12. As was the case for the American League, the pitching efficiency scores exhibited much less variation than did the batting efficiency scores.

Over the three-season period, only one batter (Boggs, American League) was on the TCF all three times. In terms of efficiency scores, Boggs maintained the highest level of performance for any player considered. There were other players, however, whose performances also

Table 19–8.   1986 National League Pitching Dominance Frontier

A. Players Defining Frontier (Efficiency Score = 1.0)

Name	ERA	H/IP	BB/SO	Comments
Alexander	3.84	1.154	.230	Lowest BB/SO
Scott	2.22	.6618	.235	Lowest H/IP
Worrell	2.08	.835	.562	Lowest ERA

B. Five Highest Efficiency Scores Not on Frontier

Name	Efficiency Score	ERA	H/IP	BB/SO
Youmans	.9995	3.53	.6621	.584
Ryan	.9880	3.34	.669	.423
Horton	.9739	2.24	.770	.531
Sanderson	.9261	4.19	.976	.298
Welch	.9241	3.28	.966	.301

C. Five Lowest Efficiency Scores

Name	Efficiency Score	ERA	H/IP	BB/SO
Welsh	.2913	4.78	1.173	1.000
Trout	.2992	4.75	1.130	1.143
Hoyt	.3685	5.15	1.069	.800
Bilecki	.3834	4.66	1.007	1.000
Carlton	.4085	5.89	1.221	.763

evidenced consistently superior achievements. For instance, Gwynn (National League) was on the TCF in both 1987 and 1988, and had an efficiency score of .9393 in 1986. This batting performance over the study period was unmatched in the National League. In the American League, there were two players in addition to Boggs who had high efficiency scores in all three years studied. These players were Canseco (on the TCF in 1986 and 1988 and with an efficiency score of .8250 in 1987) and Puckett (on the TCF in 1988 and with efficiency scores of .9389 in 1986 and .9288 in 1987).[8]

For the 1986–1988 time period, only one pitcher was on the PDF more than once. Scott (National League) was on the PDF in both 1986 and 1988 and had an efficiency score of .9772 in 1987. This set of pitching performances is the best observed over the study period. Clemens (American League) also performed at a high level over the 1986–1988 period, being on the PDF in 1988 and having efficiency scores of .9875 in

Table 19–9. 1987 American League Pitching Dominance Frontier

A. Players Defining Frontier (Efficiency Score = 1.0)

Name	ERA	H/IP	BB/SO	Comments
Eckersley	3.03	.861	.150	Lowest BB/SO
Key	2.76	.805	.410	Lowest ERA
M. Williams	3.23	.583	.729	Lowest H/IP

B. Five Highest Efficiency Scores Not on Frontier

Name	Efficiency Score	ERA	H/IP	BB/SO
Buice	.9924	3.39	.763	.367
Viola	.9856	2.90	.916	.335
Clemens	.9719	2.97	.883	.324
Eichorn	.8904	3.17	.866	.542
Saberhagen	.8809	3.36	.957	.325

C. Five Lowest Efficiency Scores

Name	Efficiency Score	ERA	H/IP	BB/SO
Schrom	.1300	6.50	1.209	.934
P. Niekro	.1942	6.10	1.163	.938
Carlton	.3018	5.74	1.089	.945
Smithson	.3112	5.94	1.156	.717
Petry	.3153	5.61	1.104	.817

1986 and .9719 in 1987. No other players exhibited pitching efficiency scores as large as these two players over the three seasons considered.

4. Team Performance Results

Team performance data were incorporated in the computation of efficiency scores, and the results for 1986–1988 are presented in tables 19–13 to 19–18, along with the teams' winning percentages for each season. As could be expected, team efficiency scores varied over a much smaller range than individual-player efficiency scores, since extremes of individual performance were averaged out when team data were considered. For example, the largest observed difference among team efficiency scores for the TCF frontier was approximately .2048 (American League, 1988). The corresponding largest observed difference for the PDF team efficiency

Table 19-10.   1987 National League Pitching Dominance Frontier

A. Players Defining Frontier (Efficiency Score = 1.0)

Name	ERA	H/IP	BB/SO	Comments
Garrelts	3.22	.660	.433	Lowest H/IP
McGaffigan	2.39	.875	.420	Second lowest ERA
Ryan	2.76	.730	.322	Lowest BB/SO
F. Williams	2.30	.962	.650	Lowest ERA

B. Five Highest Efficiency Scores Not on Frontier

Name	Efficiency Score	ERA	H/IP	BB/SO
R. Murphy	.9986	3.04	.910	.323
J. Robinson	.9929	2.85	.724	.535
B. Smith	.9827	4.37	1.093	.330
Scott	.9772	3.23	.806	.339
Heaton	.9591	4.52	1.073	.352

C. Five Lowest Efficiency Scores

Name	Efficiency Score	ERA	H/IP	BB/SO
Hawkins	.2839	5.05	1.120	.961
Mahler	.3365	4.98	1.076	.895
Maddox	.4428	5.61	1.168	.733
Ruffin	.4466	4.35	1.157	.785
Knepper	.4728	5.27	1.277	.711

scores was .3579 (National League, 1987). In contrast, the smallest observed range among individual-player TCF efficiency scores was .8095 (American League, 1988), and the smallest observed range for individual-player PDF efficiency scores was .5148 (National League, 1988).

As a check on the relevance of the computed efficiency scores, ordinary least squares (OLS) regressions were run relating the winning percentage for each team in a particular season to the computed team efficiency scores for both the TCF and the PDF for that season. One regression equation for each season by League and one pooled regression equation (incorporating both leagues and all three seasons) were run, so seven equations were estimated in all. The regression results are presented in table 19-19. Each regression had an F-score large enough to indicate in a statistical sense that the computed efficiency scores had significant value in explaining the overall performance of the team as measured by team

Table 19–11.   1988 American League Pitching Dominance Frontier

A. Players Defining Frontier (Efficiency Score = 1.0)

Name	ERA	H/IP	BB/SO	Comments
Anderson	2.45	.984	.446	Lowest ERA
Candelaria	3.38	.955	.190	Lowest BB/SO
Clemens	2.93	.822	.213	Second lowest BB/ SO
Higuera	2.46	.739	.307	Second Lowest ERA
Robinson	2.98	.703	.632	Lowest H/IP

B. Five Highest Efficiency Scores Not on Frontier

Name	Efficiency Score	ERA	H/IP	BB/SO
Viola	.9948	2.64	.924	.280
Swindell	.9617	3.20	.967	.250
Stieb	.9312	3.04	.757	.537
Gubicza	.9297	2.70	.879	.454
Nieves	.8989	4.08	.762	.685

C. Five Lowest Efficiency Scores

Name	Efficiency Score	ERA	H/IP	BB/SO
Swift	.3921	4.59	1.140	1.383
Dotson	.4153	5.00	1.041	.935
Fraser	.4167	5.41	1.043	.930
Ballard	.4463	4.40	1.089	1.024
Bailes	.4649	4.90	1.028	.868

winning percentage. Similarly, the R^2 statistics vary from a low value of .577 to a high value of .844, indicating that the efficiency scores are reasonably good at explaining the variations in team performance. All the coefficients had the expected positive sign, indicating that higher efficiency scores were indeed associated with more successful team performance. For instance, for the National League in 1988, a .10 increase in the team TCF efficiency score would have the expected result of a .037 increase in the team's winning percentage (equivalent to about six additional wins over the course of a 162 game season). A similar .10 increase in the PDF efficiency score would be associated with an expected increase of .070 in the team's winning percentage for the National League in 1988 (about 11 additional wins over an entire season). Most of the estimated coefficients (10 of 12) were significantly different from zero at conventional levels.

Table 19–12.   1988 National League Pitching Dominance Frontier

A. Players Defining Frontier (Efficiency Score = 1.0)

Name	ERA	H/IP	BB/SO	Comments
Cone	2.22	.770	.376	Second lowest ERA
Fernandez	3.03	.679	.370	Lowest H/IP
Magrane	2.18	.805	.510	Lowest ERA
Ojeda	2.88	.830	.248	Lowest BB/SO
Perez	2.44	.707	.336	Second lowest H/IP
Scott	2.92	.741	.279	Third lowest BB/SO

B. Five Highest Efficiency Scores Not on Frontier

Name	Efficiency Score	ERA	H/IP	BB/SO
Harris	.9877	2.36	.748	.732
Rijo	.9866	2.39	.741	.398
B. Smith	.9860	3.00	.904	.262
Hershiser	.9855	2.26	.779	.410
Tudor	.9516	2.32	.956	.471

C. Five Lowest Efficiency Scores

Name	Efficiency Score	ERA	H/IP	BB/SO
Forsch	.4852	4.29	1.123	.815
Rawley	.4890	4.18	1.111	.897
Z. Smith	.5068	4.30	1.524	.746
Fischer	.5339	4.61	1.073	.864
Ruffin	.5655	4.43	1.046	.976

These statistical results support the use of DEA efficiency scores as summary measures of baseball performance.

5. Summary

This chapter should be viewed as a demonstration project that shows how DEA methodology can be applied to rate athletic performance in team sports. This particular application uses statistical measures of baseball performance to trace the relevant maximally efficient frontiers for three seasons (1986–1988). Three dimensions of batting performance (BAVG, HR, RBI) were selected to compute the Triple Crown Frontier and the

Table 19–13.   1986 American League Team Winning Percentage and Efficiency Scores

Team	Winning Pct	TCF Score	PDF Score
Baltimore	.451	.598922	.675126
Boston	.590	.674216	.785277
Cleveland	.519	.709830	.445111
Detroit	.537	.684776	.606503
Milwaukee	.478	.546128	.719990
New York	.556	.676976	.675532
Toronto	.531	.684561	.756542
California	.568	.650510	.742980
Chicago	.444	.519225	.620308
Kansas City	.469	.536466	.699251
Minnesota	.438	.646555	.697947
Oakland	.469	.599152	.614809
Seattle	.414	.593940	.608239
Texas	.537	.656945	.614383

Table 19–14.   1986 National League Team Winning Percentage and Efficiency Scores

Team	Winning Pct	TCF Score	PDF Score
Chicago	.438	.562119	.613601
Montreal	.484	.530640	.660376
New York	.667	.653819	.755633
Philadelphia	.534	.610590	.556014
Pittsburgh	.395	.529600	.573278
St. Louis	.491	.458980	.673792
Atlanta	.447	.492124	.571743
Cincinnati	.531	.583590	.628082
Houston	.593	.542574	.759007
Los Angeles	.451	.511123	.730334
San Diego	.457	.587047	.536572
San Francisco	.512	.549330	.690774

corresponding efficiency scores for all batters who appeared on a full-time basis. Similarly, three dimensions of pitching performance (ERA, H/IP, BB/SO) were selected to compute the Pitching Dominance Frontier and the corresponding efficiency scores for all full-time pitchers. DEA

Table 19–15.   1987 American League Team Winning Percentage and Efficiency Scores

Team	Winning Pct	TCF Score	PDF Score
Baltimore	.414	.651850	.450347
Boston	.481	.741670	.558260
Cleveland	.377	.639810	.380617
Detroit	.605	.784260	.667759
Milwaukee	.562	.770370	.552988
New York	.549	.693520	.577288
Toronto	.593	.731480	.758972
California	.463	.657410	.599928
Chicago	.475	.651850	.598177
Kansas City	.512	.627780	.700530
Minnesota	.525	.677780	.554945
Oakland	.500	.703700	.625189
Seattle	.481	.675984	.556139
Texas	.463	.713890	.562669

Table 19–16.   1987 National League Team Winning Percentage and Efficiency Scores

Team	Winning Pct	TCF Score	PDF Score
Chicago	.472	.621188	.596010
Montreal	.562	.630599	.837960
New York	.568	.682749	.765230
Philadelphia	.494	.546121	.525365
Pittsburgh	.494	.621188	.599380
St. Louis	.586	.648962	.615631
Atlanta	.429	.600914	.480110
Cincinnati	.519	.661390	.720120
Houston	.469	.531975	.810030
Los Angeles	.451	.518763	.731290
San Diego	.401	.569807	.534353
San Francisco	.556	.625828	.730400

technology is quite flexible and could be easily adapted to consider dimensions of baseball playing ability other than those used in this study (e.g., other measures of pitching performance). Moreover, this demonstration of the value of using DEA in a team sports context opens up

Table 19–17.   1988 American League Team Winning Percentage and Efficiency Scores

Team	Winning Pct	TCF Score	PDF Score
Baltimore	.335	.459100	.544874
Boston	.549	.663898	.782507
Cleveland	.481	.543318	.702990
Detroit	.543	.547214	.717928
Milwaukee	.537	.534340	.765744
New York	.528	.611087	.686686
Toronto	.537	.607216	.693398
California	.463	.561833	.583344
Chicago	.441	.476213	.588314
Kansas City	.522	.570661	.743592
Minnesota	.562	.613874	.741145
Oakland	.642	.646581	.745811
Seattle	.422	.544211	.693605
Texas	.435	.492692	.657850

Table 19–18.   1988 National League Team Winning Percentage and Efficiency Scores

Team	Winning Pct	TCF Score	PDF Score
Chicago	.475	.670766	.708699
Montreal	.500	.600218	.792017
New York	.625	.676208	.907280
Philadelphia	.404	.542932	.608870
Pittsburgh	.531	.608547	.717518
St. Louis	.469	.566459	.732542
Atlanta	.338	.527584	.631819
Cincinnati	.540	.584518	.786285
Houston	.506	.566928	.812317
Los Angeles	.584	.593413	.833556
San Diego	.516	.575602	.777861
San Francisco	.512	.619521	.791895

the possibility of using DEA to rate athletic performance in other team sports.

Whether the computed efficiency scores measure valuable components of baseball performance was examined by computing efficiency scores on

Table 19-19. Results of Regression Analysis Relating Team Winning Percentage to Computed Efficiency Scores

League and Season[a]	Constant[b]	Coefficient for TCF Efficiency Score[b]	Coefficient for PDF Efficiency Score[b]	R^2	F-Statistic[c]
American League 1986	−.0507 (−.3445)	.1762 (3.6655)	.1258 (1.7513)	.578	7.547
National League 1986	−.3390 (−1.9704)	.8305 (3.4207)	.5907 (3.5758)	.730	12.166
American League 1987	−.1880 (−1.5631)	.6411 (3.5384)	.4174 (4.4646)	.812	23.738
National League 1987	−.0586 (−.3998)	.6913 (3.0006)	.2121 (2.0823)	.631	7.698
American League 1988	−.1732 (−1.5439)	.6586 (2.6317)	.4391 (2.0591)	.769	18.354
National League 1988	−.2495 (−1.8849)	.3695 (1.3891)	.6987 (4.8700)	.844	24.404
Pooled Regression (both leagues, all three seasons)	−.0443 (−.8112)	.4942 (7.1727)	.3673 (7.5782)	.577	51.187

[a] American League regressions use 14 observations for each year; National League regressions use 12 observations for each year.

[b] t-statistics are in parentheses.

[c] The critical values for the F-statistics are $F(.95, 2, 11) = 3.98$; $F(.95, 2, 9) = 4.26$; and $F(.95, 2, 75) = 3.13$.

aggregate measures of team performance. These efficiency scores were then used as independent variables in a regression analysis with team winning percentage as the dependent variable. The results indicated a strong positive relationship between the computed team efficiency scores and team performance as measured by winning percentage.

One might see an obvious application in the use of computed efficiency scores for individual players as inputs in an attempt to explain observed variations in salaries. However, a number of caveats should be addressed before this task is attempted. At a minimum, the following items should be considered.

1. Presumably, players are compensated on the basis of their ability to contribute to the generation of revenues for the team. There are no revenue measures included in this DEA analysis.

2. There are certainly other dimensions of performance (e.g., fielding) that are not included in the DEA computations presented here. One would expect a player's compensation to reflect ability on these other dimensions, as well as the ones included in this study.

3. The efficiency scores computed are backward-looking measures based on past performance. Compensation should be based on expectations of future performance, and the differences between these approaches could be especially pronounced where multiyear contracts are entered into.

4. Single-season efficiency scores may not indicate underlying ability if there is a transient factor (e.g., "luck") that effects observed performance. Stochastic DEA methods could be used to separate out transitory influences when a long time series of performance data exists. Further research in this area might determine the strength of the links between compensation and DEA efficiency scores, but for now it is an open question.

Acknowledgments

Thanks to Roger Cornia, Michael Dalecki, Carol Fauerbach, Sanjeev Gupta, and Cory Leach for their help in obtaining and organizing the data. Thanks also to Kuang-Wei Wen for programming, Rajiv Banker for useful discussions regarding DEA, and two anonymous referees for helpful comments. Any remaining errors are the responsibility of the author. This chapter does not represent the views of the staff of the Joint Committee of Taxation nor any member of the U.S. Congress.

Notes

1. Note, however, that a bias may still be present in that players perform half their games in their home ballpark, which may favorably or unfavorably affect their overall performance level. No attempt is made in this study to adjust for any ballpark-induced biases.

2. It is conceivable that over the course of a season, due to player turnover, a team would put more or less emphasis on certain aspects of the game. For example, as a result of trades or injuries, a team may, in midseason, begin to emphasize the power aspects of baseball over team speed. This possibility is not addressed in this chapter.

3. The DEA formulation used here is the BCC output model described in chapter 2.

4. The subset of data used in this study is available from the author on request.

5. The complete set of players' rankings is available from the author on request.

6. The lowest efficiency score computed on a TCF for the three seasons examined was .0541 (National League, 1986).

7. The lowest efficiency score computed for a PDF for the three seasons examined was .1300 (American League, 1987).

8. By way of comparison, Babe Ruth was on the TCF for 12 of the 14 seasons over the period 1918–1931.

20 SENSITIVITY ANALYSIS OF EFFICIENCY MEASURES WITH APPLICATIONS TO KANSAS FARMING AND ILLINOIS COAL MINING

Russell Thompson, P. S. Dharmapala,
and Robert M. Thrall

1. Introduction

Data envelopment analysis (DEA), as its name indicates, is data based. In view of the possibility of erroneous or misleading data, some critics of DEA have questioned the validity and stability of measures of DEA efficiency. For example, in a 1985 survey of frontier efficiency measurement approaches, Schmidt (1985–86) stated:

> I see no virtue whatsoever in a non-statistical approach to data . . . very skeptical of non-statistical efficiency measurement exercises, certainly as they are now carried out and perhaps in any way that they could be carried out.

In 1990, Bauer (1990) stated that the primary limitation of DEA is that

> . . . the calculated frontier may be warped if the data are contaminated by statistical noise.

Notably, neither Bauer nor Schmidt provided any quantified argument to justify their criticism of DEA. Clearly, it is easy to construct artificial examples where outliers or errors in or instability (over time) of data can lead to questionable inferences about efficiency.

393

However, as we shall show below, there are many important situations in which the data are quite precisely measured and, hence, only small data changes are at all likely. In response to these and other criticisms, we investigate some criteria for stability of DEA efficiency measures in this chapter, and we present both analytic and empirical approaches to sensitivity analysis utilizing recent advances in DEA theory.

Our presentation begins with an example problem to identify the fundamental features of the approach, to show how it is applied to data, and to demonstrate why DEA efficiency measures can be relatively insensitive to data errors. This example is followed by application of the sensitivity multiplier approach to one real-world data base involving 83 Kansas farms (see Thompson et al., 1990) and to another involving 15 Illinois coal mines (see Byrnes et al., 1984). The analytic approach in appendix A provides two theorems that give bounds for simultaneous changes in all the input–output data under which the most important DEA efficiency classification remains unchanged.

Our investigation of sensitivity requires a somewhat deeper theoretical exploration of DEA theory than is contained in chapters 2 and 3, and we have provided this in appendix B. Although this theory is essential for in-depth understanding, we have provided in sections 2 and 3 an approach that does not require the reader to detour to appendix B. Our approach does feature the use of nonbasic optimal dual solutions (which are not ordinarily provided by generally available linear programming software).

2. An Example

Here we provide an introduction to what follows. For this exposition, we introduce a data domain D with two inputs, one output, and six decision-making units (DMUs) defined by the data matrix

$$P = \begin{bmatrix} 1 & 1 & 1 & 1 & 1 & 1 \\ -4 & -2 & -1 & -2 & -3 & -4 \\ -1 & -2 & -4 & -3 & -2 & -4 \end{bmatrix} \quad (20.1)$$

To put this in a more general context, let

$$P_j = \begin{bmatrix} Y_j \\ -X_j \end{bmatrix}, \quad j = 1, 2, \ldots, n \quad (20.2)$$

where Y_j is the vector of outputs with $r = 1, 2, \ldots, s$ components and X_j the vector of inputs with $i = 1, \ldots, m$ components for each of $j = 1,$

..., n DMUs. For instance, the data matrix of P in equation (20.1) corresponds to the output and input matrices

$$Y = (Y_1, Y_2, Y_3, Y_4, Y_5, Y_6) = (1, 1, 1, 1, 1, 1)$$

$$X = (X_1, X_2, X_3, X_4, X_5, X_6) = \begin{pmatrix} 4 & 2 & 1 & 2 & 3 & 4 \\ 1 & 2 & 4 & 3 & 2 & 4 \end{pmatrix} \quad (20.3)$$

Evidently we can associate this matrix with points $P_1, \ldots, P_6$ where, in the example of equation (20.1), each DMU produces one unit of output, utilizing the input amounts for each of the two inputs shown for $X_1, \ldots, X_6$ in equations (20.3).

The lined region in figure 20–1 shows the intersection $\bar{E}_S$ of the plane $y = 1$ with the production possibility set E_S, defined by

$$E_S = \{p: p \leq P_1\lambda_1 + P_2\lambda_2 + P_3\lambda_3 \text{ with } \lambda_1, \lambda_2, \lambda_3 \geq 0\} \quad (20.4)$$

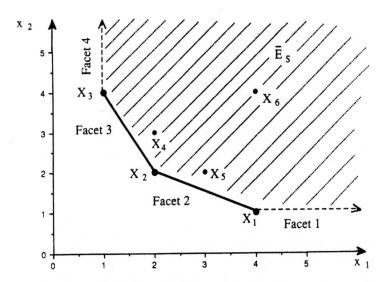

Intersection of envelopment space with plane $Y_1=1$

Figure 20–1. Envelopment space for a domain with $s = 1$, $m = 2$, $n = 6$.

$$Y = [1 \quad 1 \quad 1 \quad 1 \quad 1 \quad 1]; \ X = \begin{bmatrix} 4 & 2 & 1 & 2 & 3 & 4 \\ 1 & 2 & 4 & 3 & 2 & 4 \end{bmatrix}.$$

where $p \leqslant q$ means no output in p can exceed the corresponding output in q and the inputs of p are at least as great as those of q.

Here we have used an important property of the "corner points" (= extreme points) X_1, X_2, and X_3, which are efficient, in that the efficiency of any point in the lined region, including points on the boundary, can be evaluated in terms of these three points. This conclusion follows from the fact that any point p, observed or not, that is in the production possibility set, E_S, cannot have a greater output or a smaller input than a point generated from a nonnegative combination of P_1, P_2 and P_3.

This property of extreme efficient points is general and can be put to good use in our sensitivity analysis, since it permits us to focus on this subset, which we will symbolize as E, when we want to determine the magnitudes of data variations that can cause changes in the extreme efficiency characterization for any DMU. Moreover, this property of the set E, as represented in equation (20.4), makes it possible to study data perturbations into points with coordinate values that might be far removed from the original values, and to continue doing this until the relation in equation (20.4) is violated.

These extreme efficient points also have other important properties. For instance, not only do points like P_1, P_2, or P_3 have dual solutions that are all positive, but also their optimal dual multipliers form a set of "full dimensionality," and this property enables us to evaluate the efficiency changes that might accompany alterations in the inputs and outputs for data points in E_S, including X_1, X_2, and X_3.

These properties of efficient extreme points, along with other properties needed for our sensitivity analyses, are developed in full in appendix B. Here we simply want to provide appropriate insights and interpretations for the developments in subsequent sections of this chapter.

For instance, the following programming problem can be used to evaluate the performance of DMU_1 from the data in equation (20.1):

$$
\begin{aligned}
&\min \theta \\
&\text{subject to} \\
&1 \leqslant 1\lambda_1 + 1\lambda_2 + 1\lambda_3 + 1\lambda_4 + 1\lambda_5 + 1\lambda_6 \\
&-4\theta \leqslant -4\lambda_1 + -2\lambda_2 + -1\lambda_3 + -2\lambda_4 + -3\lambda_5 + -4\lambda_6 \\
&-\theta \leqslant -1\lambda_1 + -2\lambda_2 + -4\lambda_3 + -3\lambda_4 + -2\lambda_5 + -4\lambda_6
\end{aligned}
\tag{20.5}
$$

with all variables, except θ, constrained to be nonnegative.

The dual to problem (20.5) is

$$\max \mu$$
subject to
$$\begin{aligned}
4v_1 + v_2 &= 1 \\
\mu - 4v_1 - v_2 &\leq 0 \\
\mu - 2v_1 - 2v_2 &\leq 0 \\
\mu - v_1 - 4v_2 &\leq 0 \\
\mu - 2v_1 - 3v_2 &\leq 0 \\
\mu - 3v_1 - 2v_2 &\leq 0 \\
\mu - 4v_1 - 4v_2 &\leq 0
\end{aligned}$$
(20.6)

with $\mu, v_1, v_2 \geq 0$.

One pair of optimal solutions to these two problems is

$$\theta^* = \lambda_1^* = 1 \quad \text{and all other } \lambda_j^* = 0 \text{ (primal)}$$

$$\mu^* = 1, \quad v_1^* = \frac{1}{8}, \quad v_2^* = \frac{1}{2} \text{ (dual)}$$
(20.7)

Note that here all the optimal dual variables are positive and all six dual inequalities, except the first, have the left side negative. These properties are important because they characterize what is called a Strong Complementary Slackness Condition (SCSC) solution pair for an extreme efficient DMU (See appendix B or Charnes et al., 1991, 1986d, for more details). These properties allow us to evaluate *all* inputs and *all* outputs, and hence provide the information needed (as we shall see) to determine data variations that can be permitted without altering the efficiency (or inefficiency) characterizations initially accorded to each DMU.

To see how this is done, we record in table 20–1 the optimal dual variables when the data in equation (20.1) are used to evaluate the efficiencies of the DMUs associated with P_1, P_2, and P_3. In passing we note that the corresponding primal solutions for each of P_1, P_2, and P_3 are unique, with $\theta^* = \lambda_j^* = 1$ and all other $\lambda_j^* = 0$. The dual solutions are not necessarily unique, however, as can be seen by the values listed alongside P_1 in table 20–1, which differ from the μ^*, v_1^*, and v_2^* exhibited in equations (20.7). Although these values differ, we still find that all dual variables are positive in these alternate optima. Similarly, the dual variables are also all positive for P_2 and P_3 in table 20–1.

Now we represent the solutions in table 20–1 via the vectors

$$\omega^1 = (1, 0.10, 0.60)^T$$
$$\omega^2 = (1, 0.25, 0.25)^T$$
$$\omega^3 = (1, 0.60, 0.10)^T$$
(20.8)

where the superscript indicates whether the vector is associated with P_1, P_2, or P_3.

Table 20–1. Optimal Dual Variables

DMU	Dual Variables		
	μ^*	v_1^*	v_2^*
P_1	1.0	0.10	0.60
P_2	1.0	0.25	0.25
P_3	1.0	0.60	0.10

To develop the measures of efficiency that we will use, we next consider the following functions (introduced in chapter 2),

$$h_j(\omega) = f_j(\omega)/g_j(\omega), \quad j = 1, \ldots, n \qquad (20.9)$$

where

$$f_j(\omega) = \mu^T Y_j \text{ (for outputs) and } g_j(\omega) = v^T X_j \text{ (for inputs)}.$$

Here ω consists of an $s \times 1$ vector μ of dual output variables and an $m \times 1$ vector v of dual input variables. We then use these ratios as measures of comparative efficiency and say that $h_k(\omega) > h_j(\omega)$ means that DMU$_k$ *is more efficient than* DMU$_j$ *relative to the vector* ω *of dual variable multipliers.* In particular, we define

$$h_o(\omega) = \max_j h_j(\omega) \qquad (20.10)$$

and use this maximum value as the basis for determining the efficiencies of all $j = 1, \ldots, n$ DMUs "relative to ω" via the ratios

$$\frac{h_j(\omega)}{h_o(\omega)} \qquad (20.11)$$

Turning to our simple one-output–two-input example, for illustration, we apply the evaluators for P_1 in table 20–1 to the data in equation (20.1). For $j = 1, 2, \ldots, 6$, we then obtain

$$h_1(\omega^1) = \frac{\mu^*}{v_1^* x_{11} + v_2^* x_{12}} = \frac{1}{.4 + .6} = 1.000$$

$$h_2(\omega^1) = \frac{\mu^*}{v_1^* x_{21} + v_2^* x_{22}} = \frac{1}{.2 + 1.2} = 0.714$$

$$h_3(\omega^1) = \frac{\mu^*}{v_1^* x_{31} + v_2^* x_{32}} = \frac{1}{.1 + 2.4} = 0.400$$

$$h_4(\omega^1) = \frac{\mu^*}{v_1^* x_{41} + v_2^* x_{42}} = \frac{1}{.2 + 1.8} = 5.000$$

$$h_5(\omega^1) = \frac{\mu^*}{v_1^* x_{51} + v_2^* x_{52}} = \frac{1}{.3 + 1.2} = 0.667$$

$$h_6(\omega^1) = \frac{\mu^*}{v_1^* x_{61} + v_2^* x_{62}} = \frac{1}{.4 + 2.4} = 0.357 \qquad (20.12)$$

Evidently $h_1(\omega^1)$ is maximal, and so we designate it as the $h_0(\omega^1)$ defined in equation (20.10).

Proceeding in the same manner, we obtain the similar ratios for DMU_2 and DMU_3, which are listed in table 20–2. These are, of course, the efficiencies of the DMUs listed in the first column of table 20–2 relative to the ω^1, ω^2, and ω^3 shown at the top of the columns to which they apply. As can be seen, the extreme efficient DMUs are top ranked in each column and, as shown in appendix B, every extreme efficient DMU can be characterized by the possession of such optimal dual solutions.

Reference to table 20–2 also reveals that ranges of data variations can be accommodated without causing a change in the characterization of DMU_1, DMU_2, or DMU_3 as top ranked under ω^1, ω^2, and ω^3, respectively. To explore these ranges, we introduce 5% increases in x_1 and x_2 for DMU_1, DMU_2, and DMU_3 along with simultaneous decreases of 5% in x_1 and x_2 for DMU_4, DMU_5, and DMU_6.

Starting with iteration 0 in table 20–2, we refer to the first of these 5%

Table 20–2. Values of $h_j(\omega^k)$, given SCSC Solutions for DMU_k in E ($k = 1, 2, 3$)

DMU	DMU_1 $h_j(\omega^1)$	DMU_2 $h_j(\omega^2)$	DMU_3 $h_j(\omega^3)$
1	1.000	0.800	0.400
2	0.714	1.000	0.714
3	0.400	0.800	1.000
4	0.500	0.800	0.667
5	0.667	0.800	0.500
6	0.357	0.500	0.357

changes as involving iteration 1 with results that we can record, as in table 20–3, because the same dual evaluators remain applicable even though they are no longer solutions for the linear programs in chapter 2. In fact, continuing these iterations with 5% increments and decrements, we find that a 15% increment–decrement is needed for DMU_4 and DMU_5 to displace DMU_2 from its top-ranked status (relative to ω^2) and that simultaneous increments and decrements in excess of 20% are needed for DMU_5 to replace DMU_1 as top ranked for ω^1. Finally, an incrementing and decrementing in excess of 20% is needed for DMU_4 to replace DMU_3 as top ranked for ω^3.

As discussed in appendix A, we can also examine the situation with respect to stability by processing from the opposite side and inquiring as to the magnitudes (or percentages) minimally necessary to change the status of one or more inefficient DMUs. Here, too, our extreme efficient vectors play a critical role since, in any case, we will have

$$h_j^*(\omega^k) < h_k^*(\omega^k) \quad \text{for } k = 1, 2, 3 \text{ and all } j \neq k. \qquad (20.13)$$

Because of the continuity of the $h_j(\omega)$ in the (data) coefficients X_j and Y_j, the inequalities (20.13) are maintained under small changes in the data matrix P, and hence the E classifications of DMUs 1, 2, and 3 are preserved. This is the heart of our approach to sensitivity.

Of course, inequalities (20.13) cannot hold for any DMU not in E. For instance, the dual associated with P_4, the point associated with the inefficient DMU_4 inequality (20.1), is found by solving

Table 20–3. Values of $h_j^*(\omega^k)$, given SCSC Solutions DMU_k in E ($k = 1, 2, 3$)

DMU	DMU_1 $h_j^*(\omega^1)$	DMU_2 $h_j^*(\omega^2)$	DMU_3 $h_j^*(\omega^3)$
1	0.952	0.762	0.381
2	0.680	0.952	0.680
3	0.381	0.762	0.952
4	0.526	0.842	0.702
5	0.702	0.842	0.526
6	0.376	0.526	0.376

$$\max \mu$$

subject to

$$2v_1 + 3v_2 = 1$$
$$\mu - 4v_1 - v_2 \leq 0$$
$$\mu - 2v_1 - 2v_2 \leq 0$$
$$\mu - v_1 - 4v_2 \leq 0$$
$$\mu - 2v_1 - 3v_2 \leq 0$$
$$\mu - 3v_1 - 2v_2 \leq 0$$
$$\mu - 4v_1 - 4v_2 \leq 0 \qquad (20.14)$$

The (unique) maximizing solution for this dual is $\mu^* = 6/7$, $v_1^* = 2/7$, and $v_2^* = 1/7$. Substitution in problem (20.14) shows that all constraints are satisfied. However, inequalities 2 and 3 in (20.14) become equations with

$$\mu^* = \frac{6}{7} = 2v_1^* + 2v_2^*, \qquad (20.15)$$

so that

$$h_1(\omega^*) = \frac{\mu^*}{2v_1^* + 2v_2^*} = 1 = \frac{\mu^*}{2v_1^* + 4v_2^*} = h_2(\omega^*), \qquad (20.16)$$

and reference to figure 20–1 shows that these data are from the two extreme efficient DMUs that enter into the evaluation of X_4.

3. Our Approach to Sensitivity

The sensitivity analyses we have just completed show that DEA results tend to be robust for extreme efficient DMUs. In fact, we have here tended to understate the stability of DEA results in response to variations in the data. Later in this chapter, we will make this evaluation more precise. Here we want to note that our approach permits us to conduct stability and sensitivity analyses in a manner that allows for simultaneous variation in all data, and this makes it possible to determine where the solutions are likely to be most sensitive. It is important to note as a consequence of inequalities (20.13) that our SCSC-based sensitivity analysis requires only evaluation of the functions h_j^* for each DMU$_j$— that is, it merely requires substituting variations in the input/output data to determine the changed function h_j^*, as opposed to solving a modified LP. Thus the approach developed here differs from and greatly advances the kinds of sensitivity analyses that have heretofore been available.

A string of earlier DEA papers (Charnes et al., 1985b; Charnes and

Neralic, 1986a, 1986b, 1986c, 1987, 1988, 1989a, 1989b, 1990a, 1990b) dealt with data changes via updating the inverse of the basis matrix associated with a selected basic solution relative to the initial data for a selected efficient DMU (see Charnes and Cooper, 1968). A major limitation of this approach is that it does not do full justice to the strengths of DEA, in part because it fails by its inherent use of LP basic solutions to exploit fully the optimal multiplier (dual) space, which is the *master key* to show the robustness of the DEA efficiency measures for simultaneous changes in *all* the observational data.

Banker (1990), Banker et al. (1991), Charnes and Zlobec (1989), Charnes et al. (1990c), Land et al. (1988), and Peterson and Olesen (1989) deal with several other approaches to sensitivity analysis. However, our approach is entirely different from what is done in these references and in any of the other cited papers. For one thing, our approach uses nonbasic optimal dual solutions, which is not true of these other aproaches. Our approach is also based on modifications of the CCR input ratio form, as discussed in appendix B, and, as already noted, it can deal with simultaneous changes in all columns of P—or changes in any subset that may be of interest for analyses of DMU behavior—for guidance in data assembly, or data refinement, and so on.

4. SCSC Multipliers Applied to Sensitivity in Kansas Farming

In this section we apply the SCSC approach to a study of Kansas farming (Thompson et al., 1990). Table 20–4 summarizes the DEA efficiency analysis based on the CCR ratio model. In total, 83 farms were analyzed; 23 of them were in the set E, and 60 of them were in the set N. Instead of considering all the DMU_j in N, the "nearly" efficient set $E_c = \{DMU_j: 0.79 \leq \theta_j^o \leq 1.0\}$ was evaluated, relative to the DMU_j in E.

This analysis was made for the four inputs, namely, production costs (x_1), cropland acres farmed (x_2), labor hours applied (x_3), and depreciated investment in current/intermediate assets (x_4). It considered the following three classes of farms: class I produced dryland wheat (y_1), class II produced dryland wheat (y_1) and milo (y_2), and class III produced irrigated wheat (y_1), milo (y_2), and soybeans (y_3).

For each DMU_o in E, application of an SCSC multiplier required first finding an SCSC solution ω^o in W_o, and then the corresponding dual slack vector T_o in the respective dual (given the SCSC primal characteristics of a DMU_o in E).

Table 20–4. Summary of DEA efficiency Results in Kansas Farming Efficiency Analysis, Ratio Model

| Class | Number of DMUs | | | Efficiency Measures |
	Total	Set E	Set E_c	Set E_c
I	32	6	4	.98, .82, .95, .80.
II	23	6	3	.85, .83, .82.
III	28	11	7	.85, .98, .92, .86, .96, .97, .79.
Totals	83	23	14	

Given the computed SCSC solution for each DMU_j in E, a sensitivity analysis was made for input variations one at a time. Stepwise, for every DMU_j in E, each input was increased by 5% increments; and for each DMU_j in E_c, each corresponding input was decreased by 5% decrements. The h-functions, given the SCSC solution, were evaluated at each step for all DMU_j in the union of E and E_c to check for changes in the top ranking. This process was continued for $5\% + /5\% -$ input increments/decrements up to $30\% + /30\% -$.

4.1. Interpretative Illustration

As an aid to the reader, the tables of sensitivity results below were organized to show not only whether a switch point occurred but also where it occurred; further, the DMU replacement is identified. It is important to note that the analysis is made for each DMU_o, relative to all other DMU_j, $j \neq o$, in E and E_c. Stable Always (SA) means that the selected DMU_o in E was never replaced in any of the variations analyzed. For example, consider DMU_8 in table 20–5; in the labor row, SA indicates that DMU_8 was the top-ranked DMU_j, $j = 8, 9, 14, 15, 16, 31, 3, 10, 13, 25$, across all of the increments/decrements in the labor input evaluated; and the (switched) row below each input indicates the level of input variation that resulted in a switch in the top ranking, if one occurred. Next, consider DMU_9; in the labor row, $\rightarrow 3$ indicates that h'_3 for DMU_3 in E_c replaced h'_9 for DMU_9 in E as the top-ranked DMU_j when the level of variation in the labor input reached 5%. Similarly, DMU_3 replaced DMU_{14} and also DMU_{31}. Several double switches in top ranking also occurred.

Table 20-5.   Results of SCSC Sensitivity Analysis for Class I Farms, Six Farms in $E = \{8, 9, 14, 15, 16, 31\}$, Four Farms in $E_c = \{3, 10, 13, 25\}$

Input Varied	DMU_o in E					
	8	9	14	15	16	31
Labor (switched)	SA	→3 (5%)	→3 (5%)	SA	SA	→3 (5%)
Prod. Cost (switched)	SA	→3 (15%)	→16→3 (5%, 20%)	SA	→3 (15%)	→16→3 (10%, 20%)
Land (switched)	SA	SA	→3 (20%)	SA	SA	→14→3 (10%, 20%)
Capital (switched)	SA	SA	→9 (5%)	SA	SA	SA

SA is stable always.

→ indicates switch in h_j top ranking.

(switched) indicates the relative variation where the switch occurred.

In each case, the total number of sensitivity evaluations made is the product of the number of DMUs in E, the number of inputs (four), and the six $5\% + /5\% -$ stepwise variations. In the discussion of the results, the emphasis is directed initially to the (input, DMU_o in E) pairs to facilitate interpretation.

It is important to realize just what it means to have or not to have a switch in the column for DMU_j. If there is no switch, then ω^j remains an SCSC vector for DMU_j for all seven steps from 0% to $30\% + /30\% -$. If a switch first occurs at step q, then ω^j remains SCSC for the first $(q - 1)$ steps, i.e., from 0% to $5(q - 1)\% + /5(q - 1)\% -$. Moreover, a switch at step q means that ω^j no longer satisfies inequality (20.B12) (see appendix B), but says nothing about the possible existence of a different multiplier $\bar{\omega}^j$ that could attest (through inequality (20.B12)) to continued membership in E for DMU_j. Thus, *our procedure is "conservative" in the sense that it provides sufficient but not necessary conditions for stability of the extreme efficient characterization of a DMU.*

4.2. Results of the SCSC Analysis of Sensitivity

4.2.1. Class I Farms—Six DMUs in E and Four DMUs in E_c. Of the 24 (input, DMU_o in E) pairs analyzed, 14 were stable always for the full range of input variation analyzed (see table 20–5). Relative to the inputs, this occurred as follows: capital, 5; land, 4; labor, 3; and production cost, 2. However, in 10 of the 24 pairs, the DMU_j with the top ranking changed once seven times and twice three times. Six of the seven single switches in the top ranking involved DMU_3 in E_c, with $\theta_3^* = 0.985$, replacing DMU_o in E. The three double switches in the top ranking all involved another DMU_j in E first replacing the respective DMU_o followed by DMU_3 in E_c replacing that DMU_j.

4.2.2. Class II Farms—Six DMUs in E and Three DMUs in E_c. Of the 24 (input, DMU_o in E) pairs evaluated, 17 were stable always (see table 20–6). Six of the seven switches in top ranking were from DMU_o in E to another DMU_j in E; in the other switch, DMU_{20} in E_c replaced DMU_{14} in E with a variation in x_2 of 10%.

4.2.3. Class III Farms—11 DMUs in E and 7 DMUs in E_c. Of the 44 (input, DMU_o in E) pairs evaluated, 29 pairs were stable always (see table 20–7). The 15 pairs with switches involved 14 with one switch in the top ranking and one with two switches in the top ranking. Nine of the 14 single top-ranking switches involved a DMU_j in E replacing DMU_o in E. The other five single switches in top ranking involved four DMU_j in E_c replacing DMU_o in E as follows:

Table 20–6. Results of SCSC Sensitivity Analysis for Class II Farms, Six Farms in $E = \{4, 6, 14, 15, 18, 21\}$ and Three Farms in $E_c = \{5, 9, 20\}$

	DMU_o in E					
Input Varied	4	6	14	15	18	21
Labor (switched)	→21 (5%)	SA	→18 (5%)	SA	SA	SA
Prod. Cost (switched)	SA	SA	→18 (5%)	SA	SA	SA
Land (switched)	→21 (5%)	SA	→20 (10%)	SA	SA	SA
Capital (switched)	→21 (5%)	SA	→18 (5%)	SA	SA	SA

SA is stable always.
→ indicates switch in h_j top ranking.
(switched) indicates the relative variation where the switch occurred.

Table 20–7. Results of Sensitivity Analysis for Class III Farms, Eleven Farms in $E = \{1, 3, 5, 6, 7, 10, 15, 18, 22, 24, 27\}$ and Seven Farms in $E_c = \{4, 11, 14, 16, 17, 21, 25\}$

Input Varied	DMU$_o$ in E										
	1	3	5	6	7	10	15	18	22	24	27
Labor (switched)	→3 (15%)	SA	SA	SA	SA	SA	SA	→21 (30%)	SA	→5 (20%)	SA
Prod. Cost (switched)	→5 (30%)	SA	SA	SA	SA	SA	SA	SA	SA	→5 (5%)	SA
Land (switched)	→17 (10%)	→25 (5%)	SA	→17 (5%)	SA	→11 (10%)	SA	SA	SA	→10 (5%)	→17 (10%)
Capital (switched)	SA	→5→25 (10%, 20%)	SA	→5 (15%)	SA	SA	SA	SA	SA	→5 (15%)	→5 (15%)

SA is stable always.
→ indicates switch in h_j top ranking.
(switched) indicates the relative variation where the switch occurred.

Input	% + / % −	DMU$_j$ in E_c Replacing DMU$_o$
x_2—land	5, 5	25, 17
x_2—land	10, 10	11, 17
x_3—labor	30	21

The double switch in the top ranking involved first DMU$_5$ in E replacing DMU$_o$ in E ($10\% + /10\% -$ in x_4) and then DMU$_{25}$ in E_c replacing DMU$_5$ in E ($20\% + /20\% -$ in x_4).

4.2.4. Sensitivity Results for All Three Classes of Farms. Of the 92 (input, DMU$_o$ in E) pairs evaluated, 60 were stable always; 28 had one top-ranking switch (where 50% of the time another DMU$_j$ in E replaced DMU$_o$ in E); and only four had a double switch in top ranking (where in each case the first switch was from one member of E to another member of E).

4.3. Analysis of h_j Top Rankings Considering Institutional Factors

The institutional framework in which the decision maker operates conditions the accuracy of measurements affecting him. This is especially true for farmers participating in the Kansas Farm Management Associations (KFMA). One of the KFMA's primary objectives is to ensure accurate farm cost, revenue, and income accounting to help the farmers become more productive and to assist them in reporting (see Langemeier, 1985).

A very high percentage of these farmers participate in the U.S. Department of Agriculture (USDA) Soil Conservation and Stabilization (ASCS) program. Every participating farmer has had his farm and its major crop acres/production precisely measured. Every ASCS county office in major agricultural areas maintains farm-specific Farm Record Cards on all eligible farms. This card contains an accurate historical and current end-of-the-year acreage/yield record for all ASCS program crops, e.g., wheat and milo.

Beyond the USDA, the U.S. Department of Treasury Internal Revenue Service (IRS) requires accurate revenue, cost, and income reports for tax purposes. The National Bureau of Standards studies continuously the accuracy of all types of weights and measures. Further, every state in the nation has an institution inspecting all devices used in commercial weights and measures. For example, in Texas, the Texas Department of Agriculture inspection sticker appears prominently on every elevator scale/gasoline meter used in commerce to weigh/measure commodities bought and sold. In addition, many national, state, city, county, and township authorities have legal regulatory powers requiring accurate measures of land, labor, and capital.

Because of the significance of these institutional considerations, the data records for acreage were regarded as extremely accurate; and the data records for production costs, capital investments, and hired labor inputs were regarded as quite accurate. The least accurately measured input was believed to be each farmer's estimate of his own contributed farm labor.

In accordance with these institutional factors, reasonable acreage data-measurement errors were limited (in absolute value) to $5\%+/5\%-$ or less; similarly, production cost and capital measurement errors were limited to $10\%+/10\%-$ or less, and labor measurement errors were limited to $20\%+/20\%-$ or less. In the presence of these working premises, there were only the following seven switches in top ranking from a DMU_j in E to a DMU_j in E_c:

Class	Input	# Switches	DMU_j in E_c	DMU_j in E Replaced
I	x_1	2	3, 3	9, 16
I	x_3	3	3, 3, 3	9,
III	x_2	2	25, 17	14,
				31
				3, 6

In total, 552 sensitivity evaluations were made for the three classes of farms. Overall, 98.7% of the sensitivity evaluations made did not result in a DMU_j in E_c replacing the top ranking of a DMU_j in E. Thus, in light of the conditioning influence of institutional factors on measurement accuracy, the fundamental DEA efficiency measures were found to be very insensitive to potential input data errors in the Kansas farming study.

5. SCSC Sensitivity Analysis of Illinois Coal Mining

Byrnes et al. (1984) evaluated the efficiency of 15 Illinois coal mines; their model had one output and eight inputs, namely, dragline capacity (K_1), power-shovel capacity (K_2), wheel-excavator capacity (K_3), thickness of first-seam mined (T_1), reciprocal of depth to first-seam mined $(1/D_1)$, thickness of second-seam mined (T_2), reciprocal of depth to second-seam mined $(1/D_2)$, and labor employed. This is called here the BFG Coal Model.

Recently, Thompson et al. (1990) re-evaluated Byrnes et al.'s data and efficiency measures; some minor measurement differences were noted. Also, Thompson et al. postulated an alternative coal model (TDT Coal Model) using the variable $(T_1/D_1 + T_2/D_2)$ as an indicator of mine quality; it replaced the separate use of the four variables T_1, D_1, T_2, and D_2 in the BFG Coal Model. Thompson et al.'s efficiency measures are presented in table 20–8 for both coal models (CCR case).

In accordance with the Kansas farming application above and Thompson et al.'s efficiency measures, the SCSC sensitivity multiplier principle was applied to the efficiency results for the BFG Coal Model and also for the TDT Coal Model. The resulting presentation below is similar to the one above for Kansas farming. However, in the coal-modeling sensitivity analysis, note that the set E_c includes all the DMUs in N.

5.1. BFG Coal Model Sensitivity Results

The results of the BFG Coal Model sensitivity analysis showed extreme insensitivity of the DMUs in $E = \{1, 2, 3, 4, 10, 13, 14, 15\}$ to generally relatively large variations in the input data (see table 20–9). Notably, 95.5% (275 out of 288) of the sensitivity evaluations were stable always.

Table 20-8. DEA Efficiency Results for Illinois Coal Mines, 1978, Ratio Model Efficiency Measures

	BFG Coal Model (Original)		TDT Coal Model (Alternative)	
DMU	Efficiency	Class	Efficiency	Class
1	1.00	E	1.00	E
2	1.00	E	0.81	N
3	1.00	E	1.00	E
4	1.00	E	1.00	E
5	0.88	N	0.95	N
6	0.92	N	0.62	N
7	0.82	N	0.46	N
8	0.68	N	0.68	N
9	0.88	N	0.53	N
10	1.00	E	1.00	E
11	0.77	N	0.28	N
12	0.64	N	0.52	N
13	1.00	E	0.57	N
14	1.00	E	0.46	N
15	1.00	E	0.57	N

Table 20-9. SCSC Sensitivity Analysis Results for Illinois Coal Mines, 1978, BFG Coal Model, Ratio Model Efficiency Measures

Input Varied	DMU_o in E							
	1	2	3	4	10	13	14	15
K_1 (switched)	SA	SA	SA	SA	SA	→2 5%	→2 10%	SA
K_2	SA	SA	SA	SA	SA	SA	SA	SA
K_3	SA	SA	SA	SA	SA	SA	SA	SA
T_1	SA	SA	SA	SA	SA	SA	SA	SA
$1/D_1$ (switched)	SA	SA	SA	SA	→2 30%	→2 20%	→15 5%	→2 10%
T_2 (switched)	SA	SA	SA	SA	SA	SA	→5 15%	→5 15%
$1/D_2$	SA	SA	SA	SA	SA	SA	SA	SA
Labor (switched)	SA	SA	SA	→5 30%	→3→2 15% 25%	→2 25%	SA	→5 10%

SA is stable always.
→ indicates switch in h_j top ranking.
(switched) indicates the relative variation where the switch occurred.

5.2. TDT Coal Model Sensitivity Results

The sensitivity analysis of the TDT Coal Model was relative to four DMUs in $E = \{1, 3, 4, 10\}$ and five input variables K_1, K_2, K_3, labor, and $(T_1/D_1 + T_2/D_2)$. The h-function rankings remained unchanged in 98% (118 out of 120) of the sensitivity evaluations made (see table 20–10). Hence, for the TDT Coal Model, the DMUs in E were also found to be extremely insensitive to potential data input errors.

5.3. Institutional Considerations for Illinois Coal Mining

Similar to Kansas farming, there are many institutional considerations limiting the extent of likely potential errors in the input data for Illinois coal mining. Not only the Illinois State departments and agencies but also U.S. Federal departments and agencies, e.g., EPA and OSHA, closely monitor many of the mining activities by company. This monitoring includes a wide range of input and output characteristics. Also, the financial community commonly requires appraisals of the coal reserves before financing is extended. Limiting the data variations considered (in absolute value) to 20% +/20% − or less, which was the largest considered in the presence of institutional considerations in the Kansas farming study, we found 98% of the DMU_j in E were insensitive to potential data errors.

Table 20–10. SCSC Sensitivity Analysis Results for Illinois Coal Mines, Alternative TDT Coal Model, Ratio Model Efficiency Measures

Input Varied	DMU_o in E			
	1	3	4	10
K_1 (switched)	SA	SA	→5 30%	SA
K_2	SA	SA	SA	SA
K_3	SA	SA	SA	SA
$(T_1/D_1 + T_2/D_2)$ (switched)	SA	SA	→5 30%	SA
Labor	SA	SA	SA	SA

SA is stable always.
→ indicates switch in h_j top ranking.
(switched) indicates the relative variation where the switch occurred.

6. Summary and Conclusions

An SCSC dual solution ω for a strong efficient DMU_k yields a DEA efficiency ratio $h_k(\omega)$ strictly greater than $h_j(\omega)$ for all $j \neq k$. This inequality is the key to our SCSC approach to sensitivity analysis, which establishes the robustness under small data changes of the strong efficient classification for a DMU. This inequality is exploited in the analytic sufficient conditions for robustness of the two theorems of appendix A and also in the applications using real-world data for Kansas farming as well as for Illinois coal mining. Appendix B extends the DEA theory of chapters 2 and 3. This extension provides a foundation for a deeper understanding and possible extensions of our findings on DEA robustness. The robustness of the DEA efficiency measures found here stands in sharp contrast to the unsupported claims of some critics.

In this chapter, we have dealt primarily with the seminal CCR model of Charnes, Cooper, and Rhodes (1978). For other models and additional background material, see Banker et al. (1984), Charnes and Cooper (1985a), Farrell (1957), Sengupta (1989), and Seiford and Thrall (1990).

Acknowledgments

An earlier version of this chapter on sensitivity analysis was presented at the CORS/ORSA/TIMS National Meetings, Vancouver, May 1989. The sensitivity analysis approach provided a way to address the data irregularity issue, which is a primary concern of econometricians in their reviews of DEA contributions. This point was specifically raised at the NSF Conference on "New Uses of DEA in Management," Austin, September 1989. The authors are indebted to the helpful review comments by W. W. Cooper, Rajiv Banker, and several unknown referees.

Appendix A: Two Theorems

Here we present two theorems that provide limits on simultaneous and percentage data deviations, respectively, under which membership in the extreme efficient set E is preserved.

We consider an extreme efficient DMU_o; and for it, we consider a normalized SCSC optimal virtual multiplier ω^o for which we have

$$h_o(\omega^o) = f_o(\omega^o)/g_o(\omega^o) = f_o(\omega^o) = g_o(\omega^o) = 1 \qquad (20.A1)$$

and where by the extreme efficiency property for DMU_o, we have

$$h_j(\omega^o) < 1 \quad \text{for } j \neq o \tag{20.A2}$$

Then we may write

$$h_o(\omega^o) = 1 > d = \max_{j \neq o} h_j(\omega^o)$$

$$\text{and} \quad \delta_j = 1 - h_j(\omega^o) > 0, \quad j = 1, \ldots, n \ (j \neq o). \tag{20.A3}$$

By the SCSC property, we have

$$h_j(\omega^o) > 0, f_j(\omega^o) > 0, \quad \text{and} \quad g_j(\omega^o) > 0 \text{ for all } j \tag{20.A4}$$

We let

$$v^\dagger = \Sigma v_i^o, \quad \mu^\dagger = \Sigma \mu_r^o \tag{20.A5}$$

Next, let

$$\varepsilon_1 = \min_j g_j(\omega^o)/v^\dagger \tag{20.A6}$$

and

$$\varepsilon_2 = \min_{j \neq o} \delta_j/\{[1 + 1/g_o(\omega^o)][\mu^\dagger + v^\dagger]\} \tag{20.A7}$$

and choose ε and c so that

$$0 < \varepsilon < \min\{\varepsilon_1, \varepsilon_2\} \tag{20.A8}$$

and

$$0 < c < (1 - \sqrt{d})/(1 + \sqrt{d}) \tag{20.A9}$$

Let a modified data matrix P^1 be obtained from $P = [P_1 \ldots P_n]$ by changes in the individual data elements x_{ij} and y_{rj}.

Then we have the following two theorems:

Theorem A1: Absolute Change Case.
Suppose DMU_o is in E.
If no element of $P-P^1$ exceeds ε in absolute value, then DMU_o remains extreme efficient under P^1.

Theorem A2: Percentage Change Case.
Suppose DMU_o is in E.
If for all i, r, and j, we have

$$(1 - c)x_{ij} \leq x_{ij}^1 \leq (1 + c)x_{ij}, \text{ and } (1 - c)y_{rj} \leq y_{rj}^1 \leq (1 + c)y_{rj} \tag{20.A10}$$

Then DMU$_o$ remains extreme efficient under P^1.

Theorem A2 is not only simpler than theorem A1 but also probably more useful, since proportional changes are independent of the input and output measurement units. This is clearly not true for absolute changes.

Our proofs of the two theorems are based on a worst-case, best-case scenario. For the worst-case for DMU$_o$, consider a modification P_o^1 of P_o for which $h_o^1(\omega^o) = \min h_o^2(\omega^o)$ for all permitted P_o^2. We also consider, for each $j \neq o$, a *best-case* modification P_j^1 of P_j that maximizes $h_j^2(\omega^o)$ for all (permitted) modifications of P.

A1. Proof of Theorem A1

We note that in the proof of this theorem, we need not require that all y_{rj}^2 or x_{ij}^2 be nonnegative, since the proof of the theorem requires only that equation (20.A6) and inequality (20.A8) be satisfied.

We define P_o^1 and P_j^1 for $j \neq o$ by

$$x_o^1 = x_o + \varepsilon I_m, \quad y_o^1 = y_o - \varepsilon I_s$$
$$x_j^1 = x_j - \varepsilon I_m, \quad y_j^1 = y_j + \varepsilon I_s \qquad (20.A11)$$

where I_k is the k by 1 vector of ones.

Then, by the hypothesis of theorem A1, we have $P_o^2 \leqslant P_o^1$ and $P_j^2 \geqslant P_j^1$ for all permitted choices of P_o^2 and P_j^2.

It follows from the definition of h (see inequality (20.A2)) that

$$h_o^2(\omega^o) \geqslant h_o^1(\omega^o), \quad h_j^2(\omega^o) \leqslant h_j^1(\omega^o) \quad \text{for } j \neq o \qquad (20.A12)$$

Hence, to establish the theorem, we need only show that the choice of ε (see equation (20.A6)) assures that

$$h_o^1(\omega^o) > h_j^1(\omega^o) \quad \text{for all } j \neq o \qquad (20.A13)$$

Consider the following difference and its expression:

$$h_o^1(\omega^o) - h_j^1(\omega^o) = \frac{f_o(\omega^o) - \varepsilon\mu^\dagger}{g_o(\omega^o) + \varepsilon v^\dagger} - \frac{f_j(\omega^o) + \varepsilon\mu^\dagger}{g_j(\omega^o) - \varepsilon v^\dagger} \qquad (20.A14)$$

A direct algebraic manipulation using equations (20.A1) and (20.A3) leads to

$$h_o^1(\omega^o) - h_j^1(\omega^o) = G[\delta_j(1 + \varepsilon) - \varepsilon(\mu^\dagger + v^\dagger)(1 + 1/g_2(\omega^o))] \qquad (20.A15)$$

where

$$G = g_j(\omega^o)/(1 + \varepsilon v^\dagger)(g_j(\omega^o) - v^\dagger)$$
$$\varepsilon(\mu^\dagger + v^\dagger)(1 + (1/g_j(\omega^o))) < \varepsilon_2(\mu^\dagger + v^\dagger)(1 + (1/g_j(\omega^o))) \le \delta_j$$

$$(20.\text{A}16)$$

Hence, for all $j \neq o$,

$$h_o^1(\omega^o) - h_j^1(\omega^o) > G[\delta_j(1 + \varepsilon) - \delta_j] > o,$$

thus establishing theorem A1.

A2. Proof of Theorem A2

For this proof, we define the worst-case P_o^1 and *best-cases* P_j^1 for $j \neq o$ by

$$x_o^1 = x_o(1 + c), \quad y_o^1 = y_o(1 - c)$$
$$x_j^1 = x_j(1 - c), \quad y_j^1 = y_j(1 + c) \qquad (20.\text{A}17)$$

Following the same reasoning as in the previous proof, we need only show that inequality (20.A13) holds when c is given by inequality (20.A9). Clearly,

$$h_o^1(\omega^o) = \frac{f_o(\omega^o)(1 - c)}{g_o(\omega^o)(1 + c)} = \frac{1 - c}{1 + c} \times h_o(\omega^o) \qquad (20.\text{A}18)$$

and, for $j \neq o$,

$$h_j^1(\omega^o) = \frac{f_j(\omega^o)(1 + c)}{g_j(\omega^o)(1 - c)} = \frac{1 + c}{1 - c} \times h_j(\omega^o) \qquad (20.\text{A}19)$$

By equations (20.A1) and (20.A3) and inequality (20.A9), we have

$$\frac{h_j^1(\omega^o)}{h_o^1(\omega^o)} = ((1 + c)/(1 - c))^2 h_j(\omega^o) \le ((1 + c)/(1 - c))^2 d \qquad (20.\text{A}20)$$

From inequality (20.A9), we have

$$d < ((1 - c)/(1 + c))^2$$

so that

$$\frac{h_j^1(\omega^o)}{h_o^1(\omega^o)} < ((1 + c)/(1 - c))^2((1 - c)/(1 + c))^2 = 1$$

and theorem A2 follows.

We can readily generalize theorem A2 to cover other types of proportional changes. For example, if the changes are limited to inputs only or outputs only, then theorem A2 is valid if $\sqrt{d}$ is replaced by d in inequality (20.A9), i.e.,

$$0 < c < (1 - d)/(1 + d) \qquad (20.A21)$$

This same bound for c remains valid if both inputs and outputs for DMU_o are involved but no other P_j are changed.

If only inputs or outputs for DMU_o are involved, then the respective replacements for inequality (20.A9) are

$$0 < c < (1 - d)/d \qquad \text{(inputs only)} \qquad (20.A22)$$

and

$$0 < c < 1 - d \qquad \text{(outputs only)} \qquad (20.A23)$$

It is interesting to compare inequalities (20.A22) and (20.A23) with the results in Charnes and Neralic (1990b; see also their earlier papers—1989a, 1989b, 1990a—as well as Charnes et al., 1985b). All these papers utilize the basic dual solution

$$\omega^T = (1/3, 1/18, 1/19) \qquad (*)$$

for the data domain D defined by the matrix

$$P = \begin{bmatrix} 2 & 4 & 2 & 3 & 2 \\ -4 & -12 & -8 & -6 & -2 \\ -6 & -8 & -2 & -6 & -8 \end{bmatrix} = \begin{bmatrix} Y \\ -X \end{bmatrix} \qquad (20.A24)$$

An alternative basic solution is

$$\omega^T = (1/3, 1/9, 1/18) \qquad (**)$$

Neither equation (*) nor equation (**) is SCSC (see, e.g., Spivey and Thrall, 1970). However, the average of the solutions in equations (*) and (**),

$$\omega^{oT} = (1/3, 1/12, 1/12) \qquad (***)$$

is SCSC. For this SCSC solution,

$$[h_j(\omega^o)] = [0.8, 0.8, 0.8, 1.0, 0.8]$$

with $d = 0.8$. The corresponding values from inequalities (20.A22) and (20.A23) for c are 0.25 (input) and 0.20 (output), which agree with the values $\hat{\beta}$-1 and $\hat{\alpha}$-1 found by Charnes and Neralic (1990b, pp. 10–11). Note that our approach also gives the following upper bounds for DMU_o

($= DMU_4$): 1) $c < 0.111$ for simultaneous proportionate changes in all inputs (by inequality (20.A22)), and 2) $c < 0.050$ for proportionate changes in all inputs and outputs (by inequality (20.A9)).

For ω^o (see solution (***)), theorem A1 applies with $\varepsilon < 0.16$, and theorem A2 applies with $c < 0.0557$.

Here, we have shown the importance of using SCSC solutions to penetrate the *interior* of the $(m + s)$-dimensional multiplier space W_o. By contrast, reliance on basic solutions (see, e.g., Charnes et al., 1985b) *limits* one to the subset W_o^m, which (as is shown in appendix B) has dimension two less than that of the full multiplier space W_o.

Our approach and Charnes et al.'s (including Charnes and Neralic's and Charnes and Zlobec's) approaches are all useful. Each has its advantages and disadvantages.

Quite clearly, the power of the SCSC approach depends on how far ω^o is from the boundaries of W_o. In the above example, ω^o is very centrally located. An alternate SCSC $\omega^1 = (1/54)[4, 5, 18]$ gives the larger value $d^1 = 6/7$, with the respective input and output bounds $c < 1/6$, $c < 1/7$; these bounds are much more restrictive than those given by Charnes et al., referenced above, or by the use of ω^o of solution (***). The development of methods to identify *good* choices, if not the *best* one, for ω^o is worthy of further research.

Appendix B: Additional DEA Background

B1. DEA Domains and Efficiency Classes

We build on the concepts and notation of chapter 2 (this volume) and focus on the input-oriented CCR Primal and Dual models of chapter 2, section 5.1, and the CCR Ratio Form of chapter 2, section 6.1. Following Charnes et al. (1991), we introduce several modifications.

(M1). We generalize the input and output data vectors X_j and Y_j by permitting zero values for some (but not all) individual inputs and outputs.

(M2). We delete ε in CCR_P-I, CCR_D-I, and $CCR-IR$ and accordingly permit zero values for some (but not all) of their components v_i, μ_r.

(M3). We remove the multiplier restrictions $h_j(\mu, v) \leqslant 1$ in $CCR-IR$.

Extending the earlier notation, a DEA *data domain* D considers a set of n DMUs and a technology that is characterized by an $(s + m) \times n$ data matrix

$$P = \begin{bmatrix} Y \\ -X \end{bmatrix} = [P_1, \ldots, P_n] \qquad (20.\text{B1})$$

where $P_j = \begin{bmatrix} Y_j \\ -X_j \end{bmatrix}$ is the input/output vector for DMU_j. The minus sign accompanying the input vector X_j serves to simplify matrix formulation of concepts as in relationships (20.B2) to (20.B5) below. Observe that $p = \begin{bmatrix} y \\ -x \end{bmatrix} \geq p^* = \begin{bmatrix} y^* \\ -x^* \end{bmatrix}$ is equivalent to $y \geq y^*$ and $x \leq x^*$. In particular, $p > p^*$ means every output is increased and every input is decreased.

The data matrix P defines the *production possibility set* or *envelopment space*,

$$E_s = \left\{ p = \begin{bmatrix} y \\ -x \end{bmatrix} \middle| P \leq P\lambda \text{ for some } \lambda \geq 0 \right\} \qquad (20.\text{B2})$$

The strong Pareto boundary or *extended frontier* EFR of E_S consists of all vectors p in E_S for which the relationship

$$p' > p \quad \text{(strict dominance)} \qquad (20.\text{B3})$$

does not hold for any p' in E_S. The weak Pareto boundary or *efficiency frontier* FR (also called the envelopment surface) of E_S consists of those vectors p in T for which the relationship

$$p' \geq p \quad \text{(weak dominance)} \qquad (20.\text{B4})$$

does not hold for any p' in E_S. A DMU in EFR that is not in FR is said to be (DEA) *weak efficient*, and one in FR is said to be (DEA) *efficient* (or technically efficient).

We focus on the CCR models in input form and with ε deleted. They can be restated in more concise form as

Primal	**Dual**	
min θ	max $\omega_o = \mu^T Y_o$	(20.B5)
subject to	subject to	
$p\lambda \geq \begin{bmatrix} Y_o \\ -\theta X_o \end{bmatrix}, \lambda \geq 0$	$v^T X_o = 1, P^T \omega \leq 0, \omega = \begin{bmatrix} \mu \\ v \end{bmatrix} \geq 0$	

Next, let

$$f_j(\omega) = \mu^T Y_j, \quad g_j(\omega) = v^T X_j \tag{20.B6}$$

Then we use the ratio

$$h_j(\omega) = f_j(\omega)/g_j(\omega) \tag{20.B7}$$

as a measure of (comparative) efficiency; i.e., if $h_o(\omega) > h_j(\omega)$, we say that DMU$_o$ *is more efficient than* DMU$_j$, *relative to the multiplier* ω.

We define the efficiency of DMU$_j$ relative to ω to be

$$\theta_j(\omega) = h_j(\omega)/h_o(\omega) \tag{20.B8}$$

where

$$h_o(\omega) = \max_j h_j(\omega)$$

Then it can be shown that

$$\max_\omega \theta_j(\omega) \tag{20.B9}$$

is the DEA-efficiency $\theta_j^* = \omega_j^*$ of DMU$_j$.

DMU$_o$ lies on the extended frontier EFR if, and only if, there exists a multiplier ω for which $\theta_o(\omega) = 1$, i.e., for which

$$h_o(\omega) \geq h_j(\omega) \quad \text{for all } j \tag{20.B10}$$

If no such multiplier exists, we call DMU$_o$ *inefficient*. If DMU$_o$ is on EFR, we consider the (nonempty) set W_o of all multipliers for which inequality (20.B10) holds. We say that DMU$_o$ is *extreme efficient* if

$$\dim W_o = m + s, \tag{20.B11}$$

or, equivalently, if for some multiplier we have

$$h_o(\omega) > h_j(\omega) \quad \text{for all } j \neq o. \tag{20.B12}$$

Because of the continuity of the functions h_j in both the data coefficients X_j, Y_j and the variable multiplier ω, we see that inequality (20.B12) remains valid at least for small changes in the data and the multipliers.

We denote by E the set of all extreme efficient DMUs. A vector in W_o is said to be *normalized* if

$$h_o(\omega) = f_o(\omega) = g_o(\omega) = 1 \tag{20.B13}$$

and we denote by W_o^m the subset of all normalized ω in W_o. If ω is in W_o, then so is $\omega' = \begin{bmatrix} \alpha\mu \\ \beta\upsilon \end{bmatrix}$ for any positive numbers α and β.

In particular, if

$$\alpha = 1/f_o(\omega), \quad \beta = 1/g_o(\omega), \tag{20.B14}$$

then w' is normalized. From this it follows that

$$\dim W_o^m = \dim W_o - 2. \tag{20.B15}$$

The set E plays a central role in our sensitivity studies, in part because every extreme ray of E_S contains a unique element of E and each element of E generates an extreme ray. The elements of E thus form a minimal set of generators for the cone E_S; thus we can strengthen equation (20.B2) to

$$E_s = \left\{ p = \begin{bmatrix} Y \\ -X \end{bmatrix} \middle| p \leq p\lambda, \lambda \geq 0, \text{ where } \lambda_j \neq 0 \text{ only if DMU}_j \text{ is in } E \right\}. \tag{20.B16}$$

B2. SCSC and Primal and Dual Slacks

We combine the output and input slack vectors s^+ and s^- of chapter 2 (this volume) into a single *primal slack vector*

$$S = \begin{bmatrix} s^- \\ s^+ \end{bmatrix} = P\lambda - \begin{bmatrix} Y_o \\ -\theta X_o \end{bmatrix} \tag{20.B17}$$

We also introduce the dual slack vector

$$T = \begin{bmatrix} t_1 \\ \vdots \\ t_n \end{bmatrix} = -P^T\omega \tag{20.B18}$$

Thus

$$t_j = -Y_j^T\mu + X_j^T\upsilon \quad (j = 1, \ldots, n) \tag{20.B19}$$

Using the nonnegativity of λ, S, ω, T for any optimal pair λ, ω, of solutions to models (20.B5), the ordinary complementary slackness condition can be stated as

$$\lambda^T T = 0 \quad \text{and} \quad S^T\omega = 0 \tag{20.B20}$$

If, in addition to equations (20.B20), we have

$$\lambda + T > 0 \quad \text{and} \quad S + \omega > 0 \tag{20.B21}$$

then the *strong complementary slackness condition* is said to hold, and we say that λ *and* ω *are SCSC vectors*.

Such vectors always exist (see Spivey and Thrall, 1970), and if $P > 0$, they can be obtained as averages of any initial optimal pair λ, ω with additional optimal vectors that maximize, in turn, selected components of λ, ω, S, or T. (The case when P has some zero elements is treated by Charnes et al., 1991.)

Suppose, next, that a dual vector $\omega = \begin{bmatrix} \mu \\ \upsilon \end{bmatrix}$ is SCSC for $\mathrm{DMU_o}$, and let α, β be any positive numbers. Then we generalize the SCSC concept by saying that $\omega' = \begin{bmatrix} \alpha\mu \\ \beta\upsilon \end{bmatrix}$ is also SCSC for $\mathrm{DMU_o}$.

B3. More on Optimal Dual Solutions

We next turn to further analysis of the example domain of section 2 above, making use of the theory developed in sections B1 and B2.

Table 20–11 displays the basic optimal solutions (four in all) for the input-oriented CCR dual of the three extreme efficient DMUs in this example domain.

(Note that ω^{B1} and ω^{B4} require $\varepsilon = 0$; see **M2** above.) These solutions are illustrated in figure 20–2.

The four basic solutions in figure 20–2 correspond (respectively) to the four facets indicated in figure 20–1. Actually, the full facets are planes whose intersections with $y_1 = 1$ are displayed in figure 20–1.

The facets are described analytically in table 20–12.

Vectors on the line segment $(\omega^{B1}, \omega^{B2})$ constitute the normalized multiplier space W_1^m of all optimal dual solutions for $\mathrm{DMU_1}$. The planar region marked $\overline{W}_1$ consists all of all optimal multipliers for $\mathrm{DMU_1}$ that have $\mu_1 = 1$. The full three-dimensional multiplier space W_1 for $\mathrm{DMU_1}$ consists of all positive multiples of vectors in $\overline{W}_1$. Similarly, the segments

Table 20–11. Basic Optimal Dual Solutions

Optimal Set	ω^{B1} DMU_1	ω^{B2} $DMU_{1,2}$	ω^{B3} $DMU_{2,3}$	ω^{B4} DMU_3
μ_1	1	1	1	1
υ_1	0	1/6	1/3	1
υ_2	1	1/3	1/6	0

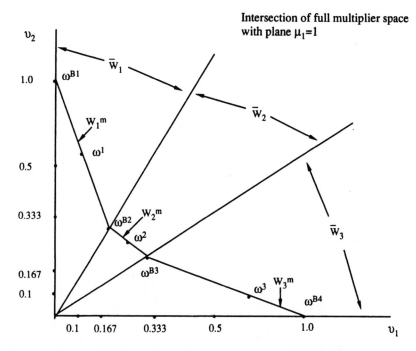

Figure 20-2. The dual (multiplier) space for the example domain.

Table 20-12. The Four Facets

Facet	1	2	3	4
$\begin{bmatrix} y_1 \\ -x_1 \\ -x_2 \end{bmatrix}$	$\begin{bmatrix} 1 \\ -1 \\ -4-\alpha \end{bmatrix} \gamma$	$\begin{bmatrix} 1 \\ -2+\beta \\ -2-2\beta \end{bmatrix} \gamma$	$\begin{bmatrix} 1 \\ -2-2\beta \\ -2+\beta \end{bmatrix} \gamma$	$\begin{bmatrix} 1 \\ -4-\alpha \\ -1 \end{bmatrix} \gamma$

where $\gamma > 0,\ \alpha \geqslant 0,\ 1 \geqslant \beta \geqslant 0$

(ω^{B2}, ω^{B3}) and (ω^{B3}, ω^{B4}) constitute W_2^m and W_3^m, respectively. Every interior point in W_j^m is SCSC for $DMU_j(j = 1, 2, 3)$; the particular solutions ω^1, ω^2, ω^3 were selected (somewhat arbitrarily) as the following linear combinations of basic solutions:

$$\omega^1 = .4\omega^{B1} + .6\omega^{B2}, \quad \omega^2 = .5\omega^{B2} + .5\omega^{B3}, \quad \omega^3 = .6\omega^{B3} + .4\omega^{B4}.$$

(20.B22)

To emphasize the need for SCSC solutions, consider a modification of D to $D^*(\alpha)$ where $P^*(\alpha)$ is the same as P except that P_2 is replaced by

$$P_2^*(\alpha) = \begin{bmatrix} 1 \\ -2 - \alpha \\ -2 \end{bmatrix} \quad \text{where } -1 \leq \alpha \leq 1 \qquad (20.\text{B}23)$$

Table 20–11 shows that ω^{B2} belongs to $W_1 \cap W_2$ in $D = D^*(0)$. However, for $\alpha \neq 0$, ω^{B2} belongs only to W_1 for $\alpha > 0$ and only to W_2 for $\alpha < 0$. This again illustrates the power of using nonbasic SCSC solutions.

For any data domain D, a positive basic solution ω for any DMU_k will have $h_j(\omega) = 1$ for at least $m + s - 1$ values of j; thus in equation (20.A3) we have $d = 1$ and $\delta_j = 0$, and in equation (20.A7) we have $\varepsilon_2 = 0$, so that neither theorem A1 or A2 is applicable. Thus, both theorems require that the solution ω^o must be SCSC. Similarly, the following sensitivity analyses of the Kansas farms and of the Illinois coal mines require starting with an SCSC dual solution ω^o for an extreme efficient DMU_o.

Our example illustrates some important general properties of facets. for any data domain D, every facet F corresponds to a basic dual solution ω^o of some extreme efficient DMU_o. If $\omega^o > 0$, we call F *interior*, and if ω^o has at least one zero component, we call F *exterior*. In our example, facets 2 and 3 are interior and facets 1 and 4 are exterior. Here the efficient frontier FR is the union of all interior facets. For every domain D, the extended frontier EFR is the union of all facets interior and exterior. Thus, for our example, FR = facet 2 $\cup$ facet 3. An interior facet will contain at least $m + s - 1$ extreme efficient DMU_j, and their corresponding dual vectors ω^j will all be proportional.

III EPILOGUE: PROCESS AND BIBLIOGRAPHY

21 THE DEA PROCESS, USAGES, AND INTERPRETATIONS

1. Introduction

As is true with the application of any analytical approach to the "art of reckoning" (Eilon, 1984), the use of data envelopment analysis (DEA) requires knowledge about formulation of models, choice of variables, underlying assumptions, data representation, interpretation of results, and knowledge of limitations. In this chapter, we discuss the process of conducting DEA studies and various uses such as exploratory data analysis, implementation of DEA solutions, and recent model formulations, as well as caveats in applying the method. It should be noted that this chapter represents the accumulated experience of many DEA practitioners and researchers in applying DEA. It represents another concrete example of how the practice of DEA not only shaped the evolution of theoretical and model development but also informed the process and understanding of DEA analysis.

2. The Basics

By now the reader should be aware that a distinguishing feature of DEA is the absence of any assumption about the underlying functional form relating the independent and dependent variables. In micro economic theory, the specification of a production function (e.g., Cobb–Douglas) determines the description of input–output relationship in an organization. The underlying assumption of such a specification is the existence of a transformation technology that determines what maximum amounts of outputs can be produced from a combination of various inputs—or alternately, the minimum combination of various inputs needed to produce a given level of outputs. However, as Seiford and Thrall (1990) observed, "This description of the production technology would be provided by the production function, *if it were known*" (pp. 7–8). In reality the production function is not known. The analyst has only data—observations about various inputs and their magnitudes and about various achieved outputs and their magnitudes. Thus the point of departure for DEA is the construction, from the observed data, of a piecewise *empirical* production frontier. Stolp (1990) recognized this distinguishing feature of DEA and noted that "by imposing the weaker assumption that the relations among production inputs and outputs are merely monotonic and concave, DEA makes it more possible for the data to '*speak for themselves*' rather than speak in the idiom of some imposed functional form" (p. 104). In DEA the data speak for themselves because the analysis is focused on maximizing each individual observation, in contrast to fitting a single regression plane that is assumed to describe the behavior of each observation "on average."

Getting started with a DEA analysis involves several issues. The first relates to choosing the DEA model to be formulated—in other words, deciding on which of the basic models described in chapter 2 (this volume) is most appropriate.

The choice of DEA model can be made by answering two questions: 1) Does the problem formulation justify an assumption of constant returns to scale (CRS)? and 2) Is the problem formulation oriented toward output maximization, input minimization, or on equal emphasis of outputs and inputs? Table 21–1 summarizes the choices available.

The scale/orientation heuristic is very useful in choosing models for most applications. It should be noted, however, that the additive model for constant returns to scale is not discussed in chapter 2 (this volume) because it is not widely known in the literature and has not been empirically applied so far (Ali and Seiford in Fried, Lovell, and Schmidt, 1993).

Data set construction involves another issue. The discussion so far has assumed that data sets of observations are already available to the analyst. Often, however, the problem to be analyzed is well understood (e.g., relative performance evaluation of restaurants in a fast food chain), but

Table 21-1. Summary of DEA Model Choices

	Orientation		
	Output	*Input*	*Output and Input*
Constat returns to scale	CCR output	CCR input	See Ali and Seiford chapter in Fried, Lovell, and Schmidt (1993)
Variable returns to scale	BCC output	BCC input	Additive

decisions must be made on what data set should be established. In general, the client organization will possess a wealth of knowledge about what it considers to be relevant output measures, and discretionary input variables (under the control of the DMU manager) and also which exogenous variables (e.g., age, demographics) or categorical variables (e.g., presence of certain competitors) should be included. The analyst, however, must be alert to several issues. Often the client organization will identify a large number of input variables or output variables that are intercorrelated, and it is the role of the analyst to help choose a set of inputs and outputs that are minimally intercorrelated. In addition, as is true for other methodologies, the inputs and outputs included in the model should be somewhat related experientially, statistically, and/or conceptually, and it is also important to have information on the direction of the relationship, whether it is positive or negative. Another criterion to be considered in choosing among variable possibilities is accuracy of the data. Because DEA solutions are sensitive to inaccuracies in the data (see later discussion on caveats and limitations), data accuracy and verification should be given careful consideration.

DEA solutions provide detailed information about the inefficient DMUs in terms of improvements in the inputs or outputs. This is another distinguishing feature of DEA that is often misinterpreted. The improvements in inputs (decreases in one or more of the inputs) and in outputs (increases in one or more of the outputs) results from the projection of the inefficient DMUs onto the empirically derived frontier.

In the literature and in practice, the DEA calculations of improvements in inputs and outputs are often treated as deterministic prescriptions. This is understandable, because the calculated DMU-specific improvements are based on the "revealed" actual best practice of comparable DMUs located on the efficient frontier. This prescriptive orientation seems to be motivated by the unstated assumption that if certain DMUs physically define the efficient frontier, then the "comparable" inefficient DMUs "should" also be able to achieve equivalent levels of performance.

3. Attention Directing

When DEA solutions are intended as a guide to managerial action (e.g., goal setting) or policymaking, it is important to recognize that the calculated improvements in inputs and/or outputs are indicative of potential performance increases by DMUs located below the efficient frontiers. In a sense, the DMU-specific solutions should be used as an attention-directing device. The use of DEA solutions for directing attention is often not appreciated in practice and can be illustrated in several ways.

In figure 1–2 (chapter 1), we illustrated some of the new insights that are obtainable for plotting DEA solutions in terms of the aggregate score and output. Figure 1–2 also illustrates how this plot directs management attention: for example, DMUs 28 and 29 become the focus of management attention because of their potential to achieve significant improvements. Similarly, DMUs 5 and 6 should be removed from management's "poor performance" list. More importantly, the DEA solutions can be used to direct management attention toward developing a deeper understanding of why some DMUs are located on the frontier and others are relatively inefficient. In the language of statistical quality control, the reason relates to establishing assignable cause. In the practice of management and organization effectiveness, management attention is directed to identifying formal structures, processes, or other organizational factors that account for the observed differences. The objective is to assign organizational meaning to the observed differences in performance and to determine the organizational changes that inefficient DMUs will need to undertake and how to implement them. In terms of Total Quality Management or continuous improvement, attention is directed toward benchmarking— describing, flow charting, documenting—the best-practice processes of DMUs located on the frontier.

4. Exploratory Data Analysis

The concept of Exploratory Data Analysis was first formalized by Tukey (1974). Tukey distinguished between *confirmation* uses of statistics, as in tests-of-significance approaches to hypothesis testing, and *exploratory* uses of statistics for discovery and hypothesis formation. As Tukey states the matter, there is no conflict between the two, and "Today, exploratory and confirmatory can—and should—proceed side by side." His objective, in a sense, was to maximize, from residual analyses, the information content of the data—that is, to let the data speak for themselves statistically. There can (and should be) a linkage between EDA and DEA, although we are not aware of any publications that report the use of DEA in EDA. Much of EDA consists of ad hoc (but useful) devices for discovering patterns underlying the data. DEA that is based on a series of economics and management concepts accompanied by rigorous mathematical support provides a different approach to exploratory data analysis. The objective in EDA is to ascertain possible patterns that will satisfy *necessary conditions* of causal connections between variables when submitted to confirmatory statistical test. DEA can handle multiple variables interacting in complex (and unknown) ways and hence can be viewed as directed to *sufficient conditions* of causality. Subsequent analyses may then be used not only to validate what was supposedly discovered in the exploratory data analysis but also to relate these results to other conditions and relations that may be present. DEA can be used to explore alternative assignable causes, such as presence of returns to scale, importance of various exogenous variables, different data representation, or segmentation of the analysis by the use of categorical (dummy) variables.

The use of dummy variables (aka categorical or control variables) in DEA requires more care than in traditional parametric analysis. In the parametric approach, the estimated parameter coefficient for each dummy variable is an average measure of the association between that variable and the dependent variable. In addition, the calculated sign of the estimated coefficient indicates the direction of the relationship. Categorical variables in DEA have the same function as in parametric analysis. In DEA calculations, they function as further constraints on establishing subsets of comparable DMUs and on determining the direction of comparisons between subsets. Specifically, as noted in chapter 3 (this volume), the analyst must have some a priori information about the direction of the disadvantage between categories. In other words, the categories have to be represented in the model in a way that ensures that each DMU is compared only to other DMUs in its category and/or to DMUs in more disadvantaged categories.

For example, in the analysis of outlets in a fast food chain, the presence of a drive-through window could be considered an important factor affecting sales. The dummy variable for "drive-through window" would be represented in the various DEA models to constrain the comparison of outlets without drive-through windows to that category only. However, outlets without drive-through windows could be in the comparison group of outlets with drive-through windows. It is important to note that if categories are not comparable, a separate DEA analysis should be performed for each category.

DEA, however, can be used to obtain relative comparison between the categories. Such an application was first illustrated by Charnes, Cooper, and Rhodes (1981) in their analyses of Program Follow Through. In the Program Follow Through DEA study, these authors used what are now called the *CCR projection formulas* to project all observations for each DMU (= school) onto their efficiency frontiers. It was then possible to ascertain whether the evidence showed Program Follow Through (as a program) to be more efficient than the non-Program-Follow-Through performances by comparing both as if all were being managed at their theoretical technical efficiency. In the process, a distinction was naturally made between *managerial efficiency comparison* within programs and *program efficiency* across programs.

Lewin and Morey (1981), in their study of operations of the U.S. Navy Recruitment Command, showed how these projections could be made to yield yet another approach to category analysis and comparisons. We can discuss this by using figure 21–1.

Figure 21–1 reproduces the organization chart for the Navy Recruitment Command at the time of the Lewin–Morey study. To compare the managerial philosophy and practices of Recruiting Area Commanders, Lewin and Morey used the following two-stage procedure. First a DEA analysis was conducted within each region to obtain estimates of technical inefficiency as a measure of the performance (i.e., the practices) within each region. CCR projections were then effected to the regional frontier, and these projections were then used to reflect the managerial philosophy (or strategy) of the area commander within each region. A second stage was then undertaken by Lewin and Morey in which the thus-adjusted regional data were pooled in order to provide evaluations of regional performance. This permitted comparisons of the *potential* for each regional commander's strategy and thus made it possible to distinguish between strategies and the manner in which the district offices performed. In this way, Lewin and Morey (1981) developed a method for performing categorical analyses in DEA as an alternative to other methods that could not be used because no natural nesting of the categories could be drawn upon.

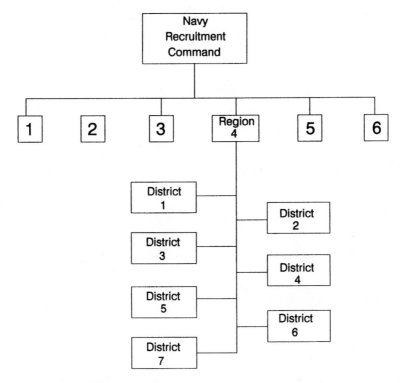

Figure 21–1.   Organization chart of Navy recruitment command. Reprinted with permission from Lewin and Morey, 1981.

5. Hybrid Modeling

The above analysis of regional vs. managerial efficiency applied DEA in a two-stage procedure but did not alter the formulation of the basic DEA model being analyzed. In contrast, hybrid modeling involves, for example, multi-stage DEA models where each DEA model is unique and where the outputs from the first model become part of the inputs for the second model and so on. Other hybrid examples involve the combining of DEA solutions with parametric analyses, models in which the output-oriented formulation differs from the input-oriented models, and the longitudinal "windows" analyses.

Charnes et al. (1986) describe a two-phase application that arose from the application of DEA in the analysis of U.S. Army Recruiting Command activities. These authors observed that advertising did not of itself produce the recruits that were wanted as final outputs. Instead, the advertising dollars expended in stage 1 produced an "awareness" in the form of "stated intentions to enlist" (as obtained from survey data), which when combined with other recruiting resources (e.g., recruiting staff) in stage 2 obtain the desired final outputs—either signed "contracts to enlist" or candidates taking qualifying examinations such as the Army Specialty Field Aptitude Battery.

Figure 21–2 portrays this two-stage model. Outputs obtained from the inputs in stage 1 (e.g., advertising expenditures) serve, in turn, as inputs to stage 2, where they can be combined with *other* inputs to produce the final desired outputs. Note that not all of the outputs from the stage 1 model need to become inputs for stage 2. Stage 1 can produce desired outputs for which no further processing is required.

The two-stage DEA model illustrates the value of decomposing the analysis of an activity into two or more linked models. A somewhat different example relates to an analysis of an activity where the output-oriented model and input-oriented model are asymmetric. Unlike the discussion in chapters 2 and 3 of this volume, which assumes a symmetry in the variable structure of both the output- and input-oriented models, applications can arise where hybrid asymmetric modeling can be advantageous.

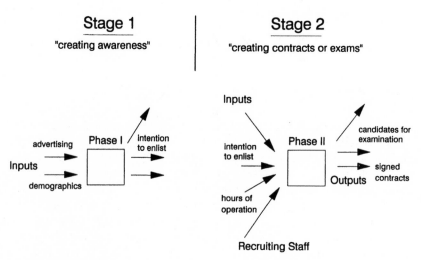

Figure 21–2. Overview of a two-stage DEA approach. From Charnes et al. (1986) (Research Reports CCS 532).

For example, in the analysis of the operations of outlets in a fast food chain, the output-oriented model needs to be formulated with input variables such as advertising, competition, territory demographics, etc. that affect sales. Similarly the input-oriented model would be formulated to minimize the resources such as direct materials, supplies, labor hours, etc. needed to achieve a given level of sales. This latter form of hybrid modeling, although not often reported in the literature, has had wide application in practice.

Combining DEA and parametric analyses represents another instant of hybrid modeling. Lovell, Walters, and Wood (chapter 17, this volume) use a three-stage DEA and ordinary least square approach in their analysis of secondary public schools. Their approach is noteworthy for three reasons. First, it involves a three-stage DEA model, which provides another example of hybrid modeling described in figure 21-2. Second, they use regression analysis to explain variations in the distribution of efficiency scores. Third, they use a modified DEA technique (MDEA) that ranks schools on a $(0, +\infty)$ scale in contrast to the conventional $(0, +1)$ scale. This is accomplished by ranking efficient DMUs by the amount by which their input vector Would *increase* while maintaining an efficiency score $\theta = 1$ and the slack values S^+ and S^- equal to zero. Charnes, Haag, Jaska, and Semple (1992) used the same logic to determine the robustness of efficiency scores.

The MDEA procedure is implemented by not including the DMU being optimized in its constraint set (see chapter 2, this volume). The net effect is that the aggregate efficiency, θ, is bounded below by zero, as always, but is not bounded from above. It can be shown that all inefficient DMUs continue to have scores below 1 (i.e., $\theta < 1$), all efficient DMUs have $\theta \geq 1$, *and* all of the slack S^+ and S^- are zero.

The primary benefit of this approach is the ability to make finer distinctions between efficient DMUs and to produce a logarithmic MDEA distribution of relative performance scores that are were approximately normally distributed. The spiked distribution characteristic of DEA scores was first noted by Charnes, Cooper, and Rhodes (1981)[1] and has always posed analytical difficulties for studying these distributions with regression techniques. By the use of MDEA, Lovell, Walter, and Wood (chapter 17) were able to explain some of the variation in the MDEA scores. In essence, their analysis of secondary schools is an example of how one can apply central-tendency methods to the study of outliers (Lewin, 1992) and discern "new truths" by explaining the variation in the distribution of external observations.

Window analysis provides another example of hybrid modeling applying DEA in longitudinal analyses. Conceptually, window analysis can be thought of as structuring the time series analysis as discrete moving averages where the analyst needs to determine the number of periods in each window. As is noted in chapter 3, the choice of W (the number of time periods) at this stage in the development of the technique is ad hoc. The analyst is advised to run window analysis with two to three different "windows" to ascertain the degree to which the DEA solutions are sensitive to the choice of W. If the DEA solutions are very sensitive to choice of W, then W should be small ($W \leq 3$). If the DEA solutions are not sensitive to W, then other considerations should enter into the choice of W.

In addition to providing trend information on the relative efficiency scores of DMUs over time (for control purposes and attention directing), window analysis can provide additional valuable insights. In particular, some of the available DEA software packages extract summary information about the number of times a specific DMU is used to evaluate the efficiency of other DMUs (including itself). This information is useful for determining which DMUs are included most often and which DMUs are consistently located below the frontier. Also, if a DMU is consistently only used as its own reference set, it needs to be further examined. It could be an outlier for which no comparable group exists (see discussion of Anheuser Busch in chapter 11).

6. Caveats and Concluding Observations

As with the application of parametric methods, the analyst user of DEA needs to be cognizant of the sensitivity of the method to certain issues. For example, as is true for regression applications, it is important to establish a priori (whether theoretically, from experience, or empirically) the existence of an association (at least a moderate relationship) between the inputs and outputs. We have also noted the need to minimize redundancies in the inputs and outputs (i.e., eliminate intercorrelations for the inputs and for the outputs). In addition, because the DEA methodology requires only a single observation for each input and output, it can be sensitive to errors in the data such as accuracy (e.g., wrong decimal point) or in measurement. It is also sensitive to outlier data in the sense that for extreme outliers (those for which DMU is only used as its own reference), the DEA solutions are not informative. These cases, however, are very rare.

There can be applications where the usual DEA applications will not be able to discriminate among the DMUs—in other words, all the DMUs are calculated to be efficient. This problem can arise in two ways, but it primarily occurs when the number of DMUs relative to the number of inputs and outputs is too small and therefore each DMU can be on the frontier. Charnes et al. (1989) have proposed a heuristic that recommends that the minimum number of DMUs be equal to or greater than three times the sum of the inputs and outputs. Thompson et al. (1990), in their analysis of Kansas farming, illustrate a procedure for bounding the multipliers that greatly increases the ability of DEA to make distinctions. The Cone Ratio approach (Charnes, Cooper, Huang, and Sun, 1990) provides another alternative for combining judgment or expertise in order to refine DEA solutions (see discussion in chapter 3).

Finally, it is important to note that DEA calculations, as with all mathematical programming calculations, can be affected by alternate optima and degeneracy. In particular, unless preventative measures are taken, cycling can prevent the algorithm from converging on an optimal solution. These problems—alternate optima, degeneracy, and cycling— are a result of implementation trade-offs in DEA software design. The DEA software packages described in chapter 5 are not guaranteed to be totally immune from these problems, but each employs computational strategies that are designed to counteract the occurrence of such difficulties. (For a discussion of these difficulties, see Ali and Seiford (1993).)

In conclusion, we firmly believe that DEA provides a new approach to organizing and analyzing data, to uncovering new production relationsnips in the data, and to letting the data speak for themselves more directly. Since the publication of the first ratio models, the theory, practice, and range of applications have grown rapidly (figure 1–3, chapter 1) and are beginning to mature. The availability of reliable DEA software packages will greatly accelerate this process, to the point that DEA will become part of the routine analytical arsenal to be applied on its own or as a complement to more traditional central-tendencies methods.

Note

1. See note 1 for chapter 17 for other studies using regression analysis to explain variation in DEA scores.

22 A DEA BIBLIOGRAPHY (1978–1992)

Lawrence M. Seiford

Since the original DEA study by Charnes, Cooper, and Rhodes (1978), there has been rapid growth in the field. Due to the interdisciplinary nature of much of the research, there is a need for a single source referencing the wide range of articles appearing in the literature. The author's intention in maintaining a bibliography of DEA-related articles is to provide such a single source and thus facilitate comprehensive growth in the field.

This version compiles 472 published articles and dissertations related to data envelopment analysis (DEA). The bibliography covers the years 1978–1992. Due to the archival nature of the publication, working papers and technical reports were excluded.

While the bibliography was compiled from various sources, it represents the effort of a single person, and consequently no claim can be made as to its completeness. Any corrections, additions, and/or suggestions will be welcomed in order that the bibliography may be revised and redistributed in a more complete and correct form.

The author wishes to thank all colleagues who have sent copies of their papers and would appreciate receiving additional DEA-related articles for incorporation into future versions of the bibliography.

Please address correspondence to:

Professor Lawrence M. Seiford
Department of Industrial Engineering and Operations Research
114 Marston Hall
The University of Massachusetts
Amherst, MA 01003 USA

Voice: (413) 545-1658
Fax: (413) 545-0724
Bitnet: Seiford@UMAECS
Internet: Seiford@ECS.UMASS.edu

Adolphson, Donald L., Cornia, Gary C., Walters, Lawrence C. Railroad Property Valuation Using Data Envelopment Analysis. *Interfaces* (1989), 19(3):18–26.

Adolphson, Donald L., Cornia, Gary C., Walters, Lawrence C. The Relative Efficiency of Railroads and Obsolescence. *Proceedings of the Seventeenth Annual Program on the Appraisal of Utilities and Railroad Property for Ad Valorem Taxation.* Wichita, KS: Wichita State University (1987), 97–130.

Adolphson, Donald L., Cornia, Gary C., Walters, Lawrence C. A Unified Framework for Classifying DEA Models. In Hugh E. Bradley (ed.), *Operational Research '90: Selected Papers from the Twelfth IFORS International Conference on Operational Research, 1990 June 25, Athens, Greece.* New York: Pergamon Press (1991), 647–657.

Afriat, S. Efficiency in Production and Consumption. In Ali Dogramaci, Rolf Färe (eds.), *Applications of Modern Production Theory: Efficiency and Productivity.* Boston: Kluwer Academic Publishers (1988), 251–268.

Ahn, Tae Sik. Efficiency and Related Issues in Higher Education: A Data Envelopment Analysis Approach. Austin, TX: Ph.D. dissertation, Graduate School of Business, University of Texas (1987).

Ahn, Tae Sik, Arnold, V., Charnes, A., Cooper, W. W. DEA and Ratio Efficiency Analyses for Public Institutions of Higher Learning in Texas. *Research in Governmental and Nonprofit Accounting* (1989), 5:165–185.

Ahn, Tae Sik, Charnes, A., Cooper, W. W. Efficiency Characterizations in Different DEA Models. *Socio-Economic Planning Sciences* (1988), 22(6): 253–257.

Ahn, Tae Sik, Charnes, A., Cooper, W. W. Some Statistical and DEA Evaluations of Relative Efficiencies of Public and Private Institutions of Higher Learning. *Socio-Economic Planning Sciences* (1988), 22(6):259–269.

Ahn, Tae Sik, Charnes, A., Cooper, W. W. Using Data Envelopment Analysis to Measure the Efficiency of Not-for-Profit Organizations: A Critical Evaluation— A Comment. *Managerial and Decision Economics* (1988), 9(3):251–253.

Ahn, Tae Sik, Seiford, Lawrence M. Sensitivity of DEA to Models and Variable Sets in a Hypothesis Test Setting: The Efficiency of University Operations. In Yuji Ijiri (ed.), *Creative and Innovative Approaches to the Science of Management*. New York: Quorum Books (1993).

Ali, Agha Iqbal. Computational Aspects of Data Envelopment Analysis. In A. Charnes, W. W. Cooper, Arie Y. Lewin, Lawrence M. Seiford, (eds.), *Data Envelopment Analysis: Theory, Methodology, and Applications*. Boston: Kluwer (1995).

Ali, Agha Iqbal. Data Envelopment Analysis: Computational Issues. *Computers, Environment and Urban Systems* (1990), 14(2):157–165.

Ali, Agha Iqbal. Streamlined Computation for Data Envelopment Analysis. *European Journal of Operational Research* (1993), 64(1).

Ali, Agha Iqbal, Charnes, A., Cooper, W. W., Divine, D., Klopp, Gerald A., Stutz, J. An Application of Data Envelopment Analysis to Management of U.S. Army Recruitment Districts. In R. L. Schultz (ed.), *Applications of Management Science, A Research Annual*.

Ali, Agha Iqbal, Cook, Wade D., Seiford, Lawrence M. Strict vs. Weak Ordinal Relations for Multipliers in Data Envelopment Analysis. *Management Science* (1991), 37(6).

Ali, Agha Iqba, Seiford, Lawrence M. The Mathematical Programming Approach to Efficiency Measurement. In H. Fried, C. A. Knox Lovell, S. Schmidt (eds.), *The Measurement of Productive Efficiency: Techniques and Applications*. London: Oxford University Press (1993).

Ali, Agha Iqbal, Seiford, Lawrence M. Translation Invariance in Data Envelopment Analysis. *Operations Research Letters* (1990), 9(6):403–405.

Anderson, David R., Sweeney, Dennis J., Williams, Thomas A. Linear Programming Applications: Data Envelopment Analysis. In *An Introduction to Management Science: Quantitative Approaches to Decision Making*. St. Paul, MN: West Publishing Company (1991), 147–152.

Austin, Melinda Jill. A Data Envelopment Analysis Approach to Measuring Relative Performance of People in Service Organizations. Mississippi State, MS: D.B.A. dissertation, Mississippi State University (1986).

Backes-Gellner, U. Okonomie der Hochschulforschung, Organisationstheoretische Uberlegungen und betriebswirtschaftliche Befunde [in German]. Wiesbaden: unpublished dissertation (1989).

Backes-Gellner, U., Zanders, E. Lehre und Forschung als Verbundproduktion: Data-Envelopment-Analysen und organisations-oekonomische Interpretationen der Realität in wirtschaftswissenschaftlichen Fachbe-reichen [in German]. *Zeitschrift fuer Betriebswirtschaft* (1989), 59(3):271–290.

Balakrishnan, P. V., Desai, Anand, Storbeck, James E. Efficiency Evaluation of Retail Outlet Networks. *Environment and Planning B: Planning and Design* (1993).

Banathy, Bela Antal. Examining Performance in Community Colleges: Data Envelopment Analysis as a Means of Increasing the Domain of Inquiry. Berkeley, CA: Ph.D. dissertation, University of California (1991).

Banker, Rajiv D. Econometric Estimation and Data Envelopment Analysis. In James L. Chan, James M. Patton (eds.), *Research in Governmental and Nonprofit Accounting* (1989), 5:231–243.

Banker, Rajiv D. Estimating Most Productive Scale Size Using Data Envelopment Analysis. *European Journal of Operational Research* (1984), 17(1):35–44.

Banker, Rajiv D. A Game Theoretic Approach to Measuring Efficiency. *European Journal of Operational Research* (1980), 5:262–266.

Banker, Rajiv D. Maximum Likelihood, Consistency and Data Envelopment Analysis: A Statistical Foundation. *Management Science* (1993).

Banker, Rajiv D. Productivity Measurement and Management Control. In P. Kleindorfer (ed.), *The Management of Productivity and Technology in Manufacturing*. New York: Plenum Press (1985), 239–257.

Banker, Rajiv D. Studies in Cost Allocation and Efficiency Evaluation. Boston, MA: D.B.A. dissertation, Graduate School of Business Administration, Harvard University (1980).

Banker, Rajiv D., Charnes, A., Clarke, Richard L., Cooper, W. W. Erratum: Constrained game formulations and interpretations for data envelopment analysis. *European Journal of Operational Research* (1989), 42.

Banker, Rajiv D., Charnes, A., Cooper, W. W. Some Models for Estimating Technical and Scale Inefficiencies in Data Envelopment Analysis. *Management Science* (1984), 30(9):1078–1092.

Banker, Rajiv D., Charnes, A., Cooper, W. W., Clarke, Richard L. Constrained Game Formulations and Interpretations for Data Envelopment Analysis. *European Journal of Operational Research* (1989), 40(3):299–308.

Banker, Rajiv D., Charnes, A., Cooper, W. W., Maindiratta, Ajay. A Comparison of DEA and Translog Estimates of Production Frontiers Using Simulated Observations From a Known Technology. In Ali Dogramaci, Rolf Färe (eds.), *Applications of Modern Production Theory: Efficiency and Productivity*. Boston: Kluwer Academic Publishers (1988).

Banker, Rajiv D., Charnes, A., Cooper, W. W., Schinnar, A. P. A Bi-Extremal Principle for Frontier Estimation and Efficiency Evaluations. *Management Science* (1981), 27(12):1370–1382.

Banker, Rajiv D., Charnes, A., Cooper, W. W., Swarts, J., Thomas, D. An Introduction to Data Envelopment Analysis with Some of Its Models and Their Uses. In James L. Chan, James M. Patton (eds.), *Research in Governmental and Nonprofit Accounting* (1989), 5:125–163.

Banker, Rajiv D., Conrad, R. F., Strauss, R. P. A Comparative Application of Data Envelopment Analysis and Translog Methods: An Illustrative Study of Hospital Production. *Management Science* (1986), 32(1):30–44.

Banker, Rajiv D., Das, S., Datar, Srikant M. Analysis of Cost Variances for Management Control in Hospitals. *Research in Governmental and Nonprofit Accounting* (1989), 5:268–291.

Banker, Rajiv D., Datar, Strikant M., Kemerer, Chris F. Factors Affecting Software Maintenance Productivity: An Exploratory Study. *Proceedings of the 8th International Conference on Information Systems.* Pittsburgh, PA (December 1987), 160–175.

Banker, Rajiv D., Datar, Strikant M., Kemerer, Chris F. A Model to Evaluate Variables Impacting the Productivity of Software Maintenance Projects. *Management Science* (1991), 37(1).

Banker, Rajiv D., Johnston, Holly Hanson. Evaluating the Impacts of Operating Strategies on Efficiency in the U.S. Airline Industry. In A. Charnes, W. W. Cooper, Arie Y. Lewin, Lawrence M. Seiford (eds.), *Data Envelopment Analysis: Theory, Methodology, and Applications.* Boston: Kluwer (1995).

Banker, Rajiv D., Kemerer, Chris F. Scale Economies in New Software Development. *IEEE Transactions on Software Engineering* (1989), 15(10):1199–1205.

Banker, Rajiv D., Maindiratta, Ajay. Erratum to: Piecewise Loglinear Estimation of Efficient Production Surfaces. *Management Science* (1986), 32(3):385.

Banker, Rajiv D., Maindiratta, Ajay. Maximum Liklihood Estimation of Monotone and Concave Production Frontiers. *The Journal of Productivity Analysis* (1992), 3(4):401–415.

Banker, Rajiv D., Maindiratta, Ajay. Nonparametic Analysis of Technical and Allocative Efficiencies in Production. *Econometrica* (1988), 56(6):1315–1332.

Banker, Rajiv D., Maindiratta, Ajay. Piecewise Loglinear Estimation of Efficient Production Surfaces. *Management Science* (1986), 32(1):126–135.

Banker, Rajiv D., Morey, Richard C. Efficiency Analysis for Exogenously Fixed Inputs and Outputs. *Operations Research* (1986a), 34(4):513–521.

Banker, Rajiv D., Morey, Richard C. Incorporating Value Judgements in Efficiency Analysis. *Research in Governmental and Nonprofit Accounting* (1989), 5:245–267.

Banker, Rajiv D., Morey, Richard C. The Use of Categorical Variables in Data Envelopment Analysis. *Management Science* (1986b), 32(12):1613–1627.

Banker, Rajiv D., Thrall, Robert M. Estimation of Returns to Scale Using Data Envelopment Analysis *European Journal of Operational Research* (1992), 62(1).

Barr, R. S., Seiford, Lawrence M., Siems, Thomas F. An Envelopment-Analysis Approach to Measuring the Managerial Quality of Banks. *Annals of Operations Research* (1993), 45:1–19.

Bauer, Paul W. Recent Developments in the Econometric Estimation of Frontiers. *Journal of Econometrics* (1990), 46(1/2):39–56.

Beasley, J. E. Comparing University Departments. *Omega* (1990), 18(2).

Beasley, J. E. OR-Library: Distributing Test Problems by Electronic Mail. *Journal of the Operational Research Society* (1990), 41(11).

Beck, M. Die Effizienz staatlicher und privater Industrieunternehmen in Polen 1987: Eine empirische Analyse mittels einer nichtparametrischen Frontier Production Function. *Zeitschrift fur bffentliche und gemeinwirtschaftliche Unternehmen* (1990), 13(4):426–443.

Bedard, Jean Catherine. Use of Data Envelopment Analysis in Accounting Applications: Evaluation and Illustration by Prospective Hospital Reimbursement. Madison, WI: Ph.D. dissertation, Graduate School of Business, University of Wisconsin (1985).

Berg, Sigbjorn Atle, Frsund, Finn R., Jansen, Eilev S. Malmquist Indices of Productivity Growth During the Deregulation of Norwegian Banking, 1980-89. *Scandinavian Journal of Economics* (1992), 94 (Supplement).

Berry, Delano Howard. An Extension of Managerial Accounting and Operational Auditing in the Public Sector: A Case Study of School Food Service Programs in Selected Local School Districts in the Commonwealth of Kentucky. Lexington, KY: Ph.D. dissertation, University of Kentucky (1991).

Bessent, Authella M., Bessent, E. Wailand. Determining the Comparative Efficiency of Schools Through Data Envelopment Analysis. *Educational Administration Quarterly* (1980), 16(2):57-75.

Bessent, Authella M., Bessent, E. Wailand. A Fractional Programming Model for Determining the Efficiency of Decision Making Units. *ERIC Clearinghouse on Educational Management*. Eugene, OR: University of Oregon (1981).

Bessent, Authella M., Bessent, E. Wailand. Productivity in Community College Programs: A Technique for Determining Relative Efficiency. Dallas TX: Community College Productivity Center, (1981).

Bessent, Authella M., Bessent, E. Wailand, Charnes, A., Cooper, W. W., Thorogood, N. Evaluation of Educational Program Proposals by Means of Data Envelopment Analysis. *Educational Administration Quarterly* (1983), 19(2):82-107.

Bessent, Authella M., Bessent, E. Wailand, Clark, Charles T., Elam, Joyce. Constrained Facet Analysis—A New Method for Evaluating Local Frontiers of Efficiency and Performance. *Air Force Journal of Logistics* (1984), 8(3):2-8.

Bessent, Authella M., Bessent, E. Wailand, Clark, Charles T., Elam, Joyce. A Microcomputer-based Productivity Support System for Increasing the Managerial Efficiency of Operating Units. In Stephen J. Andriole (ed.), *Microcomputer Decision Support Systems: Design, Implementation and Evaluation*. QED Information Sciences (1985), 219-230.

Bessent, Authella M., Bessent, E. Wailand, Clark, Charles T., Garrett, Allan W. Managerial Efficiency Measurement in School Administration. *National Forum of Educational Administration and Supervision Journal* (1987), 3(3):56-66.

Bessent, Authella M., Bessent, E. Wailand, Elam, Joyce, Clark, Charles T. Efficiency Frontier Determination by Constrained Facet Analysis. *Operations Research* (1988), 36(5):785-796.

Bessent, Authella M., Bessent, E. Wailand, Elam, Joyce, Long, D. Educational Productivity Council Employs Management Science Methods to Improve Educational Quality. *Interfaces* (1984), 14(6):1-8.

Bessent, Authella M., Bessent, E. Wailand, Kennington, J., Regan, B. An Application of Mathematical Programming to Assess Productivity in the Houston Independent School District. *Management Science* (1982), 28(12): 1355-1367.

Bitran, G. R., Valor-Sabatier, J. Some Mathematical Programming Based

Measures of Efficiency in Health Care Institutions. *Advances in Mathematical Programming and Financial Planning* (1987), 1:61-84.

Bjurek, Hans, Hjalmarsson, Lennart, Frsund, Finn R. Deterministic Parametric and Nonparametric Estimation of Efficiency in Service Production: A Comparison. *Journal of Econometrics* (1990), 46(1,2):213-227.

Bjurek, Hans, Kjulin, Urban, Gustafsson, Bjorn, Bosworth, Derek L. Efficiency, Productivity and Determinants of Inefficiency at Public Day Care Centers in Sweden—Comment. *Scandinavian Journal of Economics* (1992), 94 (Supplement).

Blair, Larry Delwood. A Comparative Analysis of the Financial Practices of School Districts Selected by Data Envelopment Analysis Efficiency Indices. Austin, TX: Ph.D. dissertation, College of Education, University of Texas (1983).

Bohnet, A., Beck, M. The Impact of the Income Tax on Work Effort and X-Inefficiency in Enterprises. In K. Weiermair, M. Perlman (eds.), *Studies in Economic Rationality: X-Efficiency Examined and Leibenstein*. Ann Arbor (1990), 227-251.

Borden, James Patrick. An Assessment of the Impact of Diagnosis Related Group (DRG)-Based Reimbursement on the Technical Efficiency of New Jersey Hospitals. Philadelphia, PA: Ph.D. dissertation, Drexel University (1986).

Borden, James Patrick. An Assessment of the Impact of Diagnosis-Related Group (DRG)-Based Reimbursement on the Technical Efficiency of New Jersey Hospitals Using Data Envelopment Analysis. *Journal of Accounting and Public Policy* (1988), 7(2):77-96.

Boussofiane, A., Dyson, R. G., Thanassoulis, E. Applied Data Envelopment Analysis. *European Journal of Operational Research* (1991), 52(1):1-15.

Bowen, William M. The Nuclear Waste Site Selection Decision—a Comparison of Two Decision-Aiding Models. Bloomington, IN: Ph.D. dissertation, (Department of Geography) Indiana University (1990).

Bowen, William M. Subjective judgements and data envelopment analysis in site selection. *Computers, Environment and Urban Systems* (1990), 14(2):133-144.

Bowlin, William F. Evaluating Performance in Governmental Organizations. *Government Accountants Journal* (1986), 35(2):50-57.

Bowlin, William F. Evaluating the Efficiency of US Air Force Real-Property Maintenance Activities. *Journal of the Operational Research Society* (1987), 38(2):127-135.

Bowlin, William F. An Intertemporal Assessment of the Efficiency of Air Force Accounting and Finance Offices. *Research in Governmental and Nonprofit Accounting* (1989), 5:293-310.

Bowlin, William F., Charnes, A., Cooper, W. W. Efficiency and Effectiveness in DEA: An Illustrative Application to Base Maintenance Activities in the U.S. Air Force. In O. A. Davis (ed.), *Papers in Cost Benefit Analysis*. Pittsburgh, PA: Carnegie-Mellon University.

Bowlin, William F., Charnes, A., Cooper, W. W., Sherman, H. David. Data Envelopment Analysis and Regression Approaches to Efficiency Estimation and Evaluation. *Annals of Operations Research* (1985), 2(1):113–138.

Bowlin, William Frank. A Data Envelopment Analysis Approach to Performance Evaluation in Not-for-profit Entities with an Illustrative Application to the U.S. Air Force. Austin, TX: Ph.D. dissertation, Graduate School of Business, University of Texas (1984).

Bowlin, William F., Wallace, J. R. II, Murphy, R. L. Efficiency-Based Budgeting. *Journal of Cost Analysis* (1989).

Boyd, G., Färe, Rolf. Measuring the Efficiency of Decision Making Units: A Comment. *European Journal of Operational Research* (1984), 15:331–332.

Brockett, Patrick L., Seiford, Lawrence M. Contributions of A. Charnes to the Area of Statistical Analysis. In Fred Y. Phillips, John J. Rousseau (eds.), *Systems and Management Science by Extremal Methods*. Boston: Kluwer Academic Publishers (1992), 69–88.

Byrnes, P. Ownership and Efficiency in the Water Supply Industry: An Application of the Nonparametric Programming Approach to Efficiency Measurement. Carbondale, IL: Ph.D. dissertation, Southern Illinois University (1985).

Byrnes, P., Färe, Rolf, Grosskopf, S., Measuring Productive Efficiency: An Application to Illinois Strip Mines. *Management Science* (1984), 30(6):671–681.

Byrnes, P., Färe, Rolf, Grosskopf, S., Lovell, C. A. Knox. The Effect of Unions of Productivity: U.S. Surface Mining of Coal. *Management Science* (1988), 34(9):1037–1053.

Byrnes, P., Grosskopf, S., Hayes, K. Efficiency and Ownership: Further Evidence. *Review of Economics and Statistics* (1986), 65:337–341.

Byrnes, P., Valdmanis, Vivian. Analyzing Technical and Allocative Efficiency of Hospitals. In A. Charnes, W. W. Cooper, Arie Y. Lewin, Lawrence M. Seiford (eds.), *Data Envelopment Analysis: Theory, Methodology, and Applications*. Boston: Kluwer (1995).

Camm, J. D., Grogan, T. J. An Application of Frontier Analysis: Handicapping Running Races. *Interfaces* (1988), 18(6):52–60.

Capettini, Robert, Dittman, David A., Morey, Richard C. Reimbursement Rate Setting for Medicaid Prescription Drugs Based on Relative Efficiencies. *Journal of Accounting and Public Policy* (1985), 4(2):83–110.

Cave, M., Hanney, S., Kogan, M., Trevet, G. *The Use of Performance Indicators in Higher Education: A Critical Analysis of Developing Practice*. London: Jessica Kingsley Publishers Ltd. (1988).

Chan, James L., Patton, James M. (eds.). *Research in Governmental and Nonprofit Accounting*, Vol. 5. Chicago: JAI Press (1989).

Chan, James J., Patton, James M. (eds.). *Research in Governmental and Nonprofit Accounting*, Vol. 6. Chicago: JAI Press (1990).

Chan, Peng S., Sueyoshi, Toshiyuki. Environmental Change, Competition, Strategy, Structure and Firm Performance. An Application of Data Envelopment Analysis in the Airline Industry. *International Journal of Systems Science* (1991), 22(9):1625–1636.

Chang, Kuo-Ping, Guh, Yeah-Yuh. Linear Production Functions and the Data Envelopment Analysis. *European Journal of Operational Research* (1991), 52(2):215–223.

Chang, Kuo-Ping, Kao, Pei-Hua. The Relative Efficiency of Public versus Private Municipal Bus Firms: An Application of Data Envelopment Analysis. *The Journal of Productivity Analysis* (1992), 3(1/2):67–84.

Chang, Yih-Long, Sueyoshi, Toshiyuki. An interactive application of data envelopment analysis in microcomputers. *Computer Science in Economics and Management* (1991), 4(1).

Charnes, A., Clark, Charles T., Cooper, W. W., Golany, Boaz. A Developmental Study of Data Envelopment Analysis in Measuring the Efficiency of Maintenance Units in the U.S. Air Forces. In Russell G. Thompson, Robert M. Thrall (eds.), *Annals of Operation Research* (1985), 2(1):95–112.

Charnes, A., Clarke, Richard L., Cooper, W. W. An Approach to Testing for Organizational Slack with R. Banker's Game Theoretic Formulation of DEA. *Research in Governmental and Nonprofit Accounting* (1989), 5:211–230.

Charnes, A., Cooper, W. W. Auditing and Accounting for Program Efficiency and Management Efficiency in Not-For-Profit Entities. *Accounting, Organizations and Society* (1980), 5(1):87–107.

Charnes, A., Cooper, W. W. Data Envelopment Analysis. In Hugh E. Bradley (ed.), *Operational Research '90: Selected Papers from the Twelfth IFORS International Conference on Operational Research* (1991), 641–646.

Charnes, A., Cooper, W. W. Management Science Relations for Evaluation and Management Accountability. *Journal of Enterprise Management* (1980), 2(2): 143–162.

Charnes, A., Cooper, W. W. Managerial Economics: Past, Present and Future. *Journal of Enterprise Management* (1978), 1(1):5–23.

Charnes, A., Cooper, W. W. The Non-Archimedean CCR Ratio for Efficiency Analysis: A Rejoinder to Boyd and Färe. *European Journal of Operational Research* (1984), 15(3):333–334.

Charnes, A., Cooper, W. W. Preface to Topics in Data Envelopment Analysis. *Annals of Operations Research* (1985), 2(1):59–94.

Charnes, A., Cooper, W. W., Divine, D., Ruefli, T. W., Thomas, D. Comparisons of DEA and Existing Ratio and Regression Systems for Effecting Efficiency Evaluations of Regulated Electric Cooperatives in Texas. *Research in Governmental and Nonprofit Accounting* (1989), 5:187–210.

Charnes, A., Cooper, W. W., Golany, Boaz, Phillips, Fred Y., Rousseau, John J. A Multi Period Analysis of Market Segments and Brand Efficiency in the Competitive Carbonated Beverage Industry. In A. Charnes, W. W. Cooper, Arie Y. Lewin, Lawrence M. Seiford (eds.), *Data Envelopment Analysis: Theory, Methodology, and Applications*. Boston: Kluwer (1995).

Charnes, A., Cooper, W. W., Golany, Boaz, Seiford, Lawrence M., Stutz, J. Foundations of Data Envelopment Analysis for Pareto-Koopmans Efficient Empirical Production Functions. *Journal of Econometrics* (1985), 30(1/2): 91–107.

Charnes, A., Cooper, W. W., Huang, Z. M., Sun, Dee Bruce. Polyhedral Cone-Ratio DEA Models with an Illustrative Application to Large Commercial Banks. *Journal of Econometrics* (1990), 46(1-2):73-91.

Charnes, A., Cooper, W. W., Huang, Z. M., Sun, Dee Bruce. Relations Between Half-Space and Finitely Generated Cones in Polyhedral Cone-Ratio DEA Models. *International Journal of Systems Science* (1991), 22(11):2057-2077.

Charnes, A., Cooper, W. W., Learner, David B., Phillips, Fred Y. Management Science and Marketing Management. *Journal of Marketing* (1985), 49(3): 93-105.

Charnes, A., Cooper, W. W., Lewin, Arie Y., Morey, Richard C., Rousseau, John J. Sensitivity and Stability Analysis in DEA. *Annals of Operations Research* (1985), 2:139-156.

Charnes, A., Cooper, W. W., Lewin, Arie Y., Seiford, Lawrence M. (eds.). *Data Envelopment Analysis: Theory, Methodology, and Applications.* Boston: Kluwer (1995).

Charnes, A., Cooper, W. W., Li, S. Using DEA to Evaluate Relative Efficiencies in the Economic Performance of Chinese Cities. *Socio-Economic Planning Sciences* (1989), 23(6):325-344.

Charnes, A., Cooper, W. W., Niehaus, R., Schinnar, A. P. *Measuring Efficiency and Tradeoffs in Attainment of EEO Goals. Work, Organizations, and Technological Change.* New York: Plenum Press (1982), 241-256.

Charnes, A., Cooper, W. W., Rhodes, Edwardo L. The Distribution of DMU Efficiency Measures. *Journal of Enterprise Management* (1980), 2(2):160-162.

Charnes, A., Cooper, W. W., Rhodes, Edwardo L. An Efficiency Opening for Managerial Accounting in Not-For-Profit Entities. In H. P. Holzer (ed.), *Management Accounting 1980: Proceedings of the University of Illinois Management Accounting Symposium.* Urbana, IL: University of Illinois (1980), 21-47.

Charnes, A., Cooper, W. W., Rhodes, Edwardo L. Evaluating Program and Managerial Efficiency: An Application of Data Envelopment Analysis to Program Follow Through. *Management Science* (1981), 27(6):668-697.

Charnes, A., Cooper, W. W., Rhodes, Edwardo L. Measuring the Efficiency of Decision Making Units. *European Journal of Operational Research* (1978), 2(6):429-444.

Charnes, A., Cooper, W. W., Rhodes, Edwardo L. Short Communication: Measuring the Efficiency of Decision Making Units. *European Journal of Operational Research* (1979), 3(4):339.

Charnes, A., Cooper, W. W., Schinnar, A. P. An Extended Cobb-Douglas Form for Use in Production Economics. In Tej K. Kaul, Jati K. Sengupta (eds.), *Essays in Honor of Karl A. Fox.* Amsterdam: Elsevier Science Publishers (1991), 99-124.

Charnes, A., Cooper, W. W., Schinnar, A. P. Transforms and Approximation in Cost and Production Function Relations. *Omega* (1982), 10(2):207-211.

Charnes, A., Cooper, W. W., Sears, M., Zlobec, S. Efficiency Evaluations in Perturbed Data Envelopment Analysis. In Jurgen Guddat, Hubertus Th

Jongen, Bernd Kummer, Frantisek Nozicka (eds.), *Mathematical Research: Proceedings of the Second International Conference on Parametric Optimization and Related Topics, 1989 June 27, Eisenach (Thuringla), GDR.* Berlin: Akademie Verlag (1991), 62:38–49.

Charnes, A., Cooper, W. W., Seiford, Lawrence M., Stutz, J. Invariant Multiplicative Efficiency and Piecewise Cobb–Douglas Envelopments. *Operations Research Letters* (1983), 2(3):101–103.

Charnes, A., Cooper, W. W., Seiford, Lawrence M., Stutz, J. A Multiplicative Model for Efficiency Analysis. *Socio-Economic Planning Sciences* (1982), 16(5):223–224.

Charnes, A., Cooper, W. W., Thrall, Robert M. Classifying and Characterizing Efficiencies and Inefficiencies in Data Development Analysis. *Operations Research Letters* (1986), 5(3):105–110.

Charnes, A., Cooper, W. W., Thrall, Robert M. A Structure for Classifying and Characterizing Efficiency and Inefficiency in Data Development Analysis. *Journal of Productivity Analysis* (1991), 2:197–237.

Charnes, A., Cooper, W. W., Wei, Quan Ling, Huang, Z. M. Cone Ratio Data Envelopment Analysis and Multi-objective Programming. *International Journal of Systems Science* (1989), 20(7):1099–1118.

Charnes, A., Cooper, W. W., Wei, Quan Ling, Huang, Z. M. Fundamental Theorems of Nondominated Solutions Associated with Cones in Normed Linear Spaces. *Journal of Mathematical Analysis and Applications* (1990), 150(1):54–78.

Charnes, A., Haag, Stephen, Jaska, Patrick V., Semple, John. Sensitivity of Efficiency Classifications in the Additive Model of Data Envelopment Analysis. *International Journal of Systems Science* (1992), 23(5):789–798.

Charnes, A., Huang, Z. M., Rousseau, John J., Wei, Quan Ling. Cone Extremal Solutions of Multi-Payoff Games with Cross-Constrained Strategy Sets. *Optimization* (1990), 21(1):51–69.

Charnes, A., Huang, Z. M., Semple, John, Song, T., Thomas, D. Origins and Research in Data Envelopment Analysis. *The Arabian Journal for Science and Engineering* (1990), 15(4B):617–625.

Charnes, A., Neralić, L. Sensitivity Analysis in Data Envelopment Analysis—Part II. *Glasnik Mathemativ cki. Serija III* (1989), 24(44).

Charnes, A., Neralić, L. Sensitivity Analysis in Data Envelopment Analysis—Part I. *Glasnik Matemativ cki. Serija III* (1989), 24(44):211–226.

Charnes, A., Neralić, L. Sensitivity Analysis of the Additive Model in Data Envelopment Analysis. *European Journal of Operational Research* (1990), 48(3):332–341.

Charnes, A., Rousseau, John J., Semple, John. Non-Archimedean Infinitesimals, Transcendentals and Categorical Inputs in Linear Programming and Data Envelopment analysis. *International Journal of Systems Science* (1992), 23(12): 2401–2406.

Charnes, A., Zlobec, S. Stability of Efficiency Evaluations in Data Envelopment Analysis. *Zeitschrift für Operations Research* (1989), 33(3):167–179.

Chattopadhyay, Sajal Kumar. Economics of Nursing Home Care in Connecticut: Financing, Cost and Efficiency. Storrs, CT: Ph.D. dissertation, University of Connecticut (1991).

Chilingerian, Jon A. Exploring Why Some Physicians' Hospital Practices Are More Efficient: Taking DEA Inside the Hospital. In A. Charnes, W. W. Cooper, Arie Y. Lewin, Lawrence M. Seiford (eds.), *Data Envelopment Analysis: Theory, Methodology, and Applications.* Boston: Kluwer (1995).

Chilingerian, Jon A. Investigating Non-Medical Factors Associated with the Technical Efficiency of Physicians in the Provision of Hospital Services: A Pilot Study. *Annual Best Paper, Proceedings of the Academy of Management* (1989), 85–89.

Chilingerian, Jon A., Sherman, H. David. Managing Physician Efficiency and Effectiveness in Providing Hospital Services. *Health Services Management Resources* (1990), 3(1):3–15.

Chismar, William Gerard. Assessing the Economic Impact of Information Systems Technology on Organizations. Pittsburgh, PA: Ph.D. dissertation, Carnegie-Mellon University (1986).

Chu, Xuehao, Fielding, G. J., Lamar, Bruce. Measuring Transit Performance using Data Envelopment Analysis. *Transportation Research, Part A (Policy and Practice)* (1992), 26A(3):223–230.

Clark, Charles Terrance. Data Envelopment Analysis and Extensions for Decision Support and Management Planning. Austin, TX: Ph.D. dissertation, Graduate School of Business, University of Texas (1983).

Clarke, Richard L. Evaluating USAF Vehicle Maintenance Productivity Over Time: An Application of Data Envelopment Analysis. *Decision Sciences* (1992), 23(2).

Clarke, Richard Lee. Effects of Repeated Applications of Data Envelopment Analysis on Efficiency of Air Force Vehicle Maintenance Units in the Tactical Air Command and a Test for the Presence of Organizational Slack Using Rajiv Banker's Game Theory Formulations. Austin, TX: Ph.D. dissertation, Graduate School of Business, University of Texas (1988).

Clarke, Richard L., Gourdin, Kent N. Measuring the Efficiency of the Logistics Process. *Journal of Business Logistics* (1991), 12(2).

Colwell, R. J., Davis, E. P. Output and Productivity in Banking. *Scandinavian Journal of Economics* (1992), 94 (Supplement).

Cook, Wade D., Johnston, D. A. Evaluating Alternative Suppliers for the Development of Complex Systems: A Multiple Criteria Approach. *Journal of the Operations Research Society* (forthcoming).

Cook, Wade D., Johnston, D. A., McCutcheon, D. Implementations of Robotics: Indentifying Efficient Implementors. *Omega: International Journal of Management Science* (1992), 20(2):227–239.

Cook, Wade D., Kazakov, Alex, Roll, Yaakov. On the Measurement of the Relative Efficiency of a Set of Decision-Making Units. In K. Weiermair, M. Perlman (eds.), *Studies in Economic Rationality: X-Efficiency Examined and*

Extolled. Essays written in the tradition of and to honor Harvey Leibenstein.
Ann Arbor: (1990), 351–368.

Cook, Wade D., Kazakov, Alex, Roll, Yaakov. On the Measurement and
Monitoring of Relative Efficiency of Highway Maintenance Patrols. In A.
Charnes, W. W. Cooper, Arie Y. Lewin, Lawrence M. Seiford (eds.), *Data
Envelopment Analysis: Theory, Methodology, and Applications.* Boston:
Kluwer (1995).

Cook, Wade D., Kazakov. Alex, Roll, Yaakov, Seiford, Lawrence M. A Data
Envelopment Approach to Measuring Efficiency: Case Analysis of Highway
Maintenance Patrols. *Journal of Socio-Economics* (1991), 20(1):83–103.

Cook, Wade D., Kress, Moshe. A Data Envelopment Model for Aggregating
Preference Rankings. *Management Science* (1990), 36(11):1302–1310.

Cook, Wade D., Kress, Moshe. A Multiple Criteria Decision Model with Ordinal
Preference Data. *European Journal of Operational Research* (1991), 54(2):
191–198.

Cook, Wade D., Kress, Moshe. *Ordinal Information and Preference Structures:
Decision Models and Applications.* Englewood Cliffs, NJ: Prentice Hall (1991).

Cook, Wade D., Kress, Moshe. Rating Players in a Tournament: An mth-
Generation Approach. In Fred Y. Phillips, John J. Rousseau (eds.), *Systems
and Management Science by Extremal Methods.* Boston: Kluwer Academic
Publishers (1992), 349–360.

Cook, Wade D., Kress, Moshe, Seiford, Lawrence M. Prioritization Models for
Frontier Decision Making Units in DEA. *European Journal of Operations
Research* (1992), 59(2).

Cook, Wade D., Roll, Yaakov. Measurement of the Relative Efficiency of
Highway Maintenance Patrols in Ontario: Final Report on Phase II—Full
Model Design. Toronto, Ontario, Canada: Ministry of Transportation (1988).

Cook, Wade D., Roll, Yaakov, Kazakov, Alex. A DEA Model for Measuring the
Relative Efficiency of Highway Maintenance Patrols. *INFOR* (1990), 28(2):
113–124.

Cook, Wade D., Roll, Yaakov, Kazakov, Alex. Measurement of the Relative
Efficiency of Highway Maintenance Patrols in Ontario. Toronto, Ontario,
Canada: Ministry of Transportation (1988).

Crane, Katie. Grading IS Performance. *Computerworld* (1990), 24(47).

Daft, R. L., Lewin, Arie Y. Can Organization Studies Begin to Break Out of the
Normal Science Straitjacket? An Editorial Essay. *Organization Science* (1990),
1(1):1–9.

Day, D. L., Lewin, Arie Y., Salazar, R. J., Li, Hongyu. Strategic Leaders in the
U.S. Brewing Industry: A Longitudinal Analysis of Outliers. In A. Charnes,
W. W. Cooper, Arie Y. Lewin, Lawrence M. Seiford (eds.), *Data Envelopment
Analysis: Theory, Methodology, and Applications* (forthcoming).

Deprins, D., Simar, L., Tulkens, H. Measuring Labor-Efficiency in Post Offices.
In M. Marchand, P. Pestieau, H. Tulkens (eds.), *The Performance of Public
Enterprises: Concepts and Measurement.* North-Holland: Elsevier Science
Publishers B.V. (1984), 243–267.

Desai, Anand. Data Envelopment Analysis: A Clarification. *Evaluation and Research in Education* (1992), 6(1):39–41.

Desai, Anand. Extension to Measures of Relative Efficiency with an Application to Educational Productivity. Philadelphia, PA: Ph.D. dissertation, University of Pennsylvania (1986).

Desai, Anand, Gulledge, Thomas R., Haynes, Kingsley E., Shroff, Homee F. E., Storbeck, James E. A DEA Approach to Siting Decision Sensitivity. *Regional Science Review* (1991), 18:71–80.

Desai, Anand, Haynes, Kingsley E., Storbeck, James E. A Spatial Efficiency Framework for the Support of Locational Decisions. In A. Charnes, W. W. Cooper, Arie Y. Lewin, Lawrence M. Seiford (eds.), *Data Envelopment Analysis: Theory, Methodology, and Applications*. Boston: Kluwer (1995).

Desai, Anand, Henderson, J. Stephen. Natural Gas Prices and Contractual Terms. *Energy Systems and Policy* (1988), 12(4):255–271.

Desai, Anand, Schinnar, A. P. Technical Issues in Measuring Scholastic Improvement due to Compensatory Education Programs. *Socio-Economic Planning Sciences* (1990), 24(2):143–153.

Desai, Anand, Storbeck, James E. A Data Envelopment Analysis for Spatial Efficiency. *Computers, Environment and Urban Systems* (1990), 14(2):145–156.

Desai, Anand, Storbeck, James E., Haynes, Kingsley E., Shroff, Homee F. E., Xiao, Yan. Extending Multiple Objective Programming for Siting Decision Sensitivity. *Modeling and Simulation* (1990), 22:153–158.

Desai, Anand, Walters, Lawrence C. Graphical Presentations of Data Envelopment Analyses: Management Implications from Parallel Axes Representations. *Decision Sciences* (1991), 22(2):335–353.

Desai, Anand, You, Min-Bong. Incentive Regulation and the Measurement of Performance. *Proceedings of the Sixth NARUC Biennial Regulatory Information Conference* (1988), 3:155–181.

DesHarnais, S., Hogan, A. J., McMahon, L. F. Jr., Fleming, S. Changes in Rates of Unscheduled Hospital Readmissions and Changes in Efficiency Following the Introduction of the Medicare Prospective Payment System. An Analysis Using Risk-Adjusted Data. *Evaluation of Health Professions* (1991), 14(2): 228–252.

Diamond, Arthur M. Jr., Medewitz, Jeanette N. Use of Data Envelopment Analysis in an Evaluation of the Efficiency of the DEEP Program for Economic Education. *Journal of Economic Education* (1990), 21(3):337–354.

Dieck-Assad, Martin Jorge. On Some Methods, Informatics and Applications of Data Envelopment Analysis. Austin, TX: Ph.D. dissertation, Graduate School of Business, University of Texas (1986).

Dittman, David A., Capettini, Robert, Morey, Richard C. Measuring Efficiency in Acute Care Hospitals: An Application of Data Envelopment Analysis. *Journal of Health and Human Resources Administrtion* (1991), 14(1):89–108.

Divine, John Douglas. Efficiency Analysis and Management of Not for Profit and Governmentally Regulated Organizations. Austin, TX: Ph.D. dissertation, Graduate School of Business, University of Texas (1986).

Dogramaci, Ali, Färe, Rolf (eds.) *Applications of Modern Production Theory: Efficiency and Productivity*. Boston: Kluwer Academic Publishers (1988).

Doyle, J. R., Green, R. H. Comparing Products using Data Envelopment Analysis. *Omega* (1991), 19(6).

Drake, Philip D. An Analysis of the Audit Services Market: The Effect of Audit Structure on Auditor Efficiency, A Data Envelopment Analysis Approach. Columbus, OH: Ph.D. dissertation, Ohio State University (1990).

Duffy, Jo Ann Miller. The Measurement of Service Productivity and Related Contextual Factors in Long Term Care Facilities. Austin, TX: Ph.D. dissertation, School of Nursing University of Texas (1987).

Dyson, R. G., Thanassoulis, E. Reducing Weight Flexibility in Data Envelopment Analysis. *Journal of the Operational Research Society* (1988), 39(6):563–576.

Easun, M. S. Identifying Inefficiencies in Resource Management; An Application of Data Envelopment Analysis to Selected School Libraries in California. Berkeley, CA: Ph.D. dissertation, School of Library and Information Studies, University of California (1992).

Eechambadi, Narasimhan Varadarajan. Efficiency Analysis of Market Response and the Marketing Mix: Extending Data Envelopment Analysis to a Competitive Environment. Austin, TX: Ph.D. dissertation, Graduate School of Business, University of Texas (1985).

Elam, Joyce, Kobielus, James. From Mysticism to Management. *Network World* (1988), 5(25):23, 34, 45.

Elam, Joyce, Thomas, J. B. Evaluating Productivity of Information Systems Organizations in State Government. *Public Productivity Review* (1989), 12(3): 263–277.

Epstein, Michael K., Henderson, John C. Data Envelopment Analysis for Managerial Control and Diagnosis. *Decision Sciences* (1989), 20(1):90–119.

Fairhall, John (Education Editor). Liverpool and Ilea Score High in Test. *Guardian*, November 13, 1987, London.

Färe, Rolf. A Dynamic Non-Parametric Measure of Output Efficiency. *Operations Research Letters* (1986), 5(2):83–85.

Färe, Rolf, Grosskopf, S. Measuring Congestion in Production. *Zeitschrift für Nationalökonomie* (1983), 43(3):257–271.

Färe, Rolf, Grosskopf, S. Measuring Output Efficiency. *European Journal of Operational Research* (1983), 13:173–179.

Färe, Rolf, Grosskopf, S., Lindgren, B., Roos, P. Productivity Changes in Swedish Pharmacies 1980–1989: A Non-Parametric Malmquist Approach. *The Journal of Productivity Analysis* (1992), 3(1/2):85–101.

Färe, Rolf, Grosskopf, S., Lindgren, B., Roos, P. Productivity Developments in Swedish Hospitals: A Malmquist Output Index Approach. In A. Charnes, W. W. Cooper, Arie Y. Lewin, Lawrence M. Seiford (eds.), *Data Envelopment Analysis: Theory, Medthodology, and Applications*. Boston: Kluwer (1995).

Färe, Rolf, Grosskopf, S., Logan, James. The Relative Efficiency of Illinois Electric Utilities. *Resources and Energy* (1983), 5(4):349–367.

Färe, Rolf, Grosskopf, S., Lovell, C. A. Knox. *The Measurement of Efficiency of*

Production. Boston: Kluwer Academic Publishers (1985).

Färe, Rolf, Grosskopf, S., Njinkeu, D. On Piecewise Reference Technologies. *Management Science* (1988), 34(12):1507–1511.

Färe, Rolf, Hunsaker, Worthen. Notions of Efficiency and Their Reference Sets. *Management Science* (1986), 32(2):237–243.

Färe, Rolf, Logan, James. The Rate of Return Regulated Version of Farrell Efficiency. *International Journal of Production Economics* (1992), 27(2): 161–165.

Färe, Rolf, Lovell, C. A. Knox. Measuring the Technical Efficiency. *Journal of Economic Theory* (1978), 19(1):150–162.

Ferrier, G. D. Ownership Type, Property Rights and Relative Efficiency. In A. Charnes, W. W. Cooper, Arie Y. Lewin, Lawrence M. Seiford (eds.), *Data Envelopment Analysis: Theory, Methodology, and Applications.* Boston: Kluwer (1995).

Ferrier, G. D., Hirschberg, J. G. Climate Control Efficiency. *Energy Journal* (1992), 13(1):37–54.

Ferrier, G. D., Lovell, C. A. Knox. Measuring Cost Efficiency in Banking: Econometric and Linear Programming Evidence. *Journal of Econometrics* (1990), 46(1/2):229–245.

Førsund, Finn R. A Comparison of Parametric and Non-Parametric Efficiency Measures: The Case of Norwegian Ferries. *The Journal of Productivity Analysis* (1992), 3(1/2):25–43.

Førsund, Finn R., Hernaes, E. A Comparative Analysis of Ferry Transport in Norway. In A. Charnes, W. W. Cooper, Arie Y. Lewin, Lawrence M. Seiford (eds.), *Data Envelopment Analysis: Theory, Methodology, and Applications.* Boston: Kluwer (1995).

Førsund, Finn R., Hjalmarsson, Lennart. *Analyses of Industrial Structure: A Putty-Clay Approach.* Stockholm, Sweden: The Industrial Institute for Economic and Social Research (1987).

Frank, Richard G. On Making the Illustration Illustrative: A Comment on Banker, Conrad and Strauss. *Management Science* (1988), 34(8):1026–1029.

Frantz, Roger. X-Efficiency and Allocative Efficiency: What Have We Learned? *AEA Papers and Proceedings* (1992), 82(2):434–438.

Fried, H., Lovell, C. A. Knox, Schmidt, S. (eds). *The Measurement of Productive Efficiency: Techniques and Applications.* London: Oxford University Press (1993).

Gallegos-Monteagudo, Jesus Armando. Strategic and Economic Performance of State-Owned Enterprises: The Case of the Latin American Airline Industry. Austin, TX: Ph.D. dissertation, Graduate School of Business, University of Texas (1991).

Ganley, Joseph A. Efficiency Measurement in the Public Sector: Applications of Data Envelopment Analysis. London: Ph.D. dissertation, Queen Mary College, University of London (1990).

Garrett, Allan Warren. Constrained Facet Analysis and Related Linear Programming Models: Tools for the Evaluation of the Efficiency, Productivity and

Effectiveness of School Classrooms. Austin, Texas: Ph.D. dissertation, College of Education, University of Texas (1985).

Gillett, Raphael, Aitkenhead, Marilyn. Rank Injustice in Academic Research. *Nature* (1987), 327:381–382.

Giokas, D. I. Bank Branch Operating Efficiency: A Comparative Application of DEA and the Loglinear Model. *Omega* (1991), 19(6).

Golany, Boaz. An Interactive MOLP Procedure for the Extension of DEA to Effectiveness Analysis. *Journal of the Operational Research Society* (1988), 39(8):725–734.

Golany, Boaz. A Note on Including Ordinal Relations Among Multipliers in Data Envelopment Analysis. *Management Science* (1988), 34(8):1029–1033.

Golany, Boaz. On Chance Constrained, Competitive and Cooperative Evaluational Methods in Some Problems of Dynamic Management. Austin, TX: Ph.D. dissertation, Graduate School of Business, University of Texas (1985).

Golany, Boaz, Learner, David B., Phillips, Fred Y., Rousseau, John J. Managing for Efficiency and Effectiveness: An Illustrative Example from Marketing. *APORS '88: Selected Papers from the First Conference of the Association of Asian-Pacific Operational Research Societies within IFORS, 1988 August, Seoul.*

Golany, Boaz, Learner, David B., Phillips, Fred Y., Rousseau, John J. Managing Service Productivity: The Data Envelopment Analysis Perspective. *Computers, Environment and Urban Systems* (1990), 14(2):89–102.

Golany, Boaz, Roll, Yaakov. An Application Procedure for DEA. *Omega* (1989), 17(3):237–250.

Golany, Boaz, Roll, Yaakov. Incorporating Standards Via Data Envelopment Analysis. In A. Charnes, W. W. Cooper, Arie Y. Lewin, Lawrence M. Seiford (eds.), *Data Envelopment Analysis: Theory, Methodology, and Applications.* Boston: Kluwer (1995).

Golany, Boaz, Rousseau, John J. Efficiency Evaluation Games. In Fred Y. Phillips, John J. Rousseau (eds), *Systems and Management Science by Extremal Methods.* Boston: Kluwer Academic Publishers (1992), 327–347.

Gold, Franklin Harold. Data Envelopment Analysis: An Application to a Savings and Loan Association. Boston, MA: M.S. thesis, Alfred P. Sloan School of Management, M.I.T. (1982).

Golden, Peggy A. Measuring Organizational Slack and an Application of the Slack Construct to the Prediction of Merger And Acquisition. Lexington, KY: D.B.A. dissertation, University of Kentucky (1989).

Goldstein, Harvey. Data Envelopment Analysis: An Exposition and Critique. *Evaluation and Research in Education* (1990), 4(1):17–20.

Gong, Byeong-Ho. Finite Sample Evidence on the Performance of Stochastic Frontier and Data Envelopment Models in the Estimation of Firm-specific Technical Efficiency Using Panel Data. Houston, TX: Ph.D. dissertation, Rice University (1987).

Gong, Byeong-Ho, Sickles, Robin C. Finite Sample Evidence on the Performance of Stochastic Frontiers and Data Envelopment Analysis Using Panel Data. *Journal of Econometrics* (1992), 51(1–2):259–284.

Granof, Michael H. New Technique May Alter Efficiency Reviews. *Government Accounting and Auditing Update* (1991), 2(6).

Greenberg, Robert, Nunamaker, Thomas R. A Generalized Multiple Criteria Model for Control and Evaluation of Nonprofit Organizations. *Financial Accountability and Management* (1987), 3(4):331–342.

Grosskopf, S. The Role of the Reference Technology in Measuring Productive Efficiency. *Economic Journal* (1986), 96:499–513.

Grosskopf, S., Valdmanis, Vivian. Measuring Hospital Performance: A Nonparametric Approach. *Journal of Health Economics* (1987), 6:89–107.

Guddat, Jurgen, Jongen, Hubertus Th, Kummer, Bernd, Nozicka, Frantisek (eds.), *Parametric Optimization and Related Topics: Papers from the Second International Conferences, 1989 June 27, Eisenach* (1991).

Gulledge, Thomas R. Book Review: Applications of Modern Production Theory: Efficiency and Productivity by Dogramaci and Färe. *Interfaces* (1990), 20(2): 87–88.

Haag, Stephen, Jaska, Patrick V., Semple, John. Assessing the Relative Efficiency of Agricultural Production Units in the Blackland Prairie, Texas. *Applied Economics* (1992), 24(5):559–565.

Hackman, Steven T. An Axiomatic Framework of Dynamic Production. *The Journal of Productivity Analysis* (1990), 1(4):309–324.

Hao, Steven Horng-Shuh. Using Data Envelopment Analysis and Translog Methods to Investigate Blood Center Operations: Efficiency, Economies of Scale, and Economies of Scope. Buffalo, NY: Ph.D. dissertation, State University of New York (1992).

Harrison, Mernoy Edward, Jr. Measuring the Comparative Technical Efficiency of Universities. Chapel Hill, NC: Ph.D. dissertation, Graduate School of Business Administration, University of North Carolina (1988).

Haynes, Kingsley E., Stough, Roger R., Shroff, Homee F. E. New Methodology in Context: Data Envelopment Analysis. *Computers, Environment and Urban Systems* (1990), 14(2):85–88.

Heffernan, Joseph. Efficiency Considerations in the Social Welfare Agency. *Administration in Social Work* (1991), 15(1,2).

Hjalmarsson, Lennart, Veiderpass, Ann. Efficiency and Ownership in Swedish Electricity Retail Distribution. *The Journal of Productivity Analysis* (1992), 3(1/2):7–23.

Hjalmarsson, Lennart, Veiderpass, Ann, Mork, Knut Anton. Productivity in Swedish Electricity Retail Distribution: Comment. *Scandinavian Journal of Economics* (1992), 94 (Supplement).

Hotes, R. W. Development of a Program for Evaluating Training Outputs using a Data Envelopment Analysis Approach. *Combined Proceedings: Sixth Annual Conference on Interactive Instruction Delivery and Third Annual Conference on Learning Technology in the Health Care Sciences, 1988 February 24, Orlando, CA, USA.* Warrenton, VA: Society for Applied Learning Technology (1988).

Huang, Yueh-Guey Laura. An Application of Data Envelopment Analysis:

Measuring the Relative Performance of Florida General Hospitals. *Journal of Medical Systems* (1990), 14(4):191–196.

Huang, Yueh-Guey Laura. An Evaluation of the Efficiency of Rural Primary Care Programs: An Application of Data Envelopment Analysis. Chapel Hill, NC: Dr. P. H. dissertation, School of Public Health, University of North Carolina (1986).

Huang, Yueh-Guey Laura. Using Mathematical Programming to Assess the Relative Performance of the Health Care Industry. *Journal of Medical Systems* (1989), 13(3):155–162.

Huang, Yueh-Guey Laura, McLaughlin, C. P. Relative Efficiency in Rural Primary Health Care: An Application of Data Envelopment Analysis. *Health Service Research* (1989), 24(2):143–158.

Jagannathan, R. An Algorithm for a Class of Nonconvex Programming Problems With Nonlinear Fractional Objectives. *Management Science* (1985), 31(7): 847–851.

Jaska, Patrick V. Sensitivity for Data Envelopment Analysis with an Application to Texas Agricultural Production. Arlington, TX: Ph.D. dissertation, University of Texas (1991).

Jesson, David. School Effectiveness and Efficiency. In *Quality in Schools*. London: National Foundation for Educational Research (1988), 5–13.

Jesson, David, Mayston, David. Information, Accountability and Educational Performance Indicators. In Carol Taylor Fitz-Gibbon (ed.), *Performance Indicators*. Clevedon, Avon, England: Bank House (1989), 77–87.

Jesson, David, Mayston, David. Measuring Performance in Authorities and Schools. In *Education and Training U.K.* Newbury, Berkshire, U.K.: Policy Journals (1989), 12–21.

Jesson, David, Mayston, David, Smith, Peter. Performance Assessment in the Education Sector: Educational and Economic Perspectives. *Oxford Review of Education* (1987), 13(3):249–266.

Johnson, Ronald W., Lewin, Arie Y. Management and Accountability Models of Public Sector Performance. In Trudi Miller (ed.), *Public Sector Performance, A Conceptual Turning Point*. Baltimore, MD: John Hopkins Press (1984), 224–250.

Johnston, Holly Hanson. Empirical Studies in Management Accounting: Three Essays on the U.S. Airline Industry, 1981–1985. Pittsburgh, PA: Ph.D. dissertation, Carnegie-Mellon University; 1990.

Joseph, D. A., Cerveny, R. P., Rhodes, Edwardo L. Application Architecture and Technologic Efficiency: A Comparative Study of Computerized Bank Transaction Systems. *Proceedings of the AIDS National Meeting* (1983).

Justinger, Maryann E. Schwab. An Efficiency Analysis of Services for Adult Students at Community Colleges. Buffalo, NY: Ed. D. dissertation, State University of New York (1986).

Kamakura, Wagner A. A Note on The Use of Categorical Variables in Data Envelopment Analysis. *Management Science* (1988), 34(10):1273–1276.

Kamakura, Wagner A., Ratchford, Brian T., Agrawal, Jagdish. Measuring Market Efficiency and Welfare Loss. *Journal of Consumer Research* (1988), 15(3).

Kao, Chiang, Yang, Yong Chi. Reorganization of Forest Districts via Efficiency Measurement. *European Journal of Operational Research* (1992), 58(3): 356–362.

Katims, Michael Allen. Using Efficiency Analysis to Evaluate Program Effects of Educational Intervention. Austin, TX: Ph.D. dissertation, College of Education, University of Texas (1985).

Kazakov, Alex, Cook, Wade D., Roll, Yaakov. Measurement of Highway Maintenance Patrol Efficiency: Model and Factors. *Transportation Research Record* (1989), 1216:39–45.

Kemerer, Chris F, Measurement of Software Development Productivity. Pittsburgh, PA: Ph.D. dissertation, Graduate School of Industrial Administration, Carnegie-Mellon University (1987).

Kemerer, Chris F. Production Process Modeling of Software Maintenance Productivity. *Proceedings of the IEEE Conference on Software Maintenance– 1988, 1988 October 24; Scottsdale, AZ, USA.* Washington, D.C.: IEEE Computer Society Press (1988), 282.

Kim, Sung-Jong. Productivity of Cities. Theory, Measurement, and Policy Implications: The Korean Case. Dallas, TX: Ph.D. dissertation, University of Texas (1992).

Kittelsen, S. A. C., Førsund, Finn R. Efficiency Analysis of Norwegian District Courts. *The Journal of Productivity Analysis* (1992), 3(3):277–306.

Kleinsorge, Ilene K. Incorporation of Quality Considerations in Measuring Relative Technical Efficiency of Nursing Homes. Lawrence, KS: Ph.D. dissertation, School of Business, University of Kansas (1988).

Kleinsorge, Ilene K., Karney D. F. Management of Nursing Homes using Data Envelopment Analysis. *Socio-Economic Planning Sciences* (1992), 26(1):57–71.

Kleinsorge, Ilene K., Schary, Phillip B., Tanner, Ray D. Evaluating Logistics Decisions. *International Journal of Physical Distribution and Materials Management* (1989), 19(12).

Kleinsorge, Ilene K., Schary, Phillip B., Tanner, Ray D. The Shipper-Carrier Partnership: A New Tool for Performance Evaluation. *Journal of Business Logistics* (1991), 12(2).

Klopp, Gerald A. The Analysis of the Efficiency of Productive Systems With Multiple Inputs and Outputs. Chicago, IL: Ph.D. dissertation, Industrial and Systems Engineering, University of Illinois (1985).

Kornbluth, J. S. H. Analysing Policy Effectiveness Using Cone Restricted Data Envelopment Analysis. *Journal of the Operational Research Society* (1991), 42(12):1097–1104.

Kusbiantoro. A Study of Urban Mass Transit Performance: Concept, Measurement, and Explanation. Philadelphia, PA: Ph.D. dissertation, University of Pennsylvania (1985).

Kwimbere, F. J. Measuring Efficiency in Not-For-Profit Organisations: An Attempt to Evaluate Efficiency in Selected U.K. University Departments Using Data Envelopment Analysis (DEA). Bath, England: M. Sc. thesis, School of Management, University of Bath (1987).

Lang, James R., Golden, Peggy A. Evaluatiny the Efficiency of SBDCs with Data Envelopment Analysis: A Longitudinal Approach. *Journal of Small Business Management* (1989), 27(2).

Learner, David B., Phillips, Fred Y. Contributions to Marketing. In Fred Y. Phillips, John J. Rousseau (eds.), *Systems and Management Science by Extremal Methods*. Boston: Kluwer Academic Publishers (1992), 29–45.

Learner, David B., Phillips, Fred Y., Rousseau, John J. Managing Marketing Productivity: Mathematical and Computational Advances Allow Improved Management of Services Productivity, with Particular Application in Marketing. *Proceedings of the 41st ESOMAR Congress on Marketing Research* (1988).

Lee, Chih-Tah. Duality of Technology and Economic Behavior in a Data Envelopment Analysis/Assurance Region Context. Houston, TX: Ph.D. dissertation, University of Houston (1988).

Leibenstein, Harvey, Maital, Shlomo. Empirical Estimation and Partitioning of X-Inefficiency: A Data-Envelopment Approach. *American Economic Review* (1992), 82(2).

Levitt, M. S., Joyce, M. A. S. *The Growth and Efficiency of Public Spending*. Cambridge: The National Institute of Economic and Social Research, Occasional Papers XLI, Cambridge University (1987).

Lewin, Arie Y. Comments on "Measuring Routine Nursing Service Efficiency: A Comparison of Cost Per Patient Day and Data Envelopment Analysis Models." *Health Services Research* (1983), 18(2, Part 1):206–208.

Lewin, Arie Y. On Learning from Outliers. In Fred Y. Phillips, John J. Rousseau (eds.), *Systems and Management Science by Extremal Methods*. Boston: Kluwer Academic Publishers (1992), 11–17.

Lewin, Arie Y., Minton, J. W. Determining Organizational Effectiveness: Another Look, and an Agenda for Research. *Management Science* (1986), 32(5): 514–538.

Lewin, Arie Y., Morey, Richard C. Measuring the Relative Efficiency and Output Potential of Public Sector Organizations: An Application of Data Envelopment Analysis. *International Journal of Policy Analysis and Information Systems* (1981), 5:267–285.

Lewin Arie Y., Morey, Richard C., Cook, T. J. Evaluating the Administrative Efficiency of Courts. *Omega* (1982), 10(4):401–411.

Ley, Eduardo. Eficiencia productiva: un estudio aplicado al sector hospitalario (with English summary). *Investigaciones Economicas* (1991), 15(1):71–88.

Ley, Eduardo. Essays on Applied Production Analysis. Ann Arbor, MI: Ph.D. dissertation, University of Michigan (1991).

Li, Hongyu. On Some Contributions to Productivity Analysis of Firms in an

Industry Over Time. Austin, TX: Ph.D. dissertation, Graduate School of Business, University of Texas (1992).

Lovell, C. A. Knox, Schmidt, P. A Comparison of Alternative Approaches to the Measurement of Productive Efficiency. In Ali Dogramaci, Rolf Färe (eds.), *Applications of Modern Production Theory: Efficiency and Productivity.* Boston: Kluwer Academic Publishers (1988), 3–32.

Lovell, C. A. Knox, Walters, Lawrence C., Wood, L. L. Stratified Models of Education Production Using Modified DEA and Regression Analysis. In A. Charnes, W. W. Cooper, Arie Y. Lewin, Lawrence M. Seiford (eds.), *Data Envelopment Analysis: Theory, Methodology, and Applications.* Boston: Kluwer (1995).

Lovell, C. A. Knox, Zieschang, K. D. The Problem of New and Disappearing Commodities in the Construction of Price Indexes. In: A. Charnes, W. W. Cooper, Arie Y. Lewin, Lawrence M. Seiford (eds.), *Data Envelopment Analysis: Theory, Methodology, and Applications.* Boston: Kluwer (1995).

Ludwin, William G., Guthrie, Thomas L. Assessing Productivity with Data Envelopment Analysis. *Public Productivity Review* (1989), 12(4).

Macmillan, W. D. The Estimation and Application of Multi-Regional Economic Planning Models Using Data Envelopment Analysis. *Papers of The Regional Science Association* (1986), 60:41–57.

Macmillan, W. D. The Measurement of Efficiency in Multiunit Public Services. *Environment and Planning A* (1987), 19:1511–1524.

Mahajan, Jayashree, A Data Envelopment Analytic Model for Assessing the Relative Efficiency of the Selling Function. *European Journal of Operational Research* (1991), 53(2):189–205.

Maindiratta, Ajay. Largest Size-Efficient Scale and Size Efficiencies of Decision-Making Units in Data Envelopment Analysis. *Journal of Econometrics* (1990), 46(1–2):57–72.

Majumdar, Sumit Kumar. The Impact of a Competitive Environment on Corporate Performance in U.S. Telecommunications Minneapolis, MN: Ph.D. dissertation, Carlton School of Mgt, University of Minnesota (1990).

Mayston, David, Jesson, David. Data Envelopment Analysis and the Generation of Management Performance Information. In C. Fitz Gibbon (ed.), *Performance Indicators—a Dialogue. . .*: Multi Lingual Matters in Education (1989).

Mayston, David, Jesson, David. Developing Models of Educational Accountability. *Oxford Review of Education* (1988), 14(3):321–339.

Mazur, M. Evaluating the Relative Efficiency of Baseball Players? In A. Charnes, W. W. Cooper, Arie Y. Lewin, Lawrence M. Seiford (eds.), *Data Envelopment Analysis: Theory, Methodology, and Applications.* Boston: Kluwer (1995).

Meyer, M., Wohlmannstetter, V. Effizienzmessung in Krankenhaeusrn. *Zeitschrift fuer Betriebswirtschaft* (1985), 55:262–280

Miliotis, Panayotis A. Data Envelopment Analysis Applied to Electricity Distribution Districts. *Journal of the Operational Research Society* (1992), 43(4).

Morey, Richard C. The Impact of Changes in the Delayed-Entry Program Policy on Navy Recruiting Cost. *Interfaces* (1991), 21(4):79-91.

Morey, Richard C., Capettini, Robert, Dittman, David A. Pareto Rate Setting Strategies: An Application to Medicaid Drug Reimbursement. *Policy Sciences* (1985), 18(2):169-200.

Morey, Richard C., Fine, D. J., Loree, S. W. Comparing the Allocative Efficiencies of Hospitals. *Omega* (1990), 18(1):71-83.

Morey, Richard C., Fine, D. J., Loree, S. W., Retzlaff-Roberts, Donna L., Tsubakitani, S. The Trade-off Between Hospital Cost and Quality of Care. An Exploratory Empirical Analysis. *Medical Care* (1992), 30(8):677-698.

Nesher, Ariela. The Effects of Public Services Provision on the Quality of Urban Life. Philadelphia, PA: Ph.D. dissertation, University of Pennsylvania (1981).

Norman, Michael, Stoker, Barry. *Data Envelopment Analysis: The Assessment of Performance.* New York: John Wiley (1991).

Nunamaker, Thomas R. Measuring Routine Nursing Service Efficiency: A Comparison of Cost Per Pttient Day and Data Envelopment Analysis Models. *Health Services Research* (1983), 18(2, Part 1):183-205.

Nunamaker, Thomas R. Using Data Envelopment Analysis to Measure the Efficiency of Non-Profit Organizations: A Critical Evaluation—Reply. *Managerial and Decision Economics* (1988), 9(3):255-256.

Nunamaker, Thomas R. Using Data Envelopment Analysis to Measure the Efficiency of Non-profit Organizations: A Critical Evaluation. *Managerial and Decision Economics* (1985), 6(1):50-58.

Nunamaker, Thomas Ray. Efficiency Measurement and Medicare Reimbursement in Nonprofit Hospitals: An Investigation of the Usefulness of Data Envelopment Analysis. Madison, WI: Ph.D. dissertation, Graduate School of Business, University of Wisconsin (1983).

Nyman, John A., Bricker, Dennis L. Profit Incentives and Technical Efficiency in the Production of Nursing Home Care. *Review of Economics and Statistics* (1989), 71(4):586-594.

Observer. Good School Guide Angers Teachers. London: June 5, 1988, 8.

Oral, Muhittin, Kettani, Ossama, Lang, Pascal. A Methodology for Collective Evaluation and Selection of Industrial R&D Projects. *Management Science* (1991), 37(7):871-885.

Oral, Muhittin, Yolalan, Reha. An Empirical Study on Measuring Operating Efficiency and Profitability of Bank Branches. *European Journal of Operational Research* (1990), 46(3):282-294.

Ozcan Y. A., Luke R. D., Haksever C. Ownership and Organizational Performance. A Comparison of Technical Efficiency Across Hospital Types. *Medical Care* (1992), 30(9):781-794.

Ozcan Yasar A. Sensitivity Analysis of Hospital Efficiency Under Alternative Output/Input and Peer Groups: A Review. *Knowledge and Policy* (1993).

Ozcan Yasar A., Lynch, Janet. Rural Hospital Closures: An Inquiry Into Efficiency. In L. F. Rossiter, R. Scheffer (eds.), *Advances in Health Economics and Health Services Research* (1993), 13.

Parkan, Celik. Calculation of Operational Performance Ratings. *International Journal of Production Economics: Proceedings of the 6th International Working Seminar on Production Economics* (1991), 24(1–2):165–173.

Parkan, Celik. Measuring the Efficiency of Service Operations: An Application to Bank Branches. *Engineering Costs and Production Economics* (1987), 12(1–4): 237–242.

Passmore, Biddy. Consultants Provide Value-for-Money Tests in Croydon. *Times Educational Supplement*. London: January 17, 1986, 8.

Pedersen, P. B., Olesen, O., Petersen, N. C. Produktivitetsevaluering ag 96 danske sygehuse: en praesentation af DEA-metoden og et eksempel pa dens anvendelse [in Danish]. *Ledelse & Erhvervsokonomi* (1987), 2:67–81.

Petersen, Niels Christian. Data Envelopment Analysis on a Relaxed Set of Assumptions. *Management Science* (1990), 36(3):305–314.

Pettypool, M. D., Troutt, M. D. Decisional Data and the Principle of Maximum Efficiency Estimation. In *Mathematical and Computer Modelling: Sixth International Conference on Mathematical Modelling, 1987 August 4, St. Louis, MO, USA* (1988), 11.

Pettypool, M. D., Troutt, M. D. Recent Improvements to Data Envelopment Analysis. *Mathematical and Computer Modelling* (1988), 11:1104–1106.

Pettypool, Majorie Diane. An Examination of Some Mathematical Programming Approaches to Productivity Ratio Estimation. Carbondale, IL: D.B.A. dissertation, Southern Illinois University (1990).

Phillips, Fred Y., Parsons, Ronald G., Donoho, Andrew. Parallel Microcomputing for Data Envelopment Analysis. *Computers, Environment and Urban Systems* (1990), 14(2):167–170.

Phillips, Fred Y., Rousseau, John J. *Proceedings of the Applied Geography Conference*. Association of American Geographers (1990).

Pina, Vicente, Torres, Lourdes. Evaluating the Efficiency of Nonprofit Organizations: An Application of Data Envelopment Analysis to the Public Health Service. *Financial Accountability and Management* (1992), 8(3).

Pollitt, Michael. The Relative Performance of Publicly Owned and Privately Owned Electric Utilities: Some International Evidence. Oxford: M. Philadelphia thesis in Economics, Brasenose College (1991).

Rangan, N., Grabowski, R., Aly, H. Y., Pasurka, C. The Technical Efficiency of US Banks. *Economics Letters* (1988), 28:169–175.

Ray, Subhash C. Data Envelopment Analysis, Nondiscretionary Inputs and Efficiency: An Alternative Interpretation. *Socio-Economic Planning Sciences* (1988), 22(4):167–176.

Ray, Subhash C. Resource-Use Efficiency in Public Schools: A Study of Connecticut Data. *Management Science* (1991), 37(12):1620–1628.

Reaves, Linda Jean. Using Data Envelopment Analysis to Operationalize the Concept of Equal Education Opportunity. Austin, TX: Ph.D. dissertation, College of Education, University of Texas (1983).

Reif, John H., Smolka, Scott A. Data Flow Analysis of Distributed Communicating Processes. *International Journal of Parallel Programming* (1990), 19(1).

Retzlaff-Roberts, Donna Lynn. Incorporating Uncertainty Into Allocative Data Envelopment Analysis. Cincinnati. OH: Ph.D. dissertation, University of Cincinnati (1990).

Rhodes, Edwardo L. An Exploratory Analysis of Variations in Performance Among U.S. National Parks. In Richard H. Silkman (ed.), *Measuring Efficiency: An Assessment of Data Envelopment Analysis*. San Francisco, Jossey Bass: American Evaluation Association (1986), 47-71.

Rhodes, Edwardo Lao. Data Envelopment Analysis and Approaches for Measuring the Efficiency of Decision-making Units with an Application to Program Follow-Through in U.S. Education. Pittsburgh, PA: Ph.D. dissertation, School of Urban and Public Affairs, Carnegie-Mellon University (1978).

Roll, Yaakov, Cook, Wade D., Golany, Boaz. Controlling Factor Weights in Data Envelopment Analysis. *IIE Transactions* (1991), 23(1):2-9.

Roll, Yaakov, Golany, Boaz. Alternate Methods of Treating Factor Weights in DEA. *Omega* (1993), 21(1):99-109.

Roll, Yaakov, Golany, Boaz, Seroussy, D. Measuring the Efficiency of Maintenance Units in the Israeli Air Force. *European Journal of Operational Research* (1989), 43(2):136-142.

Rosenberg, D. DEA (Data Envelopment Analysis) or Dubious Efficiency Assessment. *Journal of Health and Human Resources Administration* (1991), 14(1): 65-76.

Rosenberg, D. EFPF (Economic Frontier Production Function): DEA (Data Envelopment Analysis) Preview. *Journal of Health and Human Resources Administration* (1991), 14(1):77-83.

Rosenberg, D. Forget CEA (Cost Effectiveness Analysis). Use DEA (Data Envelopment Analysis)! *Journal of Health and Human Resources Administration* [1991], 14(1):101-112.

Rosenberg, D. Productivity Analysis: DEA (Data Envelopment Analysis) with Fixed Inputs. *Journal of Health and Human Resources Administration* (1991), 14(1):84-88.

Rosko, M. D. Measuring Technical Efficiency in Health Care Organizations. *Journal of Medical Systems* (1990), 14(5):307-322.

Rousseau, John J., Semple, John. Categorical Outputs in Data Envelopment Analysis. *Management Science* (1993), 39(3):384-386.

Rumsey, Hal A. Productivity Measurement by Data Envelopment Analysis and related Models: An Application to Air Force Civil Engineering. *Proceedings of the American Society for Engineering Management Annual Meeting* (1987), 110-115.

Rumsey, Hal Andrew. Organizational Validity of Constrained Facet Analysis in U.S. Air Force Civil Engineering. Rolla, MO: Ph.D. dissertation, University of Missouri (1986).

Sant, R. Mesasuring the Efficiency of Pubs for Allied Breweries Ltd Using DEA.

Coverntry, U.K.: M. Sc. thesis, University of Warwick (1989).

Sarafoglou, Nikias, Haynes, Kingsley E. Regional Efficiencies of Building Sector Research in Sweden: An Introduction. *Computers, Environment and Urban Systems* (1990), 14(2):117–132.

Schinnar, A. P. Frameworks for Social Accounting and Monitoring of Invariance, Efficiency and Heterogeneity. In Models for Alternative Development Strategies. Hague, The Netherlands: Institute of Social Studies (1980).

Sear, Alan M. Operating Characteristics and Comparative Performance of Investor-Owned Multihospital Systems. *Hospital and Health Services Administration* (1992), 37(3).

Seaver, Bill L., Triantis, Konstantinos P. A Fuzzy Clustering Approach Used in Evaluating Technical Efficiency Measures in Manufacturing. *The Journal of Productivity Analysis* (1992), 3(4):337–363.

Seiford, Lawrence M. Data Envelopment Analysis: Learning from Outliers. In *Proceedings of the First Industrial Engineering Research Conference, 1992 May 20*. Chicago: Institute of Industrial Engineers (1992).

Seiford, Lawrence M. Models, Extensions, and Applications of Data Envelopment Analysis: A Selected Reference Set. *Computers, Environment and Urban Systems* (1990), 14(2).

Seiford, Lawrence M., Thrall, Robert M. Recent Developments in DEA: The Mathematical Programming Approach to Frontier Analysis. *Journal of Econometrics* (1990), 46(1–2):7–38.

Sengupta, Jati K. The Active Approach of Stochastic Optimization with New Applications. In Jati K. Sengupta, G. K. Kadekodi (eds.), *Econometrics of Planning and Efficiency*. Dordrecht: Kluwer Academic Publishers (1988), 93–108.

Sengupta, Jati K. A Contribution to the Theory of Farrell Efficiency. In *Essays in Honor of Professor Bhabatosh Datta*. Calcutta, India (1989).

Sengupta, Jati K. Data Envelopment Analysis for Efficiency Measurement in the Stochastic Case. *Computers and Operations Research* (1987), 14(2):117–129.

Sengupta, Jati K. Data Envelopment with Maximum Correlation. *International Journal of Systems Science* (1989), 20(11):2085–2093.

Sengupta, Jati K. *Efficiency Analysis by Production Frontiers: The Nonparametric Approach*. Dordrecht: Kluwer Academic Publishers (1989).

Sengupta, Jati K. Efficiency Comparisons in Input-Output Systems. *International Journal of Systems Science* (1988), 19(7):1085–1094.

Sengupta, Jati K. Efficiency Measurement in Non-market Systems through Data Envelopment Analysis. *International Journal of Systems Science* (1987), 18(12): 2279–2304.

Sengupta, Jati K. Efficiency Measurement in Stochastic Input-Output Systems. *International Journal of Systems Science* (1982), 13:273–287.

Sengupta, Jati K. Farrell Efficiency: Some Generalizations and Econometric Implications. In *Essays in Honor Professor Karl A. Fox*. Amsterdam: North Holland (1989).

Sengupta, Jati K. A Fuzzy Systems Approach in Data Envelopment Analysis.

Computers and Mathematics with Applications (1992), 24(8-9).

Sengupta, Jati K. The Influence Curve Approach in Data Envelopment Analysis. *Mathematical Programming* (1991), 52(1):147-166.

Sengupta, Jati K. *Information and Efficiency in Economic Decision*. Dordrecht: Kluwer Academic Publishers (1985).

Sengupta, Jati K. The Measurement of Productive Efficiency: A Robust Minimax Approach. *Managerial and Decision Economics* (1989), 9:153-161.

Sengupta, Jati K. Measuring Economic Efficiency with Stochastic Input-Output Data. *International Journal of Systems Science* (1989), 20(2):203-213.

Sengupta, Jati K. Measuring Efficiency by a Fuzzy Statistical Approach. *Fuzzy Sets and Systems* (1992), 46(1).

Sengupta, Jati K. Measuring Managerial Efficiency by Data Envelopment Analysis. *Management Review* (1986), 1:3-18.

Sengupta, Jati K. Multivariate Risk Aversion with Applications. In *Information and Efficiency in Economic Decision*. Dordrecht: Kluwer Academic Publishers (1985), 351-370.

Sengupta, Jati K. Nonlinear Measures of Technical Efficiency. *Computers and Operations Research* (1989), 16(1):55-65.

Sengupta, Jati K. Nonparametric Tests of Efficiency of Portfolio Investment. *Journal of Economics* (1989).

Sengupta, Jati K. Production Frontier Estimation to Measure Efficiency: A Critical Evaluation in Light of Data Envelopment Analysis. *Managerial and Decision Economics* (1987), 8(2):93-99.

Sengupta, Jati K. Recent Nonparametric Measures of Productive Efficiency. In Jati K. Sengupta, G. K. Kadekodi (eds.), *Econometrics of Planning and Efficiency*. Dordrecht: Kluwer Academic Publishers (1988), 169-193.

Sengupta, Jati K. Risk Aversion in Decision Models. In *Information and Efficiency in Economic Decision*. Dordrecht: Kluwer Academic Publishers (1985), 397-434.

Sengupta, Jati K. Robust Decisions in Economic Models. *Computers and Operations Research* (1991), 18(2):221-232.

Sengupta, Jati K. Robust Efficiency Measures in a Stochastic Efficiency Model. *International Journal of Systems Science* (1988), 19(5):779-791.

Sengupta, Jati K. Robust Solutions in Stochastic Linear Programming. *Journal of the Operational Research Society* (1991), 42(10):857-870.

Sengupta, Jati K. Structural Efficiency in Stochastic Models of Data Envelopment Analysis. *International Journal of Systems Science* (1990), 21(6):1047-1056.

Sengupta, Jati K. Tests of Efficiency in Data Envelopment Analysis. *Computers and Operations Research* (1990), 17(2):123-132.

Sengupta, Jati K. Transformations in Stochastic DEA Models. *Journal of Econometrics* (1990), 46(1,2):109-124.

Sengupta, Jati K., Sfeir, Raymond E. Efficiency Measurement by Data Envelopment Analysis with Econometric Applications. *Applied Economics* (1988), 20(3):285-293.

Sengupta, Jati K., Sfeir, Raymod E. Production Frontier Estimates of Scale in

Public Schools in California. *Economics of Education Review* (1986), 5(3): 297–307.

Sexton, Thomas R. The Methodology of Data Envelopment Analysis. In Richard H. Silkman (ed.), *Measuring Efficiency: An Assessment of Data Envelopment Analysis*. San Francisco, Jossey Bass: American Evaluation Association (1986), 7–29.

Sexton, Thomas R., Leiken A. M., Nolan A. H., Liss S., Hogan, A. J., Silkman, Richard H. Evaluating Managerial Efficiency of Veterans Administration Medical Centers using Data Envelopment Analysis. *Medical Care* (1989), 27(12):1175–1188.

Sexton, Thomas R., Leiken, A. M., Sleeper, S., Coburn A. F. The Impact of Prospective Reimbursement on Nursing Home Efficiency. *Medical Care* (1989), 27(2):154–163.

Sexton, Thomas R., Silkman, Richard H., Hogan, A. J. Data Envelopment Analysis: Critique and Extensions. In Richard H. Silkman (ed.), *Measuring Efficiency: An Assessment of Data Envelopment Analysis*. San Francisco, Jossey Bass: American Evaluation Association (1986), 73–105.

Shakun, Melvin F., Sudit, E. F. Effectiveness, Productivity and Design of Purposeful Systems: The Profit-Making Case. *International Journal of General Systems* (1983), 9(4):205–215.

Shash, Ali H. A Probabilistic Model for U.S. Nuclear Power Construction Times. Austin, TX: Ph.D. dissertation, Department of Civil Engineering, University of Texas (1988).

Sherman, H. David. Data Envelopment Analysis as a New Managerical Audit Methodology—Test and Evaluation. *Auditing—A Journal of Practice and Theory* (1984), 4(1):35–53.

Sherman, H. David. Hospital Efficiency Measurement and Evaluation: Empirical Test of a New Technique. *Medical Care* (1984), 22(10):922–938.

Sherman, H. David. Improving the Productivity of Service Businesses. *Sloan Management Review* (1984), 25(3):11–23.

Sherman, H. David. Managing Productivity of Health Care Organizations. In Richard H. Silkman (ed.), *Measuring Efficiency: An Assessment of Data Envelopment Analysis*. San Francisco, Jossey Bass: American Evaluation Association (1986), 31–46.

Sherman, H. David. Measurement of Hospital Technical Efficiency: A Comparative Evaluation of Data Envelopment Analysis and Other Efficiency Measurement Techniques for Measuring and Locating Inefficiency in Health Care Organizations. Boston, MA: D.B.A. dissertation, Graduate School of Business Administration. Harvard University (1981).

Sherman, H. David, *Service Organization Productivity Measurement*. Hamilton, Ontario, Canada: The Society of Management Accountants of Canada (1988).

Sherman, H. David, Gold, Franklin. Bank Branch Operating Efficiency: Evaluation with Data Envelopment Analysis. *Journal of Banking and Finance* (1985), 9(2):297–315.

Shroff, Homee Farrokh E. Siting Efficiencies of Long-term Health Care Facilities: The Northern Virginia Health System. Boston, MA: Ph.D. dissertation, Boston University (1992).

Sickles, Robin C., Streitwieser, Mary L. Technical Inefficiency and Productive Decline in the U.S. Interstate Natural Gas Pipeline Industry Under the Natural Gas Policy Act. *The Journal of Productivity Analysis* (1992), 3(1/2):119–133.

Siems, Thomas F. An Envelopment Analysis Approach to Measuring Management Quality and Predicting Bank Failure. Dallas. TX: Ph.D. dissertation, Southern Methodist University (1991).

Siems, Thomas F. Quantifying Management's Role in Bank Survival. *Federal Reserve Bank of Dallas Economic Review* (1992), 29–41.

Silkman, Richard H. Editor's Notes, In Richard H. Silkman (ed.), *Measuring Efficiency: An Assessment of Data Envelopment Analysis*. San Francisco, Jossey Bass: American Evaluation Association (1986), 1–6.

Silkman, Richard H. (ed.). *Measuring Efficiency: An Assessment of Data Envelopment Analysis*. San Francisco, Jossey Bass: American Evaluation Association (1986).

Silverwood, L. Performance Measures for the NHS. Coverntry, U.K.: M. Sc. thesis, University of Warwick (1989).

Simonsen, William Steven. Resource Recovery Facilities: Production and Cost Functions, and Debt Financing Issues. New York: Ph.D. dissertation, New York University (1991).

Sinha, Kingshuk Kanti. Models for Evaluation of Complex Technological Systems: Strategic Applications in High Technology Manufacturing. Austin, TX: Ph.D. dissertation, Graduate School of Business, University of Texas (1991).

Smith, David M. *UGC Research Ratings: Pass or Fail?* Area (Institute of British Geographers) (1986), 247–250.

Smith, Peter. Data Envelopment Analysis Applied to Financial Statments. *Omega* (1990), 18(2):131–138.

Smith, Peter, Mayston, David. Measuring Efficiency in the Public Sector. *Omega* (1987), 15(3):181–189.

Smith, Peter, Sharp, Colin A., Orford, Robert J. Negative Political Feedback: An Examination of the Problem of Modelling Political Responses in Public Sector Effectiveness Auditing: Comments. *Accounting Auditing and Accountability Journal* (1992), 5(1).

Sojka, J. Dynamic Aspects of Data Envelopment Analysis. *Ekonomicko-Matematicky Obzor* (1989), 25(2).

Splitek, David Franklin. A Study of the Production Efficiency of Texas Public Elementary Schools. Austin, TX: Ph.D. dissertation, College of Education, University of Texas (1981).

Stolp, Chandler. A Framework for Evaluating the Efficiency of Health Centers in Nicaragua. In Michael E. Conroy (ed.), *NICARAGUA: Profiles of The Revolutionary Public Sector*. Boulder, Colorado: Westview Press (1987), 143–170.

Stolp, Chandler. Strengths and Weaknesses of Data Envelopment Analysis. An

Urban and Regional Perspective. *Computers, Environment and Urban Systems* (1990), 14(2):103–116.

Stone, Martha Jean. A Comparative Analysis of the Personnel Practices of School Districts Selected by Data Envelopment Analysis Efficiency Indices. Austin, TX: Ph.D. dissertation, College of Educations, University of Texas (1984).

Sueyoshi, Toshiyuki. Algorithmic Strategy for Assurance Region Analysis in DEA. *Journal of the Operations Research Society of Japan* (1992), 35(1).

Sueyoshi, Toshiyuki. Estimation of Stochastic Frontier Cost Function Using Data Envelopment Analysis: An Application to the AT&T Divestiture. *Journal of the Operational Research Society* (1991), 42(6):463–477.

Sueyoshi, Toshiyuki. Measuring Technical, Allocative and Overall Efficiencies Using a DEA Algorithm. *Journal of the Operational Research Society* (1992), 43(2):141–155.

Sueyoshi, Toshiyuki. Measuring the Industrial Performance of Chinese Cities by Data Envelopment Analysis. *Socio-economic Plannig Sciences* (1992), 26(2).

Sueyoshi, Toshiyuki. A Special Algorithm for an Additive Model in Data Envelopment Analysis. *Journal of the Operational Research Society* (1990), 41(3): 249–257.

Sueyoshi, Toshiyuki. A Study on Efficiency Analysis Using DEA [in Japanese]. *Communication of the Operations Research Society of Japan* (1990), 35(3): 167–173.

Sueyoshi, Toshiyuki, Chang, Yih-Long. Efficient Algorithm for Additive and Multiplicative Models in Data Envelopment Analysis. *Operations Research Letters* (1989), 8(4):205–213.

Sun, Dee Bruce. Evaluation of Managerial Performance in Large Commercial Banks by Data Envelopment Analysis. Austin, TX: Ph.D. dissertation, Graduate School of Business, University of Texas (1988).

Swann, G. M. P. International Differences in Product Design and Their Economic Significance. *Applied Economics* (1987), 19(2):201–213.

Tankersley, William Baxter. The Effects of Organizational Control Structure and Process on Organizational Performance. Tallahassee, FL: Ph.D. dissertation, Florida State University (1990).

Thanassoulis, E., Dyson, R. G. Estimating Preferred Target Input–Output Levels Using Data Envelopment Analysis: *European Journal of Operational Research* (1992), 56(1):80–97.

Thanassoulis, E., Dyson, R. G., Foster, M. J. Relative Efficiency Assessments Using Data Envelopment Analysis: An Application to Data on Rates Departments. *Journal of the Operational Research Society* (1987), 38(5):397–411.

Thiry, Bernard, Tulkens, Henry. Allowing for Inefficiency in Parametric Estimation of Production Functions for Urban Transit Firms. *The Journal of Productivity Analysis* (1992), 3(1/2):45–65.

Thomas, David Alan. Data Envelopment Analysis Methods in the Management of Personnel Recruitment Under Competition in the Context of U.S. Army Recruiting. Austin, TX: Ph.D. dissertation, Graduate School of Business, University of Texas (1990).

Thomas, Dennis Lee. Auditing the Efficiency of Regulated Companies Through the Use of Data Envelopment Analysis: An Application to Electric Cooperatives. Austin, TX: Ph.D. dissertation, Graduate School of Business, University of Texas (1985).

Thomas, D., Greffe, R., Grant, K. Application of Data Envelopment Analysis to Management Audits of Electric Distribution Utilities. In Robert E. Burnes (ed.), *Proceedings of the Fifth NARUC Biennial Regulatory Information Conference*. Columbus, DH: The National Regulatory Research Institute, Ohio State University (1986), 1783–1882.

Thompson, Russell G., Dharmapala, P. S., Thrall, Robert M. Sensitivity Analysis of Efficiency Measures With Applications to Kansas Farming and Illinois Coal Mining. In: A. Charnes, W. W. Cooper, Arie Y. Lewin, Lawarence M. Seiford (eds.), *Data Envelopment Analysis: Theory, Methodology, and Applications*. Boston: Kluwer (1995).

Thompson, Russell G., Langemeier, Larry N., Lee, Chih-Tah, Lee, Euntaik, Thrall, Robert M. The Role of Multiplier Bounds in Efficiency Analysis with Application to Kansas Farming. *Journal of Econometrics* (1990), 46(1,2): 93–108.

Thompson, Russell G., Lee, Euntaik, Thrall, Roert M. DEA/AR-Efficiency of U.S. Independent Oil/Gas Producers Over Time. *Computers and Operations Research* (1992), 19(5):377–391.

Thompson, Russell G., Lesso, W., Pettit, R. R., Samson, C., Sterm, L. H., Singleton, F. D. Jr., Smith, Barton A., Thrall, Robert M. *Systems Task Force Comparative Site Evaluations for the Texas SSC Project: Vol. E and Appendices*. Woodlands, TX: Houston Area Research Center (1985 January 31).

Thompson, Russell G., Singleton, F. D. Jr., Thrall, Robert M., Smith, Barton A. Comparative Site Evaluation for Locating a High-Energy Physics Lab in Texas. *Interfaces* (1986), 16(6):35–49.

Thorogood, Nellie Jean Carr. The Application and Utilization of Data Envelopment Analysis for Decision Support in the Administration of Instructional Programs for an Urban Community College. Austin, TX: Ph.D. dissertation, College of Education, University of Texas (1983).

Thrall, Robert M. Classification Transitions under Expansion of Inputs and Outputs in Data Envelopment Analysis. *Managerial and Decision Economics* (1989), 10(2):159–162.

Tomkins, Cyril; Green, R. H. An Experiment in the Use of Data Envelopment Analysis for Evaluating the Efficiency of UK University Departments of Accounting. *Financial Accountability and Management* (1988), 4(2):147–164.

Tone, K. A Comparative Study on AHP and DEA. *International Journal on Policy and Information* (1989), 13(2):57–63.

Tone, K., Sawada, T. An Efficiency Analysis of Public vs. Private Bus Transportation Enterprises. In Hugh E. Bradley (ed.), *Operational Research '90: Selected Papers from the Twelfth IFORS International Conference on Operational Research* (1991), 357–365.

Tseng, Mei-Ling. Efficiency Comparison of Nursing Homes: An Application of

Data Envelopment Analysis. Birmingham, AL: Ph.D. dissertation, University of Alabama (1990).

Turner, Leslie Daniel. Improved Measures of Manufacturing Maintenance in a Capital Budgeting Context: An Application of Data Envelopment Analysis Efficiency Measures. Lexington, KY: D.B.A. dissertation, University of Kentucky (1988).

Turner, Leslie D., DePree, Chauncey M., Jr. The Relative Efficiency of Boards of Accountancy: A Measure of the Profession's Enforcement and Disciplinary Processes. *Journal of Accounting and Public Policy* (1991), 10(1):1–13.

Valdmanis, Vivian. Hospital Care for the Poor: A Comparison of Public and Private Provision. Nashville, TN: Ph.D. dissertation, Vanderbilt University (1986).

Valdmanis, Vivian. Sensitivity Analysis for DEA Models: An Empirical Example Using Public versus NFP Hospitals. *Journal of Public Economics* (1992), 48(2).

Varian, Hal R. Goodness-of-Fit in Optimizing Models. *Journal of Econometrics* (1990) 46(1/2):125–140.

Vassdal, Terje. Effektivitetsmalinger med Ikke-Parametriske Metoder [in Norwegian]. *Norsk Okonomisk Tidsskrift* (1990), 104:113–138.

Vassdal, Terje. Maling av produktivitet: en sammenligning av ulike metoder, med spesiell vekt pa Data Envelopment Analysis [in Norwegian]. Tromsö, Norway: Ph.D. dissertation, University of Tromsö (1988).

Vassiloglou, M., Giokas, D. I. A Study of the Relative Efficiency of Bank Branches: An Application of Data Envelopment Analysis. *Journal of the Operational Research Society* (1990), 41(7).

Walters, Lawrence Clayton. How Well Are We Housed? Measuring Deficiencies in Housing Services. Philadelphia, PA: Ph.D. dissertation, University of Pennsylvania (1987).

Weber, Charles Arthur. A Decision Support System Using Multicriteria Techniques for Vendor Selection. Columbus, OH: Ph.D. dissertation, Ohio State University (1991).

Wei, Quan Ling, Lu, Gang, Yue, Ming. Some Identities for Sets of Efficient Decision-making Units of Data Envelopment Analysis in Composite Data Envelopment Analysis Modesl. *Journal of Systems Science and Mathematical Sciences* (1989), 9.

Wei, Quan Ling, Xiao, Zhi Jie. Production Functions and the Compositive Data Envelopment Analysis Model. *Journal of Systems Science and Mathematical Sciences* (1991), 11(1).

Wilby, Peter. How the Education Authorities Scored in Exams. *The Independent* London: April 21, 1989, 21.

Wong, Y.-HB. Data Envelopment Analysis. London: M. Sc. thesis, The Management School, Imperial College (1988).

Wong, Y.-HB., Beasley, J. E. Restricting Weight Flexibility in Data Envelopment Analysis. *Journal of the Operational Research Society* (1990), 41(9): 829–835.

Wu, Lifen, Xiao, Cheng-zhong. Comparative Sampling Research on Operations Management in Machine Tools Industry between China and the Countries in Western Europe [in Chineese]. *Journal of Shanghai Institute of Mechanical Engineering* (1989), 11(1):61–67.

Wu, Li-Fen, Xiao, Cheng-Zhong. Comparing Manufacturing Practices between the People's Republic of China and Countries in Western Europe. *International Manufacturing Practices Workshop*: Shanghai (May 1990).

Yue, Ming. The Data Envelopment Analysis Method for Establishing Production Functions. *Mathematics in Practice and Theory* (Chinese).

Yue, Piyu. Data Envelopment Analysis and Commercial Bank Performance: A Primer with Applicatios to Missouri Banks. *Federal Reserve Bank of St. Louis Review* (1992), 74(1):31–45.

Yue, Piyu, Two Essays on Economic Analyses. Austin, TX: Ph.D. dissertation, University of Texas (1990).

Zanders, E. Okonomie von Altenheimen: Betriebsvergleiche und Arbeitsvertrage [in German]. Frankfurt: Ph.D. dissertation (1990).

Zomorrodian, Mohammad Reza. Guidelines for Improving Efficiency in Elementary Schools in Western Massachusetts. A Data Envelopment Analysis Approach. Amherst, MA: Ed. D. Thesis, University of Massachusetts (1990).

Notes about Authors

Agha Iqbal Ali is Professor of Operations Management in the department of finance and operations management in the School of Management at The University of Massachusetts at Amherst. He received his Ph.D. in operations research from Southern Methodist University in 1980. His work in data envelopment analysis has appeared in journals such as *Operations Research Letters*, Management Science, *European Journal of Operational Research* and in books such as *The Measurement of Productive Efficiency: Techniques and Application* published by Oxford. His work in the areas of network, integer, and combinatorial programming has appeared in journals such as *Operations Research, Networks, Discrete Applied Mathematics*, and *Naval Research Logistics Quarterly*. He serves as an Associate Editor for the journal *Operations Research*.

Rajiv D. Banker is the Arthur Andersen Chair in Accounting and Information Systems at the Carlson School of Management, University of Minnesota, holding joint appointments in the departments of Accounting, Information and Decision Sciences, and Operations and Management Sciences. Graduating at the top of his class from the University of Bombay, Banker received his doctorate in business administration from Harvard University in 1980. Banker has published over 70 refereed articles in leading research journals in accounting, information systems,

471

operations management, management science and economics. His research articles have received three awards, and continue to be cited frequently in recent research in several disciplines. He has also received three awards for teaching excellence at Carnegie Mellon University and the University of Minnesota.

Patricia E. Byrnes is Assistant Professor, School of Public Policy and Management and Research Associate, Mershon Center, at Ohio State University. She received her Ph.D. in economics from Southern Illinois University, Carbondale in 1986. Her current research interests include public sector efficiency and productivity measurement and evaluation of state and local economic development program.

Abraham Charnes, internationally renowned scholar in management science and applied mathematics, died in December 1992. He was University Professor across the University of Texas System, John T. Harbin U.T. Regents Chair Emeritus, and Director of the Center for Cybernetic Studies. A Founder and Past President of TIMS, he was a Fellow of ORSA, The Econometric Society and AAAS. He published over 400 articles and eight books and lectured for Academies of Science and at universities worldwide. His many awards include finalist for the Nobel Prize in Economics (1975), U.S. Navy Medal for Distinguished Public Service by a civilian (1977), co-recipient of the von Neumann Theory Prize of TIMS and ORSA (1982), and Department of Defense Medal for Distinguished Public Service by a civilian (1992).

Jon A. Chilingerian is Associate Professor of Management and Co-Director of the Pow Doctoral Program in Health Policy at the Heller School for Advanced Studies at Brandeis University. He received his Ph.D. degree from the Massachusetts Institute of Technology's Sloan School of Management. Dr. Chilingerian's research has focused on measuring and managing physician efficiency and effectiveness. At Brandeis he teaches courses in organizational behavior, managerial accounting, and the management of health organizations.

Wade D. Cook is a Professor of Management Science in the Faculty of Administrative Studies at York University, Canada. He is a member of a number of professional societies including TIMS and CORS, and is an editor of *INFOR* and the *Journal of Productivity Analysis*. His research has appeared in a wide range of professional and academic journals, and he has recently co-authored the book *Ordinal Information and Preference Structures & Decision Models and Applications*.

W. W. Cooper is Professor of Management, Accounting and Management Science and Information Systems in the Graduate School of Business of the University of Texas at Austin. Author or co-author of more than 400 scientific-professional articles and 17 books, he is a fellow of the Econometric Society and the American Association for the Advancement of Science. He holds the John von Neumann Theory medal jointly awarded by the Institute of Management Sciences and the Operations Research Society of America as well as the Outstanding Accounting Educator Award of the American Accounting Association.

Diana L Day is on the faculty of Rutgers University, Camden, New Jersey. Prior to Rutgers, she was the Ehrenkranz/Greenwall Assistant Professor of Management at the Wharton School. Dr. Day concentrated in strategic management for her Ph.D. from Columbia University. Her dissertation in 1986, "A Contingency Theory. of Relatedness in Corporate Venturing and Venture performance," started her on her main research stream in corporate entrepreneurship, Since then she has written numerous papers in this stream dealing with issues from the entry strategies of new ventures to championing of such ventures and their location in the organization structure. Her current research focuses on the intra-industry sources of variability in firm performance. She serves on the editorial board of *Organization Science* and the *Journal of High Technology Management and Marketing* and is a member of the Academy of Management, Strategic Management Society, American Marketing Association, TIMS/ORSA, and IEEE.

Anand Desai is associate professor and associate director for doctoral studies at the School of Public Policy and Management of the Ohio State University where he teaches courses on modeling, statistics, and information systems. His research interests include mathematical modeling applied to public policy analysis. In particular, he is interested in the measurement and modeling issues related to the evaluation of the provision of public services.

Professor Roll Fare received his Docent in Economics from the University of Lund, Sweden, in 1973. He has published extensively in the area of production theory. His current research deals with inter temporal production frontiers, including dynamic Data Envelopment Analysis.

Gary D. Ferrier is Assistant Professor of Economics at the University of Arkansas. He has published a number of papers on the use of DEA and econometric techniques to measure the levels and determinants of efficiency and technological change. Professor Ferrier has also taught at Southern Methodist University as well as in Italy and Malaysia. He has a B.A. from the University of Wisconsin and a Ph.D. from the University of North Carolina.

Finn R. Forsund is professor at Department of Economics, University of Oslo, where he graduated in 1968, and got his doctor's degree on essays in production theory. He has published on production theory, on estimation of frontier functions and short-run functions, and on DEA applications and Malmquist indices in journals like *The Scandinavian Journal of Economics*, *Econometrica*, *Journal of Econometrics*, and *Journal of Productivity Analysis*. He has also published in journals and books within environmental economics, on spatial aspects, input-output applications, and on economic instruments.

Boaz Golany is an Associate Professor of Industrial Engineering and Management at the Technion-Israel Institute of Technology. He has a B.Sc. (cum laude) in Industrial Engineering and Management from the Technion (1982), and a Ph.D. from the Business School of the University of Texas at Austin (1985). Dr. Golany is an author and co-author on some 40 papers in academic and professional journals and books. His publications are in the areas of Industrial Engineering, Operations Research and Management Science. In the US he has been actively involved in various efficiency evaluation projects in military milieux as well as numerous efficiency studies in the private sector. In Israel he has been consulting on inventory control issues to companies in the oil industry including the Israeli Refineries Ltd. He is an active member in various professional societies including TIMS (US) and ORSIS (Israel).

Kingsley E. Haynes is the Director of The Institute of Public Policy, an independent university-wide doctoral granting research program, at George Mason University in Fairfax, Virginia. He is also a University Professor of Decision Science, Geography and Public Policy. Previously he served as Dean of the Graduate School at George Mason; and Chair of the Department of Geography and Faculty of Urban and Regional Analysis at Boston and Indiana Universities, respectively. Most recently his research has focused on technology led reengineering in large scale public and private organizations. He worked with Dr. A. Charnes when he was on the faculty at the LBJ School at the University of Texas at Austin (1970–1978).

Erik Hernaes is research director at the Oslo department of the Foundation for Research in Economics and Business Administration, associated with the Department of Economics, University of Oslo, from which Hernaes graduated in 1972. He has also worked at the Central Bureau of Statistics, Oslo. His main field is labour market and econometrics, in particular educational and labour force projections, earnings relations, and unemployment. He has published in a series from the National Bureau of Economic Research.

Holly H. Johnston earned her Ph.D. at the Carnegie Mellon University. Her research is interdisciplinary, involving the development of models for estimating production and cost functions and measuring productivity, productivity and managerial accounting, relationships between cost structures, managerial strategies, changing economic and regulatory environments, and market structures, and the value of information technology. She has recently published in the *Accounting Review*.

Dr. A. Kazakov is Senior Research Engineer of R & D Branch of the Ministry of Transportation of Ontario. He received the M.Sc. in Engineering Physics in 1969 and Ph.D. in theoretical physics in 1972 from Leningrad Polytechnic Institute and has worked in the areas of Physics of Solid State, Nuclear Physics in Russia. In 1976 he immigrated to Canada. Since then his major interests are in areas of practical application of Operations Research and development of Decision systems.

Arie Y. Lewin is Professor of Business Administration and Professor of Sociology at Duke University. He is the founding editor in chief of *Organization Science* and from 1986–1988 he served at the National Science Foundation as Director for the Decision, Risk and Management Science program. Professor Lewin is author of four books and his research articles have appeared or are forthcoming in many different journals. His overall research interests involve the analysis of organizational effectiveness and the design of organizations. He is presently engaged in a multi-year Japan, Germany, U.S.A. comparative study of organization transitions. He is a member of the Institute of Management Sciences, Academy of Management, Society for Judgement and Decision Making and the American Accounting Association, and serves on the editorial boards of *Technological Forecasting and Social Change*, *European Journal of Operations Research* and *Journal of Productivity Analysis*.

Dr. Hongyu Li received a Ph.D. in Operations Management from The University of Texas at Austin under supervision of Dr. Abraham Charnes in 1992. He is currently a faculty member in the Department of Decision Sciences, National University of Singapore.

Bjorn Lindgren, Ph.D., is Professor of Health Economics at Lund University, Sweden. He was Director of the Swedish Institute for Health Economics 1982–1991. He is a scientific advisor to the Swedish National Board of Health and Welfare, and he has been consultant to the OECD and the WHO. His current work includes research on productivity and efficiency in health care and care for the elderly, the economics of medical decision-making, and the economics of alcohol consumption.

C. A. Knox Lovell is the C. Herman and Mary Virginia Terry Distinguished Professor of Economics at the University of Georgia. Lovell has published widely in the field of efficiency and productivity measurement, and is the author of four books, including *The Measurement of Efficiency of Production* (with Fare & Grosskopf), Kluwer, 1985. He is Editor-in-Chief of *The Journal of Productivity Analysis*, and an Associate Editor of *Management Science*.

Mark J. Mazur is a Senior Staff Economist at the Council of Economic Advisers in the Executive Office of the President. When the paper in this volume was written, he was on the faculty of the School of Urban Affairs at Carnegie-Mellon University. Mark received a Ph.D. in Business from Stanford University in 1986.

Fred Phillips is Research Director at The University of Texas' IC^2 Institute and Associate Director of U.T.'s Center for Cybernetic Studies. He attended The University of Texas (Ph.D. 1978) and the Tokyo Institute of Technology. He has held positions at the Universities of Aston and Birmingham in England, General Motors Research Laboratories, MRCA Information Services, and St. Edward's University. His research focuses are the measurement and valuation of management information; applications of mathematical programming to statistical inference; new product development; and integrated business data and analysis services. He is a member of TIMS, the Information Industries Association, the Western Regional Science Association, and AMA.

Yaacov Roll was a professor of Industrial Engineering in the Faculty of Industrial Engineering and Management at the Technion-Israel of Technology, where he held the Gruenblat Chair in Production Engineering. He received his B.Sc. in Industrial Engineering and M.Sc. in

Operations Research at the Technion. His teaching and research interests included optimization of production systems, work system design and productivity measurement. Professor Roll is the author and co-author of numerous articles in various journals including *IIE Transactions*, *EJOR*, *IJPR*, *JPA*, and others. He has been a consultant to many private and public organizations in Israel and elsewhere. He was a member of I. Mech. E (UK) and ORSIS (Israel). Professor Roll passed away in May 1993.

Pontus Roos, Licentiate (PhL) in economics at University of Lund, Sweden. At present, he is working as a project manager at the Swedish Institute for Health Economics (IHE). At IHE, he is responsible for the programme Efficiency & Productivity. The programme conducts consultancy activities as well as research. His research interests include efficiency and productivity measurement, interactions between productivity and quality, pricing of inputs and outputs, and measurement of health care outcomes.

John J. Rousseau is Research Associate at the Center for Cybernetic Studies, Graduate School of Business, and Associate at the IC2 Institute of University of Texas at Austin. He holds a B.Sc. and M.Com. from the University of Birmingham (U.K.) and an interdisciplinary Ph.D. in Mathematics, Economics and Business Administration from the University of Texas at Austin. Member of TIMS and ORSA, he has published in applied economics, game theory, marketing research, operations research and management science.

Lawrence M. Seiford is Professor of Industrial Engineering and Operations Research at the University of Massachusetts at Amherst. He received his Ph.D. from the University of Texas under A. Charnes. His principal research interests encompass the areas of systems quality and productivity, decision theory, game theory, and computer-based decision support systems (DSS). He serves as an Editor of the *Journal of Productivity Analysis*, Associate Editor of *INFOR: Information Systems and Operational Research*, is a member of the editorial board of *The Mathematica Journal*, and a coordinator for the Productivity Analysis Research Network (PARN), a worldwide network for researchers/ research institutions in the field of productivity and frontier analysis. He has several books forthcoming and has written and coauthored over sixty articles in the areas of quality, productivity, performance measurement, game theory, and systems modeling.

James E. Storbeck is currently Director of Analytics for The Magellan Group, Austin, Texas, having previously been a professor in the College of Business at The Ohio State University from 1980–1994. He has an interdisciplinary Ph.D. (1980) in Business Administration/Public Policy/ Demography from the Center for Cybernetics at The University of Texas at Austin. Dr. Storbeck has published over 30 articles and chapters in professional journals and books, in the areas of management science, operations research and regional science. During his tenure at Ohio State, Dr. Storbeck has participated in numerous projects and research studies involving productivity and performance measurement in business and government.

Russell G. Thompson is a professor of decision and information sciences at the University of Houston and President of Decision Analysis, Inc., a data analysis and forecasting firm in Houston, Texas. He has managed many complex interdisciplinary projects. His most recent research emphasizes applications of DEA/AR methods to measure the relative efficiency and Profit ratios of private sector firms, Best-practice analyses, using DEA, have been completed to date for several Fortune 500 companies.

Robert M. Thrall, since changing to emeritus status at Rice University at the end of 1983, has spent a year as program director at NSF and has restricted his research to DEA. Over half of his DEA publications are co-authored with various teams of collaborators which frequently include at least one specialist in the application area being analyzed.

Vivian G. Valdmanis received her Ph.D. in 1986 from Vanderbilt University in Policy Development with a focus in health economics. In 1987, Dr. Valdmanis was a NCHSR post-doctoral fellow at the University of Michigan. She has been a health researcher in Washington, DC, taught at Tulane University, and is currently a faculty member at the University of Oklahoma. Her area of research include hospital economics and productivity.

Lawrence C. Walters received his Ph.D. in public policy analysis and management from the University of Pennsylvania in 1987. He has coauthored several studies extending DEA applications in transportation, education finance, property tax assessment and higher education, as well as studies of returns to scale and graphical presentations of DEA results. He is currently Associate Professor of Public Management at Brigham Young University.

Lisa L. Wood holds an M.A. and Ph.D. in Public Policy and Management from the Wharton School of the University of Pennsylvania and is Director of the Market Assessment and Forecasting program at Research Triangle Institute. Dr. Wood has led numerous market assessment studies and several projects to examine consumer preferences and decision-making behavior. She currently manages a multiyear project to develop Market TREK, a PC based software system for forecasting market penetration of new technologies, products, and services. She has published articles in *Resources and Energy Economics*, *The Journal of Forecasting*, *Interfaces*, *Defense Economics*, and *Public Choice*, as well as papers in several conference proceedings.

Kimberly D. Zieschang has been an Economist in the Statistics Department of the International Monetary Fund since October 1992. Prior to that he was Chief of the Division of Price and Index Number Research, Bureau of Labor Statistics. He completed his Ph.D. in Economics in 1978 from the University of North Carolina under the direction of C. A. Knox Lovell. He has published articles on efficiency measurement, econometrics, survey statistics, index numbers, banking services, and tax policy.

Professor Agha Iqbal Ali
University of Massachusetts at
Amherst
Department of General Business
and Finance
School of Management
Amherst, MA 01003
(413) 545-5622

Mr. Peter C. Anselmo
The University of Texas at Austin
CBA 4.202
Austin, TX 78712
(512) 471-3676

Professor Rajiv D. Banker
Accounting and Information
Systems
Carlson School of Management
University of Minnesota
Minneapolis, MN 55455

Professor Patricia Byrnes
School of Public Policy and
Management
Ohio State University
1755 College Road
202 Hagerty Hall
Columbus, OH 43210-1399
(614) 292-8696

Dr. Abraham Charnes
Center for Cybernetic Studies
University of Texas at Austin
CBA 5.202
Austin, TX 78712-1177
(512) 471-1821

Mr. Wen-Chyuan Chiang
University of Texas at Austin
Management Department
1636K West 6th Street
Austin, TX 78703
(512) 471-1670

Professor Jon A. Chilingerian
Brandeis University
Post Office Box 9110
Waltham, MA 02254-9110
(617) 736-3828

Professor Wade D. Cook
Faculty of Administrative Studies
York University
4700 Keele Street
North York, Ontario
Canada M3J 1P3
(416) 736-5074

Professor William W. Cooper
University of Texas at Austin
Graduate School of Business
Management, CBA 4.202
Austin, TX 78712-1170
(512) 471-1822

Professor Jay G. Cooprider
University of Texas at Austin
MSIS, CBA 5.202
Austin, TX 78712
(512) 471-7858

Professor Chauncey (Marc)
DePree, Jr.
University of Southern Mississippi
2108 Sunset Drive
Hattiesburg, MS 39402
(601) 266-4644

Professor Anand Desai
School of Public Policy and
Management
Ohio State University
1775 College Road
Columbus, OH 43210-1399
(614) 292-0826

Ms. May T. Dobal
University of Texas at Austin
1700 Red River
Austin, TX 78701-1499
(512) 471-7311 or (512) 471-3676

Professor Philip D. Drake
Accounting
Southern Methodist University
Post Office Box 333
Dallas, TX 75275
(214) 692-2186

Mr. Tony Eff
University of Texas at Austin
ECB 1.116
Austin, TX 78712
(512) 471-3211

Professor Joyce J. Elam
Florida International University
Decision Sciences & Information
Systems
University Park
Miami, FL 33199
(305) 348-2719

Professor Gary D. Ferrier
Univ. of Arkansas
Department of Economics
402 BADM
Fayetteville, AR 72701-1201
501-575-6223

Professor James A. Fitzsimmons
University of Texas at Austin
Department of Management
Austin, TX 78712
(512) 471-9453

Professor Finn Forsund
University of Oslo
Box 1095, 0317 Blindern
Oslo, Norway
47-2-455127

Ms. Vandana M. Gadh
School of Urban and Public Affairs
Carnegie Mellon University
Pittsburgh, PA 15213-3890
(412) 268-8766

Professor Armando Gallegos
ESAN (Escuela de Administracion
de Negocios para Graduados)
Lima, Peru

Mr. Paul Garner
Manager, Performance Audit
Division
Texas State Auditor's Office
Post Office Box 12067
Austin, TX 78711-2067
(512) 479-4765

Mr. James H. Gerberman
University of Texas at Austin
1104 Brushy Bend Drive
Austin, TX 78681
(512) 929-2016

Dr. Boaz Golany
Senior Lecturer
Technion-Israel Institute of
Technology
Faculty of Industrial Engineering
and Management
Technion City–Haifa 32000
Israel
972-4-294512

Mr. Michael W. Gray
University of Texas at Austin
Department of Accounting
2913 Patriot Avenue
Lago Vista, TX 78645
(512) 267-1625

Dr. Betsy Greenberg
University of Texas at Austin
CBA 5.202
Austin, TX 78712
(512) 471-1756

Professor Steven T. Hackman
School of ISYE
Georgia Institute of Technology
Industrial and Systems Engineering
Atlanta, GA 30332-0205
(404) 894-2327

Dr. Kingsley E. Haynes
Institute of Public Policy
George Mason University
4400 University Drive
Fairfax, VA 22030
(703) 993-2280

Professor Lennart Hjalmarsson
Department of Economics
Gothenburg School of Economics
Gothenburg University
Viktoriagatan 30
S-411 25 Goteborg, Sweden
(46-31) 631345

Professor Charles Holt
University of Texas at Austin
Management
Graduate School of Business
Austin, TX 78712
(512) 471-9450

Professor Laura Y. Huang
Department of Public Health
Chang Gung Medical School
259 Wen-Hwa 1st Rd
Kwei-Schan, Tao-Yuan
Taiwan

Professor George P. Huber
Department of Management, CBA
4.202
The University of Texas at Austin
Austin, TX 78712
(512) 471-9604

Professor David L. Huff
University of Texas at Austin
CBA 7.242
Austin, TX 78712
(512) 471-1128

Mr. Jeff Inman
The University of Texas at Austin
Marketing Department CBA 7.202
Austin, TX 78712
(512) 471-1128

Professor David Jesson
Education Research Centre
University of Sheffield
Sheffield SIO 2TN
United Kingdom
(44-742) 768555 (X4724)

Mr. Charles M. Johnson
Marketing Department
University of Texas at Austin
Austin, TX 78712
(512) 471-1128

Dr. George Kozmetsky
Director, IC2 Institute
2815 San Gabriel
Austin, TX 78705
(512) 478-4081

Professor Kenneth C. Land
Department of Sociology
Duke University
Durham, NC 27706
(919) 684-4141

Mr. Reiner Lang
Center for Business Decision
Analysis
University of Texas at Austin
2103 Nueces
Austin, TX 78705
(512) 471-5183

Professor Arie Y. Lewin
Duke University
Fuqua School of Business
Durham, NC 27706
(919) 684-5383

Professor Shanling Li
Faculty of Management
McGill University
1001 Sherbrooke Street West
Montreal, PQ
Canada H3A 1G5

Professor Bjorn Lindgren
The Swedish Institute for Health
Economics
Post Office Box 1207
Lund, SWEDEN 221 05
46 46 11 70 75

Professor Knox Lovell
Economics Department
University of Georgia
Athens, GA 30602
(706) 542-3689

Mr. Cheng H. Mah
EDP Auditor
Texas State Auditor's Office
Post Office Box 12067
Austin, TX 78711-2067
(512) 479-4871

Mark J. Mazur
Executive Office of the President
Council of Economic Advisors
Washington, DC 20500
202-395-5147

Professor Richard C. Morey
Tulane University
Department of Health Systems
Mgt
School of Public Health
New Orleans, LA 70122

Professor Paul E. Nelson
Purdue University
Krannert School of Management
West Lafayette, IN 47907
(317) 494-4404

Alfred L. Norman
University of Texas at Austin
Department of Economics
ECB 3.148
Austin, TX 78712
(512) 471-3211

Mr. Ole B. Olesen
Research Scholar
Department of Management
Odense University
5230 Odense M
Denmark

Professor Niels Christian Petersen
Department of Management
Odense University
Campusvej 55, 5230 Odense M
Denmark
(66) 158600-3267

Dr. Fred Y. Phillips
Research Programs Director
IC2 Institute
2815 San Gabriel
Austin TX 78705
(512) 478-4081

Professor Edwardo L. Rhodes
Indiana University
School of Public and Environmental
Affairs
Room 260
Bloomington, IN 47405
(812) 855-3107

Mr. Brad Richards
Booz-Allen & Hamilton
4330 East-West Highway
Bethesda, MD 20814
(301) 951-2973

Professor Yaakov Roll
Technion-Israel Institute of
Technology
Faculty of Industrial Engineering
and Management
Technion City–Haifa 32000
Israel
(416) 736-5074

Mr. Pontus Roos
The Swedish Institute for Health
Economics
Post Office Box 1207
Lund, Sweden 221 05
46 46 11 70 75

Dr. John Rousseau
Senior Research Scientist
Information Services Research
MRCA Information Services
3001 N. Lamar Blvd. #107
Austin, TX 78705
(512) 478-4588

Professor R. Robert Russell
Graduate School of Management
University of California Riverside
Riverside, CA 92521
(714) 787-4325

Professor Ronald Salazar
Management
University of Houston
College of Business Administration
Houston, TX 77004-6283
(713) 749-6718

Mr. Robert W. Samohyl
Visiting Professor
University of Texas at Austin
ECB 2.134C
Austin, TX 78712
(512) 471-3211

Professor Lawrence Seiford
University of Massachusetts
Industrial Engineering and Opera-
tions Research
Amherst, MA 01003
(413) 545-1658
Seiford @ ECS. UMASS. edn

Professor H. David Sherman
Northeastern University
College of Business Administration
404 Hayden Hall
Boston, MA 02115
(617) 437-4640

Professor Robin C. Sickles
Economics
Rice University
6100 South Main
Post Office Box 1892
Houston, TX 77251
(713) 527-8101

Raymond W. Smilor
Vice President
Center for Entrepreneurial
Leadership
Ewing Marion Kauffman
Foundation
4900 Oak
Kansas City, MO 64112-2776
(816) 932-1094

Professor J. Reed Smith
Department of Accounting
CBA 4M.202
The University of Texas at Austin
Austin, TX 78712-1172
(512) 471-5215

Professor Vernon L. Smith
Regents' Professor of Economics
Economic Science Laboratory
University of Arizona
Tucson, AZ 85721
(602) 621-4747

Professor William Spelman
LBJ School of Public Affairs
Drawer Y, University Station
Austin, TX 78713-7450
(512) 471-8953

Professor Rajendra K. Srivastava
Marketing
The University of Texas at Austin
CAB 7.202
Austin, TX 78712
(512) 471-1128

Professor Sara Stokes
The University of Texas at Austin
CBA 5.202
Austin, TX 78712
(512) 471-5216

Professor Chandler Stolp
LBJ School of Public Affairs
University of Texas at Austin
Austin, TX 78713
(512) 471-8954

Professor Toshiyuki Sueyoshi
The Ohio State University
School of Public Administration
1775 College Road
Columbus, OH 43210
(614) 292-8226

Mr. David Sullivan
University of Texas at Austin
Management Science
1408 W. 51st
Austin, TX 78756
(512) 451-9354

Professor Edward L. Summers
University of Texas at Austin
Department of Accounting, CBA
4M.202
Austin, TX 78712-1172
(512) 471-5330

Professor Dee Bruce Sun
Department of Information
Systems
School of Business Administration
California State University
Long Beach, CA 90840

Dr. Emmanuel Thanassoulis
Lecturer
University of Warwick
Business School
Coventry, United Kingdom
CV47AL
(0203) 523523 (x2145)

Professor Russell Thompson
University of Houston
Decision and Information Sciences
CBA
4800 Calhoun Road
Houston, TX 77004
(713) 749-6767 or 528-3158

Dr. Sten Thore
IC2 Institute
2815 San Gabriel
Austin, TX 78705
(512) 478-4081

Dr. Robert M. Thrall
12003 Pebble Hill Drive
Houston, TX 77024
(713) 464-9165

Mr. Noam Tractinsky
University of Texas at Austin
1648-Q West 6th Street
Austin, TX 78703
(713) 471-3322

Professor Konstantinos P. Triantis
Virginia Polytechnic Institute and
State University
Northern Virginia Graduate
Center
Department of IEOR
2990 Telestar Court
Falls Church, VA 22042
(703) 698-6086 or 6019

Professor Henry G. Tulkens
CORE–Universite Catholique de
Louvain
34 Voie du Roman Pays
1348 Louvain-La-Neuve, Belgium
(3210) 47 43 21 or 47 43 32

Professor Leslie D. Turner
Department of Accounting
BEP 462
Northern Kentucky University
Highland Heights, KY 41076
(606) 572-6381

Professor Vivian Valdmanis
Dept of Health Systems
Management
School of Public Health
Univ. of Oklahoma
Oklahoma City, OK 73190

Professor Lawrence Walters
Brigham Young University
Department of Political Science
760 TNRB
Provo, UT 84602
(801) 378-7495

Dr. Don Warren
Director, Technical Resources
Section
Texas Department of Human
Services
Mail Code 232-E1
P.O. Box 149030
Austin, TX 78714-9030
(512) 450-3679

Ms. Harriet Warren
Systems Analyst
Department of Veteran Affairs
Post Office Box 426
Buda, TX 78610
(512) 482-7417

Dr. Lisa L. Wood
Center for Economics Research
Research Triangle Institute
Research Triangle Park, NC 27709

Mr. Martin Wright
The University of Texas at Austin
9810 Oak Hollow Drive
Austin, TX 78758
(512) 471-3322

Professor Suthathip Yaisawarng
Department of Economics
Union College
Schenectady, NY 12308-2365
(518) 370-6228

Dr. Kimberly D. Zieschang
Associate Commissioner
Bureau of Labor Statistics
2 Massachusetts Ave, NE
Washington, DC 20212-0001
(202) 623-6300

REFERENCES

Annual Market Development Report, World Airline Fleets. *Air Transport World*, May issues (1980–1986).

Aaron, H., Schwartz, W. *The Painful Prescription: Rationing Hospital Care.* Washington, D.C.: The Brookings Institute (1984).

Afriat, S. Efficiency Estimation of Production Functions. *International Economic Review* (1972), 13:568–598.

Ahn, T., Charnes, A., Cooper, W. W. A Note on the Efficiency Characterizations Obtained in Different DEA Models. *Socio-Economic Planning Sciences* (1989), 22(6):253–257.

Ahn, T., Charnes, A., Cooper, W. W. Some Statistical and DEA Evaluations of Relative Efficiencies of Public and Private Institutions of Higher Learning. *Socio-Economic Planning Sciences* (1988), 22(6):259–269.

Ahn, T., Seiford, L. M. Sensitivity of DEA to Models and Variable Sets in a Hypothesis Test Setting: The Efficiency of University Operations. In Y. Ijiri (ed.), *Creative and Innovative Approaches to the Science of Management.* New York: Quorum Books (1993).

Aigner, D. J., Chu, S. F. On Estimating the Industry Production Function. *American Economic Review* (1968), 58:826–839.

Aigner, D. J., Lovell, C. A. K., Schmidt, P. Formulation and Estimation of Stochastic Frontier Production Models. *Journals of Econometrics* (1977), 6: 21–37.

Alchian, A. A. Some Economics of Property Rights. *Il Politico* (1965), 30:816–829.

Ali, A. I. Computational Aspects of DEA. Chapter 4, this book.

Ali, A. I. Streamlined Computation for Data Envelopment Analysis. *European Journal of Operational Research* (1992), 64(1).

Ali, A. I. Data Envelopment Analysis: Computational Issues. *Computers, Environment, and Urban Systems* (1990), 14:157–165.

Ali, A. I., Cook, W. D., Seiford, L. M. Strict vs. Weak Ordinal Relations For Multipliers in Data Envelopment Analysis. *Management Science* (1991), 37(6):733–738.

Ali, A. I., Seiford, L. M. Translation Invariance in Data Envelopment Analysis. *Operations Research Letters* (1990), 9(5):403–405.

Ali, A. I., Seiford, L. M. Computational Accuracy and Infinitesimals in Data Envelopment Analysis. INFOR (1993), 31(4):290–297.

Amato, L. Firm Size, Leading Firms and Mobility. *Studies in Economic Analysis* (1984), 8:5–24.

Amel, D. F., Rhoades, S. A. Strategic Groups in Banking. *Review of Economics and Statistics* (1988), 7:685–689.

Anderson, D. R., Sweeney, D. J., Williams, T. A. *An Introduction to Management Science: Quantitative Approaches to Decision Making*, 6th ed. St. Paul, MN: West Publishing Company (1991).

Andersen, P., Petersen, N. C. A Procedure for Ranking Efficient Units in Data Envelopment Analysis. Management Science (1993), 39:1261–1264.

Archibald, R. On the Theory of Industrial Price Measurement: Output Price Indexes. *Annals of Economic and Social Measurement* (1977), 6:57–72.

Ashby, W. R. Variety, Constraint, and the Law of Requisite Variety. In Walter Buckley (ed.), *Modern Systems Research for Behavioral Scientists*. Chicago: Aldine (1969), 129–136.

Ashton, P. K., Dalton, J. A. Strategic Behavior and Performance in the Semiconductor Industry. *Texas Business Review* (1983), 57:57–61.

Bailey, E. E., Graham, D. R., Kaplan, D. P. *Deregulating the Airlines: An Economic Analysis*. Cambridge, MA: MIT Press (1985).

Bailey, E. E., Williams, J. R. Sources of Economic Rent in the Deregulated Airline Industry. *Journal of Law and Economics* (1988), 31:173–198.

Baird, I. S., Surdharshan, D., Thomas, H. Addressing Temporal Change in Strategic Groups Analysis: A Three-Mode Factor Analysis Approach. *Journal of Management* (1988), 14:425–439.

Banker, R. D. Estimating Most Productive Scale Size Using Data Envelopment Analysis. *European Journal of Operational Research* (1984), 17(1):35–44.

Banker, R. D. Maximum Likelihood, Consistency and Data Envelopment Analysis: A Statistical Foundation. *Management Science* (1993).

Banker, R. D. Stochastic Data Envelopment Analysis. Working Paper (1990).

Banker, R. D., Charnes, A., Cooper, W. W. Some Models for Estimating Technical and Scale Inefficiencies in Data Envelopment Analysis. *Management Science* (1984), 30(9):1078–1092.

Banker, R. D., Charnes, A., Cooper, W. W., Maindiratta, A. A Comparison of DEA and Translog Estimates of Production Frontiers Using Simulated Observations From a Known Technology. In A. Dogramaci, R. Färe (eds.), *Applications of Modern Production Theory: Efficiency and Productivity*. Boston: Kluwer Academic Publishers (1988).

Banker, R. D., Charnes, A., Cooper, W. W., Schinnar, A. A Bi-extremal Principle for Frontier Estimation and Efficiency Evaluation. *Management Science* (1981), 27(12):1370–1382.

Banker, R. D., Charnes, A., Cooper, W. W., Swarts, J., Thomas, D. An Introduction to Data Envelopment Analysis with Some of its Models and Their Uses. *Research in Governmental and Nonprofit Accounting* (1989), 5:125–163.

Banker, R. D., Conrad, R., Strauss, R. A Comparative Application of Data Envelopment Analysis and Translog Methods: An Illustrative Study of Hospital Production. *Management Science* (1986), 32(1):30–44.

Banker, R. D., Datar, S. M., Kemerer, C. F. A Model to Evaluate Variables Impacting the Productivity of Software Maintenance Projects. *Management Science* (1991), 37(1):1–18.

Banker, R. D., Johnston, H. H. Cost Driver Analysis in the Service Sector: An Empirical Study of the U.S. Airlines. Accounting Review (1993):576–606.

Banker, R. D., Johnston, H. H. Evaluating the Impacts of Operating Strategies on Efficiency in the U.S. Airline Industry. Chapter 6, this book.

Banker, R. D., Maindiratta, A. Nonparametric Analysis of Technical and Alloctive Efficiencies in Production. *Econometrica* (1988), 56(6):1315–1332.

Banker, R. D., Maindiratta, A. Piecewise Loglinear Estimation of Efficient Production Surfaces. *Management Science* (1986), 32(1):126–135.

Banker, R. D., Maindiratta, A. Erratum to: Piecewise Loglinear Estimation of Efficient Production Surfaces. *Management Science* (1986), 32(3): 385.

Banker, R. D., Morey, R. Efficiency Analysis for Exogenously Fixed Inputs and Outputs. *Operations Research* (1986a), 34(4):513–521.

Banker, R. D., Morey, R. The Use of Categorical Variables in Data Envelopment Analysis. *Management Science* (1986b), 32(12):1613–1627.

Banker, R. D., Thrall, R. Estimation of Returns to Scale Using Data Envelopment Analysis. European Journal of Operations Research (1992), 21(1).

Barney, J., Hoskisson, R. Strategic Groups: Untested Assertions and Research Proposals. *Managerial and Decision Economics* (forthcoming).

Bauer, P. W. Recent Developments in the Econometric Estimation of Frontiers. *Journal of Econometrics* (1990), 46(1/2):39–56.

Belsey, D. A., Kuh, E., Welsch, R. S. *Regression Diagnostics*. New York: John Wiley and Sons (1980).

Berg, S. A., Førsund, F. R., Jansen, E. S. Malmquist Indices of Productivity Growth During the Deregulation of Norwegian Banking 1980–89. *Scandinavian Journal of Economics* (1992), 94: Supplement, 211–228.

Berg. S. A., Førsund, F. R., Jansen, E. S. Technical Efficiency of Norwegian Banks: The Non-parametric Approach to Efficiency Measurement. *Journal of Productivity Analysis* (1991), 2:127–142.

Bessent, A., Bessent, W., Kennington, J., Regan, B. An Application of Mathematical Programming to Assess Productivity in the Houston Independent School District. *Management Science* (1982), 28(12):1355–1367.

Boardman, A. E., Vining, A. R. Ownership and Performance in Competitive Environments: A Comparison of the Performance of Private, Mixed, and State-Owned Enterprises. *Journal of Law and Economics* (1989), 32:1–33.

Boles, J. N. Efficiency Squared—Efficient Computation of Efficiency Indexes. *Western Farm Economic Association Proceedings* (1966), 137–142.

Bowen, J. T. Development of a Taxonomy of Services to Gain Strategic Marketing Insight. College Station, TX: unpublished doctoral dissertation, Texas A&M University.

Bowlin, W. F., Charnes, A., Cooper, W. W., Sherman, H. D. Data Envelopment Analysis and Regression Approaches to Efficiency Estimation and Evaluation. *Annals of Operations Research* (1985), 2:113–138.

Breusch, T. S., Pagan, A. R. A Simple Test for Heteroscedasticity and Random Coefficient Variation. *Econometrica* (1979), 47:1287–1294.

Brewster, A., Jacobs, C., Bradbury, R. Classifying Severity of Illness by Using Clinical Findings. *Health Care Financing Review*, 1984 Supplement, HCFA Pub. No. 03194, Office of Research and Demonstrations, Health Care Financing Adminstration. Washington, D.C.: U.S. Government Printing Office (November 1984).

Brewster, A. C., et al. Medis Groups: A Clinically Based Approach to Classifying Hospital Patients at Admission. *Inquiry* (1985), 22:377–387.

Breyer, F. The Specification of a Hospital Cost Function: A Comment on the Recent Literature. *Journal of Health Economics* (1987), 6(2):147–157.

Brill, E. The Use of Optimization Models in Public-Sector-Planning. *Management Science* (1979), 25:413–422.

Brill, E., Chang, S., Hopkins, L. Modeling to Generate Alternatives: The HSJ Approach and an Illustration Using a Problem in Land Use Planning. *Management Science* (1982), 28:221–235.

Bureau of Labor Statistics. *BLS Handbook of Methods*, Bulletin 2285. Washington, D.C.: U.S. Government Printing Office (1988).

Byrnes, P., Färe, R., Grosskopf, S. Measuring Productive Efficiency: An Application to Illinois Strip Mines. *Management Science* (1984), 30(6):671–681.

Byrnes, P., Färe, R., Grosskopf, S., Lovell, C. A. K. The Effect of Unions on Productivity: U.S. Surface Mining of Coal. *Management Science* (1988), 34:1037–1053.

Byrnes, P., Grosskopf, S., Hayes, K. Efficiency and Ownership: Further Evidence. *Review of Economic and Statistics* (1986), 68:337–341.

Byrnes, P., Valdmanis, V. Variable Cost Frontiers: An Investigation of Labor Costs in Hospitals. In T. R. Gulledge, Jr., L. A. Litteral (eds.), *Cost Analysis Applications of Economics and Operations Research*. Berlin: Springer Verlag (1989).

Calori, R., Effective Strategies in Emerging Industries. *Long Range Planning* (1985), 18:55–61.

Cameron, B. J. Higher Education Efficiency Measurement Using DEA. Working Paper, Darling Downs Institute of Advanced Education, Toowoomba, Queensland, Australia (May 1989).

Campbell, D. M. Why Do Physicians In Neonatal Care Units Differ In Their Admission Threshold? Social Science and Medicine (1984), 18:365-374.

Catron, B. Price Measurement for Computer Hardware: A Demonstration of Quality Adjustment Techniques. Division of Producer Prices and Price Indexes. Washington, D.C.: Bureau of Labor Statistics (April 1988).

Caves, D. W., Christensen, L. R., Diewert, W. E. The Economic Theory of Index Numbers and the Measurement of Input, Output, and Productivity. Econometrica (1982a), 50:1393-1414.

Caves, D. W., Christensen, L. R., Diewert, W. E. Multilateral Comparisons of Output, Input, and Productivity Using Superlative Index Numbers. Economic Journal (1982b), 92:73-86.

Caves, D. W., Christensen, L. R., Swanson, J. A. Productivity Growth, Scale Economies, and Capacity Utilization in U.S. Railroads, 1955-1974. American Economic Review (1981), 71:994-1002.

Caves, D. W., Christensen, L. R., Tretheway, M. W. Economies of Density versus Economies of Scale: Why Trunk and Local Service Airline Costs Differ. Rand Journal of Economics (1984), 15(4):471-489.

Caves, R. E., Petersen, B. C. Cooperatives Tax Advantages: Growth, Retained Earnings, and Equity Rotation. American Journal of Agricultural Economics (1986), 68(2):207-213.

Caves, R. J. Economic Analysis and the Quest For Competitive Advantage. American Economic Review (1984), 74:127-132.

Charnes, A., Clark, T., Cooper, W. W., Golany, B. A Developmental Study of Data Envelopment Analysis in Measuring the Efficiency of Maintenance Units in the U.S. Air Force. In R. Thompson and R. M. Thrall (eds.), Annals of Operation Research (1985), 2:95-112.

Charnes, A., Cooper, W. W. Preface to Topics in Data Envelopment Analysis. Annals of Operations Research (1985), 2:59-94.

Charnes, A, Cooper, W. W. The Non-Archimedean CCR Ratio for Efficiency Analysis: A Rejoinder to Boyd and Färe. European Journal of Operational Research (1984), 15(3):333-334.

Charnes, A., Cooper, W. W. Managerial Economics: Past, Present and Future. Journal of Enterprise Management (1978), 1(1):5-23.

Charnes, A., Cooper, W. W. Structural Sensitivity Analysis in Linear Programming and an Exact Product Form Left Inverse. Naval Research Logistic Quarterly (1968), 15:517-522.

Charnes, A., Cooper, W. W. Programming with Linear Fractional Functionals. Naval Research Logistics Quarterly (1962), 9(3/4):181-185.

Charnes, A., Cooper, W. W. Management Models and Industrial Applications of Linear Programming. Management Science (1957), 4(1):38-91.

Charnes, A., Cooper, W. W., Divine, D., Ruefli, T. W., Thomas, D. Comparisons of DEA and Existing Ratio and Regression Systems for Effecting

Efficiency Evaluations of Regulated Electric Cooperatives in Texas. *Research in Governmental and Nonprofit Accounting* (1989), 5:187–210.

Charnes, A., Cooper, W. W., Golany, B., Halek, R., Klopp, G., Schmitz, E., Thomas, D. Two-Phase Data Envelopment Analysis Approaches to Policy Evaluation and Management of Army Recruiting Activities: Tradeoffs Between Joint Services and Army Advertising. Research Report CCS #532, Center for Cybernetic Studies, University of Texas at Austin, Austin, TX (March 1986).

Charnes, A., Cooper, W. W., Golany, B., Seiford, L., Stutz, J. Foundations of Data Envelopment Analysis for Pareto-Koopmans Efficient Empirical Production Functions. *Journal of Econometrics (Netherlands)* (1985). 30(1/2):91–107.

Charnes, A., Cooper, W. W., Golany, B., Seiford, L., Stutz, J. A Dimensionless Efficiency Measure for Departures from Pareto Optimality. Research Report CCS 480, Center for Cybernetic Studies, The University of Texas at Austin, Austin, TX (February 1984).

Charnes, A., Cooper, W. W., Li, Shanling. Using DEA to Evaluate the Efficiency of Economic Performance by Chinese Cities. *Socio-Economic Planning Sciences* (1989), 23:325–344.

Charnes, A., Cooper, W. W., Learner, D. B., Phillips, F. Y., Golany, B., Eechambadi, N. Efficiency Analysis of Response Under Competition. Research Report CCS 469, Center for Cybernetic Studies, The University of Texas at Austin, Austin, TX (1984).

Charnes, A., Cooper, W. W., Lewin, A. Y., Morey, R. C., Rousseau, J. Sensitivity and Stability Analysis in DEA. *Annals of Operations Research* (1985), 2:139–156.

Charnes, A., Cooper, W. W., Rhodes, E. Evaluating Program and Managerial Efficiency: An Application of Data Envelopment Analysis to Program Follow Through. *Management Science* (1981), 27(6):668–697.

Charnes, A., Cooper, W. W., Rhodes, E. Short Communication: Measuring the Efficiency of Decision Making Units. *European Journal of Operational Research* (1979), 3(4):339.

Charnes, A., Cooper, W. W., Rhodes, E. Measuring the Efficiency of Decision Making Units. *European Journal of Operational Research* (1978), 2(6): 429–444.

Charnes, A., Cooper, W. W., Rhodes, E. Management Science Relations for Evaluation and Management Accountability. *Journal of Enterprise Management 2* (1980):143–162.

Charnes, A., Cooper, W. W., Rousseau, J., Semple, J. Data Envelopment Analysis and Axiomatic Nations of Efficiency and Reference Sets. Research Report CCS 558, Center for Cybernetic Studies, The University of Texas at Austin, Austiny TX (January 1987).

Charnes, A., Cooper, W. W., Seiford, L., Stutz, J. Invariant Multiplicative Efficiency and Piecewise Cobb–Douglas Envelopments. *Operations Research Letters* (1983), 2(3):101–103.

Charnes, A., Cooper, W. W., Seiford, L., Stutz, J. A Multiplicative Model for Efficiency Analysis. *Socio-Economic Planning Sciences* (1982), 16(5):223–224.

Charnes, A., Cooper, W. W., Sun, D. B., Huang, Z. M. Polyhedral Cone-Ratio DEA Models With An Illustrative Application to Large Commercial Banks. *Journal Of Econometrics* (1990), 46:73–91.

Charnes, A., Cooper, W. W., Thrall, R. M. Classifying and Characterizing Efficiencies and Inefficiencies in Data Envelopment Analysis. *Operations Research Letters* (1986), 5(3):105–110.

Charnes, A., Cooper, W. W., Thrall, R. M. A Structure for Classifying and Characterizing Efficiencies and Inefficiencies in Data Envelopment Analysis. *Journal of Productivity Analysis* (1991), 2:197–237.

Charnes, A., Cooper, W. W., Wei, Q. L. A Semi-Infinite Multicriteria Programming Approach to Data Envelopment Analysis With Infinitely Many Decision-Making Units. Research Report CCS 551, Center for Cybernetic Studies, The University of Texas at Austin, Austin, TX (January 1987).

Charnes, A., Cooper, W. W., Wei, Q. L., Huang, Z. M. Cone Ratio Data Envelopment Analysis and Multi-Objective Programming. *International Journal of Systems Science* (1989), 20(7):1099–1118.

Charnes, A., Cooper, W. W., Zlobec, S. Efficiency Evaluations in Perturbed Data Envelopment Analysis. In J. Guddat (ed.), *Parametric Optimization and Related Topics II*. Berlin: Akademic-Verlag (1990).

Charnes, A., Haag, S., Jaska, P., Semple, J. Sensitivity of Efficiency Calculations in the Additive Model of Data Envelopment Analysis. *International Journal of Systems Science* (1992), 23(5):789–798.

Charnes, A., Neralic, L. Sensitivity Analysis of the Additive Model in Data Envelopment Analysis. *European Journal of Operations Research* (1990a), 48:332–341.

Charnes, A., Neralic, L. Sensitivity Analysis in Data Envelopment Analysis 1. *Glasnik Mathematicki* (1989a), 24(44):211–226.

Charnes, A., Neralic, L. Sensitivity Analysis in Data Envelopment Analysis 2. *Glasnik Mathematicki* (1989b), 24(44:2/3), 449–463.

Charnes, A., Neralic, L. Sensitivity Analysis of the Proportionate Change of Inputs or Outputs. In *Data Envelopment Analysis*, presented at IFORS '90, Athens, Greece (June 1990b).

Charnes, A., Zlobec, S. Stability of Efficiency Evaluations in Data Envelopment Analysis. *Zeitschrift für Operations Research* (1989), 33:167–179.

Childs, M. D., Hunter, D. Non Medical Factors Influencing Use of Diagnostic X-Ray By Physicians. *Medical Care* (July–August 1972).

Chilingerian, J. A. On Estimating the Decision-Making Efficiency of Temporary Firms: A Research Note of Data Envelopment Analysis. Working Paper #88-102, Heller School, Brandeis University, Waltham, MA (1988).

Chilingerian, J. A., Sherman, D. For-Profit vs. Non-Profit Hospitals: The Effect of the Profit Motive on the Management of Operations. *Financial Accountability and Management* (1987), 3(3).

Chilingerian, J. A., Sherman, D. Managing Physicians' Efficiency and Effectiveness in Providing Hospital Services. *Health Services Management Research* (1990), 3(1).

Christensen, L. R., Jorgenson, D. W. The Measurement of U.S. Real Capital Input, 1929–1967. *The Review of Income and Wealth* (1969), 14(4, Series 15):293–320.

Church, R., Huber, D. On Determining Many Close to Optimal Configurations for Single and Multiple Objective Location Problems. Research Series No. 34, Department of Civil Engineering, University of Tennessee, Knoxville (July 1979).

Church, R., Roberts, K. Generalized Coverage Models and Public Facility Location. *Papers of the Regional Science Association* (1983), 53:117–135.

Church, R., Current, J., Storbeck, J. A Bicriterion Maximal Covering Location Formulation which Considers the Satisfaction of Uncovered Demand. *Decision Sciences* (1991), 22:38–52.

Coate, M. B., Allen, R. F. Efficiency, Market Power and Profitability in American Manufacturing: Comment/Reply. *Southern Economic Journal* (1984), 51:274–281.

Coleman, J. S., et al. *Equality of Educational Opportunity*. Washington, D.C.: USGPO (1966).

Conklin, J. E., Lieberman, J. V., Barnes, C., Louis, D. Z. Disease Staging: Implications for Hospital Reimbursement and Management. *Health Care Financing Review* (November 1984, annual supplement).

Cook, W., Kazakov, A., Roll, Y., Seiford, L. A Data Analysis Approach to Measuring Efficiency: Case Analysis of Highway Maintenance Patrols. *Journal of Socio Economics* (1991), 20(1):83–104.

Cook, W., Roll, Y., Kazakov, A. Measurement of the Relative Efficiency of Highway Maintenance Patrols in Ontario. Report #ECN-88-01, Ministry of Transportation, Ontario, Canada (1988).

Cook, W., Roll, Y., Kazakov, K: Measurement of the Relative Efficiency of Highway Maintenance Patrols in Ontario, Phase II: Full Model Design. Report #2311-9088-260, Ministry of Transportation, Ontario, Canada (1988).

Cool, K. Strategic Group Formation and Strategic Group Shifts. A Longitudinal-Analysis of the U.S. Pharmaceutical Industry 1963–1982. West Lafayette, IN: unpublished doctoral dissertation, Purdue University (1985).

Cool, K., Schendel, D. Performance Differences Among Strategic Group Members. *Strategic Management Journal* (1988), 9:207–223.

Cool, K., Schendel, D. Strategic Group Formation and Performance: The Case of the U.S. Pharmaceutical Industry 1963–1982. *Management Science* (1987), 33:1102–1124.

Cowing, T., Holtman, A. Multi-product Short-Run Hospital Cost Functions: Empirical Evidence and Policy Implications from Cross-Sectional Data. *Southern Economic Journal* (1983), 49:637–653.

Cowing, T., Reifschneider, D., Stevenson, R. E. A Comparison of Alternative Frontier Cost Function Specifications. In A. Dogramaci (ed.), *Development in Econometric Analyses of Productivity*. Boston, MA: Kluwer-Nijhoff (1982).

Cromwell, J. Hospital Productivity Trends in Short-Term General Non-Teaching

Hospitals. *Inquiry* (1974), 11:181–186.

Cyert, R. M., March, J. G. *A Behavorial Theory of the Firm*. Englewood Cliffs, NJ: Prentice-Hall, (1963).

Day, D., Lewin, A. Y., Salazar, R., Li, H. Strategic Leaders in the U.S. Brewing Industry: A Longitudinal Analysis of Outliers. Chapter 11, this book.

DeAlessi, L. The Economics of Property Rights: A Review of the Evidence. In R. O. Serbe, Jr. (ed.), Research in Law and Economics, Vol. 2. Greenwich, CT: JAI Press (1980), 1–47.

De Bondt, R., Sleuwaegen, L., Veugelers, R. Innovative Strategic Groups in Multinational Industries. *European Economic Review* (1988), 32:905–925.

Debreu, G. The Coeficient of Resource Utilization. Econometrica (1951), 19: 273–292.

Dess, G. G., Davis, P. S., Porter's (1980) Generic Strategies as Determinants of Strategic Group Membership and Organizational Performance. *Academy of Management Journal* (1984), 27:467–488.

Deprins, D., Simar, L., Tulkens, H. Measuring Labor-Efficiency in Post Offices. In M. Marchand, P. Pestieau, H. Tulkens (eds.), *The Performance of Public Enterprises. Concept and Measurement*. Amsterdam: North-Holland (1984), 243–267.

Desai, A., Extensions to the Measurement of Relative Efficiency with an Application to Educational Productivity. Philadelphia, PA: unpublished Ph.D. dissertation, Department of Public Policy and Management, Wharton School, University of Pennsylvania.

Desai, A., Storbeck, J. A Data Envelopment Analysis for Spatial Efficiency. *Computers, Environment and Urban Systems* (1990), 14:145–156.

Diewert, W. E. Fisher Ideal Output, Input, and Productivity Indexes Revisited. *Journal of Productivity Analysis* (1992), 3(3):211–248.

Diewert, W. E. Exact and Superlative Index Numbers. *Journal of Econometrics* (1976), 4:115–145.

Drucker, P. Management and the World's Work. *Harvard Business Review*, (1988), 66(5):65–76.

Drucker, P. F. *The Practice of Management*. New York: Harper and Brothers (1954).

Dyson, R. G., Thanassoulis, E. Reducing Weight Flexibility in Data Envelopment Analysis. *Journal of the Operational Research Society* (1988), 39(6):563–576.

Eakin, B., Kniesner, T. Estimating a Non-Minimum Cost Function for Hospitals. *Sourthern Economic Journal* (1988), 54:583–597.

Efron, B. *The Jackknife, the Bootstrap, and Other Resampling Plans*. Philadelphia: SIAM (1982).

Eisenberg, J. *Doctors' Decisions and the Cost of Medical Care*. Ann Arbor: Health Administration Press (1986).

Eisenberg, J., Nicklin, D. Use of Diagnostic Services by Physicians in Community Practice. *Medical Care* (1981), 19(3):297–309.

Enthoven, A. *Health Plan*. Reading, MA: Addison-Wesley (1980).

Everitt, B. S. *The Analysis of Contingency Tables*. New York: John Wiley and Sons (1980).

Färe, R. *Fundamentals of Production Theory*. Berlin: Springer-Verlag (1988).

Färe, R., Fukuyama, H., Primont, D. Estimating Returns to Scale via Shepard's (Input) Distance Function. Working Paper, Southern Illinois University. Carbondale, IL (1988).

Färe, R., Grosskopf, S. A Nonparametric Cost Approach to Scale Efficiency. *The Scandinavian Journal of Economics* (1985), 87:594–604.

Färe, R., Grosskopf, S., Logan, J. The Relative Performance of Publicy-Owned and Privately-Owned Electric Utilities. *Journal of Public Economics* (1985), 26:89–106.

Färe, R., Grosskopf, S., Lovell, C. A. K. *The Measurement of Efficiency of Production*. Boston, MA: Kluwer-Nijhoff Publishing (1985).

Färe, R., Lyon, V. The Determinateness Test and Economic Price Indices. *Econometrica* (1981), 49:209–214.

Färe, R., Grosskopf, S., Lovell, C. A. K., Yaisawarng, S. Derivation of Shadow Prices for Undersirable Outputs: A Distance Function Approach. *Review of Economics and Statistics* (1993), 75:374–380.

Färe, R., Zieschang, K. D. Determining Output Shadow Prices for a Cost-Constrained Technology. *Journal of Economics (Zeitschrift für Nationalökonomie)* (1991), 54(2):143–155.

Farrell, M. J. The Measurement of Productive Efficiency. *Journal of the Royal Statistical Society, Series A* (1957), 120(3):253–290.

Ferrier, G., Lovell, C. A. K. Measuring Cost Efficience in Banking. *Journal of Econometrics* (1990), 46:229–245.

Fetter, R. B., Freeman, J. Diagnostic Related Groups: Product Line Management Within Hospitals. *Academy of Management Review* (1986), 11(1):41–54.

Fiegenbaum, A. *Dynamic Aspects of Strategic Groups and Competitive Strategy Concepts and Empirical Examination in the Insurance Industry*. Urbana, IL: unpublished doctoral dissertation, University of Illinois at Urbana-Champaing (1987).

Fiegenbaum, A., Surdharshan, D., Thomas, H. The Concept of Stable Strategic Time Periods in Strategic Group Research. *Managerial and Decision Economics* (1987), 8:139–148.

Fiegenbaum, A., McGee, J., Thomas, H. Exploring the Linkage Between Strategic Groups and Competitive Strategy. *International Studies of Management and Organization* (1988), 18:6–25.

Fishbane, M., Starfield, B. Child Health Care in The United States. *The New England Journal Of Medicine* (1981), 305(10).

Fisher, F. M., Shell, K. *The Economic Theory of Price Indices*. New York: Academic Press (1972).

Fisher, H., Rushton, G. Spatial Efficiency of Service Locations and the Regional Development Process. *Papers of the Regional Science Association* (1979), 42:83–97.

Fombrun, C. J., Zajac, E. J. Structural and Perceptual Influences on Intraindustry, Stratification. *Academy of Management Journal* (1987), 30:33–50.

Førsund, F. R. A Comparison of Parametric and Non-parametric Efficiency Measures: The Case of Norwegian Ferries. *Journal of Productivity Analysis* (1992), 3(1/2):25–43.

Førsund, F. R. Malmquist Indices of Productivity Growth: An Application To Norwegian Ferries. In H. O. Fried, A. K. Lovell, S. S. Schmidt (eds.), *The Measurement of Productive Efficiency: Techniques and Applications*. Oxford: Oxford University Press (1993):352–373.

Førsund, F. R., Hjalmarsson, L. *Analyses of Industrial Structure: A Putty-clay Approach*. The Industrial Institute for Economic and Social Research. Stockholm: Almquist and Wiksell International (1987).

Førsund, F. R., Hjalmarsson, L. Generalised Farrell Measures of Efficiency: An Application to Milk Processing in Swedish Dairies. *Economic Journal* (1979), 89:294–315.

Førsund, F. R., Hjalmarsson, L. On the Measurement of Productive Efficiency. *Swedish Journal of Economics* (1974), 76:141–154.

Franklin County Mental Health Board, *Community Mental Health Centers Location by Zip Code*. Memorandum (February 19, 1988).

Frazier, G. L., Howell, R. D. Business Definition and Performance. *Journal of Marketing* (1987), 47:59–67.

Fried, H. O., Lovell, C. A. K., Schmidt, S. (eds.). *The Measurement of Productive Efficiency: Techniques and Applications*. Oxford: Oxford University Press (1993).

Fried, H. O., Lovell, C. A. K., Vanden Eeckaut, P. Evaluating the Performance of U.S. Credit Unions. Journal of Banking and Finance (1993), 17:251–265.

Frisch, R. Necessary and Sufficient Conditions Regarding the Form of an Index Number Which Shall Meet Certain of Fisher's Tests. *Journal of the American Statistical Association* (1930), 25:297–406.

Garber, A., Fuchs, V. R., Silverman, J. F. Differences Between Faculty and Community Services in a University Hospital. *New England Journal of Medicine* (1984), 310:1231–1237.

Ghazanfar, A. Analysis of Competition in the Office Reprographics Industry in the U.K. London: unpublished doctoral dissertation, London Business School, University of London (1984).

Ghosh, A., McLafferty, S. *Location Strategies for Retail and Service Firms*. Lexington, MA: Lexington Books (1987).

GML Corporation. *Microcomputer Review*. Lexington, MA: Lexington Books (1988).

Golany, B., Learner, D. B., Phillips, F. Y., Rousseau, J. J. Efficiency and Effectiveness in Marketing Management. In B. H. Ahn (ed.), *Asian-Pacific Operations Research APORS '88*. Amsterdam: North Holland (1990a), 495–508.

Golany, B., Learner, D. B., Phillips, F. Y., Rousseau, J. J. Managing Service Productivity: The Data Envelopment Analysis Perspective. *Computers, Environment, and Urban Systems* (1990b), 14(2):89–102.

Golany, B., Phillips, F. Y., Rousseau, J. J. (1989) Models for Improved Effectiveness Based on DEA Efficiency Results. *IIE Transactions* (forthcoming).

Golany, B., Roll, Y. An Application Procedure for DEA. *Omega* (1989), 17(3): 237–250.

Golany, B., Roll, Y., Rybak, D. Measuring Efficiency of Power Plants in the Israeli Electric Corporation By Data Envelopment Analysis. IEEE Transactions on Engineering Management (1994), 41(3):1–14.

Gong, B., Sickles, R. C. Finite Sample Evidence on the Performance of Stochastic Frontiers and Data Envelopment Analysis Using Panel Data. *Journal of Econometrics* (1992), 51(1/2):259–284.

Good, D., Nadiri, M. I., Sickles, R. C. The Structure of Production, Technical Change and Efficiency in a Multiproduct Industry: An Application to the U.S. Airlines. Working Paper, Rice University, Houston, TX (1989).

Graham, D. R., Kaplan, D. P. Competition and the Airlines: An Evaluation of Deregulation. Staff Report, Office of Economic Analysis, U.S. Civil Aeronautics Board, Washington, D.C. (December 1982).

Greening, T. Diversification, Strategic Groups and the Structure–Conduct–Performance Relationship: A Synthesis. *Review of Economics and Statistics* (1980), 62:475–477.

Grosskopf, S. The Role of the Reference Technology in Measuring Productive Efficiency. *Economic Journal* (1986), 96:499–513.

Grosskopf, S., Valdmanis, V. Measuring Hospital Performance: A Non-parametric Approach. *Journal of Health Economics* (1987), 6:89–107.

Hansen, G. S. *Determinants of Firm Performance: An Integration of Economic and Organizational Factors*. Ann Arbor, MI: unpublished doctoral dissertation, The University of Michigan (1987).

Hanushek, E. The Impact of Differential Expenditures on School Performance. *Educational Research* (1989), 18(4):45–62.

Hanushek, E. The Economics of Schooling: Production and Efficiency in Public Schools. *Journal of Economic Literature* (1986), 24(3):1141–1171.

Harrigan, K. R. An Application of Clustering For Strategic Group Analysis. *Strategic Management Journal* (1985), 6:55–73.

Harris, J. E. The Internal Organization of Hospitals: Some Economic Implications. *The Bell Journal of Economics*, 467–482.

Hatten, K. J. *Strategic Models in the Brewing Industry*. West LaFayette, IN: unpublished doctoral dissertation, Purdue University (1984).

Hatten, K. J., Hatten, M. L. Strategic Groups, Asymmetrical Mobility Barriers and Contestability. *Strategic Management Journal* (1987), 8:329–342.

Hatten, K. J., Hatten, M. L. Some Empirical Insights for Strategic Marketers: The Case of Beer. In H. Thomas, D. Gardner (eds.), *Strategic Marketing and Management*. London: John Wiley & Sons (1985).

Hawes, J. M. An Analysis of The Marketing Strategies Employed By Food Retailers For Generic Brand Grocery Products. Fayetteville, AK: unpublished doctoral dissertation, University of Arkansas (1981).

Hawes, J. M., Crittenden, F. W. Taxonomy of Competitive Retailing Strategies. *Strategic Management Journal* (1984), 5:275–287.

Hayes, S. L. III, Spence, A. M., Marks, D. V. P. *Competition in The Investment Banking Industry*. Cambridge, MA: Harvard University Press (1983).

Heggestad, A., Rhoades, S. Multi-Market Interdependence and Local Market Competition in Banking. *Review of Economics and Statistics* (1978), 60:417–427.

Hergert, M. The Incidence and Implications of Strategic Grouping in U.S. Manufacturing Industries. Cambridge, MA: unpublished doctoral dissertation, Harvard University (1983).

Hicks, J. R. The Valuation of Social Income. *Economica* (1940), 7:105–124.

Hlatky, M. A., et al. Diagnostic Test Use in Different Practice Settings. *Archives of Internal Medicine* (1983), 143.

Hollas, D. R., Stansell, S. R. An Examination of the Effect of Ownership Form on Price Efficiency: Proprietary, Cooperative and Municipal Electric Utilities. *Southern Economic Journal* (1988), 55:336–350.

Hunt, M. S. Competition in the Major House Appliance Industry 1960–1970. Cambridge, MA: unpublished doctoral dissertation, Harvard University (1972).

International Data Corporation. *The Gray Sheet; Computer Industry Report* (1988), 23(21):5.

Jensen, M. C., Meckling, W. H. Rights and Production Functions: An Application to Labor-Managed Firms and Codetermination. *Journal of Business* (1979), 52:469–506.

Johnson, W. E. *Strategic Groups and Market Rivalry*. Columbia, SC: unpublished doctoral dissertation, University of South Carolina (1985).

Judge, G. G., Griffiths, W. E., Hill, R. C., Lutkepohl, H., Lee, T. *The Theory and Practice of Econometrics*, 2nd ed. New York: John Wiley and Sons (1985).

Kalirajan, K. P., Shand, R. T. Testing Causality Between Technical and Allocative Efficiencies. Working Paper No. 8816, Research School of Pacific Studies, The Australian National University, Canberra, ACT, Australia (1988).

Kamakura, W. A. A Note on The Use of Categorical Variables in Data Envelopment Analysis. *Management Science* (1988), 34(10):1273–1276.

Keithahn, C. F. The Brewing Industry. Staff Report of the Bureau of Economics, Federal Trade Commission. Washington, D.C.: U.S. Government Printing Office (1978).

Kennedy, P. Logarithmic Dependent Variables and Prediction Bias. *Oxford Bulletin of Economics and Statistics* (1983), 45:389–392.

Kim, S. J. Strategic Opportunities in the Property and Liability Insurance Industry: Relationship Among Strategy, Regulation, and Performance. Madison, WI: unpublished doctoral dissertation, The University of Wisconsin–Madison (1985).

Kimura, Y. Competitive Strategies and Strategic Groups in the Japanese Semiconductor Industry (Industrial Organizations, Advantages, Innovations, Joined Economic Activities Management). New York: unpublished doctoral dissertation, Graduate School of Business Administration, New York University (1986).

Kirby, M. G. Airline Economics of "Scale" and Australian Domestic Air Transport Policy. *Journal of Transport Economics and Policy* (September 1986), 339–352.

Kmenta, J., Gilbert, R. F. Estimation of Seemingly Unrelated Regressions with Autoregressive Disturbances. *Journal of the American Statistical Association* (1970), 65(329):186–197.

Knoke, D., Burke, P. J. *Log-Linear Models.* Sage University Paper Series on Quantitative Applications in the Social Sciences, series no. 07-001. Beverly Hills and London: Sage Publications (1990).

Kogut, B. Normative Observations on the International Value-Added Chain and Strategic Groups. *Journal of International Business Studies* (1984), 15:151–167.

Koopmans, T. C. Analysis of Production as an Efficient Combination of Activities. In T. C. Koopmans (ed.), Activity Analysis of Production and Allocation. New York, Wiley (1951).

Kumar, K. R. The Relationship Between Mixed Strategies and Strategic Groups. *Managerial and Decision Economics* (1987), 8:235–242.

Lahti, A. *Strategy and Performance of a Firm: An Empirical Investigation in the Knitwear Industry in Finland in 1969–1981.* Helsinki: unpublished doctoral dissertation, Helsinki School of Economics (1983).

Landstingsförbundet (The Federation of Swedish County Councils), Läkarförbundet (The Swedish Medical Association) and Socialstyrelsen (The Swedish National Board of Health and Welfare). *Läkares arbetstider och Tjänstor (Doctors Working Time and Situation).* Socialstyrelsen (The Swedish National Board of Health and Welfare) (different years).

Langemeier, L. N. *Annual Report: 1985, Management Information, Kansas Farm Management Associations.* Manhattan, KA: Department of Agriculture Economics, Coop. Ext. Service, Kansas State University (1985).

Lecraw, D. J. Diversification Strategy and Performance. *Journal of Industrial Economics* (1984), 33:179–198.

Leibenstein, H., Maital, S. Empirical Estimation and Partitioning of X-Ineffiency: A Data-Envelopment Approach. *American Economic Review* (1992), 82(2):428–433.

LeVay, C. Agricultural Co-operatives Theory: A Review. *Journal of Agricultural Economics* (1983), 34:1–44.

LeVay, C., Bateman, D. I. Why Aid Agricultural Co-operatives? *Agricultural Administration* (1980), 8:97–107.

Lewin, A. Y., Minton, J. W. Determining Organizational Effectiveness: Another Look, and An Agenda for Research. *Management Science* (1986), 32(5):514–538.

Lindgren, B., Roos, P. *Produktions-, Kostnads-och produktivitetsutveckling inom offentligt bedriven hälso-och sjukvård 1960–1980 (Changes in the Production, Costs and Productivity of Public Health Services).* Finansdepartementet (Ministry of Finance), DsFi 1985:3 (1985).

Lovell, C. A. K., Walters, L., Wood, L. Stratefied Models of Education Production Using Modified DEA and Regression Analysis. Chapter 17, this book.

Lubatkin, M., Pitts, M. PIMPS: Fact or Folklore. *Journal of Business Strategy* (1983), 3:38–43.

Luft, H. S. Assessing The Evidence on HMO Performance. *Milbank Memorial Fund Quarterly* (1980), 58(4).

Maddala, G. S. *Limited-Dependent and Qualitative Variables in Econometrics.* New York: Cambridge University Press (1983).

Malmquist, S. Index Numbers and Indifference Surfaces. *Trabajos de Estatistica* (1953), 4:209–242.

March, J. G., Simon, H. A. *Organizations.* New York: John Wiley and Sons (1958).

Mascarenhas, B. Strategic Group Dynamics. *Academy of Management Journal* (1989), 32:333–352.

Mascarenhas, B., Aakar, D. A. Strategy Over the Business Cycle. *Strategic Management Journal* (1989), 10:199–210.

McArthur, A. W. *An Empirical Investigation of Strategic Groups and Performance in the Airline Industry 1979–1981.* Eugene, OR: unpublished doctoral dissertation, University of Oregon (1984).

McGee, J. Strategic Groups: A Useful Linkage Between Industry Structure and Strategic Management. In H. Thomas, D. G. Gardner (eds.), *Strategic Marketing and Management.* New York: John Wiley (1985).

McGee, J., Thomas, H. Strategic Groups: Theory, Research and Taxonomy. *Management Journal* (1986), 7:141–160.

Meeusen, W., van den Broeck, J. Efficiency Estimation from Cobb–Douglas Production Functions with Composed Error. *International Economic Review* (1977), 18:435–444.

Mester, L. J. Testing for Expense Preference Behavior: Mutual versus Stock Savings and Loans. *RAND Journal of Economics* (1989), 20:483–498.

Miles, R., Snow, C. *Organizational Strategy, Structure, and Process.* New York: McGraw-Hill (1978).

Miller, D., Friesen, P. H. *Organizations: A Quantum View.* Englewood Cliffs, NJ: Prentice-Hall (1984).

Miller, R. Strategic Pathways to Growth in Retailing. *Journal of Business Strategy* (1981), 1:16–29.

Mintzberg, H. Patterns of Strategy Formulation. *Management Science* (1978), 934–948.

Mintzberg, H., McHugh, A. Strategy Formation in an Adhocracy. *Administrative Science Quarterly* (1985), 3:160–197.

Murtagh, B. A. *Advanced Linear Programming.* New York: McGraw-Hill (1981).

National Commission on Excellence in Education. *A Nation at Risk: The Imperative for Educational Reform.* Washington, D.C.: USGPO (1983).

Nayyar, P., McGee, J., Thomas, H. Research Notes and Communications Strategic Groups: A Comment; a Further Comment. *Strategic Management*

Journal (1989), 10:101–107.

Newman, H. H. Strategic Groups and the Structure-Performance Relationship. *Review of Economics and Statistics* (1978), 60:471–427.

Newman, H. H. Strategic Groups and the Structure/Performance Relationship: A Study with Respect to the Chemical Process Industries. Cambridge, MA: unpublished doctoral dissertation, Harvard University (1974).

Nishimizu, M., Page, J. M. Total Factor Productivity Growth, Technological Progress and Technical Efficiency Change: Dimensions of Productivity Change in Yugoslavia 1965–78. *Economic Journal* (1982), 92:920–936.

Norman, M., Stoker, B. *Data Envelopment Analysis: The Assessment of Performance*. New York: John Wiley & Sons (1991).

Nunamaker, T. Using Data Envelopment Analysis to Measure the Efficiency of Non-Profit Organizations: A Critical Evaluation. *Managerial and Decision Economics* (1985), 6(1):50–58.

Oster, S. Intraindustry Structure and the Ease of Strategic Change. *Review of Economics and Statistics* (1982), 64:376–383.

Pareto, U. Manuel d'economie politique, 2nd ed. Paris, Marcerl Giard (1927).

Park, R. E., Mitchell, B. M. Estimating the Autocorrelated Error Model with Trended Data. *Journal of Econometrics* (1980), 13:185–201.

Parkan, C. Measuring the Efficiency of Service Operations: An Application to Bank Branches. *Engineering Costs and Production Economics* (1987), 12: 237–242.

Parker, T. H. *Toward Integrating Strategic Process and Strategy Content: Conceptual Foundations and Empirical Results from Commercial Banking*. Lincoln, NE: unpublished doctoral dissertation, The University of Nebraska–Lincoln (1987).

Parks, R. W. Efficient Estimation of a System of Regression Equations When Disturbances Are Both Serially and Contemporaneously Correlated. *Journal of The American Statistical Association* (June 1967), 500–509.

Paschke, P., Taylor, L. A., Thor, C. G. Measuring the Productivity of a Hospital's Clinical Laboratory. *Journal of Medical Systems* (1984), 8(4):265–277.

Pauly, M. V. *Doctors and Their Workshops: Economic Models of Physician Behavior*. Chicago: The University of Chicago Press (1980).

Pauly, M. V., Wilson, P. Hospital Output Forecasts and the Costs of Empty Hospital Beds. *Health Services Research* (1986), 3:403–428.

Pedersen, P. B., Olsesen, O., Petersen, N. C. Produktivitets-evaluering af 96 danske sygehus (Measuring Productivity of 96 Danish Hospitals). *Ledelse & Erhvervsøkonomi (The Danish Journal of Management Research)* (1987), 2:67–81.

Petersen, N. C. Data Envelopment Analysis on a Relaxed Set of Assumptions. *Management Science* (1990), 20(3):305–314.

Petersen, N. C. Data Envelopment Analysis on a Relaxed Set of Assumptions. *Management Science* (1990), 36(3):305–314.

Pineault, R. The Effect of Medical Training Factors on Physician Utilization Behavior. *Medical Care* (January 1977).

Porter, M. E. The Structure Within Industries and Companies Performance. *Review of Economics and Statistics* (1979), 61:214–227.

Porter, M. E. Competitive Advantage: Creating and Sustaining Superior Performance. New York: The Free Press (1985).

Porter, M. E. *Competitive Strategy: Techniques for Analyzing Industries and Competitors*. New York: The Free Press (1980).

Porter, M. E. *Consumer Behavior, Retailer Power, and Manufactures Strategy in Consumer Goods Industries*. Cambridge, MA: unpublished doctoral dissertation, Harvard University (1973).

Porter, P. K., Scully, G. W. Economic Efficiency in Cooperatives. *Journal of Law and Economics* (1987), 30:489–512.

Primeaux, W. J. A Method for Determining Strategic Groups and Life Stages of an Industry. In H. Thomas, D. M. Gardner (eds.), *Strategic Marketing and Management*. New York: John Wiley (1985).

Ramsler, M. *Strategic Groups and Foreign Market Entry in Global Banking Competition*. Cambridge, MA: unpublished dissertation, Harvard University (1982).

Ratza, C. The Strategic Marketing Process: A Practical Framework for Analytic Market Planning and Analysis. *Managerial Planning* (1985), 33:41–45.

Ray, S. C. Resource-Use Efficiency in Public Schools: A Study of Connecticut Data. *Management Science* (1991), 37(12):1620–1629.

Ray, S. C. Data Envelopment Analysis, Nondiscretionary Inputs and Efficiency: An Alternative Interpretation. *Socio-Economic Planning Sciences* (1988), 22(4):167–176.

Rhoades, S. A Further Evaluation of the Effect of Diversification on Industry Profit Performance. *Review of Economics and Statistics* (1974), 56:557–558.

Rhoades, S. The Effect of Diversification on Industry Profit Preformance in 241 Manufacturing Industries: 1963. *Review of Economics and Statistics* (1973), 55:146–155.

Rhodes, Edwardo. Data Envelopment Analysis and Approaches for Measuring the Efficiency of Decision-making Units with an Application to Program Follow-through in U.S. Education. Pittsburgh, PA: Ph.D. dissertation. School of Urban & Public Affairs, Carnegie Mellow Univ (1978).

Rhodes, E. L., Southwick, L. Jr. Comparison of University Performance Differences Over Time. Working Paper, School of Public and Environmental Affairs, Indiana University, Bloomington, IN (1989).

Roll, Y., Cook, W., Golany, B. Controlling Factor Weights in Data Envelopment Analysis. *IIE Transactions* (1991), 23(1):2–9.

Roll, Y., Moran. Hospital Productivity Measurement: An Engineering Approach. *Omega* (1984), 12(5):449–455.

Roll, Y., Sachish, A. Producitivity Measurement at the Plant Level. *Omega* (1981), 9(1):37–42.

Rushton, G. Selecting the Objective Function in Location-Allocation Analysis. In A. Ghosh, G. Rushton (eds.), *Spatial Analysis and Location-Allocation Models*. New York: Van Nostrand Reinhold (1987), 345–364.

Ryans, A. B., Wittink, D. R. Security Reruns as a Basis for Estimating the Competitive Structure in an Industry. In H. Thomas, D. M. Gardner (eds.), *Strategic Marketing and Management*. Chichester and New York: John F. Wiley & Sons.

Salvatore, T. Competitor Analysis in Health Care Marketing. *Strategic Management Journal* (1984), 4:11–16.

Schilling, D., McGarity, A., ReVelle, C. Hidden Attributes and the Display of Information in Multiobjective Analysis. *Management Science* (1982), 28: 236–242.

Schmidt, P. Frontier Production Functions. *Econometric Review* (1985–86), 4(2): 289–328.

Schmidt, P. On the Statistical Estimation of Parametric Frontier Production Functions. *Review of Economics and Statistics* (May 1976), 238–239.

Seiford, L. M. Models, Extensions, and Applications of Data Envelopment Analysis: A Selected Reference Set. *Computers, Environment, and Urban Systems* (1990), 14(2).

Seiford, L. M., Thrall, R. M. Recent Developments in DEA: The Mathematical Programming Approach To Frontier Analysis. *Journal of Econometrics* (1990), 46(1/2):7–38.

Sengupta, J. T. *Efficiency Analysis by Production Frontiers: The Nonparametric Approach*. Dordrecht: Kluwer Academic Publishers (1989).

Sengupta, J. K. Data Envelopment Analysis for Efficiency Measurement in the Stochastic Case. *Computers and Operations Research* (1987), 14:117–169.

Sexton, T., Silkman, R., Hogan, A. Data Envelopment Analysis: Critique and Extensions. In R. Silkman (ed.) *Measuring Efficiency: An Assessment of Data Envelopment Analysis. New Directions for Program Evaluation*. San Francisco: Jossey-Bass (1986).

Shephard, R. W. *Indirect Production Functions*. Meisenheim am Glan: Verlag Anton Bain (1974).

Shephard, R. W. *Theory of Cost and Production Functions*. Princeton, NJ: Princeton University Press (1970).

Sherman, H. D. *Service Organization Productivity Measurement*. Hamilton, Ontario, Canada: The Society of Management Accountants of Canada (1988).

Sherman, H. D. Improving the Productivity of Service Businesses. *Sloan Management Review* (1984), 25(3):11–23.

Sherman, H. D. Hospital Efficiency Measurement and Evaluation. *Medical Care* (1984), 22(10):922–938.

Sickles, R. C. A Nonlinear Multivariate Error Components Analysis of Technology and Specific Factor Productivity Growth with an Application to the U.S. Airlines. *Journal of Econometrics* (1985), 27:61–78.

Sickles, R. C., Good, D., Johnson, R. L. Allocative Distortions and the Regulatory Transition of the U.S. Airline Industry. *Journal of Econometrics* (1986), 33:143–163.

Silkman, R. H. (ed.). *Measuring Efficiency: An Assessment of Data Envelopment*

Analysis. Publication No. 32 in the series New Directions for Program Evaluation, A Publication of the American Evaluation Association. San Francisco: Jossey Bass (1986).

Simon, H. A. On the Concept of Organizational Goals. *Administrative Science Quarterly* (1964), 9:1–22.

Sinclair, J., Catron, B. New Price Index for the Computer Industry. *Monthly Labor Review* (1990), 113(10):16–24.

Sitorus, B. L. Productive Efficiency and Redundant Factors of Production in Traditional Agriculture of Underdeveloped Countries. *Proceedings of the Thirty Ninth Annual Meeting of the Western Farm Economics Association* (1966), 153–158.

Sloan, F., Steniwald, B. *Insurance, Regulation, and Hospital Costs.* Lexington, MA: Lexington Books (1980).

Spivey, W. A., Thrall, R. M. *Linear Optimization.* New York: Holt, Rinehart and Winston (1970).

Statistiska Centralbyrån (The Central Statistical Bureau). *Arbetikraftsunder-sökningarna (The Labour Force Surveys).* Statistiska Centralbyrån (The Central Statistical Bureau) (different years).

Stephens, M. S. EDF Statistics for Goodness of Fit and Some Comparisons. *Journal of the American Statistical Association* (1974), 69(347):730–737.

Tassey, G. Competitive Strategies and Performance in Technology-Based Industries. *Journal of Economics and Business* (1983), 21–40.

Thomas, H., Venkatraman, N. Research on Strategic Groups: Progress and Prognosis. *Journal of Management Studies* (1988), 25:537–555.

Thompson, R., Singleton, F., Thrall, R., Smith, B. Comparative Site Evaluations for Locating a High-Energy Physics Lab in Texas. *Interfaces* (1986), 16(6): 35–49.

Thompson, R. G., Dharmapala, P. S., Thrall, R. Sensitivity Analysis of Efficiency Measures with Applications to Kansas Farming and Illinois Coal Mining. Chapter 20, this book.

Thompson, R. G., Langemeier, L. N., Lee, C. T., Thrall, R. M. The Role of Multiplier Bounds in Efficiency Analysis with Application to Kansas Farming. *Journal of Econometrics* (1990), 46(1/2):93–108.

Thrall, R. M. Classification Transitions Under Expansion of Inputs and Outputs in Data Envelopment Analysis. *Managerial and Decision Economics* (1989), 10:159–162.

Tremblay, V. J. Strategic Groups and the Demand for Beer. *Journal of Industrial Economics* (1985), 34:183–198.

Tremblay, V. J. *The Effect of Firm Behavior and Technology on Firm Size: A Case Study of the U.S. Brewing Industry.* Pullman, WA: unpublished doctoral dissertation, Washington State University (1983).

Triplett, J. The Economic Interpretation of Hedonic Methods. *Survey of Current Business.* Washington, D.C.: U.S. Government Printing Office (1986).

Triplett, J. Concepts of Quality in Input and Output Price Measures: A Resolution of the User-Value Resource-Cost Debate. In M. Foss (ed.), *The U.S. National Income and Product Accounts: Selected Topics*. Chicago: University of Chicago Press (1983).

Tulkens, H. On FDH Efficiency Analysis: Some Methodological Issues and Applications to Retail Banking, Courts, and Urban Transit. *Journal of Productivity Analysis* (forthcoming).

Ulrich, D. Specifying External Relations: Definition of and Actors in an Organization's Environment. *Human Relations* (1984), 37:245–262.

U.S. Department of Education, Center for Education Statistics. *High School and Beyond, 1980 Sophomore Cohort, Third Follow-up (1986)*. National Opinion Research Center Contractor Report. Washington, D.C.: Department of Education (1987).

U.S. General Accounting Office. *Deregulation: Increased Competition is Making Airlines More Efficient and Responsive to Consumers*. Washington, D.C.: U.S. Government Printing Office (November 6, 1985).

Varian, H. Goodness-of-fit in Optimizing Models. *Journal of Econometrics* (1990), 46:125–140.

Vickers, J., Yarrow, G. *Privatization: An Economic Analysis*. Cambridge, MA: MIT Press (1988).

White, H. A Heteroscedasticity-consistent Covariance Matrix Estimator and a Direct Test for Heteroscedasticity. *Econometrica* (1980), 48(4):817–838.

Wong, Y., Beasley, J. E. Restricting Weight Flexibility in Data Envelopment Analysis. Journal of the Operational Research Society (1990), 41(9):829–835.

Wood, L. L. Measuring the Relative Efficiency of Schools in the Philadelphia School District Using Data Envelopment Analysis. Philadelphia, PA: Masters Paper, Department of Public Policy and Management, Wharton School, University of Pennsylvania (1983).

Wyckoff, J. H., Lavigne, J. The Technical Inefficiency of Public Elementary Schools in New York. Working Paper, Graduate School of Public Affairs, State University of New York at Albany (1992).

Yelin, E., et al. A Comparison of the Treatment of Rheumatoid Arthritis in HMO's and Fee-For-Service Practices. *The New England Journal of Medicine* (1985), 312(15).

Young, D., Saltman, R. B. Preventive Medicine for Hospital Costs. *Harvard Business Review* (1983), 61.

Zellner, A. An Efficient Method of Estimating Seemingly Unrelated Regressions and Tests for Aggregation Bias. *Journal of the American Statistical Association* (1962), 58:977–992.

Zieschang, K. The Characteristics Approach to the Problem of New and Disappearing Goods in Price Indexes. BLS Working Paper 183. Washington, D.C.: Bureau of Labor Statistics (1988).

Zieschang, K. Output Price Measurement When Product Design is Endogenous. BLS Working Paper 150. Washington, D.C.: Bureau of Labor Statistics (1985).

INDEX

509

Department of Agricultural Economics
and Rural Sociology
The Pennsylvania State University
103 Armsby Building
University Park, PA 16802-5600